Matching Supply with Demand

**An Introduction to
Operations Management**

Gérard Cachon
*The Wharton School,
University of Pennsylvania*

Christian Terwiesch
*The Wharton School,
University of Pennsylvania*

McGraw-Hill
Irwin

Boston   Burr Ridge, IL   Dubuque, IA   Madison, WI   New York   San Francisco   St. Louis
Bangkok   Bogotá   Caracas   Kuala Lumpur   Lisbon   London   Madrid   Mexico City
Milan   Montreal   New Delhi   Santiago   Seoul   Singapore   Sydney   Taipei   Toronto

McGraw-Hill Irwin

MATCHING SUPPLY WITH DEMAND: AN INTRODUCTION TO OPERATIONS MANAGEMENT
Published by McGraw-Hill/Irwin, a business unit of The McGraw-Hill Companies, Inc., 1221 Avenue of the
Americas, New York, NY, 10020. Copyright © 2006 by The McGraw-Hill Companies, Inc. All rights reserved.
No part of this publication may be reproduced or distributed in any form or by any means, or stored in a
database or retrieval system, without the prior written consent of The McGraw-Hill Companies, Inc., including,
but not limited to, in any network or other electronic storage or transmission, or broadcast for distance learning.

Some ancillaries, including electronic and print components, may not be available to customers outside the
United States.

This book is printed on acid-free paper.

4 5 6 7 8 9 0 CCW/CCW 0 9 8 7

ISBN-13: 978-0-07-291899-1
ISBN-10: 0-07-291899-3

Editorial director: *Brent Gordon*
Executive editor: *Scott Isenberg*
Developmental editor: *Cynthia Douglas*
Senior marketing manager: *Douglas Reiner*
Senior media producer: *Victor Chiu*
Project manager: *Harvey Yep*
Production supervisor: *Gina Hangos*
Senior designer: *Mary E. Kazak*
Senior photo research coordinator: *Jeremy Cheshareck*
Senior supplement producer: *Rose M. Range*
Senior digital content specialist: *Brian Nacik*
Cover design: *Allison Traynham*
Typeface: *10/12 Times New Roman*
Compositor: *Carlisle Communications, Ltd.*
Printer: *Courier Westford*

Library of Congress Cataloging-in-Publication Data
Cachon, Gérard.
   Matching supply with demand : an introduction to operations management / Gérard
Cachon, Christian Terwiesch.
      p. cm.
   Includes bibliographical references and index.
   ISBN 0-07-291899-3 (alk. paper)
   1. Production management. I. Terwiesch, C. (Christian) II. Title.
TS155.C13 2006
   658.3—dc22

                                                                    2004057918

www.mhhe.com

To the teachers, colleagues and professionals who shared with us their knowledge.

About the Cover

The Chinese words on the cover are "change," "balance," and "harmony." "Qualität" is German for quality, "flusso" is Italian for flow, and "la demande" is French for demand. These words, together with the fulcrum symbol, visualize the book's objective of changing an organization so that it is able to match (balance) supply with demand. The cover was designed by Gérard Cachon, Christian Terwiesch, and Karl Ulrich together with the McGraw-Hill designer, Allison Traynham.

About the Authors

Gérard Cachon *The Wharton School, University of Pennsylvania*

Professor Cachon is an Associate Professor of Operations and Information Management at the Wharton School of the University of Pennsylvania, where he teaches a variety of courses including the core MBA course in operations management, an MBA elective on marketing and operations integration, and a Ph.D. course in operations management. Professor Cachon's research focuses on supply chain management; in particular, how new technologies enable better performing supply chain designs and how the application of novel incentive schemes enhances supply chain coordination. His articles have appeared in *Harvard Business Review, Management Science, Manufacturing and Service Operations Management* and *Operations Research.* He is on the editorial review board of five of the leading journals in operations management. He has consulted with a wide range of companies on supply chain management, including 4R Systems, Ahold, Americold, Campbell Soup, IBM, Medtronic and O'Neill.

Before joining the Wharton School in July, 2000, Professor Cachon was on the faculty at the Fuqua School of Business, Duke University. He received a Ph.D. from The Wharton School in 1995.

He is an avid proponent of bicycle commuting and other environmentally friendly modes of transportation. Along with his wife and four children he enjoys hiking, skiing, fishing, snorkeling, and scuba diving.

Christian Terwiesch *The Wharton School, University of Pennsylvania*

Professor Terwiesch teaches MBA and executive classes in the areas of operations management and product development at The Wharton School of the University of Pennsylvania, where he is an Associate Professor of Operations and Information Management. He also has held a visiting appointment at INSEAD in Fontainebleau, France, where he received his PhD in 1997. His research on product development and supply chain management appears in many of the leading academic journals, including *Management Science, Operations Research, Marketing Science, Organization Science,* and the *Journal of Product Innovation Management.* He is active on various editorial boards for journals such as *Management Science, Production and Operations Management,* and *IEEE Transactions.*

Professor Terwiesch has done research for and consulted with various organizations. His consulting projects include concurrent engineering for BMW, supply chain management for Intel and Medtronic, R&D pipeline management for Merck, and operations improvements for several large hospitals.

He is a cycling fanatic and is still racing long distance triathlon races in Europe and the US. Along with his wife and three children, he enjoys spending summers in Europe.

Preface

This book represents our view of the essential body of knowledge for an introductory operations management course. In the years that we have been teaching operations at The Wharton School, our students have repeatedly asked us for recommended readings to go along with the cases and lectures in our courses. Unfortunately, our students found all our suggestions either too remote from the real world (fictitious companies with unrealistic assumptions) or too technical (measured by the number of Greek letters per page).

Given those shortcomings of existing textbooks, our guiding principle in the development of *Matching Supply with Demand* has always been "real operations, real simple." "Real operations" means that most of the chapters in this book are written from the perspective of a specific company. The reason for this is twofold. First, we hope that the arguably somewhat dry material will come to life by discussing it in a real-world context. Companies and products are simply easier to remember than numbers and equations. We have chosen a wide variety of companies, small and large, representing services, manufacturing, and retailing alike. While obviously not fully representative, we believe that—taken together—these cases provide a realistic picture of operations management problems today.

Second, we do not want equations and models to merely provide students with mathematical gymnastics for the sake of an intellectual exercise. We feel that professional training, even in a rigorous academic setting, requires tools and strategies that students can implement in practice. We achieve this by demonstrating how to apply our models from start to finish in a realistic operational setting. For example, we do not assume the existence of inputs such as a demand forecast or a cost parameter, we actually explain how these inputs can be obtained in practice. Furthermore, we openly address the implementation challenges of each model/strategy we discuss so that students know what to expect when the "rubber hits the pavement."

As important as "real operations" is "real simple." But "real simple" does not mean plenty of "blah-blah" without any analytical rigor. Quite to the contrary, instead of ducking the challenge, this text actually pushes the boundary of what is generally viewed as teachable to students in a first course on operations management. To us, "real simple" means hard analysis that is made easy to learn. This is crucial for an operations text. Our objective is to teach business leaders, not tacticians. Thus, we need students to be able to quickly develop a foundation of formal models so that they have the time to explore the big picture, that is, how operations can be transformed to provide an organization with sustainable competitive advantage and/or superior customer service. Students that get bogged down in details, equations, and analysis are not fully capturing the valuable insights they will need in their future career.

So how do we strive for "real simple"? First, we recognize that not every student comes to this material with an engineering/math background. As a result, we tried to use as little mathematical notation as possible, to provide many real-world examples, and to adhere to consistent terminology and phrasing. Second, we provide various levels of detail for each analysis. For example, every little step in an analysis is described in the text via an explicit example; then a summary of the process is provided in a "how to" exhibit, a brief listing of key notation and equations is provided at the end of each chapter, and, finally, solved practice problems are offered to reinforce learning. While we do humbly recognize, given the quantitative sophistication of this text, that "much simpler" might be more accurate than "real simple," we nevertheless hope that students will be pleasantly surprised to discover that their analytical capabilities are even stronger than they imagined.

The initial version of *Matching Supply with Demand* made its debut in portions of the operations management core course at Wharton in the 2002–2003 academic year. The subsequent version was fully implemented and integrated into the 12 sections of the Wharton daytime core as well as the 4 sections of the Wharton Executive MBA core in the 2003–2004 academic year. This version incorporates the feedback we have received over the last two years from students, from our colleagues at Wharton, and from many colleagues at other institutions.

Although this book has been designed with MBA students in mind (regular and executive), this should not rule out its appeal to an undergraduate curriculum. Moreover, while you will probably not find this book in any airport bookstore (it is not that simple), we firmly believe that professionals in areas such as process analysis, supply chain management, and service operations also will benefit from its content.

We teach the importance of quality in operations, and so we took quality quite seriously with this text. We checked and rechecked numbers ourselves, but we also engaged several students to check every number. Errors were found and corrected, and fortunately, fewer errors were found on each iteration of each chapter. While we hope this text is defect free, realistically, we are sure there must be additional errors. If any additional corrections are needed, we welcome hearing about them.

Gérard Cachon

Christian Terwiesch

Acknowledgements

Although this book is still a work in progress, it is important to us to acknowledge the many people who have already helped with this project.

We begin with the 2004 MBA class that weathered through our initial version of the text. It is not practical for us to name every student that shared comments with us, but we do wish to name the students who took the time to participate in our focus groups: Gregory Ames, Maria Herrada-Flores, Justin Knowles, Karissa Kruse, Sandeep Naik, Jeremy Stackowitz, Charlotte Walsh, and Thomas (TJ) Zerr. The 2005 MBA class enjoyed a much more polished manuscript, but nevertheless contributed numerous suggestions and identified remaining typos and errors (much to our chagrin). In addition to Wharton students, we have received helpful feedback from students at Texas A&M, the University of Toronto, and INSEAD.

Along with our students, we would like to thank our co-teachers in the core: Krishnan Anand, Morris Cohen, Marshall Fisher, Serguei Netessine, Kathy Pearson, Stephan Spinler, Anita Tucker, Karl Ulrich, and Yu-Sheng Zheng. In addition to useful pedagogical advice and quality testing, they shared many of their own practice problems and questions.

This book is not the first book in Operations Management, nor will it be the last. We hope we have incorporated the best practices of existing books while introducing our own innovations. The book by Anupindi et al. as well as the article by Harrison and Loch were very helpful to us, as they developed the process view of operations underlying Chapters 2 to 6. We apply definitions and terminology from those sources whenever possible without sacrificing our principle of "real operations, real simple." We also credit the book by Chase and Aquilano especially for Chapter 8.

We also have received some indirect and direct assistance from faculty at other universities. Garrett van Ryzin's (Columbia) and Xavier de Groote's (INSEAD) inventory notes were influential in the writing of Chapters 2 and 11 and the revenue management note by Serguei Netessine (Wharton) and Rob Shumsky (Rochester) was the starting point for Chapter 13. The process analysis, queuing, and inventory notes and articles written by Martin Lariviere (Northwestern), Michael Harrison (Stanford), and Christoph Loch (INSEAD) were also influential in several of our chapters. Martin, being a particularly clever question designer, was kind enough to share many of his questions with us. Several brave souls actually read the entire manuscript and responded with detailed comments. These reviewers included Stephen Chick (INSEAD), Karen Donohue (University of Minnesota), Mark Ferguson (Georgia Tech), Matthew Keblis (Texas A&M), Joe Milner (University of Toronto), Erica Plambeck (Stanford University), Eric Svaan (University of Michigan), Noel Watson (Harvard University), and Rachel Zhang (Cornell University).

Our PhD student "volunteers," Karan Girotra, Marcelo Olivares, and Fuqiang Zhang, as well as Ruchika Lal and Bernd Terwiesch, took on the tedious job of quality testing. Greg Neubecker and Bethany Schwartz helped to collect and analyze data and could frequently solve practice problems faster than we could. The text is much cleaner due to their efforts.

The many cases and practical examples that illustrate the core concepts of this book reflect our extensive collaboration with several companies, including the University of Pennsylvania Hospital System in the Philadelphia region, the Circored plant in Trinidad, the Xootr factory in New Hampshire, the An-ser call center in Wisconsin, the operations group at O'Neill in California, and the supply chain group at Medtronic in Minnesota. We have benefited from countless visits and meetings with their management teams. We thank the people of these organizations, whose role it is to match supply and demand in the "real world," for sharing their knowledge, listening to our ideas, and challenging our models.

Special thanks go to Jeff Salomon and his team (Interventional Radiology) Karl Ulrich (Xootr), Allan Fromm (An-ser), Cherry Chu and John Pope (O'Neill), and Frederic Marie and John Grossman (Medtronic). Allan Fromm deserves extra credit as he was not only willing to share with us his extensive knowledge of service operations that he gathered as a CEO of a call center company but also proofread the entire manuscript and tackled most of the practice problems.

We especially thank our friend, colleague, and cycling partner Karl Ulrich, who has been involved in various aspects of the book, starting from its initial idea to the last details of the design process, including the cover design.

We thank Scott Isenberg, Cynthia Douglas, Colin Kelley, and Harvey Yep at McGraw-Hill for providing guidance, motivation, and insights.

Finally, we thank our family members, some of whom were surely unwilling reviewers who nevertheless performed their family obligation with a cheerful smile.

Gérard Cachon

Christian Terwiesch

Brief Contents

Table of Contents

1

Introduction

A central premise in economics is that prices adjust to match supply with demand: if there is excess demand, prices rise; if there is excess supply, prices fall. But while an economist may find comfort with this theory, managers in practice often do not. To them excess demand means lost revenue and excess supply means wasted resources. They fully understand that matching supply with demand is extremely difficult and requires more tools than just price adjustments.

Consider the following examples:

Great Story

- When Sony launched the Playstation 2 in 2000, many consumers eager to buy were able to purchase the product only by waiting several weeks. Yet, when Microsoft launched the X-box, a product that was expected to be at least equally successful, it had to discount its prices by over $100 per unit a year after launch as retailers kept more than 100,000 of the units on their shelves.

- In early 2002, a victim of a car crash in Germany died in a rescue helicopter after the medical team together with their dispatcher had unsuccessfully attempted to find a slot in an operating room at eight different hospitals. In the United States, every day there are thousands of patients requiring emergency care, who cannot be transported to the nearest emergency room and/or have to wait considerable time before receiving care.

- Mass-customization advocates promise consumers purchasing new vehicles that they soon would be able to receive a product built to their exact orders. Mass-customization continues to be happening "definitely next year" for more than 20 years now, while in practice the lots of dealers are full of unpopular vehicles, forcing the automotive industry to provide hefty discounts on each new vehicle purchase.

- A customer calling into most call centers is likely to spend a significant time waiting on the line before talking to a customer service representative. The same call center, at another moment in the day, is likely to have numerous representatives waiting unproductively for consumers to call.

- There were 95 million doses of the flu vaccine produced for the 2002–2003 flu season in the United States. Unfortunately, 12 million doses were not used and had to be destroyed (a vaccine is good only for one flu season). Only 87 million doses of the flu vaccine were produced for the next season, 2003–2004. (Not coincidentally, $95 - 12 = 87$.) Unfortunately, in that season there were widespread shortages, leading to flu-related deaths, especially in Colorado.

All of these cases have in common that they suffer from a mismatch between demand and supply, with respect either to their timing or to their quantities.

This book is about how firms can design their operations to better match supply with demand. Our motivation is simply stated: By better matching supply with demand, a firm gains a significant competitive advantage over its rivals. A firm can achieve this better match through the implementation of the rigorous models and the operational strategies we outline in this book.

To somewhat soften our challenge to economic theory, we do acknowledge it is possible to mitigate demand–supply mismatches by adjusting prices. For example, Microsoft did cut prices with its video-game console when faced with weak demand. But this price adjustment came only after committing to a large inventory investment. In other words, we view that price adjustment as a symptom of a problem, rather than evidence of a healthy system. Moreover, in many other cases, price adjustments are impossible. The time period between the initiation of demand and the fulfillment through supply is too short or there are too few buyers and sellers in the market. There simply is no market for emergency care in operating rooms, waiting times in call centers, or an item missing on the shelf in a grocery store.

Why is matching supply with demand difficult? The short answer is that demand can vary, either in predictable or unpredictable ways, and supply is inflexible. On average an organization might have the correct amount of resources (people, product, and/or equipment), but most organizations find themselves frequently in situations with resources in the wrong place, at the wrong time, and/or in the wrong quantity. Furthermore, shifting resources across locations or time is costly, hence the inflexibility in supply. For example, physicians are not willing to rush back and forth to the hospital as they are needed and retailers cannot afford to immediately move product from one location to another. While it is essentially impossible to always achieve a perfect match between supply and demand, successful firms continually strive for that goal.

Table 1.1 provides a sample of industries that we will discuss in this book and describes their challenge to match supply with demand. Take the airline industry (first column in Table 1.1.). British Airways achieves a 70.3 percent utilization of their aircrafts; that is, a 300-seat aircraft will have, on average, 89 seats flying empty. If British Airways could have one more passenger travel on a flight, that is, increase its utilization by 0.33 percent, its corporate profits would increase by close to $65 million, which approximately corresponds to the airline's quarterly profits for quarter two of 2001. This illustrates a critical lesson: Even a seemingly small improvement in operations, for example, a utilization increase of 0.33 percent, can have a significant effect on a firm's profitability precisely because, for most firms, their profit (if they have a profit) is a relatively small percentage of their revenue. Hence, improving the match between supply and demand is a critically important responsibility for a firm's management.

The other examples in Table 1.1 are drawn from a wide range of settings: health care delivery and devices, retailing, and heavy industry. Each suffers significant consequences due to demand–supply mismatches, and each requires specialized tools to improve and manage its operations.

To conclude our introduction, we strongly believe that effective operations management is about effectively matching supply with demand. Organizations that take the design of their operations seriously and aggressively implement the tools of operations management will enjoy a significant performance advantage over their competitors. This lesson is especially relevant for senior management given the razor-thin profit margins firms must deal with in modern competitive industries.

1.1 Learning Objectives and Framework

In this book we look at organizations as entities that must match the supply of what they produce with the demand for their product. In this process, we will introduce a number of

TABLE 1.1   Examples of Supply–Demand Mismatches

	Air Travel	Emergency Room	Retailing	Iron Ore Plant	Pacemakers
Supply	Seats on specific flight	Medical service	Consumer electronics	Iron ore	Medical equipment
Demand	Travel for specific time and destination	Urgent need for medical service	Consumers buying a new video system	Steel mills	Heart surgeon requiring pacemaker at exact time and location
Supply exceeds demand	Empty seat	Doctors, nurses, and infrastructure are underutilized	High inventory costs; few inventory turns	Prices fall	Pacemaker sits in inventory
Demand exceeds supply	Overbooking; customer has to take different flight (profit loss)	Crowding and delays in the ER; potential diversion of ambulances	Forgone profit opportunity; consumer dissatisfaction	Prices rise	Forgone profit (typically not associated with medical risk)
Actions to match supply and demand	Dynamic pricing; booking policies	Staffing to predicted demand; priorities	Forecasting; quick response	If prices fall too low, production facility is shut down	Distribution system holding pacemakers at various locations
Managerial importance	About 30% of all seats fly empty; a 1–2% increase in seat utilization makes difference between profits and losses	Delays in treatment or transfer have been linked to death	Per unit inventory costs for consumer electronics retailing commonly exceed net profits	Prices are so competitive that the primary emphasis is on reducing the cost of supply	Most products (valued $20k) spend 4–5 months waiting in a trunk of a salesperson before being used
Reference	Chapter 13, Revenue Management with Capacity Controls	Chapter 6, Variability and Its Impact on Process Performance: Waiting Time Problems; Chapter 7, The Impact of Variability on Process Performance: Throughput Losses	Chapter 9, Betting on Uncertain Demand: The Newsvendor Model; Chapter 2, The Process View of the Organization; Chapter 10, Make-to-Order and Quick Response with Reactive Capacity	Chapter 3, Understanding the Supply Process: Evaluating Process Capacity Chapter 4, Estimating and Reducing Labor Costs	Chapter 11, Service Levels and Lead Time in Supply Chains: The Order-Up-to Inventory Model

quantitative models and qualitative strategies, which we collectively refer to as the "tools of operations management." By "quantitative model" we mean some mathematical procedure or equation that takes inputs (such as a demand forecast, a processing rate, etc.) and outputs a number that either instructs a manager on what to do (how much inventory to buy, how many nurses to have on call, etc.) or informs a manager about a relevant performance measure (e.g., the average time a customer waits for service, the average number of patients in the emergency room, etc.). By "qualitative strategy" we mean a guiding principle: for example, increase the flexibility of your production facilities, decrease the variety of products offered, serve customers in priority order, and so forth. The next section gives a brief description of the key models and strategies we cover. Our learning objective for this book, put as succinctly as we can, is to teach students how and when to implement the tools of operations management.

Just as the tools of operations management come in different forms, they can be applied in different ways:

1. Operations management tools can be applied to ensure that resources are used as efficiently as possible; that is, the most is achieved with what we have.
2. Operations management tools can be used to make desirable trade-offs between competing objectives.
3. Operations management tools can be used to redesign or restructure our operations so that we can improve performance along multiple dimensions simultaneously.

We view our diverse set of tools as complementary to each other. In other words, our focus is neither exclusively on the quantitative models nor exclusively on the qualitative strategies. Without analytical models it is difficult to move beyond the "blah-blah" of strategies, and without strategies it is easy to get lost in the minutia of tactical models. Put another way, we have designed this book to provide a rigorous operations management education for a strategic, high-level manager or consultant.

We will apply operations tools to firms that produce services and goods in a variety of environments—from apparel to health care, from call centers to pacemakers, and from kick scooters to iron ore fines. We present many diverse settings precisely because there does not exist a "standard" operational environment. Hence, there does not exist a single tool that applies to all firms. By presenting a variety of tools and explaining their pros and cons, students will gain the capability to apply this knowledge no matter what operational setting they encounter.

Consider how operations tools can be applied to a call center. A common problem in this industry is to find an appropriate number of customer service representatives to answer incoming calls. The more representatives we hire, the less likely incoming calls will have to wait; thus, the higher will be the level of service we provide. However, labor is the single largest driver of costs in a call center, so, obviously, having more representatives on duty also will increase the costs we incur per call.

The first use of operations management tools is to ensure that resources are used as effectively as possible. Assume we engage in a benchmarking initiative with three other call

FIGURE 1.1
Local Improvement of Operations by Eliminating Inefficiencies

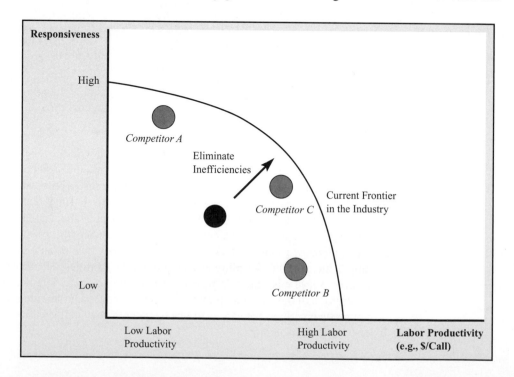

centers and find that the performance of our competitors behaves according to Figure 1.1: Competitor A is providing faster response times but also has higher costs. Competitor B has longer response times but has lower costs. Surprisingly, we find that competitor C outperforms us on both cost and service level. How can this be?

It must be that there is something that competitor C does in the operation of the call center that is smarter than what we do. Or, in other words, there is something that we do in our operations that is inefficient or wasteful. In this setting, we need to use our tools to move the firm toward the frontier illustrated in Figure 1.1. The frontier is the line that includes all benchmarks to the lower left; that is, no firm is outside the current frontier. For example, a premium service might be an important element of our business strategy, so we may choose not to compromise on service. And, we could have a target that at least 90 percent of the incoming calls will be served within 10 seconds or less. But given that target, we should use our quantitative tools to ensure that our labor costs are as low as possible, that is, that we are at least on the efficiency frontier.

The second use of operations management tools is to find the right balance between our competing objectives, high service and low cost. This is similar to what is shown in Figure 1.2. In such a situation, we need to quantify the costs of waiting as well as the costs of labor and then recommend the most profitable compromise between these two objectives.

Moving to the frontier of efficiency and finding the right spot on the frontier are surely important. But outstanding companies do not stop there. The third use for our operations management tools is to fundamentally question the design of the current system itself. For example, a call center might consider merging with or acquiring another call center to gain scale economies. Alternatively, a call center might consider an investment in the development of a new technology leading to shorter call durations.

In such cases, a firm pushes the envelope, that is, moves the frontier of what previously was feasible (see Figure 1.3). Hence, a firm is able to achieve faster responsiveness and higher labor productivity. But, unfortunately, there are few free lunches: while we have improved both customer service and labor productivity, pushing out the frontier generally

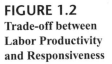

FIGURE 1.2
Trade-off between Labor Productivity and Responsiveness

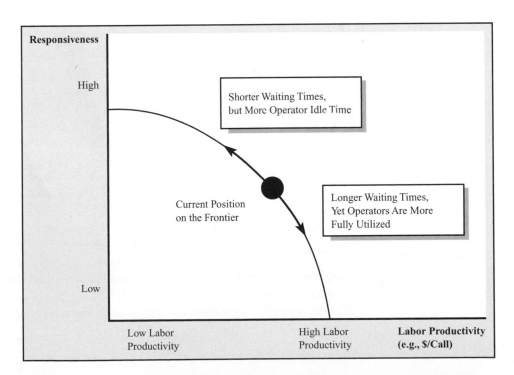

FIGURE 1.3
Redesigning the
Process to Operate at
an Improved Frontier

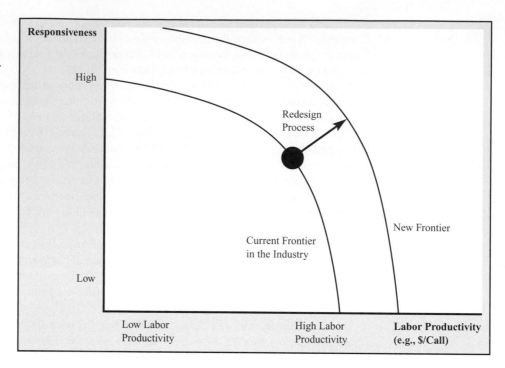

requires some investments in time and effort. Hence, we need to use our tools to quantify the improvements we can achieve so that we can decide whether the effort is justifiable. It is easy to tell a firm that investing in technology can lead to shorter call durations, faster service, and higher labor productivity, but is that investment worthwhile? Our objective is to educate managers so that they can provide "big ideas" and can back them up with rigorous analysis.

1.2   Road Map of the Book

This book can be roughly divided into five clusters of closely related chapters.

The first cluster, Chapters 2–5, analyzes business processes (the methods and procedures by which a service is completed or a good is produced). For the most part, the view taken in those chapters is one of process without variability in service times, production times, demand arrival, quality, and so forth. Hence, the objective is to organize the business process to maximize supply given the resources available to the firm.

Chapters 6–8 introduce variability into business process analysis. Issues include the presence of waiting times, lost demand due to poor service, and lost output due to poor quality. This cluster concludes with an overview of the Toyota Production System.

Chapters 9–12 discuss inventory control, information management, and process flexibility. Issues include demand forecasting, stocking quantities, performance measures, product design, and production flexibility.

Chapter 13 departs from a focus on the supply process and turns attention to the demand process. In particular, the chapter covers the tools of revenue management that allow a firm to better match its demand to its fixed supply.

Chapter 14 concludes the book with key issues in the management and coordination of the supply chain.

Table 1.2 summarizes these clusters.

TABLE 1.2
A High-Level
Grouping of
Chapters

Chapters	Theme
2–5	Process analysis without variability in service times, production rates, demand arrival, quality, etc.
6–8	Process analysis with variability in service times, production rates, demand arrival, quality, etc.
9–12	Inventory control, information management, process flexibility
13	Revenue management
14	Supply chain management

The following provides a more detailed summary of the contents of each chapter:

• Chapter 2 defines a process, introduces the basic process performance metrics, and provides a framework for characterizing processes (the product–process matrix). Little's Law is introduced, an essential formula for understanding business processes and the link between operations management and financial accounting.

• Chapter 3 introduces process analysis tools from the perspective of a manager (as opposed to an engineer): how to determine the capacity of a process and how to compute process utilization.

• Chapter 4 looks at assembly operations with a specific focus on labor costs, an extremely important performance metric. It frequently drives location decisions (consider the current debate related to offshoring) and has—especially in service operations—a major impact on the bottom line. We define measures such as labor content, labor utilization, and idle time. We also introduce the concept of line balancing.

• Chapter 5 studies production in the presence of setup times and setup costs (the EOQ model). A key issue is the impact of product variety on production performance.

• Chapter 6 explores the consequences of variability on a process. As we will discuss in the context of a call center, variability can lead to long customer waiting times and thereby is a key enemy in all service organizations. We discuss how an organization should handle the trade-off between a desire for minimizing the investment into capacity (e.g., customer service representatives) while achieving a good service experience for the customer.

• Chapter 7 continues the discussion of variability and its impact on service quality. As we will discuss in the context of emergency medicine, variability frequently can lead to situations in which demand has to be turned away because of insufficient capacity. This has substantial implications, especially in the health care environment.

• Chapter 8 details the tools of quality management (e.g., statistical process control) and describes how Toyota, via its world-famous collection of production strategies called the Toyota Production System, achieves high quality and low costs.

• Chapter 9 focuses on the management of seasonal goods with only one supply opportunity. The newsvendor model allows a manager to strike the correct balance between too much supply and too little supply.

• Chapter 10 expands upon the setting of the previous chapter by allowing additional supply to occur in the middle of the selling season. This "reactive capacity" allows a firm to better respond to early season sales information.

• Chapter 11 continues the discussion of inventory management with the introduction of lead times. The order-up-to model is used to choose replenishment quantities that achieve target availability levels (such as an in-stock probability or a fill rate).

• Chapter 12 highlights numerous risk-pooling strategies to improve inventory management within the supply chain: for example, location pooling, product pooling, universal design, delayed differentiation (also known as postponement), and capacity pooling.

• Chapter 13 covers revenue management. In particular, the focus is on the use of booking limits and overbooking to better match demand to supply when supply is fixed.

• Chapter 14 identifies the bullwhip effect as a key issue in the effective operation of a supply chain and offers coordination strategies for firms to improve the performance of their supply chain.

Some of the chapters are designed to be "entry level" chapters, that is, chapters that can be read independently from the rest of the text. Other chapters are more advanced, so they at least require some working knowledge of the material in another chapter. Table 1.3 summarizes the contents of the chapters and indicates prerequisite chapters.

TABLE 1.3   Chapter Summaries and Prerequisites

Chapter	Managerial Issue	Key Qualitative Framework	Key Quantitative Tool	Prerequisite Chapters
2: The Process View of the Organization	Understanding business processes at a high level; process performance measures inventory, flow time, and flow rate	Product–process matrix; focus on process flows	Little's law Inventory turns and inventory costs	None
3: Understanding the Supply Process: Evaluating Process Capacity	Understanding the details of a process	Process flow diagram; finding and removing a bottleneck	Computing process capacity and utilization	Chapter 2
4: Estimating and Reducing Labor Costs	Labor costs	Line balancing; division of labor	Computing labor costs, labor utilization Minimizing idle time	Chapters 2, 3
5: Batching and Other Flow Interruptions: Set-up Times and the Economic Order Quantity Model	Set-up time and set-up costs; managing product variety	Achieving a smooth process flow; deciding about set-ups and ordering frequency	EOQ model Determining batch sizes	Chapters 2, 3
6: Variability and Its Impact on Process Performance: Waiting Time Problems	Waiting times in service processes	Understanding congestion; pooling service capacity	Waiting time formula	None
7: The Impact of Variability on Process Performance: Throughput Losses	Lost demand in service processes	Role of service buffers; pooling	Erlang loss formula Probability of diverting demand	Chapter 6
8: Quality Management and the Toyota Production System	Defining and improving quality	Statistical process control; six sigma; Toyota Production System	Computing process capability; creating a control chart	None
9: Betting on Uncertain Demand: The Newsvendor Model	Choosing stocking levels for seasonal-style goods	Improving the forecasting process	Forecasting demand The newsvendor model for choosing stocking quantities and evaluating performance measures	None

(continued)

TABLE 1.3 Continued

Chapter	Managerial Issue	Key Qualitative Framework	Key Quantitative Tool	Prerequisite Chapters
10: Make-to-Order and Quick Response with Reactive Capacity	How to use reactive capacity to reduce demand–supply mismatch costs	Value of better demand information; assemble-to-order and make-to-order strategies	Reactive capacity models	Chapter 9
11: Service Levels and Lead Times in Supply Chains: The Order-up-to Model	Inventory management with numerous replenishments	Impact of lead times on performance; how to choose an appropriate objective function	The order-up-to model for inventory management and performance measure evaluation	Chapter 9 is highly recommended
12: Risk Pooling Strategies to Reduce and Hedge Uncertainty	How to better design the supply chain or a product or a service to better match supply with demand	Quantifying, reducing, avoiding, and hedging uncertainty	Newsvendor and order-up-to models	Chapters 9 and 11
13: Revenue Management with Capacity Controls	How to manage demand when supply is fixed	Reserving capacity for high-paying customers; accepting more reservations than available capacity	Booking limit/protection level model; overbooking model	Chapter 9
14: Supply Chain Coordination	How to manage demand variability and inventory across the supply chain	Bullwhip effect; supply chain contracts	Supply chain contract model	Chapter 9

2

The Process View of the Organization

Matching supply and demand would be easy if business processes would be instantaneous and could immediately create any amount of supply to meet demand. Understanding the questions of "Why are business processes not instantaneous?" and "What constrains processes from creating more supply?" is thereby at the heart of operations management. To answer these questions, we need to take a detailed look at how business processes actually work. In this chapter, we introduce some concepts fundamental to process analysis. The key idea of the chapter is that it is not sufficient for a firm to create great products and services; the firm also must design and improve its business processes that supply its products and services.

To get more familiar with the process view of a firm, we now take a detailed look behind the scenes of a particular operation, namely the Department of Interventional Radiology at Presbyterian Hospital in Philadelphia.

2.1   Presbyterian Hospital Philadelphia

Interventional radiology is a subspecialty field of radiology that uses advanced imaging techniques such as real-time X-rays, ultrasound, computed tomography, and magnetic resonance imaging to perform minimally invasive procedures.

Over the past decade, interventional radiology procedures have begun to replace an increasing number of standard "open surgical procedures" for a number of reasons. Instead of being performed in an operating room, interventional radiology procedures are performed in an angiography suite (see Figure 2.1). Although highly specialized, these rooms are less expensive to operate than conventional operating rooms. Interventional procedures are often safer and have dramatically shorter recovery times compared to traditional surgery. Also, an interventional radiologist is often able to treat diseases such as advanced liver cancer that cannot be helped by standard surgery.

Although we may not have been in the interventional radiology unit, many, if not most, of us have been in a radiology department of a hospital at some point in our life. From the perspective of the patient, the following steps need to take place before the patient can go home or return to his or her hospital unit. In process analysis, we refer to these steps as *activities:*

- Registration of the patient.
- Initial consultation with a doctor; signature of the consent form.
- Preparation for the procedure.

FIGURE 2.1
**Example of a
Procedure in an
Interventional
Radiology Unit**

Reprinted with permission of
Arrow International, Inc.

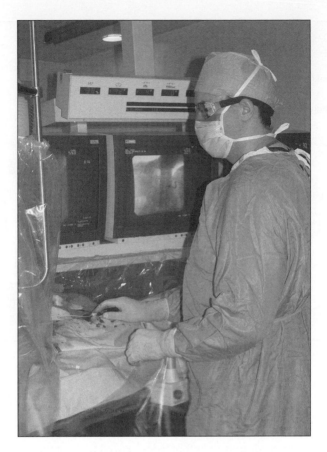

- The actual procedure.
- Removal of all equipment.
- Recovery in an area outside the angiography suite.
- Consultation with the doctor.

Figure 2.2 includes a graphical representation of these steps, called a *Gantt diagram* (named after the 19th century industrialist Henry Gantt). It provides several useful pieces of information.

First, the Gantt chart allows us to see the process steps and their durations, which are also called *activity times*. The duration simply corresponds to the length of the corresponding bars. Second, the Gantt diagram also illustrates the dependence between the various process activities. For example, the consultation with the doctor can only occur once the patient has arrived and been registered. In contrast, the preparation of the angiography suite can proceed in parallel to the initial consultation.

You might have come across Gantt charts in the context of project management. Unlike process analysis, project management is typically concerned with the completion of one single project. The most well-known concept of project management is the *critical path*. The critical path is composed of all those activities that—if delayed—would lead to a delay in the overall completion time of the project, or—in this case—the time the patient has completed his or her stay in the radiology unit.

In addition to the eight steps described in the Gantt chart of Figure 2.2, most of us associate another activity with hospital care: waiting. Strictly speaking, waiting is not really

FIGURE 2.2
Gantt Chart Summarizing the Activities for Interventional Radiology

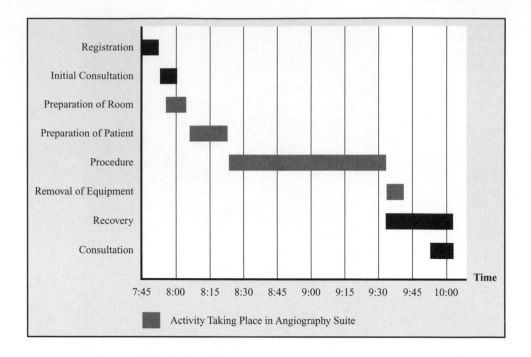

an activity, as it does not add any value to the process. However, waiting is nevertheless relevant. It is annoying for the patient and can complicate matters for the hospital unit. For this reason, waiting times take an important role in operations management. Figure 2.3 shows the actual durations of the activities for a patient arriving at 12:30, as well as the time the patient needs to wait before being moved to the angiography suite.

But why is there waiting time? Waiting is—to stay in the medical language for the moment—a symptom of supply–demand mismatch. If supply would be unlimited, our visit to the hospital would be reduced to the duration of the activities outlined in Figure 2.2 (the critical path). Imagine visiting a hospital in which all the nurses, technicians, doctors, and hospital administrators would just care for you!

Given that few of us are in a position to receive the undivided attention of an entire hospital unit, it is important that we not only take the egocentric perspective of the patient, but look at the hospital operations more broadly. From the perspective of the hospital, there are many patients "flowing" through the process.

The people and the equipment necessary to support the interventional radiology process deal with many patients, not just one. We refer to these elements of the process as the *process resources.* Consider, for example, the perspective of the nurse and how she/he spends her/his time in the department of interventional radiology. Obviously, radiology from the viewpoint of the nurse is not an exceptional event, but a rather repetitive endeavor. Some of the nurse's work involves direct interaction with the patient; other work—while required for the patient—is invisible to the patient. This includes the preparation of the angiography suite and various aspects of medical record keeping.

Given this repetitive nature of work, the nurse as well as the doctors, technicians, and hospital administrators think of interventional radiology as a process, not a project. Over the course of the day, they see many patients come and go. Many hospitals, including the Presbyterian Hospital in Philadelphia, have a "patient log" that summarizes at what times patients arrive at the unit. This patient log provides a picture of demand on the corresponding day. The patient log for December 2, 2002, is summarized by Table 2.1.

FIGURE 2.3
Gantt Chart
Summarizing the
Activities for a
Patient Arriving at
12:30

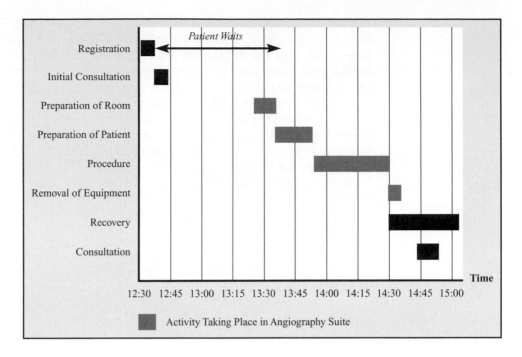

Many of these arrivals were probably scheduled some time in advance. Our analysis here focuses on what happens to the patient once he/she has arrived in the interventional radiology unit. A separate analysis could be performed, looking at the process starting with a request for diagnostics up to the arrival of the patient.

Given that the resources in the interventional radiology unit have to care for 11 patients on December 2, they basically need to complete the work according to 11 Gantt charts of the type outlined in Figure 2.2. This—in turn—can lead to waiting times. Waiting times arise when several patients are "competing" for the same limited resource, which is illustrated by the following two examples.

First, observe that the critical path for a typical patient takes about 2 hours. Note further that we want to care for 11 patients over a 10-hour workday. Consequently, we will have to take care of several patients at once. This would not be a problem if we had unlimited resources, nurses, doctors, space in the angiography suites, and so forth. However, given the resources that we have, if the Gantt charts of two patients are requesting the same resource

TABLE 2.1
Patient Log on
December 2, 2002

Number	Patient Name	Arrival Time	Room Assignment
1		7:35	Main room
2		7:45	
3		8:10	
4		9:30	Main room
5		10:15	Main room
6		10:30	Main room
7		11:05	
8		12:35	Main room
9		14:30	Main room
10		14:35	
11		14:40	

simultaneously, waiting times result. For example, the second patient might require the initial consultation with the doctor at a time when the doctor is in the middle of the procedure for patient 1. Note also that patients 1, 4, 5, 6, 8, and 9 are assigned to the same room (the unit has a main room and a second room used for simpler cases), and thus they are also potentially competing for the same resource.

A second source of waiting time lies in the unpredictable nature of many of the activities. Some patients will take much longer in the actual procedure than others. For example, patient 1 spent 1:30 hours in the procedure, while patient 9 was in the procedure for 2:15 hours (see Figure 2.4). As an extreme case, consider patient 5, who refused to sign the consent form and left the process after only 15 minutes.

Such uncertainty is undesirable for resources, as it leaves them "flooded" with work at some moments in the day and "starved" for work at other moments. Figure 2.5 summarizes at what moments in time the angiography suite was used on December 2.

By now, we have established two views to the interventional radiology:

• The view of the patient for whom the idealized stay is summarized by Figure 2.2. Mismatches between supply and demand from the patient's perspective means having a unit of demand (i.e., the patient) wait for a unit of supply (a resource).

• The view of the resources (summarized by Figure 2.5), which experience demand–supply mismatches when they are sometimes "flooded" with work, followed by periods of no work.

As these two perspectives are ultimately two sides of the same coin, we are interested in bringing these two views together. This is the fundamental idea of process analysis.

FIGURE 2.4
Time Patient Spent in the Interventional Radiology Unit (for Patients Treated in Main Room Only), Including Room Preparation Time

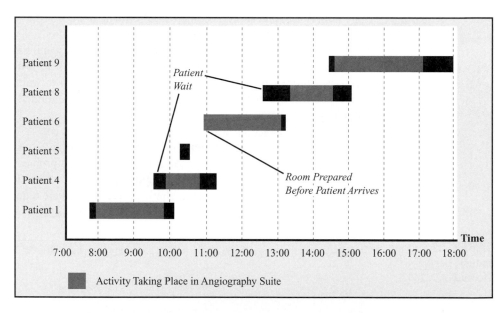

FIGURE 2.5
Usage of the Main Room

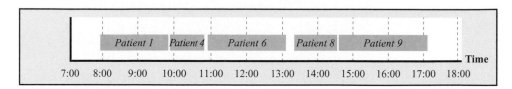

2.2 Three Measures of Process Performance

At the most aggregate level, a process can be thought of as a "black box" that uses *resources* (labor and capital) to transform *inputs* (undiagnosed patients, raw materials, unserved customers) into *outputs* (diagnosed patients, finished goods, served customers). This is shown in Figure 2.6. Chapter 3 explains the details of constructing figures like Figure 2.6, which are called *process flow diagrams.* When analyzing the processes that lead to the supply of goods and services, we first define our unit of analysis.

In the case of the interventional radiology unit, we choose patients as our *flow unit.* Choosing the flow unit is typically determined by the type of product or service the supply process is dealing with; for example, vehicles in an auto plant, travelers for an airline, or gallons of beer in a brewery.

As suggested by the term, flow units flow through the process, starting as input and later leaving the process as output. With the appropriate flow unit defined, we next can evaluate a process based on three fundamental process performance measures:

• The number of flow units contained within the process is called the *inventory* (in a production setting, it is referred to as *work in process, WIP*). Given that our focus is not only on production processes, inventory could take the form of the number of insurance claims or the number of tax returns at the IRS. There are various reasons why we find inventory in processes, which we discuss in greater detail below. While many of us might initially feel uncomfortable with the wording, the inventory in the case of the interventional radiology unit is a group of patients.

• The time it takes a flow unit to get through the process is called the *flow time.* The flow time takes into account that the item (flow unit) may have to wait to be processed because there are other flow units (inventory) in the process potentially competing for the same resources. Flow time is an especially important performance metric in service environments or in other business situations that are sensitive to delays, such as make-to-order production, where the production of the process only begins upon the arrival of the customer order. In a radiology unit, flow time is something that patients are likely to care about: it measures the time from their arrival at the interventional radiology unit to the time patients can go home or return to their hospital unit.

• Finally, the rate at which the process is delivering output (measured in [flow units/unit of time], e.g., units per day) is called the *flow rate* or the *throughput rate.* The maximum rate with which the process can generate supply is called the *capacity* of the process. For December 2, the throughput of the interventional radiology unit was 11 patients per day.

Table 2.2 provides several examples about processes and their corresponding flow rates, inventory levels, and flow times.

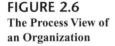

FIGURE 2.6
The Process View of an Organization

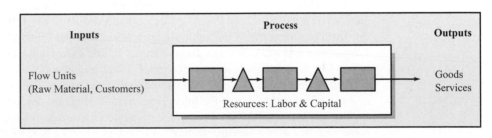

TABLE 2.2
**Examples of Flow
Rates, Inventories,
and Flow Times**

	U.S. Immigration	Champagne Industry	MBA Program	Large PC Manufacturer
Flow unit	Application for immigration benefit	Bottle of champagne	MBA student	Computer
Flow rate/ throughput	Approved or rejected visa cases: 6.3 million per year	260 million bottles per year	600 students per year	5,000 units per day
Flow time	Average processing time: 7.6 months	Average time in cellar: 3.46 years	2 years	10 days
Inventory	Pending cases: 4.0 million cases	900 million bottles	1,200 students	50,000 computers

You might be somewhat irritated that we have moved away from the idea of supply and demand mismatch for a moment. Moreover, we have not talked about profits so far. However, note that increasing the maximum flow rate (capacity) avoids situations where we have insufficient supply to match demand. From a profit perspective, a higher flow rate translates directly into more revenues (you can produce a unit faster and thus can produce more units), assuming your process is currently *capacity constrained,* that is, there is sufficient demand that you could sell any additional output you make.

Shorter flow times reduce the time delay between the occurrence of demand and its fulfillment in the form of supply. Shorter flow times therefore also typically help to reduce demand–supply mismatches. In many industries, shorter flow times also result in additional unit sales and/or higher prices, which makes them interesting also from a broader management perspective.

Lower inventory results in lower working capital requirements as well as many quality advantages that we explore later in this book. A higher inventory also is directly related to longer flow times (explained below). Thus, a reduction in inventory also yields a reduction in flow time. As inventory is the most visible indication of a mismatch between supply and demand, we will now discuss it in greater detail.

2.3   Little's Law

At the end of October 2001, there was approximately $1.16 trillion of inventory in the United States, and the inventory-to-sales ratio was 1.39. About one-third of that inventory was held by retailers, one-fifth by wholesalers, and the remainder by manufacturers. Over one-fourth of retail inventory is in the motor vehicle industry. The good news is that the inventory-to-sales ratio has been dropping over the last decade, from about 1.53 in 1992. The bad news is that there is still an enormous amount of capital tied up in inventory.

Accountants view inventory as an asset, but from an operations perspective, inventory often should be viewed as a liability. This is not a snub on accountants; inventory *should* be an asset on a balance sheet, given how accountants define an asset. But in common speech, the word *asset* means "a desirable thing to have" and the dictionary defines *liability* as "something that works to one's disadvantage." In this sense, inventory can clearly be a liability. This is most visible in a service process such as a hospital unit, where patients in the waiting room obviously cannot be counted toward the assets of the health care system.

Let's take another visit to the interventional radiology unit. Even without much medical expertise, we can quickly find out which of the patients are currently undergoing care from some resource and which are waiting for a resource to take care of them. Similarly, if we took a quick walk through a factory, we could identify which parts of the inventory serve

FIGURE 2.7
Cumulative Inflow and Outflow

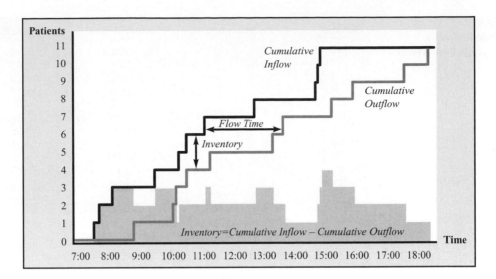

as raw materials, which ones are work-in-process, and which ones have completed the production process and now take the form of finished goods inventory.

However, taking a single walk through the process—dishwasher factory or interventional radiology unit—will not leave us with a good understanding of the underlying operations. All it will give us is a snapshot of what the process looked like at one single moment in time. Unfortunately, it is this same snapshot approach that underlies most management (accounting) reports: balance sheets itemize inventory into three categories (raw materials, WIP, finished goods); hospital administrators typically distinguish between pre- and postoperative patients. But such snapshots do not tell us *why* these inventories exist in the first place! Thus, a static, snapshot approach neither helps us to analyze business processes (why is there inventory?) nor helps us to improve them (is this the right amount of inventory?).

Now, imagine that instead of our single visit to the hospital unit, we would be willing to stay for some longer period of time. We arrive early in the morning and make ourselves comfortable at the entrance of the unit. Knowing that there are no patients in the interventional radiology unit overnight, we then start recording any arrival or departure of patients. In other words, we collect data concerning the patient inflow and outflow.

At the end of our stay, we can plot a graph similar to Figure 2.7. The upper of the two curves illustrates the cumulative number of patients who have entered the unit. The curve begins at time zero (7:00) and with zero patients. If we had done the same exercise in a unit with overnight patients, we would have recorded our initial patient count there. The lower of the two curves indicates the cumulative number of patients who have left the unit. Figure 2.7 shows us that by noon, seven patients have arrived, of which five have left the unit again.

At any given moment in time, the *vertical distance* between the upper curve and the lower curve corresponds to the number of patients in the interventional radiology unit, or—abstractly speaking—the inventory level. Thus, although we have not been inside the interventional radiology unit this day, we are able to keep track of the inventory level by comparing the cumulative inflow and outflow. For example, the inventory at noon consisted of two patients.

We also can look at the *horizontal distance* between the two lines. If the patients leave the unit in the same order they entered it, the horizontal gap would measure the exact amount of time each patient spent in the interventional radiology unit. More generally,

TABLE 2.3
Calculation of
Average Flow Time

Number	Patient Name	Arrival Time	Departure Time	Flow Time
1		7:35	8:50	1:15
2		7:45	10:05	2:20
3		8:10	10:10	2:00
4		9:30	11:15	1:45
5		10:15	10:30	0:15
6		10:30	13:35	3:05
7		11:05	13:15	2:10
8		12:35	15:05	2:30
9		14:30	18:10	3:40
10		14:35	15:45	1:10
11		14:40	17:20	2:40
			Average	2:04:33

given that the length of stay might vary across patients and patients do not necessarily leave the unit in the exact same sequence in which they entered it, the average gap between the two lines provides the average length of stay.

Thus, Figure 2.7 includes all three of the basic process performance measures we discussed on the previous page: flow rate (the slope of the two graphs), inventory (the vertical distance between the two graphs), and flow time (the horizontal distance between the two graphs).

Based on either the graph or the patient log, we can now compute these performance measures for December 2. We already know that the flow rate was 11 patients/day.

Next, consider inventory. Inventory changes throughout the day, reflecting the differences between inflow and outflow of patients. A "brute force" approach to compute average inventory is to count the inventory at every moment in time throughout the day, say every five minutes, and then take the average. For December 2, this computation yields an average inventory of 2.076 patients.

Next, consider the flow time, the time a patient spends in the unit. To compute that information, we need to add to the patient log, Table 2.1, the time each patient left the interventional radiology unit. The difference between arrival time and departure time would be the flow time for a given patient, which in turn would allow us to compute the average flow time across patients. This is shown in Table 2.3 and is in many ways similar to the two graphs in Figure 2.7. We can easily compute that on December 2, the average flow time was 2 hours, 4 minutes, and 33 seconds, or 2.076 hours.

At this point, you might ask: "Does the average inventory always come out the same as the average flow time?" The answer to this question is a profound *no*. However, the fact that the average inventory was 2.076 patients and the average flow time was 2.076 hours is no coincidence either.

To see how inventory and flow time relate to each other, let us review the three performance measures, flow rate, flow time, and inventory:

- Flow rate = 11 patients per day, which is equal to one patient per hour.
- Flow time = 2.076 hours.
- Inventory = 2.076 patients.

Thus, while inventory and flow time do not have to—and in fact rarely are—equal, they are linked in another form. We will now introduce this relationship as Little's Law (named after John D. C. Little).

$$\text{Average inventory} = \text{Average flow rate} \times \text{Average flow time} \quad \text{(Little's Law)}$$

Many people think of this relationship as trivial. However, it is not. Its proof is rather complex for the general case (which includes—among other nasty things—variability) and by mathematical standards is very recent.

Little's Law is useful in finding the third performance measure when the other two are known. For example, if you want to find out how long patients in a radiology unit spend waiting for their chest X-ray, you could do the following:

1. Observe the inventory of patients at a couple of random points during the day, giving you an average inventory. Let's say this number is seven patients: four in the waiting room, two already changed and waiting in front of the procedure room, and one in the procedure room.

2. Count the procedure slips or any other records showing how many patients were treated that day. This is the day's output. Let's say there were 60 patients over a period of 8 hours; we could say that we have a flow rate of 60/8 = 7.5 patients/hour.

3. Use Little's Law to compute Flow time = Inventory/Flow rate = 7/7.5 = 0.933 hour = 56 minutes. This tells us that, on average, it takes 56 minutes from the time a patient enters the radiology unit to the time his or her chest X-ray is completed. Note that this information would otherwise have to be computed by collecting additional data (e.g., see Table 2.3).

When does Little's Law hold? The short answer is *always*. For example, Little's Law does not depend on the sequence in which the flow units (e.g., patients) are served (remember FIFO and LIFO from your accounting class?). (However, the sequence could influence the flow time of a particular flow unit, e.g., the patient arriving first in the morning, but not the average flow time across all flow units.) Furthermore, Little's Law does not depend on randomness: it does not matter if there is variability in the number of patients or in how long treatment takes for each patient; all that matters is the average flow rate of patients and the average flow time.

In addition to the direct application of Little's Law, for example, in the computation of flow time, Little's Law is also underlying the computation of inventory costs as well as a concept known as inventory turns. This is discussed in the following section.

2.4 Inventory Turns and Inventory Costs

Using physical units as flow units (and, hence, as the inventory measure) is probably the most intuitive way to measure inventory. This could be vehicles at an auto retailer, patients in the hospital, or tons of oil in a refinery.

However, working with physical units is not necessarily the best method for obtaining an aggregate measure of inventory across different products: there is little value to saying you have 2,000 units of inventory if 1,000 of them are paper clips and the remaining 1,000 are computers. In such applications, inventory is often measured in some monetary unit, for example, $5 million worth of inventory.

Measuring inventory in a common monetary unit facilitates the aggregation of inventory across different products. This is why total U.S. inventory is reported in dollars. To illustrate the notion of monetary flow units, consider Kmart, a large U.S. retailer. Instead of thinking of Kmart's stores as sodas, toys, clothes, and bathroom tissues (physical units), we can think of its stores as processes transforming goods valued in monetary units into sales, which also can be evaluated in the form of monetary units.

As can easily be seen from Kmart's balance sheet, on January 29, 2002, the company held an inventory valued at $4.825 billion (see Table 2.4). Given that our flow unit now is the "individual dollar bill," we want to measure the flow rate through Kmart's operation.

TABLE 2.4 **Excerpts from Financial Statements of Kmart and Wal-Mart**

Source: Taken from 10-K filings.

	January 28, 1998	January 27, 1999	January 26, 2000	January 31, 2001	January 29, 2002
Kmart Corp.					
Inventory	$6,367,000,000	$6,536,000,000	$6,350,000,000	$5,796,000,000	$4,825,000,000
Income					
Total operating					
revenue	$33,674,000,000	$35,925,000,000	$37,028,000,000	$36,151,000,000	$30,762,000,000
Cost of goods sold	$26,319,000,000	$28,161,000,000	$29,732,000,000	$29,853,000,000	$26,258,000,000
Net income	$518,000,000	$364,000,000	($268,000,000)	($2,446,000,000)	($3,219,000,000)
Wal-Mart Stores Inc.					
Inventory	$16,497,000,000	$17,076,000,000	$19,793,000,000	$21,644,000,000	$22,749,000,000
Income					
Net sales	$117,958,000,000	$137,634,000,000	$165,013,000,000	$191,329,000,000	$217,799,000,000
Total operating					
revenue	$119,299,000,000	$139,208,000,000	$166,809,000,000	$193,295,000,000	$219,812,000
Cost of goods sold	$93,438,000,000	$108,725,000,000	$129,664,000,000	$150,255,000,000	$171,562,000,000
Net income	$3,526,000,000	$4,430,000,000	$5,377,000,000	$6,295,000,000	$6,671,000,000

The direct approach would be to take "sales" as the resulting flow. Yet, this measure is inflated by Kmart's gross profit margin; that is, a dollar of sales is measured in sales dollars, while a dollar of inventory is measured, given the present accounting practice, in a cost dollar. Thus, the appropriate measure for flow rate is the cost of goods sold, or COGS for short.

With these two measures—flow rate and inventory—we can apply Little's Law to compute what initially might seem a rather artificial measure: how long does the average flow unit (dollar bill) spend within the Kmart system before being turned into sales, at which point the flow units will trigger a profit intake. This corresponds to the definition of flow time.

$$\text{Flow rate} = \text{Cost of goods sold} = \$26{,}258 \text{ million/year}$$

$$\text{Inventory} = \$4{,}825 \text{ million}$$

Hence, we can compute flow time via Little's Law as

$$\text{Flow time} = \frac{\text{Inventory}}{\text{Flow rate}}$$

$$= \$4{,}825 \text{ million}/\$26{,}258 \text{ million/year} = 0.18 \text{ year} = 67 \text{ days}$$

Thus, we find that it takes Kmart—on average—67 days to translate a dollar investment into a dollar of—hopefully profitable—revenues. Note that if we conducted a similar analysis for the previous years, we would find that Kmart has improved this metric considerably from 1998 to 2002 (e.g., it took 88 days in 1998).

This calculation underlies the definition of another way of measuring inventory, namely in terms of *days of supply*. We could say that Kmart has 67 days of inventory in their process. In other words, the average item we find at Kmart spends 67 days in Kmart's supply chain.

Alternatively, we could say that Kmart turns over its inventory 365 days/year/67 days = 5.44 times per year. This measure is called *inventory turns*. Inventory turns is a common benchmark in the retailing environment and other supply chain operations:

$$\text{Inventory turns} = \frac{1}{\text{Flow time}}$$

To illustrate this application of Little's Law further, consider Wal-Mart, Kmart's strongest competitor. Repeating the same calculations as outlined on the previous page, we find the following data about Wal-Mart:

Cost of goods sold $= \$171,562$ million/year

Inventory $= \$22,749$ million

Flow time $= \$22,749$ million/$\$171,562$ million/year

$= 0.13$ year $= 48.4$ days

Inventory turns $= 1/48.4$ turns/day

$= 365$ days/year $\times 1/48.4$ turns/day $= 7.54$ turns per year

Thus, we find that Wal-Mart is able to achieve substantially higher inventory turns than Kmart. Table 2.5 summarizes inventory turn data for various segments of the retailing industry. Table 2.5 also provides information about gross margins in various retail settings (keep them in mind the next time you haggle for a new sofa or watch!).

Inventory requires substantial financial investments: the debt service on $1.16 trillion in the U.S. economy is obviously rather substantial even if the inventory is financed at an attractive rate of 10 percent. Yet, most companies would not be happy with a return on assets of 10 percent. Moreover, the inventory holding cost is substantially higher than the mere financial holding cost for a number of reasons:

- Inventory might become obsolete (think of the annual holding cost of a microprocessor).
- Inventory might physically perish (you don't want to think of the cost of holding fresh roses for a year).
- Inventory might disappear (also known as theft or shrink).
- Inventory requires storage space and other overhead cost (insurance, security, real-estate, etc).
- There are other less tangible costs of inventory that result from increased wait times (because of Little's Law, to be discussed in chapter 6) and lower quality (to be discussed in chapter 8).

Given an annual cost of inventory (e.g., 30 percent per year) and the inventory turn information as computed above, we can compute the per-unit inventory cost that a process (or

TABLE 2.5
Inventory Turns and Margins for Selected Retail Segments

Source: Based on Gaur et al. 2002.

Retail Segment	Examples	Annual Inventory Turns	Gross Margin
Apparel and accessory	Ann Taylor, GAP	4.57	37%
Catalog, mail-order	Spiegel, Lands End	8.60	39%
Department stores	Sears, JCPenney	3.87	34%
Drug and proprietary stores	Rite Aid, CVS	5.26	28%
Food stores	Albertson's, Safeway	10.78	26%
Hobby, toy/game stores	Toys R Us	2.99	35%
Home furniture/equipment	Bed Bath & Beyond, Linens N' Things	5.44	40%
Jewelry	Tiffany	1.68	42%
Radio, TV, consumer electronics	Best Buy, Circuit City, CompUSA	4.10	31%
Variety stores	Kmart, Wal-Mart, Target	4.45	29%

Exhibit 2.1

CALCULATING INVENTORY TURNS AND PER-UNIT INVENTORY COSTS

1. Look up the value of inventory from the balance sheet.
2. Look up the cost of goods sold (COGS) from the earnings statement; do *not* use sales!
3. Compute inventory turns as

$$\text{Inventory turns} = \frac{\text{COGS}}{\text{Inventory}}$$

4. Compute per-unit inventory costs as

$$\text{Per-unit inventory costs} = \frac{\text{Annual inventory costs}}{\text{Inventory turns}}$$

Note: The annual inventory cost needs to account for the cost of financing the inventory, the cost of depreciation, and other inventory-related costs the firm considers relevant (e.g., storage, theft).

a supply chain) incurs. To do this, we take the annual holding cost and divide it by the number of times the inventory turns in a year:

$$\text{Per-unit inventory cost} = \frac{\text{Annual inventory costs}}{\text{Annual inventory turns}}$$

For example, a company that works based on a 20 percent annual inventory cost and that turns its inventory six times per year incurs per-unit inventory costs of

$$\frac{20\% \text{ per year}}{6 \text{ turns per year}} = 3.33\%$$

In the case of Kmart (we earlier computed that the inventory turns 5.44 times per year), and assuming annual holding costs of 20 percent per year, this translates to inventory costs of more than 3.68 percent of the cost of goods sold (20%/5.44 = 3.68). The calculations to obtain per unit inventory costs are summarized in Exhibit 2.1.

To stay in the retailing context a little longer, consider a retailer of consumer electronics who has annual inventory costs of 30 percent (driven by financial costs and obsolescence). Assuming the retailer turns its inventory about four times per year (see Table 2.5.), we obtain a per-unit inventory cost of 30%/4 = 7.5%. Consider a TV in the retailer's assortment that is on the shelf with a price tag of $300 and is procured by the retailer for $200. Based on our calculation, we know that the retailer incurs a $200 × 7.5% = $15 inventory cost for each such TV that is sold. To put this number into perspective, consider Figure 2.8.

Figure 2.8 plots the relationship between gross margin and inventory turns for consumer electronics retailers (based on Gaur et al. 2002). Note that this graph does not imply causality in this relationship. That is, the model does not imply that if a firm increases its gross margin, its inventory turns will decline commensurately. Instead, the way to look at Figure 2.8 is to think of gross margin for a given set of products as being fixed by the competitive environment. We can then make two interesting observations:

FIGURE 2.8
Relationship between Inventory Turns and Gross Margin

Source: Based on Gaur et al. 2002.

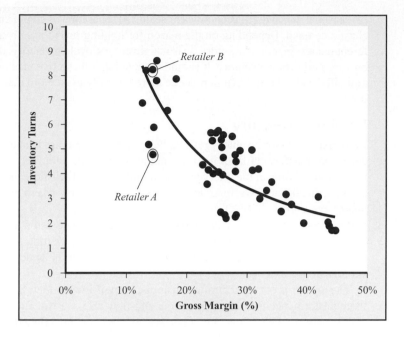

- A retailer can decide to specialize in products that turn very slowly to increase its margins. For example, Radio Shack is known for its high margins, as they carry many products in their assortment that turn only once or twice a year. In contrast, Best Buy is carrying largely very popular items, which exposes the company to stiffer competition and lower gross margins.

- For a given gross margin, we observe dramatic differences concerning inventory turns. For example, inventory turns vary between four and nine times for a 15 percent gross margin. Consider retailer A and assume that all retailers work with a 30 percent annual holding cost. Based on the annual inventory turns of 4.5, retailer A faces a 6.66 percent per-unit inventory cost. Now, compare this to competing retailer B, who turns its inventory eight times per year. Thus, retailer B operates with 3.75 percent per-unit inventory costs, almost a 3 percent cost advantage over retailer A. Given that net profits in this industry segment are around 2 percent of sales, such a cost advantage can make the difference between profits and bankruptcy.

2.5   Five Reasons to Hold Inventory

While Little's Law allows us to compute the average inventory in the process (as long as we know flow time and flow rate), it offers no help in answering the question we raised previously: Why is there inventory in the process in the first place? To understand the need for inventory, we can no longer afford to take the black-box perspective and look at processes from the outside. Instead, we have to look at the process in much more detail.

As we saw from Figure 2.7, inventory reflected a deviation between the inflow into a process and its outflow. Ideally, from an operations perspective, we would like Figure 2.7 to take the shape of two identical, straight lines, representing process inflow and outflow. Unfortunately, such straight lines with zero distance between them rarely exist in the real world. De Groote (1994) discusses five reasons for holding inventory, that is, for having the inflow line differ from the outflow line: (1) the time a flow unit spends in the process;

(2) seasonal demand; (3) economies of scale; (4) separation of steps in a process; and (5) stochastic demand. Depending on the reason for holding inventory, inventories are given different names: pipeline inventory, seasonal inventory, cycle inventory, decoupling inventory/buffers, and safety inventory. It should be noted that these five reasons are not necessarily mutually exclusive and that in practice there typically exist more than one reason for holding inventory.

Pipeline Inventory

This first reason for inventory reflects the time a flow unit has to spend in the process in order to be transformed from input to output. Even with unlimited resources, patients still need to spend time in the interventional radiology unit; their flow time would be the length of the critical path. We refer to this basic inventory on which the process operates as *pipeline inventory.*

For the sake of simplicity, let's assume that every patient would have to spend exactly 1.5 hours in the interventional radiology unit, as opposed to waiting for a resource to become available, and that we have one patient arrive every hour. How do we find the pipeline inventory in this case?

The answer is obtained through an application of Little's Law. Since we know two of the three performance measures, flow time and flow rate, we can figure out the third, in this case inventory: with a flow rate of one patient per hour and a flow time of 1.5 hours, the average inventory is

$$\text{Inventory} = 1[\text{patients/hour}] \times 1.5[\text{hours}] = 1.5 \text{ patients}$$

which is the number of patients undergoing some value-adding activity. This is illustrated by Figure 2.9.

In certain environments, you might hear managers make statements of the type "we need to achieve zero inventory in our process." If we substitute Inventory = 0 into Little's Law, the immediate result is that a process with zero inventory is also a process with zero flow rate (unless we have zero flow time, which means that the process does not do anything to the flow unit). Thus, as long as it takes an operation even a minimum amount of time to work on a flow unit, the process will always exhibit pipeline inventory. There can be no hospital without patients and no factory can operate without some work in process!

Little's Law also points us toward the best way to reduce pipeline inventory. As reducing flow rate (and with it demand and profit) is typically not a desirable option, the *only* other way to reduce pipeline inventory is by reducing flow time.

FIGURE 2.9
Pipeline Inventory

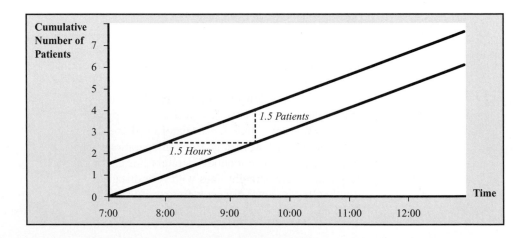

Seasonal Inventory

Seasonal inventory occurs when capacity is rigid and demand is variable. Two examples illustrate this second reason for inventory. Campbell's Soup sells more chicken noodle soup in January than in any other month of the year (see Chapter 14)—not primarily because of cold weather, but because Campbell's discounts chicken noodle soup in January. June is the next biggest sales month, because Campbell's increases its price in July.

So much soup is sold in January that Campbell's starts production several months in advance and builds inventory in anticipation of January sales. Campbell's could wait longer to start production and thereby not build as much inventory, but it would be too costly to assemble the needed capacity (equipment and labor) in the winter only to dismantle that capacity at the end of January when it is no longer needed.

In other words, as long as it is costly to add and subtract capacity, firms will desire to smooth production relative to sales, thereby creating the need for seasonal inventory.

An extreme case of seasonal inventory can be found in the agricultural and food processing sector. Due to the nature of the harvesting season, Monitor Sugar, a large sugar cooperative in the U.S. Midwest, collects all raw material for their sugar production over a period of six weeks. At the end of the harvesting season, they have accumulated—in the very meaning of the word—a pile of sugar beets, about 1 million tons, taking the form of a 67-acre sugar beet pile.

Given that food processing is a very capital-intense operation, the process is sized such that the 1.325 million tons of beets received and the almost 1 million tons of inventory that is built allow for a nonstop operation of the production plant until the beginning of the next harvesting season. Thus, as illustrated by Figure 2.10, the production, and hence the product outflow, is close to constant, while the product inflow is zero except for the harvesting season.

Cycle Inventory

Throughout this book, we will encounter many situations in which it is economical to process several flow units collectively at a given moment in time to take advantage of scale economies in operations.

The scale economics in transportation processes provide a good example for the third reason for inventory. Whether a truck is dispatched empty or full, the driver is paid a fixed amount and a sizeable portion of the wear and tear on the truck depends on the mileage driven, not on the load carried. In other words, each truck shipment incurs a fixed cost that is independent of the amount shipped. To mitigate the sting of that fixed cost, it is

FIGURE 2.10
Seasonal Inventory—Sugar

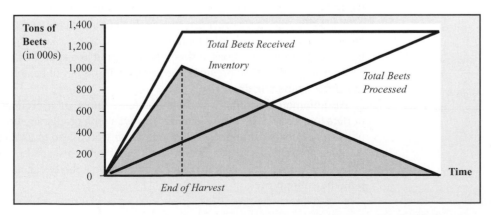

FIGURE 2.11
Cycle Inventory

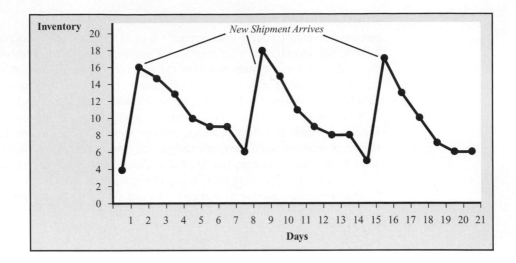

tempting to load the truck completely, thereby dividing the fixed cost across the largest number of units.

In many cases this indeed may be a wise decision. But a truck often carries more product than can be immediately sold. Hence, it takes some time to sell off the entire truck delivery. During that interval of time, there will be inventory. This inventory is labeled *cycle inventory* as it reflects that the transportation process follows a certain shipment cycle (e.g., a shipment every week).

Figure 2.11 plots the inventory level of a simple tray that is required during the operation in the interventional radiology unit. As we can see, there exists a "lumpy" inflow of units, while the outflow is relatively smooth. The reason for this is that—due to the administrative efforts related to placing orders for the trays—the hospital only places one order per week.

The major difference between cycle inventory and seasonal inventory is that seasonal inventory is due to temporary imbalances in supply and demand due to variable demand (soup) or variable supply (beets) while cycle inventory is created due to a cost motivation.

Decoupling Inventory/Buffers

Inventory between process steps can serve as buffers. An inventory buffer allows management to operate steps independently from each other. For example, consider two workers in a garment factory. Suppose the first worker sews the collar onto a shirt and the second sews the buttons. A buffer between them is a pile of shirts with collars but no buttons. Because of that buffer, the first worker can stop working (e.g., to take a break, repair the sewing machine, or change thread color) while the second worker keeps working. In other words, buffers can absorb variations in flow rates by acting as a source of supply for a downstream process step, even if the previous operation itself might not be able to create this supply at the given moment in time.

An automotive assembly line is another example of a production process that uses buffers to decouple the various stations involved with producing the vehicle. In the absence of such buffers, a disruption at any one station would lead to a disruption of all the other stations, upstream and downstream. Think of a bucket brigade to fight a fire: There are no buffers between firefighters in a bucket brigade, so nobody can take a break without stopping the entire process.

FIGURE 2.12
Safety Inventory at
a Blood Bank

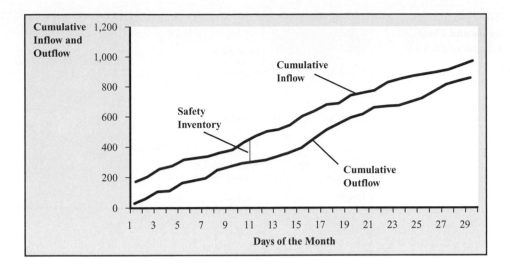

Safety Inventory

The final reason for inventory is probably the most obvious, but also the most challenging: stochastic demand. Stochastic demand refers to the fact that we need to distinguish between the predicted demand and the actually realized demand. In other words, we typically face variation in demand relative to our demand prediction. Note that this is different from variations in predictable demand, which is called *seasonality,* like a sales spike of Campbell's chicken noodle soup in January. Furthermore, stochastic demand can be present along with seasonal demand: January sales can be known to be higher than that for other months (seasonal demand) and there can be variation around that known forecast (stochastic demand).

Stochastic demand is an especially significant problem in retailing environments or at the finished goods level of manufacturers. Take a book retailer that must decide how many books to order of a given title. The book retailer has a forecast for demand, but forecasts are (at best) correct on average. Order too many books and the retailer is faced with leftover inventory. Order too few and valuable sales are lost. This trade-off can be managed, as we will discover in Chapter 9, but not eliminated (unless there are zero forecast errors).

The resulting inventory thereby can be seen as way to hedge against the underlying demand uncertainty. It might reflect a one-shot decision, for example, in the case of a book retailer selling short-life-cycle products such as newspapers or magazines. If we consider a title with a longer product life cycle (e.g., children's books), the book retailer will be able to replenish books more or less continuously over time.

Figure 2.12 shows the example of the blood bank in the Presbyterian Hospital in Philadelphia. While the detailed inflow and consumption of blood units vary over the course of the month, the hospital always has a couple of days of blood in inventory. Given that blood perishes quickly, the hospital wants to keep only a small inventory at its facility, which it replenishes from the regional blood bank operated by the Red Cross.

2.6   The Product–Process Matrix

Processes leading to the supply of goods or services can take many different forms. Some processes are highly automated, while others are largely manual. Some processes resemble the legendary Ford assembly line, while others resemble more the workshop in your local

TABLE 2.6 Process
Types and Their
Characteristics

	Examples	Number of Different Product Variants	Product Volume (units/year)
Job shop	• Design company • Commercial Printer • Formula 1 race car	High (100+)	Low (1–100)
Batch process	• Apparel sewing • Bakery • Semiconductor wafers	Medium (10–100)	Medium (100–100k)
Worker-paced line flow	• Auto assembly • Computer assembly	Medium (1–50)	High (10k–1M)
Machine-paced line flow	• Large auto assembly	1–10	High (10k–1M)
Continuous process	• Paper mill • Oil refinery • Food processing	Low (1–10)	Very high

bike store. Empirical research in operations management, which has looked at thousands of processes, has identified five "clusters" or types of processes. Within each of the five clusters, processes are very similar concerning variables such as the number of different product variants they offer or the production volume they provide. Table 2.6 describes these different types of processes.

By looking at the evolution of a number of industries, Hayes and Wheelwright (1979) observed an interesting pattern, which they referred to as the product–process matrix (see Figure 2.13). The product–process matrix stipulates that over its life cycle, a product typically is initially produced in a job shop process. As the production volume of the product increases, the production process for the product moves from the upper left of the matrix to the lower right.

For example, the first automobiles were produced using job shops, typically creating one product at a time. Most automobiles were unique; not only did they have different colors or add-ons, but they differed in size, geometry of the body, and many other aspects. Henry Ford's introduction of the assembly line corresponded to a major shift along the diagonal of the product–process matrix. Rather than producing a couple of products in a job shop, Ford produced thousands of vehicles on an assembly line.

Note that the "off-diagonals" in the product–process matrix (the lower left and the upper right) are empty. This reflects that it is neither economical to produce very high volumes in a job shop (imagine if all of the millions of new vehicles sold in the United States every year were handcrafted in the same manner as Gottlieb Daimler created the first automobile) nor does it make sense to use an assembly line in order to produce only a handful of products a year.

We have to admit that few companies—if any—would be foolish enough to produce a high-volume product in a job shop. However, identifying a process type and looking at the product–process matrix is more than an academic exercise in industrial history. The usefulness of the product–process matrix lies in two different points:

1. Similar process types tend to have similar problems. For example, as we will discuss in Chapter 4, assembly lines tend to have the problem of line balancing (some workers working harder than others). Batch-flow processes tend to be slow in responding to customer demand (see Chapter 5). Thus, once you know a process type, you can quickly de-

FIGURE 2.13
Product–Process Matrix

Source: Hayes and Wheelwright (1979).

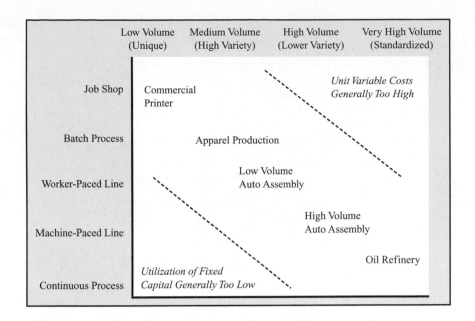

termine what type of problems the process is likely to face and what solution methods are most appropriate.

2. The "natural drift" of industries toward the lower right of Figure 2.13 enables you to predict how processes are likely to evolve in a particular industry. Consider, for example, the case of eye surgery. Up until the 1980s, corrective eye surgery was done in large hospitals. There, doctors would perform a large variety of very different eye-related cases. Fifteen years later, this situation had changed dramatically. Many highly specialized eye clinics have opened, most of them focusing on a limited set of procedures. These clinics achieve high volume and, because of the high volume and the lower variety of cases, can operate at much higher levels of efficiency. Similarly, semiconductor production equipment used to be assembled on a one-by-one basis, while now companies such as Applied Materials and Kulicke & Soffa operate worker-paced lines.

2.7 Summary

In this chapter, we emphasized the importance of looking at the operations of a firm not just in terms of the products that the firm supplies, but also at the processes that generate the supply. Looking at processes is especially important with respect to demand–supply mismatches. From the perspective of the product, such mismatches take the form of waiting times; from the perspective of the process, they take the form of inventory.

For any process, we can define three fundamental performance measures: inventory, flow time, and flow rate. The three measures are related by Little's Law, which states that the average inventory is equal to the average flow time multiplied by the average flow rate.

Little's Law can be used to find any of the three performance measures, as long as the other two measures are known. This is specifically important with respect to flow time, which is in practice frequently difficult to observe directly.

A measure related to flow time is inventory turns. Inventory turns, measured by 1/(flow time), captures how fast the flow units are transformed from input to output. It is an important benchmark in many industries, especially retailing. Inventory turns are also the basis of computing the inventory costs associated with one unit of supply.

2.8 Further Readings

De Groote (1994) is a very elegant note describing the basic roles of inventory. This note, as well as many other notes and articles by de Groote, takes a very "lean" perspective to operations management, resembling much more the tradition of economics as opposed to engineering.

Gaur, Fisher, and Raman (2002) provide an extensive study of retailing performance. They present various operational measures, including inventory turns, and show how they relate to financial performance measures.

The Hayes and Wheelwright (1979) reference is widely recognized as a pioneering article linking operations aspects to business strategy. Subsequent work by Hayes, Wheelwright, and Clark (1988) established operations as a key source for a firm's competitive advantage.

2.9 Practice Problems

Q 2.1*   **(Dell)** What percentage of cost of a Dell computer reflects inventory costs? Assume Dell's yearly inventory cost is 40 percent to account for the cost of capital for financing the inventory, the warehouse space, and the cost of obsolescence. In other words, Dell incurs a cost of $40 for a $100 component that is in the company's inventory for one entire year. In 2001, Dell's 10-k reports showed that the company had $400 million in inventory and COGS of $26,442 million.

Q 2.2   **(Airline)** Consider the baggage check-in of a small airline. Check-in data indicate that from 9 A.M. to 10 A.M., 255 passengers checked in. Moreover, based on counting the number of passengers waiting in line, airport management found that the average number of passengers waiting for check-in was 35. How long did the average passenger have to wait in line?

Q 2.3   **(Inventory Cost)** A manufacturing company producing medical devices reported $60,000,000 in sales over the last year. At the end of the same year, the company had $20,000,000 worth of inventory of ready-to-ship devices.

a. Assuming that units in inventory are valued (based on COGS) at $1,000 per unit and are sold for $2,000 per unit, how fast does the company turn its inventory? The company uses a 25 percent per year cost of inventory. That is, for the hypothetical case that one unit of $1,000 would sit exactly one year in inventory, the company charges its operations division a $250 inventory cost.

b. What—in absolute terms—is the per unit inventory cost for a product that costs $1,000?

Q 2.4   **(Apparel Retailing)** A large catalog retailer of fashion apparel reported $100,000,000 in revenues over the last year. On average, over the same year, the company had $5,000,000 worth of inventory in their warehouses. Assume that units in inventory are valued based on cost of goods sold (COGS) and that the retailer has a 100 percent markup on all products.

a. How many times each year does the retailer turn its inventory? The company uses a 40 percent per year cost of inventory. That is, for the hypothetical case that one item of $100 COGS would sit exactly one year in inventory, the company charges itself a $40 inventory cost.

b. What is the inventory cost for a $30 (COGS) item? You may assume that inventory turns are independent of the price.

Q 2.5   **(LaVilla)** LaVilla is a village in the Italian Alps. Given its enormous popularity among Swiss, German, Austrian, and Italian skiers, all of its beds are always booked in the winter season and there are, on average, 1,200 skiers in the village. On average, skiers stay in LaVilla for 10 days.

a. How many new skiers are arriving—on average—in LaVilla every day?

b. A study done by the largest hotel in the village has shown that skiers spend on average $50 per person on the first day and $30 per person on each additional day in local restaurants. The study also forecasts that—due to increased hotel prices—the average length of stay for the 2003/2004 season will be reduced to five days. What will be the percentage change in revenues of local restaurants compared to last year (when skiers still stayed for 10 days)? Assume that hotels continue to be fully booked!

Q 2.6   **(Highway)** While driving home for the holidays, you can't seem to get Little's Law out of your mind. You note that your average speed of travel is about 60 miles per hour. Moreover,

(* indicates that the solution is at the end of the book)

the traffic report from the WXPN traffic chopper states that there is an average of 24 cars going in your direction on a one-quarter mile part of the highway. What is the flow rate of the highway (going in your direction) in cars per hour?

Q 2.7   **(Industrial Baking Process)** Strohrmann, a large-scale bakery in Pennsylvania, is laying out a new production process for their packaged bread, which they sell to several grocery chains. It takes 12 minutes to bake the bread. How large an oven is required so that the company is able to produce 4,000 units of bread per hour (measured in the number of units that can be baked simultaneously)?

Q 2.8   **(Mt. Kinley Consulting)** Mt. Kinley is a strategy consulting firm that divides its consultants into three classes: associates, managers, and partners. The firm has been stable in size for the last 20 years, ignoring growth opportunities in the 90s, but also not suffering from a need to downsize in the recession at the beginning of the 21st century. Specifically, there have been—and are expected to be—200 associates, 60 managers, and 20 partners.

The work environment at Mt. Kinley is rather competitive. After four years of working as an associate, a consultant goes "either up or out"; that is, becomes a manager or is dismissed from the company. Similarly, after six years a manager either becomes a partner or is dismissed. The company recruits MBAs as associate consultants; no hires are made at the manager or partner level. A partner stays with the company for another 10 years (a total of 20 years with the company).

a. How many new MBA graduates does Mt. Kinley have to hire every year?

b. What are the odds that a new hire at Mt. Kinley will become partner (as opposed to being dismissed after 4 years or 10 years)?

Chapter

3

Understanding the Supply Process: Evaluating Process Capacity

In the attempt to match supply with demand, an important measure is the maximum amount that a process can produce in a given unit of time, a measure referred to as the *process capacity.* To determine the process capacity of an operation, we need to analyze the operation in much greater detail compared to the previous chapter. Specifically, we need to understand the various activities involved in the operation and how these activities contribute toward fulfilling the overall demand.

In this chapter, you will learn how to perform a process analysis. Unlike Chapter 2, where we felt it was sufficient to treat the details of the operation as a black box and merely focus on the performance measures inventory, flow time, and flow rate, we now will focus on the underlying process in great detail.

Despite this increase in detail, this chapter (and this book) is not taking the perspective of an engineer at operations. In fact, in this chapter you will learn how to take a fairly technical and complex operation and simplify it to a level suitable for managerial analysis. This includes preparing a process flow diagram, finding the capacity and the bottleneck of the process, computing the utilization of various process steps, and computing a couple of other performance measures.

We will illustrate this new material with the Circored plant, a joint venture between the German engineering company Lurgi AG and the U.S. iron ore producer Cleveland Cliffs. The Circored plant converts iron ore (in the form of iron ore fines) into direct reduced iron (DRI) briquettes. Iron ore fines are shipped to the plant from mines in South America; the briquettes the process produces are shipped to various steel mills in the United States.

The example of the Circored process is particularly useful for our purposes in this chapter. The underlying process is complex and in many ways a masterpiece of process engineering (see Terwiesch and Loch [2002] for further details). At first sight, the process is so complex that it seems impossible to understand the underlying process behavior without a detailed background in engineering and metallurgy. This challenging setting allows us to demonstrate how process analysis can be used to "tame the beast" and create a managerially useful view of the process, avoiding any unnecessary technical details.

3.1 How to Draw a Process Flow Diagram

The best way to begin any analysis of an operation is by drawing a *process flow diagram*. A process flow diagram is a graphical way to describe the process and it will help us to structure the information that we collect during the case analysis or process improvement project. Before we turn to the question of how to draw a process flow diagram, first consider alternative approaches to how we could capture the relevant information about a process.

Looking at the plant from above (literally), we get a picture as is depicted in Figure 3.1. At the aggregate level, the plant consists of a large inventory of iron ore (input), the plant itself (the resource), and a large inventory in finished briquettes (output). In many ways, this corresponds to the black box approach to operations taken by economists and many other managerial disciplines.

In an attempt to understand the details of the underlying process, we could turn to the engineering specifications of the plant. Engineers are interested in a detailed description of the various steps involved in the overall process and how these steps are functioning. Such descriptions, typically referred to as specifications, were used in the actual construction of the plant. Figure 3.2 provides one of the numerous specification drawings for the Circored process.

Unfortunately, this attempt to increase our understanding of the Circored process is also only marginally successful. Like the photograph, this view of the process is also a rather static one: It emphasizes the equipment, yet provides us with little understanding of how the iron ore moves through the process. In many ways, this view of a process is similar to taking the architectural drawings of a hospital and hope that this would lead to insights about what happens to the patients in this hospital.

In a third—and final—attempt to get our hands around this complex process, we change our perspective from the one of the visitor to the plant (photo in Figure 3.1) or the engineers who built the plant (drawing in Figure 3.2) to the perspective of the iron ore itself and how it flows through the process. Thus, we define a unit of iron ore—a ton, a pound, or a molecule—as our flow unit and "attach" ourselves to this flow unit as it makes

FIGURE 3.1
Photo of the Circored Plant

Source: Terwiesch and Loch (2002).

FIGURE 3.2 Engineering Drawing

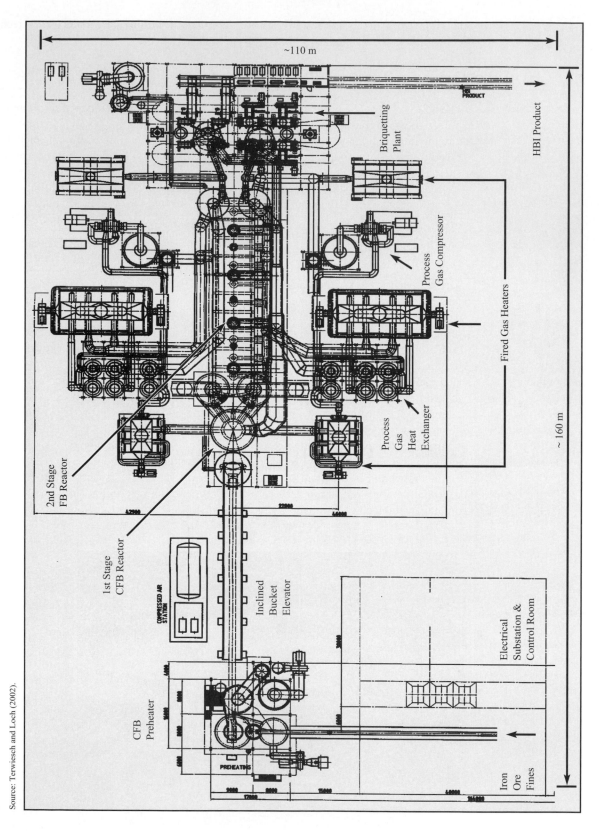

~110 m

HBI Product

Briquetting Plant

Process Gas Compressor

Fired Gas Heaters

Process Gas Heat Exchanger

~160 m

2nd Stage FB Reactor

1st Stage CFB Reactor

COMPRESSED AIR STATION

Inclined Bucket Elevator

Electrical Substation & Control Room

CFB Preheater

PREHEATING

Iron Ore Fines

Source: Terwiesch and Loch (2002).

34

its journey through the process. This is similar to taking the perspective of the patient in a hospital, as opposed to taking the perspective of the hospital resources.

To draw a process flow diagram, we first need to focus on a part of the process that we want to analyze in greater detail; that is, we need to define the *process boundaries* and an appropriate level of detail. The placement of the process boundaries will depend on the project we are working on. For example, in the operation of a hospital, one project concerned with patient waiting time might look at what happens to the patient waiting for a lab test (e.g., check-in, waiting time, encounter with the nurse). In this project, the encounter with the doctor who requested the lab test would be outside the boundaries of the analysis. Another project related to the quality of surgery, however, might look at the encounter with the doctor in great detail, while either ignoring the lab or treating it with less detail.

A process operates on flow units, which are the entities flowing through the process (e.g., patients in a hospital, cars in an auto plant, insurance claims at an insurance company). A process flow diagram is a collection of boxes, triangles, and arrows (see Figure 3.3). Boxes stand for process activities, where the operation adds value to the flow unit. Depending on the level of detail we choose, a process step (a box) can itself be a process.

Triangles represent waiting areas or *buffers* holding inventory. In contrast to a process step, inventories do not add value; thus, a flow unit does not have to spend time in them. However, as discussed in the previous chapter, there are numerous reasons why the flow unit might spend time in inventory even if it will not be augmented to a higher value there.

The arrows between boxes and triangles represent the route the flow unit takes through the process. If there are different flow units that take different routes through the process, it can be helpful to use different colors for the different routes. An example of this is given at the end of this chapter.

FIGURE 3.3
Elements of a Process

Source: Terwiesch and
Loch (2002).

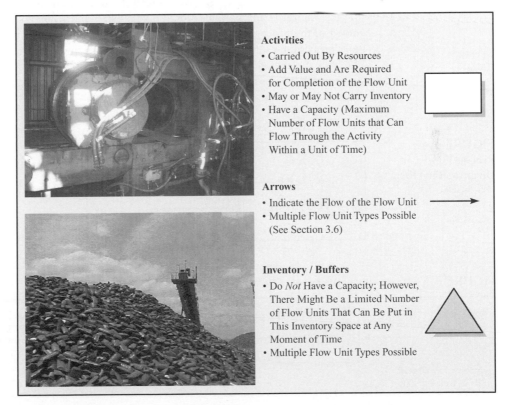

Activities
- Carried Out By Resources
- Add Value and Are Required for Completion of the Flow Unit
- May or May Not Carry Inventory
- Have a Capacity (Maximum Number of Flow Units that Can Flow Through the Activity Within a Unit of Time)

Arrows
- Indicate the Flow of the Flow Unit
- Multiple Flow Unit Types Possible (See Section 3.6)

Inventory / Buffers
- Do *Not* Have a Capacity; However, There Might Be a Limited Number of Flow Units That Can Be Put in This Inventory Space at Any Moment of Time
- Multiple Flow Unit Types Possible

In the Circored plant, the first step the flow unit encounters in the process is the *preheater,* where the iron ore fines (which have a texture like large-grained sand) are dried and heated. The heating is achieved through an inflow of high-pressured air, which is blown into the preheater from the bottom. The high-speed air flow "fluidizes" the ore, meaning that the mixed air–ore mass (a "sandstorm") circulates through the system as if it was a fluid, while being heated to a temperature of approximately 850–900°C.

However, from a managerial perspective, we are not really concerned with the temperature in the preheater or the chemical reactions happening therein. For us, the preheater is a resource that receives iron ore from the initial inventory and processes it. In an attempt to take record of what the flow unit has experienced up to this point, we create a diagram similar to Figure 3.4.

From the preheater, a large bucket elevator transports the ore to the second process step, the *lock hoppers.* The lock hoppers consist of three large containers, separated by sets of double isolation valves. Their role is to allow the ore to transition from an oxygen-rich environment to a hydrogen atmosphere.

Following the lock hoppers, the ore enters the *circulating fluid bed reactor* (CFB, 1st reactor), where the actual reduction process begins. The reduction process requires the ore to be in the reactor for 15 minutes.

After this first reduction, the material flows into the *stationary fluid bed reactor* (FB, 2nd reactor). This second reaction takes about four hours. The reactor is the size of a medium two-family home and contains 400 tons of the hot iron ore at any given moment in time. In the meantime, our diagram from Figure 3.4. has extended to something similar to Figure 3.5.

A couple of things are worth noting at this point:

• When creating Figure 3.5, we decided to omit the bucket elevator. There is no clear rule on when it is appropriate to omit a small step and when a step would have to be included in the process flow diagram. A reasonably good rule of thumb is to only include those process steps that are likely to affect the process flow or the economics of the process. The bucket elevator is cheap, the flow units spend little time on it, and this transportation step never becomes a constraint for the process. So it is not included in our process flow diagram.

FIGURE 3.4
Process Flow Diagram, First Step

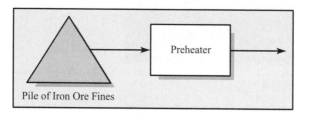

Pile of Iron Ore Fines | Preheater

FIGURE 3.5 Process Flow Diagram (to Be Continued)

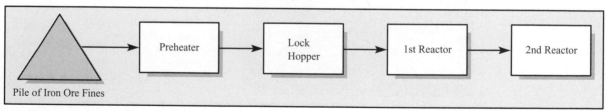

Pile of Iron Ore Fines | Preheater | Lock Hopper | 1st Reactor | 2nd Reactor

- The reaction steps are boxes, not triangles, although there is a substantial amount of ore in them, that is, they do hold inventory. The reduction steps are necessary, value-adding steps. No flow unit could ever leave the system without spending time in the reactors. This is why we have chosen boxes over triangles here.

Following the fluid bed reactor, the reduced iron enters the *flash heater,* in which a stream of high-velocity hydrogen carries the DRI to the top of the plant while simultaneously reheating it to a temperature of 685°C.

After the flash heater, the DRI enters the *pressure let-down system (discharger).* As the material passes through the discharger, the hydrogen atmosphere is gradually replaced by inert nitrogen gas. Pressure and hydrogen are removed in a reversal of the lock hoppers at the beginning. Hydrogen gas sensors assure that material leaving this step is free of hydrogen gas and, hence, safe for briquetting.

Each of the three *briquetting* machines contains two wheels that turn against each other, each wheel having the negative of one-half of a briquette on its face. The DRI is poured onto the wheels from the top and is pressed into briquettes, or iron bars, which are then moved to a large pile of finished goods inventory.

This completes our journey of the flow unit through the plant. The resulting process flow diagram that captures what the flow unit has experienced in the process is summarized in Figure 3.6.

When drawing a process flow diagram, the sizes and the exact locations of the arrows, boxes, and triangles do not carry any special meaning. For example, in the context of Figure 3.6, we chose a "U-shaped" layout of the process flow diagram, as otherwise we would have had to publish this book in a larger format.

In the absence of any space constraints, the simplest way to draw a process flow diagram for a process such as Circored's is just as one long line. However, we should keep in mind that there are more complex processes; for example, a process with multiple flow units or a flow unit that visits one and the same resource multiple times. This will be discussed further at the end of the chapter.

Another alternative in drawing the process flow diagram is to stay much closer to the physical layout of the process. This way, the process flow diagram will look familiar for engineers and operators who typically work off the specification drawings (Figure 3.2) and it might help you to find your way around when you are visiting the "real" process. Such an approach is illustrated by Figure 3.7.

FIGURE 3.6 **Completed Process Flow Diagram for the Circored Process**

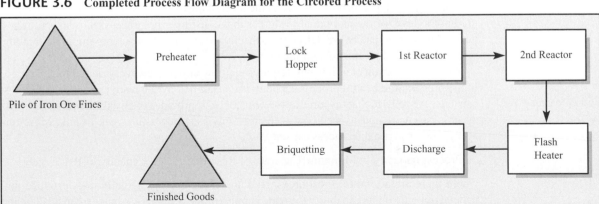

FIGURE 3.7   **Completed Process Flow Diagram for the Circored Process**

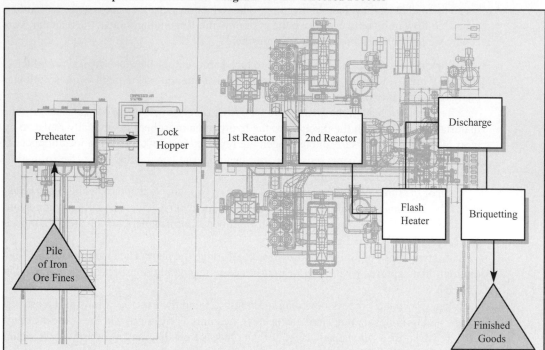

3.2   Bottleneck, Process Capacity, and Flow Rate (Throughput)

From a supply perspective, the most important question that arises is how much direct reduced iron a process can supply in a given unit of time, say one day. This measure is called the *process capacity.*

Note that the process capacity measures how much the process *can* produce, opposed to how much the process actually *does* produce. For example, consider a day where—due to a breakdown or another external event—the process does not operate at all. Its capacity would be unaffected by this, yet the flow rate would reduce to zero. This is similar to your car, which might be able to drive at 130 miles per hour (capacity), but typically—or better, hopefully—only drives at 65 miles per hour (flow rate).

Not only can capacity be measured at the level of the overall process, it also can be measured at the level of the individual resources that constitute the process. Similar to how we defined process capacity, we define the capacity of a resource as the maximum amount the resource can produce in a given time unit.

As the completion of a flow unit requires the flow unit to visit every one of the resources in the process, the overall process capacity is determined by the resource with the smallest capacity. We refer to that resource as the *bottleneck.* It provides the weakest link in the overall process chain, and, as we know, a chain is only as strong as its weakest link. More formally, we can write the process capacity as

Process capacity = Mininum{Capacity of Resource 1, . . ., Capacity of Resource *n*}

where there are a total of *n* resources. How much the process actually does produce will depend not only on its capability to create supply (process capacity), but also on the demand for its output as well as the availability of its input.

Thus, the flow rate or throughput of the process is determined as

$$\text{Flow rate} = \text{Minimum}\{\text{Available Input, Demand, Process Capacity}\}$$

If demand is lower than supply (i.e., there is sufficient input available and the process has enough capacity), the process would produce at the rate of demand, independent of the process capacity. We refer to this case as *demand-constrained*. Note that in this defi-nition demand also includes any potential requests for the accumulation of inventory. For example, while the demand for Campbell's chicken noodle soup might be lower than process capacity for the month of November, the process would not be demand-constrained if management decided to accumulate finished goods inventory in prepara-tion for the high sales in the month of January. Thus, demand in our analysis refers to everything that is demanded from the process at a given time.

If demand exceeds supply, the process is *supply-constrained*. Depending on what limits product supply, the process is either input-constrained or capacity-constrained.

Figure 3.8 summarizes the concepts of process capacity and flow rate, together with the notion of demand- versus supply-constrained processes. In the case of the supply-constrained operation, there is sufficient input; thus, the supply constraint reflects a capac-ity constraint.

To understand how to find the bottleneck in a process and thereby determine the process capacity, consider each of the Circored resources. Note that all numbers are referring to tons of process output. The actual, physical weight of the flow unit might change over the course of the process.

Finding the bottleneck in many ways resembles the job of a detective in a crime story; each activity is a "suspect," in the sense that it could potentially constrain the overall sup-ply of the process:

- The preheater can process 120 tons per hour.
- The lock hoppers can process 110 tons per hour.
- The analysis of the reaction steps is somewhat more complicated. We first observe that at any given moment of time, there can be, at maximum, 28 tons in the CFB reactor. Given that the iron ore needs to spend 15 minutes in the reactor, we can use Little's Law (see Chap-ter 2) to see that the maximum amount of ore that can flow through the reactor—and spend 15 minutes in the reactor—is

$$28 \text{ tons} = \text{Flow rate} \times 0.25 \text{ hour} => \text{Flow rate} = 112 \text{ tons/hour}$$

FIGURE 3.8   **Supply-Constrained (left) and Demand-Constrained (right) Processes**

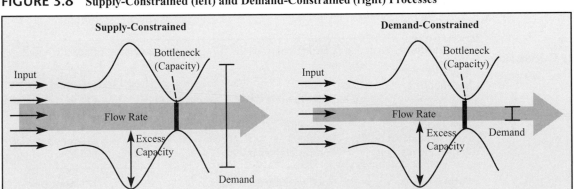

Thus, the capacity of the first reactor is 112 tons per hour. Note that a shorter reaction time in this case would translate to a higher capacity.

- We can apply a similar logic for the stationary reactor, which can hold up to 400 tons:

$$400 \text{ tons} = \text{Flow rate} \times 4 \text{ hours} => \text{Flow rate} = 100 \text{ tons/hour}$$

Thus, the capacity (the maximum possible flow rate through the resource) of the second reactor is 100 tons per hour.

- The flash heater can process 135 tons per hour.
- The pressure let-down system has a capacity of 118 tons per hour.
- Each of the three briquetting machines has a capacity of 55 tons per hour. As the briquetting machines collectively form one resource, the capacity at the briquetting machines is simply 3×55 tons per hour = 165 tons per hour.

The capacity of each process step is summarized in Table 3.1. Note that similar to the crime story example, every process can only have one bottleneck.

Following the logic outlined above, we can now identify the stationary reactor as the bottleneck of the Circored process. The overall process capacity is computed as the minimum of the capacities of each resource (all units are in tons per hour):

$$\text{Process capacity} = \text{Minimum}\{120, 110, 112, 100, 135, 118, 165\} = 100$$

3.3 How Long Does It Take to Produce a Certain Amount of Supply?

There are many situations where we need to compute the amount of time required to create a certain amount of supply. For example, in the Circored case, we might ask, "How long does it take for the plant to produce 10,000 tons?" Once we have determined the flow rate of the process, this calculation is fairly straightforward. Let X be the amount of supply we want to fulfill. Then,

$$\text{Time to fullfill } X \text{ units} = \frac{X}{\text{Flow rate}}$$

To answer our question,

$$\text{Time to produce 10,000 tons} = \frac{10,000 \text{ tons}}{100 \text{ tons/hour}} = 100 \text{ hours}$$

Note that this calculation assumes the process is already producing output, that is, the first unit in our 10,000 tons flows out of the process immediately. If the process started empty, it would take the first flow unit time to flow through the process. Chapter 4 provides the calculations for that case.

TABLE 3.1
Capacity Calculation

Process Step	Calculations	Capacity
Preheater		120 tons per hour
Lock hoppers		110 tons per hour
CFB	Little's Law: Flow rate = 28 tons/0.25 hour	112 tons per hour
Stationary reactor	Little's Law: Flow rate = 400 tons/4 hours	100 tons per hour
Flash heater		135 tons per hour
Pressure let-down system		118 tons per hour
Briquetting machine	Consists of three machines 3×55 tons per hour	165 tons per hour
Total process	Based on bottleneck, which is the stationary reactor	**100 tons per hour**

Note that in the previous equation we use flow rate, which in our case is capacity because the system is supply-constrained. However, if our system were demand-constrained, then the flow rate would equal the demand rate.

3.4 Process Utilization and Capacity Utilization

Given the first-of-its-kind nature of the Circored process, the first year of its operation proved to be extremely difficult. In addition to various technical difficulties, demand for the product (reduced iron) was not as high as it could be, as the plant's customers (steel mills) had to be convinced that the output created by the Circored process would be of the high quality required by the steel mills.

While abstracting from details such as scheduled maintenance and inspection times, the plant was designed to achieve a process capacity of 876,000 tons per year (100 tons per hour $\times$ 24 hours/day $\times$ 365 days/year, see above), the demand for iron ore briquettes was only 657,000 tons. Thus, there existed a mismatch between demand and potential supply (process capacity).

A common measure of performance that quantifies this mismatch is process utilization. We define the utilization of a process as

$$\text{Process utilization} = \frac{\text{Flow rate}}{\text{Process capacity}}$$

Thus, to measure process utilization, we look at how much the process actually *does produce* relative to how much it *can produce* if it were running at full speed. This is in line with the example of a car driving at 65 miles per hour (flow rate), despite being able to drive at 130 miles per hour (capacity): the car utilizes 65/130 = 50 percent of its potential.

For the Circored case, the resulting utilization is

$$\text{Process utilization} = \frac{657,000 \text{ tons per year}}{876,000 \text{ tons per year}} = 0.75 = 75\%$$

In general, there are several reasons why a process might not produce at 100 percent utilization:

- If demand is less than supply, the process typically will not run at full capacity, but only produce at the rate of demand.
- If there is insufficient supply of the input of a process, the process will not be able to operate at capacity.
- If one or several process steps only have a limited availability (e.g., maintenance and breakdowns), the process might operate at full capacity while it is running, but then go into periods of not producing any output while it is not running.

As we did with process capacity and the capacity of individual resources, we can define utilization not only at the level of the entire process, but also at the level of the individual resources. The utilization of a resource is defined as follows:

$$\text{Utilization of resource} = \frac{\text{Flow rate}}{\text{Capacity of resource}}$$

Given that the bottleneck is the resource with the lowest capacity and that the flow rate through all resources is identical, the bottleneck is the resource with the highest utilization.

In the case of the Circored plant, the corresponding utilizations are provided by Table 3.2. Note that all resources in a process with only one flow unit have the same flow rate, which is equal to the overall process flow rate. In this case, this is a flow rate of 657,000 tons per year.

TABLE 3.2
Utilization of the Circored Process Steps Including Downtime

Process Step	Calculations	Utilization
Preheater	657,000 tons/year/[120 tons/hour × 8,760 hours/year]	62.5%
Lock hoppers	657,000 tons/year/[110 tons/hour × 8,760 hours/year]	68.2%
CFB	657,000 tons/year/[112 tons/hour × 8,760 hours/year]	66.9%
Stationary reactor	657,000 tons/year/[100 tons/hour × 8,760 hours/year]	75%
Flash heater	657,000 tons/year/[135 tons/hour × 8,760 hours/year]	55.6%
Discharger	657,000 tons/year/[118 tons/hour × 8,760 hours/year]	63.6%
Briquetting	657,000 tons/year/[165 tons/hour × 8,760 hours/year]	45.5%
Total process	657,000 tons/year/[100 tons/hour × 8,760 hours/year]	**75%**

FIGURE 3.9   Utilization Profile

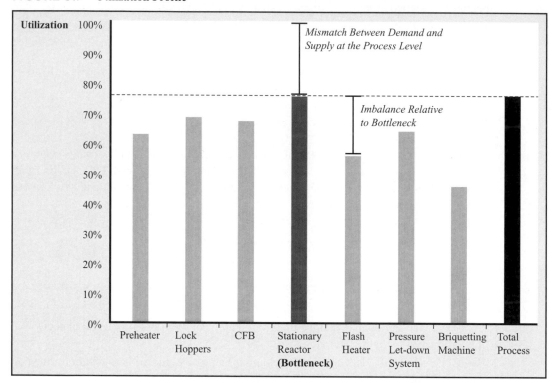

Measuring the utilization of equipment is particularly common in capital-intensive industries. Given limited demand and availability problems, the bottleneck in the Circored process did not operate at 100 percent utilization. We can summarize our computations graphically, by drawing a utilization profile. This is illustrated by Figure 3.9.

The utilization profile of the Circored process points at a small imbalance between various resources. In the next chapter, we will look at a process environment, which is labor-intensive, where we will track the utilization of labor. All of the definitions we have seen up to this point are independent of whether the resource is a worker or a piece of equipment.

Utilization is a performance measure that should be handled with a great deal of care. Specifically, it should be emphasized that the objective of most businesses is to maximize profit, not to maximize utilization. As can be seen in Figure 3.9, there are two reasons in the Circored case for why an individual resource might not achieve 100 percent utilization, thus exhibiting excess capacity.

TABLE 3.3
Utilization of the Circored Process Steps Assuming Unlimited Demand and No Downtime

Process Step	Calculations	Utilization
Preheater	100/120	83.3%
Lock hoppers	100/110	90.9%
CFB	100/112	89.3%
Stationary reactor	100/100	100%
Flash heater	100/135	74.1%
Pressure let-down system	100/118	84.7%
Briquetting machine	100/165	60.6%
Total process	**100/100**	**100%**

• First, given that no resource can achieve a higher utilization than the bottleneck, every process step other than the bottleneck will have a utilization gap relative to the bottleneck.

• Second, given that the process might not always be capacity-constrained, but rather be input- or demand-constrained, even the bottleneck might not be 100 percent utilized. In this case, every resource in the process has a "base level" of excess capacity, corresponding to the difference between the flow rate and the bottleneck capacity.

Note that the second reason disappears if there is sufficient market demand and full resource availability. In this case, only the bottleneck achieves a 100 percent utilization level. If the bottleneck in the Circored plant were utilized 100 percent, we would obtain an overall flow rate of 876,000 tons per year, or, equivalently 100 tons per hour. The resulting utilization levels in that case are summarized in Table 3.3.

3.5 Workload and Implied Utilization

Given the way we defined utilization (the ratio between flow rate and capacity), utilization can never exceed 100 percent. Thus, utilization only carries information about excess capacity, in which case utilization is strictly less than 100 percent. In contrast, we cannot infer from utilization by how much demand exceeds the capacity of the process. This is why we need to introduce an additional measure.

We define the *implied utilization* of a resource as

$$\text{Implied utilization} = \frac{\text{Capacity requested by demand}}{\text{Available capacity}}$$

The implied utilization captures the mismatch between the capacity requested from a resource by demand (also called the *workload*) and the capacity currently available at the resource.

Assume that demand for the Circored ore would increase to 1,095,000 tons per year (125 tons per hour). Table 3.4 calculates the resulting levels of implied utilization for the Circored resources.

Several points in the table deserve further discussion:

• Unlike utilization, implied utilization can exceed 100 percent. Any excess over 100 percent reflects that a resource does not have the capacity available to meet demand.

• The fact that a resource has an implied utilization above 100 percent does not make it the bottleneck. As we see in Table 3.4, it is possible to have several resources with an implied utilization above 100 percent. However, there is only one bottleneck in the process! This is the resource where the implied utilization is the highest. In the Circored case, this

TABLE 3.4
Implied Utilization of the Circored Process Steps Assuming a Demand of 125 Tons per Hour and No Downtime

Process Step	Calculations	Implied Utilization	Utilization
Preheater	125/120	104.2%	83.3%
Lock hoppers	125/110	113.6%	90.9%
CFB	125/112	111.6%	89.3%
Stationary reactor	125/100	125%	100%
Flash heater	125/135	92.6%	74.1%
Pressure let-down system	125/118	105.9%	84.7%
Briquetting machine	125/165	75.8%	60.6%
Total process	**125/100**	**125%**	**100%**

is—not surprisingly—the stationary reactor. Would it make sense to say that the process has several bottlenecks? No! Given that we can only operate the Circored process at a rate of 100 tons per hour (the capacity of the stationary reactor), we have ore flow through every resource of the process at a rate of 100 tons per hour. Thus, while several resources have an implied utilization above 100 percent, all resources other than the stationary reactor have excess capacity (their utilizations in Table 3.4 are below 100 percent). That is why we should not refer to them as bottlenecks.

• Having said this, it is important to keep in mind that in the case of a capacity expansion of the process, it might be worthwhile to add capacity to these other resources as well, not just to the bottleneck. In fact, depending on the margins we make and the cost of installing capacity, we could make a case to install additional capacity for all resources with an implied utilization above 100 percent. In other words, once we add capacity to the current bottleneck, our new process (with a new bottleneck) could still be capacity-constrained, justifying additional capacity to other resources.

3.6   Multiple Types of Flow Units

Choosing an appropriate flow unit is an essential step when preparing a process flow diagram. While, for the examples we have discussed so far, this looked relatively straightforward, there are many situations that you will encounter where this choice requires more care. The two most common complications are

• The flow of the unit moving through the process breaks up into multiple flows. For example, in an assembly environment, following an inspection step, good units continue to the next processing step, while bad units require rework.

• There are multiple types of flow units, representing, for example, different customer types. In an emergency room, life-threatening cases follow a different flow than less-complicated cases.

Consider the following example involving multiple product or customer types. An employment verification agency receives resumés from consulting firms and law firms with the request to validate information provided by their job candidates.

Consider the process flow diagram shown in Figure 3.10, which describes the process of handling the applicant's resumés. Note that while the three customer types share the first step and the last step in the process (filing and sending confirmation letter), they differ with respect to other steps:

• For internship positions, the agency provides information about the law school/business school the candidate is currently enrolled in as well as previous institutions of higher education and, to the extent possible, provides information about the applicant's course choices and honors.

FIGURE 3.10   Process Flow Diagram with Multiple Product Types

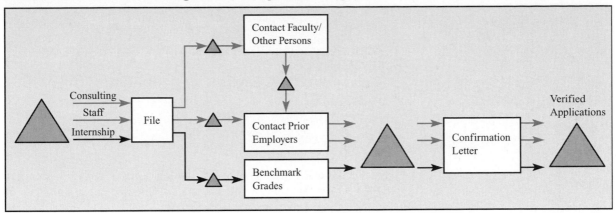

• For staff positions, the agency contacts previous employers and analyzes the letters of recommendation from those employers.

• For consulting/lawyer positions, the agency attempts to call former supervisors and/or colleagues in addition to contacting the previous employers and analyzes the letters of recommendation from those employers.

This *product mix* (different types of customers flowing through one process) complicates the process analysis. It is important to understand that the capacity of the process crucially depends on the product mix. For example, the process step "contact persons who have worked with the candidate" might have a very long activity time, resulting in a low capacity for this activity. However, if only 1 out of 100 applicants applies for a consulting position, this low capacity would not be a problem. Thus, the product mix can determine which resource is the bottleneck.

Thus, to find the bottleneck and to determine capacity in a multiproduct situation, we need to compare the available capacity with the requested capacity. The analysis is given in Table 3.5. Numbers that are raw data (i.e., that you would find in the case or by observing the real process) are printed in **bold.** Numbers that are derived by analysis are printed in *italics.*

We assume the demand is **180** applications a day, of which there are

• **30** for consulting positions,
• **110** for staff, and
• **40** for internship positions.

Assuming that the working day is 10 hours, demand is *3* consulting applications per hour, *11* staff applications per hour, and *4* applications for internships per hour.

When computing the workload of a given resource (requested capacity of a resource) as shown in Table 3.5, it is important to remember that some activities (e.g., filing the applications) are requested by all product types, whereas others (e.g., contacting faculty and former colleagues) are requested by one product type. This is (hopefully) clear by looking at the process flow diagram.

By dividing the requested capacity by the available capacity, we compute the implied utilization of the resource (see previous section). This allows us to find the "busiest" resource. In this case, this is "contact prior employers." As this ratio is above 100 percent, the process is capacity-constrained and, unless we can work overtime (i.e., add extra hours at the end of the day, in which case our available capacity would go up), we will not be able to process all the incoming applications.

TABLE 3.5 Finding the Bottleneck in the Multiproduct Case

	Activity Time	Number of Workers	Available Capacity	Requested Capacity [Applications/Hour] Workload				Implied Utilization
				Consulting	Staff	Interns	Total	
File	**3** [min./appl.]	**1**	1/3 [appl./min.] = 20 [appl./hour]	3	11	4	18	18/20=90%
Contact persons	**20** [min./appl.]	**2**	2/20 [appl./min.] =6 [appl./hour]	3	0	0	3	3/6=50%
Contact employers	**15** [min./appl.]	**3**	3/15 [appl./min.] =12 [appl./hour]	3	11	0	14	14/12=117%
Grade/ school analysis	**8** [min./appl.]	**2**	2/8 [appl./min.] =15 [appl./hour]	0	0	4	4	4/15 =27%
Confirmation letter	**2** [min./appl.]	**1**	1/2 [appl./min.] =30 [appl./hour]	3	11	4	18	18/30=60%

As discussed previously, defining the flow unit in the presence of a product mix is somewhat more complicated. One approach to defining a flow unit is as follows:

• The flow is a "random" application.

• The application is a consulting application with probability 3/18, a staff position with 11/18 probability, and an internship application with 4/18 probability.

Alternatively, we could define the flow unit as "one minute of work." Then, we can compute the available capacity as (number of workers) × 60[minutes/hour]. When we look at the requested capacity, we look at how many applications of a different type have to be processed within an hour and how many minutes of work each application requires at a given process step. For example, when we look at the process step File and staff applications, we know that

• There are 11 staff applications to be processed every hour.

• Each of them corresponds to three minutes of work.

Thus, there is a requested capacity (workload) of 33 minutes/hour for staff applications at process step File. In contrast, there is no requested capacity of staff applications for the process step Contact persons.

Table 3.6 summarizes the calculations for this alternative approach. Note that the two procedures to find the bottleneck in the case of a product mix are equivalent; that is, they yield the same bottleneck and the same levels of implied utilization.

There are two guiding principles to keep in mind when defining the flow unit:

• The capacity for each resource can be expressed in terms of that flow unit.

• Each type of demand can be expressed in terms of the number of flow units it requests.

For example, if the flow unit is "one application," then we can evaluate the capacity for each resource in terms of the number of applications processed per unit time. Furthermore, each demand type is exactly one application, so we can express the total number of applications requested for each resource. If the flow unit is "one minute of work," then we express the capacity of each resource in terms of the number of "minutes of work" per unit time, and, similarly, each demand type can be expressed in terms of number of "minutes of work" it requests from the resource.

TABLE 3.6 Using "One Minute of Work" as the Flow Unit to Find the Bottleneck in the Multiproduct Case

| | Activity Time | Number of Workers | Available Capacity | Requested Capacity [Minutes/Hour] Workload | | | | Implied Utilization |
				Consulting	Staff	Interns	Total	
File	**3** [min./appl.]	**1**	60 [min./hour]	3×3	11×3	4×3	54	54/60=*90%*
Contact persons	**20** [min./appl.]	**2**	120 [min./hour]	3×20	0	0	60	60/120=*50%*
Contact employers	**15** [min./appl.]	**3**	180 [min./hour]	3×15	11×15	0	210	210/180= *117%*
Grade/ school analysis	**8** [min./appl.]	**2**	120 [min./hour]	0	0	4×8	32	32/120=*27%*
Confirmation letter	**2** [min./appl.]	**1**	60 [min./hour]	3×2	11×2	4×2	36	36/60=*60%*

Neither of these two approaches is superior. As we have just seen, they lead to the same results. Thus, you can simply choose the approach that you find more intuitive or that seems easier to apply in a given setting.

3.7 Summary

Figure 3.11 is a summary of the major steps graphically. Exhibits 3.1 and 3.2 summarize the steps required to do the corresponding calculations for a single flow unit and multiple flow units respectively.

Any process analysis should begin with the creation of a process flow diagram. This is especially important for the case of multiple flow units, as their flows are typically more complex.

Next, we need to identify the bottleneck of the process. As long as there exists only one type of flow unit, this is simply the resource with the lowest capacity. However, for more general cases, we need to perform some extra analysis. Specifically, if there is a product mix, we have to compute the requested capacity (workload) at each resource and then compare it to the available capacity. This corresponds to computing the implied utilization, and we identify the bottleneck as the resource with the highest implied utilization.

Finally, once we have found the bottleneck, we can compute a variety of performance measures. As in the previous chapter, we are interested in finding the flow rate. The flow rate also allows us to compute the process utilization as well as the utilization profile across resources. Utilizations, while not necessarily a business goal by themselves, are important measures in many industries, especially capital-intensive industries.

FIGURE 3.11 Summary of Process Analysis

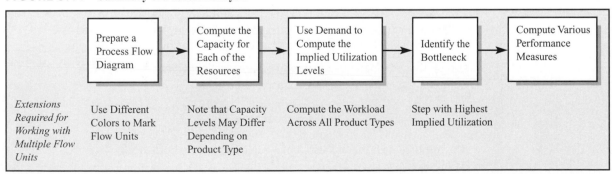

Exhibit 3.1

STEPS FOR BASIC PROCESS ANALYSIS WITH ONE TYPE OF FLOW UNIT

1. Find the capacity of every resource; if there are multiple resources performing the same activity, add their capacities together.
2. The resource with the lowest capacity is called the *bottleneck*. Its capacity determines the capacity of the entire process (*process capacity*).
3. The flow rate is found based on

$$\text{Flow Rate} = \text{Minimum \{Available input, Demand, Process capacity\}}$$

4. We find the utilization of the process as

$$\text{Process utilization} = \frac{\text{Flow rate}}{\text{Process capacity}}$$

Similarly, we find the utilization of each resource as

$$\text{Utilization of resource} = \frac{\text{Flow rate}}{\text{Capacity of resource}}$$

Exhibit 3.2

STEPS FOR BASIC PROCESS ANALYSIS WITH MULTIPLE TYPES OF FLOW UNITS

1. For each resource, compute the number of minutes that the resource can produce; this is 60[min./hour] × Number of resources within the resource pool.
2. Create a process flow diagram, indicating how the flow units go through the process; use multiple colors to indicate the flow of the different flow units.
3. Create a table indicating how much workload each flow unit is consuming at each resource:

   - The rows of the table correspond to the resources in the process.
   - The columns of the table correspond to the different types of flow units.
   - Each cell of the table should contain one of the following:
     If flow unit does not visit the corresponding resource, $\varnothing$;
     Otherwise, demand per hour of the corresponding flow unit × activity time.

4. Add up the workload of each resource across all flow units.
5. Compute the implied utilization of each resource as

$$\text{Implied utilization} = \frac{\text{Result of step 3}}{\text{Result of step 1}}$$

The resource with the highest implied utilization is the bottleneck.

The above approach is based on Table 3.6; that is, the flow unit is "one minute of work."

3.8 Practice Problems

Q 3.1* (**Process Analysis with One Flow Unit**) Consider a process consisting of three resources:

Resource	Activity Time [Min./Unit]	Number of Workers
1	10	2
2	6	1
3	16	3

What is the bottleneck? What is the process capacity? What is the flow rate if demand is eight units per hour? What is the utilization of each resource if demand is eight units per hour?

Q 3.2* (**Process Analysis with Multiple Flow Units**) Consider a process consisting of five resources that are operated eight hours per day. The process works on three different products, A, B, and C:

Resource	Number of Workers	Activity Time for A [Min./Unit]	Activity Time for B [Min./Unit]	Activity Time for C [Min./Unit]
1	2	5	5	5
2	2	3	4	5
3	1	15	0	0
4	1	0	3	3
5	2	6	6	6

Demand for the three different products is as follows: product A, 40 units per day; product B, 50 units per day; and product C, 60 units per day.

What is the bottleneck? What is the flow rate for each flow unit assuming that demand must be served in the mix described above (i.e., for every four units of A, there are five units of B and six units of C)?

Q 3.3 (**Cranberries**) International Cranberry Uncooperative (ICU) is a competitor to the National Cranberry Cooperative (NCC). At ICU, barrels of cranberries arrive on trucks at a rate of 150 barrels per hour and are processed continuously at a rate of 100 barrels per hour. Trucks arrive at a uniform rate over eight hours, from 6:00 A.M. until 2:00 P.M. Assume the trucks are sufficiently small so that the delivery of cranberries can be treated as a continuous inflow. The first truck arrives at 6:00 A.M. and unloads immediately, so processing begins at 6:00 A.M. The bins at ICU can hold up to 200 barrels of cranberries before overflowing. If a truck arrives and the bins are full, the truck must wait until there is room in the bins.

a. What is the maximum number of barrels of cranberries that are waiting on the trucks at any given time?

b. At what time do the trucks stop waiting?

c. At what time do the bins become empty?

d. ICU is considering using seasonal workers in addition to their regular workforce to help with the processing of cranberries. When the seasonal workers are working, the processing rate increases to 125 barrels per hour. The seasonal workers would start working at 10:00 A.M. and finish working when the trucks stop waiting. At what time would ICU finish processing the cranberries using these seasonal workers?

Q 3.4 (**Western Pennsylvania Milk Company**) The Western Pennsylvania Milk Company is producing milk at a fixed rate of 5,000 gallons/hour. The company's clients request 100,000 gallons of milk over the course of one day. This demand is spread out uniformly from 8 A.M. to 6 P.M. If there is no milk available, clients will wait until enough is produced to satisfy their requests.

The company starts producing at 8 A.M. with 25,000 gallons in finished goods inventory. At the end of the day, after all demand has been fulfilled, the plant keeps on producing until the finished goods inventory has been restored to 25,000 gallons.

(*indicates that the solution is at the end of the book)

When answering the following questions, treat trucks/milk as a continuous flow process. Begin by drawing a graph indicating how much milk is in inventory and how much milk is "back-ordered" over the course of the day.

a. At what time during the day will the clients have to start waiting for their requests to be filled?

b. At what time will clients stop waiting?

c. Assume that the milk is picked up in trucks that hold 1,250 gallons each. What is the maximum number of trucks that are waiting?

d. Assume the plant is charged $50 per hour per waiting truck. What are the total waiting-time charges on a day?

Q 3.5 **(Bagel Store)** Consider a bagel store selling three types of bagels that are produced according to the process flow diagram outlined below. We assume the demand is **180** bagels a day, of which there are **30** grilled veggie, **110** veggie only, and **40** cream cheese. Assume that the workday is 10 hours long and each resource is staffed with one worker.

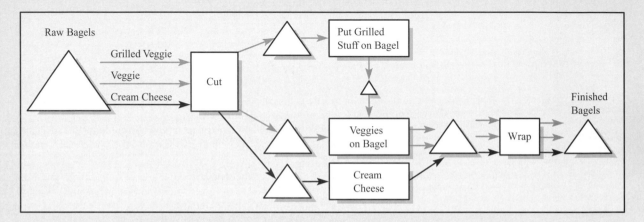

Moreover, we assume the following activity times:

	Cut	Grilled Stuff	Veggies	Cream Cheese	Wrap
Activity time	**3** [min./bagel]	**10** [min./bagel]	**5** [min./bagel]	**4** [min./bagel]	**2** [min./bagel]

Activity times are independent of which bagel type is processed at a resource (for example, cutting a bagel takes the same time for a cream cheese bagel as for a veggie bagel).

a. Where in the process is the bottleneck?

b. How many units can the process produce within one hour, assuming the product mix has to remain constant?

Q 3.6 **(Process with Rework)** Consider the following three-stage production process of glass ceramics, which is operated as a worker-paced line.

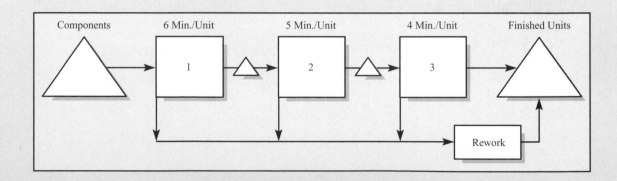

The process is experiencing severe quality problems related to insufficiently trained workers. Specifically, 20 percent of the parts going through operation 1 are badly processed by the operator. Rather than scrapping the unit, it is moved to a highly skilled rework operator, who can correct the mistake and finish up the unit completely within 15 minutes.

The same problem occurs at station 2, where 10 percent of the parts are badly processed, requiring 10 minutes of rework. Station 3 also has a 10 percent ratio of badly processed parts, each of them requiring 5 minutes by the rework operator.

a. What is the utilization of station 2 if work is released into the process at a rate of five units per hour?

b. Where in the process is the bottleneck? Why? (Remember, the bottleneck is the resource with the lowest capacity, independent of demand.)

c. What is the process capacity?

Q 3.7 **(Valley Forge Income Tax Advice)** VF is a small accounting firm supporting wealthy individuals in their preparation of annual income tax statements. Every December, VF sends out a short survey to their customers, asking for the information required for preparing the tax statements. Based on 24 years of experience, VF categorizes their cases into the following groups:

- Group 1 (new customers, easy): 15 percent of cases
- Group 2 (new customers, complex): 5 percent of cases
- Group 3 (repeat customers, easy): 50 percent of cases
- Group 4 (repeat customers, complex): 30 percent of cases

Here, "easy" versus "complex" refers to the complexity of the customer's earning situation.

In order to prepare the income tax statement, VF needs to complete the following set of activities. Activity times (and even which activities need to be carried out) depend on which group a tax statement falls into. All of the following activity times are expressed in minutes per income tax statement.

Group	Filing	Initial Meeting	Preparation	Review by Senior Accountant	Writing
1	20	30	120	20	50
2	40	90	300	60	80
3	20	No meeting	80	5	30
4	40	No meeting	200	30	60

The activities are carried out by the following three persons:

- Administrative support person: filing and writing.
- Senior accountant (who is also the owner): initial meeting, review by senior accountant.
- Junior accountant: preparation.

Assume that all three persons work eight hours per day and 20 days a month. For the following questions, assume the product mix as described above. Assume that there are 50 income tax statements arriving each month.

a. Which of the three persons is the bottleneck?

b. What is the (implied) utilization of the senior accountant? The junior accountant? The administrative support person?

c. You have been asked to analyze which of the four product groups is the most profitable. Which factors would influence the answer to this?

d. How would the process capacity of VF change if a new word processing system would reduce the time to write the income tax statements by 50 percent?

Chapter

4

Estimating and Reducing Labor Costs

The objective of any process should be to create value (make profits), not to maximize the utilization of every resource involved in the process. In other words, we should not attempt to produce more than what is demanded from the market, or from the resource downstream in the process, just to increase the utilization measure. Yet, the underutilization of a resource, human labor or capital equipment alike, provides opportunities to improve the process. This improvement can take several forms, including

• If we can reduce the excess capacity at some process step, the overall process becomes more efficient (lower cost for the same output).

• If we can use capacity from underutilized process steps to increase the capacity at the bottleneck step, the overall process capacity increases. If the process is capacity-constrained, this leads to a higher flow rate.

In this chapter, we discuss how to achieve such process improvements. Specifically, we discuss the concept of line balancing, which strives to avoid mismatches between what is supplied by one process step and what is demanded from the following process step (referred to as the process step downstream). In this sense, line balancing attempts to match supply and demand within the process itself.

We use Novacruz Inc. to illustrate the concept of line balancing and to introduce a number of more general terms of process analysis. Novacruz is the producer of a high-end kick scooter, known as the Xootr (pronounced "zooter"), displayed in Figure 4.1.

4.1 Analyzing an Assembly Operation

With the increasing popularity of kick scooters in general, and the high-end market segment for kick-scooters in particular, Novacruz faced a challenging situation in terms of organizing their production process. While the demand for their product was not much higher than 100 scooters per week in early March 2000, it grew dramatically, soon reaching 1,200 units per week in the fall of 2000. This demand trajectory is illustrated in Figure 4.2.

First consider March 2000, during which Novacruz faced a demand of 125 units per week. At this time, the assembly process was divided between three workers (resources) as illustrated by Figure 4.3.

The three workers performed the following activities. In the first activity, the first 30 of the overall 80 parts are assembled, including the fork, the steer support, and the t-handle.

FIGURE 4.1
The Xootr by Novacruz

Given the complexity of this assembly operation, it takes about 13 minutes per scooter to complete this activity. We refer to 13 minutes/unit as the *activity time*. Note that in the current process, each activity is staffed with exactly one worker.

In the second activity, a worker assembles the wheel, the brake, and some other parts related to the steering mechanism. The second worker also assembles the deck. This step is somewhat faster, and its activity time is 11 minutes per unit. The scooter is completed by the third worker, who wipes off the product, applies the decals and grip tape, and conducts the final functional test. The activity time is about 8 minutes per unit.

FIGURE 4.2
Lifecycle Demand Trajectory for Xootrs

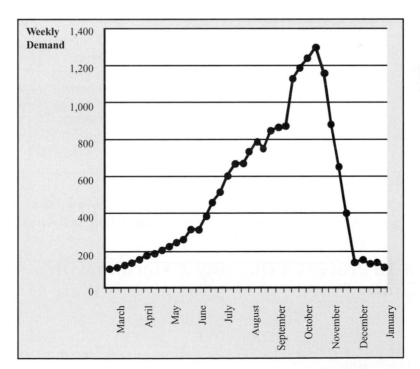

FIGURE 4.3
**Current process
layout**

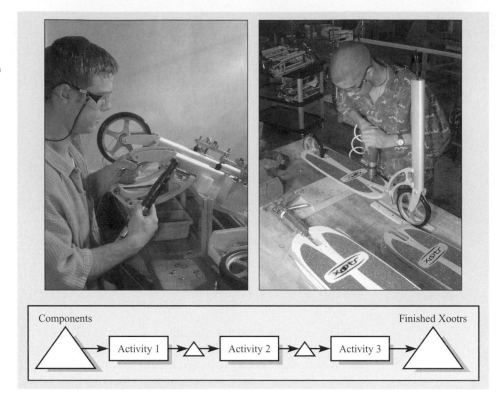

To determine the capacity of an individual resource or a group of resources performing the same activity, we write:

$$\text{Capacity} = \frac{\text{Number of resources}}{\text{Activity time}}$$

This is intuitive, as the capacity grows proportionally with the number of workers. For example, for the first activity, which is performed by one worker, we write:

$$\text{Capacity} = \frac{1}{13 \text{ minutes/scooter}} = 0.0769 \text{ scooter/minute}$$

which we can rewrite as

$$0.0769 \text{ scooter/minute} \times 60 \text{ minutes/hour} = 4.6 \text{ scooters/hour}$$

Similarly, we can compute capacities of the second worker to be 5.45 scooters/hour and of the third worker to be 7.5 scooters/hour.

As we have done in the preceding chapter, we define the bottleneck as the resource with the lowest capacity. In this case the bottleneck is the first resource, resulting in a process capacity of 4.6 scooters/hour.

4.2   Time to Process a Quantity *X* Starting with an Empty Process

Imagine Novacruz received a very important rush order of 100 scooters, which would be assigned highest priority. Assume further that this order arrives early in the morning and there are no scooters currently in inventory, neither between the resources (work-in-process, WIP) nor in the finished goods inventory (FGI). How long will it take to fulfill this order?

As we are facing a large order of scooters, we will attempt to move as many scooters through the system as possible. Therefore, we are capacity-constrained and the flow rate of the process is determined by the capacity of the bottleneck (one scooter every 13 minutes). The time between the completions of two subsequent flow units is called the *cycle time* of a process and will be defined more formally in the next section.

We cannot simply compute the time to produce 100 units as 100 units/0.0769 unit/minute = 1,300 minutes because that calculation assumes the system is producing at the bottleneck rate, one unit every 13 minutes. However, that is only the case once the system is "up and running." In other words, the first scooter of the day, assuming the system starts the day empty (with no work in process inventory), takes even longer than 13 minutes to complete. How much longer depends on how the line is paced.

The current system is called a *worker-paced* line because each worker is free to work at his or her own pace: if the first worker finishes before the next worker is ready to accept the parts, then the first worker puts the completed work in the inventory between them. Eventually the workers need to conform to the bottleneck rate; otherwise, the inventory before the bottleneck would grow too big for the available space. But that concern is not relevant for the first unit moving through the system, so the time to get the first scooter through the system is $13 + 11 + 8 = 32$ minutes. More generally:

Time through an empty worker-paced process = Sum of the activity times

An alternative to the worker-paced process is a machine-paced process as depicted in Figure 4.4. In a machine-paced process all of the steps must work at the same rate even with the first unit through the system. Hence, if a machine-paced process were used, then the first Xootr would be produced after 3×13 minutes, as the conveyor belt has the same speed at all three process steps (there is just one conveyor belt, which has to be paced to the slowest step). More generally,

Time through an empty machine-paced process
= Number of resources in sequence × Activity time of the bottleneck step

Now return to our worker-paced process. After waiting 32 minutes for the first scooter, it only takes an additional 13 minutes until the second scooter is produced and from then onwards, we obtain an additional scooter every 13 minutes. Thus, scooter 1 is produced after 32 minutes, scooter 2 after $32 + 13 = 45$ minutes, scooter 3 after $32 + (2 \times 13) = 58$ minutes, scooter 4 after $32 + (3 \times 13) = 71$ minutes, and so on.

More formally, we can write the following formula. The time it takes to finish X units starting with an empty system is

Time to finish X units starting with an empty system
$$= \text{Time through an empty process} + \frac{X - 1 \text{ unit}}{\text{Flow rate}}$$

You may wonder whether it is always necessary to be so careful about the difference between the time to complete the first unit and all of the rest of the units. In this case it is because the number of scooters is relatively small, so each one matters. But imagine a

FIGURE 4.4
A Machine-Paced Process Layout
(Note: conveyor belt is only shown for illustration)

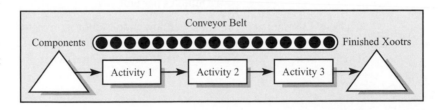

Exhibit 4.1

TIME TO PROCESS A QUANTITY *X* STARTING WITH AN EMPTY PROCESS

1. Find the time it takes the flow unit to go through the empty system:

   - in worker-paced line, this is the sum of the activity times
   - in machine-paced line, this is the cycle time × the number of stations

2. Compute the capacity of the process (see previous methods). Since we are producing *X* units as fast as we can, we are capacity-constrained; thus,

$$\text{Flow rate} = \text{Process capacity}$$

3. Time to finish *X* units

$$= \text{Time through empty process} + \frac{X - 1 \text{ unit}}{\text{Flow rate}}$$

Note: If the process is a continuous process, we can use *X* instead.

continuous-flow process such as a cranberry processing line. Suppose you want to know how long it takes to produce five tons of cranberries. Let's say a cranberry weighs one gram, so five tons equals five million cranberries. Now how long does it take to produce five million cranberries? Strictly speaking, we would look at the time it takes the first berry to flow through the system and then add the time for the residual 4,999,999 berries. However, for all computational purposes, five million minus one is still five million, so we can make our life a little easier by just ignoring this first berry:

$$\text{Time to finish } X \text{ units with a continuous-flow process}$$
$$= \text{Time through an empty process} + \frac{X \text{ units}}{\text{Flow rate}}$$

Exhibit 4.1 summarizes the calculations leading to the time it takes the process to produce *X* units starting with an empty system.

4.3 Labor Content and Idle Time

What is the role of labor cost in the production of the Xootr? Let's look first at how much actual labor is involved in the assembly of the Xootr. Towards this end, we define the *labor content* as the sum of the activity times of the three workers. In this case we compute a labor content of

$$\text{Labor content} = \text{Sum of activity times with labor}$$
$$= 13 \text{ minutes/unit} + 11 \text{ minutes/unit} + 8 \text{ minutes/unit}$$
$$= 32 \text{ minutes per unit}$$

These 32 minutes per unit reflect how much labor is invested into the production of one scooter. We could visualize this measure as follows. Let's say there would be a slip of paper attached to a Xootr and each worker would write the amount of time spent working on the Xootr on this slip. The sum of all numbers entered on the slip is the labor content.

Assume that the average hourly rate of the assembly employees is $12 per hour (and thus $0.20 per minute). Would the resulting cost of labor then be 32 minutes/unit × 0.20/minute = 6.40/unit? The answer is a clear *no*! The reason for this is that the labor content is a measure that takes the perspective of the flow unit but does not reflect any information about how the process is actually operated.

Assume—for illustrative purposes—that we would hire an additional worker for the second activity. As worker 2 is not a constraint on the overall output of the process, this would probably not be a wise thing to do (and that is why we call it an illustrative example). How would the labor content change? Not at all! It would still require the same 32 minutes of labor to produce a scooter. However, we have just increased our daily wages by 33 percent, which should obviously be reflected in our cost of direct labor.

To correctly compute the cost of direct labor, we need to look at two measures:

- The number of scooters produced per unit of time (the flow rate).
- The amount of wages we pay for the same time period.

Above, we found that the process has a capacity of 4.6 scooters an hour, or 161 scooters per week (we assume the process operates 35 hours per week). Given that demand is currently 125 scooters per week (we are demand-constrained), our flow rate is at 125 scooters per week.

Now, we can compute the cost of direct labor as

$$
\begin{aligned}
\text{Cost of direct labor} &= \frac{\text{Total wages per unit of time}}{\text{Flow rate per unit of time}} \\
&= \frac{\text{Wages per week}}{\text{Scooters produced per week}} \\
&= \frac{3 \times \$12/\text{h} \times 35\ \text{h/week}}{125\ \text{scooters/week}} \\
&= \frac{\$1{,}260/\text{week}}{125\ \text{scooters/week}} = \$10.08/\text{scooter}
\end{aligned}
$$

Why is this number so much higher than the number we computed based on the direct labor content? The difference between the two numbers reflects underutilization, or what we will refer to as *idle time*. In this case, there are two sources of idle time:

• The process is never able to produce more than its bottleneck. In this case, this means one scooter every 13 minutes. However, if we consider worker 3, who only takes eight minutes on a scooter, this translates into a 5-minute idle time for every scooter built.

• If the process is demand-constrained, even the bottleneck is not operating at its full capacity, and consequently also exhibits idle time. Given a demand rate of 125 scooters/week, that is, 3.57 scooters/hour or one scooter every 16.8 minutes, all three workers get an extra 3.8 minutes of idle time for every scooter they make.

This reflects the utilization profile and the sources of underutilization that we discussed in Chapter 3 with the Circored process.

Note that this calculation assumes the labor cost is fixed. If it were possible to shorten the workday from the current 7 hours of operations to 5 hours and 25 minutes (25 scooters a day × one scooter every 13 minutes), we would eliminate the second type of idle time.

More formally, define the following:

$$\text{Cycle time} = \frac{1}{\text{Flow rate}}$$

Cycle time provides an alternative measure of how fast the process is creating output. As we are producing one scooter every 16.8 minutes, the cycle time is 16.8 minutes. Similar to what we did intuitively above, we can now define the idle time for worker i as the following:

Idle time for a single worker = Cycle time − Activity time of the single worker

Note that this formula assumes that every activity is staffed with exactly one worker. The idle time measures how much unproductive time a worker has for every unit of output produced. These calculations are summarized by Table 4.1.

If we add up the idle time across all workers, we obtain the total idle time that is incurred for every scooter produced:

$$3.8 + 5.8 + 8.8 = 18.4 \text{ minutes/unit}$$

Now, apply the wage rate of $12 per hour ($0.20/minute × 18.4 minutes/unit), and, voilà, we obtain exactly the difference between the labor cost we initially expected based on the direct labor content alone ($6.40 per unit) and the actual cost of direct labor computed above.

As a final measure of process efficiency, we can look at the average labor utilization of the workers involved in the process. We can obtain this number by comparing the labor content with the amount of labor we have to pay for (the labor content and the idle time):

$$\text{Average labor utilization} = \frac{\text{Labor content}}{\text{Labor content} + \text{Sum of idle times across workers}}$$

$$= \frac{32[\text{minutes per unit}]}{32[\text{minutes per unit}] + 18.4[\text{minutes per unit}]}$$

TABLE 4.1
Basic Calculations Related to Idle Time

	Worker 1	Worker 2	Worker 3
Activity time	13 minutes/unit	11 minutes/unit	8 minutes/unit
Capacity	$\frac{1}{13}$ unit/minutes = 4.61 units/hour	$\frac{1}{11}$ unit/minutes = 5.45 units/hour	$\frac{1}{8}$ unit/minutes = 7.5 units/hour
Process capacity	Minimum {4.61 units/h, 5.45 units/h, 7.5 units/h} = 4.61 units/hour		
Flow rate	Demand = 125 units/week = 3.57 units/hour Flow rate = Minimum {demand, process capacity} = 3.57 units/hour		
Cycle time	1/3.57 hours/unit = 16.8 minutes/unit		
Idle time	16.8 minutes/unit − 13 minutes/unit = 3.8 minutes/unit	16.8 minutes/unit − 11 minutes/unit = 5.8 minutes/unit	16.8 minutes/unit − 8 minutes/unit = 8.8 minutes/unit
Utilization	3.57/4.61 = 77%	3.57/5.45 = 65.5%	3.57/7.5 = 47.6%

Exhibit 4.2

SUMMARY OF LABOR COST CALCULATIONS

1. Compute the capacity of all resources; the resource with the lowest capacity is the bottleneck (see previous methods) and determines the process capacity.
2. Compute Flow rate = Min {Available input, Demand, Process capacity};

$$\text{compute Cycle time} = \frac{1}{\text{Flow rate}}$$

3. Compute the total wages (across all workers) that are paid per unit of time:

$$\text{Cost of direct labor} = \frac{\text{Total wages}}{\text{Flow rate}}$$

4. Compute the idle time of each worker for each unit:

Idle time for worker at resource i = Cycle time $\times$ (Number of workers at resource i) $-$ Activity time at resource i

5. Compute the labor content of the flow unit: this is the sum of all activity times involving direct labor.
6. Add up the idle times across all resources (total idle time); then compute

$$\text{Average labor utilization} = \frac{\text{Labor content}}{\text{Labor content} + \text{Total idle time}}$$

An alternative way to compute the same number is by averaging the utilization level across the three workers:

$$\text{Average labor utilization} = \tfrac{1}{3} \times (\text{Utilization}_1 + \text{Utilization}_2 + \text{Utilization}_3) = 63.4\%$$

where Utilization$_i$ denotes the utilization of the ith worker. Exhibit 4.2 summarizes the calculations related to our analysis of labor costs. It includes the possibility that there are multiple workers performing the same activity.

4.4   Increasing Capacity by Line Balancing

Comparing the utilization levels in Table 4.1 reveals a strong imbalance between workers: while worker 1 is working 77 percent of the time, worker 3 is only active about half of the time (47.6 percent to be exact). Imbalances within a process provide micro-level mismatches between what could be supplied by one step and what is demanded by the following steps. *Line balancing* is the act of reducing such imbalances. It thereby provides the opportunity to

- Increase the efficiency of the process by better utilizing the various resources, in this case labor.
- Increase the capacity of the process (without adding more resources to it) by reallocating either workers from underutilized resources to the bottleneck or work from the bottleneck to underutilized resources.

While based on the present demand rate of 125 units per week and the assumption that all three workers are a fixed cost for 35 hours per week, line balancing would change neither the flow rate (process is demand-constrained) nor the cost of direct labor (assuming the 35 hours per week are fixed); this situation changes with the rapid demand growth experienced by Novacruz.

Consider now a week in May, by which, as indicated by Figure 4.1, the demand for the Xootr had reached a level of 200 units per week. Thus, instead of being demand constrained, the process now is capacity-constrained, specifically, the process now is constrained by worker 1, who can produce one scooter every 13 minutes, while the market demands scooters at a rate of one scooter every 10.5 minutes (200 units/week / 35 hours/week = 5.714 units/hour).

Given that worker 1 is the constraint on the system, all her idle time is now eliminated and her utilization has increased to 100 percent. Yet, workers 2 and 3 still have idle time:

- The flow rate by now has increased to one scooter every 13 minutes or $\frac{1}{13}$ unit per minute (equals $\frac{1}{13} \times 60 \times 35 = 161.5$ scooters per week) based on worker 1.
- Worker 2 has a capacity of one scooter every 11 minutes, that is, $\frac{1}{11}$ unit per minute. Her utilization is thus Flow rate/Capacity$_2 = \frac{1}{13}/\frac{1}{11} = \frac{11}{13} = 84.6\%$.
- Worker 3 has a capacity of one scooter every 8 minutes. Her utilization is thus $\frac{1}{13}/\frac{1}{8} = \frac{8}{13} = 61.5\%$.

Note that the increase in demand not only has increased the utilization levels across workers (the average utilization is now $\frac{1}{3} \times (100\% + 84.6\% + 61.5\%) = 82\%$), but also has reduced the cost of direct labor to

$$\text{Cost of direct labor} = \frac{\text{Total wages per unit of time}}{\text{Flow rate per unit of time}}$$

$$= \frac{\text{Wages per week}}{\text{Scooters produced per week}}$$

$$= \frac{3 \times \$12/\text{hour} \times 35 \text{ hours/week}}{161.5 \text{ scooters/week}}$$

$$= \frac{\$1,260/\text{week}}{161.5 \text{ scooters/week}} = \$7.80/\text{scooter}$$

Now, back to the idea of line balancing. Line balancing attempts to evenly (fairly!) allocate the amount of work that is required to build a scooter across the three process steps.

In an ideal scenario, we could just take the amount of work that goes into building a scooter, which we referred to as the labor content (32 minutes/unit), and split it up evenly between the three workers. Thus, we would achieve a perfect line balance if each worker could take 32/3 minutes/unit; that is, each would have an identical activity time of 10.66 minutes/unit.

Unfortunately, in most processes it is not possible to divide up the work that evenly. Specifically, the activities underlying a process typically consist of a collection of *tasks* that cannot easily be broken up. A closer analysis of the three activities in our case reveals the task structure shown in Table 4.2.

For example, consider the last task of worker 1 (assemble handle cap), which takes 118 seconds per unit. These 118 seconds per unit of work can only be moved to another worker in their entirety. Moreover, we cannot move this task around freely, as it obviously would not be feasible to move the "assemble handle cap" task to after the "seal carton" task.

TABLE 4.2
Task Durations

Worker	Tasks	Task Duration [seconds/unit]
Worker 1	Prepare cable	30
	Move cable	25
	Assemble washer	100
	Apply fork, threading cable end	66
	Assemble socket head screws	114
	Steer pin nut	49
	Brake shoe, spring, pivot bolt	66
	Insert front wheel	100
	Insert axle bolt	30
	Tighten axle bolt	43
	Tighten brake pivot bolt	51
	Assemble handle cap	118
		Total: 792
Worker 2	Assemble brake lever and cable	110
	Trim and cap cable	59
	Place first rib	33
	Insert axles and cleats	96
	Insert rear wheel	135
	Place second rib and deck	84
	Apply grip tape	56
	Insert deck fasteners	75
		Total: 648
Worker 3	Inspect and wipe off	95
	Apply decal and sticker	20
	Insert in bag	43
	Assemble carton	114
	Insert Xootr and manual	94
	Seal carton	84
		Total: 450

However, we could move the 118 seconds per unit from worker 1 to worker 2. In this case, worker 1 would now have an activity time of 674 seconds per unit and worker 2 (who would become the new bottleneck) would have an activity time of 766 seconds per unit. The overall process capacity is increased, we would produce more scooters, and the average labor utilization would move closer to 100 percent.

But can we do better? Within the scope of this book, we only consider cases where the sequence of tasks is given. Line balancing becomes more complicated if we can resequence some of the tasks. For example, there exists no technical reason why the second to last task of worker 2 (apply grip tape) could not be switched with the subsequent task (insert deck fasteners). There exist simple algorithms and heuristics that support line balancing in such more complex settings. Yet, their discussion would derail us from our focus on managerial issues.

But even if we restrict ourselves to line balancing solutions that keep the sequence of tasks unchanged, we can further improve upon the 766-second cycle time we outlined above. Remember that the "gold standard" of line balancing, the even distribution of the labor content across all resources, suggested an activity time of 10.66 minutes per unit, or 640 seconds per unit.

Moving the "assemble handle cap" task from worker 1 to worker 2 was clearly a substantial step in that direction. However, worker 2 has now 126 seconds per unit (766 seconds/unit – 640 seconds/unit) more than what would be a balanced workload. This situation can be improved if we take the worker's last two tasks, (apply grip tape, insert deck fasteners) and move the corresponding 56 + 75 seconds/unit = 131 seconds/unit to worker 3.

The new activity times would be as follows:

- Worker 1: 674 seconds per unit (792 − 118 seconds/unit).
- Worker 2: 635 seconds per unit (648 + 118 − 56 − 75 seconds/unit).
- Worker 3: 581 seconds per unit (450 + 56 + 75 seconds/unit).

Are they optimal? No! We can repeat similar calculations and further move work from worker 1 to worker 2 (tighten brake pivot bolt, 51 seconds per unit) and from worker 2 to worker 3 (place second rib and deck, 84 seconds per unit). The resulting (final) activity times are now

- Worker 1: 623 seconds per unit (674 − 51 seconds/unit).
- Worker 2: 602 seconds per unit (635 + 51 − 84 seconds/unit).
- Worker 3: 665 seconds per unit (581 + 84 seconds/unit).

To make sure we have not "lost" any work on the way, we can add up the three new activity times and obtain the same labor content (1,890 seconds per unit) as before. The resulting labor utilization would be improved to

$$\text{Average labor utilization} = \text{Labor content(Labor content} + \text{Total idle time)}$$

$$= 1{,}890/(1{,}890 + 42 + 63 + 0) = 94.7\%$$

The process improvement we have implemented based on line balancing is sizeable in its economic impact. Based on the new bottleneck (worker 3), we see that we can produce one Xootr every 665 seconds, thereby having a process capacity of $\frac{1}{665}$ units/second × 3,600 seconds/hour × 35 hours/week = 189.5 units per week. Thus, compared to the unbalanced line (161.5 units per week), we have increased process capacity (and flow rate) by 17 percent (28 units) without having increased our weekly spending rate on labor. Moreover, we have reduced the cost of direct labor to $6.65/unit.

Figure 4.5 summarizes the idea of line balancing by contrasting cycle time and task allocation of the unbalanced line (before) and the balanced line (after).

4.5   Scale Up to Higher Volume

As indicated by Figure 4.2, demand for the Xootr increased dramatically within the next six months and, by July, had reached a level of 700 units per week. Thus, in order to maintain a reasonable match between supply and demand, Novacruz had to increase its process capacity (supply) further.

To increase process capacity for a worker-paced line, in this case from 189.5 units/week (see balanced line with three workers above) to 700 units per week, additional workers are needed. While the fundamental steps involved in building a Xootr remain unchanged, we have several options to lay out the new, high-volume process:

- Using the exact same layout and staffing plan, we could replicate the—now balanced—process and add another (and another, . . .) worker-paced line with three workers each.
- We could assign additional workers to the three process steps, which would increase the capacity of the steps and hence lead to a higher overall process capacity.
- We could divide up the work currently performed by three workers, thereby increasing the specialization of each step (and thus reducing activity times and hence increasing capacity).

We will quickly go through the computations for all three approaches. The corresponding process flow diagrams are summarized in Figure 4.6.

FIGURE 4.5
Graphical
Illustration of
Line Balance

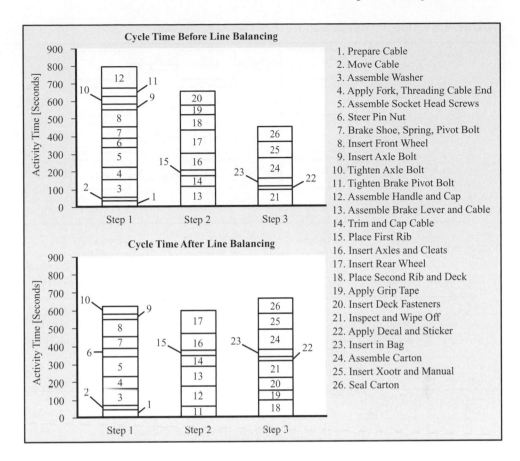

Increasing Capacity by Replicating the Line

As the capacity of the entire operation grows linearly with the number of replications, we could simply add three replications of the process to obtain a new total capacity of 4 × 189.5 units/week = 758 units per week.

The advantage of this approach is that it would allow the organization to benefit from the knowledge it has gathered from their initial process layout. The downside of this approach is that it keeps the ratio of workers across the three process steps constant (in total, four people do step 1, four at step 2, and four at step 3), while this might not necessarily be the most efficient way of allocating workers to assembly tasks (it keeps the ratio between workers at each step fixed).

Alternatively, we could just add two replications and obtain a process capacity of 568.5 units per week and make up for the remaining 131.5 units (700 − 568.5 units/week) by adding overtime. Given that the 131.5 units to be produced in overtime would be spread over the three lines, each line would have to produce 131.53 = 43.83 units per week, corresponding to 8.1 hours of overtime per week (43.83 units/week / 5.41 units/hour).

Under the assumption that we could use overtime, the average labor utilization would remain unchanged at 94.7 percent.

Increasing Capacity by Selectively Adding Workers

While the first approach assumed the number of workers at each process step to be the same, such a staffing might not necessarily be optimal. Specifically, we observe that (after the rebalancing) the third step is the bottleneck (activity time of 665 seconds per unit). Thus, we feel tempted to add over-proportionally more workers to this step than to the first two.

FIGURE 4.6   **Three Process Layouts for High-Volume Production**

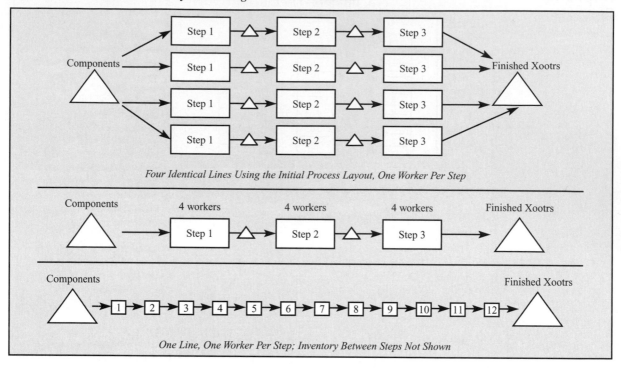

Four Identical Lines Using the Initial Process Layout, One Worker Per Step

One Line, One Worker Per Step; Inventory Between Steps Not Shown

Given that we defined the capacity at each resource as the number of workers divided by the corresponding activity time, we can write the following:

$$\text{Requested capacity} = \frac{\text{Number of workers}}{\text{Activity time}}$$

For step 1, this calculation yields (700 units per week at 35 hours per week is 0.00555 unit per second):

$$0.00555 \text{ unit/second} = \frac{\text{Number of workers}}{623 \text{ seconds per unit}}$$

Thus, the number of workers required to meet the current demand is $0.00555 \times 623 = 3.46$ workers. Given that we cannot hire half a worker (and ignoring overtime for the moment), this means we have to hire four workers at step 1. In the same way, we find that we need to hire 3.34 workers at step 2 and 3.69 workers at step 3.

The fact that we need to hire a total of four workers for each of the three steps reflects the good balance that we have achieved above. If we would do a similar computation based on the initial numbers (792,648,450 seconds/unit for workers 1, 2, and 3 respectively; see Table 3.2), we would obtain the following:

• At step 1, we would hire 0.00555 unit/second = Number of workers/792 seconds/unit; therefore, Number of workers = 4.4.

• At step 2, we would hire 0.00555 unit/second = Number of workers/648 seconds/unit; therefore, Number of workers = 3.6.

• At step 3, we would hire 0.00555 unit/second = Number of workers/450 seconds/unit; therefore, Number of workers = 2.5.

Thus, we observe that a staffing that allocates extra resources to activities with longer activity times (5 workers for step 1 versus 4 for step 2 and 3 for step 3) provides an alternative way of line balancing.

Note also that if we had just replicated the unbalanced line, we would have had to add four replications as opposed to the three replications of the balanced line (we need five times step 1). Thus, line balancing, which at the level of the individual worker might look like "hair-splitting," debating about every second of worker time, at the aggregate level can achieve very substantial savings in direct labor cost.

At several places throughout the book, we will discuss the fundamental ideas of the Toyota Production System, of which line balancing is an important element. In the spirit of the Toyota Production System, idle time is considered as waste (*muda*), and therefore should be eliminated from the process to the extent possible.

Increasing Capacity by Further Specializing Tasks

Unlike the previous two approaches to increase capacity, the third approach fundamentally alters the way the individual tasks are assigned to workers. As we noted in our discussion of line balancing, we can think of each activity as a set of individual tasks. Thus, if we increase the level of specialization of workers, and now have each worker only be responsible for one or two tasks (opposed to previously an activity consisting of 5 to 10 tasks), we would be able to reduce activity time and thereby increase the capacity of the line.

Specifically, we begin our analysis by determining a targeted cycle time based on demand: in this case we want to produce 700 units per week, which means 20 scooters per hour or one scooter every three minutes. How many workers does it take to produce one Xootr every three minutes?

The answer to this question is actually rather complicated. The reason for this complication is as follows. We cannot compute the capacity of an individual worker without knowing which tasks this worker will be in charge of. At the same time, we cannot assign tasks to workers, as we do not know how many workers we have.

To break this circularity, we start our analysis with the staffing we have obtained under the previous approaches, that is, 12 workers for the entire line. Table 4.3 shows how we can assign the tasks required to build a Xootr across these 12 workers.

Following this approach, the amount of work an individual worker needs to master is reduced to a maximum of 180 seconds. We refer to this number as the *span of control*. Given that this span of control is much smaller than under the previous approaches (665 seconds), workers will be able to perform their tasks with significantly less training. Workers are also likely to improve upon their activity times more quickly as specialization can increase the rate of learning.

The downside of this approach is its negative effect on labor utilization. Consider what has happened to labor utilization:

$$\text{Average labor utilization} = \frac{\text{Labor content}}{\text{Labor content} + \text{Sum of idle time}}$$

$$= \frac{1890}{1{,}890 + 25 + 0 + 65 + 7 + 11 + 11 + 51 + 45 + 40 + 10 + 3 + 2} = 87.5\%$$

Note that average labor utilization was 94.7 percent (after balancing) with three workers. Thus, specialization (smaller spans of control) makes line balancing substantially more complicated. This is illustrated by Figure 4.7.

The reason for this decrease in labor utilization, and thus the poorer line balance, can be found in the granularity of the tasks. Since it is not possible to break up the individual tasks further, moving a task from one worker to the next becomes relatively more significant. For example, when we balanced the three-worker process, moving a 51-second-per-unit task to another step accounted for just 8 percent of the step's work (671 seconds per unit). In a 12-step process, however, moving the same 51-second-per-unit task is now relative to a

TABLE 4.3
Activity Times and Task Allocation under Increased Specialization

Worker	Tasks	Task Duration [seconds/unit]
Worker 1	Prepare cable	30
	Move cable	25
	Assemble washer	100
		Total: 155
Worker 2	Apply fork, threading cable end	66
	Assemble socket head skrews	114
		Total: 180
Worker 3	Steer pin nut	49
	Brake shoe, spring, pivot bolt	66
		Total: 115
Worker 4	Insert front wheel	100
	Insert axle bolt	30
	Tighten axle bolt	43
		Total: 173
Worker 5	Tighten brake pivot bolt	51
	Assemble handle cap	118
		Total: 169
Worker 6	Assemble brake lever and cable	110
	Trim and cap cable	59
		Total: 169
Worker 7	Place first rib	33
	Insert axles and cleats	96
		Total: 129
Worker 8	Insert rear wheel	135
		Total: 135
Worker 9	Place second rib and deck	84
	Apply grip tape	56
		Total: 140
Worker 10	Insert deck fasteners	75
	Inspect and wipe off	95
		Total: 170
Worker 11	Apply decal and sticker	20
	Insert in bag	43
	Assemble carton	114
		Total: 177
Worker 12	Insert Xootr and manual	94
	Seal carton	84
		Total: 178
	Total labor content	1,890

169-second-per-unit workload for the step, thereby accounting for 30 percent of work. For this reason, it is difficult to further improve the allocation of tasks to workers relative to what is shown in Figure 4.7.

The observation that line balancing becomes harder with an increase in specialization can best be understood if we "turn this reasoning on its head": line balancing becomes easier with a decrease in specialization. To see this, consider the case of having one single worker do all the tasks in the process. The corresponding labor utilization would be 100

FIGURE 4.7
Line Balance in a
Highly Specialized
Line
(Different shades
represent different
tasks)

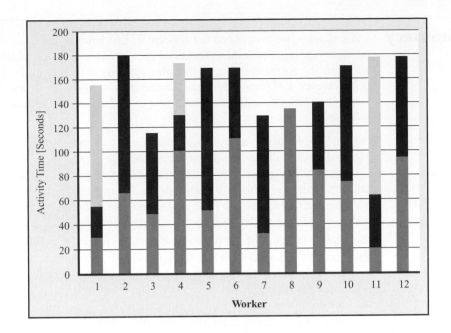

percent (assuming there is enough demand to keep at least one worker busy), as, by definition, this one person would also be the bottleneck.

The idea of having one resource perform all activities of the process is referred to as a work cell. The process flow diagram of a work cell is illustrated by Figure 4.8. Since the activity time at a work cell with one worker is the same as the labor content, we would have a capacity per work cell of $\frac{1}{1,890}$ unit per second $= 1.9048$ units per hour, or 66.66 units per week. Already 11 work cells would be able to fulfill the demand of 700 Xootrs per week. In other words, the improved balance that comes with a work cell would allow us to further improve efficiency.

Again, the downside of this approach is that it requires one worker to master a span of control of over 30 minutes, which requires a highly trained operator. Moreover, Novacruz found that working with the 12-person line and the corresponding increase in specialization led to a substantial reduction in activity times.

FIGURE 4.8
Parallel Work Cells
(Only three work-
cells are shown)

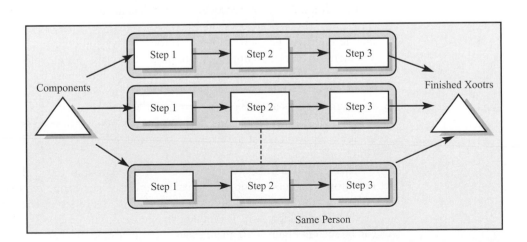

4.6 Summary

In this chapter, we introduced the concept of line balancing. Line balancing attempts to eliminate idle time from the process and thereby increase labor utilization. At first sight, line balancing seems to belong in the same category as "hair-splitting" and "penny-counting." However, it is important to understand the managerial role that line balancing plays in operations. Specifically, it is important to understand the following three managerial benefits:

• First of all, while it is always more tempting to talk about dollars rather than pennies, pennies do matter in many industries. Consider, for example, the computer industry. All PC manufacturers purchase from the same pool of suppliers of processors, disk drives, optical devices, and so forth. Thus, while the $10 of labor cost in a computer might seem small relative to the purchase price of the computer, those $10 are under our managerial control, while most of the other costs are dictated by the market environment.

• Second, in the spirit of the Toyota Production System (TPS), idle time is waste and thereby constitutes what in TPS is known as *muda*. The problem with *muda*/idle time is that it not only adds to the production costs, but has the potential to hide many other problems. For example, a worker might use idle time to finish or rework a task that she could not complete during the allocated activity time. While this does not lead to a direct, out-of-pocket cost, it avoids the root cause of the problem, which, when it surfaces, can be fixed.

• Third, while the $10 labor cost in the assembly operation of a PC manufacturer discussed above might seem like a low number, there is much more labor cost involved in the PC than $10. What appears as procurement cost for the PC maker is to some extent labor cost for the suppliers of the PC maker. If we "roll up" all operations throughout the value chain leading to a PC, we find that the cost of labor is rather substantial. This idea is illustrated in Figure 4.9 for the case of the automotive industry: while for a company like DaimlerChrysler assembly labor costs seem to be only a small element of costs, the 70 percent of costs that are procurement costs themselves include assembly labor costs from suppliers, subsuppliers, and so forth. If we look at all costs in the value chain (from DaimlerChrysler to their fifth-tier supplier), we see that about a quarter of costs in the automotive supply chain are a result of labor costs. A consequence of this observation is that it is not enough to improve our own operations internally, but to spread such improvements throughout the supplier network, as this is where the biggest improvement opportunities are hidden. This concept of supplier development is another fundamental concept of the Toyota Production System.

In addition to these three factors, line balancing also illustrates an important—and from a managerial perspective very attractive—property of operations management. Line balancing improves per-unit labor cost (productivity) and does not require any financial investments in assets! To improve labor productivity, we would typically attempt to automate parts of the assembly, which would lower the per-unit labor cost, but at the same time require a higher investment of capital. Such an approach would be most likely if we operated in a high wage location such as Germany or France. In contrast, we could try to operate the process with little or no automation but have a lot of labor time invested in the process. Such an approach would be more likely if we moved the process to a low-wage location such as China or Taiwan.

This tension is illustrated by Figure 4.10. The horizontal axis of Figure 4.10. shows the return on the assets tied up in the manufacturing process. High returns are desirable, which could be achieved by using little automation and a lot of labor. The vertical axis shows the productivity of labor, which would be maximized if the process were highly automated. As can be seen in Figure 4.10, there exists a tension (trade-off) between the dimensions, visible

FIGURE 4.9
Sources of Cost in the Supply Chain

Source: Whitney 2004, based on DaimlerChrysler.

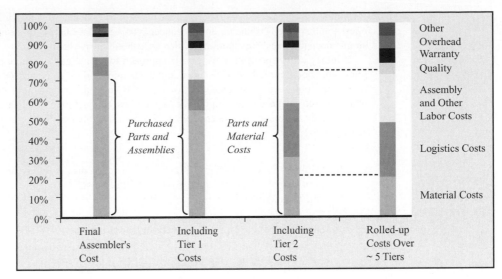

in the form of an efficient frontier. Thus, changes with respect to the level of automation would move the process up or down the frontier. One dimension is traded against the other.

In contrast, the effect of line balancing in the context of Figure 4.10 is very different. Line balancing improves labor productivity without any additional investment. To the extent that line balancing allows the firm to eliminate some currently underutilized resources using production equipment, line balancing also reduces the required assets. Thus, what from a strategic perspective seems like a simple, one-dimensional positioning problem along the technology frontier now has an additional dimension. Rather than simply taking the current process as given and finding a good strategic position, the firm should attempt to improve its process capability and improve along both performance dimensions simultaneously.

FIGURE 4.10
Trade-off between Labor Productivity and Capital Investment

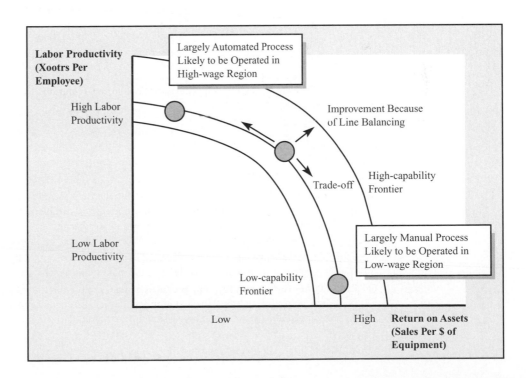

4.7 Further Readings

Bartholdi and Eisenstein (1996) develop the concept of a bucket brigade, which corresponds to a line operation that is self-balancing. In this concept, workers move between stations and follow relatively simple decision rules that determine which task should be performed next.

Whitney (2004) presents a systematic approach to design and production of mechanical assemblies. This book introduces mechanical and economic models of assemblies and assembly automation. The book takes a system view of assembly, including the notion of product architecture, feature-based design, computer models of assemblies, analysis of mechanical constraint, assembly sequence analysis, tolerances, system-level design for assembly and JIT methods, and economics of assembly automation.

4.8 Practice Problems

Q4.1*   **(Empty System, Labor Utilization)** Consider a process consisting of three resources in a worker-paced line and a wage rate of $10 per hour. Assume there is unlimited demand for the product.

Resource	Activity Time (minutes)	Number of Workers
1	10	2
2	6	1
3	16	3

a. How long does it take the process to produce 100 units starting with an empty system?

b. What is the average labor content?

c. What is the average labor utilization?

d. What is the cost of direct labor?

Q4.2   **(Assign Tasks to Workers)** Consider the following six tasks that must be assigned to 4 workers on a conveyor-paced assembly line (i.e., a machine-paced line flow). Each worker must perform at least one task.

	Time to Complete Task (seconds)
Task 1	30
Task 2	25
Task 3	35
Task 4	40
Task 5	15
Task 6	30

The current conveyor-paced assembly line configuration assigns the workers in the following way:

• Worker 1: Task 1

• Worker 2: Task 2

• Worker 3: Tasks 3, 4

• Worker 4: Tasks 5, 6

a. What is the capacity of the current line?

b. Now assume that tasks are allocated to maximize capacity of the line, subject to the conditions that (1) a worker can only perform two adjacent operations and (2) all tasks need to be done in their numerical order. What is the capacity of this line now?

c. Now assume that tasks are allocated to maximize capacity of the line and that tasks can be performed in any order. What is the maximum capacity that can be achieved?

Q4.3   **(PowerToys)** PowerToys Inc. produces a small remote-controlled toy truck on a conveyor belt with nine stations. Each station has, under the current process layout, one worker assigned to it. Stations and processing times are summarized in the following table:

(* indicates that the solution is at the end of the book)

Station	Task	Processing Times (seconds)
1	Mount battery units	75
2	Insert remote control receiver	85
3	Insert chip	90
4	Mount front axle	65
5	Mount back axle	70
6	Install electric motor	55
7	Connect motor to battery unit	80
8	Connect motor to rear axle	65
9	Mount plastic body	80

a. What is the bottleneck in this process?

b. What is the capacity, in toy trucks per hour, of the assembly line?

c. What is the direct labor cost for the toy truck with the current process if each worker receives $15/hour, expressed in dollars per toy truck?

d. What would be the direct labor cost for the toy truck if work would be organized in a work cell, that is, one worker performs all tasks? Assume that the activity times would remain unchanged (i.e., there are no specialization gains).

e. What is the utilization of the worker in station 2?

Because of a drastically reduced forecast, the plant management has decided to cut staffing from nine to six workers per shift. Assume that (i) the nine tasks in the above table cannot be divided; (ii) the nine tasks are assigned to the six workers in the most efficient way possible; and (iii) if one worker is in charge of two tasks, the tasks have to be adjacent (i.e., one worker cannot work on tasks 1 and 3).

f. How would you assign the nine tasks to the six workers?

g. What is the new capacity of the line (in toy trucks per hour)?

Q4.4 **(12 Tasks to 4 Workers)** Consider the following tasks that must be assigned to four workers on a conveyor-paced assembly line (i.e., a machine-paced line flow). Each worker must perform at least one task. There is unlimited demand.

Time to Complete Task (seconds)	
Task 1	30
Task 2	25
Task 3	15
Task 4	20
Task 5	15
Task 6	20
Task 7	50
Task 8	15
Task 9	20
Task 10	25
Task 11	15
Task 12	20

The current conveyor-paced assembly-line configuration assigns the workers in the following way:

- Worker 1: Tasks 1, 2, 3
- Worker 2: Tasks 4, 5, 6
- Worker 3: Tasks 7, 8, 9
- Worker 4: Tasks 10, 11, 12

a. What is the capacity of the current line?

b. What is the direct labor content?

c. What is the average labor utilization (do not consider any transient effects, such as the line being emptied before breaks or shift changes)?

d. How long would it take to produce 100 units, starting with an empty system?

The firm is hiring a fifth worker. Assume that tasks are allocated to the five workers to maximize capacity of the line, subject to the conditions that (i) a worker can only perform adjacent operations and (ii) all tasks need to be done in their numerical order.

e. What is the capacity of this line now?

Again, assume the firm has hired a fifth worker. Assume further that tasks are allocated to maximize capacity of the line and that tasks can be performed in any order.

f. What is the maximum capacity that can be achieved?

g. What is the minimum number of workers that could produce at an hourly rate of 72 units? Assume the tasks can be allocated to workers as described in the beginning (i.e., tasks cannot be done in any order).

Q4.5 (**Geneva Watch**) The Geneva Watch Corporation manufactures watches on a conveyor belt with six stations. One worker stands at each station and performs the following tasks:

Station	Tasks	Processing Time (seconds)
A: Preparation 1	Heat-stake lens to bezel	14
	Inspect bezel	26
	Clean switch holes	10
	Install set switch in bezel	18
	Total time for A	68
B: Preparation 2	Check switch travel	23
	Clean inside bezel	12
	Install module in bezel	25
	Total time for B	60
C: Battery installation	Install battery clip on module	20
	Heat-stake battery clip on module	15
	Install 2 batteries in module	22
	Check switch	13
	Total time for C	70
D: Band installation	Install band	45
	Inspect band	13
	Total time for D	58
E: Packaging preparation	Cosmetic inspection	20
	Final test	55
	Total time for E	75
F: Watch packaging	Place watch and cuff in display box	20
	Place cover in display box base	14
	Place owner's manual, box into tub	30
	Total time for F	64

These six workers begin their workday at 8:00 A.M. and work steadily until 4:00 P.M. At 4:00, no new watch parts are introduced into station A and the conveyor belt continues until all of the work-in-process inventory has been processed and leaves station F. Thus, each morning the workers begin with an empty system.

a. What is the bottleneck in this process?

b. What is the capacity, in watches per hour, of the assembly line (ignore the time it takes for the first watch to come off the line)?

c. What is the direct labor content for the processes on this conveyor belt?

d. What is the utilization of the worker in station B (ignore the time it takes for the first watch to come off the line)?

e. How many minutes of idle time will the worker in station C have in one hour (ignore the time it takes for the first watch to come off the line)?

f. What time will it be (within one minute) when the assembly line has processed 193 watches on any given day?

Q4.6   (**Super Sonic**) The Super Sonic Corporation assembles circuit boards at its Chicago facility for its line of consumer electronics products. The Chicago facility produces boards for televisions, VCRs, and stereo systems, which are then assembled at different plants throughout North America. Each line at the Chicago board plant is dedicated to a particular product line.

The television circuit board assembly line consists of 10 stations connected by a conveyor belt and automated material-handling equipment. The line operates for eight hours per day and can sell every unit it produces. See the table below for a summary of the process. Note that the inventory numbers refer to the number of flow units that are currently processed at the resource. For example, the inspection step takes up five slots at the assembly line, five times as much as the solder screen step.

- **Solder screen:** Raw boards are fed into the screen machine. The machine then applies paste prior to placement of all surface-mount parts. A single operator tends the machine and makes sure that it is always fed with the appropriate amounts of input materials.

- **Position parts:** A fully automated pick and place robot positions each surface mount component at the appropriate site on the board. The machines are fed by reels of components and are programmed automatically to synchronize placements with the design of each board being processed.

- **Through-hole part assembly:** This is an entirely manual process. Workers place larger and more delicate through-hole components (each CPU chip) on the board.

- **Convection ovens:** Each oven heats a board to reflow solder that has been applied to the surface-mount parts. Operators position thermal sensors on each board to ensure that the correct amount of heat is applied to different sectors of the board. The operators also load and unload boards from the ovens.

- **Wave solder:** The operator attaches each board to a rack and then loads and unloads racks that are fed into the machine on a conveyor belt. The machine is used to connect through-hole components to each board by passing the board over a pool of molten solder.

- **Board cleaning:** Boards are cleaned in automated washing machines that rinse off all debris and residues associated with the placement and soldering steps. Workers load and unload boards into the machines. Each machine runs one board at a time on a preset wash/rinse cycle.

- **Inspect:** This is a manual process. Each board is examined to ensure that all components are properly placed and soldered.

- **Burn-in test:** Each board is connected to an automated testing machine. The boards are powered up and their output is monitored over the test period. Operators load and unload boards and remove defective boards for rework.

- **Functionality and performance test:** This is another manual operation. Testers test the functionality of each board against a preprogrammed protocol.

- **Package and ship:** Boards are shipped with electrostatic protective materials.

Station	Task	Activity Time (per board)	Labor Content (per board)	Number of Resources	Inventory (boards)
1	Solder screen	2 minutes	2 minutes	1 worker	1
2	Position parts	5 minutes	0 minute	3 machines	3
3	Through-hole part assembly	9 minutes	9 minutes	4 workers	4
4	Convection ovens	15 minutes	2 minutes	7 ovens 2 workers	7
5	Wave solder	1.5 minutes	0.5 minute	1 worker	1
6	Board cleaning	12 minutes	2 minutes	6 machines 2 workers	6
7	Inspect	8 minutes	8 minutes	5 inspection workers	5
8	Burn-in test	20 minutes	3 minutes	9 machines 2 workers	9
9	Functionality and performance test	10 minutes	10 minutes	5 testers	5
10	Package and ship	6 minutes	6 minutes	3 workers	3

a. What is the bottleneck activity?

b. What is the process capacity of the line?

c. What is the direct labor content of a board?

d. What is the utilization of station 1, the solder screen operation?

e. What is the flow time of the process (i.e., the average time to get one board through the line), assuming that the process is capacity-constrained?

f. Approximately how long would it take Super Sonic to complete an order for 500 boards? Assume that the factory is empty when the order arrives.

g. Super Sonic is interested in increasing the capacity of the line without investing in any additional equipment. They think they can do so by reassigning workers on the line. What would be the impact on line capacity of decreasing the number of inspectors in activity 7 (inspect) from five to four people and reassigning that inspector optimally, that is, to the activity that would provide the greatest increment in capacity?

Chapter 5

Batching and Other Flow Interruptions: Setup Times and the Economic Order Quantity Model

Up to this point, we were working under the assumption that during every X units of time, one flow unit would enter the process and one flow unit would leave the process. We defined X as the process cycle time. In the scooter example of the previous chapter, we established a cycle time of three minutes in conjunction with Table 4.3, allowing us to fulfill demand of 700 scooters per week.

In an ideal process, a cycle time of three minutes would imply that every resource receives one flow unit as an input each three-minute interval and creates one flow unit of output each three-minute interval. Such a smooth and constant flow of units is the dream of any operations manager, yet it is rarely feasible in practice. There are several reasons for why the smooth process flow is interrupted, the most important ones being setups and variability in processing times or quality levels. The focus of this chapter is on setups, which are an important characteristic of batch-flow operations. Problems related to variability are discussed in Chapters 6 and 7. And quality problems are discussed in Chapter 8.

Unlike mass production systems with their highly specialized tools, batch operations typically use general-purpose technology to produce a larger variety of products in production runs. Given the general nature of the production technology and the high level of product variety, the production resources in a batch-flow operation commonly have to be set up before beginning work on a specific product.

We define a production batch as a collection of flow units that are processed before the resource (usually the equipment being used at that step) needs to go through another setup. Such a setup might involve changing the equipment configuration from producing product A to producing product B (in which case, we also speak of a changeover time), an example common in low-volume, high-variety manufacturing. A setup also might be the result of some other, recurring flow interruption, such as breaks for workers or downtime for machines.

In this chapter, we continue our discussion of the Xootr production process. While the assembly operations discussed in Chapter 3 do not include any setup times, the CNC milling machine that produces the steer support as well as the ribs required for final assembly of the Xootr follow a batch operation (see Figure 5.1). Specifically, the milling machine must undergo a one-hour setup whenever it is switched from producing steer support parts to ribs and, similarly, a one-hour setup whenever it is switched back to producing steer support parts. Every Xootr includes one steer support unit and two ribs.

5.1   The Impact of Setups on Capacity

The objective of our analysis remains to predict the three basic performance measures of a process: inventory, flow rate, and flow time. Toward that end, we need to be able to identify the bottleneck of the process, which requires the computation of the capacity for each of the various process steps.

However, in determining the capacity of each process step, it is important to not only count the per-unit activity times, but also to include the effect of setup times on capacity. As no output is produced while the resource is in setup mode, it is fairly intuitive that frequent setups lead to lower capacity.

Shigeo Shingo, one of the most influential thought leaders in manufacturing, is quoted as saying, "The flow must go on," when he witnessed changeover times of more than an hour in an automotive plant he studied. The idea of "the flow must go on" is helpful to us for two reasons. First, it illustrates that setups are interruptions of the process flow. They thereby "steal" capacity. Second, while we can do many things to choose batch sizes intelligently—which will be explained in the following pages—there fundamentally exists only one response to setups: eliminate them, or at least try to reduce the time it takes to perform the setup. Shigeo Shingo developed a powerful technique toward that end, which we revisit at the end of this chapter.

To understand how setups reduce the capacity of a process, consider Figure 5.2. The impact of setups on capacity is fairly intuitive. As nothing is produced at a resource during setup, the more frequently a resource is set up, the lower its capacity. As discussed above, the milling machine underlying the example of Figure 5.2 has the following activity times/setup times:

- It takes one minute to produce one steer support unit (of which there is one per Xootr).

FIGURE 5.1   **Milling Machine (left) and Steer Support Parts (right)**

FIGURE 5.2 **The Impact of Setup Times on Capacity**

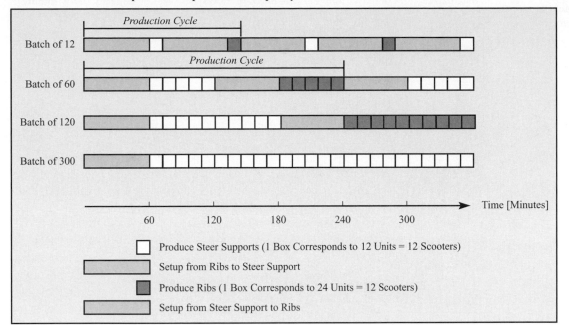

• It takes 60 minutes to change over the milling machine from producing steer supports to producing ribs (setup time).

• It takes 0.5 minute to produce one rib; since there are two ribs in a Xootr, this translates to one minute/unit.

• Finally, it takes another 60 minutes to change over the milling machine back to producing steer supports.

Now consider the impact that varying the batch size has on capacity. Recall that we defined capacity as the maximum flow rate at which a process can operate. If we produce in small batches of 12 scooters per batch, we spend a total of two hours of setup time (one hour to set up the production for steer supports and one hour to set up the production of ribs) for every 12 scooters we produce. These two hours of setup time are lost for regular production.

The capacity of the resource can be increased by increasing the batch size. If the machine is set up every 60 units, the capacity-reducing impact of setup can be spread out over 60 units. This results in a higher capacity for the milling machine. Specifically, for a batch size of 60, the milling machine could produce at 0.25 scooter per minute. Table 5.1 summarizes the capacity calculations for batch sizes of 12, 60, 120, and 300.

Generalizing the computations in Table 5.1, we can compute the capacity of a resource with setups as a function of the batch size:

$$\text{Capacity given batch size} = \frac{\text{Batch size}}{\text{Setup time} + \text{Batch size} \times \text{Time per unit}}$$

Basically, the above equation is spreading the "unproductive" setup time over the members of a batch. To use the equation, we need to be careful how exactly we define the batch size, the setup time, and the time per unit:

• The batch size is the number of scooters that are produced in one "cycle" (i.e., before the process repeats itself, see Figure 5.2). Let's say the batch size would be $B = 100$ scooters.

Batch Size	Time to Complete One Batch [minutes]	Capacity [units/minute]
TABLE 5.1 **The Impact of Setups on Capacity**		
12	60 minutes (set up steering support) + 12 minutes (produce steering supports) + 60 minutes (set up ribs) + 12 minutes (produce ribs) 144 minutes	12/144 = 0.0833
60	60 minutes (set up steering support) + 60 minutes (produce steering supports) + 60 minutes (set up ribs) + 60 minutes (produce ribs) 240 minutes	60/240 = 0.25
120	60 minutes (set up steering support) + 120 minutes (produce steering supports) + 60 minutes (set up ribs) + 120 minutes (produce ribs) 360 minutes	120/360 = 0.333
300	60 minutes (set up steering support) + 300 minutes (produce steering supports) + 60 minutes (set up ribs) + 300 minutes (produce ribs) 720 minutes	300/720 = 0.4166

• The setup time includes all setups within a production cycle. In this case, this includes $S = 60$ minutes $+ 60$ minutes $= 120$ minutes.

• The time per unit includes all production time that is needed to produce one complete unit of output at the milling machine. In this case, this includes 1 minute/unit for the steer support as well as two times 0.5 minute/unit for the two ribs. The total time per unit is thus $p = 1$ minute/unit $+ 2 \times 0.5$ minute/unit $= 2$ minutes/unit.

With these more careful definitions, we can now use the above equation to compute the capacity of the milling machine as

$$\text{Capacity (for B} = 100) = \frac{\text{Batch size}}{\text{Setup time} + \text{Batch size} \times \text{Time per unit}}$$

$$= \frac{100 \text{ units}}{120 \text{ minutes} + 100 \text{ units} \times 2 \text{ minutes/unit}}$$

$$= 0.3125 \text{ unit/minute}$$

No matter how large a batch size we choose, we will never be able to produce faster than one unit every p units of time. Thus, $1/p$ can be thought of as the maximum capacity the process can achieve. This is illustrated in Figure 5.3.

5.2 Interaction between Batching and Inventory

Given the desirable effect that large batch sizes increase capacity, why not choose the largest possible batch size to maximize capacity? While large batch sizes are desirable from a capacity perspective, they typically require a higher level of inventory, either within the process or at the finished goods level. Holding the flow rate constant, we can infer from Little's Law that such a higher inventory level will also lead to longer flow times. This is

FIGURE 5.3
Capacity as a
Function of the
Batch Size

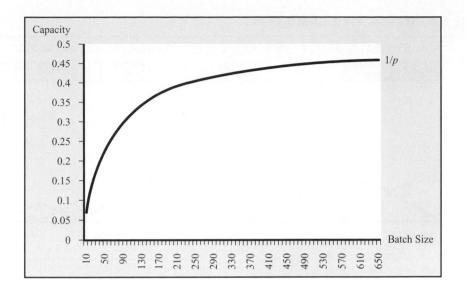

why batch-flow operations generally are not very fast in responding to customer orders (remember the last time you bought furniture?).

The interaction between batching and inventory is illustrated by the following two examples. First, consider an auto manufacturer producing a sedan and a station wagon on the same assembly line. For simplicity, assume both models have the same demand rate, 400 cars per day each. The metal stamping steps in the process preceding final assembly are characterized by especially long setup times. Thus, to achieve a high level of capacity, the plant runs large production batches and produces sedans from the first of a month to the 15th and station wagons from the 16th to the end of the month.

However, it seems fairly unrealistic to assume that customers only demand sedans at the beginning of the month and station wagons at the end of the month. In other words, producing in large batches leads to a mismatch between the rate of supply and the rate of demand.

Thus, in addition to producing enough to cover demand in the first half of the month, to satisfy demand for sedans the company needs to produce 15 days of demand to inventory, which then fulfills demand while the line produces station wagons. This is illustrated by the left side of Figure 5.4. Observe that the average level of inventory is 3,000 cars for each of the two models. Now, ignoring setup times for a moment, consider the case in which the firm produces 400 station wagons and 400 sedans a day. In this setting, one would only need to carry 0.5 day of cycle inventory, a dramatic reduction in inventory. This is illustrated by the right side of Figure 5.4. Thus, smaller batches translate to lower inventory levels!

In the ideal case, which has been propagated by Toyota Production Systems under the word *heijunka* or *mixed model* production, the company would alternate between producing one sedan and producing one station wagon, thereby producing in batch sizes of one. This way, a much better synchronization of the demand flow and the production flow is achieved and cycle inventory is eliminated entirely.

Second, consider a furniture maker producing chairs in batch sizes of 100. Starting with the wood-cutting step and all the way through the finishing process, the batch of 100 chairs would stay together as one entity.

Now, take the position of one chair in the batch. What is the most dominant activity throughout the process? Waiting! The larger the batch size, the longer the time the flow unit waits for the other "members" of the same batch—a situation comparable with going to the

FIGURE 5.4 The Impact of Batch Sizes on Inventory

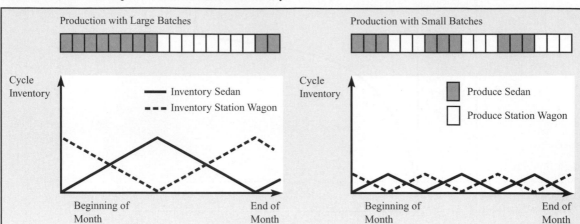

barber with an entire class of children. Given Little's Law, this increase in wait time (and thereby flow time) leads to a proportional increase in inventory.

With these observations, we can turn our attention back to the milling machine at Nova Cruz. Similar to Figure 5.4, we can draw the inventory of components (ribs and steer supports) over the course of a production cycle. Remember that the assembly process following the milling machine is requiring a supply of one unit every three minutes. This one unit consists, from the view of the milling machine, of two ribs and a steer support unit. If we want to ensure a sufficient supply to keep the assembly process operating, we have to produce a sufficient number of ribs such that during the time we do not produce ribs (e.g., setup time and production of steer support) we do not run out of ribs. If we assume, for the moment, a batch size of $B = 200$, the inventory of ribs changes as follows:

• During the production of ribs, inventory accumulates. As we produce one unit per minute, but only supply 0.33 unit per minute to the assembly process, rib inventory accumulates at a rate of 0.66 unit per minute.

• Because we produce for 200 minutes, the inventory at the end of the production run of ribs will be at 200 minutes × 0.66 unit per minute = 133 units.

• How long do 133 units of inventory last? The inventory ensures supply to the assembly for 400 minutes (cycle time of assembly operations was three minutes). After these 400 minutes, we need to start producing ribs again. During these 400 minutes, we have to accommodate two setups (together 120 minutes) and 200 minutes for producing the steer supports.

The resulting production plan as well as the corresponding inventory levels are summarized by Figure 5.5.

5.3 Choosing a Batch Size in Presence of Setup Times

When choosing an appropriate batch size for a process flow, it is important to balance the conflicting objectives: capacity and inventory. Large batches lead to large inventory; small batches lead to losses in capacity.

In balancing these two conflicting objectives, we benefit from the following two observations:

FIGURE 5.5 **The Impact of Setup Times on Capacity**

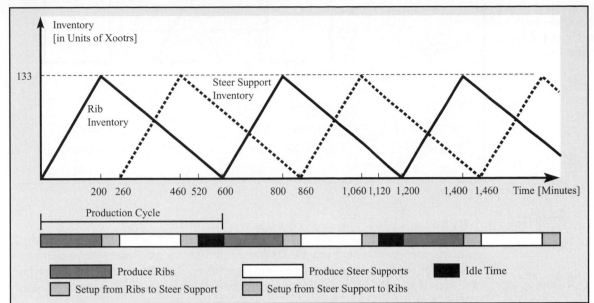

- Capacity at the bottleneck step is extremely valuable (as long as the process is capacity-constrained, i.e., there is more demand than capacity) as it constrains the flow rate of the entire process.
- Capacity at a nonbottleneck step is free as it does not provide a constraint on the current flow rate.

This has direct implications for choosing an appropriate batch size at a process step with setups.

- If the setup occurs at the bottleneck step (and the process is capacity-constrained), it is desirable to increase the batch size, as this results in a larger process capacity and, therefore, a higher flow rate.
- If the setup occurs at a nonbottleneck step (or the process is demand-constrained), it is desirable to decrease the batch size, as this decreases inventory as well as flow time.

The scooter example summarized by Figure 5.6 illustrates these two observations and how they help us in choosing a good batch size. Remember that B denotes the batch size, S the setup time, and p the per unit activity time.

The process flow diagram in Figure 5.6 consists of only two activities: the milling machine and the assembly operations. We can combine the assembly operations into one activity, as we know that its slowest step (bottleneck of assembly) can create one Xootr every three minutes.

To determine the capacity of the milling machine for a batch size of 12, we apply the formula

$$\text{Capacity } (B) = \frac{\text{Batch size}}{\text{Setup time} + \text{Batch size} \times \text{Time per unit}}$$

$$= \frac{B}{S + B \times p} = \frac{12}{120 + 12 \times 2} = 0.0833 \text{ unit/minute}$$

FIGURE 5.6
Data from the
Scooter Case about
Setup Times and
Batching

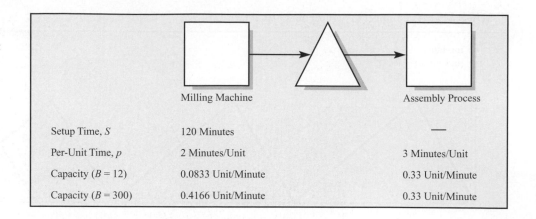

	Milling Machine	Assembly Process
Setup Time, S	120 Minutes	—
Per-Unit Time, p	2 Minutes/Unit	3 Minutes/Unit
Capacity ($B = 12$)	0.0833 Unit/Minute	0.33 Unit/Minute
Capacity ($B = 300$)	0.4166 Unit/Minute	0.33 Unit/Minute

The capacity of the assembly operation is easily computed based on its bottleneck capacity of $\frac{1}{3}$ unit per minute. Note that for $B = 12$, the milling machine is the bottleneck.

Next consider, what happens to the same calculations if we increase the batch size from 12 to 300. While this does not affect the capacity of the assembly operations, the capacity of the milling machine now becomes

$$\text{Capacity } (B) = \frac{B}{S + B \times p} = \frac{300}{120 + 300 \times 2} = 0.4166 \text{ unit/minute}$$

Thus, we observe that the location of the bottleneck has shifted from the milling machine to the assembly operation, just by modifying the batch size. Now which of the two batch sizes is the "better" one, 12 or 300?

• The batch size of 300 is clearly too large. The milling machine incurs idle time as the overall process is constrained by the (substantially) smaller capacity of the assembly operations (note, based on Figure 5.5, we know that even for the smaller batch size of $B = 200$, there exists idle time at the milling machine). This large batch size is likely to create unnecessary inventory problems as described above.

• The batch size of 12 is likely to be more attractive in terms of inventory. Yet, the process capacity has been reduced to 0.0833 unit per minute, leaving the assembly operation starved for work.

As a batch size of 12 is too small and a batch size of 300 is too large, a good batch size is "somewhere in between." Specifically, we are interested in the smallest batch size that does not adversely affect process capacity.

To find this number, we equate the capacity of the step with setup (in this case the milling machine) with the capacity of the step from the remaining process that has the smallest capacity (in this case, the assembly operations):

$$\frac{B}{120 + B \times 2} = \frac{1}{3}$$

and solve this equation for B:

$$\frac{B}{120 + B \times 2} = \frac{1}{3}$$

$$3 \times B = 120 + 2 \times B$$

$$B = 120$$

which gives us, in this case, $B = 120$. This algebraic approach is illustrated by Figure 5.7. If you feel uncomfortable with the calculus outlined above (i.e., solving the equation for the batch size B), or you want to program the method directly into Excel or another software package, you can use the following equation:

$$\text{Recommended batch size} = \frac{\text{Flow rate} \times \text{Setup time}}{1 - \text{Flow rate} \times \text{Time per unit}}$$

which is equivalent to the analysis performed above. To see this, simply substitute Setup time = 120 minutes, Flow rate = 0.333 unit per minute, and Time per unit = 2 minutes per unit and obtain

$$\text{Recommended batch size} = \frac{\text{Flow rate} \times \text{Setup time}}{1 - \text{Flow rate} \times \text{Time per unit}} = \frac{0.333 \times 120}{1 - 0.333 \times 2} = 120$$

Figure 5.7 shows the capacity of the process step with setup, which increases with the batch size B, and for very high values of batch size B approaches $1/p$ (similar to the graph in Figure 5.3). As the capacity of the assembly operation does not depend on the batch size, it corresponds to a constant (flat line).

The overall process capacity is—in the spirit of the bottleneck idea—the minimum of the two graphs. Thus, before the graphs intersect, the capacity is too low and flow rate is potentially given up. After the intersection point, the assembly operation is the bottleneck and any further increases in batch size yield no return. Exhibit 5.1 provides a summary of the computations leading to the recommended batch size in the presence of setup times.

FIGURE 5.7
Choosing a "Good" Batch Size

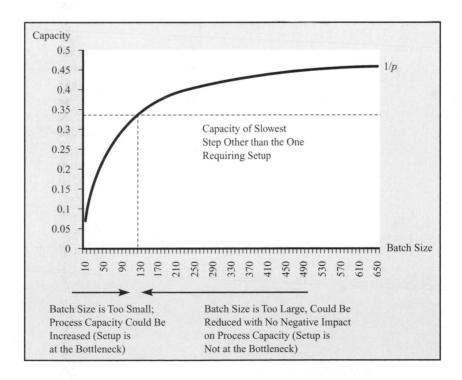

Exhibit 5.1

FINDING A GOOD BATCH SIZE IN PRESENCE OF SETUP TIMES

1. Compute Flow rate = Minimum {Available input, Demand, Process capacity}.
2. Define the production cycle, which includes the processing and setups of all flow units before the resource starts processing the first type of flow units again.
3. Compute the time in a production cycle that the resource is in setup; setup times are those times that are independent of the batch size.
4. Compute the time in a production cycle that the resource is processing; this includes all the activity times that are incurred per unit (i.e., are repeated for every member of the batch).
5. Compute the capacity of the resource with setup for a given batch size:

$$\text{Capacity } (B) = \frac{B}{\text{Setup time} + B \times \text{Time per unit}}$$

6. We are looking for the batch size that leads to the lowest level of inventory without affecting flow rate; we find this by solving the equation

$$\text{Capacity } (B) = \text{Flow rate}$$

for the batch size B. This also can be done directly using the following formula:

$$\text{Recommended batch size} = \frac{\text{Flow rate} \times \text{Setup time}}{1 - \text{Flow rate} \times \text{Time per unit}}$$

5.4 Balancing Setup Costs with Inventory Costs: The EOQ Model

Up to now, our focus has been on the role of setup times, as opposed to setup costs. Specifically, we have seen that setup time at the bottleneck leads to an overall reduction in process capacity. Assuming that the process is currently capacity-constrained, setup times thereby carry an opportunity cost reflecting the overall lower flow rate (sales).

Independent of such opportunity costs, setups frequently are associated with direct (out-of-pocket) costs. In these cases, we speak of setup costs (as opposed to setup times). Consider, for example, the following settings:

• The setup of a machine to process a certain part might require scrapping the first 10 parts that are produced after the setup. Thus, the material costs of these 10 parts constitute a setup cost.

• Assume that we are charged a per-time-unit usage fee for a particular resource (e.g., for the milling machine discussed above). Thus, every minute we use the resource, independent of whether we use it for setup or for real production, we have to pay for the resource. In this case, "time is money" and the setup time thereby translates directly into setup costs. However, as we will discuss below, one needs to be very careful when making the conversion from setup times to setup costs.

• When receiving shipments from a supplier, there frequently exists a fixed shipment cost as part of the procurement cost, which is independent of the purchased quantity. This is similar to the shipping charges that a consumer pays at a catalog or online retailer. Shipping costs are a form of setup costs.

All three settings reflect *economies of scale:* the more we order or produce as part of a batch, the more units there are in a batch over which we can spread out the setup costs.

If we can reduce per-unit costs by increasing the batch size, what keeps us from using infinitely (or at least very large) batches? Similar to the case of setup times, we again need to balance our desire for large batches (fewer setups) with the cost of carrying a large amount of inventory.

In the following analysis, we need to distinguish between two cases:

• If the quantity we order is produced or delivered by an outside supplier, all units of a batch are likely to arrive at the same time.

• In other settings, the units of a batch might not all arrive at the same time. This is especially the case when we produce the batch internally.

Figure 5.8 illustrates the inventory levels for the two cases described above. The lower part of Figure 5.8 shows the case of the outside supplier and all units of a batch arriving at the same moment in time. The moment a shipment is received, the inventory level jumps up by the size of the shipment. It then falls up to the time of the next shipment.

The upper part of Figure 5.8 shows the case of units created by a resource with (finite) capacity. Thus, while we are producing, the inventory level increases. Once we stop production, the inventory level falls. Let us consider the case of an outside supplier first (lower part of Figure 5.8). Specifically, consider the case of the Xootr handle caps that Nova Cruz sources from a supplier in Taiwan for $0.85 per unit. Note that the maximum inventory of handle caps occurs at the time we receive a shipment from Taiwan. The inventory is then depleted at the rate of the assembly operations, that is, at a flow rate, R, of 700 units (pairs of handle caps) per week, which is equal to one unit every three minutes.

For the following computations, we make a set of assumptions. We later show that these assumptions do not substantially alter the optimal decisions.

• We assume that production of Xootrs occurs at a constant rate of one unit every three minutes. We also assume our orders arrive on time from Taiwan. Under these two assumptions, we can deplete our inventory all the way to zero before receiving the next shipment.

• There is a fixed setup cost per order that is independent of the amount ordered. In the Xootr case, this largely consists of a $300 customs fee.

The purchase price is independent of the number of units we order, that is, there are no quantity discounts. We talk about quantity discounts in the next section.

The objective of our calculations is to minimize the cost of inventory and ordering with the constraint that we must never run out of inventory (i.e., we can keep the assembly operation running).

We have three costs to consider: purchase costs, delivery fees, and holding costs. We use 700 units of handle caps each week no matter how much or how frequently we order. Thus, we have no excuse for running out of inventory and there is nothing we can do about our purchase costs of

$$\$0.85/\text{unit} \times 700 \text{ units/week} = \$595 \text{ per week}$$

So when choosing our ordering policy (when and how much to order), we focus on minimizing the sum of the other two costs, delivery fees and inventory costs.

The cost of inventory depends on how much it costs us to hold one unit in inventory for a given period of time, say one week. We can obtain the number by looking at the annual inventory costs and dividing that amount by 52. The annual inventory costs need to account for financing the inventory (cost of capital, especially high for a start-up like Nova Cruz),

FIGURE 5.8
Different Patterns
of Inventory Levels

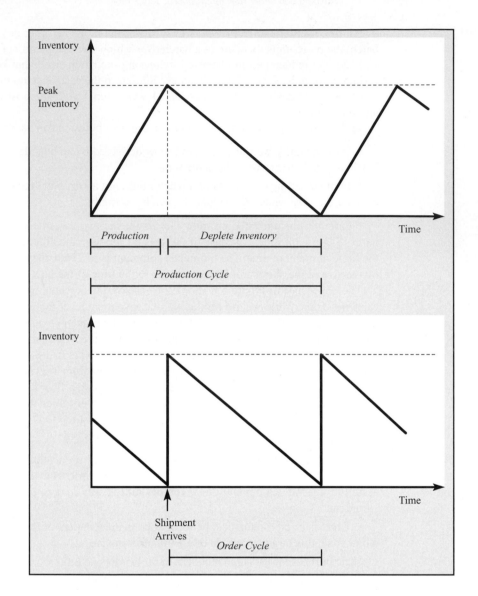

costs of storage, and costs of obsolescence. Nova Cruz uses an annual inventory cost of 40 percent. Thus, it costs Nova Cruz 0.7692 percent to hold a piece of inventory for one week. Given that a handle cap costs $0.85 per unit, this translates to an inventory cost of $h = 0.007692 \times \$0.85/\text{unit} = \$0.006538$ per unit and week. Note that the annual holding cost needs to include the cost of capital as well as any other cost of inventory (e.g., storage, theft, etc).

How many handle caps will there be, on average, in Nova Cruz's inventory? As we can see in Figure 5.8, the average inventory level is simply

$$\text{Average inventory} = \frac{\text{Order quantity}}{2}$$

If you are not convinced, refer in Figure 5.8 to the "triangle" formed by one order cycle. The average inventory during the cycle is half of the height of the triangle, which is half the order quantity, $Q/2$. Thus, for a given inventory cost, h, we can compute the inventory cost per unit of time (e.g., inventory costs per week):

FIGURE 5.9 **Inventory and Ordering Costs for Different Order Sizes**

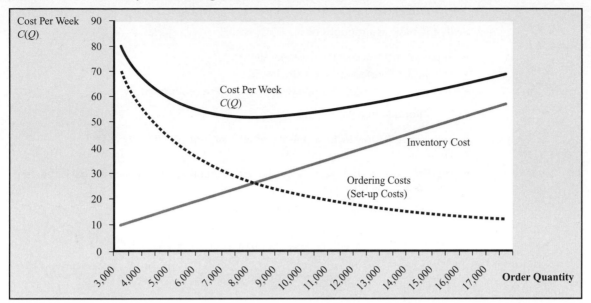

$$\text{Inventory costs [per unit of time]} = \frac{1}{2} \text{ Order quantity} \times h = \frac{1}{2} Q \times h$$

Before we turn to the question of how many handle caps to order at once, let's first ask ourselves how frequently we have to place an order. Say at time 0 we have *I* units in inventory and say we plan our next order to be *Q* units. The *I* units of inventory will satisfy demand until time *I*/*R* (in other words, we have *I*/*R* weeks of supply in inventory). At this time our inventory will be zero if we don't order before then. We would then again receive an order of *Q* units (if there is a lead time in receiving this order, we simply would have to place this order earlier).

Do we gain anything by receiving the *Q* handle caps earlier than at the time when we have zero units in inventory? Not in this model: demand is satisfied whether we order earlier or not and the delivery fee is the same too. But we do lose something by ordering earlier: we incur holding costs per unit of time the *Q* units are held.

Given that we cannot save costs by choosing the order time intelligently, we must now work on the question of how much to order (the order quantity). Let's again assume that we order *Q* units with every order and let's consider just one order cycle. The order cycle begins when we order *Q* units and ends when the last unit is sold, *Q*/*R* time units later. For example, with *Q* = 1,000, an order cycle lasts 1,000 units/700 units per week = 1.43 weeks. We incur one ordering fee (setup costs), *K*, in that order cycle, so our setup costs per week are

$$\text{Setup costs [per unit of time]} = \frac{\text{Setup cost}}{\text{Length of order cycle}}$$

$$= \frac{K}{Q/R} = \frac{K \times R}{Q}$$

Let *C*(*Q*) be the sum of our average delivery cost per unit time and our average holding cost per unit time (per week):

$$\text{Per unit of time cost } C(Q) = \text{Setup costs} + \text{Inventory costs}$$

$$= \frac{K \times R}{Q} + \frac{1}{2} \times h \times Q$$

Exhibit 5.2

FINDING THE ECONOMIC ORDER QUANTITY

1. Verify the basic assumptions of the EOQ model:

   - Replenishment occurs instantaneously.
   - Demand is constant and not stochastic.
   - There is a fixed setup cost K independent of the order quantity.

2. Collect information on

   - Setup cost, K (only include out-of-pocket cost, not opportunity cost).
   - Flow rate, R.
   - Holding cost, h (not necessarily the yearly holding cost; needs to have the same time unit as the flow rate).

3. For a given order quantity Q, compute

$$\text{Inventory costs [per unit of time]} = \frac{1}{2} Q \times h$$

$$\text{Setup costs [per unit of time]} = \frac{K \times R}{Q}$$

4. The economic order quantity minimizes the sum of the inventory and the setup costs and is

$$Q^* = \sqrt{\frac{2 \times K \times R}{h}}$$

The resulting costs are

$$C(Q^*) = \sqrt{2 \times K \times R \times h}$$

Note that purchase costs are not included in $C(Q)$ for the reasons discussed earlier. From the above we see that the delivery fee per unit time decreases as Q increases: we amortize the delivery fee over more units. But as Q increases, we increase our holding costs.

Figure 5.9 graphs the weekly costs of delivery, the average weekly holding cost, and the total weekly cost, $C(Q)$. As we can see, there is a single order quantity Q that minimizes the total cost $C(Q)$. We call this quantity Q^*, the economic order quantity, or EOQ for short. Hence the name of the model.

From Figure 5.9 it appears that Q^* is the quantity at which the weekly delivery fee equals the weekly holding cost. In fact, that is true, as can be shown algebraically. Further, using calculus it is possible to show that

$$\text{Economic order quantity} = \sqrt{\frac{2 \times \text{Setup cost} \times \text{Flow rate}}{\text{Holding cost}}}$$

$$Q^* = \sqrt{\frac{2 \times K \times R}{h}}$$

As our intuition suggests, as the setup costs K increase, we should make larger orders, but as holding costs h increase, we should make smaller orders.

We can use the above formula to establish the economic order quantity for handle caps:

$$Q^* = \sqrt{\frac{2 \times \text{Setup cost} \times \text{Flow rate}}{\text{Holding cost}}}$$

$$= \sqrt{\frac{2 \times 300 \times 700}{0.006538}} = 8{,}014.69$$

The steps required to find the economic order quantity are summarized by Exhibit 5.2.

5.5 Observations Related to the Economic Order Quantity

If we always order the economic order quantity, our cost per unit of time, $C(Q^*)$ can be computed as

$$C(Q^*) = \frac{K \times R}{Q^*} + \frac{1}{2} \times h \times Q^* = \sqrt{2 \times K \times R \times h}$$

While we have done this analysis to minimize our average cost for a single order, it should be clear that Q^* would minimize our average cost per unit (given that the rate of purchasing handle caps is fixed). The cost per unit can be computed as

$$\text{Cost per unit} = \frac{C(Q^*)}{R} = \sqrt{\frac{2 \times K \times h}{R}}$$

As we would expect, the per-unit cost is increasing with the ordering fee K as well as with our inventory costs. Interestingly, the per-unit cost is decreasing with the flow rate R. Thus, if we doubled our flow rate, our ordering costs increase by less than a factor of 2. In other words, there are economies of scale in the ordering process: the per-unit ordering cost is decreasing with the flow rate R. Put yet another way, an operation with setup and inventory holding costs becomes more efficient as the demand rate increases.

While we have focused our analysis on the time period when Nova Cruz experienced a demand of 700 units per week, the demand pattern changed drastically over the product life cycle of the Xootr. As discussed in Chapter 4, Nova Cruz experienced a substantial demand growth from 200 units per week to over 1,000 units per week. Table 5.2 shows how increases in demand rate impact the order quantity as well as the per-unit cost of the handle caps. We observe that, due to scale economies, ordering and inventory costs are decreasing with the flow rate R.

A nice property of the economic order quantity is that the cost function, $C(Q)$, is relatively flat around its minimum Q^* (see graph in Figure 5.9). This suggests that if we were to order Q units instead of Q^*, the resulting cost penalty would not be substantial as long as Q is reasonably close to Q^*. Suppose we order only half of the optimal order quantity, that is, we order $Q^*/2$. In that case, we have

$$C(Q^*/2) = \frac{K \times R}{Q^*/2} + \frac{1}{2} \times h \times Q^*/2 = \frac{5}{4} \times \sqrt{2 \times K \times R \times h} = \frac{5}{4} \times C(Q^*)$$

Thus, if we order only half as much as optimal (i.e., we order twice as frequently as optimal), then our costs increase only by 25 percent. The same holds if we order double the economic order quantity (i.e., we order half as frequently as optimal).

TABLE 5.2
Scale Economies in
the EOQ Formula

Flow Rate R	Economic Order Quantity Q^*	Per-Unit Ordering and Inventory Cost $C(Q^*)/R$	Ordering and Inventory Costs as a Percentage of Total Procurement Costs
200	4,284	0.14 [$/unit]	14.1%
400	6,058	0.10	10.4%
600	7,420	0.08	8.7%
800	8,568	0.07	7.6%
1,000	9,579	0.06	6.8%

This property has several important implications:

• Consider the optimal order quantity $Q^* = 8{,}014$ established above. However, now also assume that our supplier is only willing to deliver in predefined quantities (e.g., in multiples of 5,000). The robustness established above suggests that an order of 10,000 will only lead to a slight cost increase (increased costs can be computed as $C(Q = 10{,}000) = \$53.69$, which is only 2.5 percent higher than the optimal costs).

• Sometimes, it can be difficult to obtain exact numbers for the various ingredients in the EOQ formula. Consider, for example, the ordering fee in the Nova Cruz case. While this fee of $300 was primarily driven by the $300 for customs, it also did include a shipping fee. The exact shipping fee in turn depends on the quantity shipped and we would need a more refined model to find the order quantity that accounts for this effect. Given the robustness of the EOQ model, however, we know that the model is "forgiving" with respect to small misspecifications of parameters.

A particularly useful application of the EOQ model relates to *quantity discounts*. When procuring inventory in a logistics or retailing setting, we frequently are given the opportunity to benefit from quantity discounts. For example:

• We might be offered a discount for ordering a full truckload of supply.

• We might receive a free unit for every five units we order (just as in consumer retailing settings of "buy one, get one free").

• We might receive a discount for all units ordered over 100 units.

• We might receive a discount for the entire order if the order volume exceeds 50 units (or say $2,000).

We can think of the extra procurement costs that we would incur from not taking advantage of the quantity discount—that is, that would result from ordering in smaller quantities—as a setup cost. Evaluating an order discount therefore boils down to a comparison between inventory costs and setup costs (savings in procurement costs), which we can do using the EOQ model.

If the order quantity we obtain from the EOQ model is sufficiently large to obtain the largest discount (the lowest per-unit procurement cost), then the discount has no impact on our order size. We go ahead and order the economic order quantity. The more interesting case occurs when the EOQ is less than the discount threshold. Then we must decide if we wish to order more than the economic order quantity to take advantage of the discount offered to us.

Let's consider one example to illustrate how to think about this issue. Suppose our supplier of handle caps gives us a discount of 5 percent off the entire order if the order exceeds

10,000 units. Recall that our economic order quantity was only 8,014. Thus, the question is "should we increase the order size to 10,000 units in order to get the 5 percent discount, yet incur higher inventory costs, or should we simply order 8,014 units?"

We surely will not order more than 10,000; any larger order does not generate additional purchase cost savings but does increase inventory costs. So we have two choices: either stick with the EOQ or increase our order to 10,000. If we order $Q^* = 8,014$ units, our total cost per unit time is

$$700 \text{ units/week} \times \$0.85/\text{unit} + C(Q^*)$$

$$= \$595/\text{week} + \$52.40/\text{week}$$

$$= \$647.40/\text{week}$$

Notice that we now include our purchase cost per unit time of 700 units/week $\times$ \$0.85/unit. The reason for this is that with the possibility of a quantity discount, our purchase cost now depends on the order quantity.

If we increase our order quantity to 10,000 units, our total cost per unit time would be

$$700 \text{ units/week} \times \$0.85/\text{unit} \times 0.95 + C(10,000)$$

$$= \$565.25/\text{week} + \$53.69/\text{week}$$

$$= \$618.94/\text{week}$$

where we have reduced the procurement cost by 5 percent (multiplied by 0.95) to reflect the quantity discount. Given that the cost per week is lower in the case of the increased order quantity, we want to take advantage of the quantity discount.

After analyzing the case of all flow units of one order (batch) arriving simultaneously, we now turn to the case of producing the corresponding units internally (upper part of Figure 5.8).

All computations we performed above can be easily transformed to this more general case (see, e.g., Nahmias 2000). Moreover, given the robustness of the economic order quantity, the EOQ model leads to reasonably good recommendations even if applied to production settings with setup costs. Hence, we will not discuss the analytical aspects of this. Instead, we want to step back for a moment and reflect on how the EOQ model relates to our discussion of setup times at the beginning of the chapter.

A common mistake is to rely too much on setup *costs* as opposed to setup *times*. For example, consider the case of Figure 5.6 and assume that the monthly capital cost for milling machine 1 is \$9,000, which corresponds to \$64 per hour (assuming four weeks of 35 hours each). Thus, when choosing the batch size, and focusing primarily on costs, Nova Cruz might shy away from frequent setups. Management might even consider using the economic order quantity established above and thereby quantify the impact of larger batches on inventory holding costs.

There are two major mistakes in this approach:

• This approach to choosing batch sizes ignores the fact that the investment in the machine is already sunk.

• Choosing the batch size based on cost ignores the effect setups have on process capacity. As long as setup costs are a reflection of the cost of capacity—as opposed to direct financial setup costs—they should be ignored when choosing the batch size. It is the overall process flow that matters, not an artificial local performance measure! From a capacity perspective, setups at nonbottleneck resources are free. And if the setups do occur at the bottleneck, the corresponding setup costs not only reflect the capacity costs of the local resource, but of the entire process!

Thus, when choosing batch sizes, it is important to distinguish between setup costs and setup times. If the motivation behind batching results from setup times (or opportunity costs of capacity), we should focus on optimizing the process flow. Section 5.3 provides the appropriate way to find a good batch size. If we face "true" setup costs (in the sense of out-of-pocket costs) and we only look at a single resource (as opposed to an entire process flow), the EOQ model can be used to find the optimal order quantity.

Finally, if we encounter a combination of setup times and (out-of-pocket) setup costs, we should use both approaches and compare the recommended batch sizes. If the batch size from the EOQ is sufficiently large so that the resource with the setup is not the bottleneck, minimizing costs is appropriate. If the batch size from the EOQ, however, makes the resource with the setups the bottleneck, we need to consider increasing the batch size beyond the EOQ recommendation.

5.6   Transfer Batches

Up to this point we have assumed that a batch would stay together as a collection of flow units throughout the process. However, in many settings, processed units are forwarded to the next process step, although some of the flow units in the same batch are still in process at the previous step. The following definitions are useful distinctions.

• For process steps involving setups, we can define a *production batch* as a collection of flow units that is produced between two setups.

• We can define a *transfer batch* as a collection of flow units that is transferred as an entity or group from one process step to another.

Both production and transfer batches reflect setups/economies of scale. Just as we have seen from Table 5.1 that it is not economical to produce in batch sizes of one when there are setups, similarly, material handling and transportation aspects of the process become increasingly complex and costly with smaller batch sizes. For example, a forklift transferring five cases of goods takes as long for the transportation time as a forklift with 50 cases.

If the nature of the transportation steps permits, it might be possible to reduce the transfer batch size significantly below the production batch size. In this case, flow units of the same production batch would be processed at a downstream step, while some of their "peers" are still being produced at the step with setup. Working with smaller transfer batches has the direct benefit of shortened flow time and thereby—because of Little's Law—of lower overall inventory.

It is also important to keep in mind that internal transportation processes are not adding any value to the customer. Hence, one should look for opportunities to eliminate the need for internal transportation by grouping resources with flows between them physically close to each other. The extreme case of this is an assembly-line layout.

However, even if not organized as an assembly line (e.g., the milling machine in the Xootr example), a firm should always attempt to transfer flow units one by one. This is the only way to have "the flow go on" (or, in the spirit of the book, have a flow rate matching the demand rate). The Toyota Production System also advocates the idea of piece-by-piece transfer of parts under the word *ikko-nagashi.*

5.7   Setup Time Reduction

Despite improvement potential from the use of "good" batch sizes and smaller transfer batches, setups remain a source of disruption of a smooth process flow. For this reason, rather than taking setups as "God-given" constraints and finding ways to accommodate them, we should find ways that directly address the root cause of the disruption.

This is the basic idea underlying the single minute exchange of die (SMED) method. The creators of the SMED method referred to any setup exceeding 10 minutes as an unacceptable source of process flow disruption. The 10-minute rule is not necessarily meant to be taken literally: the method was developed in the automotive industry, where setup times used to take as much as four hours. The SMED method helps to define an aggressive, yet realistic setup time goal and to identify potential opportunities of setup time reduction.

The basic underlying idea of SMED is to carefully analyze all tasks that are part of the setup time and then divide those tasks into two groups, *internal* setup tasks and *external* setup tasks.

- Internal setup tasks are those tasks that can only be executed while the machine is stopped.

- External setup tasks are those tasks that can be done while the machine is still operating, meaning they can be done *before* the actual changeover occurs.

Experience shows that companies are biased toward using internal setups and that, even without making large investments, internal setups can be translated into external setups.

Similar to our discussion about choosing a good batch size, the biggest obstacles to overcome are ineffective cost accounting procedures. Consider, for example, the case of a simple heat treatment procedure in which flow units are moved on a tray and put into an oven. Loading and unloading of the tray is part of the setup time. The acquisition of an additional tray that can be loaded (or unloaded) while the other tray is still in process (before the setup) allows the company to convert internal setup tasks to external ones. Is this a worthwhile investment?

The answer is, as usual, it depends. SMED applied to nonbottleneck steps is not creating any process improvement at all. As discussed previously, nonbottleneck steps have excessive capacity and therefore setups are entirely free (except for the resulting increase in inventory). Thus, investing in any resource, technical or human, is not only wasteful, but it also takes scarce improvement capacity/funds away from more urgent projects. However, if the oven in the previous example were the bottleneck step, almost any investment in the acquisition of additional trays suddenly becomes a highly profitable investment.

The idea of internal and external setups as well as potential conversion from internal to external setups is best visible in car racing. Any pit stop is a significant disruption of the race car's flow toward the finish line. At any point and any moment in the race, an entire crew is prepared to take in the car, having prepared for any technical problem from tire changes to refueling. While the technical crew might appear idle and underutilized throughout most of the race, it is clear that any second they can reduce from the time the car is in the pit (internal setups) to a moment when the car is on the race track is a major gain (e.g., no race team would consider mounting tires on wheels during the race; they just put on entire wheels).

5.8   Other Flow Interruptions: Buffer or Suffer

In addition to illustrating the SMED method, the race car example also helps to illustrate how the concept of batching can be applied to *continuous process flows,* as opposed to discrete manufacturing environments. First of all, we observe that the calculation of the average speed of the race car is nothing but a direct application of the batching formula introduced at the beginning of this chapter:

$$\text{Average speed (number of miles between stops)} = \frac{\text{Number of miles between stops}}{\text{Duration of the stop} + \text{Time to cover one mile} \times \text{Number of miles between stops}}$$

In continuous flow processes, the quantity between two flow interruptions is frequently referred to as a production run.

Consider the production of orange juice, which is produced in a continuous flow process. At an abstract level, orange juice is produced in a three-step process: extraction, filtering, and bottling. Given that the filter at the second process step has to be changed regularly, the process needs to be stopped for 30 minutes following every four hours of production. While operating, the step can produce up to 100 barrels per hour.

To determine the capacity of the filtering step, we use

$$\text{Capacity}(B) = \frac{B}{S + B \times p}$$

$$= \frac{\text{Amount processed between two stops}}{\text{Duration of stop} + \text{Time to produce one barrel} \times \text{Amount processed between two stops}}$$

$$= \frac{400 \text{ barrels}}{30 \text{ minutes} + 400 \text{ barrels} \times 60/100 \text{ minutes per barrel}}$$

$$= \frac{400 \text{ barrels}}{270 \text{ minutes}}$$

$$= 1.48 \; barrels/minute \; = 88.88 \; barrels/hour$$

While in the case of batch flow operations we have allowed for substantial buffer sizes between process steps, the process as described in Figure 5.10 is currently operating without buffers. This has substantial implications for the overall flow rate.

Analyzing each step in isolation would suggest that the extraction step is the bottleneck, which would give us a process capacity of 80 barrels per hour. However, in the absence of buffers, the extraction step needs to stop producing the moment the filtering step is shut down. Thus, while running, the process is constrained by the extraction step, producing an output of 80 barrels per hour, and while being shut down, the process step is constrained by the filtering step (at 0 barrel per hour).

Previously, we considered the setup step in isolation from the rest of the process. That is a valid analysis if the setup step indeed works in isolation from the rest of the process, that is, if there is sufficient inventory (buffers) between steps. That assumption is violated here: The filtering step cannot operate at 88 barrels per hour because it is constrained by the extraction step of 80 barrels per hour.

For this reason, when we use our equation

$$\text{Capacity} = \frac{\text{Amount processed between two stops}}{\text{Duration of stop} + \text{Time to produce one barrel} \times \text{Amount processed between two stops}}$$

FIGURE 5.10

Data for the Production of Orange Juice

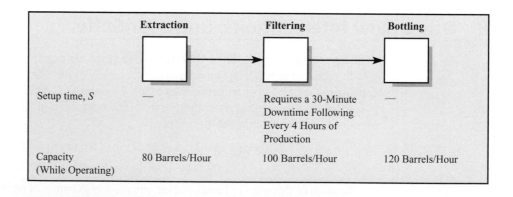

	Extraction	Filtering	Bottling
Setup time, S	—	Requires a 30-Minute Downtime Following Every 4 Hours of Production	—
Capacity (While Operating)	80 Barrels/Hour	100 Barrels/Hour	120 Barrels/Hour

it is important that we acknowledge that we are producing at a rate of 80 barrels per hour (i.e., $\frac{1}{80}$ hour per barrel) while we are at the filtering step. This leads to the following computation of process capacity:

$$\text{Capacity} = \frac{320 \text{ barrels}}{0.5 \text{ hour} + 320 \text{ barrels} \times \frac{1}{80} \text{ hour per barrel}}$$

$$= 320 \text{ barrels}/4.5 \text{ hours}$$

$$= 71.11 \text{ barrels/hour}$$

This prompts the following interesting observation: In the presence of flow interruptions, buffers can increase process capacity. Practitioners refer to this phenomenon as "buffer or suffer," indicating that flow interruptions can be smoothed out by introducing buffer inventories. In the case of Figure 5.10, the buffer would need to absorb the outflow of the extraction step during the downtime of the reduction step. Thus, adding a buffer between these two steps would indeed increase process capacity up to the level where, with 80 barrels per hour, the extraction step becomes the bottleneck.

5.9 Summary

Setups are interruptions of the supply process. These interruptions on the supply side lead to mismatches between supply and demand, visible in the form of inventory and—where this is not possible (see orange juice example)—lost throughput.

While in this chapter we have focused on inventory of components (handle caps), work-in-process (steer support parts), or finished goods (station wagons versus sedans, Figure 5.4), the supply–demand mismatch also can materialize in an inventory of waiting customer orders. For example, if the product we deliver is customized and built to the specifications of the customer, holding an inventory of finished goods is not possible. Similarly, if we are providing a substantial variety of products to the market, the risk of holding completed variants in finished goods inventory is large (this will be further discussed in the Chapter 12). Independent of the form of inventory, a large inventory corresponds to long flow times (Little's Law). For this reason, batch processes are typically associated with very long customer lead times.

FIGURE 5.11 **Summary of Batching**

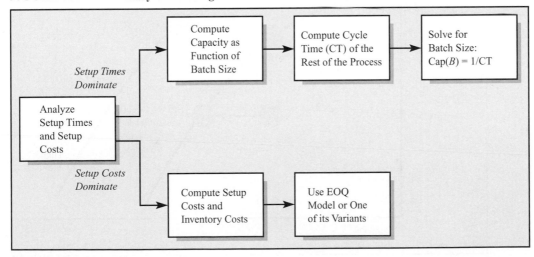

In this chapter, we discussed tools to choose a batch size. We distinguished between setup times and setup costs. To the extent that a process faces setup times, we need to extend our process analysis to capture the negative impact that setups have on capacity. We then want to look for a batch size that is large enough to not make the process step with the setup the bottleneck, while being small enough to avoid excessive inventory.

To the extent that a process faces (out-of-pocket) setup costs, we need to balance these costs against the cost of inventory. We discussed the EOQ model for the case of supply arriving in one single quantity (sourcing from a supplier), as well as the case of internal production. Figure 5.11 provides a summary of the major steps you should take when analyzing processes with flow interruptions, including setup times, setup costs, or machine downtimes. There are countless extensions to the EOQ model to capture, among other things, quantity discounts, perishability, learning effects, inflation, and quality problems.

Our ability to choose a "good" batch size provides another example of process improvement. Consider a process with significant setup times at one resource. As a manager of this process, we need to balance the conflicting objectives of

• Fast response to customers (short flow times, which correspond, because of Little's Law, to low inventory levels), which results from using small batch sizes.

• Cost benefits that result from using large batch sizes. The reason for this is that large batch sizes enable a high throughput, which in turn allows the firm to spread out its fixed costs over a maximum number of flow units.

This tension is illustrated by Figure 5.12. Similar to the case of line balancing, we observe that adjustments in the batch size are not trading in one performance measure against the other, but allow us to improve by reducing current inefficiencies in the process.

Despite our ability to choose batch sizes that mitigate the tension between inventory (responsiveness) and costs, there ultimately is only one way to handle setups: eliminate them wherever possible or at least shorten them. Setups do not add value and are therefore wasteful.

Methods such as SMED are powerful tools that can reduce setup times substantially. Similarly, the need for transfer batches can be reduced by locating the process resources according to the flow of the process.

FIGURE 5.12
Choosing a Batch Size

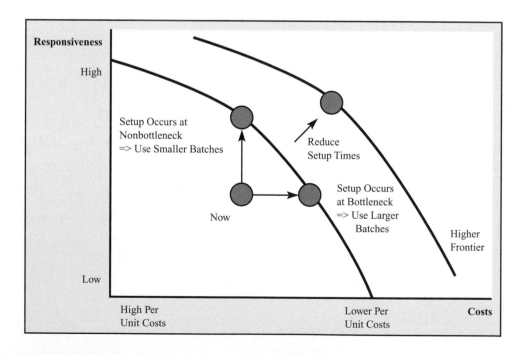

5.10 Further Reading

Nahmias (2000) is a widely used textbook in operations management that discusses, among other things, many variants of the EOQ model.

5.11 Practice Problems

Q5.1*   **(Window Boxes)** Metal window boxes are manufactured in two process steps: stamping and assembly. Each window box is made up of three pieces: a base (one part A) and two sides (two part Bs).

  The parts are fabricated by a single stamping machine that requires a setup time of 120 minutes whenever switching between the two part types. Once the machine is set up, the activity time for each part A is one minute while the activity time for each part B is only 30 seconds.

  Currently, the stamping machine rotates its production between one batch of 360 for part A and one batch of 720 for part B. Completed parts move from the stamping machine to the assembly only after the entire batch is complete.

  At assembly, parts are assembled manually to form the finished product. One base (part A) and two sides (two part Bs), as well as a number of small purchased components, are required for each unit of final product. Each product requires 27 minutes of labor time to assemble. There are currently 12 workers in assembly. There is sufficient demand to sell every box the system can make.

  a. What is the capacity of the stamping machine?

  b. What batch size would you recommend for the process?

Q5.2   **(Simple Setup)** Consider the following batch flow process consisting of three process steps performed by three machines:

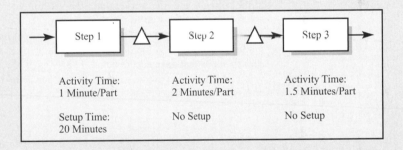

Work is processed in batches at each step. Before a batch is processed at step 1, the machine has to be set up. During a setup, the machine is unable to process any product.

  a. Assume that the batch size is 50 parts. What is the capacity of the process?

  b. For a batch size of 10 parts, which step is the bottleneck for the process?

  c. Using the current production batch size of 50 parts, how long would it take to produce 20 parts starting with an empty system? Assume that the units in the batch have to stay together (no smaller transfer batches allowed) when transferred to step 2 and to step 3. A unit can leave the system the moment it is completed at step 3. Assume step 1 needs to be set up before the beginning of production.

  d. Using the current production batch size of 50 parts, how long would it take to produce 20 parts starting with an empty system? Assume that the units in the batch do *not* have to stay together; specifically, units are transferred to the next step the moment they are completed at any step. Assume step 1 needs to be set up before the beginning of production.

  e. What batch size would you choose, assuming that all units of a batch stay together for the entire process?

(* indicates that the solution is at the end of the book)

Q5.3   (**Setup Everywhere**) Consider the following batch-flow process consisting of three process steps performed by three machines:

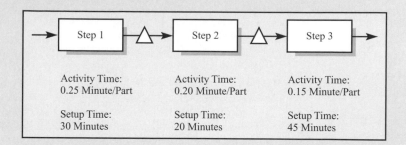

Work is processed in batches at each step. Before a batch is processed at a step, the machine at that step must be set up. (During a setup, the machine is unable to process any product.) Assume that there is a dedicated setup operator for each machine (i.e., there is always someone available to perform a setup at each machine.)

   a. What is the capacity of step 1 if the batch size is 35 parts?

   b. For what batch sizes is step 1 (2, 3) the bottleneck?

Q5.4   (**Bubba Chump Shrimp**) The Bubba Chump Shrimp Company processes and packages shrimp for sale to wholesale seafood distributors. The shrimp are transported to the main plant by trucks that carry 1,000 pounds (lbs.) of shrimp. Once the continuous flow processing of the shrimp begins, *no* inventory is allowed in buffers due to spoilage and all of the shrimp must be processed within 12 hours to prevent spoilage. The processing begins at the sorter, where the trucks dump the shrimp onto a conveyor belt that feeds into the sorter, which can sort up to 500 lbs. per hour. The shrimp then proceed to the desheller, which can process shrimp at the rate of 400 lbs. per hour. However, after 3 hours and 45 minutes of processing, the desheller must be stopped for 15 minutes to clean out empty shrimp shells that have accumulated. The veins of the shrimp are then removed in the deveining area at a maximum rate of 360 lbs. per hour. The shrimp proceed to the washing area, where they are processed at 750 lbs. per hour. Finally, the shrimp are packaged and frozen.

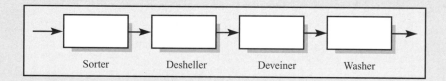

Note: All unit weights given are in "final processed shrimp." You do *not* need to account for the weight of the waste in the deshelling area. The plant operates continuously for 12 hours per day beginning at 8:00 A.M. Finally, there is negligible time to fill the system in the morning.

   a. What is the daily process capacity of the desheller (in isolation of the other processes)?

   b. What is the daily process capacity of the deveiner (in isolation of the other processes)?

   c. What is the daily process capacity of the processing plant (excluding the packaging and freezing)?

   d. If five trucks arrive one morning at 8:00 A.M., what is the total number of pounds of shrimp that must be wasted?

Q5.5   (**Cat Food**) Cat Lovers Inc. (CLI) is the distributor of a very popular blend of cat food that sells for $1.25 per can. CLI experiences demand of 500 cans per week on average. They order the cans of cat food from the Nutritious & Delicious Co. (N&D). N&D sells cans to CLI at $0.50 per can and charges a flat fee of $7 per order for shipping and handling.

CLI uses the economic order quantity as their fixed order size. Assume that the opportunity cost of capital and all other inventory cost is 15 percent annually and that there are 50 weeks in a year.

a. How many cans of cat food should CLI order at a time?

b. What is CLI's total order cost for one year?

c. What is CLI's total holding cost for one year?

d. What is CLI's weekly inventory turns?

Q5.6　**(Millenium Liquors)** Millennium Liquors is a wholesaler of sparkling wines. Their most popular product is the French Bete Noire 1989. Weekly demand is for 45 cases. Assume demand occurs over 50 weeks per year. The wine is shipped directly from France. Millennium's annual cost of capital is 15 percent, which also includes all other inventory-related costs. Below are relevant data on the costs of shipping and handling. These costs include the usual ordering and handling costs, plus the cost of refrigeration, which includes a fixed component (mainly depreciation of the cooling equipment) and a variable component that depends on the number of cases in inventory.

- Cost per case: $120
- Shipping cost (for any size shipment): $290
- Cost of labor to place and process an order: $10
- Cost of labor to place cases into warehouse: $2/case
- Cost of labor to pick case when sold: $2/case
- Fixed cost for refrigeration: $75/week
- Variable cost for refrigeration: $3/case/week

a. Calculate the weekly holding cost for one case of wine.

b. Use the EOQ model to find the number of cases per order and the average number of orders per year.

c. Currently orders are placed by calling France and then following up with a letter. Millennium and its supplier may switch to a simple ordering system using the Internet. The new system will require much less labor. What would be the impact of this system on the ordering pattern?

Q5.7　**(Powered by Koffee)** Powered by Koffee (PBK) is a new campus coffee store. PBK uses 50 bags of whole bean coffee every month, and you may assume that demand is perfectly steady throughout the year.

PBK has signed a year-long contract to purchase its coffee from a local supplier, Phish Roasters, for a price of $25 per bag and a $85 fixed cost for every delivery independent of the order size. The holding cost due to storage is $1 per bag per month. PBK managers figure their cost of capital is approximately 2 percent per month.

a. What is the optimal order size, in bags?

b. Given your answer in (a), how many times a year does PBK place orders?

c. Given your answer in (a), how many months of supply of coffee does PBK have on average?

d. On average, how many dollars per month does PBK spend to hold coffee (including cost of capital)?

Suppose that a South American import/export company has offered PBK a deal for the next year. PBK can buy a years' worth of coffee directly from South America for $20 per bag and a fixed cost for delivery of $2,000. Assume the estimated cost for inspection and storage is $1 per bag per month and the cost of capital is approximately 2 percent per month.

e. Should PBK order from Phish Roasters or the South America import/export company? Quantitatively justify your answer.

Q5.8*　**(Beer Distributor)** A beer distributor finds that it sells on average 100 cases a week of regular 12-oz. Budweiser. For this problem assume that demand occurs at a constant rate over a 50-week year. The distributor currently purchases beer every two weeks at a cost of $8 per case. The inventory-related holding cost (capital, insurance, etc.) for the distributor

(* indicates that the solution is at the end of the book)

equals 25 percent of the dollar value of inventory per year. Each order placed with the supplier costs the distributor $10. This cost includes labor, forms, postage, and so forth.

a. Assume the distributor can choose any order quantity it wishes. What order quantity minimizes the distributor's total inventory-related costs (holding and ordering)?

For the next three parts, assume the distributor selects the order quantity specified in part (a).

b. What are the distributor's inventory turns per year?

c. What is the inventory-related cost per case of beer sold?

d. Assume the brewer is willing to give a 5 percent quantity discount if the distributor orders 600 cases or more at a time. If the distributor is interested in minimizing its total cost (i.e., purchase and inventory-related costs), should the distributor begin ordering 600 or more cases at a time?

Chapter

6

Variability and Its Impact on Process Performance: Waiting Time Problems

For consumers, one of the most visible—and probably annoying—forms of supply–demand mismatches is waiting time. As consumers, we seem to spend a significant portion of our life waiting in line, be it in physical lines (supermarkets, check-in at airports) or in "virtual" lines (listening to music in a call center, waiting for a response e-mail).

It is important to distinguish between different types of waiting time:

• Waiting time predictably occurs when the expected demand rate exceeds the expected supply rate for some limited period of time. This happens especially in cases of constant capacity levels and demand that exhibits seasonality. This leads to implied utilization levels of over 100 percent for some time period. Queues forming at the gate of an airport after the flight is announced are an example of such queues.

• As we will see in the next section, in the presence of variability, queues also can arise if the implied utilization is below 100 percent. Such queues can thereby be fully attributed to the presence of variability, as there exists, on average, enough capacity to meet demand.

While the difference between these two types of waiting time probably does not matter much to the customer, it is of great importance from the perspective of operations management. The root cause for the first type of waiting time is a capacity problem; variability is only a secondary effect. Thus, when analyzing this type of a problem, we first should use the tools outlined in Chapters 3, 4, and 5 instead of focusing on variability.

The root cause of the second type of waiting time is variability. This makes waiting time unpredictable, both from the perspective of the customer as well as from the perspective of the operation. Sometimes, it is the customer (demand) waiting for service (supply) and, sometimes, it is the other way around. Demand just never seems to match supply in these settings.

Analyzing waiting times and linking these waiting times to variability require the introduction of new analytical tools, which we present in this chapter. We will discuss the tools for analyzing waiting times based on the example of An-ser Services, a call-center operation in Wisconsin that specializes in providing answering services for financial services, insurance companies, and medical practices. Specifically, the objective of this chapter is to

- Predict waiting times and derive some performance metrics capturing the service quality provided to the customer.
- Recommend ways of reducing waiting time by choosing appropriate capacity levels, redesigning the service system, and outlining opportunities to reduce variability.

6.1   Motivating Example: A Somewhat Unrealistic Call Center

For illustrative purposes, consider a call center with just one employee from 7 A.M. to 8 A.M. Based on prior observations, the call-center management estimates that, on average, a call takes 4 minutes to complete (e.g., giving someone driving directions) and there are, on average, 12 calls arriving in a 60-minute period, that is, on average, one call every 5 minutes.

What will be the average waiting time for a customer before talking to a customer service representative? From a somewhat naïve perspective, there should be no waiting time at all. Since the call center has a capacity of serving 60/4 = 15 calls per hour and calls arrive at a rate of 12 calls per hour, supply of capacity clearly exceeds demand. If anything, there seems to be excess service capacity in the call center since its utilization, which we defined previously (Chapter 3) as the ratio between flow rate and capacity, can be computed as

$$\text{Utilization} = \frac{\text{Flow rate}}{\text{Capacity}} = \frac{12 \text{ calls per hour}}{15 \text{ calls per hour}} = 80\%$$

First, consider the arrivals and service times as depicted in Figure 6.1. A call arrives exactly every 5 minutes and then takes exactly 4 minutes to be served. This is probably the weirdest call center that you have ever seen! No need to worry, we will return to "real operations" momentarily, but the following thought experiment will help you grasp how variability can lead to waiting time.

Despite its almost robotlike service times and the apparently very disciplined customer service representative ("sorry, 4 minutes are over; thanks for your call"), this call center has one major advantage: no incoming call ever has to wait.

FIGURE 6.1
A Somewhat Odd Service Process

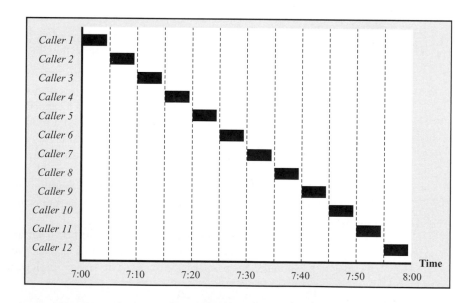

Assuming that calls arrive like kick scooters at an assembly line and are then treated by customer service representatives that act like robots reflects a common mistake managers make when calculating process performance. These calculations look at the process at an aggregate level and consider how much capacity is available over the entire hour (day, month, quarter), yet ignore how the requests for service are spaced out within the hour.

If we look at the call center on a minute-by-minute basis, a different picture emerges. Specifically, we observe that calls do not arrive like kick scooters appear at the end of the assembly line, but instead follow a much less systematic pattern, which is illustrated by Figure 6.2.

Moreover, a minute-by-minute analysis also reveals that the actual service durations also vary across calls. As Figure 6.2 shows, while the average service time is 4 minutes, there exist large variations across calls, and the actual activity times range from 2 minutes to 7 minutes.

Now, consider how the hour from 7:00 A.M. to 8:00 A.M. unfolds. As can be seen in Figure 6.2, the first call comes in at 7:00 A.M. This call will be served without waiting time, and it takes the customer service representative 5 minutes to complete the call. The following 2 minutes are idle time from the perspective of the call center (7:05–7:07). At 7:07, the second call comes in, requiring a 6-minute service time. Again, the second caller does not have to wait and will leave the system at 7:13. However, while the second caller is being served, at 7:09 the third caller arrives and now needs to wait until 7:13 before beginning the service.

Figure 6.3 shows the waiting time and service time for each of the 12 customers calling between 7:00 A.M. and 8:00 A.M. Specifically, we observe that

- Most customers do have to wait a considerable amount of time (up to 10 minutes) before being served. This waiting occurs, although, on average, there is plenty of capacity in the call center.

- The call center is not able to provide a consistent service quality, as some customers are waiting, while others are not.

- Despite long waiting times and—because of Little's Law—long queues (see lower part of Figure 6.3), the customer service representative incurs idle time repeatedly over the time period from 7 A.M. to 8 A.M.

Why does variability not average out over time? The reason for this is as follows. In the call center example, the customer service representative can only serve a customer if there is

FIGURE 6.2 Data Gathered at a Call Center

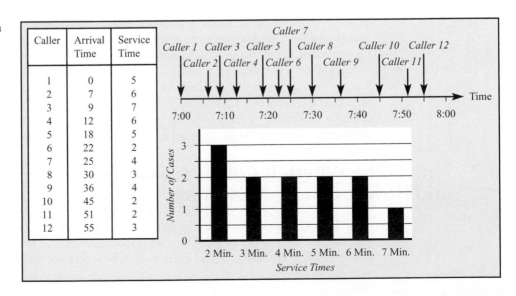

FIGURE 6.3
Detailed Analysis of
Call Center

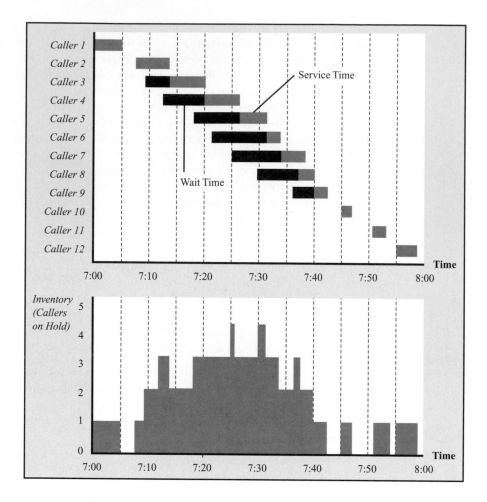

capacity *and* demand at the same moment in time. Therefore, capacity can never "run ahead" of demand. However, demand can "run ahead" of capacity, in which case the queue builds up. The idea that inventory can be used to decouple the supply process from demand, thereby restoring the flow rate to the level achievable in the absence of variability, is another version of the "buffer or suffer" principle that we already encountered in Chapter 5. Thus, if a service organization attempts to achieve the flow-rate levels feasible based on averages, long waiting times will result (unfortunately, in those cases, it is the customer who gets "buffered" and "suffers").

Taking the perspective of a manager attempting to match supply and demand, our objectives have not changed. We are still interested in calculating the three fundamental performance measures of an operation: inventory, flow rate, and flow time. Yet, as the above example illustrated, we realize that the process analysis tools we have discussed up to this point in the book need to be extended to appropriately deal with variability.

6.2 Variability: Where It Comes From and How It Can Be Measured

As a first step toward restoring our ability to understand a process's basic performance measures in the presence of variability, we take a more detailed look at the concept of variability itself. Specifically, we are interested in the sources of variability and how to measure variability.

FIGURE 6.4
**Variability and
Where It Comes
From**

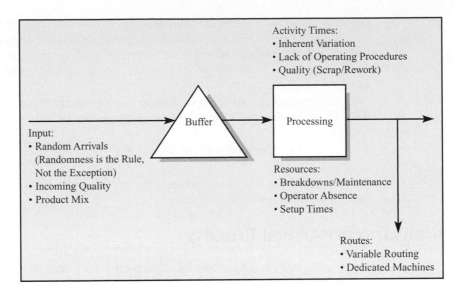

Why is there variability in a process to begin with? Drawing a simple (the most simple) process flow diagram suggests the following four sources of variability (these four sources are summarized in Figure 6.4):

• Variability from the inflow of flow units. The biggest source of variability in service organizations comes from the market itself. While some patterns of the customer-arrival process are predictable (e.g., in a hotel there are more guests checking out between 8 and 9 A.M. than between 2 and 3 P.M.), there always remains uncertainty about when the next customer will arrive.

• Variability in activity times. Whenever we are dealing with human operators at a resource, it is likely that there will be some variability in their behavior. Thus, if we would ask a worker at an assembly line to repeat a certain activity 100 times, we would probably find that some of these activities were carried out faster than others. Another source of variability in activity times that is specific to service environment is that in most service operations, the customer him/herself is involved in many of the tasks constituting the activity time. At a hotel front desk, some guests might require extra time (e.g., the guest requires an explanation for items appearing on his or her bill), while others check out faster (e.g., simply use the credit card that they used for the reservation and only return their room key).

• Random availability of resources. If resources are subject to random breakdowns, for example, machine failures in manufacturing environments or operator absenteeism in service operation, variability is created.

• Random routing in case of multiple flow units in the process. If the path a flow unit takes through the process is itself random, the arrival process at each individual resource is subject to variability. Consider, for example, an emergency room in a hospital. Following the initial screening at the admissions step, incoming patients are routed to different resources. A nurse might handle easy cases, more complex cases might be handled by a general doctor, and severe cases are brought to specific units in the hospital (e.g., trauma center). Even if arrival times and service times are deterministic, this random routing alone is sufficient to introduce variability.

In general, any form of variability is measured based on the standard deviation. In our case of the call center, we could measure the variability of call durations based on collecting some data and then computing the corresponding standard deviation. The problem with this approach is that the standard deviation provides an *absolute* measure of variability. Does a standard deviation of 5 minutes indicate a high variability? A 5-minute standard deviation for call durations (activity times) in the context of a call center seems like a large number. In the context of a 2-hour surgery in a trauma center, a 5-minute standard deviation seems small.

For this reason, it is more appropriate to measure variability in *relative* terms. Specifically, we define the *coefficient of variation* of a random variable as

$$\text{Coefficient of variation} = \text{CV} = \frac{\text{Standard deviation}}{\text{Mean}}$$

As both the standard deviation and the mean have the same measurement units, the coefficient of variation is a unitless measure.

6.3 Analyzing an Arrival Process

Any process analysis we perform is only as good as the information we feed into our analysis. For this reason, Sections 6.3 and 6.4 focus on data collection and data analysis for the upcoming mathematical models. As a manager intending to apply some of the following tools, this data analysis is essential. However, as a student with only a couple of hours left to the final exam, you might be better off jumping straight to Section 6.5.

Of particular importance when dealing with variability problems is an accurate representation of the demand, which determines the timing of customer arrivals.

Assume we got up early and visited the call center of An-ser; say we arrived at their offices at 6:00 A.M. and we took detailed notes of what takes place over the coming hour. We would hardly have had the time to settle down when the first call comes in. One of the An-ser staff takes the call immediately. Twenty-three seconds later, the second call comes in; another 1:24 minutes later the third call; and so on.

We define the time at which An-ser receives a call as the *arrival time.* Let AT_i denote the arrival time of the ith call. Moreover, we define the time between two consecutive arrivals as the *interarrival time,* IA. Thus, $\text{IA}_i = \text{AT}_{i+1} - \text{AT}_i$. Figure 6.5 illustrates these two definitions.

If we continue this data collection, we accumulate a fair number of arrival times. Such data are automatically recorded in call centers, so we could simply download a file that looks like Table 6.1.

Before we can move forward and introduce a mathematical model that predicts the effects of variability, we have to invest in some simple, yet important, data analysis. A major risk related to any mathematical model or computer simulation is that these tools always provide us with a number (or a set of numbers), independent of the accuracy with which the inputs we enter into the equation reflect the real world.

FIGURE 6.5 The Concept of Interarrival Times

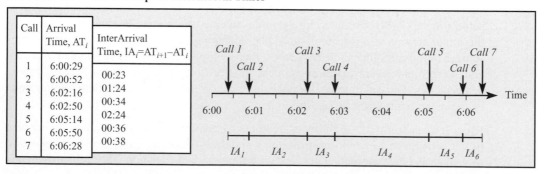

TABLE 6.1 Call Arrivals at An-ser on April 2, 2002, from 6:00 A.M. to 10:00 A.M.

6:00:29	6:52:39	7:17:57	7:33:51	7:56:16	8:17:33	8:28:11	8:39:25	8:55:56	9:21:58
6:00:52	6:53:06	7:18:10	7:34:05	7:56:24	8:17:42	8:28:12	8:39:47	8:56:17	9:22:02
6:02:16	6:53:07	7:18:17	7:34:19	7:56:24	8:17:50	8:28:13	8:39:51	8:57:42	9:22:02
6:02:50	6:53:24	7:18:38	7:34:51	7:57:39	8:17:52	8:28:17	8:40:02	8:58:45	9:22:30
6:05:14	6:53:25	7:18:54	7:35:10	7:57:51	8:17:54	8:28:43	8:40:09	8:58:49	9:23:13
6:05:50	6:54:18	7:19:04	7:35:13	7:57:55	8:18:03	8:28:59	8:40:23	8:58:49	9:23:29
6:06:28	6:54:24	7:19:40	7:35:21	7:58:26	8:18:12	8:29:06	8:40:34	8:59:32	9:23:45
6:07:37	6:54:36	7:19:41	7:35:44	7:58:41	8:18:21	8:29:34	8:40:35	8:59:38	9:24:10
6:08:05	6:55:06	7:20:10	7:35:59	7:59:12	8:18:23	8:29:38	8:40:46	8:59:45	9:24:30
6:10:16	6:55:19	7:20:11	7:36:37	7:59:20	8:18:34	8:29:40	8:40:51	9:00:14	9:24:42
6:12:13	6:55:31	7:20:26	7:36:45	7:59:22	8:18:46	8:29:45	8:40:58	9:00:52	9:25:07
6:12:48	6:57:25	7:20:27	7:37:07	7:59:22	8:18:53	8:29:46	8:41:12	9:00:53	9:25:15
6:14:04	6:57:38	7:20:38	7:37:14	7:59:36	8:18:54	8:29:47	8:41:26	9:01:09	9:26:03
6:14:16	6:57:44	7:20:52	7:38:01	7:59:50	8:18:58	8:29:47	8:41:32	9:01:31	9:26:04
6:14:28	6:58:16	7:20:59	7:38:03	7:59:54	8:19:20	8:29:54	8:41:49	9:01:55	9:26:23
6:17:51	6:58:34	7:21:11	7:38:05	8:01:22	8:19:25	8:30:00	8:42:23	9:02:25	9:26:34
6:18:19	6:59:41	7:21:14	7:38:18	8:01:42	8:19:28	8:30:01	8:42:51	9:02:30	9:27:02
6:19:11	7:00:50	7:21:46	7:39:00	8:01:56	8:20:09	8:30:08	8:42:53	9:02:38	9:27:04
6:20:48	7:00:54	7:21:56	7:39:17	8:02:08	8:20:23	8:30:23	8:43:24	9:02:51	9:27:27
6:23:33	7:01:08	7:21:58	7:39:35	8:02:26	8:20:27	8:30:23	8:43:28	9:03:29	9:28:25
6:24:25	7:01:31	7:23:03	7:40:06	8:02:29	8:20:44	8:30:31	8:43:47	9:03:33	9:28:37
6:25:08	7:01:39	7:23:16	7:40:23	8:02:39	8:20:54	8:31:02	8:44:23	9:03:38	9:29:09
6:25:19	7:01:56	7:23:19	7:41:34	8:02:47	8:21:12	8:31:11	8:44:49	9:03:51	9:29:15
6:25:27	7:04:52	7:23:48	7:42:20	8:02:52	8:21:12	8:31:19	8:45:05	9:04:11	9:29:52
6:25:38	7:04:54	7:24:01	7:42:33	8:03:06	8:21:25	8:31:20	8:45:10	9:04:33	9:30:47
6:25:48	7:05:37	7:24:09	7:42:51	8:03:58	8:21:28	8:31:22	8:45:28	9:04:42	9:30:58
6:26:05	7:05:39	7:24:45	7:42:57	8:04:07	8:21:43	8:31:23	8:45:31	9:04:44	9:30:59
6:26:59	7:05:42	7:24:56	7:43:23	8:04:27	8:21:44	8:31:27	8:45:32	9:04:44	9:31:03
6:27:37	7:06:37	7:25:01	7:43:34	8:05:53	8:21:53	8:31:45	8:45:39	9:05:22	9:31:55
6:27:46	7:06:46	7:25:03	7:43:43	8:05:54	8:22:19	8:32:05	8:46:24	9:06:01	9:33:08
6:29:32	7:07:11	7:25:18	7:43:44	8:06:43	8:22:44	8:32:13	8:46:27	9:06:12	9:33:45
6:29:52	7:07:24	7:25:39	7:43:57	8:06:47	8:23:00	8:32:19	8:46:40	9:06:14	9:34:07
6:30:26	7:07:46	7:25:40	7:43:57	8:07:07	8:23:02	8:32:59	8:46:41	9:06:41	9:35:15
6:30:32	7:09:17	7:25:46	7:45:07	8:07:43	8:23:12	8:33:02	8:47:00	9:06:44	9:35:40
6:30:41	7:09:34	7:25:48	7:45:32	8:08:28	8:23:30	8:33:27	8:47:04	9:06:48	9:36:17
6:30:53	7:09:38	7:26:30	7:46:22	8:08:31	8:24:04	8:33:30	8:47:06	9:06:55	9:36:37
6:30:56	7:09:53	7:26:38	7:46:38	8:09:05	8:24:17	8:33:40	8:47:15	9:06:59	9:37:23
6:31:04	7:09:59	7:26:49	7:46:48	8:09:15	8:24:19	8:33:47	8:47:27	9:08:03	9:37:37
6:31:45	7:10:29	7:27:30	7:47:00	8:09:48	8:24:26	8:34:19	8:47:40	9:08:33	9:37:38
6:33:49	7:10:37	7:27:36	7:47:15	8:09:57	8:24:39	8:34:20	8:47:46	9:09:32	9:37:42
6:34:03	7:10:54	7:27:50	7:47:53	8:10:39	8:24:48	8:35:01	8:47:53	9:10:32	9:39:03
6:34:15	7:11:07	7:27:50	7:48:01	8:11:16	8:25:03	8:35:07	8:48:27	9:10:46	9:39:10
6:36:07	7:11:30	7:27:56	7:48:14	8:11:30	8:25:04	8:35:25	8:48:48	9:10:53	9:41:37
6:36:12	7:12:02	7:28:01	7:48:14	8:11:38	8:25:07	8:35:29	8:49:14	9:11:32	9:42:58
6:37:21	7:12:08	7:28:17	7:48:50	8:11:49	8:25:16	8:36:13	8:49:19	9:11:37	9:43:27
6:37:23	7:12:18	7:28:25	7:49:00	8:12:00	8:25:22	8:36:14	8:49:20	9:11:50	9:43:37
6:37:57	7:12:18	7:28:26	7:49:04	8:12:07	8:25:31	8:36:23	8:49:40	9:12:02	9:44:09
6:38:20	7:12:26	7:28:47	7:49:48	8:12:17	8:25:32	8:36:23	8:50:19	9:13:19	9:44:21
6:40:06	7:13:16	7:28:54	7:49:50	8:12:40	8:25:32	8:36:29	8:50:38	9:14:00	9:44:32
6:40:11	7:13:21	7:29:09	7:49:59	8:12:41	8:25:45	8:36:35	8:52:11	9:14:04	9:44:37
6:40:59	7:13:22	7:29:27	7:50:13	8:12:42	8:25:48	8:36:37	8:52:29	9:14:07	9:44:44
6:42:17	7:14:04	7:30:02	7:50:27	8:12:47	8:25:49	8:37:05	8:52:40	9:15:15	9:45:10
6:43:01	7:14:07	7:30:07	7:51:07	8:13:40	8:26:01	8:37:11	8:52:41	9:15:26	9:46:15
6:43:05	7:14:49	7:30:13	7:51:31	8:13:41	8:26:04	8:37:12	8:52:43	9:15:27	9:46:44
6:43:57	7:15:19	7:30:50	7:51:40	8:13:52	8:26:11	8:37:35	8:53:03	9:15:36	9:49:48
6:44:02	7:15:38	7:30:55	7:52:05	8:14:04	8:26:15	8:37:44	8:53:08	9:15:40	9:50:19
6:45:04	7:15:41	7:31:24	7:52:25	8:14:41	8:26:28	8:38:01	8:53:19	9:15:40	9:52:53
6:46:13	7:15:57	7:31:35	7:52:32	8:15:15	8:26:28	8:38:02	8:53:30	9:15:40	9:53:13
6:47:01	7:16:28	7:31:41	7:53:10	8:15:25	8:26:37	8:38:10	8:53:32	9:15:41	9:53:15
6:47:10	7:16:36	7:31:45	7:53:18	8:15:39	8:26:58	8:38:15	8:53:44	9:15:46	9:53:50
6:47:35	7:16:40	7:31:46	7:53:19	8:15:48	8:27:07	8:38:39	8:54:25	9:16:12	9:54:24
6:49:23	7:16:45	7:32:13	7:53:51	8:16:09	8:27:09	8:38:40	8:54:28	9:16:34	9:54:48
6:50:54	7:16:50	7:32:16	7:53:52	8:16:10	8:27:17	8:38:44	8:54:49	9:18:02	9:54:51
6:51:04	7:17:08	7:32:16	7:54:04	8:16:18	8:27:26	8:38:49	8:55:05	9:18:06	9:56:40
6:51:17	7:17:09	7:32:34	7:54:16	8:16:26	8:27:29	8:38:57	8:55:05	9:20:19	9:58:25
6:51:48	7:17:09	7:32:34	7:54:26	8:16:39	8:27:35	8:39:07	8:55:14	9:20:42	9:59:19
6:52:17	7:17:19	7:32:57	7:54:51	8:17:16	8:27:54	8:39:20	8:55:22	9:20:44	
6:52:17	7:17:22	7:33:13	7:55:13	8:17:24	8:27:57	8:39:20	8:55:25	9:20:54	
6:52:31	7:17:22	7:33:36	7:55:35	8:17:28	8:27:59	8:39:21	8:55:50	9:21:55	

Answering the following two questions before proceeding to any other computations improves the predictions of our models substantially.

• Is the arrival process *stationary;* that is, is the expected number of customers arriving in a certain time interval constant over the period we are interested in?

• Are the interarrival times *exponentially distributed,* and therefore form a so-called *Poisson* arrival process?

We now define the concepts of stationary arrivals and exponentially distributed interarrival times. We also describe how these two questions can be answered, both in general as well as in the specific setting of the call center described previously. We also discuss the importance of these two questions and their impact on the calculations in this and the next chapter.

Stationary Arrivals

Consider the call arrival pattern displayed in Table 6.1. How tempting it is to put these data into a spreadsheet, compute the mean and the standard deviation of the interarrival times over that time period, and end the analysis of the arrival pattern at this point, assuming that the mean and the standard deviation capture the entire behavior of the arrival process. Five minutes with Excel, and we could be done!

However, a simple graphical analysis (Figure 6.6) of the data reveals that there is more going on in the arrival process than two numbers can capture. As we can see graphically in Figure 6.6, the average number of customers calling within a certain time interval (e.g., 15 minutes) is not constant over the day.

To capture such changes in arrival processes, we introduce the following definitions:

• An arrival process is said to be *stationary* if, for any time interval (e.g., an hour), the expected number of arrivals in this time interval only depends on the length of the time interval, not on the starting time of the interval (i.e., we can move a time interval of a fixed length forth and back on a time line without changing the expected number of arrivals). In the context of Figure 6.6, we see that the arrival process is not stationary. For example, if

FIGURE 6.6
Seasonality over the Course of a Day

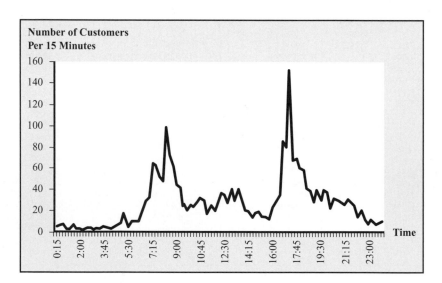

we take a 3-hour interval, we see that there are many more customers arriving from 6 to 9 A.M. than there are from 1 to 4 A.M.

- An arrival process exhibits *seasonality* if it is not stationary.

When analyzing an arrival process, it is important that we distinguish between changes in demand (e.g., the number of calls in 15 minutes) that are a result of variability and changes in demand that are a result of seasonality. Both variability and seasonality are unpleasant from an operations perspective. However, the effect of seasonality alone can be perfectly predicted ex ante, while this is not possible for the case of variability (we might know the expected number of callers for a day, but the actual number is a realization of a random variable).

Based on the data at hand, we observe that the arrival process is not stationary over a period of several hours. In general, a simple analysis determines whether a process is stationary.

1. Sort all arrival times so that they are increasing in time (label them as $AT_1 \ldots AT_n$).
2. Plot a graph with ($x = AT_i$; $y = i$) as illustrated by Figure 6.7.
3. Add a straight line from the lower left (first arrival) to the upper right (last arrival).

If the underlying arrival process is stationary, there will be no significant deviation between the graph you plotted and the straight line. In this case, however, in Figure 6.7 (left) we observe several deviations between the straight line and the arrival data. Specifically, we observe that for the first hour, fewer calls come in compared to the average arrival rate from 6 A.M. to 10 A.M. In contrast, around 8:30 A.M., the arrival rate becomes much higher than the average. Thus, our analysis indicates that the arrival process we face is not stationary.

FIGURE 6.7 **Test for Stationary Arrivals**

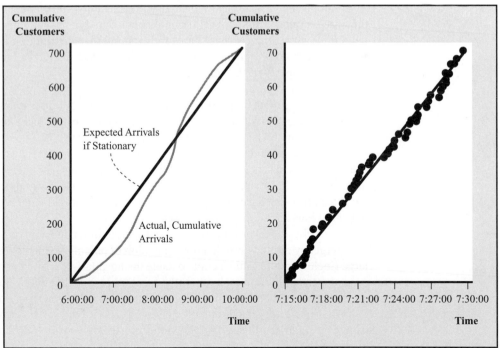

When facing nonstationary arrival processes, the best way to proceed is to divide up the day (the week, the month) into smaller time intervals and have a separate arrival rate for each interval. If we then look at the arrival process within the smaller intervals—in our case, we use 15-minute intervals—we find that the seasonality within the interval is relatively low. In other words, within the interval, we come relatively close to a stationary arrival stream. The stationary behavior of the interarrivals within a 15-minute interval is illustrated by Figure 6.7 (right).

Figure 6.7 (left) is interesting to compare with Figure 6.7 (right): the arrival process behaves as stationary "at the micro-level" of a 15-minute interval, yet exhibits strong seasonality over the course of the entire day, as we observed in Figure 6.6. Note that the peaks in Figure 6.6 correspond to those time slots where the line of "actual, cumulative arrivals" in Figure 6.7 grows faster than the straight line "predicted arrivals."

In most cases in practice, the context explains this type of seasonality. For example, in the case of An-ser, the spike in arrivals corresponds to people beginning their day, expecting that the company they want to call (e.g., a doctor's office) is already "up and running." However, since many of these firms are not handling calls before 9 A.M., the resulting call stream is channeled to the answering service.

Exponential Interarrival Times

Interarrival times commonly are distributed following an *exponential distribution.* If IA is a random interarrival time and the interarrival process follows an exponential distribution, we have

$$\text{Probability } \{\text{IA} \leq t\} = 1 - e^{-\frac{t}{a}}$$

where a is the average interarrival time as defined above. Exponential functions are frequently used to model interarrival time in theory as well as practice, both because of their good fit with empirical data as well as their analytical convenience. If an arrival process has indeed exponential interarrival times, we refer to it as a *Poisson arrival process.*

It can be shown analytically that customers arriving independently from each other at the process (e.g., customers calling into a call center) form a demand pattern with exponential interarrival times. The shape of the cumulative distribution function for the exponential distribution is given in Figure 6.8. The average interarrival time is in minutes. An important property of the exponential distribution is that the standard deviation is also equal to the average, a.

Another important property of the exponential distribution is known as the *memoryless property.* The memoryless property simply states that the number of arrivals in the next time slot (e.g., 1 minute) is independent of when the last arrival has occurred.

To illustrate this property, consider the situation of an emergency room. Assume that, on average, a patient arrives every 10 minutes and no patients have arrived for the last 20 minutes. Does the fact that no patients have arrived in the last 20 minutes increase or decrease the probability that a patient arrives in the next 10 minutes? For an arrival process with exponential interarrival times, the answer is *no.*

Intuitively, we feel that this is a reasonable assumption in many settings. Consider, again, an emergency room. Given that the population of potential patients for the ER is extremely large (including all healthy people outside the hospital), we can treat new patients as arriving independently from each other (the fact that Joan Wiley fell off her mountain bike has nothing to do with the fact that Joe Hoop broke his ankle when playing basketball).

Because it is very important to determine if our interarrival times are exponentially distributed, we now introduce the following four-step diagnostic procedure:

FIGURE 6.8   **Distribution Function of the Exponential Distribution (left) and an Example of a Histogram (right)**

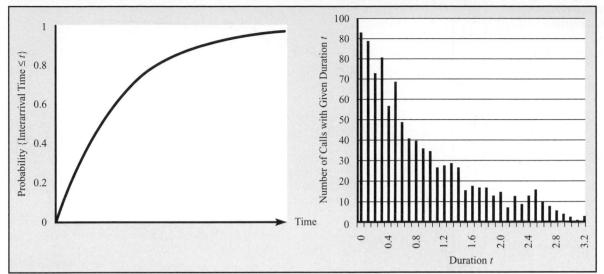

1. Compute the interarrival times $IA_1 \ldots IA_n$.
2. Sort the interarrival times in increasing order; let a_i denote the ith smallest interarrival time (a_1 is the smallest interarrival time; a_n is the largest).
3. Plot pairs ($x = a_i$, $y = i/n$). The resulting graph is called an empirical distribution function.
4. Compare the graph with an exponential distribution with "appropriately chosen parameter." To find the best value for the parameter, we set the parameter of the exponential distribution equal to the average interarrival time we obtain from our data. If a few observations from the sample are substantially remote from the resulting curve, we might adjust the parameter for the exponential distribution "manually" to improve fit.

Figure 6.9 illustrates the outcome of this process. If the underlying distribution is indeed exponential, the resulting graph will resemble the analytical distribution as in the case of Figure 6.9. Note that this procedure of assessing the goodness of fit works also for any other distribution function.

Nonexponential Interarrival Times

In some cases, we might find that the interarrival times are not exponentially distributed. For example, we might encounter a situation where arrivals are scheduled (e.g., every hour), which typically leads to a lower amount of variability in the arrival process.

While in the case of the exponential distribution the mean interarrival time is equal to the standard deviation of interarrival times and, thus, one parameter is sufficient to characterize the entire arrival process, we need more parameters to describe the arrival process if interarrival times are not exponentially distributed.

Following our earlier definition of the coefficient of variation, we can measure the variability of an arrival (demand) process as

$$CV_a = \frac{\text{Standard deviation of interarrival time}}{\text{Average interarrival time}}$$

FIGURE 6.9
Empirical versus
Exponential
Distribution for
Interarrival Times

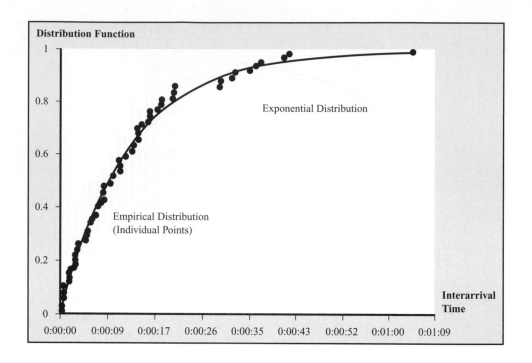

Given that for the exponential distribution the mean is equal to the standard deviation, its coefficient of variation is equal to 1.

Summary: Analyzing an Arrival Process

Figure 6.10 provides a summary of the steps required to analyze an arrival process. It also shows what to do if any of the assumptions required for the following models (Chapters 6 and 7) are violated.

FIGURE 6.10
How to Analyze a
Demand/Arrival
Process

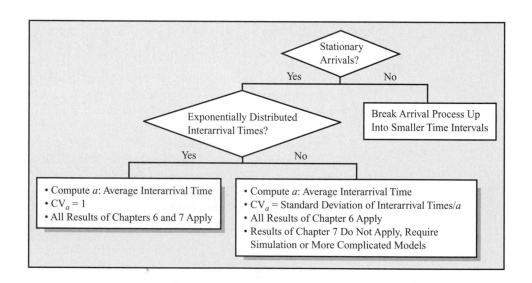

6.4   Service Time Variability

Just as exact arrival time of an individual call is difficult to predict, so is the actual duration of the call. Thus, service processes also have a considerable amount of variability from the supply side. Figure 6.11 provides a summary of call durations (service times from the perspective of the customer service representative) for the case of the An-ser call center.

We observe that the variability in service times is substantial. While some calls were completed in less than a minute, others took more than 10 minutes! Thus, in addition to the variability of demand, variability also is created within the process.

There have been reports of numerous different shapes of activity time distributions. For the purposes of this book, we focus entirely on their mean and standard deviation. In other words, when we collect data, we do not explicitly model the distribution of the service times, but assume that the mean and standard deviation capture all the relevant information. This information is sufficient for all computations in Chapters 6 and 7.

Based on the data summarized in Figure 6.11, we compute the mean call time as 120 seconds and the corresponding standard deviation as 150 seconds. As we have done with the interarrival times, we can now define the coefficient of variation, which we obtain by

$$CV_p = \frac{\text{Standard deviation of activity time}}{\text{Average activity time}}$$

As with the arrival process, we need to be careful not to confuse variability with seasonality. Seasonality in service times refers to known patterns of call durations as a function of the day of the week or the time of the day (as Figure 6.12 shows, calls take significantly longer on weekends than during the week). Call durations also differ depending on the time of the day.

The models we introduce in Chapters 6 and 7 require a stationary service process (in the case of seasonality in the service process, just divide up the time line into smaller intervals, similar to what we did with the arrival process) but do not require any other properties (e.g., exponential distribution of service time). Thus, the standard deviation and mean of the service time are all we need to know.

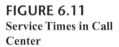

FIGURE 6.11
Service Times in Call Center

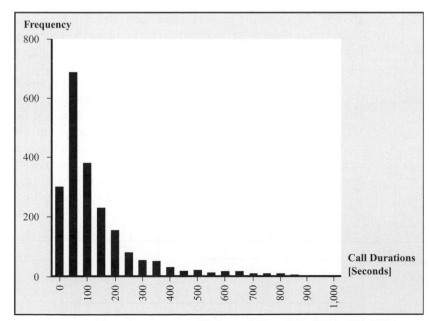

FIGURE 6.12
Average Call Durations: Weekday versus Weekend

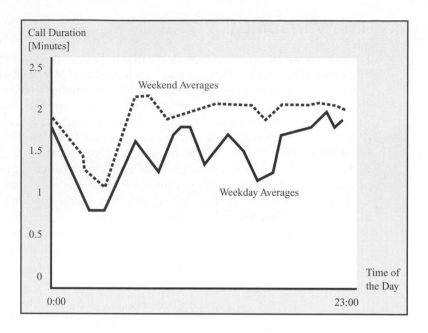

6.5   Predicting the Average Waiting Time for the Case of One Resource

Based on our measures of variability, we now introduce a simple formula that restores our ability to predict the basic process performance measures: inventory, flow rate, and flow time.

In this chapter, we restrict ourselves to the most basic process diagram, consisting of one buffer with unlimited space and one single resource. This process layout corresponds to the call center example discussed above. Figure 6.13 shows the process flow diagram for this simple system.

Flow units arrive to the system following a demand pattern that exhibits variability. On average, a flow unit arrives every a time units. We labeled a as the average interarrival time. This average reflects the mean of interarrival times IA_1 to IA_n. After computing the standard deviation of the IA_1 to IA_n, interarrival times we can compute the coefficient of variation CV_a of the arrival process as discussed previously.

Assume that it takes on average p units of time to serve a flow unit. Similar to the arrival process, we can define p_1 to p_n as the empirically observed activity times and compute the coefficient of variation for the processing times, CV_p, accordingly. Given that there is only one single resource serving the arriving flow units, the capacity of the server can be written as $1/p$.

As discussed in the introduction to this chapter, we are considering cases in which the capacity exceeds the demand rate; thus, the resulting utilization is strictly less than 100 percent. If the utilization were above 100 percent, inventory would predictably build up and we would not need any sophisticated tools accounting for variability to predict that flow units

FIGURE 6.13
A Simple Process with One Queue and One Server

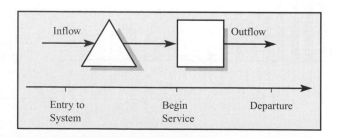

will incur waiting times. However, the most important insight of this chapter is that flow units incur waiting time even if the server utilization is below 100 percent.

Given that capacity exceeds demand and assuming we never lose a customer (i.e., once a customer calls, he or she never hangs up), we are demand-constrained and, thus, the flow rate R is the demand rate. (Chapter 7 deals with the possibility of lost customers.) Specifically, since a customer arrives, on average, every a units of time, the flow rate $R = 1/a$. Recall that we can compute utilization as

$$\text{Utilization} = \frac{\text{Flow rate}}{\text{Capacity}} = \frac{1/a}{1/p} = p/a < 100\%$$

Note that, so far, we have not applied any concept that went beyond the deterministic process analysis we discussed in Chapters 3 to 5.

Now, take the perspective of a flow unit moving through the system (see Figure 6.14). A flow unit can spend time waiting in the queue (in a call center, this is the time when you listen to Music of the '70s). Let T_q denote the time the flow unit has to spend in the queue waiting for the service to begin. The subscript q denotes that this is only the time the flow unit waits in the queue. Thus, T_q does *not* include the actual service time, which we defined as p. Based on the waiting time in the queue T_q and the average service time p, we can compute the flow time (the time the flow unit will spend in the system) as

$$\text{Flow time} = \text{Time in queue} + \text{Activity time}$$

$$T = T_q + p$$

Instead of taking the perspective of the flow unit, we also can look at the system as a whole, wondering how many flow units will be in the queue and how many will be in service. Let I_q be defined as the inventory (number of flow units) that are in the queue and I_p be the number of flow units in process. Since the inventory in the queue I_q and the inventory in process I_p are the only places we can find inventory, we can compute the overall inventory in the system as $I = I_q + I_p$.

As long as there exists only one resource, I_p is a number between zero and one: sometimes there is a flow unit in service ($I_p = 1$); sometimes there is not ($I_p = 0$). The probability that at a random moment in time the server is actually busy, working on a flow unit, corresponds to the utilization. For example, if the utilization of the process is 30 percent, there exists a .3 probability that at a random moment in time the server is busy. Alternatively, we can say that over the 60 minutes in an hour, the server is busy for

$$.3 \times 60 \text{ [minutes/hour]} = 18 \text{ minutes}$$

FIGURE 6.14
A Simple Process with One Queue and One Server

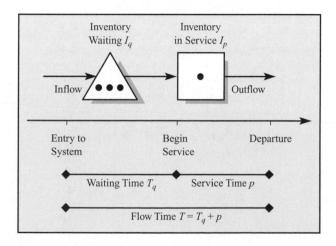

While the inventory in service I_p and the activity time p are relatively easy to compute, this is unfortunately not the case for the inventory in the queue I_q or the waiting time in the queue T_q.

Based on the activity time p, the utilization, and the variability as measured by the coefficients of variation for the interarrival time CV_a and the processing time and CV_p, we can compute the average waiting time in the queue using the following formula:

$$\text{Time in queue} = \text{Activity time} \times \left(\frac{\text{Utilization}}{1 - \text{Utilization}} \right) \times \left(\frac{CV_a^2 + CV_p^2}{2} \right)$$

The formula does not require that the service times or the interarrival times follow a specific distribution. Yet, for the case of nonexponential interarrival times, the formula only approximates the expected time in the queue, as opposed to being 100 percent exact. The formula should be used only for the case of a stationary process (see Section 6.3 for the definition of a stationary process as well as for what to do if the process is not stationary).

The above equation states that the waiting time in the queue is the product of three factors:

- The waiting time is expressed as multiples of the activity time. However, it is important to keep in mind that the activity time also directly influences the utilization (as Utilization = Activity time/Interarrival time). Thus, one should not think of the waiting time as increasing linearly with the activity time.

- The second factor captures the utilization effect. Note that the utilization has to be less than 100 percent. If the utilization is equal to or greater than 100 percent, the queue continues to grow. This is not driven by variability, but simply by not having the requested capacity. We observe that the utilization factor is nonlinear and becomes larger and larger as the utilization level is increased closer to 100 percent. For example, for Utilization = 0.8, the utilization factor is $0.8/(1 - 0.8) = 4$; for Utilization = 0.9, it is $0.9/(1 - 0.9) = 9$; and for Utilization = 0.95, it grows to $0.95/(1 - 0.95) = 19$.

- The third factor captures the amount of variability in the system, measured by the average of the coefficient of variation of interarrival times CV_a and activity times CV_p. Since CV_a and CV_p neither affect the average activity time p nor the utilization u, we observe that the waiting time grows with the variability in the system.

The best way to familiarize ourselves with this newly introduced formula is to apply it and "see it in action." Toward that end, consider the case of the An-ser call center at 2:00 A.M. in the morning. An-ser is a relatively small call center and they receive very few calls at this time of the day (see Section 6.3 for detailed arrival information), so at 2:00 A.M., there is only one person handling incoming calls.

From the data we collected in the call center, we can quickly compute that the average activity time at An-ser at this time of the day is around 90 seconds. Given that we found in the previous section that the activity time does depend on the time of the day, it is important that we use the service time data representative for these early morning hours: Activity time $p = 90$ seconds.

Based on the empirical service times we collected in Section 6.4, we now compute the standard deviation of the service time to be 120 seconds. Hence, the coefficient of variation for the activity time is

$$CV_p = 120 \text{ seconds}/90 \text{ seconds} = 1.3333$$

From the arrival data we collected (see Figure 6.6), we know that at 2:00 A.M. there are 3 calls arriving in a 15-minute interval. Thus, the interarrival time is $a = 5$ minutes = 300 seconds. Given the activity time and the interarrival time, we can now compute the utilization as

$$\text{Utilization} = \text{Activity time/Interarrival time} \ (= p/a)$$

$$= 90 \text{ seconds}/300 \text{ seconds} = 0.3$$

Concerning the coefficient of variation of the interarrival time, we can take one of two approaches. First, we could take the observed interarrival times and compute the standard deviation empirically. Alternatively, we could view the arrival process during the time period as random. Given the good fit between the data we collected and the exponential distribution (see Figure 6.9), we assume that arrivals follow a Poisson process (interarrival times are exponentially distributed). This implies a coefficient of variation of

$$CV_a = 1$$

Substituting these values into the waiting time formula yields

$$\text{Time in queue} = \text{Activity time} \times \left(\frac{\text{Utilization}}{1 - \text{Utilization}} \right) \times \left(\frac{CV_a^2 + CV_p^2}{2} \right)$$

$$= 90 \times \frac{0.3}{1 - 0.3} \times \frac{1^2 + 1.333^2}{2}$$

$$= 53.57 \text{ seconds}$$

Note that this result captures the average waiting time of a customer before getting served. To obtain the customer's total time spent for the call, including waiting time and service time, we need to add the activity time p for the actual service. Thus, the flow time can be computed as

$$T - T_q + p = 53.57 \text{ seconds} + 90 \text{ seconds} = 143.57 \text{ seconds}$$

It is important to point out that the value 53.57 seconds provides the average waiting time. The actual waiting times experienced by individual customers vary. Some customers get lucky and receive service immediately; others have to wait much longer than 53.57 seconds. This is discussed further below.

Waiting times computed based on the methodology outlined above need to be seen as long-run averages. This has the following two practical implications:

• If the system would start empty (e.g., in a hospital lab, where there are no patients before the opening of the waiting room), the first couple of patients are less likely to experience significant waiting time. This effect is transient: Once a sufficient number of patients have arrived, the system reaches a "steady-state." Note that given the 24-hour operation of An-ser, this is not an issue in this specific case.

• If we observe the system for a given time interval, it is unlikely that the average waiting time we observe within this interval is exactly the average we computed. However, the longer we observe the system, the more likely the expected waiting time T_q will indeed coincide with the empirical average. This resembles a casino, which cannot predict how much money a specific guest will win (or typically lose) in an evening, yet can well predict the economics of the entire guest population over the course of a year.

Now that we have accounted for the waiting time T_q (or the flow time T), we are able to compute the resulting inventory. With $1/a$ being our flow rate, we can use Little's Law to compute the average inventory I as

$$I = R \times T = \frac{1}{a} \times (T_q + p)$$

$$= 1/300 \times (53.57 + 90) = 0.479$$

Thus, there is, on average, about half a customer in the system (it is 2:00 A.M. after all . . .). This inventory includes the two subsets we defined as inventory in the queue (I_q) and inventory in process (I_p):

• I_q can be obtained by applying Little's Law, but this time, rather than applying Little's Law to the entire system (the waiting line and the server), we apply it only to the waiting line in isolation. If we think of the waiting line as a mini process in itself (the corresponding process flow diagram consists only of one triangle), we obtain a flow time of T_q. Hence,

$$I_q = 1/a \times T_q = 1/300 \times 53.57 = 0.179$$

• At any given moment in time, we also can look at the number of customers that are currently talking to the customer service representative. Since we assumed there would only be one representative at this time of the day, there will never be more than one caller at this stage. However, there are moments in time when no caller is served, as the utilization of the employee is well below 100 percent. The average number of callers in service can thus be computed as

$$I_p = \text{Probability}\{0 \text{ callers talking to representative}\} \times 0$$
$$+ \text{Probability}\{1 \text{ caller talking to representative}\} \times 1$$

$$I_p = (1 - u) \times 0 + u \times 1 = u$$

In this case, we obtain $I_p = 0.3$.

6.6 Predicting the Average Waiting Time for the Case of Multiple Resources

After analyzing waiting time in the presence of variability for an extremely simple process, consisting of just one buffer and one resource, we now turn to more complicated operations. Specifically, we analyze a waiting time model of a process consisting of one waiting area (queue) and a process step performed by multiple, identical resources.

We continue our example of the call center. However, now we consider time slots at more busy times over the course of the day, when there are many more customer representatives on duty in the An-ser call center. The basic process layout is illustrated in Figure 6.15.

Let m be the number of parallel servers we have available. Given that we have m servers working in parallel, we now face a situation where the average service time is likely to be much longer than the average interarrival time. Taken together, the m resources have a ca-

FIGURE 6.15
A Process with One Queue and Multiple, Parallel Servers ($m = 5$)

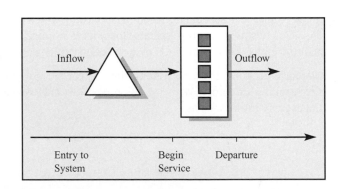

pacity of m/p, while the demand rate continues to be given by $1/a$. We can compute the utilization u of the service process as

$$\text{Utilization} = \frac{\text{Flow rate}}{\text{Capacity}} = \frac{1/\text{Interarrival time}}{(\text{Number of resources}/\text{Activity time})}$$

$$= \frac{1/a}{m/p} = \frac{p}{a \times m}$$

Similar to the case with one single resource, we are only interested in the cases of utilization levels below 100 percent.

The flow unit will initially spend T_q units of time waiting for service. It then moves to the next available resource, where it spends p units of time for service. As before, the total flow time is the sum of waiting time and service time:

$$\text{Flow time} = \text{Waiting time in queue} + \text{Activity time}$$

$$T = T_q + p$$

Based on the activity time p, the utilization u, the coefficients of variation for both service (CV_p) and arrival process (CV_a) as well as the number of resources in the system (m), we can compute the average waiting time T_q using the following formula:[1]

$$\text{Time in queue} = \left(\frac{\text{Activity time}}{m} \right) \times \left(\frac{\text{Utilization}^{\sqrt{2(m+1)}-1}}{1 - \text{Utilization}} \right) \times \left(\frac{CV_a^2 + CV_p^2}{2} \right)$$

As in the case of one single resource, the waiting time is expressed as the product of the activity time, a utilization factor, and a variability factor. We also observe that for the special case of $m = 1$, the above formula is exactly the same as the waiting time formula for a single resource. Note that all other performance measures, including the flow time (T), the inventory in the system (I), and the inventory in the queue (I_q), can be computed as discussed before.

While the above expression does not necessarily seem an inviting equation to use, it can be programmed without much effort into a spreadsheet. Furthermore, it provides the average waiting time for a system that otherwise could only be analyzed with much more sophisticated software packages.

Unlike the waiting time formula for the single resource case, which provides an exact quantification of waiting times as long as the interarrival times follow an exponential distribution, the waiting time formula for multiple resources is an approximation. The formula works well for most settings we encounter, specifically if the ratio of utilization u to the number of servers m is large (u/m is high).

Now that we have computed waiting time, we can again use Little's Law to compute the average number of flow units in the waiting area I_q, the average number of flow units in service I_p, and the average number of flow units in the entire system $I = I_p + I_q$. Figure 6.16 summarizes the key performance measures.

Note that in the presence of multiple resources serving flow units, there can be more than one flow unit in service simultaneously. If u is the utilization of the process, it is also the utilization of each of the m resources, as they process demand at the same rate. We can compute the expected number of flow units at any of the m resources *in isolation* as

$$u \times 1 + (1 - u) \times 0 = u$$

---

[1]Hopp and Spearman (1996); the formula initially had been proposed by Sakasegawa (1977) and used successfully by Whitt (1983). For $m = 1$, the formula is exactly the same as in the previous section. The formula is an approximation for $m > 1$. An exact expression for this case does not exist.

Exhibit 6.1

SUMMARY OF WAITING TIME CALCULATIONS

1. Collect the following data:

   - Number of servers, m
   - Activity time, p
   - Interarrival time, a
   - Coefficient of variation for interarrival (CV_a) and processing time (CV_p)

2. Compute utilization: $u = \dfrac{p}{a \times m}$

3. Compute expected waiting time:

$$T_q = \left(\frac{\text{Activity time}}{m} \right) \times \left(\frac{\text{Utilization}^{\sqrt{2(m+1)}-1}}{1 - \text{Utilization}} \right) \times \left(\frac{CV_a^2 + CV_p^2}{2} \right)$$

4. Based on T_q, we can compute the remaining performance measures as

$$\text{Flow time } T = T_q + p$$

$$\text{Inventory in service } I_p = m \times u$$

$$\text{Inventory in the queue } I_q = T_q/a$$

$$\text{Inventory in the system } I = I_p + I_q$$

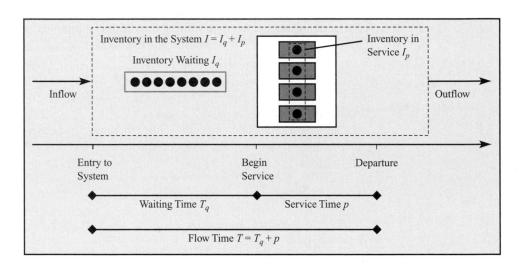

FIGURE 6.16
Summary of Key Performance Measures

Adding up across the m resources then yields

$$\text{Inventory in process} = \text{Number of resources} \times \text{Utilization}$$

$$I_p = m \times u$$

We illustrate the methodology using the case of An-ser services. Assuming we would work with a staff of 10 customer service representatives (CSRs) for the 8:00 A.M. to 8:15 A.M. time slot, we can compute the utilization as follows:

$$\text{Utilization } u = \frac{p}{a \times m} = \frac{90 \, [\text{seconds/call}]}{10 \times 11.39 \, [\text{seconds/call}]} = 0.79$$

where we obtained the interarrival time of 11.39 seconds between calls by dividing the length of the time interval (15 minutes = 9,000 seconds) by the number of calls received over the interval (79 calls). This now allows us to compute the average waiting time as

$$T_q = \left(\frac{p}{m}\right) \times \left(\frac{u^{\sqrt{2(m+1)}-1}}{1-u}\right) \times \left(\frac{CV_a^2 + CV_p^2}{2}\right)$$

$$= \left(\frac{90}{10}\right) \times \left(\frac{0.79^{\sqrt{2(10+1)}-1}}{1-0.79}\right) \times \left(\frac{1+1.33^2}{2}\right) = 24.94 \text{ seconds}$$

The most important calculations related to waiting times caused by variability are summarized in Exhibit 6.1.

6.7   Service Levels in Waiting Time Problems

So far, we have focused our attention on the average waiting time in the process. However, a customer requesting service from our process is not interested in the average time he or she waits in queue or the average total time to complete his or her request (waiting time T_q and flow time T respectively), but in the wait times that he or she experiences personally.

Consider, for example, a caller who has just waited for 15 minutes listening to music while on hold. This caller is likely to be unsatisfied about the long wait time. Moreover, the response from the customer service representative of the type "we are sorry for your delay, but our average waiting time is only 4 minutes" is unlikely to reduce this dissatisfaction.

Thus, from a managerial perspective, we not only need to analyze the average wait time, but also the likelihood that the wait time exceeds a certain *target wait time* (*TWT*). More formally, we can define the *service level* for a given target wait time as the percentage of customers that will begin service in TWT or less units of waiting time:

$$\text{Service level} = \text{Probability}\{\text{Waiting time} \leq \text{TWT}\}$$

This service level provides us with a way to measure to what extent the service is able to respond to demand within a consistent waiting time. A service level of 95 percent for a target waiting time of TWT = 2 minutes means that 95 percent of the customers are served in less than 2 minutes of waiting time.

Figure 6.17 shows the empirical distribution function (see Section 6.3 on how to create this graph) for waiting times at the An-ser call center for a selected time slot. Based on the graph, we can distinguish between two groups of customers. About 65 percent of the customers did not have to wait at all and received immediate service. The remaining 35 percent of the customers experienced a waiting time that strongly resembles an exponential distribution.

We observe that the average waiting time for the entire calling population (not just the ones who had to wait) was, for this specific sample, about 10 seconds. For a target wait time TWT = 30 seconds, we find a service level of 90 percent; that is, 90 percent of the callers had to wait 30 seconds or less.

Service levels as defined above are a common performance measure for service operations in practice. They are used internally by the firm in charge of delivering a certain

FIGURE 6.17
Empirical
Distribution of
Waiting Times
at An-ser

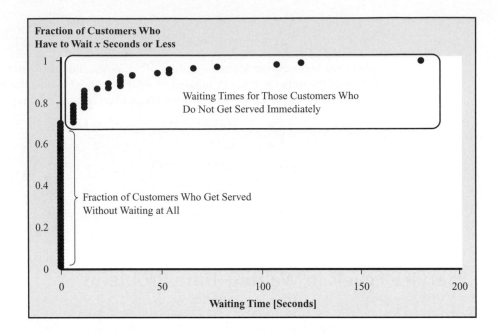

service. They also are used frequently by firms that want to outsource a service, such as a call center, as a way to contract (and track) the responsiveness of their service provider.

There is no universal rule of what service level is right for a given service operation. For example, responding to large public pressure, the German railway system (Deutsche Bundesbahn) has recently introduced a policy that 80 percent of the calls to their customer complaint number should be handled within 20 seconds. Previously, only 30 percent of the calls were handled within 20 seconds. How fast you respond to calls depends on your market position and the importance of the incoming calls for your business. A service level that worked for the German railway system in 2003 (30 percent within 20 seconds) is likely to be unacceptable in other, more competitive environments.

6.8   Economic Implications: Generating a Staffing Plan

So far, we have focused purely on analyzing the call center for a given number of customer service representatives (CSRs) on duty and predicted the resulting waiting times. This raises the managerial question of how many CSRs An-ser should have at work at any given moment in time over the day. The more CSRs we schedule, the shorter the waiting time, but the more we need to pay in terms of wages.

When making this trade-off, we need to balance the following two costs:

- Cost of waiting, reflecting increased line charges for 1-800 numbers and customer dissatisfaction (line charges are incurred for the actual talk time as well as for the time the customer is on hold).
- Cost of service, resulting from the number of CSRs available.

Additional costs that could be factored into the analysis are

- Costs related to customers calling into the call center but who are not able to gain access even to the waiting line, that is, they receive a busy signal (blocked customers; this will be discussed further in Chapter 7).
- Costs related to customers who hang up while waiting for service.

FIGURE 6.18
Economic
Consequences
of Waiting

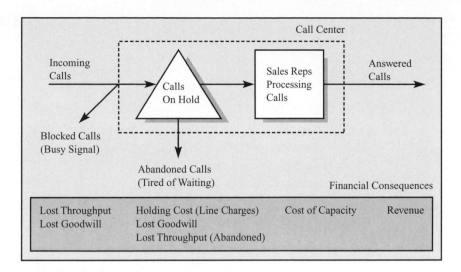

TABLE 6.2
Determining the
Number of CSRs
to Support Target
Walt Time

Number of CSRs, m	Utilization $u = p/(a \times m)$	Expected Wait Tme T_q [seconds] Based on Waiting Time Formula
8	0.99	1221.23
9	0.88	72.43
10	0.79	24.98
11	0.72	11.11
12	0.66	5.50
13	0.61	2.89
14	0.56	1.58

In the case of An-ser, the average salary of a CSR is $10 per hour. Note that CSRs are paid independent of being idle or busy. Variable costs for a 1-800 number are about $0.05 per minute. A summary of various costs involved in managing a call center—or service operations in general—is given by Figure 6.18.

When deciding how many CSRs to schedule for a given time slot, we first need to decide on how responsive we want to be to our customers. For the purpose of our analysis, we assume that the management of An-ser wants to achieve an average wait time of 10 seconds. Alternatively, we could also set a service level and then staff according to a TWT constraint, for example, 95 percent of customers to be served in 20 seconds or less.

Now, for a given arrival rate, we need to determine the number of CSRs that will correspond to an average wait time of 10 seconds. Again, consider the time interval from 8:00 to 8:15 A.M. Table 6.2 shows the utilization level as well as the expected wait time for different numbers of customer service representatives. Note that using fewer than 8 servers would lead to a utilization above one, which would mean that queues would build up independent of variability, which is surely not acceptable.

Table 6.2 indicates that adding CSRs leads to a reduction in waiting time. For example, while a staff of 8 CSRs would correspond to an average waiting time of about 20 minutes, the average waiting time falls below 10 seconds once a twelfth CSR has been added. Thus, working with 12 CSRs allows An-ser to meet its target of an average wait time of 10 seconds. In this case, the actual service would be even better and we expect the average wait time for this specific time slot to be 5.50 seconds.

Providing a good service level does come at the cost of increased labor. The more CSRs are scheduled to serve, the lower is their utilization. In Chapter 4 we defined the cost of direct labor as

$$\text{Cost of direct labor} = \frac{\text{Total wages per unit of time}}{\text{Flow rate per unit of time}}$$

where the total wages per unit of time are determined by the number of CSRs m times their wage rate (in our case $10 per hour or 16.66 cents per minute) and the flow rate is determined by the arrival rate. Therefore,

$$\text{Cost of direct labor} = \frac{m \times 16.66 \text{ cents/minute}}{1/a} = a \times m \times 16.66 \text{ cents/minute}$$

An alternative way of writing the cost of labor uses the definition of utilization ($u = p/(a \times m)$). Thus, in the above equation, we can substitute p/u for $a \times m$ and obtain

$$\text{Cost of direct labor} = \frac{p \times 16.66 \text{ cents/minute}}{u}$$

This way of writing the cost of direct labor has a very intuitive interpretation: The actual activity time p is inflated by a factor of 1/Utilization to appropriately account for idle time. For example, if utilization were 50 percent, we are charged a $1 of idle time penalty for every $1 we spend on labor productively. In our case, the utilization is 66 percent; thus, the cost of direct labor is

$$\text{Cost of direct labor} = \frac{1.5 \text{ minutes/call} \times 16.66 \text{ cents/minute}}{0.66} = 37 \text{ cents/call}$$

This computation allows us to extend Table 6.2 to include the cost implications of the various staffing scenarios (our calculations do not consider any cost of lost goodwill). Specifically, we are interested in the impact of staffing on the cost of direct labor per call as well as in the cost of line charges.

Not surprisingly, we can see in Table 6.3 that moving from a very high level of utilization of close to 99 percent (using 8 CSRs) to a more responsive service level, for example, as provided by 12 CSRs, leads to a significant increase in labor cost.

At the same time, though, line charges drop from over $1 per call to almost $0.075 per call. Note that $0.075 per call is the minimum charge that can be achieved based on staffing changes, as it corresponds to the pure talk time.

Adding line charges and the cost of direct labor allows us to obtain total costs. In Table 6.3, we observe that total costs are minimized when we have 10 CSRs in service.

TABLE 6.3
Economic Implications of Various Staffing Levels

Number of Servers	Utilization	Cost of Labor per Call	Cost of Line Charges per Call	Total Cost per Call
8	0.988	0.2531	1.0927	1.3458
9	0.878	0.2848	0.1354	0.4201
10	0.790	0.3164	0.0958	0.4122
11	0.718	0.3480	0.0843	0.4323
12	0.658	0.3797	0.0796	0.4593
13	0.608	0.4113	0.0774	0.4887
14	0.564	0.4429	0.0763	0.5193
15	0.527	0.4746	0.0757	0.5503

However, we need to be careful in labeling this point as the optimal staffing level, as the total cost number is a purely internal measure and does not take into account any information about the customer's cost of waiting. For this reason, when deciding on an appropriate staffing level, it is important to set acceptable service levels for waiting times as done in Table 6.2 and then staffing up to meet these service levels (opposed to minimizing internal costs).

If we repeat the analysis that we have conducted for the 8:00 to 8:15 A.M. time slot over the 24 hours of the day, we obtain a staffing plan. The staffing plan accounts for both the seasonality observed throughout the day as well as the variability and the resulting need for extra capacity. This is illustrated by Figure 6.19.

When we face a nonstationary arrival process as in this case, a common problem is to decide into how many intervals one should break up the time line to have close to a stationary arrival process within a time interval (in this case 15 minutes). While we cannot go into the theory behind this topic, the basic intuition is this: It is important that the time intervals are large enough so that

- We have enough data to come up with reliable estimates for the arrival rate of the interval (e.g., if we had worked with 30-second intervals, our estimates for the number of calls arriving within a 30-second time interval would have been less reliable).

- Over the course of an interval, the queue needs sufficient time to reach a "steady state"; this is achieved if we have a relatively large number of arrivals and service completions within the duration of a time interval (more than 10).

In practice, finding a staffing plan can be somewhat more complicated, as it needs to account for

- Breaks for the operators.

- Length of work period. It is typically not possible to request an operator to show up for work for only a one-hour time slot. Either one has to provide longer periods of time or one would have to temporarily route calls to other members of the organization (supervisor, back-office employees).

Despite these additional complications, the analysis outlined above captures the most important elements typical for making supply-related decisions in service environments.

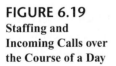

FIGURE 6.19
Staffing and Incoming Calls over the Course of a Day

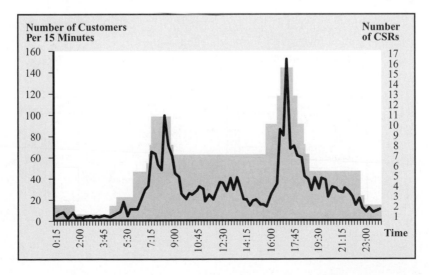

6.9   Impact of Pooling: Economies of Scale

Consider a process that currently corresponds to two (m) demand arrival processes that are processed by two (m) identical servers. If demand cannot be processed immediately, the flow unit waits in front of the server where it initially arrived. An example of such a system is provided in Figure 6.20 (left).

Here is an interesting question: Does combining the two systems into a single system with one waiting area and two (m) identical servers lead to lower average waiting times? We refer to such a combination of multiple resources into one "mega-resource" as *pooling*.

Consider, for example, two small food services at an airport. For simplicity, assume that both of them have a customer arrival stream with an average interarrival time a of 4 minutes and a coefficient of variation equal to one. The activity time p is three minutes per customer and the coefficient of variation for the service process also is equal to one. Consequently, both food services face a utilization of $p/a = 0.75$.

Using our waiting time formula, we compute the average waiting time as

$$T_q = \text{Activity time} \times \left(\frac{\text{Utilization}}{1 - \text{Utilization}} \right) \times \left(\frac{CV_a^2 + CV_p^2}{2} \right)$$

$$= 3 \times \left(\frac{0.75}{1 - 0.75} \right) \times \left(\frac{1 + 1}{2} \right)$$

$$= 3 \times (0.75/0.25) = 9 \text{ minutes}$$

Now compare this with the case in which we combine the capacity of both food services to serve the demand of both services. The capacity of the pooled process has increased by a factor of two and now is $\frac{2}{3}$ unit per minute. However, the demand rate also has doubled: If there was one customer every four minutes arriving for service 1 and one customer every four minutes arriving for service 2, the pooled service experiences an arrival rate of one customer every $a = 2$ minutes (i.e., two customers every four minutes is the same as one customer every two minutes).

We can compute the utilization of the pooled process as

$$u = \frac{p}{a \times m}$$

$$= 3/(2 \times 2) = 0.75$$

Observe that the utilization has not changed compared to having two independent services. Combining two processes with a utilization of 75 percent leads to a pooled system with a 75 percent utilization. However, a different picture emerges when we look at the waiting

FIGURE 6.20
The Concept of Pooling

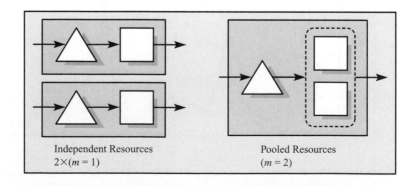

Independent Resources
$2 \times (m = 1)$

Pooled Resources
$(m = 2)$

time of the pooled system. Using the waiting time formula for multiple resources, we can write

$$T_q = \left(\frac{\text{Activity time}}{m} \right) \times \left(\frac{\text{Utilization}^{\sqrt{2(m+1)}-1}}{1 - \text{Utilization}} \right) \times \left(\frac{CV_a^2 + CV_p^2}{2} \right)$$

$$= \left(\frac{3}{2} \right) \times \left(\frac{0.75^{\sqrt{2(2+1)}-1}}{1 - 0.75} \right) = 3.95 \text{ minutes}$$

In other words, the pooled process on the right of Figure 6.20 can serve the same number of customers using the same service time (and thereby having the same utilization), but in only *half* the waiting time!

While short of being a formal proof, the intuition for this result is as follows. The pooled process uses the available capacity more effectively, as it prevents the case that one resource is idle while the other faces a backlog of work (waiting flow units). Thus, pooling identical resources balances the load for the servers, leading to shorter waiting times. This behavior is illustrated in Figure 6.21.

Figure 6.21 illustrates that for a given level of utilization, the waiting time decreases with the number of servers in the resource pool. This is especially important for higher levels of utilization. While for a system with one single server waiting times tend to "go through the roof" once the utilization exceeds 85 percent, a process consisting of 10 identical servers can still provide reasonable service even at utilizations approaching 95 percent.

Given that a pooled system provides better service than individual processes, a service organization can benefit from pooling identical branches or work groups in one of two forms:

- The operation can use pooling to reduce customer waiting time without having to staff extra workers.
- The operation can reduce the number of workers while maintaining the same responsiveness.

These economic benefits of pooling can be illustrated nicely within the context of the Anser case discussed above. In our analysis leading to Table 6.2, we assumed that there would be 79 calls arriving per 15-minute time interval and found that we would need 12 CSRs to serve customers with an average wait time of 10 seconds or less.

FIGURE 6.21
How Pooling Can Reduce Waiting Time

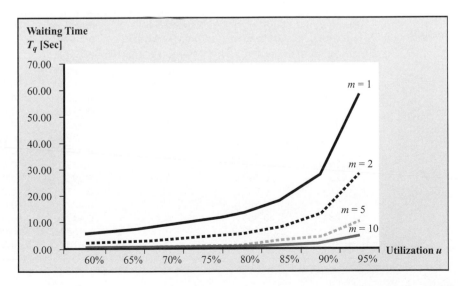

Assume we could pool An-ser's call center with a call center of comparable size; that is, we would move all CSRs to one location and merge both call centers' customer populations. Note that this would not necessarily require the two call centers to "move in" with each other; they could be physically separate as long as the calls are routed through one joint network.

Without any consolidation, merging the two call centers would lead to double the number of CSRs and double the demand, meaning 158 calls per 15-minute interval. What would be the average waiting time in the pooled call center? Or, alternatively, if we maintained an average waiting time of 10 seconds or less, how much could we reduce our staffing level? Table 6.4 provides the answers to these questions.

First, consider the row of 24 CSRs, corresponding to pooling the entire staff of the two call centers. Note specifically that the utilization of the pooled call center is not any different from what it was in Table 6.2. We have doubled the number of CSRs, but we also have doubled the number of calls (and thus cut the interarrival time by half). With 24 CSRs, we expect an average waiting time of 1.2 seconds (compared to almost 6 seconds before).

Alternatively, we could take the increased efficiency benefits resulting from pooling by reducing our labor cost. We also observe from Table 6.4 that a staff of 20 CSRs would be able to answer calls with an average wait time of 10 seconds. Thus, we could increase utilization to almost 80 percent, which would lower our cost of direct labor from $0.3797 to $0.3165. Given an annual call volume of about 700,000 calls, such a saving would be of significant impact for the bottom line.

Despite the nice property of pooled systems outlined above, pooling should not be seen as a silver bullet. Specifically, pooling benefits are much lower than expected (and potentially negative) in the following situations:

• Pooling benefits are significantly lower when the systems that are pooled are not truly independent. Consider, for example, the idea of pooling waiting lines before cash registers in supermarkets, similar to what is done at airport check-ins. In this case, the individual queues are unlikely to be independent, as customers in the current, nonpooled layout will intelligently route themselves to the queue with the shortest waiting line. Pooling in this case will have little, if any, effect on waiting times.

• Similar to the concept of line balancing we introduced earlier in this book, pooling typically requires the service workforce to have a broader range of skills (potentially leading

TABLE 6.4
Pooling Two Call Centers

Number of CSRs	Utilization	Expected Wait Time [seconds]	Labor Cost per Call	Line Cost per Call	Total Cost
16	0.988	588.15	0.2532	0.5651	0.8183
17	0.929	72.24	0.2690	0.1352	0.4042
18	0.878	28.98	0.2848	0.0992	0.3840
19	0.832	14.63	0.3006	0.0872	0.3878
20	0.790	8.18	0.3165	0.0818	0.3983
21	0.752	4.84	0.3323	0.0790	0.4113
22	0.718	2.97	0.3481	0.0775	0.4256
23	0.687	1.87	0.3639	0.0766	0.4405
24	0.658	1.20	0.3797	0.0760	0.4558
25	0.632	0.79	0.3956	0.0757	0.4712
26	0.608	0.52	0.4114	0.0754	0.4868
27	0.585	0.35	0.4272	0.0753	0.5025
28	0.564	0.23	0.4430	0.0752	0.5182
29	0.545	0.16	0.4589	0.0751	0.5340
30	0.527	0.11	0.4747	0.0751	0.5498

to higher wage rates). For example, an operator sufficiently skilled that she can take orders for hiking and running shoes, as well as provide answering services for a local hospital, will likely demand a higher wage rate than someone who is just trained to do one of these tasks.

• In many service environments, customers value being treated consistently by the same person. Pooling several lawyers in a law firm might be desirable from a waiting-time perspective but ignores the customer desire to deal with one point of contact in the law firm.

• Similarly, pooling can introduce additional setups. In the law-firm example, a lawyer unfamiliar with the situation of a certain client might need a longer time to provide some quick advice on the case and this extra setup time mitigates the operational benefits from pooling.

• Pooling can backfire if pooling combines different customer classes because this might actually increase the variability of the service process. Consider two clerks working in a retail bank, one of them currently in charge of simple transactions (e.g., activity time of 2 minutes per customer), while the other one is in charge of more complex cases (e.g., activity time of 10 minutes). Pooling these two clerks makes the service process more variable and might actually increase waiting time.

6.10   Priority Rules in Waiting Lines

Choosing an appropriate level of capacity helps to prevent waiting lines from building up in a process. However, in a process with variability, it is impossible to eliminate waiting lines entirely. Given, therefore, that at some point in time some customers will have to wait before receiving service, we need to decide on the order in which we permit them access to the server. This order is determined by a *priority rule,* sometimes also referred to as a queuing discipline.

Customers are assigned priorities by adding a (small) step at the point in the process where customers arrive. This process step is called the *triage step.* At triage, we collect information about some of the characteristics of the arriving customer, which we use as input for the priority rule. Below we discuss priority rules based on the following characteristics:

• The service time or the expected service time of the customer (service-time-dependent priority rules).
• Service-time-independent priority rules, including priority rules based on customer arrival time and priority rules based on customer importance or urgency.

Service-Time-Dependent Priority Rules

If it is possible to observe the customer's service time or his or her expected service time prior to initiating the service process, this information should be incorporated when assigning a priority to the customer. The most commonly used service-time-dependent priority rule is the shortest processing time (SPT) rule.

Under the SPT rule, the next available server is allocated to the customer with the shortest (expected) processing time of all customers currently in the waiting line. The SPT rule is extremely effective and performs well, with respect to the expected waiting time as well as to the variance of the waiting time. If the service times are not depending on the sequence with which customers are processed, the SPT rule can be shown to lead to the shortest average flow time. Its basic intuition is summarized by Figure 6.22.

Service-Time-Independent Priority Rules

In many cases it is difficult or impossible to assess the service time or even the expected service time prior to initiating the service process. Moreover, if customers are able to

FIGURE 6.22   The Shortest Processing Time (SPT) Rule (used in the right case)

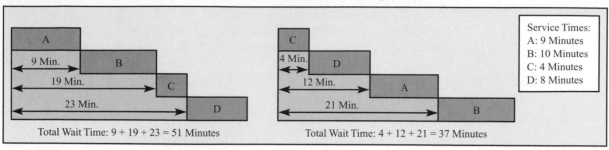

Service Times:
A: 9 Minutes
B: 10 Minutes
C: 4 Minutes
D: 8 Minutes

Total Wait Time: 9 + 19 + 23 = 51 Minutes   Total Wait Time: 4 + 12 + 21 = 37 Minutes

misrepresent their service time, then they have an incentive to suggest that their service time is less than it really is when the SPT rule is applied (e.g., "Can I just ask a quick question? . . ."). In contrast, the customer arrival time is easy to observe and difficult for the customer to manipulate.

For example, a call center receiving calls for airline reservations knows the sequence with which callers arrive but does not know which customer has already gathered all relevant information and is ready to order and which customer still requires explanation and discussion.

The most commonly used priority rule based on arrival times is the first-come, first-served (FCFS) rule. With the FCFS rule, the next available server is allocated to the customer in the waiting line with the earliest arrival time.

In addition to using arrival time information, many situations in practice require that characteristics such as the urgency or the importance of the case are considered in the priority rule. Consider the following two examples:

• In an emergency room, a triage nurse assesses the urgency of each case and then assigns a priority to the patient. Severely injured patients are given priority, independent of their arrival times.

• Customers calling in for investor services are likely to experience different priorities, depending on the value of their invested assets. Customers with an investment of greater than $5 million are unlikely to wait, while customers investing only several thousand dollars might wait for 20 minutes or more.

Such urgency-based priority rules are also independent of the service time. In general, when choosing a service-time-independent priority rule, the following property should be kept in mind: Whether we serve customers in the order of their arrival, in the reverse order of their arrival (last-come, first-served), or even in alphabetical order, the expected waiting time does not change. Thus, higher priority service (shorter waiting time) for one customer always requires lower priority (longer waiting time) for other customers.

From an implementation perspective, one last point is worth noting. Using priority rules other than FCFS might be perceived as unfair by the customers who arrived early and are already waiting the longest. Thus, while the average waiting time does not change, serving latecomers first increases the variance of the waiting time. Since variability in waiting time is not desirable from a service-quality perspective, the following property of the FCFS rule is worth remembering: Among service-time-independent priority rules, the FCFS rule minimizes the variance of waiting time and flow time.

6.11 Reducing Variability

In this chapter, we have provided some new methods to evaluate the key performance measures of flow rate, flow time, and inventory in the presence of variability. We also have seen that variability is the enemy of all operations (none of the performance measures improves as variability increases). Thus, in addition to just taking variability as given and adjusting our models to deal with variability, we should always think about ways to reduce variability.

Ways to Reduce Arrival Variability

One—somewhat obvious—way of achieving a match between supply and demand is by "massaging" demand such that it corresponds exactly to the supply process. This is basically the idea of *appointment systems* (also referred to as reservation systems in some industries).

Appointment systems have the potential to reduce the variability in the arrival process as they encourage customers to arrive at the rate of service. However, one should not overlook the problems associated with appointment systems, which include

- Appointment systems do not eliminate arrival variability. Customers do not perfectly arrive at the scheduled time (and some might not arrive at all, "no-shows"). Consequently, any good appointment system needs ways to handle these cases (e.g., extra charge or extra waiting time for customers arriving late). However, such actions are typically very difficult to implement, due to what is perceived to be "fair" and/or "acceptable," or because variability in service times prevents service providers from always keeping on schedule (and if the doctor has the right to be late, why not the patient?).
- What portion of the available capacity should be reserved in advance. Unfortunately, the customers arriving at the last minute are frequently the most important ones: emergency operations in a hospital do not come through an appointment system and business travelers paying 5 to 10 times the fare of low-price tickets are not willing to book in advance (this topic is further explored in the revenue management chapter, Chapter 13).

The most important limitation, however, is that appointment systems might reduce the variability of the arrival process as seen by the operation, but they do not reduce the variability of the true underlying demand. Consider, for example, the appointment system of a dental office. While the system (hopefully) reduces the time the patient has to wait before seeing the dentist on the day of the appointment, this wait time is not the only performance measure that counts, as the patient might already have waited for three months between requesting to see the dentist and the day of the appointment. Thus, appointment systems potentially hide a much larger supply–demand mismatch and, consequently, any good implementation of an appointment system includes a continuous measurement of both of the following:

- The inventory of customers who have an appointment and are now waiting for the day they are scheduled to go to the dentist.
- The inventory of customers who wait for an appointment in the waiting room of the dentist.

In addition to the concept of appointment systems, we can attempt to influence the customer arrival process (though, for reasons similar to the ones discussed, not the true underlying demand pattern) by providing incentives for customers to avoid peak hours. Frequently observed methods to achieve this include

- Early-bird specials at restaurants or bars.

- Price discounts for hotels during off-peak days (or seasons).
- Price discounts in transportation (air travel, highway tolls) depending on the time of service.
- Pricing of air travel depending on the capacity that is already reserved.

It is important to point out that, strictly speaking, the first three items do not reduce variability; they level expected demand and thereby reduce seasonality (remember that the difference between the two is that seasonality is a pattern known already ex ante). The fourth item refers to the concept of revenue management, which is discussed in Chapter 13.

Ways to Reduce Service Time Variability

In addition to reducing variability by changing the behavior of our customers, we also should consider how to reduce internal variability. However, when attempting to standardize activities (reducing the coefficient of variation of the service times) or shorten activity times, we need to find a balance between operational efficiency (call durations) and the quality of service experienced by the customer (perceived courtesy).

Figure 6.23 compares five of An-ser's operators for a specific call service along these two dimensions. We observe that operators NN, BK, and BJ are achieving relatively short call durations while being perceived as friendly by the customers (based on recorded calls). Operator KB has shorter call durations, yet also scores lower on courtesy. Finally, operator NJ has the longest call durations and is rated medium concerning courtesy.

Based on Figure 6.23, we can make several interesting observations. First, observe that there seems to exist a frontier capturing the inherent trade-off between call duration and courtesy. Once call durations for this service go below 2.5 minutes, courtesy seems hard to maintain. Second, observe that operator NJ is away from this frontier, as he is neither overly friendly nor fast. Remarkably, this operator also has the highest variability in call durations,

FIGURE 6.23
Operator Performance Concerning Call Duration and Courtesy

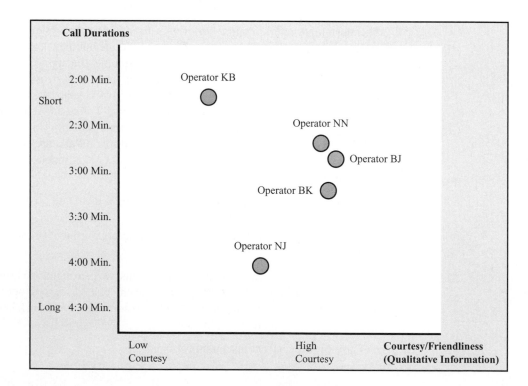

which suggests that he is not properly following the operating procedures in place (this is not visible in the graph).

To reduce the inefficiencies of operators away from the frontier (such as NJ), call centers invest heavily in training and technology. For example, technology allows operators to receive real-time instruction of certain text blocks that they can use in their interaction with the customer (scripting). Similarly, some call centers have instituted training programs in which operators listen to tapes of other operators or have operators call other operators with specific service requests. Such steps reduce both the variability of service times as well as their means and, therefore, represent substantial improvements in operational performance.

There are other improvement opportunities geared primarily toward reducing the variability of the service times:

- Although in a service environment (or in a make-to-order production setting) the operator needs to acknowledge the idiosyncrasy of each customer, the operator still can follow a consistent process. For example, a travel agent in a call center might use predefined text blocks (scripts) for his or her interaction with the customer (welcome statement, first question, potential up-sell at the end of the conversation). This approach allowed operators NN, BK, and BJ in Figure 6.23 to be fast and friendly. Thus, being knowledgeable about the process (when to say what) is equally important as being knowledgeable about the product (what to say).

- Activity times in a service environment—unlike activity times in a manufacturing context—are not under the complete control of the resource. The customer him/herself plays a crucial part in the activity at the resource, which automatically introduces a certain amount of variability (e.g., having the customer provide his or her credit card number, having the customer bag the groceries, etc.) What is the consequence of this? At least from a variability perspective, the answer is clear. Reduce the involvement of the customer during the service at a scarce resource wherever possible (note that if the customer involvement does not occur at a scarce resource, having the customer be involved and thereby do part of the work might be very desirable, e.g., in a self-service setting).

- Variability in service times frequently reflects quality problems. In manufacturing environments, this could include reworking a unit that initially did not meet specifications. However, rework also occurs in service organizations (e.g., a patient who is released from the intensive care unit but later on readmitted to intensive care can be thought of as rework).

Many of these concepts are discussed further in Chapter 8.

6.12 Summary

In this chapter, we have analyzed the impact of variability on waiting times. As we expected from our more qualitative discussion of variability in the beginning of this chapter, variability causes waiting times, even if the underlying process operates at a utilization level of less than 100 percent. In this chapter, we have outlined a set of tools that allows us to quantify this waiting time, with respect to both the average waiting time (and flow time) as well as the service level experienced by the customer.

There exists an inherent tension between resource utilization (and thereby cost of labor) and responsiveness: Adding service capacity leads to shorter waiting times but higher costs of labor (see Figure 6.24). Waiting times grow steeply with utilization levels. Thus, any responsive process requires excess capacity. Given that capacity is costly, it is important that only as much capacity is installed as is needed to meet the service objective in place for the process. In this chapter, we have outlined a method that allows a service operation to find the point on the frontier that best supports their business objectives (service levels).

FIGURE 6.24
Balancing Efficiency with Responsiveness

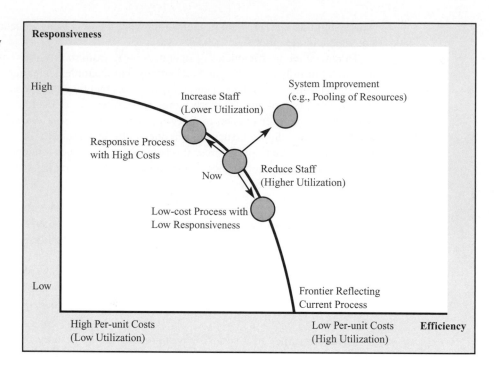

However, our results should be seen not only as a way to predict/quantify the waiting time problem. They also outline opportunities for improving the process. Improvement opportunities can be broken up into capacity-related opportunities and system-design-related opportunities, as summarized below.

Capacity-Related Improvements
Operations benefit from flexibility in capacity, as this allows management to adjust staffing level to predicted demand. For example, the extent to which a hospital is able to have more doctors on duty at peak flu season is crucial in conducting the staffing calculations outlined in this chapter. A different form of flexibility is given by the operation's ability to increase capacity in the case of unpredicted demand. For example, the extent to which a bank can use supervisors and front-desk personnel to help with unexpected spikes in inbound calls can make a big difference in call center waiting times. This leads to the following two improvement opportunities:

• Demand (and sometimes supply) can exhibit seasonality over the course of the day. In such cases, the waiting time analysis should be done for individual time intervals over which the process behaves relatively stationary. System performance can be increased to the extent the organization is able to provide time-varying capacity levels that mirror the seasonality of demand (e.g., Figure 6.19).

• In the presence of variability, a responsive process cannot avoid excess capacity, and thereby will automatically face a significant amount of idle time. In many operations, this idle time can be used productively for tasks that are not (or at least are less) time critical. Such work is referred to as background work. For example, operators in a call center can engage in outbound calls during times of underutilization.

System-Design-Related Improvements
Whenever we face a trade-off between two conflicting performance measures, in this case between responsiveness and efficiency, finding the right balance between the measures is

important. However, at least equally important is the attempt to improve the underlying process, shifting the frontier and allowing for higher responsiveness and lower cost (see Figure 6.24). In the context of services suffering from variability-induced waiting times, the following improvement opportunities should be considered:

- By combining similar resources into one joint resource pool (pooling resources), we are able to either reduce wait times for the same amount of capacity or reduce capacity for the same service level. Processes that face variability thereby exhibit very strong scale economies.
- Variability is not exogenous and we should remember to reduce variability wherever possible.
- By introducing a triage step before the actual service process that sequences incoming flow units according to a priority rule (service-time-dependent or service-time-independent), we can reduce the average wait time, assign priority to the most important flow units, or create a waiting system that is perceived as fair by customers waiting in line.

6.13 Further Reading

Gans, Koole and Mandelbaum (2002) is a recent overview on call-center management from a queuing theory perspective. Further quantitative tools on queueing can be found in Hillier and Lieberman (2002).

Hall (1997) is a very comprehensive and real-world-focused book that provides numerous tools related to variability and its consequences in services and manufacturing.

6.14 Practice Problems

Q6.1* **(Online Retailer)** Customers send e-mails to a help desk of an online retailer every 2 minutes, on average, and the standard deviation of the interarrival time is also 2 minutes. The online retailer has three employees answering e-mails. It takes on average 4 minutes to write a response e-mail. The standard deviation of the service times is 2 minutes.

a. Estimate the average customer wait before being served.

b. How many e-mails would there be, on average, that have been submitted to the online retailer but not yet answered?

Q6.2 **(My-law.com)** My-law.com is a recent start-up trying to cater to customers in search of legal services who are intimidated by the idea of talking to a lawyer or simply too lazy to enter a law office. Unlike traditional law firms, My-law.com allows for extensive interaction between lawyers and their customers via telephone and the Internet. This process is used in the upfront part of the customer interaction, largely consisting of answering some basic customer questions prior to entering a formal relationship.

In order to allow customers to interact with the firm's lawyers, customers are encouraged to send e-mails to my-lawyer@My-law.com. From there, the incoming e-mails are distributed to the lawyer who is currently "on call." Given the broad skills of the lawyers, each lawyer can respond to each incoming request.

E-mails arrive from 8 A.M. to 6 P.M. at a rate of 10 e-mails per hour (coefficient of variation for the arrivals is 1). At each moment in time, there is exactly one lawyer "on call," that is, sitting at his or her desk waiting for incoming e-mails. It takes the lawyer, on average, 5 minutes to write the response e-mail. The standard deviation of this is 4 minutes.

a. What is the average time a customer has to wait for the response to his/her e-mail, ignoring any transmission times? *Note:* This includes the time it takes the lawyer to start writing the e-mail *and* the actual writing time.

b. How many e-mails will a lawyer have received at the end of a 10-hour day?

(* indicates that the solution is at the end of the book)

c. When not responding to e-mails, the lawyer on call is encouraged to actively pursue cases that potentially could lead to large settlements. How much time on a 10-hour day can a My-law.com lawyer dedicate to this activity (assume the lawyer can instantly switch between e-mails and work on a settlement)?

To increase the responsiveness of the firm, the board of My-law.com proposes a new operating policy. Under the new policy, the response would be highly standardized, reducing the standard deviation for writing the response e-mail to 0.5 minute. The average writing time would remain unchanged.

d. How would the amount of time a lawyer can dedicate to the search for large settlement cases change with this new operating policy?

e. How would the average time a customer has to wait for the response to his/her e-mail change? *Note:* This includes the time until the lawyer starts writing the e-mail *and* the actual writing time.

Q6.3   **(Car Rental Company)** The airport branch of a car rental company maintains a fleet of 50 SUVs. The interarrival time between requests for an SUV is 2.4 hours, on average, with a standard deviation of 2.4 hours. There is no indication of a systematic arrival pattern over the course of a day. Assume that, if all SUVs are rented, customers are willing to wait until there is an SUV available. An SUV is rented, on average, for 3 days, with a standard deviation of 1 day.

a. What is the average number of SUVs parked in the company's lot?

b. Through a marketing survey, the company has discovered that if it reduces its daily rental price of $80 by $25, the average demand would increase to12 rental requests per day and the average rental duration will become 4 days. Is this price decrease warranted? Provide an analysis!

c. What is the average time a customer has to wait to rent an SUV? Please use the initial parameters rather than the information in (b).

d. How would the waiting time change if the company decides to limit all SUV rentals to *exactly* 4 days? Assume that if such a restriction is imposed, the average interarrival time will increase to 3 hours, with the standard deviation changing to 3 hours.

Q6.4   **(Tom Opim)** The following situation refers to Tom Opim, a first-year MBA student. In order to pay the rent, Tom decides to take a job in the computer department of a local department store. His only responsibility is to answer telephone calls to the department, most of which are inquiries about store hours and product availability. As Tom is the only person answering calls, the manager of the store is concerned about queuing problems.

Currently, the computer department receives an average of one call every 3 minutes, with a standard deviation in this interarrival time of 3 minutes.

Tom requires an average of 2 minutes to handle a call. The standard deviation in this activity time is 1 minute.

The telephone company charges $5.00 per hour for the telephone lines whenever they are in use (either while a customer is in conversation with Tom or while waiting to be helped).

Assume that there are no limits on the number of customers that can be on hold and that customers do not hang up even if forced to wait a long time.

a. For one of his courses, Tom has to read a book (*The Pole,* by E. Silvermouse). He can read 1 page per minute. Tom's boss has agreed that Tom could use his idle time for studying, as long as he drops the book as soon as a call comes in. How many pages can Tom read during an 8-hour shift?

b. How long does a customer have to wait, on average, before talking to Tom?

c. What is the average total cost of telephone lines over an 8-hour shift? Note that the department store is billed whenever a line is in use, including when a line is used to put customers on hold.

Q6.5   **(Atlantic Video)** Atlantic Video, a small video rental store in Philadelphia, is open 24 hours a day, and—due to its proximity to a major business school—experiences customers arriving around the clock. A recent analysis done by the store manager indicates that there are

30 customers arriving every hour, with a standard deviation of interarrival times of 2 minutes. This arrival pattern is consistent and is independent of the time of day. The checkout is currently operated by one employee, who needs on average 1.7 minutes to check out a customer. The standard deviation of this check-out time is 3 minutes, primarily as a result of customers taking home different numbers of videos.

a. If you assume that every customer rents at least one video (i.e., has to go to the checkout), what is the average time a customer has to wait in line before getting served by the checkout employee, not including the actual checkout time (within 1 minute)?

b. If there are no customers requiring checkout, the employee is sorting returned videos, of which there are always plenty waiting to be sorted. How many videos can the employee sort over an 8-hour shift (assume no breaks) if it takes exactly 1.5 minutes to sort a single video?

c. What is the average number of customers who are at the checkout desk, either waiting or currently being served (within 1 customer)?

d. Now assume *for this question only* that 10 percent of the customers do not rent a video at all and therefore do not have to go through checkout. What is the average time a customer has to wait in line before getting served by the checkout employee, not including the actual checkout time (within 1 minute)? Assume that the coefficient of variation for the arrival process remains the same as before.

e. As a special service, the store offers free popcorn and sodas for customers waiting in line at the checkout desk. (*Note:* The person who is currently being served is too busy with paying to eat or drink.) The store owner estimates that every minute of customer waiting time costs the store 75 cents because of the consumed food. What is the optimal number of employees at checkout? Assume an hourly wage rate of $10 per hour.

Q6.6 **(RentAPhone)** RentAPhone is a new service company that provides European mobile phones to American visitors to Europe. The company currently has 80 phones available at Charles de Gaulle Airport in Paris. There are, on average, 25 customers per day requesting a phone. These requests arrive uniformly throughout the 24 hours the store is open. (*Note:* This means customers arrive at a faster rate than 1 customer per hour.) The corresponding coefficient of variation is 1.

Customers keep their phones on average 72 hours. The standard deviation of this time is 100 hours.

Given that RentAPhone currently does not have a competitor in France providing equally good service, customers are willing to wait for the telephones. Yet, during the waiting period, customers are provided a free calling card. Based on prior experience, RentAPhone found that the company incurred a cost of $1 per hour per waiting customer, independent of day or night.

a. What is the average number of telephones the company has in its store?

b. How long does a customer, on average, have to wait for the phone?

c. What are the total monthly (30 days) expenses for telephone cards?

d. Assume RentAPhone could buy additional phones at $1,000 per unit. Is it worth it to buy one additional phone? Why?

e. How would waiting time change if the company decides to limit all rentals to *exactly* 72 hours? Assume that if such a restriction is imposed, the number of customers requesting a phone would be reduced to 20 customers per day.

7

The Impact of Variability on Process Performance: Throughput Losses

After having analyzed waiting times caused by variability, we now turn to a second undesirable impact variability has on process performance: *throughput loss*. Throughput losses occur in the following cases, both of which differ from the case of flow units patiently waiting for service discussed in Chapter 6:

- There is a limited buffer size and demand arriving when this buffer is full is lost.
- Flow units are impatient and unwilling or unable to spend too much time waiting for service, which leads to flow units leaving the buffer before being served.

Analyzing processes with throughput losses is significantly more complicated compared to the case of patient customers discussed in Chapter 6. For this reason, we focus our analysis on the simplest case of throughput loss, which assumes that the buffer size is zero, that is there is no buffer. We will introduce a set of analytical tools and discuss their application to time-critical emergency care provided by hospitals, especially trauma centers. In these settings, waiting times are not permissible and, when a trauma center is fully utilized, incoming ambulances are diverted to other hospitals.

There exist more general models of variability that allow for buffer sizes larger than zero, yet due to their complexity, we only discuss those models conceptually. Again, we start the chapter with a small motivating example.

7.1 Motivating Examples: Why Averages Do Not Work

Consider a street vendor who sells custom-made sandwiches from his truck parked along the sidewalk. Demand for these sandwiches is, on average, one sandwich in a five-minute time slot. However, the actual demand varies, and thus sometimes no customer places an order, while at other times the owner of the truck faces one or two orders. Customers are not willing to wait for sandwiches and leave to go to other street vendors if they cannot be served immediately.

TABLE 7.1
Street Vendor Example of Variability

Scenario	Demand	Capacity	Flow Rate
A	0	0	0
B	0	1	0
C	0	2	0
D	1	0	0
E	1	1	1
F	1	2	1
G	2	0	0
H	2	1	1
I	2	2	2
Average	1	1	$\frac{5}{9}$

The capacity leading to the supply of sandwiches over a five-minute time slot also varies and can take the values 0, 1, or 2 with equal probabilities (the variability of capacity might reflect different order sizes or operator absenteeism). The average capacity therefore is one, just as is the average demand.

From an aggregate planning perspective, demand and supply seem to match, and on average, the truck should be selling at a flow rate of one sandwich every five minutes:

$$\text{Flow rate} = \text{Minimum}\{\text{Demand, Capacity}\} = \text{Minimum}\{1,1\} = 1$$

Now, consider an analysis that is conducted at the more detailed level. If we consider the potential outcomes of both the demand and the supply processes, we face nine possible scenarios, which are summarized in Table 7.1.

Consider each of the nine scenarios. But instead of averaging demand and capacity and then computing the resulting flow rate (as done above, leading to a predicted flow rate of one), we compute the flow rate for each of the nine scenarios and then take the average across scenarios. The last column in Table 7.1 provides the corresponding calculations.

Note that for the first three scenarios (Demand = 0), we are not selling a single sandwich. However, if we look at the last three scenarios (Demand = 2), we cannot make up for this loss, as we are constrained by capacity. Thus, even while demand is booming (Demand = 2), we are selling on average one sandwich every five minutes.

If we look at the average flow rate that is obtained this way, we observe that close to half of the sales we expected to make based on our aggregate analysis do not materialize! The explanation for this is as follows: In order to sell a sandwich, the street vendor needed demand (a customer) and supply (the capacity to make a sandwich) at the same moment in time. Flow rate could have been improved if the street vendor could have moved some supply to inventory and thereby stored it for periods of time in which demand exceeded supply, or, vice versa, if the street vendor could have moved some demand to a backlog of waiting customers and thereby stored demand for periods of time in which supply exceeded demand: another example of the "buffer or suffer" principle.

7.2   Ambulance Diversion

Now, let's move from analyzing a "cooked-up" food-truck to a problem of much larger importance, with respect to both its realism as well as its relevance. Over the last couple of years, reports have shown a substantial increase in visits to emergency departments. At the same time many hospitals, in response to increasing cost pressure, have downsized important resources that are part of the emergency care process. This has led to a decrease in the number of hours hospitals are "open" for emergency patients arriving by helicopter or ambulance.

Under U.S. federal law, all hospitals that participate in Medicare are required to screen—and, if an emergency condition is present, stabilize—any patient who comes to the emergency department, regardless of the individual's ability to pay.[1] Under certain circumstances where a hospital lacks staffing or facilities to accept additional emergency patients, the hospital may place itself on "diversion status" and direct en route ambulances to other hospitals.

In total, the General Accounting Office estimates that about two of every three hospitals went on diversion at least once during the fiscal year 2001. Moreover, the study estimates that about 2 in every 10 of these hospitals were on diversion for more than 10 percent of the time, and about 1 in every 10 was on diversion for more than 20 percent of the time—or about five hours per day.

We focus our analysis on trauma cases, that is, the most severe and also the most urgent type of emergency care. A triage system evaluates the patients while they are in the ambulance/helicopter and directs the arrival to the emergency room (less severe cases) or the trauma center (severe cases). Thus, the trauma center only receives patients who have had a severe trauma.

7.3   Throughput Loss for a Queue with One Single Resource

Consider the following situation of a trauma center in a hospital in the Northeastern United States. Incoming patients are moved into one of three trauma bays. On average, patients spend two hours in the trauma bay. During that time the patients are diagnosed and, if possible, stabilized. The most severe cases, which are difficult or impossible to stabilize, spend very little time in a trauma bay and are moved directly to the operating room.

Given the severe conditions of patients coming into the trauma center, any delay of care can have fatal consequences for the patient. Thus, having patients wait for service is not an option in this setting. If, as a result of either frequent arrivals or long service times, all three trauma bays are utilized, the trauma center has to move to the ambulance diversion status defined above.

We model the trauma center as a process flow diagram consisting of no buffer and multiple parallel resources (see Figure 7.1). Given that we have three trauma bays (and corresponding staff) available, there can be a maximum of three patients in the process. Once all three bays are in use, the trauma center informs the regional emergency system that it has

FIGURE 7.1
Process Flow Diagram for Trauma Center

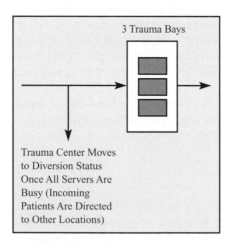

3 Trauma Bays

Trauma Center Moves to Diversion Status Once All Servers Are Busy (Incoming Patients Are Directed to Other Locations)

---

[1] The following definitions and statistics are taken from the report "Hospital Emergency Departments" given by the General Accounting Office to the U.S. Senate.

to go on diversion status; that is, any patients needing trauma services at that time are transported to other hospitals in the region.

The trauma center we analyze handles about 2,000 cases per year. For our analysis, we focus on the late evening hours, during which, on average, a new patient arrives every three hours. In addition to traffic rush hour, the late evening hours are among the busiest for the trauma center, as many of the incoming cases are results of vehicle accidents (alcohol-induced car accidents tend to happen in the evening) and victims of violence (especially in the summer months, many violent crimes occur in the evening hours).

Thus, we have a new patient every $a = 3$ hours and it takes, on average, $p = 2$ hours of time to get the patient out of the trauma center. In our analysis, we assume that the trauma bays are the resources and that there is sufficient staff to operate all three bays simultaneously, if the need arises.

Given that there are three trauma bays available, the capacity of the trauma center is

$$\text{Capacity} = \frac{\text{Number of resources}}{\text{Activity time}} = \frac{3}{2 \text{ hours/patient}}$$

$$= 1.5 \text{ patients per hour}$$

Since incoming patients arrive randomly, we use exponential interarrival times and consequently face a coefficient of variation of CV_a equal to one. The coefficient of variation of the service time in this case turns out to be above one (many medical settings are known to have extremely high variability). However, as we will see below, the following computations do not depend on the service time variability and apply to any service time distribution.

We are interested in analyzing the following performance measures:

- What percent of the time will the trauma center have to go on diversion status? Similarly, how many patients are diverted because all three trauma bays are utilized?

- What is the flow rate through the trauma center, that is, how many patients are treated every unit of time (e.g., every day)?

The most difficult, yet also most important step in our analysis is computing the probability with which the process contains m patients, P_m. This probability is of special importance, as once m patients are in the trauma center, the trauma center needs to divert any incoming requests until it has discharged a patient. The probability of having all m servers busy, P_m, depends on two variables:

- The *implied utilization.* Given that some patients are not admitted to the process (and thereby do not contribute to throughput), we no longer need to impose the condition that the capacity exceeds the demand rate ($1/a$). This assumption was necessary in the previous chapter, as otherwise the waiting line would have "exploded." In a system that automatically "shuts down" the process in case of high demand, this does not happen. Hence, u now includes the case of a utilization above 100 percent, which is why we speak of the implied utilization (Demand rate/Capacity) as opposed to utilization (Flow rate/Capacity).

- The number of resources (trauma bays) m.

We begin our analysis by computing the implied utilization:

$$u = \frac{\text{Demand rate}}{\text{Capacity}} = \frac{0.3333 \text{ patients per hour}}{1.5 \text{ patients per hour}} = 0.2222$$

Based on the implied utilization u and the number of resources m, we can use the following method to compute the probability that all m servers are busy, P_m. Define $r = u \times m = p/a$. Thus, $r = 0.67$.

We can then use the *Erlang loss formula* table (Appendix B) to look up the probability that all m resources are utilized and hence a newly arriving flow unit has to be rejected. First, we find the corresponding row heading in the table ($r = 0.67$) indicating the ratio of activity time to interarrival time (see Table 7.2). Second, we find the column heading ($m = 3$) indicating the number of resources. The intersection of that row with that column is

$$\text{Probability\{all } m \text{ servers busy\}} = P_m(r) = 0.0255 \qquad \text{(Erlang loss formula)}$$

Thus, we find that our trauma center, on average, will be on diversion for 2.5 percent of the time, which corresponds to about 0.6 hour per day and about 18 hours per month.

A couple of remarks are in order to explain the impact of the activity time-to-interarrival-time ratio r and the number of resources m on the probability that all servers are utilized:

• The probability $P_m(r)$ and hence the analysis does not require the coefficient of variation for the service process. The analysis only applies to the (realistic) case of exponentially distributed interarrival times; therefore, we implicitly assume that the coefficient of variation for the arrival process is equal to one.

• The formula underlying the table in Appendix B is attributed to the work of Agner Krarup Erlang, a Danish engineer who invented many (if not most) of the models that we use in Chapters 6 and 7 for his employer, the Copenhagen Telephone Exchange. In this context, the arrivals were incoming calls for which there was either a telephone line available or not (in which case the calls were lost, which is why the formula is also known as the *Erlang loss formula*).

• At the beginning of Appendix B, we provide the formula that underlies the Erlang loss formula table. We can use the formula directly to compute the probability $P_m(r)$ for a given activity-time-to-interarrival-time ratio r and the number of resources m.

In addition to the probability that all resources are utilized, we also can compute the number of patients that will have to be diverted. Since demand for trauma care continues at a rate of $1/a$ independent of the diversion status of the trauma center, we obtain our flow rate as

$$\text{Flow rate} = \text{Demand rate} \times \text{Probability that not all servers are busy}$$

$$= 1/a \times (1 - P_m) = \tfrac{1}{3} \times 0.975 = 0.325 \text{ patient per hour}$$

Similarly, we find that we divert $\tfrac{1}{3} \times 0.025 = 0.0083$ patient per hour $= 0.2$ patient per day.

TABLE 7.2
Finding the Probability $P_m(r)$ Using the Erlang Loss Table from Appendix B

			Erlang Loss Table				
				m			
		1	2	3	4	5	6 . . .
	0.10	0.0909	0.0045	0.0002	0.0000	0.0000	0.0000
	0.20	0.1667	0.0164	0.0011	0.0001	0.0000	0.0000
	0.25	0.2000	0.0244	0.0020	0.0001	0.0000	0.0000
	0.30	0.2308	0.0335	0.0033	0.0003	0.0000	0.0000
r	0.33	0.2500	0.0400	0.0044	0.0004	0.0000	0.0000
	0.40	0.2857	0.0541	0.0072	0.0007	0.0001	0.0000
	0.50	0.3333	0.0769	0.0127	0.0016	0.0002	0.0000
	0.60	0.3750	0.1011	0.0198	0.0030	0.0004	0.0000
	0.67	0.4000	0.1176	0.0255	0.0042	0.0006	0.0001
	0.70	0.4118	0.1260	0.0286	0.0050	0.0007	0.0001
	0.75	0.4286	0.1385	0.0335	0.0062	0.0009	0.0001
	. . .						

The case of the trauma center provides another example of how variability needs to be accommodated in a process by putting excess capacity in place. A utilization level of 22 percent in an environment of high fixed costs seems like the nightmare of any administrator. Yet, from the perspective of a person in charge of creating a responsive process, absolute utilization numbers should always be treated with care: The role of the trauma center is not to maximize utilization; it is to help people in need and ultimately save lives.

One main advantage of the formula outlined above is that we can quickly evaluate how changes in the process affect ambulance diversion. For example, we can compute the probability of diversion that would result from an increased utilization. Such a calculation would be important, both to predict diversion frequencies, as well as to predict flow rate (e.g., number of patients served per month).

Consider, for example, a utilization of 50 percent. Such a case could result from a substantial increase in arrival rate (e.g., consider the case that a major trauma center in the area closes because of the financial problems of its hospital).

Based on the increased implied utilization, $u = 0.5$, and the same number of trauma bays, $m = 3$, we compute $r = u \times m = 1.5$. We then use the Erlang loss formula table to look up the probability $P_m(r)$ that all m servers are utilized:

$$P_3(1.5) = 0.1343$$

Thus, this scenario of increased utilization would lead to ambulance diversion more than 13 percent of the time, corresponding to close to 100 hours of diversion every month.

Figure 7.2 shows the relationship between the level of implied utilization and the probability that the process cannot accept any further incoming arrivals. As we can see, similar to waiting time problems, there exist significant scale economies in loss systems: While a 50 percent utilization would lead to a diversion probability of 30 percent with one server ($m = 1$), it only leads to a 13 percent diversion probability with three servers and less than 2 percent for 10 servers.

Exhibit 7.1 summarizes the computations required for the Erlang loss formula.

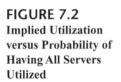

FIGURE 7.2
Implied Utilization versus Probability of Having All Servers Utilized

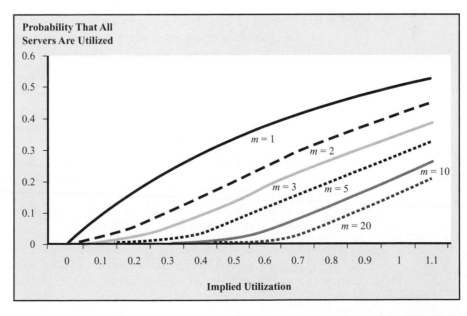

Exhibit 7.1

USING THE ERLANG LOSS FORMULA

1. Define $r = \dfrac{p}{a}$ where p is the activity time and a is the interarrival time

2. Use the Erlang loss formula table in Appendix B to look up the probability that all servers are busy:

$$\text{Probability \{all } m \text{ servers are busy\}} = P_m(r)$$

3. Compute flow rate based on

$$\text{Flow rate} = \text{Demand rate} \times \text{Probability that not all servers are busy}$$
$$R = 1/a \times (1 - P_m)$$

4. Compute lost customers as

$$\text{Customers lost} = \text{Demand rate} \times \text{Probability that all servers are busy}$$
$$= 1/a \times P_m$$

7.4 Customer Impatience and Throughput Loss

In Chapter 6 we analyzed a process in which flow units patiently waited in a queue until it was their turn to be served. In contrast, in the case of the trauma center, we have analyzed a process in which flow units never waited but, when all servers were busy, were turned immediately into lost flow units (were routed to other hospitals).

These two cases, a waiting problem on one side and a loss problem on the other side, are important, yet they also are extreme cases concerning the impact of variability on process performance. Many interesting applications that you might encounter are somewhere in between these two extremes. Without going into a detailed analysis, it is important that we at least discuss these intermediate cases at the conceptual level.

The first important intermediate case is a waiting problem in which there is a buffer that allows a limited number of flow units to wait for service. The limit of the buffer size might represent one of these situations:

- In a call center, there exists a maximum number of calls that can be on hold simultaneously; customers calling in when all these lines are in use receive a busy signal (i.e., they don't even get to listen to the 70s music!). Similarly, if one thinks of a queue in front of a drive-through restaurant, there exist a maximum number of cars that can fit in the queue; once this maximum is reached, cars can no longer line up.

- Given that, as a result of Little's Law, the number of customers in the queue can be translated into an expected wait time, a limit on the queue size might simply represent a maximum amount of time customers would be willing to wait. For example, customers looking at a queue in front of a movie theater might simply decide that the expected wait time is not justified by the movie they expect to see.

Although we will not discuss them in this book, there exist mathematical models to analyze this type of problem and for a given maximum size of the buffer, we can compute the usual performance measures, inventory, flow rate, and wait time (see, e.g., Hillier and Liebermann (2002)).

For the case of a single server, Figure 7.3 shows the relationship between the number of available buffers and the probability that all buffers are full; that is, the probability that the process can no longer accept incoming customers. As we can see, this probability is quickly decreasing as we add more and more buffer space. Note that the graph shifts up as we increase the level of utilization, which corresponds to the intuition from earlier chapters.

Since we can compute the throughput of the system as

$$(1 - \text{Probability that all buffers are full}) \times \text{Demand rate}$$

we also can interpret Figure 7.3 as the throughput loss. The right part of Figure 7.3 shows the impact of buffer size on throughput. Even for a single server and a utilization of 90 percent, we need more than 10 buffers to come close to restoring the throughput we would expect in the absence of variability.

The second intermediate case between a waiting problem and a loss problem resembles the first case but is different in the sense that customers always enter the system (opposed to not even joining the queue), but then leave the queue unserved as they become tired of waiting. The technical term for this is "customers *abandon* the queue" or the customers *balk*. This case is very common in call centers that have very long wait times. However, for call centers with high service levels for short target wait times, such as in the case of the An-ser call center discussed in Chapter 6, there are very few abandonment cases (this is why we could safely ignore customers abandoning the queue for our analysis in Chapter 6).

Figure 7.4 shows an example of call center data (collected by Gans et al. (2002)) in a setting with long waiting times. The horizontal axis shows how long customers had to wait before talking to an agent. The vertical axis represents the percentage of customers hanging up without being served. We observe that the longer customers have to wait, the larger the proportion of customers lost due to customer impatience.

There are three types of improvement opportunities for the two intermediate cases, limited buffer space and abandoning customers:

• Reduce wait times. Similar to our prior analysis, anything we can do to reduce wait times (intelligently choose capacity, reduce variability, etc.) helps reduce throughput losses resulting from customer impatience.

FIGURE 7.3
Impact of Buffer Size on the Probability P_m for Various Levels of Implied Utilization as Well as on the Throughput of the Process in the Case of One Single Server

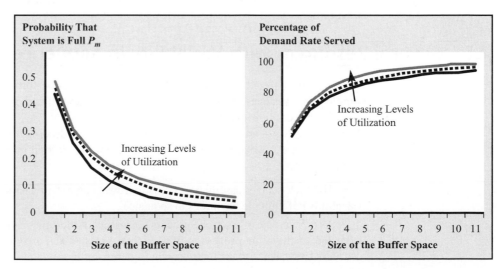

FIGURE 7.4
Impact of Waiting Time on Customer Loss

Source: Gans et al 2002

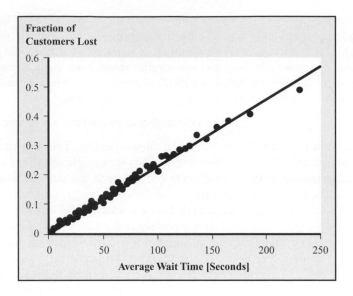

• Increase the maximum number of flow units that can be in the buffer. This can be achieved by either altering the actual buffer (adding more space, buying more telephone lines) or increasing the customers' willingness to tolerate waiting.

• Avoid customers leaving that have already waited. Having customers wait and then leave is even worse than having customers leave immediately, so it is important to avoid this case as much as possible. One way of achieving this is to reduce the perceived waiting duration by giving customers meaningful tasks to do (e.g., key in some information, help reduce the actual service time) or by creating an environment where waiting is not too painful (two generations of operations managers were told to install mirrors in front of elevators, so we are not going to repeat this suggestion). Obviously, mirrors at elevators and playing music in call centers alone do not solve the problem entirely; however, these are changes that are typically relatively inexpensive to implement. A more meaningful (and also low-cost) measure would be to communicate the expected waiting time upfront to the customer (e.g., as done in some call centers or in Disney's theme parks). This way, customers have expectations concerning the wait time and can make a decision whether or not to line up for this service (Disney case) or can even attempt to run other errands while waiting for service (call center case).

7.5   Several Resources with Variability in Sequence

After having analyzed variability and its impact on process performance for the case of very simple processes consisting of just one resource, we now extend our analysis to more complicated process flow diagrams.

Specifically, we analyze a sequence of resources as described in the process flow diagram in Figure 7.5. Such processes are very common, both in manufacturing and service environments:

• The kick-scooter assembly process that we analyzed in Chapter 3 consists (ignoring variability) of multiple resources in sequence.

• As an example of a service process consisting of multiple resources in sequence, consider the immigration process at most U.S. airports. When arriving in the United States, travelers first have to make their way through the immigration authority and then line up at customs.

FIGURE 7.5
A Serial Queuing System with Three Resources

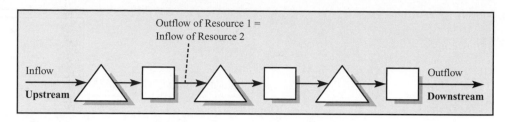

A complicating factor in the analysis of such processes is that the subsequent resources do not operate independently from each other: The departure process of the first resource is the arrival process of the second resource, and so forth. Thus, the variability of the arrival process of the second resource depends on the variability of the arrival process of the first resource and on the variability of the service process of the first resource. What a mess!

Independent of our ability to handle the analytical challenges related to such processes, which also are referred to as tandem queues, we want to introduce some basic intuition of how such processes behave.

The Role of Buffers

Similar to what we have seen in the example of impatient customers and limited buffer space (Figure 7.3), buffers have the potential to improve the flow rate through a process. While, in the case of a single resource, buffers increase flow rate as they reduce the probability that incoming units are denied access to the system, the impact of buffers in *tandem queues* is somewhat more complicated. When looking at a tandem queue, we can identify two events that lead to reductions in flow rate (see Figure 7.6):

• A resource is *blocked* if it is unable to release the flow unit it has just completed as there is no buffer space available at the next resource downstream.

• A resource is *starved* if it is idle and the buffer feeding the resource is empty.

In the trauma center example discussed at the beginning of the chapter, blocking is the most important root cause of ambulance diversion. The actual time the trauma surgeon needs to care for a patient in the trauma bay is only, on average, one hour. However, on average, patients spend one additional hour in the trauma bay waiting for a bed in the intensive care unit (ICU) to become available. Since, during this time, the trauma bay cannot be used for newly arriving patients, a full ICU "backs up" and blocks the trauma center. The study of the General Accounting Office on emergency room crowding and ambulance diversion, mentioned above, pointed to the availability of ICU beds as the single largest source leading to ambulance diversion.

It is important to understand that the effects of blocking can snowball from one resource to additional resources upstream. This can be illustrated in the hospital setting outlined above. Consider a patient who is ready to be discharged from a general care unit at 11 A.M. However, as the patient wants to be picked up by a family member, the patient can only leave at 5 P.M. Consequently, the unit cannot make the bed available to newly arriving patients, including those who come from the ICU. This, in turn, can lead to a patient in the ICU who is ready to be discharged but now needs to wait in the ICU bed. And, yes, you guessed right, this in turn can lead to a patient in the trauma center, who could be moved to the ICU, but now has to stay in the trauma bay. Thus, in a process with limited buffer space, all resources are dependent on another. This is why we defined buffers that help management to relax these dependencies as *decoupling inventory* (Chapter 2).

Blocking and starving can be easily avoided by adding buffers. The buffers would have to contain a sufficient number of flow units so as to avoid starvation of the downstream resource. At the same time, the buffer should have enough space to prevent the resource

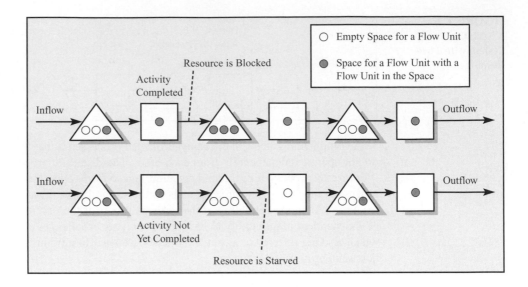

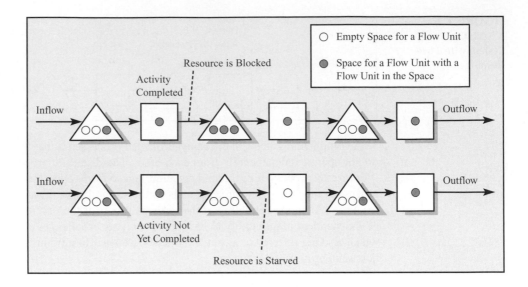

148 *Chapter 7*

FIGURE 7.6
The Concepts of Blocking and Starving

upstream from ever being blocked. Several hospitals have recently experimented with introducing discharge rooms for patients who are ready to go home from a general care unit: Even a buffer at the end of the process (healthy patient) will reduce the probability that an incoming trauma patient has to be diverted because of a fully utilized trauma center.

In addition to the probability of not being able to admit newly arriving flow units, an important performance measure for our process continues to be the flow rate. Figure 7.7 uses simulation to compare four process layouts of three resources with variability. This situation corresponds to a worker-paced line, with one worker at every resource. The activity times are exponentially distributed with means of 6.5 minutes/unit, 7 minutes/unit, and 6 minutes/unit respectively.

Based on averages, we would expect the process to produce one unit of output every seven minutes. However, in the absence of any buffer space, the process only produces at a rate of one unit every 11.5 minutes (upper left). The process does not realize its full capacity, as the bottleneck is frequently blocked (station 2 has completed a flow unit but cannot forward it to station 3) or starved (station 2 wants to initiate production of the next flow unit but does not receive any input from upstream).

If we introduce buffers to this process, the flow rate improves. Even just allowing for one unit in buffer before and after the bottleneck increases the output to one unit every 10 minutes (lower left). If we put no limits on buffers, the process is able to produce the expected flow rate of one unit every seven minutes (upper right). Yet, we also observe that the buffer between the first and the second step will grow very rapidly.

Finally, the lower-right part of Figure 7.7 outlines an alternative way to restore the flow rate, different from the concept of "buffer or suffer" (in fact, the flow rate is even a little larger than in the case of the upper right). By combining the three activities into one activity, we eliminate starving and blocking entirely. At the same time, we only have one unit of inventory in process, which is very desirable for reasons discussed below. This concept is called *horizontal pooling,* as it resembles the concept of pooling identical activities and their previously separate arrival streams that we discussed in Chapter 6. Observe further the similarities between horizontal pooling and the concept of a work cell discussed in Chapter 4.

Given the cost of inventory as well as its detrimental impact on quality discussed in Chapter 8, we need to be careful in choosing where and how much inventory (buffer space) we allow in the process. Since the bottleneck is the constraint limiting the flow rate through the

FIGURE 7.7 **Flow Rate Compared at Four Configurations of a Queuing System**

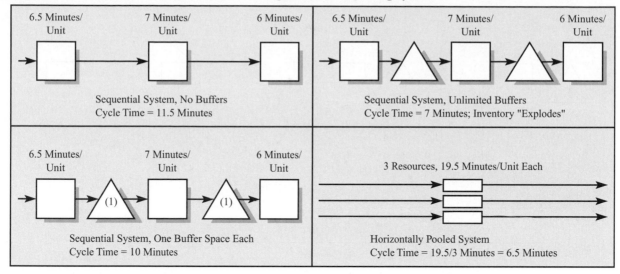

process (assuming sufficient demand), we want to avoid the bottleneck being either starved or blocked. Consequently, buffers are especially helpful right before and right after the bottleneck.

7.6 Summary

Variability not only impacts inventory and wait time but potentially also leads to losses in throughput. In this chapter, we have presented and analyzed the simplest case of such loss systems, consisting of multiple parallel resources with no buffer. The key computations for this case can be done based on the Erlang loss formula.

We then extended our discussion to the case in which customers potentially wait for service but are sufficiently impatient that a loss in throughput can still occur.

Figure 7.8 shows an overview of the various types of scenarios we discussed and, at least partially, analyzed. On the very left of the figure is the waiting problem of Chapter 6; on the very right is the no-buffer loss system (Erlang loss system) presented at the beginning of this chapter. In between are the intermediate cases of impatient customers. Observe that the four process types share a lot of similarities. For example, a wait system with limited, but large, buffer size is likely to behave very similar to a pure waiting problem. Similarly, as the buffer size approaches zero, the system behavior approaches the one of the pure loss system. Finally, we also looked at the case of several resources in series, forming a sequence of queues.

From a managerial perspective, the primary objective continues to be to reduce variability wherever possible. All concepts we discussed in Chapter 6 still apply, including the ideas to reduce the variability of service times through standardization and training.

However, since we cannot reduce variability entirely, it is important that we create processes that are robust enough so that they can accommodate as much of the remaining variability as possible. The following should be kept in mind to address throughput loss problems resulting from variability:

- *Use Buffers.* Nowhere else in this book is the concept of "buffer or suffer" so visible as in this chapter. To protect process resources, most importantly the bottleneck, from variability, we need to add buffers to avoid throughput losses of the magnitude in the example of Figure 7.7. In a sequence of resources, buffers are needed right before and right after the bottleneck to avoid the bottleneck either starving or becoming blocked.

FIGURE 7.8 **Different Types of Variability Problems**

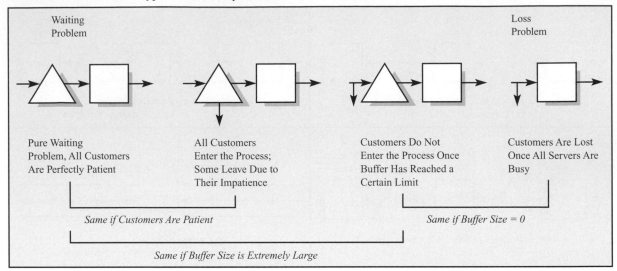

- *Keep track of demand.* A major challenge in managing capacity-related decisions in a process with customer loss is to collect *real* demand information, which is required to compute the implied utilization level. Why is this difficult? The moment our process becomes sufficiently full that we cannot admit any new flow units (all trauma bays are utilized, all lines are busy in the call center), we lose demand, and, even worse, we do not even know how much demand we lose (i.e., we also lose the demand information). A common mistake that can be observed in practice is that managers use flow rate (sales) and utilization (Flow rate/Capacity) when determining if they need additional capacity. As we have discussed previously, utilization is by definition less than 100 percent. Consequently, the utilization measure always gives the impression that there is sufficient capacity in place. The metric that really matters is demand divided by capacity (implied utilization), as this reveals what sales could be if there were sufficient capacity.

- *Use background work.* Similar to what we discussed in Chapter 6 with respect to waiting time problems, we typically cannot afford to run a process at the low levels of utilization discussed in the trauma care setting. Instead, we can use less time-critical work to use potential idle time in a productive manner. However, a word of caution is in order. To qualify as background work, this work should not interfere with the time-critical work. Thus, it must be possible to interrupt or delay the processing of a unit of background work. Moreover, we have to ensure that background work does not compete for the same resource as time-critical work further downstream. For example, it has been reported that elective surgery (at first sight a great case of background work for a hospital) can lead to ambulance diversion, as it competes with trauma care patients for ICU capacity.

7.7 Further Reading

Gans, Koole, and Mandelbaum (2002), referenced in Chapter 6, is also a great reading with respect to customer loss patterns. Again, we refer the interested readers to Hillier and Lieberman (2002) and Hall (1997) for additional quantitative methods.

7.8 Practice Problems

Q7.1* **(Loss System)** Flow units arrive at a demand rate of 55 units per hour. It takes, on average, six minutes to serve a flow unit. Service is provided by seven servers.

a. What is the probability that all seven servers are utilized?

b. How many units are served every hour?

c. How many units are lost every hour?

Q7.2 **(Home Security)** A friend of yours approaches you with the business idea of a private home security service. This private home security service guarantees to either dispatch one of their own five guards immediately if one of their customers sends in an alarm or, in the case that all five guards are responding to other calls, direct the alarm to the local police. The company receives 12 calls per hour, evenly distributed over the course of the day.

The local police charges the home security company $500 for every call that the police responds to. It takes a guard, on average, 90 minutes to respond to an alarm.

a. What fraction of the time are incoming alarms directed to the police?

b. How much does the home security company have to pay the local police every month?

Q7.3 **(Video Store)** A small video store has nine copies of the DVD *Captain Underpants, The Movie* in its store. There are 15 customers every day who request this movie for their children. If the movie is not on the shelf, they leave and go to a competing store. Customers arrive evenly distributed over 24 hours.

The average rental duration is 36 hours.

a. What is the likelihood that a customer going to the video store will find the movie available?

b. Assume each rental is $5. How much revenue does the store make per day from the movie?

c. Assume each child that is not able to obtain the movie will receive a $1 bill. How much money would the store have to give out to children requesting *Captain Underpants* every day?

d. Assume the demand for the movie will stay the same for another six months. What would be the payback time (not considering interest rates) for purchasing an additional copy of the movie at $50? Consider the extra revenues related to question b and the potential cost savings (question c).

Q7.4 **(Gas Station)** Consider the situation of Mr. R. B. Cheney, who owns a large gas station at a highway in Vermont. In the afternoon hours, there are, on average, 1,000 cars per hour passing by the gas station, of which 2 percent would be willing to stop for refueling. However, since there are several other gas stations with similar prices at the highway, potential customers are not willing to wait and bypass Cheney's gas station.

The gas station has six spots that can be used for filling up vehicles and it takes a car, on average, five minutes to free up the spot again (includes filling up and any potential delay caused by the customer going to the gas station).

a. What is the probability that all six spots are taken?

b. How many customers are served every hour?

Q7.5 **(Two Workstations)** Suppose a process contains two workstations that operate with no buffer between them.

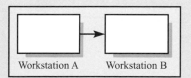

(* indicates that the solution is at the end of the book)

Now consider the three possible scenarios below:

Scenario	Processing Time of Workstation A	Processing Time of Workstation B
Scenario 1	5 minutes	5 minutes
Scenario 2	5 minutes	4 minutes or 6 minutes equally likely
Scenario 3	5 minutes	3 minutes or 5 minutes equally likely

a. Which of the three scenarios will have, on average, the highest flow rate?

b. Which of the three scenarios will have, on average, the lowest flow time?

Chapter

Quality Management and the Toyota Production System

Many production and service processes suffer from quality problems. Airlines lose baggage, computer manufacturers ship laptops with defective disk drives, pharmacies distribute wrong medications to patients, and postal services lose or misdeliver articles of mail. In addition to these quality problems directly visible to consumers, many quality problems remain hidden from the perspective of the consumer, as they are detected and corrected within the boundaries of the process. For example, products arriving at the end of an assembly process might not pass final inspection, requiring that components be disassembled, reworked, and put together again. Although hidden to the consumer, such quality problems have a profound impact on the economics of business processes.

The main purpose of this chapter is to understand quality problems and to improve business processes with respect to quality. We will do this in five steps:

1. We first introduce the methodology of statistical process control, a powerful method that allows an organization to detect quality problems and to measure the effectiveness of process improvement efforts.

2. We introduce various ways to measure the capability of a process, including the concept of six sigma.

3. We then discuss how quality problems impact the process flow, thereby extending the process analysis discussion we started in Chapters 3 and 4. Specifically, we analyze how quality problems affect flow rate as well as the location of the bottleneck.

4. One of the arch enemies of quality is inventory. Funny enough, adding inventory is also the most prominent way organizations attempt to manage quality problems. We discuss the inventory–quality relationship and define the concept of kanban, and more generally of pull systems, which can reduce inventory and improve quality.

5. Finally, we integrate these points—as well as many other points from previous chapters—by explaining the success of a specific organizational system that is frequently (and rightfully) associated with mastering quality problems, the Toyota Production System (TPS).

8.1 Controlling Variation: Practical Motivation

Variation is the root cause of all quality problems. To see this, imagine a process without any variation. In this case, the process would either always function as desired, in which case we would not need a chapter on quality, or it would never function as desired, in which case it would be unlikely that our organization would be in business to begin with. We might face variation with respect to durations, as we have discussed in Chapters 6 and 7, but also could encounter variation with respect to other measures, such as the courtesy of a customer service representative in a call center or the physical dimensions of a manufactured component. Thus, (once again) understanding variation, including its sources and its measurement, is essential to improve our operation.

As an example, consider the production of the steer support for the Xootr kick scooter discussed in Chapter 4.[1] The component is obtained via extrusion from aluminum and subsequent refinement at a computer-controlled machine tool (CNC machine). Figures 8.1 and 8.2 show the engineering drawing and the component in the assembly. Despite the fact that every steer support component is refined by the CNC machine, there still exists some variation with respect to the exact geometry of the output. This variation is the result of many

FIGURE 8.1 **Engineering Drawing of the Steer Support, a Critical Component of the Xootr Scooter**
The height of the steer support is specified by the dimensions (shown in the lower center portion of the drawing) as falling between 79.900 and 80.000 mm.

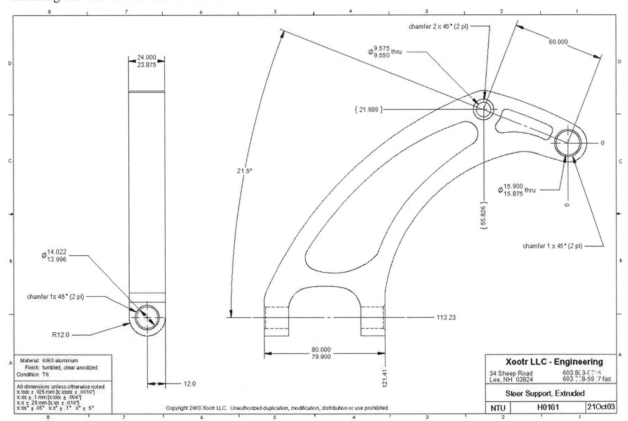

[1] The authors thank Karl Ulrich of Xootr LLC for his invaluable input.

FIGURE 8.2
Steer Support within Xootr Scooter Assembly
The height of the steer support must closely match the opening in the lower handle.

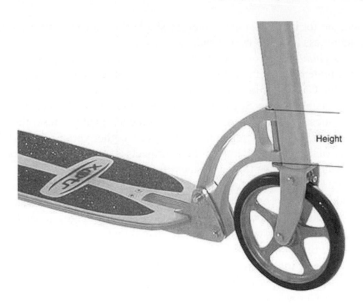

Height

causes, including differences in raw materials, the way the component is placed in the machine, the temperature of the room at the time of the processing, an occasional mistake in programming the CNC machine, or some of the many other factors that we discuss further below.

According to the design of the product, the ideal steer support would measure 79.950 mm; the drawing specifies that the height must fall between 79.900 mm and 80.000 mm. If the height is less than 79.900 mm, the part may rattle excessively because it fits loosely. If the height is greater than 80.000 mm then the part may not fit in the available gap in the handle assembly.

Given that variation of the steer support's height can cause quality problems, the engineers of the company (Xootr LLC) monitor the height very carefully. Every day, a sample of components is taken and measured accurately. Xootr engineers use *statistical process control (SPC)* to achieve the following:

• The company wants to achieve a consistent process that meets the specification as often as possible. SPC allows Xootr LLC to define performance measures that objectively describe the company's ability to produce according to their specifications.

• While a certain amount of variation seems natural, SPC allows Xootr LLC to quickly identify any "abnormally" large variation or changes in the underlying geometry.

8.2   The Two Types of Variation

Before we introduce the method of SPC, it is helpful to reflect a little more about the potential sources of variation. Following the work by W. A. Shewhart and W. E. Deming, we distinguish between two types of variation. *Common causes* of variation refer to constant variation reflecting pure randomness in the process. At the risk of being overly poetic for an operations management textbook, let us note that no two snowflakes are alike and no two flowers are exactly identical. In the same way, there is inherent variation in any business process and consequently no two steer support parts that Xootr can build will be exactly identical. Given that common-cause variation corresponds to "pure" randomness, a plot of the heights for a sample of steer support parts would have a shape similar to the normal distribution. Thus, for the case of common-cause variation, we cannot predict the exact outcome for the randomness in every single flow unit, yet we can describe the underlying randomness in the form of a statistical distribution.

Assignable causes of variation are those effects that result in changes of the parameters of the underlying statistical distribution of the process. For example, a mistake in programming the CNC machine, an operator error, or wear and tear of the extrusion machine would be assignable causes. Such causes are not common for all steer support parts; they only affect a subset. For those parts affected by the assignable cause, the distribution of heights looks statistically different and might have a higher variance or a different mean. The objective of many process improvement projects is to "assign" changes in process behavior to such causes and then to prevent them from recurring in the future.

To understand the notion of common causes of variation and how they differ from assignable causes, consider the following illustrative example. Take a piece of paper and write three rows, each containing the capital letter R eight times. Use your "normal" writing hand for the first row. Then, switch hands and write the eight Rs in the second row with the hand that you typically do not write with. Finally, for the last row, use your "normal" writing hand for the first four Rs and then switch hands for the last four. The outcome is likely to resemble what is shown in Figure 8.3.

The first row of Rs looks relatively consistent. While not every letter is exactly the same, there exists some (common-cause) variation from one letter to the next. In the second row, we observe a much larger (common-cause) variation with respect to the shape of the eight Rs. However, just as in the first row, there exists no obvious pattern that would allow us to predict the shape of the next letter (e.g., it is not possible to predict the shape of the sixth letter based on the first five letters in the same row). The pattern of letters in the last row is different. Following the fourth R, the process changes substantially. This variation can be clearly assigned to the cause of switching hands.

The distinction between common causes of variation and assignable causes is not a universal truth; it depends on the degree of knowledge of the observer. For example, to a layman, the movement of the Dow Jones Industrial Index might appear totally random, while an experienced trader can easily point to specific causes (earnings announcements, information releases by the government or rating agencies) that explain certain patterns of the market. Thus, just as the layman might learn and understand patterns that currently appear random to her, a process observer will discover new assignable causes in variation that she previously fully attributed to common causes.

FIGURE 8.3
Examples for Variation Types

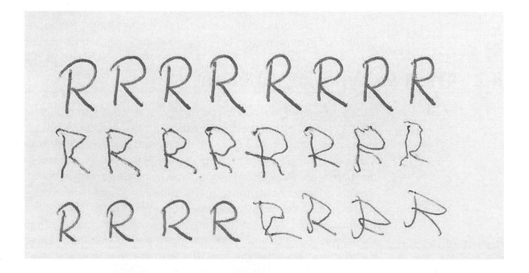

The objective of statistical process control is to

• Alert management to assignable causes (i.e., in the case of the third row, we want to set off an alarm as soon after the fifth letter as possible). However, we do not want to alert management to the small variation from one letter to the next in the first two rows.

• Measure the amount of variation in the process, creating an objective measure of consistency (i.e., we want some way to measure that the first row is "better" than the second row).

• Assign causes to variation that currently is perceived as pure randomness and subsequently control these causes, leading to reduced variation and a higher consistency in outcomes.

8.3   Constructing Control Charts

Control charts are graphical tools to statistically distinguish between assignable and common causes of variation. Control charts visualize variation, thereby enabling the user to judge whether the observed variation is due to common causes or assignable causes, such as the breakdown of a machine or an operator mistake.

Control charts are part of a larger set of tools known as statistical process control, a quality movement that goes back to the 1930s, and over the decades included the "quality gurus" W. A. Shewart, W. E. Deming, and J. M. Juran. Control charts have recently become fashionable again as they are an integral part of the six-sigma movement, introduced by Motorola and publicized widely by General Electric. Although their origin lies in the manufacturing domain, control charts are applicable to service processes equally well. At the end of this section, we discuss an application of control charts in a call center setting.

In order to distinguish between assignable and common causes of variation concerning a specific process outcome, control charts track the process outcome over time. Such process outcomes could be the physical size of a component that is assembled into a scooter or the time it takes a customer service representative to answer a call.

Given that data collection in many environments is costly, control charts are frequently based on samples taken from the process, as opposed to assessing every individual flow unit. Common sample sizes for control charts range between 2 and 10. The advantage of working with a sample as opposed to individual observations lies in the fact that the sample mean approximately follows a normal distribution. When constructing a control chart, a sample is drawn in each of several time periods for typically 20 to 50 time periods. In the Xootr case, we will create a control chart based on one month of data and five units sampled every day.

Control charts plot data over time in a graph similar to what is shown in Figure 8.4. The x-axis of the control chart captures the various time periods at which samples from the process are taken. For the two types of control chart that we discuss in this section, the y-axis plots one of the following two metrics:

• In the $\overline{X}$ *chart* (pronounce "X-bar chart"), the y-axis corresponds to the mean of each sample. $\overline{X}$ charts can be used to document trends over time and to identify unexpected drifts (e.g., resulting from the wear of a tool) or jumps (e.g., resulting from a new person operating a process step), corresponding to assignable causes of variation.

$$\overline{X} = \frac{x_1 + x_2 + \cdots + x_n}{n}$$

where n is the sample size in each period.

FIGURE 8.4
A Generic Control Chart

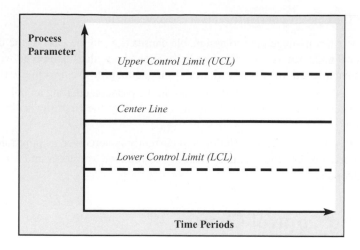

- In the R (range) chart, the y-axis corresponds to the range of each sample. The range is the difference between the highest value in the sample and the lowest value in the sample. Thus,

$$R = \max\{x_1, x_2, \ldots x_n\} - \min\{x_1, x_2, \ldots x_n\}$$

Instead of using the range of the sample, an alternative measure of variability is the standard deviation. The main reason why control charts have historically focused on the range instead of the standard deviation lies in its simplicity with respect to computation and explanation to a broad set of people in an organization.

To familiarize ourselves with the control chart methodology introduced up to this point, consider the data, displayed in Table 8.1, the Xootr engineers collected related to the height of the steer support component. The data show five data points for each day over a 25-day period. Based on the above definitions of $\overline{X}$ and R, we can compute the last two columns of the table.

For example, for day 14, $\overline{X}$ is computed as

$$\overline{X} = (79.973 + 79.986 + 79.942 + 79.978 + 79.979)/5 = 79.972$$

Similarly, for day 14, R is computed as

$$R = \max\{79.973, 79.986, 79.942, 79.978, 79.979\}$$
$$- \min\{79.973, 79.986, 79.942, 79.978, 79.979\} = 0.044$$

After computing the mean and the range for every period, we proceed to compute the average range and the average $\overline{X}$ across all days. The average across all $\overline{X}$s is frequently called $\overline{\overline{X}}$ (pronounced "X-double bar"), reflecting that it is an average across averages, and the average range is called $\overline{R}$ (pronounced "R-bar"). As we can see at the bottom of Table 8.1, we have

$$\overline{\overline{X}} = 79.951 \quad \text{and} \quad \overline{R} = 0.0402$$

In creating the $\overline{X}$ chart, we use the computed value of $\overline{\overline{X}}$ as a center line and plot the values of $\overline{X}$ for each day in the sample. For the R-chart, we plot the value of R in a chart that uses the average range, $\overline{R}$, as the center line.

Finally, we have to include the control limits into the charts. We set the control limits such that when we observe an entry for $\overline{X}$ or R outside the control limits (i.e., above the upper control or below the lower control), we can say with 99.7 percent confidence that the

TABLE 8.1
Measurements of
Steer Support
Dimension in Groups
of Five Observations

Period	X_1	X_2	X_3	X_4	X_5	Mean	Range
1	79.941	79.961	79.987	79.940	79.956	79.957	0.047
2	79.953	79.942	79.962	79.956	79.944	79.951	0.020
3	79.926	79.986	79.958	79.964	79.950	79.957	0.059
4	79.960	79.970	79.945	79.967	79.967	79.962	0.025
5	79.947	79.933	79.932	79.963	79.954	79.946	0.031
6	79.950	79.955	79.967	79.928	79.963	79.953	0.039
7	79.971	79.960	79.941	79.962	79.918	79.950	0.053
8	79.970	79.952	79.946	79.928	79.970	79.953	0.043
9	79.960	79.957	79.944	79.945	79.948	79.951	0.016
10	79.936	79.945	79.961	79.958	79.947	79.949	0.025
11	79.911	79.954	79.968	79.947	79.918	79.940	0.057
12	79.950	79.955	79.992	79.964	79.940	79.960	0.051
13	79.952	79.945	79.955	79.945	79.952	79.950	0.010
14	79.973	79.986	79.942	79.978	79.979	79.972	0.044
15	79.931	79.962	79.935	79.953	79.937	79.944	0.031
16	79.966	79.943	79.919	79.958	79.923	79.942	0.047
17	79.960	79.941	80.003	79.951	79.956	79.962	0.061
18	79.954	79.958	79.992	79.935	79.953	79.959	0.057
19	79.910	79.950	79.947	79.915	79.994	79.943	0.083
20	79.948	79.946	79.943	79.935	79.920	79.939	0.028
21	79.917	79.949	79.957	79.971	79.968	79.952	0.054
22	79.973	79.959	79.971	79.947	79.949	79.960	0.026
23	79.920	79.961	79.937	79.935	79.934	79.937	0.041
24	79.937	79.934	79.931	79.934	79.964	79.940	0.032
25	79.945	79.954	79.957	79.935	79.961	79.950	0.026
					Average	**79.951**	**0.0402**

TABLE 8.2
Control Chart
Parameters for 99.7
percent Confidence

Number of Observations in Subgroup (n)	Factor for X-Bar Chart (A_2)	Factor for Lower Control Limit in R Chart (D_3)	Factor for Upper Control Limit in R chart (D_4)	Factor to Estimate Standard Deviation (d_2)
2	1.88	0	3.27	1.128
3	1.02	0	2.57	1.693
4	0.73	0	2.28	2.059
5	0.58	0	2.11	2.326
6	0.48	0	2.00	2.534
7	0.42	0.08	1.92	2.704
8	0.37	0.14	1.86	2.847
9	0.34	0.18	1.82	2.970
10	0.31	0.22	1.78	3.078

process has gone "out of control." Given the parameters displayed for various sample sizes in Table 8.2, we compute the control limits based on the following equations:

$$\text{Upper control limit for } \overline{X} = \overline{\overline{X}} + A_2 \times \overline{R} = 79.951 + 0.58 \times 0.0402 = 79.974$$

$$\text{Lower control limit for } \overline{X} = \overline{\overline{X}} - A_2 \times \overline{R} = 79.951 - 0.58 \times 0.0402 = 79.928$$

$$\text{Upper control limit for } R = D_4 \times \overline{R} = 2.11 \times 0.0402 = 0.0848$$

$$\text{Lower control limit for } R = D_3 \times \overline{R} = 0 \times 0.0402 = 0$$

The control charts obtained this way allow for a visual assessment of the variation of the process. The definition of control limits implies that 99.7 percent of the sample points are

FIGURE 8.5
X-bar Chart
and *R* Chart

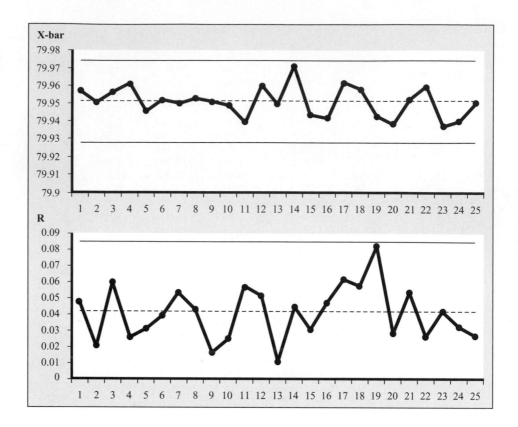

expected to fall between the upper and lower control limits. Thus, if any point falls outside the control limits, we can claim with a 99.7 percent confidence level that the process has gone "out of control," that is, that an assignable cause has occurred.

In addition to an observation $\bar{X}$ falling above the upper control limit or below the lower control limit, a sequence of eight subsequent points above (or below) the center line also should be seen as a warning sign justifying further investigation (in the presence of only common causes of variation, the probability of this happening is simply $(0.5)^8 = 0.004$, which corresponds to a very unlikely event).

Figure 8.5 shows the control charts for the Xootr. We observe that the production process for the steer support is well in control. There seems to be an inherent randomness in the exact size of the component. Yet, there is no systemic pattern, such as a drift or a sudden jump outside the control limits.

8.4   Control Chart Example from a Service Setting

To illustrate an application of control charts in a service setting, we turn back to the case of the An-ser call center, the answering service in Wisconsin that we discussed in conjunction with the waiting time formula in Chapter 6. An-ser is interested in an analysis of call durations for a particular type of incoming call, as both mean and variance of call durations impact the customer waiting time (see Chapter 6).

To analyze call durations for this particular type of incoming call, An-ser collected the data displayed in Table 8.3 over a period of 27 days. Similar to the Xootr case, we can compute the mean and the range for each of the 27 days. From this, we can then compute the overall mean:

$$\bar{\bar{X}} = 3.81 \text{ minutes}$$

TABLE 8.3
Data for a Control Chart at An-ser

Period	X_1	X_2	X_3	X_4	X_5	Mean	Range
1	1.7	1.7	3.7	3.6	2.8	2.7	2
2	2.7	2.3	1.8	3.0	2.1	2.38	1.2
3	2.1	2.7	4.5	3.5	2.9	3.14	2.4
4	1.2	3.1	7.5	6.1	3.0	4.18	6.3
5	4.4	2.0	3.3	4.5	1.4	3.12	3.1
6	2.8	3.6	4.5	5.2	2.1	3.64	3.1
7	3.9	2.8	3.5	3.5	3.1	3.36	1.1
8	16.5	3.6	2.1	4.2	3.3	5.94	14.4
9	2.6	2.1	3.0	3.5	2.1	2.66	1.4
10	1.9	4.3	1.8	2.9	2.1	2.6	2.5
11	3.9	3.0	1.7	2.1	5.1	3.16	3.4
12	3.5	8.4	4.3	1.8	5.4	4.68	6.6
13	29.9	1.9	7.0	6.5	2.8	9.62	28.0
14	1.9	2.7	9.0	3.7	7.9	5.04	7.1
15	1.5	2.4	5.1	2.5	10.9	4.48	9.4
16	3.6	4.3	2.1	5.2	1.3	3.3	3.9
17	3.5	1.7	5.1	1.8	3.2	3.06	3.4
18	2.8	5.8	3.1	8.0	4.3	4.8	5.2
19	2.1	3.2	2.2	2.0	1.0	2.1	2.2
20	3.7	1.7	3.8	1.2	3.6	2.8	2.6
21	2.1	2.0	17.1	3.0	3.3	5.5	15.1
22	3.0	2.6	1.4	1.7	1.8	2.1	1.6
23	12.8	2.4	2.4	3.0	3.3	4.78	10.4
24	2.3	1.6	1.8	5.0	1.5	2.44	3.5
25	3.8	1.1	2.5	4.5	3.6	3.1	3.4
26	2.3	1.8	1.7	11.2	4.9	4.38	9.5
27	2.0	6.7	1.8	6.3	1.6	3.68	5.1
					Average	3.81	5.85

and the average range

$$\overline{R} = 5.85 \text{ minutes}$$

We then compute the control limits using the constants from Table 8.2:

$$\text{Upper control limit for } \overline{X} = \overline{\overline{X}} + A_2 \times \overline{R} = 3.81 + 0.58 \times 5.85 = 7.20$$

$$\text{Lower control limit for } \overline{X} = \overline{\overline{X}} - A_2 \times \overline{R} = 3.81 - 0.58 \times 5.85 = 0.42$$

$$\text{Upper control limit for } R = D_4 \times \overline{R} = 2.11 \times 5.85 = 12.34$$

$$\text{Lower control limit for } R = D_3 \times \overline{R} = 0 \times 5.85 = 0$$

Combining the control limits with the values of the mean, $\overline{X}$, and the range, R, we obtain the control charts shown in Figure 8.6.

As we can see in Figure 8.6, the call durations exhibit a fair amount of variation. This leads to a large average range, R-bar (lower part of Figure 8.6), and explains the large interval between the upper and lower control limits. Despite these relatively "forgiving" control limits, we observe that the process moves out of control on day 13, when the mean, $\overline{X}$, jumps up to 9.62 (upper part of Figure 8.6). There are also two additional days when the R chart indicates an abnormally large variation in the process.

Going back to the data we collected (Table 8.3), we see that this exceptionally large mean is driven by one long call duration of almost half an hour. Despite having one observation drive the result, we know with 99.7 percent confidence that this long duration was not just "bad luck" but indeed reflects an underlying problem in the process. Thus, further investigation is warranted.

In this particular case, An-ser management discovered that several calls on the days in question were handled by an operator that typically handled different types of calls. Further data analysis revealed large operator-to-operator variation for the exact same type of call. This is visible in Table 8.4. Note that all calls are of the same type, so that the duration difference can fully be attributed to the operator. Table 8.4 indicates that customer service representative 1 (CSR 1) has the lowest mean call durations. She also has the lowest standard deviation, indicating that she has the most control over her calls. In fact, listening to a sample of randomly recorded calls indicates that CSR 1 fully complies with the script for the call type. In contrast, CSR 3 takes more than twice as long when answering the same calls. Moreover, her standard deviation is seven times as large. Listening to a sample of recorded calls from CSR 3 confirms a lack of consistency and large deviations with respect to the established script.

FIGURE 8.6
Control Charts for the An-ser Case

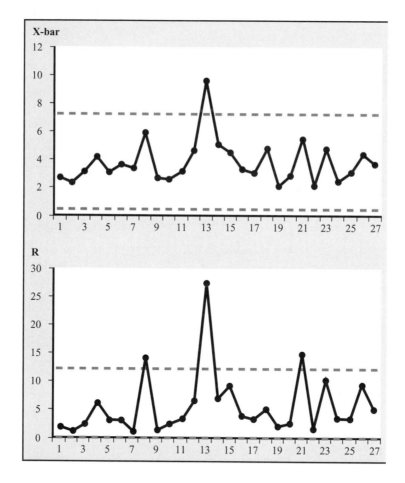

TABLE 8.4
Comparison of Operators

	CSR 1	CSR 2	CSR 3	CSR 4	CSR 5
Mean	2.95	3.23	7.63	3.08	4.26
Standard deviation	0.96	2.36	7.33	1.87	4.41

8.5   Design Specifications and Process Capability

So far, we have focused our discussion on the question to what extent the process is "in control." However, it is important to understand that a process that is in control might still fail to deliver the quality demanded from the customer or a downstream operation in the process. The reason for this lies in the definition of the control limits. Consider again the Xootr example. Since we set the control limits of 79.928 and 79.974 according to how the process performed in the past (25 days in the case above), we only measure to what extent the process is operating in line with its historical behavior (in the spirit of the letter R in Figure 8.3, the first two rows were "in control," despite the poor handwriting in the second row). This, however, contains little information about the degree to which the process is meeting the design specifications of 79.900 mm to 80.000 mm.

The consistency requirement from the customer typically takes the form of a design specification. A design specification includes

- A target value (79.950 mm in the case of the steer support component).
- A tolerance level, describing the range of values that are acceptable from the customer's perspective, [79.900 mm, 80.000 mm] for the steer support.

Again, note that design specifications are driven by the needs of the downstream process or by the end customer, while control limits are driven by how the process step has been operating in the past. Thus, it is very well possible that a process is "in control" yet incapable of providing sufficiently tight tolerances demanded by the customer. Vice versa, we say that a process, while being "in control," is capable if it can produce output according to the design specifications.

So, how do we know if a given process is capable of meeting the tolerance level established by the design specifications? This depends on

- The tightness of the design specification, which we can quantify as the difference between the upper specification level (USL) and the lower specification level (LSL).
- The amount of variation in the current process, which we can estimate based on the range R. For small sample sizes, we can translate the range R into an estimator of the standard deviation using the following equation:

$$\hat{\sigma} = \overline{R}/d_2$$

where $\hat{\sigma}$ stands for the estimated standard deviations and the values of d_2 are summarized in Table 8.2. For the steer support point, we have:

$$\hat{\sigma} = \overline{R}/d_2$$

$$= \frac{0.0402}{2.326} = 0.017283$$

Note that one also can estimate the standard deviation using a traditional statistical approach.

Thus, to increase the capability of the process in meeting a given set of design specifications, we either have to increase the tolerance level or decrease the variability in the process. We can combine these two measures into a single score, which is frequently referred to as the process capability index:

$$C_p = \frac{\text{USL} - \text{LSL}}{6\hat{\sigma}}$$

FIGURE 8.7
Comparison of Three-Sigma and Six-Sigma Process Capability

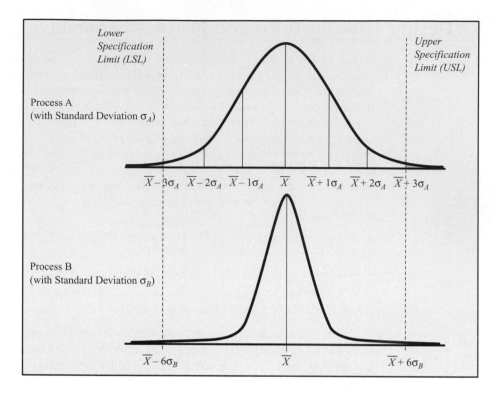

Thus, the process capability index C_p measures the allowable tolerance relative to the actual variation of the process. Figure 8.7 compares different values of C_p for a given set of design specifications. As we can see, the much lower variation (σ_B) of the process in the lower part of the figure will make it less likely that a defect will occur; that is, that the process creates a flow unit that falls above the upper specification limit or below the lower specification limit.

For the steer support component, we compute the process capability measure as follows:

$$C_p = \frac{USL - LSL}{6\hat{\sigma}} = \frac{80.000 - 79.900}{6 \times 0.017283} = 0.964345$$

A capability index of $C_p = 1$ would correspond to a process that meets the quality requirements 99.7 percent of the time. In other words, the process would have 28 defects per 10,000 units.

Traditionally, quality experts have recommended a minimum process capability index of 1.33. However, Motorola, as part of its six-sigma program, now postulates that all efforts should be made to obtain a process capability C_p of 2.0 at every individual step. This is statistically equivalent to requiring that the USL is six standard deviations above the mean and the LSL is six standard deviations below the mean. This explains the name "six-sigma" (see Figure 8.7).

Xootr LLC uses process capability scores to compare different production technologies. For example, recently, the company considered streamlining its production process for the steer support component. Instead of extruding the part and then machining it, management suggested eliminating the machining step and using the extruded part directly for production.

Xootr LLC conducted a formal analysis of this proposal based on the process capability index C_p. Collecting data similar to Table 8.1, the company found that eliminating the machining step would lead to a dramatic increase in defects, reflecting a much lower process capability index (the design specifications have not changed and there is a much higher variation in height in absence of the machining step), and hence decided not to pursue this potentially cheaper production process.

8.6   Attribute Control Charts

Rather than collecting data concerning a specific variable and then comparing this variable with specification limits to determine if the associated flow unit is defective or not, it is frequently desirable to track the percentage of defective items in a given sample. This is especially the case if it is difficult to come up with a single variable, such as length or duration, that captures the degree of specification conformance. This is the idea behind *attribute control charts.*

To construct an attribute control chart, we need to be able to distinguish defective from nondefective flow units. In contrast to variable control charts, this distinction does not have to be made based on a single dimension. It could be the result of many variables with specification limits and even qualitative factors, as long as they can be measured consistently.

Sample sizes for attribute control charts tend to be larger, typically ranging from 50 to 200. Larger sample sizes are especially necessary if defects are relatively rare events. Samples are collected over several periods, just as in the case of variable control charts.

Also the other control chart computations for attribute-based control charts strongly resemble the computations for variable control charts discussed previously. We first compute the percentage of defective items in each sample. Let p denote this percentage.

We then compute the average percentage of defects over all samples, which we call $\bar{p}$. This "average across averages" is the center line in our attribute control chart, just as we used $\bar{X}$ as the center line for variable control charts.

In order to compute the control limits, we first need to obtain an estimate of the standard deviation of defects. This estimate is given by the following equation:

$$\text{Estimated standard deviation} = \sqrt{\frac{\bar{p}(1 - \bar{p})}{\text{Sample size}}}$$

We then compute the upper and lower control limits:

$$\text{UCL} = \bar{p} + 3 \times \text{Estimated standard deviation}$$

$$\text{LCL} = \bar{p} - 3 \times \text{Estimated standard deviation}$$

Thus, we again set control limits such that the process is allowed to vary three standard deviations in each direction from the mean.

Whether one should use a variable control chart or an attribute control chart depends on the type of problem at hand.

- If there exists a single, measurable variable that determines if a unit is defective or not, one should always use variable control charts. The advantage of the variable control chart is that it makes use of valuable information that is discarded in attribute control charts. For example, if three sampled units were all very close to (yet still below) the upper specification limit, they would be classified as "nondefective" in the spirit of attribute control charts. In contrast, the variable control chart would use this information as leading to an increased estimated probability that a future unit might be above the upper control limit.

- If there are many potential causes of defects, variable-based control charts are difficult to implement. Thus, when measuring defects in activities such as order entry in a call center, baggage handling for an airline, or drug handling in a pharmacy, attribute-based control charts should be used.

FIGURE 8.8
Order Entry
Mistakes at Xootr

Cause of Defect	Absolute Number	Percentage	Cumulative Percentage
Browser error	43	0.39	0.39
Order number out of sequence	29	0.26	0.65
Product shipped, but credit card not billed	16	0.15	0.80
Order entry mistake	11	0.10	0.90
Product shipped to billing address	8	0.07	0.97
Wrong model shipped	3	0.03	1.00
Total	110		

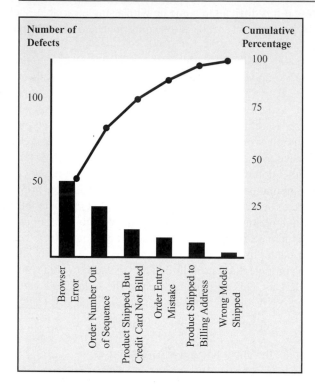

Given the multiple potential root causes of a defect in attribute-based control charts, it is frequently desirable to find which of these root causes accounts for the majority of the problems. The Pareto diagram is a graphical way of identifying the most important causes of process defects. To create a Pareto diagram, we need to collect data on the number of defect occurrences as well as the associated defect types. We can then plot simple bars with heights indicating the relative occurrences of the defect types. It is also common to plot the cumulative contribution of the defect types. An example of a Pareto diagram is shown in Figure 8.8. The figure categorizes defects related to customer orders at Xootr LLC.

The *Pareto principle* was postulated by J. M. Juran, who observed that managers spent too much time trying to fix "small" problems while not paying enough attention to "big" problems. The Pareto principle, also referred to as the 80-20 rule, postulates that 20 percent of causes account for 80 percent of the problems. In the context of quality, the Pareto principle implies that a few defect types account for the majority of defects.

8.7   Impact of Yields and Defects on Process Flow

Defects, as described in the previous section, have a profound impact on the process flow. In this section we discuss processes consisting of a sequence of process steps, of which at least one step suffers from detectable quality problems. In other words, there exists at least one step at which units are separated into "good units" and "defective units." Whereas good items can continue processing at the next operation, defective units either have to be *reworked* or are *eliminated from the process* (known as scrapped in the manufacturing context).

• In the case of the Xootr, the company scraps all steer support parts that do not meet the specifications as discussed previously.

• In contrast, Xootr LLC reworks Xootrs that require adjustments in the brake assembly. These Xootrs are rerouted to a separate operator in charge of rework. This (highly skilled) operator disassembles the brake (typically scrapping the brake cable) and adjusts the brake as needed, thereby creating a sellable Xootr.

The following examples help illustrate that the ideas of rework and flow unit elimination are by no means restricted to manufacturing processes:

• Following heart surgery, patients typically spend time recovering in the intensive care unit. While most patients can then be moved to a regular unit (and ultimately be sent home), some patients are readmitted to the intensive care unit in case of complications.

• The recruitment process of large firms, most prominently that of consulting companies, also exhibits a large percentage of flow units that are eliminated before the end of the process. For every offer made, consulting firms process hundreds of resumés and interview dozens of job candidates (possibly staged in several rounds).

• Pharmaceutical development analyzes thousands of chemical compounds for every new drug that enters the market. The initial set of compounds is reduced through a series of tests, many of which are very costly. After a test, some units are allowed to proceed to the next phase, while others are discarded for the clinical indication the company is looking for.

We define the yield of a resource as

$$\text{Yield of resource} = \frac{\text{Flow rate of units processed correctly at the resource}}{\text{Flow rate}}$$

$$= 1 - \frac{\text{Flow rate of defects at the resource}}{\text{Flow rate}}$$

Thus, the yield of a resource measures the percentage of good units that are processed at this resource. Similarly, we can define the yield at the level of the overall process:

$$\text{Process yield} = \frac{\text{Flow rate of units processed correctly}}{\text{Flow rate}} = 1 - \frac{\text{Flow rate of defects}}{\text{Flow rate}}$$

Obviously, the words *defects* and *rework* sound harsh in some of the examples described above, especially if we are dealing with human flow units. However, the following concepts and calculations apply equally well for disk drives that have to be reworked because they did not meet the specifications of final tests and patients that have to be readmitted to intensive care because they did not recover as quickly as required to safely stay in a regular hospital unit.

It also should be pointed out that a defect does not always reflect the failure of a process step, but can reflect inherent randomness (common-cause variation) in the process or differences with respect to the flow units at the beginning of the process. For example, dismissing a chemical compound as a potential cure for a given disease does not imply that previous development steps did not do their job correctly. Similarly, it lies in the nature of a recruiting process that its yield (percentage of applications resulting in a job) is well below 100 percent.

Rework

Rework means that some steps prior to the detection of the problem must be redone, or some additional process steps are required to transform a defective unit into a good unit. Two examples of rework are shown in Figure 8.9 (inventory locations are left out for simplicity).

In the upper part of the figure, defective units are taken out of the regular process and moved to a separate rework operation. This is common in many production processes such as in the Xootr example discussed above. If the rework step is always able to turn a defective unit into a good unit, the process yield would return to 100 percent. In the lower part of the figure, defective units are reworked by the same resource that previously processed the unit. The readmission of a patient to the intensive care unit corresponds to such a case.

As we can see directly from the process flow diagrams, rework changes the utilization profile of the process, and potentially the location of the bottleneck. Thus, when analyzing the influence of yields (and rework) on process capacity, we need to distinguish between bottleneck and nonbottleneck resources. If rework involves only nonbottleneck machines with a large amount of idle time, it has a negligible effect on the overall process capacity (note that it still has cost implications, reflecting costs of material and extra labor at the rework step).

In many cases, however, rework is severe enough to make a resource a bottleneck (or, even worse, rework needs to be carried out on the bottleneck). As the capacity of the bottleneck equals the capacity of the overall process, all capacity invested in rework at the bottleneck is lost from the perspective of the overall process.

Eliminating Flow Units from the Process

In many cases, it is not possible or not economical to rework a flow unit and thereby transform a defective unit into a good unit. Once the Xootr machine has produced a defective steer support unit, it is almost impossible to rework this unit into a nondefective unit. Instead, despite an approximate material cost of $12 for the unit, the company scraps the unit and produces a replacement for it.

Similarly, a consulting firm searching for a new hire prefers to simply reject the application, instead of investing in training to improve the job candidate's skills. If defective units are eliminated from the process, final output of good units is correspondingly reduced.

Strictly speaking, eliminating flow units from the process is a special form of rework, where all operations between the step where the defective unit leaves the process and the beginning of the process have to be reworked. Given that all operations up to the point of defect detection have to be reworked, the earlier we can detect and eliminate the corresponding flow unit, the less wasted capacity. This wasted capacity reflects that more units

FIGURE 8.9
Two Processes with Rework

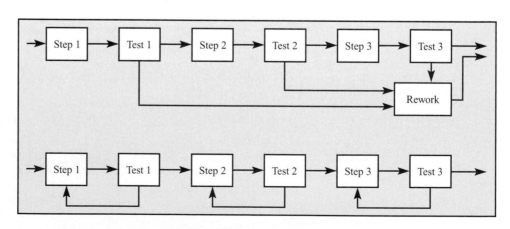

need to be started in the process than are finished. For example, in order to get 100 good units at the end of the process, we have to start with

Number of units started to get 100 good units = 100/Process yield

at the beginning of the process.

Two examples of processes in which defective units are eliminated are shown in Figure 8.10. In the upper part of the figure, defects are only detected at the end, and thereby have wasted capacity of every resource in the process. In the lower part of the figure, a test is conducted after every process step, which allows for the early elimination of defective parts, leading to less wasted capacity.

In a process in which defective units are eliminated, we can write the process yield as

$$\text{Process yield} = y_1 \times y_2 \times \ldots \times y_m$$

where m is the number of resources in the sequence and y_i is the yield of the ith resource.

Cost Economics and Location of Test Points

In addition to their effect on capacity, yields determine the value that a good unit has at various stages in the process. What is the value of a good unit in the process? The answer to this question differs depending on whether we are *capacity-constrained* or *demand-constrained*.

Consider the demand-constrained case first. At the beginning of the process, the value of a good item equals its input cost (the cost of raw material in the case of production). The value of a good unit increases as it moves through the process, even if no additional material is being added. Again, let y_n be the yield at the nth stage. The value leaving resource n is approximately $1/y_n$ times the sum of the value entering stage n plus any variable costs we incur at stage n.

The capacity-constrained case is fundamentally different. At the end of the process, the marginal extra revenue of the unit determines the value of a good unit. Yet, at the beginning of the process, the value of a good unit still equals its input costs. So should the valuation of a good unit be cost-based working forward or price-based working backwards? The discontinuity between these two approaches comes at the bottleneck operation. After the bottleneck, value is based on selling price; before the bottleneck, it is based on cost.

For example, assume that Xootr LLC is currently demand-constrained and we want to value a flow unit as it moves through the process. We should do this using a cost-based calculation, as—independent of a defect in this flow unit—we will achieve the same sales rate (i.e., we fulfill demand). In contrast, if Xootr LLC is capacity-constrained, we have to factor in the marginal extra revenue for those flow units that have already passed the bottleneck.

As a consequence of this, the costs that arise with detecting a defect dramatically increase as a flow unit moves through the process to market. Consider the case of a nonreworkable defect occurring at a prebottleneck resource, as depicted in Figure 8.11. If the defect is detected before the bottleneck, the costs of this defect are simply the costs of the

FIGURE 8.10
Process with Scrap

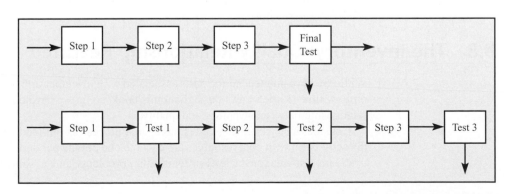

FIGURE 8.11
Cost of a Defect as
a Function of Its
Detection Location
Assuming a Capacity-
Constrained Process

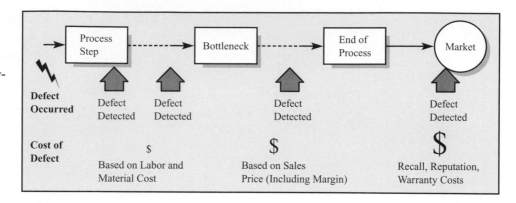

materials that went into the unit up to the detection of the defect. However, if the defect is detected after the bottleneck, the unit is almost as valuable as a complete unit. In the extreme case, if the defect is detected on the market, we are likely to incur major costs related to warranty, field repair, liability, and so forth.

This observation underlies the concept of *quality at the source,* an element of the Toyota Production System emphasizing that defects should be detected right when and where they occur, as opposed to being detected in a remote final inspection step. In addition to the cost benefits discussed above, another advantage of quality at the source is that the correction of the root cause that led to the defect is typically much easier to identify at the place and time when the defect is made. While a worker in charge of a process step that leads to a defect is likely to remember the context of the defect, figuring out what went wrong with a unit at a final inspection step is typically much harder.

Defects and Variability

Quality losses and yield-related problems not only change the capacity profile of a process, but they also cause variability. A yield of 90 percent means not that every 10th flow unit is defective, but that there is a 10 percent probability of a defect occurring. Thus, yield losses increase variability, which, as we have seen in Chapters 6 and 7, is the enemy of capacity.

Consider again the process flow diagram in the lower part of Figure 8.9, that is, a process where defective units are immediately reworked by repeating the operation. Even if the actual activity time is deterministic, yield losses force items into multiple visits at the same resource, and thus make the effective activity time for a *good* item a random variable.

Capacity losses due to variability can be partially compensated by allowing inventory after each operation with yields below 100 percent. The larger these buffers, the more the capacity-reducing impact of variability is reduced. However, additional inventory increases costs and flow times; it also can hurt the detection and solution of quality problems, as we discuss further below.

8.8   The Inventory–Quality Relationship Revisited

While we have pointed out the costs associated with inventory and the impact inventory has on flow time (Little's Law) throughout this book, so far we have only briefly discussed the relationship between inventory and quality.

Consider a sequence of two resources in a process as outlined in Figure 8.12. Assume the activity times at both resources are equal to one minute per unit. Assume further that the upstream resource (on the left) suffers quality problems, and, at some random point in time,

FIGURE 8.12
Information
Turnaround Time
and Its Relationship
with Buffer Size

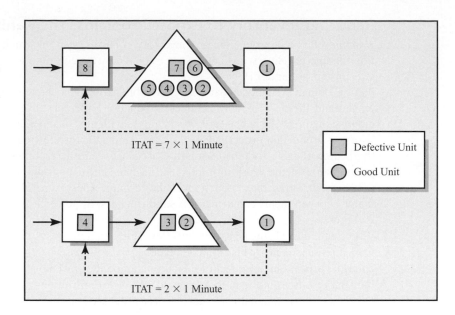

starts producing bad output. In Figure 8.12, this is illustrated by the resource producing squares instead of circles. The numbers in the squares or circles illustrate the sequence of the flow units. How long will it take until a quality problem is discovered? If there is a large buffer between the two resources (upper part of Figure 8.12.), the downstream resource will continue to receive good units from the buffer. In this example, it will take seven minutes before the downstream resource detects the defective flow unit. This gives the upstream re-source seven minutes to continue producing defective parts that need to be either scrapped or reworked.

Thus, the time between when the problem occurred at the upstream resource and the time it is detected at the downstream resource depends on the size of the buffer between the two resources. This is a direct consequence of Little's Law. We refer to the time between creating a defect and receiving the feedback about the defect as the *information turnaround time (ITAT)*. Note that we assume in this example that the defect is detected in the next resource downstream. The impact of inventory on quality is much worse if defects only get detected at the end of the process (e.g., at a final inspection step). In this case, the ITAT is driven by all inventory downstream from the resource producing the defect.

Given that buffers lead to longer ITAT, they complicate the quality improvement efforts of an operation. Consider the case of a long production line (e.g., automotive assembly) in which quality is only inspected at the end of the process. This leads to a long ITAT, for ex-ample, four hours. What happens if the inspection step detects a defective flow unit? Ide-ally, we want to find the root cause of the defect. However, in this case this is likely to be difficult, as we are looking for an event that happened many hours ago (thus, potentially in a different shift) and at a remote location. Thus, large buffers, which lead to long ITATs, cover up defects.

The idea of quality at the source is to detect and correct every defect right when and where it occurs. This is when and where fixing the problem should be easiest and all rele-vant information should be available. To achieve this, we need to turn the effect of inven-tory hiding quality problems on its head. Specifically, we want to reduce inventory to expose defects and then fix the underlying root cause of the defect. This is a fundamental element of the Toyota Production System, specifically its kanban system.

Reducing Inventory to Expose Problems: The Kanban System

Kanban refers to a production and inventory control system in which production instructions and parts delivery instructions are triggered by the consumption of parts at the downstream step (Fujimoto 1999).

In a kanban system, standardized returnable parts containers circulate between the upstream and the downstream resources. Production orders are triggered by the arrival of empty containers. A kanban card, which travels with the container, automatically issues delivery or production orders. For this reason, kanban cards are frequently called work authorization forms. If kanban cards are used between all resources in the process, they provide an effective, easy-to-implement mechanism of tying the demand of the process (downstream) with the production of the resources upstream. They therefore enforce a match between supply and demand. A simplified description of a kanban system is provided by Figure 8.13.

Observe that a kanban system *pulls* flow units through the system (downstream requests work from upstream). This is in contrast to a *push system,* where flow units are allowed to enter the process independent of the current amount of inventory in process. Especially if the first resources in the process have low levels of utilization—and are thereby likely to flood the downstream with inventory—push systems can lead to substantial inventory in the process.

The main advantage of a kanban system is that there can never be more inventory between two resources than what has been authorized by the Kanban cards. Thus, unlike in a push system, where inventory simply "happens" to management (e.g., think of the plant manager walking through the process and saying "wow, we have a lot of inventory at this step today"), in a kanban system inventory becomes a managerial decision variable. This decision variable is controlled via the number of kanban cards in the process.

One key objective of the kanban system is to gradually reduce inventory and thereby to expose quality problems. The kanban system and its approach to buffers is demonstrated with the following metaphor. Consider a boat sailing on a canal that has numerous rocks in it, shown in Figure 8.14. The freight of the boat is very valuable, so the company operating the canal wants to make sure that the boat never hits a rock.

One approach to this situation is to increase the water level in the canal. This way, there is plenty of water over the rocks and the likelihood of an accident is low. In a production setting, the rocks correspond to quality problems (defects), setup times, blocking or starving, breakdowns, or other problems in the process and the ship hitting a rock corresponds

FIGURE 8.13
Simplified Mechanics of a Kanban System

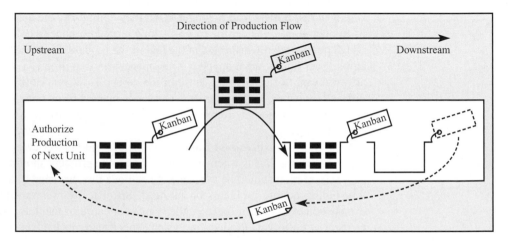

FIGURE 8.14   More or Less Inventory? A Simple Metaphor

Source: Stevenson

to lost throughput. The amount of water corresponds to the amount of inventory in the process (i.e., the number of kanban cards), which brings us back to our previous "buffer or suffer" discussion.

An alternative way of approaching the problem is this: Instead of covering the rocks with water, we also could consider reducing the water level in the canal (reduce the number of kanban cards). This way, the highest rocks are exposed (i.e., we observe a process problem), which provides us with the opportunity of removing them from the canal. Once this has been accomplished, the water level is lowered again until, step by step, all rocks are removed from the canal. Despite potential short-term losses in throughput, the advantage of this approach is that it moves the process to a better frontier (i.e., it is better along multiple dimensions).

This approach to inventory reduction is outlined in Figure 8.15. We observe that we first need to accept a short-term loss in throughput, reflecting the reduction of inventory (we stay on the efficient frontier, as we now have less inventory). Once the inventory level is lowered, we are able to identify the most prominent problems in the process (rocks in the water). Once identified, these problems are solved, thereby moving the process to a more desirable frontier.

In both the metaphor and our ITAT discussion above, inventory is the key impediment to learning and process improvement. Since with kanban cards management is in control of the inventory level, it can proactively manage the tension between the short-term need of a high throughput and the long-term objective of improving the process.

An alternative tool that management can use if it shies away from the short-term throughput loss, yet still wants to obtain the long-run benefits of learning and process improvement, was introduced by R. Jaikumar and is known as the *E-lot system* (see Bohn and Jaikumar (1992)).

The E-lot system locates small buffer inventories at specific points in the process. When a contingency arises (e.g., a defective part or a machine breakdown), a unit from the E-lot is used to maintain the normal flow and the rejected item is shifted to the E-lot for analysis. The number of units taken out of the E-lot is tracked graphically, using the control chart technique introduced in Section 8.3. The graphs are analyzed statistically on a continuous basis, which allows management to identify small quality problems as in the case of a starved resource without paying the price of lost throughput. In case of larger problems, the E-lots are depleted and the overall system comes to a stop. This is similar to the concept of the Toyota Production System, which also aims at stopping the process from producing as long as there exist unsolved quality problems. E-lots are therefore a powerful tool for directing managerial attention toward improving the process (Bohn and Jaikumar (1992)).

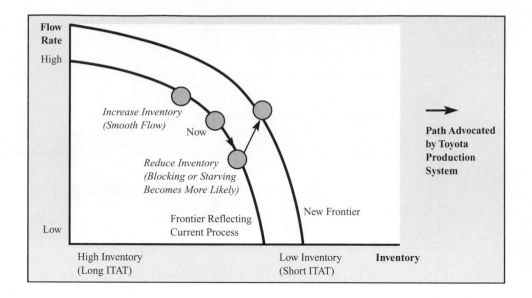

In addition to kanban (E-lots), another powerful technique to expose (and fix) problems is known as *jidoka.* Jidoka, in the narrow sense, means a specific type of machine that can automatically detect defects and shut itself down automatically. The basic idea is that shutting down the machine forces human intervention in the process, which in turn triggers process improvement (Fujimoto 1999). The jidoka concept has been generalized to include any mechanism that stops production in response to quality problems. The most well-known form of jidoka is the *Andon cord,* a cord running adjacent to assembly lines that enables workers to stop production if they detect a defect. Just like the jidoka automatic shutdown of machines, this procedure dramatizes manufacturing problems and acts as a pressure for process improvements.

8.9   The Toyota Production System

The Japanese automotive company Toyota is frequently associated with high quality as well as overall operational excellence. Various elements of the company's famous *Toyota Production System (TPS)* have been covered throughout the book. While a full description of TPS is beyond the scope of this section, the objective of this section is to

- Review and summarize the ideas from previous chapters and explain a few additional concepts that have not been discussed.
- Illustrate how the various elements of TPS are intertwined, thereby making it difficult to adapt some elements while not adapting others.

Readers who want to learn more about TPS are referred to excellent readings, such as Fujimoto (1999) and Ohno (1976), from which many of the following definitions are taken.

While TPS is frequently associated with certain buzzwords, such as JIT, kanban, and kaizen, one should not assume that simply implementing any of these concepts would lead to the level of operational excellence at Toyota. TPS is not a set of off-the-shelf solutions for various operational problems; instead it is a complex configuration of various routines ranging from human resource management to the management of production processes.

Given the introductory nature of this section, we only focus on some operational aspects of TPS. Table 8.5 summarizes a set of five principles that frequently are referred to

TABLE 8.5
Principles and Methods of the Toyota Production System

Principles	Methods

• Zero defects
• Zero breakdowns
• Zero inventory (just-in-time)
• Zero non-value-added (eliminate muda)
• Zero setup (SMED)
	• Product flow synchronized to demand
	   Pull instead of push
	      Kanban
	      Synchronized production
	   Mixed-model production (*heijunka*)
	   Match production with dealer volume
	   Piece-by-piece transfer (*ikko-nagashi*)
	• Line balancing to reduce Muda
	   Cross-trained workers
	   U-shaped line
	   Multitask assignment (*takotei-mochi*)
	• Quality methods to reduce defects
	   Foolproofing (poka-yoke)
	   Defect detection (jidoka)
	      Defects at machines (original jidoka)
	      Defects in assembly (Andon cord)
	   Build in quality (*tsukurikomi*)
	   Worker involvement/improvement (kaizen)
	      Quality circles
	      Structured problem solving
	• Human resource practices

as the "Five Zeroes of TPS," together with a set of intertwined methods that help support these principles. There exist strong interdependencies among the five principles as well as between the principles and the various methods outlined in the right column of Table 8.5. For example, to be able to achieve "zero inventory" while maintaining an economically meaningful flow rate, one needs to achieve "zero defects" (see the buffer or suffer discussion in Chapter 7 & Section 8.8) as well as "zero setup times" (see batching discussion in Chapter 5).

TPS postulates the elimination of non-value-added activities, which are also referred to as *muda*. There are different types of muda, according to T. Ohno, one of the thought leaders with respect to TPS. Muda can take the form of idle time, reflecting a poorly balanced process flow (see Chapter 4). A particular severe case of muda lies in the accumulation of inventory. Not only is inventory non-value-adding, it also hides other problems in the process as it leads to long information turnaround times and eases the pressure to find and eliminate underlying root causes (ITAT, see Section 8.8).

To achieve zero inventory, TPS advocates two forms of replenishment, both of which trigger component or subassembly deliveries based on the consumption of downstream resources (pull systems). Kanban cards circulate between resources and provide work authorizations for resources upstream (see Section 8.8). For more complex subassemblies, TPS typically uses a method known as synchronized production, which is "even more just-in-time" than kanban. With synchronized production, an internal or external supplier operates at exactly the same schedule and delivers flow units in the exact same sequence as required by Toyota's assembly line. This eliminates the need for inventory at the shipping dock of the supplier as well as at the receiving end at Toyota's plants.

TPS eliminates finished goods inventory by operating its production process in synchronization with the orders it receives from dealers (note that unlike other companies operating pull systems, such as computer manufacturer Dell, for most regional markets, Toyota does not synchronize its production with consumer demand). This is true both for the overall number of flow units produced as well as with respect to the mix of flow units across various product variants. Production plans avoid large batches of one and the same variant. Instead, product variants are mixed in the assembly line (mixed-model production, *heijunka)*, as discussed in Chapter 5. In order to avoid large capacity losses due to many set-ups, TPS requires fast changeover time (see SMED method in Section 5.7) and achieves setup times (for body panels) well below 10 minutes. In addition to eliminating production batches, TPS also requires the elimination of transfer batches. In TPS, the process should be laid out such that flow units can flow one at a time from one resource to the next *(ikko-nagashi)*.

Given that there typically exist fluctuations in demand from the end market, TPS attempts to create processes with sufficient flexibility to meet such fluctuations. Since forecasts are more reliable at the aggregate level across models or components (see discussion of pooling in Chapter 6 and again in Chapter 10), TPS requests workers be skilled in handling multiple machines. When production volume has to be decreased for a product because of low demand, TPS attempts to assign some workers to processes creating other products, and to have the remaining workers handle multiple machines simultaneously for the process with the low-demand product. Such multitask flexibility of workers also can help decrease idle time in cases of activities that require some worker involvement but are otherwise largely automated. In these cases, a worker can load one machine and, while this machine operates, instead of being idle, can operate another machine along the process flow *(takotei-mochi)*. This is facilitated if the process flow is arranged in a U-shaped manner, in which case a worker can not only share tasks with the upstream and the downstream resource, but also with another set of tasks in the process.

To achieve zero defects, TPS relies on defect prevention, rapid defect detection, and a strong worker responsibility with respect to quality. Defects can be prevented by fool-proofing many assembly operations, that is, by making mistakes in assembly operations physically impossible *(poka-yoke)*. Components are designed in a way that there exists one single way of assembling them. If, despite defect prevention, a problem occurs, TPS attempts to discover and isolate this problem as quickly as possible. This is achieved through the jidoka concept.

The idea of jidoka is to pause the process immediately whenever a defect is detected. While initially jidoka referred to machines that would stop operating once they sensed a defect, the concept is now more broadly applied to include nonautomated tasks. Most prominently, in the case of an assembly line, the jidoka philosophy is implemented based on the workers' ability to halt the line. When encountering a defect, a Toyota worker can use the An-don cord to stop the process flow and indicate the presence of a problem. This is in sharp contrast to other organizations that would leave the detection of defects to a final inspection step. In TPS, "the next step is the customer" and every resource should only let those flow units move downstream that have been inspected and evaluated as good parts. Hence, quality inspection is "built in" *(tsukurikomi)* and happens at every step in the line, as opposed to relying on a final inspection step alone (see quality at the source discussion in Section 8.7).

To support the worker's responsibility for quality, TPS strongly emphasizes quality control. Quality circles bring workers together to jointly solve production problems and to continuously improve the process *(kaizen)*. Problem solving is very data driven and follows a standardized process, including control charts, fish-bone (Ishikawa) diagrams, the "Five Whys," and other problem-solving tools.

Ishikawa diagrams (also known as *fishbone diagrams* or cause–effect diagrams) graphically represent variables that are causally related to a specific outcome, such as an increase in variation or a shift in the mean. When drawing a fishbone diagram, we typically start with a horizontal arrow that points at the name of the outcome variable we want to analyze. Diagonal lines then lead to this arrow representing main causes. Smaller arrows then lead to these causality lines, creating a fishbone-like shape. An example of this is given by Figure 8.16. Ishikawa diagrams are simple yet powerful problem-solving tools that can be used to structure brainstorming sessions and to visualize the causal structure of a complex system.

FIGURE 8.16   Example of an Ishikawa Diagram

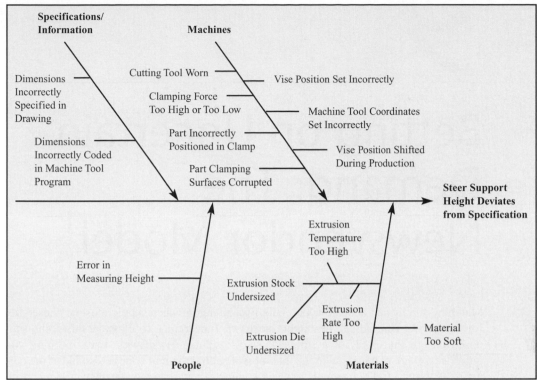

A related tool that also helps in developing causal models is known as the "Five Whys." The tool is prominently used in Toyota's organization when workers search for the root cause of a quality problem. The basic idea of the "Five Whys" is to continually question ("Why did this happen") whether a potential cause is truly the root cause or is merely a symptom of a deeper problem.

In addition to these operational principles, TPS includes a range of human resource management practices, including stable employment ("lifetime employment") for the core workers combined with the recruitment of temporary workers; a strong emphasis on skill development, which is rewarded financially through skill-based salaries; and various other aspects relating to leadership and people management.

8.10 Further Reading

Bohn and Jaikumar (1992) is a classic reading that challenges the traditional, optimization-focused paradigm of operations management. Their work stipulates that companies should not focus on optimizing decisions for their existing business processes, but rather should create new processes that can operate at higher levels of performance.

Bohn and Terwiesch (1999) provide a framework for analyzing the economics of yield-driven processes, which we used as the foundation for the discussion of rework and scrap.

Fujimoto (1999) describes the evolution of the Toyota Production System. While not a primary focus of the book, it also provides excellent descriptions of the main elements of the Toyota Production System.

Wadsworth et al. (1986) provide an excellent overview of various control charting methods. Their book also includes several examples of implementation. Breyfogle (1999) provides a detailed overview of many tools and definitions underlying six sigma. Interested readers also should look at the initial Motorola document about six sigma, which is summarized in Motorola (1987). More details on quality can be found in the earlier work by Juran (1951) or his more recent work (Juran 1989).

Betting on Uncertain Demand: The Newsvendor Model[1]

Matching supply and demand is particularly challenging when supply must be chosen before observing demand and demand is stochastic (uncertain). To illustrate this point, suppose you are the owner of a simple business: selling newspapers. Each morning you purchase a stack of papers with the intention of selling them at your newsstand at the corner of a busy street. Even though you have some idea regarding how many newspapers you can sell on any given day, you never can predict demand for sure. Some days you sell all of your papers, while other days end with unsold newspapers to be recycled. As the newsvendor you must decide how many papers to buy at the start of each day. Because you must decide how many newspapers to buy before demand occurs, unless you are very lucky, you will not be able to match supply to demand. A decision tool is needed to make the best out of this difficult situation. The *newsvendor model* is such a tool.

You will be happy to learn that the newsvendor model applies in many more settings than just the newsstand business. The essential issue is that you must take a firm bet (how much inventory to order) before some random event occurs (demand) and then you learn that you either bet too much (demand was less than your order) or you bet too little (demand exceeded your order). This trade-off between "doing too much" and "doing too little" occurs in other settings. Consider a technology product with a long lead time to source components and only a short life before better technology becomes available. Purchase too many components and you risk having to sell off obsolete technology. Purchase too few and you may forgo sizable profits. A notable example of the latter occurred to IBM in the early 1990s. IBM's laptops were more popular than they initially imagined. But due to shortages in components, IBM estimated that they were unable to satisfy $100 million in demand, a sizeable amount even for IBM.

This chapter begins with a description of the production challenge faced by O'Neill Inc., a sports apparel manufacturer. O'Neill's decision also closely resembles the newsvendor's task. We then describe the newsvendor model in detail and apply it to O'Neill's problem. We also show how to use the newsvendor model to forecast a number of performance measures relevant to O'Neill.

[1] Data in this chapter have been disguised to protect confidential information.

9.1 O'Neill Inc.

O'Neill Inc. is a designer and manufacturer of apparel, wetsuits, and accessories for water sports: surf, dive, waterski, wake-board, triathlon, and wind surf. Their product line ranges from entry-level products for recreational users, to wetsuits for competitive surfers, to sophisticated dry suits for professional cold-water divers (e.g., divers that work on oil platforms in the North Sea). O'Neill divides the year into two selling seasons: Spring (February through July) and Fall (August through January). Some products are sold in both seasons, but the majority of their products sell primarily in a single season, for example, waterski is active in the Spring season whereas recreational surf products sell well in the Fall season. Some products are not considered fashionable (i.e., they have little cosmetic variety and they sell from year to year), for example, standard neoprene black booties. With product names like "Animal," "Epic," "Hammer," "Inferno," and "Zen," O'Neill clearly also has products that are subject to the whims of fashion. For example, color patterns on surf suits often change from season to season to adjust to the tastes of the primary user (15–30-year-old California males).

O'Neill operates its own manufacturing facility in Mexico, but it does not produce all of its products there. Some items are produced by the TEC Group, O'Neill's contract manufacturer in Asia. While TEC provides many benefits to O'Neill (low cost, sourcing expertise, flexible capacity, etc.), they do require a three-month lead time on all orders. For example, if O'Neill orders an item on November 1, then O'Neill can expect to have that item at its distribution center in San Diego, California, ready for shipment to customers, only on January 31.

To better understand O'Neill's production challenge, let's consider a particular wetsuit used by surfers and newly redesigned for the upcoming spring season, the Hammer 3/2. (The "3/2" signifies the thickness of the neoprene on the suit: 3 mm thick on the chest and 2 mm everywhere else.) Figure 9.1 displays the Hammer 3/2 and O'Neill's logo. O'Neill has decided to let TEC manufacture the Hammer 3/2. Due to TEC's three-month lead time, O'Neill needs to submit an order to TEC in November before the start of the spring season. Using past sales data for similar products and the judgment of its designers and sales representatives, O'Neill developed a forecast of 3,200 units for total demand during the spring season for the Hammer 3/2. Unfortunately, there is considerable uncertainty in that forecast despite the care and attention placed on the formation of the forecast. For example, it is O'Neill's experience that 50 percent of the time the actual demand deviates from their initial forecast by more than 25 percent of the forecast. In other words, only 50 percent of the time is the actual demand between 75 percent and 125 percent of their forecast.

Although O'Neill's forecast in November is unreliable, O'Neill will have a much better forecast for total season demand after observing the first month or two of sales. At that time, O'Neill can predict whether the Hammer 3/2 is selling slower than forecast, in which case O'Neill is likely to have excess inventory at the end of the season, or whether the Hammer 3/2 is more popular than predicted, in which case O'Neill is likely to stock out. In the latter case, O'Neill would love to order more Hammers, but the long lead time from Asia prevents O'Neill from receiving those additional Hammers in time to be useful. Therefore, O'Neill essentially must "live or dive" with its single order placed in November.

Fortunately for O'Neill, the economics on the Hammer are pretty good. O'Neill sells the Hammer to retailers for $180 while it pays TEC $110 per suit. If O'Neill has leftover inventory at the end of the season, it is O'Neill's experience that they are able to sell that inventory with a 50 percent discount. Figure 9.2 summarizes the time line of events and the economics for the Hammer 3/2.

So how many units should O'Neill order from TEC? You might argue that O'Neill should order the forecast for total demand, 3,200, because 3,200 is the most likely outcome. The

FIGURE 9.1
O'Neill's Hammer
3/2 Wetsuit and Logo
for the Surf Market

forecast is also the value that minimizes the expected absolute difference between the actual demand and the production quantity; that is, it is likely to be close to the actual demand. Alternatively, you may be concerned that forecasts are always biased and therefore suggest an order quantity less than 3,200 would be more prudent. Finally, you might argue that because the gross margin on the Hammer is nearly 40 percent $((180 - 110)/180 = 0.39)$, O'Neill should order more than 3,200 in case the Hammer is a hit. We next define the newsvendor model and then discuss what the newsvendor model recommends for an order quantity.

9.2   An Introduction to the Newsvendor Model

The newsvendor model considers a setting in which you have only one production or procurement opportunity. Because that opportunity occurs well in advance of a single selling season, you receive your entire order just before the selling season starts. Stochastic demand occurs during the selling season. If demand exceeds your order quantity, then you sell your entire order. But if demand is less than your order quantity, then you have leftover inventory at the end of the season.

There is a fixed cost per unit ordered: for the Hammer 3/2, Cost = 110. It is important that Cost includes only costs that depend on the number of units ordered; amortized fixed costs should not be included because they are unaffected by our order quantity decision. In other words, this cost figure should include all costs that vary with the order quantity and no costs that do not vary with the order quantity. There is a fixed price for each unit you sell; in this case, Price = 180.

FIGURE 9.2
Time Line of Events and Economics for O'Neill's Hammer 3/2 Wetsuit

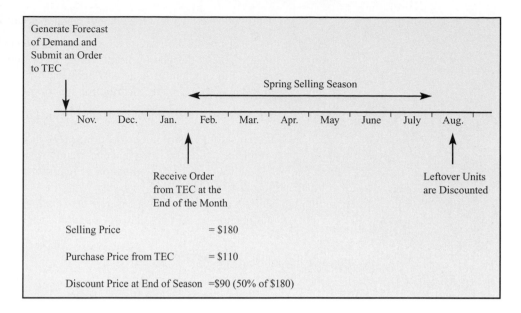

If there is leftover inventory at the end of the season, then there is some value associated with that inventory. To be specific, there is a fixed *Salvage value* that you earn on each unit of leftover inventory: with the Hammer, the Salvage value = 50% × 180 = 90. It is possible that leftover inventory has no salvage value whatsoever, that is, Salvage value = 0. It is also possible leftover inventory is costly to dispose, in which case the salvage value may actually be a salvage cost. For example, if the product is a hazardous chemical, then there is a cost for disposing of leftover inventory; that is, Salvage value < 0 is possible.

To guide your production decision, you need a forecast for demand. O'Neill's initial forecast for the Hammer is 3,200 units for the season. But it turns out (for reasons that are explained later) you need much more than just a number for a forecast. You need to have a sense of how accurate your forecast is; you need a forecast on your forecast error! For example, in an ideal world, there would be absolutely no error in your forecast: if the forecast is 3,200 units, then 3,200 units is surely the demand for the season. In reality, there will be error in the forecast, but forecast error can vary in size. For example, it is better to be 90 percent sure demand will be between 3,100 and 3,300 units than it is to be 90 percent sure demand will be between 2,400 and 4,000 units. Intuition should suggest that you might want to order a different amount in those two situations.

To summarize, the newsvendor model represents a situation in which a decision maker must make a single bet (e.g., the order quantity) before some random event occurs (e.g., demand). There are costs if the bet turns out to be too high (e.g., leftover inventory that is salvaged for a loss on each unit). There are costs if the bet turns out to be too low (the opportunity cost of lost sales). The newsvendor model's objective is to bet an amount that correctly balances those opposing forces. To implement the model, we need to identify our costs and how much demand uncertainty we face. We have already identified our costs, so the next section focuses on the task of identifying the uncertainty in Hammer 3/2 demand.

9.3 Constructing a Demand Forecast

The newsvendor model balances the cost of ordering too much against the cost of ordering too little. To do this, we need to understand how much demand uncertainty there is for the Hammer 3/2, which essentially means we need to be able to answer the following question:

What is the probability demand will be less than or equal to Q units?

for whatever Q value we desire. In short, we need a *distribution function.* Recall from statistics, every random variable is defined by its distribution function, $F(Q)$, which is the probability the outcome of the random variable is Q or lower. In this case the random variable is demand for the Hammer 3/2 and the distribution function is

$$F(Q) = \text{Prob}\{\text{Demand is less than or equal to } Q\}$$

For convenience, we refer to the distribution function, $F(Q)$, as our demand forecast because it gives us a complete picture of the demand uncertainty we face. The objective of this section is to explain how we can use a combination of intuition and data analysis to construct our demand forecast.

Distribution functions come in two forms. *Discrete distribution functions* can be defined in the form of a table: There is a set of possible outcomes and each possible outcome has a probability associated with it. The following is an example of a simple discrete distribution function with three possible outcomes:

Q	F(Q)
2,200	0.25
3,200	0.75
4,200	1.00

The Poisson distribution is an example of a discrete distribution function that we will use extensively. With *continuous distribution functions* there are an unlimited number of possible outcomes. Both the exponential and the normal are continuous distribution functions. They are defined with one or two parameters. For example, the normal distribution is defined by two parameters: its mean and its standard deviation. We use μ to represent the mean of the distribution and σ to represent the standard deviation. (μ is the Greek letter mu and σ is the Greek letter sigma). This notation for the mean and the standard deviation is quite common, so we adopt it here.

In some situations a discrete distribution function provides the best representation of demand, whereas in other situations a continuous distribution function works best. Hence, we work with both types of distribution functions.

Now that we know two ways to express our demand forecast, let's turn to the complex task of actually creating the forecast. As mentioned in Section 9.1, the Hammer 3/2 has been redesigned for the upcoming spring season. As a result, actual sales in the previous season might not be a good guide for expected demand in the upcoming season. In addition to the product redesign, factors that could influence expected demand include the pricing and marketing strategy for the upcoming season, changes in fashion, changes in the economy (e.g., is demand moving toward higher or lower price points), changes in technology, and overall trends for the sport. To account for all of these factors, O'Neill surveyed the opinion of a number of individuals in the organization on their personal demand forecast for the Hammer 3/2. The survey's results were averaged to obtain the initial 3,200 unit forecast. This represents the "intuition" portion of our demand forecast. Now we need to analyze O'Neill's available data to further develop the demand forecast.

Table 9.1 presents data from O'Neill's previous spring season with wetsuits in the surf category. Notice that the data include both the original forecasts for each product as well as its actual demand. The original forecast was developed in a process that was comparable to the one that led to the 3,200-unit forecast for the Hammer 3/2 for this season. For example, the forecast for the Hammer 3/2 in the previous season was 1,300 units, but actual demand was 1,696 units.

TABLE 9.1
Forecasts and Actual Demand Data for Surf Wetsuits from the Previous Spring Season

Product Description	Forecast	Actual Demand	Error*	A/F Ratio**
JR ZEN FL 3/2	90	140	−50	1.56
EPIC 5/3 W/HD	120	83	37	0.69
JR ZEN 3/2	140	143	−3	1.02
WMS ZEN-ZIP 4/3	170	163	7	0.96
HEATWAVE 3/2	170	212	−42	1.25
JR EPIC 3/2	180	175	5	0.97
WMS ZEN 3/2	180	195	−15	1.08
ZEN-ZIP 5/4/3 W/HOOD	270	317	−47	1.17
WMS EPIC 5/3 W/HD	320	369	−49	1.15
EVO 3/2	380	587	−207	1.54
JR EPIC 4/3	380	571	−191	1.50
WMS EPIC 2MM FULL	390	311	79	0.80
HEATWAVE 4/3	430	274	156	0.64
ZEN 4/3	430	239	191	0.56
EVO 4/3	440	623	−183	1.42
ZEN FL 3/2	450	365	85	0.81
HEAT 4/3	460	450	10	0.98
ZEN-ZIP 2MM FULL	470	116	354	0.25
HEAT 3/2	500	635	−135	1.27
WMS EPIC 3/2	610	830	−220	1.36
WMS ELITE 3/2	650	364	286	0.56
ZEN-ZIP 3/2	660	788	−128	1.19
ZEN 2MM S/S FULL	680	453	227	0.67
EPIC 2MM S/S FULL	740	607	133	0.82
EPIC 4/3	1,020	732	288	0.72
WMS EPIC 4/3	1,060	1,552	−492	1.46
JR HAMMER 3/2	1,220	721	499	0.59
HAMMER 3/2	1,300	1,696	−396	1.30
HAMMER S/S FULL	1,490	1,832	−342	1.23
EPIC 3/2	2,190	3,504	−1,314	1.60
ZEN 3/2	3,190	1,195	1,995	0.37
ZEN-ZIP 4/3	3,810	3,289	521	0.86
WMS HAMMER 3/2 FULL	6,490	3,673	2,817	0.57

*Error = Forecast − Actual demand
**A/F ratio = Actual demand divided by Forecast

So how does O'Neill know actual demand for a product that stocks out? For example, how does O'Neill know that actual demand was 1,696 for last year's Hammer 3/2 if they only ordered 1,500 units? Because retailers order via phone or fax, O'Neill can keep track of each retailer's initial order, that is, the retailer's demand before the retailer knows a product is unavailable. (However, life is not perfect: O'Neill's phone representatives do not always record a customer's initial order into the computer system, so there is even some uncertainty with that figure. We'll assume this is a minor issue and not address it in our analysis.) In other settings, a firm may not be able to know actual demand with that level of precision. For example, a retailer of O'Neill's products probably does not get to observe what demand could be for the Hammer 3/2 once the Hammer is out of stock at the retailer. However, that retailer would know when during the season the Hammer stocked out, and hence could use that information to forecast how many additional units could have been sold during the remainder of the season. Therefore, even if a firm cannot directly observe lost sales, a firm should be able to obtain a reasonable estimate for what demand could have been.

As can be seen from the data, the forecasts ranged from a low of 90 units to a high of 6,490 units. There was also considerable forecast error: O'Neill goofed with the Women's Hammer 3/2 Full suit with a forecast nearly 3,000 units above actual demand, while the forecast for the Epic 3/2 suit was about 1,300 units too low. Figure 9.3 gives a scatter plot of forecasts and actual demand. If forecasts were perfect, then all of the observations would lie along the diagonal line.

While the absolute errors for some of the bigger products are dramatic, the forecast errors for some of the smaller products are also significant. For example, the actual demand for the Juniors Zen Flat Lock 3/2 suit was more than 150 percent greater than forecast. This suggests that we should concentrate on the relative forecast errors instead of the absolute forecast errors.

Relative forecast errors can be measured with the *A/F ratio:*

$$\text{A/F ratio} = \frac{\text{Actual demand}}{\text{Forecast}}$$

An accurate forecast has an A/F ratio = 1, while an A/F ratio above 1 indicates the forecast was too low and an A/F ratio below 1 indicates the forecast was too high. Table 9.1 displays the A/F ratios for our data in the last column.

Those A/F ratios provide a measure of the forecast accuracy from the previous season. To illustrate this point, Table 9.2 sorts the data in ascending A/F order. Also included in the table is each product's A/F rank in the order and each product's percentile, the fraction of products that have that A/F rank or lower. (For example, the product with the fifth A/F ratio has a percentile of 5/33 = 15.2 percent because it is the fifth product out of 33 products in the data.) We see from the data that actual demand is less than 80 percent of the forecast for one-third of the products (the A/F ratio 0.8 has a percentile of 33.3) and actual demand is greater than 125 percent of the forecast for 27.3 percent of the products (the A/F ratio 1.25 has a percentile of 72.7).

FIGURE 9.3

Forecasts and Actual Demand for Surf Wetsuits from the Previous Season

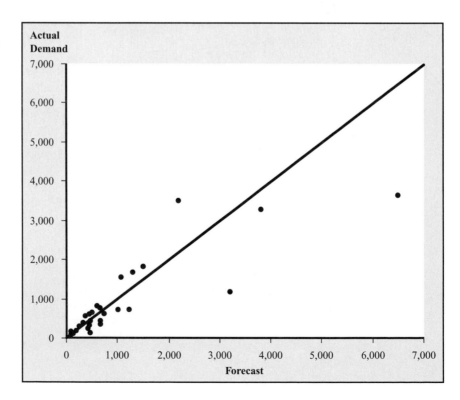

Given that the A/F ratios from the previous season reflect forecast accuracy in the previous season, maybe the current season's forecast accuracy will be comparable. For example, according to Table 9.2, there is a 3.0 percent chance demand is 25 percent of the forecast. Hence, if this season's forecast error is similar to last season's forecast error, then there is a 3.0 percent chance demand will be 800 units or fewer ($0.25 \times 3{,}200 = 800$). Similarly, from Table 9.2 we see there is a 90.9 percent chance demand is 150 percent of the forecast or lower. Translating that to the Hammer 3/2 means there is a 90.9 percent chance demand will be 4,800 units or lower ($1.5 \times 3{,}200 = 4{,}800$). For each A/F ratio we observed in our historical data set, we are able to derive the corresponding demand level for the Hammer 3/2 and the probability we should observe that demand or lower. These calculations are provided in Table 9.3.

The demand forecast represented by Table 9.3 is a discrete distribution function, but we will also refer to it as an *empirical distribution function* (because it is the distribution function constructed with the empirically observed data). Exhibit 9.1 summarizes the process of constructing an empirical distribution function.

TABLE 9.2
Sorted A/F Ratios for Surf Wetsuits from the Previous Spring Season

Product Description	Forecast	Actual Demand	A/F Ratio*	Rank	Percentile**
ZEN-ZIP 2MM FULL	470	116	0.25	1	3.0
ZEN 3/2	3,190	1,195	0.37	2	6.1
ZEN 4/3	430	239	0.56	3	9.1
WMS ELITE 3/2	650	364	0.56	4	12.1
WMS HAMMER 3/2 FULL	6,490	3,673	0.57	5	15.2
JR HAMMER 3/2	1,220	721	0.59	6	18.2
HEATWAVE 4/3	430	274	0.64	7	21.2
ZEN 2MM S/S FULL	680	453	0.67	8	24.2
EPIC 5/3 W/HD	120	83	0.69	9	27.3
EPIC 4/3	1,020	732	0.72	10	30.3
WMS EPIC 2MM FULL	390	311	0.80	11	33.3
ZEN FL 3/2	450	365	0.81	12	36.4
EPIC 2MM S/S FULL	740	607	0.82	13	39.4
ZEN-ZIP 4/3	3,810	3,289	0.86	14	42.4
WMS ZEN-ZIP 4/3	170	163	0.96	15	45.5
JR EPIC 3/2	180	175	0.97	16	48.5
HEAT 4/3	460	450	0.98	17	51.5
JR ZEN 3/2	140	143	1.02	18	54.5
WMS ZEN 3/2	180	195	1.08	19	57.6
WMS EPIC 5/3 W/HD	320	369	1.15	20	60.6
ZEN-ZIP 5/4/3 W/HOOD	270	317	1.17	21	63.6
ZEN-ZIP 3/2	660	788	1.19	22	66.7
HAMMER S/S FULL	1,490	1,832	1.23	23	69.7
HEATWAVE 3/2	170	212	1.25	24	72.7
HEAT 3/2	500	635	1.27	25	75.8
HAMMER 3/2	1,300	1,696	1.30	26	78.8
WMS EPIC 3/2	610	830	1.36	27	81.8
EVO 4/3	440	623	1.42	28	84.8
WMS EPIC 4/3	1,060	1,552	1.46	29	87.9
JR EPIC 4/3	380	571	1.50	30	90.9
EVO 3/2	380	587	1.54	31	93.9
JR ZEN FL 3/2	90	140	1.56	32	97.0
EPIC 3/2	2,190	3,504	1.60	33	100.0

*A/F ratio = Actual demand divided by Forecast
**Percentile = Rank divided by total number of wetsuits (33)

Exhibit 9.1

A PROCESS FOR USING HISTORICAL A/F RATIOS TO CONSTRUCT AN EMPIRICAL DISTRIBUTION FUNCTION

Step 1.   Assemble a data set of products for which the forecasting task is comparable to the product of interest. In other words, the data set should include products that you expect would have similar forecast error to the product of interest. (They may or may not be similar products.) The data should include an *initial forecast* of demand and the actual demand for each item. We also need an initial forecast for the product for the upcoming season. Your data table should be similar in form to Table 9.1.

Step 2.   Evaluate the A/F ratio for each product in the data set.

Step 3.   Sort the data in ascending A/F ratio order and rank the items from 1 to *N*, where *N* is the number of items in the data set. (See Table 9.2.)

Step 4.   There are *N* items in the empirical distribution function. The quantity of the *i*th item equals the initial forecast times the A/F ratio of the *i*th item in the sorted data set. The probability of the *i*th item equals *i/N*. (See Table 9.3.)

An attractive feature of the empirical distribution function in Table 9.3 is that it reflects our historical forecasting capability. A disadvantage of this demand forecast is that it predicts only a limited number of possible outcomes. For example, according to the table, it is possible that demand for the Hammer 3/2 will be 800 or 1,184 units, but 1,000 units is not possible. Hence, it can be desirable to fit a continuous distribution function to the data so that a broader range of outcomes are possible.

As an alternative to the empirical distribution function, let's use the well-known normal distribution. Given that there are an infinite number of potential normal distributions (essentially any mean and standard deviation combination), our challenge is to find a normal distribution that fits our data in Table 9.2.

Take the definition of the A/F ratio and rearrange terms to get

$$\text{Actual demand} = \text{A/F ratio} \times \text{Forecast}$$

TABLE 9.3
Discrete/Empirical Distribution Function for the Hammer 3/2 Using Historical A/F Ratios

A/F Ratio	Q	F(Q)	A/F Ratio	Q	F(Q)	A/F Ratio	Q	F(Q)
0.25	800	0.0303	0.81	2,592	0.3636	1.23	3,936	0.6970
0.37	1,184	0.0606	0.82	2,624	0.3939	1.25	4,000	0.7273
0.56	1,792	0.0909	0.86	2,752	0.4242	1.27	4,064	0.7576
0.56	1,792	0.1212	0.96	3,072	0.4545	1.30	4,160	0.7879
0.57	1,824	0.1515	0.97	3,104	0.4848	1.36	4,352	0.8182
0.59	1,888	0.1818	0.98	3,136	0.5152	1.42	4,544	0.8485
0.64	2,048	0.2121	1.02	3,264	0.5455	1.46	4,672	0.8788
0.67	2,144	0.2424	1.08	3,456	0.5758	1.50	4,800	0.9091
0.69	2,208	0.2727	1.15	3,680	0.6061	1.54	4,928	0.9394
0.72	2,304	0.3030	1.17	3,744	0.6364	1.56	4,992	0.9697
0.80	2,560	0.3333	1.19	3,808	0.6667	1.60	5,120	1.0000

Q = A/F ratio times the initial sales forecast, 3,200 units
$F(Q)$ = Probability demand is less than or equal to the quantity Q

For the Hammer 3/2, the forecast is 3,200 units. Note that the forecast is not random, but the A/F ratio is random. Hence, the randomness in actual demand is directly related to the randomness in the A/F ratio. Using standard results from statistics and the above equation, we get the following results:

$$\text{Expected actual demand} = \text{Expected A/F ratio} \times \text{Forecast}$$

and

$$\text{Standard deviation of actual demand} = \text{Standard deviation of A/F ratios} \times \text{Forecast}$$

Expected actual demand, or *expected demand* for short, is what we should choose for the mean for our normal distribution, μ. The average A/F ratio in Table 9.2 is 0.9975. Therefore, expected demand for the Hammer 3/2 in the upcoming season is $0.9976 \times 3,200 = 3,192$ units. In other words, if the initial forecast is 3,200 units and the future A/F ratios are comparable to the past A/F ratios, then the mean of actual demand is 3,192 units. So let's choose 3,192 units as our mean of the normal distribution.

This decision may raise some eyebrows: If our initial forecast is 3,200 units, why do we not instead choose 3,200 as the mean of the normal distribution? Because 3,192 is so close to 3,200, assigning 3,200 as the mean probably would lead to a good order quantity as well. However, suppose the average A/F ratio were 0.90, that is, on average, actual demand is 90 percent of the forecast. It is quite common for people to have overly optimistic forecasts, so an average A/F ratio of 0.90 is possible. In that case, expected actual demand would only be $0.90 \times 3,200 = 2,880$. Because we want to choose a normal distribution that represents actual demand, in that situation it would be better to choose a mean of 2,880 even though our initial forecast is 3,200. (Novice golfers sometimes adopt an analogous strategy. If a golfer consistently hooks the ball to the right on her drives, then she should aim to the left of the flag. In an ideal world, there would be no hook to her shot nor a bias in the forecast. But if the data say there is a hook, then it should not be ignored. Of course, the golfer and the forecaster also should work on eliminating the bias.)

Now that we have a mean for our normal distribution, we need a standard deviation. The second equation above tells us that the standard deviation of actual demand equals the standard deviation of the A/F ratios times the forecast. The standard deviation of the A/F ratios in Table 9.2 is 0.369. (Use the "stdev()" function in Excel.) So the standard deviation of actual demand is the standard deviation of the A/F ratios times the initial forecast: $0.369 \times 3,200 = 1,181$. Hence, for the second way to express our demand forecast for the Hammer 3/2, we can use a normal distribution with a mean of 3,192 and a standard deviation of 1,181. See Exhibit 9.2 for a summary of the process of choosing a mean and a standard deviation for a normal distribution forecast.

With a discrete distribution function, it is easy to find $F(Q)$ because we need only look it up in a table. But now we need to find $F(Q)$ with a normal distribution demand forecast. There are two ways this can be done. The first way is to use spreadsheet software. For example, in Excel use the function Normdist(Q, 3192, 1181, 1). The second way, which does not require a computer, is to use the Standard Normal Distribution Function Table in Appendix B.

The *standard normal* is a particular normal distribution: its mean is 0 and its standard deviation is 1. To introduce another piece of common Greek notation, let $\Phi(z)$ be the distribution function of the standard normal. Even though the standard normal is a continuous distribution, it can be "chopped up" into pieces to make it into a discrete distribution. The Standard Normal Distribution Function Table is exactly that; that is, it is the discrete

Exhibit 9.2

A PROCESS FOR USING HISTORICAL A/F RATIOS TO CHOOSE A MEAN AND STANDARD DEVIATION FOR A NORMAL DISTRIBUTION FORECAST

Step 1. Assemble a data set of products for which the forecasting task is comparable to the product of interest. In other words, the data set should include products that you expect would have similar forecast error to the product of interest. (They may or may not be similar products.) The data should include an initial forecast of demand and the actual demand. We also need an initial forecast for the item for the upcoming season.

Step 2. Evaluate the A/F ratio for each product in the data set. Evaluate the average of the A/F ratios (that is, the expected A/F ratio) and the standard deviation of the A/F ratios.

Step 3. The mean and standard deviation of the normal distribution that we will use as the forecast can now be evaluated with the following two equations:

$$\text{Expected demand} = \text{Expected A/F ratio} \times \text{Forecast}$$

$$\text{Standard deviation of demand} = \text{Standard deviation of A/F ratios} \times \text{Forecast}$$

where the forecast in the above equations is the initial forecast.

version of the standard normal distribution. The full table is in Appendix B, but Table 9.4 reproduces a portion of the table.

Although the Standard Normal Distribution Function Table is surely a table, its format makes it somewhat tricky to read. For example, suppose you wanted to know the probability that the outcome of a standard normal is 0.51 or lower. We are looking for the value of $\Phi(z)$ with $z = 0.51$. To find that value, pick the row and column in the table such that the first number in the row and the first number in the column add up to the z value you seek. With $z = 0.51$, we are looking for the row that begins with 0.50 and the column that begins with 0.01, because the sum of those two values equals 0.51. The intersection of that row with that column gives $\Phi(z)$; from Table 9.4 we see that $\Phi(0.51) = 0.6950$. Therefore, there is a 69.5 percent probability the outcome of a standard normal is 0.51 or lower.

But it is unlikely that our demand forecast will be a standard normal distribution. So how can we use the standard normal to find $F(Q)$; that is, the probability demand will be Q or lower given that our demand forecast is some other normal distribution? The answer is that we convert the quantity we are interested in, Q, into an equivalent quantity for the standard normal. In other words, we find a z such that $F(Q) = \Phi(z)$; that is, the probability demand

TABLE 9.4

A Portion of the Standard Normal Distribution Function Table, $\Phi(z)$

z	0	0.01	0.02	0.03	0.04	0.05	0.06	0.07	0.08	0.09
0	0.5000	0.5040	0.5080	0.5120	0.5160	0.5199	0.5239	0.5279	0.5319	0.5359
0.1	0.5398	0.5438	0.5478	0.5517	0.5557	0.5596	0.5636	0.5675	0.5714	0.5753
0.2	0.5793	0.5832	0.5871	0.5910	0.5948	0.5987	0.6026	0.6064	0.6103	0.6141
0.3	0.6179	0.6217	0.6255	0.6293	0.6331	0.6368	0.6406	0.6443	0.6480	0.6517
0.4	0.6554	0.6591	0.6628	0.6664	0.6700	0.6736	0.6772	0.6808	0.6844	0.6879
0.5	0.6915	0.6950	0.6985	0.7019	0.7054	0.7088	0.7123	0.7157	0.7190	0.7224
0.6	0.7257	0.7291	0.7324	0.7357	0.7389	0.7422	0.7454	0.7486	0.7517	0.7549
0.7	0.7580	0.7611	0.7642	0.7673	0.7704	0.7734	0.7764	0.7794	0.7823	0.7852

is less than or equal to Q is the same as the probability the outcome of a standard normal is z or lower. That z is called the *z-statistic*. Once we have the appropriate z-statistics, we then just look up $\Phi(z)$ in the Standard Normal Distribution Function Table to get our answer.

To convert Q into the equivalent z-statistic, use the following equation:

$$z = \frac{Q - \mu}{\sigma}$$

For example, suppose we are interested in the probability that demand for the Hammer 3/2 will be 4,000 units or lower, that is, $Q = 4,000$. With a normal distribution that has mean 3,192 and standard deviation 1,181, the quantity $Q = 4,000$ has a z-statistic of

$$z = \frac{4,000 - 3,192}{1,181} = 0.68$$

Therefore, the probability demand for the Hammer 3/2 is 4,000 units or lower is $\Phi(0.68)$; that is, it is the same as the probability the outcome of a standard normal is 0.68 or lower. According to the Standard Normal Distribution Function Table (see Table 9.4 for convenience), $\Phi(0.68) = 0.7517$. In other words, there is just over a 75 percent probability that demand for the Hammer 3/2 will be 4,000 or fewer units. Exhibit 9.3 summarizes the process of finding the probability demand will be less than or equal to some Q (or more than Q).

In the remainder of this chapter, we will work with both demand forecasts, the discrete/empirical distribution and the normal distribution. We study the empirical distribution function because the techniques we apply to it extend exactly to any other discrete distribution function, such as the Poisson or the negative binomial. We study the normal because it is a widely applied distribution (rightfully so). Furthermore, the techniques used with the normal distribution are actually quite similar to those used with the empirical distribution.

You may recall that it has been O'Neill's experience that demand deviated by more than 25 percent from their initial forecast for 50 percent of their products. We can now check whether that experience is consistent with our normal distribution forecast for the Hammer 3/2. Our initial forecast is 3,200 units. So a deviation of 25 percent or more implies demand is either less than 2,400 units or more than 4,000 units. The z-statistic for $Q = 2,400$ is $z = (2400 - 3192)/1181 = -0.67$, and from the Standard Normal Distribution Function Table, $\Phi(-0.67) = 0.2514$. (Find the row with -0.60 and the column with -0.07.) If there is a 25.14 percent probability demand is less than 2,400 units and a 75.17 percent probability that demand is less than 4,000 units, then there is a $75.17 - 25.14 = 50.03$ percent probability that demand is between 2,400 and 4,000 units. Hence, O'Neill's initial assertion regarding forecast accuracy is consistent with our normal distribution forecast of demand.

To summarize, the objective in this section is to develop a detailed demand forecast. A single "point forecast" (e.g., 3,200 units) is not sufficient. We need to quantify the amount of variability that may occur about our forecast; that is, we need a distribution function. We first constructed a discrete distribution function table with the empirical observed historical demand (Table 9.3) and then we fit a normal distribution to our historical forecast performance data.

Now that we can evaluate the distribution function of Hammer 3/2 demand, we can see how well our chosen normal distribution fits our data. Figure 9.4 combines the empirical distribution function in Table 9.3 with the normal distribution function. The figure shows that they match closely, which suggests that they are roughly equivalent. Furthermore, it suggests that the normal distribution is a good representation of our actual demand.

Exhibit 9.3

A PROCESS FOR EVALUATING THE PROBABILITY DEMAND IS EITHER LESS THAN OR EQUAL TO Q (WHICH IS F(Q)) OR MORE THAN Q (WHICH IS 1 − F(Q))

If the demand forecast is a normal distribution with mean μ and standard deviation σ, then follow steps A and B:

A. Evaluate the z-statistic that corresponds to Q:

$$z = \frac{Q - \mu}{\sigma}$$

B. The probability demand is less than or equal to Q is $\Phi(z)$. With Excel $\Phi(z)$ can be evaluated with the function Normsdist(z); otherwise, look up $\Phi(z)$ in the Standard Normal Distribution Function Table in Appendix B. If you want the probability demand is greater than Q, then your answer is $1 - \Phi(z)$.

If the demand forecast is a discrete distribution function table (as with an empirical distribution function), then look up $F(Q)$, which is the probability demand is less than or equal to Q. If you want the probability demand is greater than Q, then the answer is $1 - F(Q)$.

FIGURE 9.4
Discrete/Empirical Distribution Function (diamonds) and Normal Distribution Function with Mean 3,192 and Standard Deviation 1,181 (solid line)

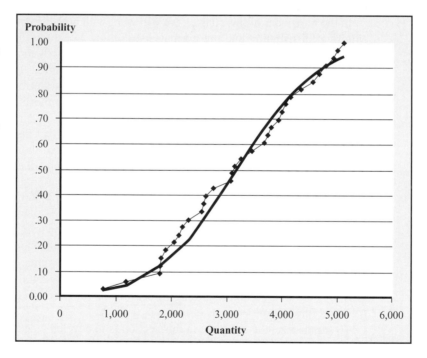

9.4 The Expected Profit-Maximizing Order Quantity

The next step after assembling all of our inputs (selling price, cost, salvage value, and demand forecast) is to choose an order quantity. The first part in that process is to decide what is our objective. A natural objective is to choose our production/procurement quantity to maximize our expected profit. This section explains how to do this. Section 9.6 considers other possible objectives.

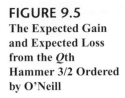

FIGURE 9.5
The Expected Gain and Expected Loss from the *Q*th Hammer 3/2 Ordered by O'Neill

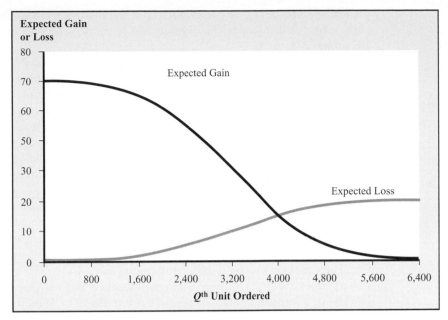

Before revealing the actual procedure for choosing an order quantity to maximize expected profit, it is helpful to explore the intuition behind the solution. Consider again O'Neill's Hammer 3/2 ordering decision. Should we order one unit? If we do, then there is a very good chance we will sell the unit: With a forecast of 3,192 units, it is likely we sell at least one unit. If we sell the unit, then the gain from that unit equals $180 − $110 = $70 (the selling price minus the purchase cost). The *expected* gain from the first unit, which equals the probability of selling the first unit times the gain from the first unit, is then very close to $70. However, there is also a slight chance that we do not sell the first unit, in which case we incur a loss of $110 − $90 = $20. (The loss equals the difference between the purchase cost and the discount price.) But since the probability we do not sell that unit is quite small, the *expected* loss on the first unit is nearly $0. Given that the expected gain from the first unit clearly exceeds the expected loss, the profit from ordering that unit is positive. In this case it is a good bet to order at least one unit.

After deciding whether to order one unit, we can now consider whether we should order two units, and then three units, and so forth. Two things happen as we continue this process. First, the probability that we sell the unit we are considering decreases, thereby reducing the expected gain from that unit. Second, the probability we do not sell that unit increases, thereby increasing the expected loss from that unit. Now imagine we order the 6,400th unit. The probability of selling that unit is quite low, so the expected gain from that unit is nearly zero. In contrast, the probability of *not* selling that unit is quite high, so the expected loss is nearly $20 on that unit. Clearly it makes no sense to order the 6,400th unit. This pattern is illustrated in Figure 9.5. We see that from some unit just above 4,000 the expected gain on that unit equals its expected loss.

Let's formalize this intuition some more. In the newsvendor model, there is a trade-off between ordering too much (which could lead to costly leftover inventory) and ordering too little (which could lead to the opportunity cost of lost sales). To balance these forces, it is useful to think in terms of a cost for ordering too much and a cost for ordering too little. Maximizing expected profit is equivalent to minimizing those costs.

To be specific, let C_o be the *overage cost,* the loss incurred when a unit is ordered but not sold. In other words, the overage cost is the per-unit cost of overordering. For the Hammer 3/2, we have $C_o = 20$.

In contrast to C_o, let C_u be the *underage cost,* the opportunity cost of not ordering a unit that could have been sold. The following is an equivalent definition for C_u: C_u is the gain from selling a unit. In other words, the underage cost is the per-unit opportunity cost of underordering. For the Hammer 3/2, $C_u = 70$. Note that the overage and underage costs are defined for a *single unit.* In other words, C_o is not the total cost of all leftover inventory, instead, C_o is the cost per unit of leftover inventory. The reason for defining C_o and C_u for a single unit is simple: We don't know how many units will be left over in inventory; or how many units of demand will be lost, but we do know the cost of each unit left in inventory and the opportunity cost of each lost sale.

Now that we have defined the overage and underage costs, we need to choose Q to strike the balance between them that results in the maximum expected profit. Based on our previous reasoning, we should keep ordering additional units until the expected loss equals the expected gain.

The expected loss on a unit is the cost of having the unit in inventory (the overage cost) times the probability it is left in inventory. For the Qth unit, that probability is $F(Q)$: It is left in inventory if demand is less than Q.[2] Therefore, the expected loss is $C_o \times F(Q)$. The expected gain on a unit is the benefit of selling a unit (the underage cost) times the probability the unit is sold, which in this case occurs if demand is greater than Q. The probability demand is greater than Q is $(1 - F(Q))$. Therefore, the expected gain is $C_u \times (1 - F(Q))$.

It remains to find the order quantity Q that sets the expected loss on the Qth unit equal to the expected gain on the Qth unit:

$$C_o \times F(Q) = C_u \times (1 - F(Q))$$

If we rearrange terms in the above equation, we get

$$F(Q) = \frac{C_u}{C_o + C_u} \qquad (9.1)$$

The profit-maximizing order quantity is the order quantity that satisfies the above equation. If you are familiar with calculus and would like to see a more mathematically rigorous derivation of the optimal order quantity, see Appendix D.

So how can we use equation (9.1) to actually find Q? Let's begin by just reading it. It says that the order quantity that maximizes expected profit is the order quantity Q such that demand is less than or equal to Q with probability $C_u/(C_o + C_u)$. That ratio with the underage and overage costs is called the *critical ratio.* We now have an explanation for why our forecast must be a distribution function. To choose the profit-maximizing order quantity, we need to find the quantity such that demand will be less than that quantity with a particular probability (the critical ratio). The mean alone (i.e., just a sales forecast) is insufficient to do that task.

---

[2] That statement might bother you. You might recall that $F(Q)$ is the probability demand is Q or lower. If demand is exactly Q, then the Qth unit will not be left in inventory. Hence, you might argue that it is more precise to say that $F(Q-1)$ is the probability the Qth unit is left in inventory. However, the normal distribution assumes demand can be any value, including values that are not integers. If you are willing to divide each demand into essentially an infinite number of fractional pieces, as is assumed by the normal, then $F(Q)$ is indeed the probability there is leftover inventory. With the empirical distribution function, we get the same answer, but it requires a slightly more complex logic that is beyond the scope of this text.

Let's begin with the easy part. We know for the Hammer 3/2 that $C_u = 70$ and $C_o = 20$, so the critical ratio is

$$\frac{C_u}{C_o + C_u} = \frac{70}{20 + 70} = 0.7778$$

We are making progress, but now comes the tricky part: We need to find the order quantity Q such that there is a 77.78 percent probability that demand is Q or lower.

Suppose we use the discrete distribution function from Table 9.3 as our demand forecast. Reading down the table, we see that $F(4{,}064) = 0.7576$ and $F(4{,}160) = 0.7879$. Therefore, the probability we are seeking, 0.7778, falls between two entries in the table, one that corresponds to an order quantity of 4,064 units, and the other that corresponds to 4,160 units. What should we do? The rule is simple, which we will call the *round-up rule:*

Round-up rule. Whenever you are looking up a target value in a table and the target value falls between two entries, choose the entry that leads to the larger order quantity.

In this case the larger quantity is 4,160 units. So if we use the discrete distribution function as our demand forecast, then the profit-maximizing order quantity is 4,160 units.

At this point you might not be entirely comfortable with the round-up rule. What if the critical ratio were 0.7577, which is just a hair above 0.7576? Your intuition might suggest ordering the lower entry value, 4,064 units. At the very least, maybe we should extrapolate. For example, suppose the critical ratio were 0.7728, which is half-way between 0.7576 and 0.7879. Extrapolation suggests ordering the average of the two quantities, 4,112 units. Nevertheless, there are two reasons why we should stick with the round-up rule. First, if the two quantities are reasonably close together (as they are here), then the difference in expected profit among these different order quantities is generally quite small. Second, in some cases extrapolation is not even feasible. For example, suppose the two quantities were 4 units and 5 units. It makes no sense to order 4.5 units. In those cases it can be shown that the higher order quantity always generates a higher expected profit. Thus, stick with the round-up rule and you will be fine.

So we have identified the optimal order quantity if the discrete distribution function is our demand forecast. Let's next consider what the optimal order is if the normal distribution is our demand forecast. This process with the normal distribution is quite similar to the process with a discrete distribution function. The only difference is that it has one additional step.

First, let's find the optimal order quantity if the standard normal is our demand forecast. Because the Standard Normal Distribution Function Table is a table like any other discrete distribution function, we already know how to do this. Just as before, we need to find the z in the table that satisfies the following equation: $\Phi(z) = C_u/(C_o + C_u)$, which is $\Phi(z) = 0.7778$ for the Hammer 3/2. In the table we see that $\Phi(0.76) = 0.7764$ and $\Phi(0.77) = 0.7794$, so we use the round-up rule and pick the larger z value, 0.77. So the optimal order quantity is 0.77 if the demand forecast is a standard normal.

Now that we have an answer for the standard normal distribution, we need to convert that answer into an order quantity for the actual normal distribution. (This is the additional step.) That conversion is done with the following equation:

$$Q = \mu + z \times \sigma$$

where μ = Mean of the normal distribution

σ = Standard deviation of the normal distribution

With the Hammer 3/2 we use the above to obtain $Q = 3{,}192 + 0.77 \times 1{,}181 = 4{,}101$. Exhibit 9.4 summarizes how to find the optimal order quantity.

Exhibit 9.4

A PROCEDURE TO FIND THE ORDER QUANTITY THAT MAXIMIZES EXPECTED PROFIT IN THE NEWSVENDOR MODEL

Step 1: Evaluate the critical ratio: $\dfrac{C_u}{C_o + C_u}$. In the case of the Hammer 3/2, the underage cost is $C_u = \text{Price} - \text{Cost}$ and the overage cost is $C_o = \text{Cost} - \text{Salvage value}$.

Step 2: If the demand forecast is a normal distribution with mean μ and standard deviation σ, then follow steps A and B:

A. Find the optimal order quantity if demand had a standard normal distribution. One method to achieve this is to find the z value in the Standard Normal Distribution Function Table such that

$$\Phi(z) = \frac{C_u}{C_o + C_u}$$

(If the critical ratio value does not exist in the table, then find the two z values that it falls between. For example, the critical ratio 0.7778 falls between $z = 0.76$ and $z = 0.77$. Then choose the larger of those two z values.) A second method is to use the Excel function Normsinv: $z = \text{Normsinv(Critical ratio)}$.

B. Convert z into the order quantity that maximizes expected profit, Q: $Q = \mu + z \times \sigma$

If the demand forecast is a discrete distribution function table (as with an empirical distribution function), then find the quantity in the table such that $F(Q) = \text{Critical ratio}$. If the critical ratio falls between two entries in the table, then choose the entry with the larger quantity.

An alternative to the process we just described is to use Excel to find the optimal order quantity. Just as before, the first step is to find the optimal order quantity for a standard normal via Excel's Normsinv function:

$$z = \text{Normsinv(Critical ratio)}$$

where the critical ratio is $C_u/(C_o + C_u)$. The second step is the same as before: Convert z into Q with the equation $Q = \mu + z \times \sigma$. Due to rounding issues, the Excel process might lead to a slightly different order quantity. For example, in Excel we get Normsinv(7/9) = 0.7647 and then $Q = 3{,}192 + 0.7647 \times 1{,}181 = 4{,}095.12$. The small difference between an order quantity of 4,101 and 4,095 should not matter much.

To summarize this section, we determined the key equation (9.1) for finding the order quantity that maximizes expected profit: With the profit-maximizing order quantity, the critical ratio is the probability demand will be that quantity or lower. Using the discrete distribution function table (Table 9.3), we found our target probability (the critical ratio) fell between two entries in the table. We used the round-up rule to choose the larger quantity. We also evaluated the optimal order quantity if our demand forecast is a normal distribution: Look up in the Standard Normal Distribution Function Table the optimal order quantity z as if demand follows a standard normal distribution and then convert z into the order quantity for the actual normal distribution. The first step in that process is identical to the process we use with the discrete distribution function, that is, look up z in the

Standard Normal Distribution Function Table just as you would look up Q in the discrete distribution function table. The second step (converting z into Q) is specific to the normal distribution.

9.5 Performance Measures

The previous section showed us how to find the order quantity that maximizes our expected profit. This section shows us how to evaluate a number of relevant performance measures. As Figure 9.6 indicates, these performance measures are closely related. For example, to evaluate expected leftover inventory, you first evaluate expected lost sales (which has up to three inputs: the order quantity, the loss function table, and the standard deviation of demand), then expected sales (which has two inputs: expected lost sales and expected demand), and then expected leftover inventory (which has two inputs: expected sales and the order quantity).

These performance measures can be evaluated for any order quantity, not just the expected profit-maximizing order quantity. To emphasize this point, this section evaluates these performance measures assuming 3,500 Hammer 3/2s are ordered. See Table 10.1 for the evaluation of these measures with the optimal order quantity, 4,101 units.

Expected Lost Sales

Let's begin with *expected lost sales,* which is the expected number of units demand (a random variable) exceeds the order quantity (a fixed threshold). (Because order quantities are measured in physical units, sales and lost sales are measured in physical units as well, not in monetary units.) For example, if we order 3,500 units of the Hammer but demand could have been high enough to sell 3,821 units, then we would lose $3,821 - 3,500 = 321$ units

FIGURE 9.6
The Relationships between Initial Input Parameters (boxes) and Performance Measures (ovals)
Note: Some performance measures require other performance measures as inputs; for example, expected sales requires expected demand and expected lost sales as inputs.

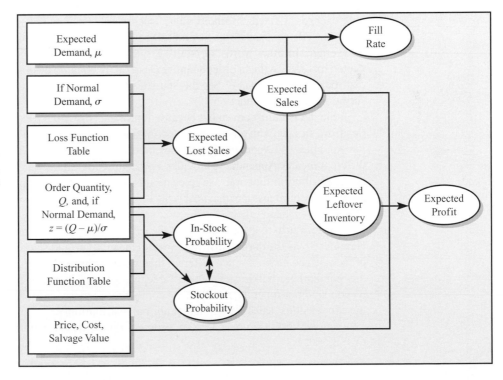

TABLE 9.5
Hammer 3/2's
Empirical
Distribution
and Loss Function

Q	F(Q)	L(Q)	Q	F(Q)	L(Q)	Q	F(Q)	L(Q)
800	0.0303	2392	2,592	0.3636	841	3,936	0.6970	191
1,184	0.0606	2020	2,624	0.3939	821	4,000	0.7273	171
1,792	0.0909	1448	2,752	0.4242	744	4,064	0.7576	154
1,792	0.1212	1448	3,040	0.4545	578	4,160	0.7879	131
1,824	0.1515	1420	3,104	0.4848	543	4,352	0.8182	90
1,888	0.1818	1366	3,136	0.5152	526	4,544	0.8485	55
2,048	0.2121	1235	3,264	0.5455	464	4,672	0.8788	36
2,144	0.2424	1160	3,456	0.5758	377	4,800	0.9091	20
2,208	0.2727	1111	3,680	0.6061	282	4,928	0.9394	8
2,304	0.3030	1041	3,744	0.6364	257	4,992	0.9697	5
2,560	0.3333	863	3,808	0.6667	233	5,120	1.0000	1

Q = Order quantity
$F(Q)$ = Probability demand is less than or equal to the order quantity
$L(Q)$ = Loss function (the expected amount demand exceeds Q)

of demand. Expected lost sales is the amount of demand that is not satisfied, which should be of interest to a manager even though the opportunity cost of lost sales does not show up explicitly on any standard accounting document.

Note that we are interested in the *expected* lost sales. Demand can be less than our order quantity, in which case lost sales is zero, or demand can exceed our order quantity, in which case lost sales is positive. Expected lost sales is the average of all of those events (the cases with no lost sales and all cases with positive lost sales).

How do we find expected lost sales for any given order quantity? Let's first suppose the discrete distribution function in Table 9.3 is our demand forecast. Table 9.5 replicates Table 9.3 and adds a column with the *loss function, L(Q)*, for each order quantity. The loss function of a random variable is the expected amount by which the outcome of the random variable exceeds a fixed threshold value, such as Q. For example, if O'Neill orders 2,592 Hammer 3/2s, then, according to Table 9.5, demand exceeds the order quantity by 841 units on average. In other words, O'Neill's expected lost sales is 841 units. To summarize, expected lost sales with an order quantity Q is exactly equal to the loss function of the demand distribution evaluated at Q. See the Statistics Tutorial in Appendix A for a more detailed description of the loss function.

Table 9.5 is quite convenient because it provides us with the expected lost sales with little effort. In fact, with any discrete distribution function, we need a loss function table similar to Table 9.5. Appendix B provides the loss function for the Poisson distribution with different means. Appendix C provides a procedure to evaluate the loss function for any discrete distribution function. We relegate this procedure to the appendix because it is computationally burdensome; that is, it is the kind of calculation you want to do on a spreadsheet rather than by hand.

Now let's turn to the evaluation of the expected lost sales if our demand forecast for the Hammer 3/2 is the normal distribution with mean 3,192 and standard deviation 1,181. That process is actually not much different than what we have already done: First we look up in the Standard Normal Loss Function Table the expected lost sales for the z-statistic that corresponds to our quantity, and then we convert the standard normal expected lost sales into the expected lost sales for our actual normal distribution.

Assume 3,500 Hammer 3/2s are ordered. First find the z-statistic that corresponds to $Q = 3,500$:

$$z = \frac{Q - \mu}{\sigma} = \frac{3,500 - 3,192}{1,181} = 0.26$$

Exhibit 9.5

EXPECTED LOST SALES EVALUATION PROCEDURE

If the demand forecast is a normal distribution with mean μ and standard deviation σ, then follow steps A through D:

A. Evaluate the z-statistic for the order quantity Q: $z = \dfrac{Q - \mu}{\sigma}$.

B. Use the z-statistic to look up in the Standard Normal Loss Function Table the expected lost sales, $L(z)$, with the standard normal distribution.

C. Expected lost sales $= \sigma \times L(z)$.

D. With Excel, expected lost sales can be evaluated with the following equation:

$$\text{Expected lost sales} = \sigma * (\text{Normdist}(z,0,1,0) - z * (1 - \text{Normsdist}(z)))$$

If the demand forecast is a discrete distribution function table (as with an empirical distribution function), then expected lost sales equals the loss function for the chosen order quantity, $L(Q)$. If the table does not include the loss function, then see Appendix C for how to evaluate it.

Now use the Standard Normal Loss Function Table in Appendix B to look up the expected lost sales if the order quantity is $z = 0.26$, $L(0.26) = 0.2824$. To convert the standard normal expected lost sales into the expected lost sales with our actual normal distribution, use the following equation:

$$\text{Expected lost sales} = \sigma \times L(z)$$

where $\qquad \sigma$ = Standard deviation of the normal distribution representing demand

$\qquad\qquad\qquad L(z)$ = Loss function with the standard normal distribution

Therefore, with 3,200 Hammer 3/2s we can expect to lose $1,181 \times 0.2824 = 334$ units of demand.

If you wish to avoid the Standard Normal Loss Function Table, then you can evaluate the loss function for the normal distribution in Excel with the following equation:

$$L(z) = \text{Normdist}(z,0,1,0) - z * (1 - \text{Normsdist}(z))$$

(If you are curious about the derivation of the above function, see Appendix D.) The process of evaluating expected lost sales for both a discrete distribution and the normal distribution is summarized in Exhibit 9.5.

Expected Sales

Expected sales is clearly something of interest to a manager. Each unit of demand results in either a sale or a lost sale, so

$$\text{Expected Sales} + \text{Expected lost Sales} = \text{Expected demand}$$

We already know expected demand: It is the mean of the demand distribution, μ. Rearrange terms in the above equation and we get

$$\text{Expected sales} = \mu - \text{Expected lost sales}$$

Therefore, the procedure to evaluate expected sales begins by evaluating expected lost sales. See Exhibit 9.6 for a summary of this procedure.

Exhibit 9.6

EXPECTED SALES, EXPECTED LEFTOVER INVENTORY, EXPECTED PROFIT, AND FILL RATE EVALUATION PROCEDURES

Step 1. Evaluate expected lost sales (see Exhibit 9.5). All of these performance measures can be evaluated directly in terms of expected lost sales and several known parameters: μ = Expected demand; Q = Order quantity; Price; Cost; and Salvage value.

Step 2. Use the following equations to evaluate the performance measure of interest.

$$\text{Expected sales} = \mu - \text{Expected lost sales}$$

$$\text{Expected leftover inventory} = Q - \text{Expected sales}$$

$$= Q - \mu + \text{Expected lost sales}$$

$$\text{Expected profit} = [(\text{Price} - \text{Cost}) \times \text{Expected sales}]$$

$$- [(\text{Cost} - \text{Salvage value}) \times \text{Expected leftover inventory}]$$

$$\text{Fill rate} = \text{Expected Sales}/\mu = 1 - (\text{Expected lost sales}/\mu)$$

Let's evaluate expected sales if 3,500 Hammers are ordered and the normal distribution is our demand forecast. We already evaluated expected lost sales to be 334 units. Therefore, Expected sales = 3,192 − 334 = 2,858 units.

Notice that expected sales is always less than expected demand (because expected lost sales is never negative). In other words, you can never expect to sell your demand forecast: While you might get lucky and sell more than the mean demand, on average you cannot sell more than the mean demand.

Expected Leftover Inventory

Expected leftover inventory is the average amount that demand (a random variable) is less than the order quantity (a fixed threshold). (In contrast, expected lost sales is the average amount by which demand exceeds the order quantity.)

Leftover inventory is a visibly explicit cost associated with a mismatch between demand and supply. Because every unit purchased is either sold or left over in inventory at the end of the season, the following equation is true:

$$\text{Expected sales} + \text{Expected leftover inventory} = Q$$

We know the right-hand side of the above equation, the quantity purchased Q. Therefore, we can easily evaluate expected leftover inventory once we have evaluated expected sales. See Exhibit 9.6 for a summary of this procedure.

If the demand forecast is a normal distribution and 3,500 Hammers are ordered, then expected leftover inventory is 3,500 − 2,858 = 642 units, because we evaluated expected sales to be 2,858 units.

It may seem surprising that expected leftover inventory and expected lost sales can both be positive. While in any particular season there is either leftover inventory or lost sales, but not both, we are interested in the expectation of those measures over all possible outcomes. Therefore, each *expectation* can be positive.

Expected Profit

We have already shown how to evaluate the order quantity that maximizes expected profit, so it is natural that we should also be able to evaluate the expected profit. We earn Price − Cost on each unit sold and we lose Cost − Salvage value on each unit we do not sell, so our expected profit is

$$\text{Expected Profit} = [(\text{Price} - \text{Cost}) \times \text{Expected sales}]$$

$$- [(\text{Cost} - \text{Salvage value}) \times \text{Expected leftover inventory}]$$

Therefore, we can evaluate expected profit after we have evaluated expected sales and leftover inventory. See Exhibit 9.6 for a summary of this procedure.

With an order quantity of 3,500 units and a normal distribution demand forecast, the expected profit for the Hammer 3/2 is

$$\text{Expected Profit} = (\$70 \times 2{,}858) - (\$20 \times 642) = \$187{,}221$$

Fill Rate

The fill rate is the expected ratio of satisfied demand (i.e., sales) to total demand:

$$\text{Fill rate} = \frac{\text{Expected sales}}{\text{Expected demand}} = \frac{\text{Expected sales}}{\mu}$$

In other words, the fill rate is the percentage of demand that is satisfied. The fill rate is a measure of customer service: The higher the fill rate, the more likely a customer will find a unit available to purchase. See Exhibit 9.6 for the procedure to evaluate the fill rate. With an order of 3,500 Hammer 3/2s and the normal distribution demand forecast, O'Neill's fill rate is 2,858/3,192 = 89.6 percent.

In-Stock Probability and Stockout Probability

The fill rate is one measure of customer service, but it is not the only potential measure of customer service. The in-stock probability is the probability the firm ends the season having satisfied all demand. (Equivalently, the in-stock probability is the probability the firm has stock available for every customer.) That occurs if demand is less than the order quantity,

$$\text{In-stock probability} = F(Q)$$

The stockout probability is the probability the firm stocks out for some customer during the selling season (i.e., a lost sale occurs). Because the firm stocks out if demand exceeds the order quantity,

$$\text{Stockout probability} = 1 - F(Q)$$

(The firm either stocks out or it does not, so the stockout probability equals 1 minus the probability demand is Q or lower.) We also can see that the stockout probability and the in-stock probability are closely related:

$$\text{Stockout probability} = 1 - \text{In-stock probability}$$

See Exhibit 9.7 for a summary of the procedure to evaluate these probabilities. With an order quantity of 3,500 Hammers, the z-statistic is $z = (3{,}500 - 3{,}192)/1{,}181 = 0.26$. From the Standard Normal Distribution Function Table, we find $\Phi(0.26) = 0.6026$, so the in-stock probability is 60.26 percent. The stockout probability is $1 - 0.6026 = 39.74$ percent.

Exhibit 9.7

IN-STOCK PROBABILITY AND STOCKOUT PROBABILITY EVALUATION

If the demand forecast is a normal distribution with mean μ and standard deviation σ, then follow steps A through D:

A. Evaluate the z-statistic for the order quantity: $z = \dfrac{Q - \mu}{\sigma}$.

B. Use the z-statistic to look up in the Standard Normal Distribution Function Table the probability the standard normal demand is z or lower, $\Phi(z)$.

C. In-stock probability $= \Phi(z)$ and Stockout probability $= 1 - \Phi(z)$.

D. In Excel, In-stock probability $=$ Normsdist(z) and Stockout probability $= 1 -$ Normsdist(z).

If the demand forecast is a discrete distribution function table (as with an empirical distribution function), then In-stock probability $= F(Q)$ and Stockout probability $= 1 - F(Q)$, where $F(Q)$ is the probability demand is Q or lower.

Notice that O'Neill satisfies nearly 90 percent of its demand (the fill rate) with the order quantity 3,500, but stocks out with nearly a 40 percent probability and only has an in-stock probability of 60 percent. Figure 9.7 displays the in-stock probability and fill rate for a wide range of order quantities for the Hammer 3/2, assuming the normal distribution is the demand forecast.

How is it possible for the in-stock probability to be so low while the fill rate is so high? The in-stock probability is approximately the fill rate at the very end of the season: It is the probability that a customer's demand can be satisfied at the end of the season. Most of the customers during the season can be satisfied (resulting in a high fill rate) even if the poor customer at the end of the season experiences a stockout (resulting in a low in-stock probability).

FIGURE 9.7

In-Stock Probability and Fill Rate for the Hammer 3/2 with a Normal Distribution Demand Forecast

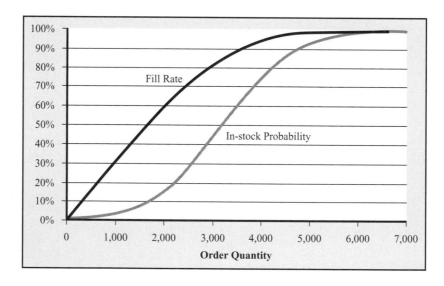

This discussion raises the following question: Which is the better measure of customer service, the fill rate or the in-stock probability? The fill rate is a good measure of average customer service since it treats each customer as equally important. The in-stock probability is a conservative measure of customer service because it is the fill rate when the fill rate is expected to be at its worst, that is, at the end of the season. Therefore, neither measure dominates the other in all situations. A catalog retailer's customers probably do not expect a high fill rate late in the Christmas season, so a stockout the week before Christmas might not have a significant long-run impact on customer goodwill. However, a grocery retailer probably does not want to be out of stock on most items at the end of the day, because certain customers are only able to do their grocery shopping at that time. Therefore, the fill rate may be more appropriate for the catalog retailer, whereas the in-stock probability may be more appropriate for the grocery retailer.

9.6   Other Objectives for Choosing an Order Quantity

Maximizing expected profit is surely a reasonable objective for choosing an order quantity, but it is not the only objective. As we saw in the previous section, the expected profit-maximizing order quantity may generate an unacceptable fill rate or in-stock probability from the firm's customer service perspective. This section explains how to determine an order quantity that satisfies a customer service objective, in terms of either a minimum fill rate or in-stock probability.

Let's begin with the objective of choosing an order quantity to achieve a target fill rate. For example, suppose O'Neill insists that all products have a 99 percent fill rate. In that case, we need to find the order quantity for the Hammer 3/2 that generates a 99 percent fill rate.

In the previous section we started with an order quantity and evaluated the fill rate. Now we need to reverse that process, that is, start with a fill rate and end up with an order quantity. This requires a couple of algebraic gymnastics. Let's start with the fill rate equation,

$$\text{Fill rate} = \frac{\text{Expected sales}}{\mu}$$

Recall that

$$\text{Expected sales} = \mu - \text{Expected lost sales}$$

If we combine the above two equations and rearrange terms, we get

$$\text{Expected lost sales} = \mu \times (1 - \text{Fill rate}) \tag{9.2}$$

Suppose the discrete distribution is our demand forecast (Table 9.5). We can evaluate the right-hand side of the above equation: $(1 - 0.99) \times 3{,}192 = 31.92$. Therefore, we want to find a Q such that the expected lost sales with that quantity is 31.92 units. Looking at Table 9.5, we see that $L(4{,}672) = 36$ and $L(4{,}800) = 20$. Therefore, an order quantity of 4,672 would yield an expected lost sales slightly above our target (36 versus 31.92), while the larger order quantity of 4,800 would yield an expected lost sales slightly below our target (20 versus 31.92). We again shall follow our round-up rule: When the target value falls between two values in a table, choose the entry with the larger quantity. In this case, we round up to the order quantity 4,800. Therefore, if we order 4,800 Hammer 3/2s and the discrete distribution is our demand forecast, then our fill rate will be at least 99 percent.

Exhibit 9.8

A PROCEDURE TO DETERMINE AN ORDER QUANTITY THAT SATISFIES A TARGET FILL RATE

If the demand forecast is a normal distribution with mean μ and standard deviation σ, then follow steps A through C:

A. Evaluate the target $L(z)$,

$$L(z) = \left(\frac{\mu}{\sigma}\right) \times (1 - \text{Fill rate})$$

B. Find the z-statistic in the Standard Normal Loss Function Table that corresponds to the target $L(z)$. If $L(z)$ falls between two z values in the table, choose the higher z value.

C. Convert the chosen z-statistic into the order quantity that satisfies our target fill rate, $Q = \mu + z \times \sigma$.

If the demand forecast is a discrete distribution function table (as with an empirical distribution function), then follow steps D and E:

D. Evaluate the target expected lost sales:

$$\text{Expected lost sales} = \mu \times (1 - \text{Fill rate})$$

E. Find the order quantity in the expected lost sales table that generates the target expected lost sales evaluated in step D. If the target expected lost sales falls between two entries in the table, choose the entry with the larger order quantity. If your table does not include expected lost sales, use the procedure in Appendix C to evaluate them.

Just to double-check our decision, we can evaluate the fill rate with the order quantity 4,800 and discover that we indeed make our target:

$$\text{Fill rate} = \frac{\text{Expected sales}}{\mu} = \frac{\mu - \text{Expected lost sales}}{\mu} = \frac{3{,}192 - 20}{3{,}192} = 99.37 \text{ percent}$$

How do we find an order quantity if our demand forecast is a normal distribution? Again, the process is quite similar, but we need to work with the standard normal. Remember that with a normal distribution

$$\text{Expected lost sales} = \sigma \times L(z)$$

If we combine the above equation with equation (9.2) and rearrange terms, we get

$$L(z) = \left(\frac{\mu}{\sigma}\right) \times (1 - \text{Fill rate})$$

Therefore, we first evaluate the right-hand side of the above equation, then look up $L(z)$ in the Standard Normal Loss Function Table, and then convert our z back into Q. The right-hand side of the above equation is $(3{,}192/1{,}181) \times (1 - 0.99) = 0.0270$. We now need to find a z-statistic such that $L(z) = 0.0270$. Looking in the Standard Normal Loss Function Table, we see that $L(1.53) = 0.0274$ and $L(1.54) = 0.0267$. Use our round-up rule again and choose $z = 1.54$, which generates $L(1.54) = 0.0267$. To finish our process, convert our z-statistic into an order quantity with the equation $Q = \mu + z \times \sigma$, so our order quantity is $3{,}192 + 1.54 \times 1{,}181 = 5{,}011$. In other words, if our demand forecast is

Exhibit 9.9

the normal distribution, then we need to order 5,011 Hammer 3/2s to achieve a 99 percent fill rate. Exhibit 9.8 summarizes the process for finding an order quantity to satisfy a target fill rate.

As we have already discovered, the fill rate and the in-stock probability are not the same for any order quantity. Therefore, a firm may prefer the more conservative in-stock probability requirement. For example, let's now suppose O'Neill wants to find the order quantity that generates a 99 percent in-stock probability with the Hammer 3/2. It turns out that this objective is easier to work with than the target fill rate objective.

The in-stock probability is $F(Q)$. So we need to find an order quantity such that there is a 99 percent probability that demand is that order quantity or lower. If the discrete distribution function is our demand forecast, then we look in Table 9.3 (or Table 9.5) and see $F(4,992) = 0.9697$ and $F(5,120) = 1.0000$. The round-up rule suggests that we need to order 5,120 Hammer 3/2s to achieve a 99 percent in-stock probability.

If our demand forecast is normally distributed, then we first find the z-statistic that achieves our objective with the standard normal distribution. In the Standard Normal Distribution Function Table, we see that $\Phi(2.32) = 0.9898$ and $\Phi(2.33) = 0.9901$. Again, we choose the higher z-statistic, so our desired order quantity is now $Q = \mu + z \times \sigma = 3,192 + 2.33 \times 1,181 = 5,944$. Notice that a substantially higher order quantity is needed to generate a 99 percent in-stock probability than a 99 percent fill rate (5,944 vs. 5,011) and both order quantities are substantially higher than the one that maximizes expected profit (4,101). Exhibit 9.9 summarizes the process for finding an order quantity to satisfy a target fill rate.

9.7 Managerial Lessons

Now that we have detailed the process of implementing the newsvendor model, it is worthwhile to step back and consider the managerial lessons it implies.

With respect to the forecasting process, there are three key lessons.

• For each product, it is insufficient to have just a forecast of expected demand. We also need a forecast for how variable demand will be about the forecast. That uncertainty in the forecast is captured by the standard deviation of demand.

• It is important to track actual demand. Two common mistakes are made with respect to this issue. First, do not forget that actual demand may be greater than actual sales due to an inventory shortage. If it is not possible to track actual demand after a stockout occurs, then you should attempt a reasonable estimate of actual demand. Second, actual demand includes potential sales only at the regular price. If you sold 1,000 units in the previous season, but 600 of them were at the discounted price at the end of the season, then actual demand is closer to 400 than 1,000.

• You need to keep track of past forecasts and forecast errors in order to assess the standard deviation of demand. Without past data on forecasts and forecast errors, it is very difficult to choose reasonable standard deviations; it is hard enough to forecast the mean of a distribution, but forecasting the standard deviation of a distribution is nearly impossible with just a "gut feel." Unfortunately, many firms fail to maintain the data they need to implement the newsvendor model correctly. They might not record the data because it is an inherently undesirable task to keep track of past errors: Who wants to have a permanent record of the big forecasting goofs? Alternatively, firms may not realize the importance of such data and therefore do not go through the effort to record and maintain it.

There are also a number of important lessons from the order quantity choice process.

• The profit-maximizing order quantity generally does not equal expected demand. If the underage cost is greater than the overage cost (i.e., it is more expensive to lose a sale than it is to have leftover inventory), then the profit-maximizing order quantity is larger than expected demand. (Because then the critical ratio is greater than 0.50.) On the other hand, some products may have an overage cost that is larger than the underage cost. For such products, it is actually best to order less than the expected demand.

• The order quantity decision should be separated from the forecasting process. The goal of the forecasting process is to develop the best forecast for a product's demand and therefore should proceed without regard to the order quantity decision. This can be frustrating for some firms. Imagine the marketing department dedicates considerable effort to develop a forecast and then the operations department decides to produce a quantity above the forecast. The marketing department may feel that their efforts are being ignored or their expertise is being second-guessed. In addition, they may be concerned that they would be responsible for ensuring that all of the production is sold even though their forecast was more conservative. The separation between the forecasting and the order quantity decision also implies that two products with the same mean forecast may have different expected profit-maximizing order quantities, either because they have different critical ratios or because they have different standard deviations.

• Explicit costs should not be overemphasized relative to opportunity costs. Inventory at the end of the season is the explicit cost of a demand–supply mismatch, while lost sales are the opportunity cost. Overemphasizing the former relative to the latter will cause you to order less than the profit-maximizing order quantity.

• It is important to recognize that choosing an order quantity to maximize expected profit is only one possible objective. It is also a very reasonable objective, but there can be situations in which a manager way wish to consider an alternative objective. For example, maximizing expected profit is wise if you are not particularly concerned with the variability of profit. If you are managing many different products so that the realized profit from any one product cannot cause undue hardship on the firm, then maximizing expected profit is a good objective to adopt. But if you are a startup firm with a single product and limited capital, then you might not be able to absorb a significant profit loss. In situations in which the variability of profit matters, it is prudent to order less than the profit-maximizing order quantity. The expected profit objective also does not consider customer service explicitly in its objective. With the expected profit-maximizing order quantity for the Hammer 3/2, the fill rate is about 95 percent and the in-stock probability is about 78 percent. Some managers may feel this is an unacceptable level of customer service, fearing that unsatisfied customers will switch to a competitor.

- Finally, while it is impossible to perfectly match supply and demand when supply must be chosen before random demand, it is possible to make a smart choice that balances the cost of ordering too much with the cost of ordering too little. In other words, uncertainty should not invite ad hoc decision making.

9.8
Summary

The newsvendor model is a tool for making a decision when there is a "too much–too little" challenge: Bet too much and there is a cost (e.g., leftover inventory), but bet too little and there is a different cost (e.g., the opportunity cost of lost sales). (See Table 9.6 for a summary of the key notation and equations.) To make this trade-off effectively, it is necessary to have a complete forecast of demand. It is not enough to just have a single sales forecast; we need to know the potential variation about that sales forecast.

In the case of O'Neill's Hammer 3/2 wetsuit, we discovered that there exists an order quantity that maximizes expected profit, but that quantity might not lead to a desirable level of customer service. In other words, there is a trade-off between profit and service. This trade-off is illustrated in Figure 9.8. While the newsvendor optimal quantity leads to an outcome in the upper-left-hand side of the trade-off curve, we also developed methods for moving down and to the right along the curve, that is, to a higher service level, albeit at a lower profit level. We see that achieving a very high in-stock probability can be quite expensive, but because the curve is relatively flat at its top, it is possible to increase service without much of a profit sacrifice. This curve allows a manager to determine the correct position for the firm.

TABLE 9.6
Summary of Key Notation and Equations in Chapter 9

Q = Order quantity C_u = Underage cost C_o = Overage cost   Critical ratio = $\dfrac{C_u}{C_o + C_u}$

μ = Expected demand σ = Standard deviation of demand

$F(Q)$: Distribution function $\Phi(Q)$: Distribution function of the standard normal

Expected actual demand = Expected A/F ratio $\times$ Forecast

Standard deviation of actual demand = Standard deviation of A/F ratios $\times$ Forecast

Expected profit-maximizing order quantity: $F(Q) = \dfrac{C_u}{C_o + C_u}$

z-statistic or normalized order quantity: $z = \dfrac{Q - \mu}{\sigma}$

$Q = \mu + z \times \sigma$

$L(z)$ = Expected lost sales with the standard normal distribution

Expected lost sales = $\sigma \times L(z)$ Expected sales = μ − Expected lost sales

Expected leftover inventory = Q − Expected sales

Expected profit = [(Price − Cost) $\times$ Expected sales]
        − [(Cost − Salvage value) $\times$ Expected leftover inventory]

Fill rate = Expected sales/μ

In-stock probability = $F(Q)$ Stockout probability = 1 − In-stock probability

To achieve a fill rate with normally distributed demand, $L(z) = (\mu/\sigma) \times (1 − \text{Fill Rate})$,

otherwise, target expected lost sales = $\mu \times (1 − \text{Fill Rate})$

FIGURE 9.8
The Trade-off between Profit and Service with the Hammer 3/2
The circle indicates the in-stock probability and the expected profit of the optimal order quantity, 4,101 units.

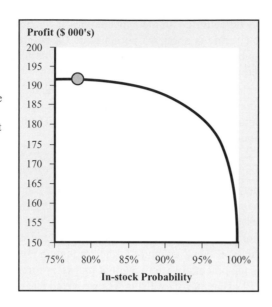

9.9 Further Reading

The newsvendor model is one of the most extensively studied models in operations management. It has been extended theoretically along numerous dimensions (e.g., multiple periods have been studied, the pricing decision has been included, the salvage values could depend on the quantity salvaged, the decision maker's tolerance for risk can be incorporated into the objective function, etc.)

Several textbooks provide more technical treatments of the newsvendor model than this chapter. See Nahmias (2001), Porteus (2002), or Silver, Pyke, and Peterson (1998).

For a review of the theoretical literature on the newsvendor model, with an emphasis on the pricing decision in a newsvendor setting, see Petruzzi and Dada (1999).

9.10 Practice Problems

Q9.1* **(McClure Books)** Dan McClure owns a thriving independent bookstore in artsy New Hope, Pennsylvania. He must decide how many copies to order of a new book, *Power and Self-Destruction*, an exposé on a famous politician's lurid affairs. Interest in the book will be intense at first and then fizzle quickly as attention turns to other celebrities. The book's retail price is $20 and the wholesale price is $12. The publisher will buy back the retailer's leftover copies at a full refund, but McClure Books incurs $4 in shipping and handling costs for each book returned to the publisher. Dan believes his demand forecast can be represented by a normal distribution with mean 200 and standard deviation 80.

a. Dan will consider this book to be a blockbuster for him if it sells more than 400 units. What is the probability *Power and Self-Destruction* will be a blockbuster?

b. Dan considers a book a "dog" if it sells less than 50 percent of his mean forecast. What is the probability this exposé is a "dog"?

c. What is the probability demand for this book will be within 20 percent of the mean forecast?

d. What order quantity maximizes Dan's expected profit?

e. Dan prides himself on good customer service. In fact, his motto is "McClure's got what you want to read." What order quantity should he choose to satisfy a 95 percent fill rate?

f. How many books should Dan order if he wants to achieve a 95 percent in-stock probability?

(* indicates that the solution is in Appendix E)

g. If Dan orders the quantity chosen in part f to achieve a 95 percent in-stock probability, then what is the probability that "Dan won't have what some customer wants to read" (i.e., what is the probability some customer won't be able to purchase a copy of the book)?

h. Suppose Dan orders 300 copies of the book. What would Dan's expected profit be in this case?

i. Suppose Dan orders 150 copies of the book. What would Dan's fill rate be in this case?

j. Being an introspective chap, Dan decided to evaluate his forecasting skills in his spare time. He collected the following data on recent books he felt matched the characteristics of *Power and Self-Destruction*. If Dan used these data to construct an empirical distribution function, then what would be his optimal order quantity? (Assume Dan's initial forecast is 200 units.)

Book	Actual Demand	Forecast	A/F Ratio	Book	Actual Demand	Forecast	A/F Ratio
1	27	100	0.27	9	88	100	0.88
2	209	170	1.23	10	57	70	0.81
3	83	160	0.52	11	188	140	1.34
4	77	100	0.77	12	157	130	1.21
5	205	150	1.37	13	65	110	0.59
6	228	190	1.20	14	135	170	0.79
7	12	60	0.20	15	155	160	0.97
8	88	60	1.47	16	82	90	0.91

Q 9.2* **(Pony Express Creations)** Pony Express Creations Inc. (www.pony-ex.com) is a manufacturer of party hats, primarily for the Halloween season. (80 percent of their yearly sales occur over a six-week period.) One of their popular products is the Elvis wig, complete with sideburns and metallic glasses. The Elvis wig is produced in China, so Pony Express must make a single order well in advance of the upcoming season. Ryan, the owner of Pony Express, expects demand to be 25,000 and the following is his entire demand forecast:

Q	Prob(D = Q)	F(Q)	L(Q)
5,000	0.0183	0.0183	20,000
10,000	0.0733	0.0916	15,092
15,000	0.1465	0.2381	10,550
20,000	0.1954	0.4335	6,740
25,000	0.1954	0.6289	3,908
30,000	0.1563	0.7852	2,052
35,000	0.1042	0.8894	978
40,000	0.0595	0.9489	425
45,000	0.0298	0.9787	170
50,000	0.0132	0.9919	63
55,000	0.0053	0.9972	22
60,000	0.0019	0.9991	8
65,000	0.0006	0.9997	4
70,000	0.0002	0.9999	2
75,000	0.0001	1.0000	2

Prob($D = Q$) = Probability demand D equals Q
$F(Q)$ = Probability demand is Q or lower
$L(Q)$ = Expected lost sales if Q units are ordered

The Elvis wig retails for $25, but Pony Express's wholesale price is $12. Their production cost is $6. Leftover inventory can be sold to discounters for $2.50.

a. Suppose Pony Express orders 40,000 Elvis wigs. What is the chance they have to liquidate 10,000 or more wigs with a discounter?

b. What order quantity maximizes Pony Express's expected profit?

c. If Pony Express wants to have a 90 percent fill rate, then how many Elvis wigs should be ordered?

d. If Pony Express orders the quantity chosen in part c, what is Pony Express's actual fill rate?

e. If Pony Express wants to have a 90 percent in-stock probability, then how many Elvis wigs should be ordered?

f. If Pony Express orders 50,000 units, then how many wigs can they expect to have to liquidate with discounters?

g. If Pony Express insists on a 100 percent in-stock probability for its customers, then what is its expected profit?

Q 9.3* **(Flextrola)** Flextrola, Inc., an electronics systems integrator, is planning to design a key component for their next-generation product with Solectrics. Flextrola will integrate the component with some software and then sell it to consumers. Given the short life cycles of such products and the long lead times quoted by Solectrics, Flextrola only has one opportunity to place an order with Solectrics prior to the beginning of its selling season. Flextrola's demand during the season is normally distributed with a mean of 1,000 and a standard deviation of 600.

Solectrics' production cost for the component is $52 per unit, and it plans to sell the component for $72 per unit to Flextrola. Flextrola incurs essentially no cost associated with the software integration and handling of each unit. Flextrola sells these units to consumers for $121 each. Flextrola can sell unsold inventory at the end of the season in a secondary electronics market for $50 each. The existing contract specifies that once Flextrola places the order, no changes are allowed to it. Also, Solectrics does not accept any returns of unsold inventory, so Flextrola must dispose of excess inventory in the secondary market.

a. What is the probability that Flextrola's demand will be within 25 percent of its forecast?

b. What is the probability that Flextrola's demand will be more than 40 percent greater than its forecast?

c. Under this contract, how many units should Flextrola order to maximize its expected profit?

For parts d through i, assume Flextrola orders 1,200 units.

d. What is Flextrola's expected sales?

e. How many units of inventory can Flextrola expect to sell in the secondary electronics market?

f. What is Flextrola's expected gross margin percentage, which is (Revenue – Cost)/ Revenue?

g. What is Flextrola's expected profit?

h. What is Solectrics' expected profit?

i. What is the probability that Flextrola has lost sales of 400 units or more?

j. A sharp manager at Flextrola noticed the demand forecast and became wary of assuming that demand is normally distributed. She plotted a histogram of demands from previous seasons for similar products and concluded that demand is better represented by the log normal distribution. Figure 9.9 plots the density function for both the log normal and the normal distribution, each with mean of 1,000 and standard deviation of 600. Figure 9.10 plots the distribution function for both the log normal and the normal. Using the more accurate forecast (i.e., the log normal distribution), approximately how many units should Flextrola order to maximize its expected profit?

FIGURE 9.9
Density Function

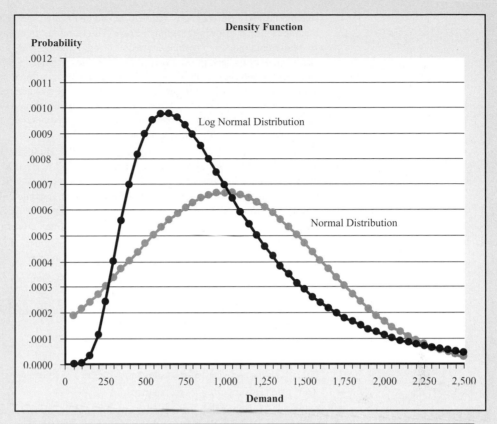

FIGURE 9.10
Distribution Function

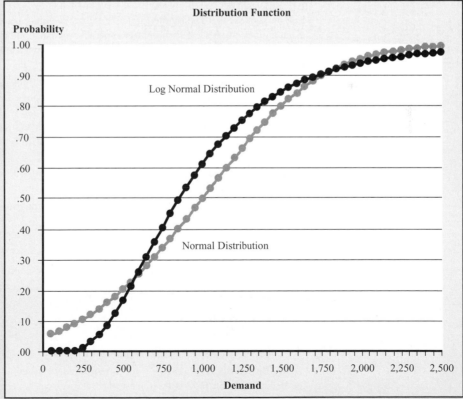

Q 9.4   **(Fashionables)** Fashionables is a franchisee of The Limited, the well-known retailer of fashionable clothing. Prior to the winter season, The Limited offers Fashionables the choice of five different colors of a particular sweater design. The sweaters are knit overseas by hand, and because of the lead times involved, Fashionables will need to order its assortment in advance of the selling season. As per the contracting terms offered by The Limited, Fashionables also will not be able to cancel, modify, or reorder sweaters during the selling season. Demand for each color during the season is normally distributed with a mean of 500 and a standard deviation of 200. Further, you may assume that the demands for each sweater are independent of those for a different color.

The Limited offers the sweaters to Fashionables at the wholesale price of $40 per sweater, and Fashionables plans to sell each sweater at the retail price of $70 per unit. The Limited delivers orders placed by Fashionables in truckloads at a cost of $2,000 per truckload. The transportation cost of $2,000 is borne by Fashionables. Assume unless otherwise specified that all the sweaters ordered by Fashionables will fit into one truckload. Also assume that all other associated costs, such as unpacking and handling, are negligible.

The Limited does not accept any returns of unsold inventory. However, Fashionables can sell all of the unsold sweaters at the end of the season at the fire-sale price of $20 each.

a. How many units of each sweater type should Fashionables order to maximize its expected profit?

b. If Fashionables wishes to ensure a 97.5 percent in-stock probability, what should its order quantity be for each type of sweater?

c. If Fashionables wishes to ensure a 97.5 percent fill rate, what should its order quantity be for each type of sweater?

For parts d through f, assume Fashionables orders 725 of each sweater.

d. What is Fashionables' expected profit?

e. What is Fashionables' expected fill rate for each sweater?

f. What is the stockout probability for each sweater?

g. Now suppose that The Limited announces that the unit of truckload capacity is 2,500 total units of sweaters. If Fashionables orders more than 2,500 units in total (actually, from 2,501 to 5,000 units in total), it will have to pay for two truckloads. What now is Fashionables' optimal order quantity for each sweater?

Q 9.5   **(Teddy Bower Parkas)** Teddy Bower is an outdoor clothing and accessories chain that purchases a line of parkas at $10 each from its Asian supplier, TeddySports. Unfortunately, at the time of order placement, demand is still uncertain. Teddy Bower forecasts that its demand is normally distributed with mean of 2,100 and standard deviation of 1,200. Teddy Bower sells these parkas at $22 each. Unsold parkas have little salvage value; Teddy Bower simply gives them away to a charity.

a. What is the probability this parka turns out to be a "dog," defined as a product that sells less than half of the forecast?

b. How many parkas should Teddy Bower buy from TeddySports to maximize expected profit?

c. If Teddy Bower wishes to ensure a 98.5 percent fill rate, how many parkas should it order?

d. If Teddy Bower wishes to ensure a 98.5 percent in-stock probability, how many parkas should it order?

For parts e through g, assume Teddy Bower orders 3,000 parkas.

e. Evaluate Teddy Bower's expected profit.

f. Evaluate Teddy Bower's fill rate.

g. Evaluate Teddy Bower's stockout probability

Q 9.6   **(Teddy Bower Boots)** To ensure a full line of outdoor clothing and accessories, the marketing department at Teddy Bower insists that they also sell waterproof hunting boots. Unfortunately, neither Teddy Bower nor TeddySports has expertise in manufacturing those kinds of boots. Therefore, Teddy Bower contacted several Taiwanese suppliers to request quotes. Due to competition, Teddy Bower knows that it cannot sell these boots for more than $54. However, $40 per boot was the best quote from the suppliers. In addition, Teddy Bower anticipates excess inventory will need to be sold off at a 50 percent discount at the end of the season. Given the $54 price, Teddy Bower's demand forecast is for 400 boots, with a standard deviation of 300.

a. If Teddy Bower decides to include these boots in its assortment, how many boots should it order from its supplier?

b. Suppose Teddy Bower orders 380 boots. What would its fill rate be?

c. Suppose Teddy Bower orders 380 boots. What would its expected profit be?

d. The marketing department will not be happy with the planned order quantity (from part a). They are likely to argue that Teddy Bower is a service-oriented company that requires a high fill rate. In particular, they insist that Teddy Bower order enough boots to have at least a 98 percent fill rate. What order quantity yields a 98 percent fill rate for Teddy Bower?

e. What would Teddy Bower's expected profit be with the order quantity from part d?

f. John Briggs, a buyer in the procurement department, overheard at lunch a discussion of the "boot problem." He suggested that Teddy Bower ask for a quantity discount from the supplier. After following up on his suggestion, the supplier responded that Teddy Bower could get a 10 percent discount if they were willing to order at least 800 boots. If the objective is to maximize expected profit, how many boots should it order given this new offer?

g. After getting involved with the "boot problem," John Briggs became curious about using A/F ratios to forecast. He directed his curiosity to another product, Teddy Bower's standard hunting boot, which has a demand forecast for 1,000 units. This boot sells for $55, and because of Teddy Bower's volume, the supplier of this boot only charges $30. The standard hunting boot never goes out of style (therefore, all leftover boots will be sold next year, but it is a seasonal product). It costs Teddy Bower $2.50 to hold a boot over from one season to the season in the following year. Furthermore, Teddy Bower anticipates that the selling price and procurement cost of this boot will be the same next year (i.e., $55 and $30, respectively). He collected the following data on 20 items that he felt were similar in nature to hunting boots. Using these data collected by John Briggs, what is Teddy Bower's profit-maximizing order quantity?

Item	Actual Demand	Forecast	A/F Ratio	Item	Actual Demand	Forecast	A/F Ratio
1	2,512	2,041	1.23	11	1,317	1,667	0.79
2	1,003	916	1.09	12	366	1,216	0.30
3	32	264	0.12	13	1,009	1,266	0.80
4	829	1,471	0.56	14	1,501	778	1.93
5	95	1,946	0.05	15	1,918	1,599	1.20
6	2,122	1,184	1.79	16	2,306	2,042	1.13
7	165	418	0.39	17	2,058	1,170	1.76
8	769	1,514	0.51	18	794	1,607	0.49
9	1,120	595	1.88	19	552	323	1.71
10	762	872	0.87	20	638	801	0.80

Q 9.7   (**Land's End**) Geoff Gullo owns a small firm that manufactures "Gullo Sunglasses." He has the opportunity to sell a particular seasonal model to Land's End. Geoff offers Land's End two purchasing options:

• Option 1.   Geoff offers to set his price at $65 and agrees to credit Land's End $53 for each unit Land's End returns to Geoff at the end of the season (because those units did not sell). Since styles change each year, there is essentially no value in the returned merchandise.

- Option 2.   Geoff offers a price of $55 for each unit, but returns are no longer accepted. In this case, Land's End throws out unsold units at the end of the season.

This season's demand for this model will be normally distributed with mean of 200 and standard deviation of 125. Land's End will sell those sunglasses for $100 each. Geoff's production cost is $25.

a.   How much would Land's End buy if they chose option 1?

b.   How much would Land's End buy if they chose option 2?

c.   Which option will Land's End choose?

d.   Suppose Land's End chooses option 1 and orders 275 units. What is Geoff Gullo's expected profit?

Q 9.8   **(Three Kings)** Erica Zhang is the chief buyer for housewares at a large department store. Unfortunately, her store faces stiff competition from specialty retailers that carry imported cooking and dining articles. To meet this competitive challenge, Erica has reorganized her housewares department to create a "store within a store" that has the same ambiance as her competitors'. To kick off her concept, she plans a one-month promotion that features a sale on several special items, including an imported Three Kings baking dish. (The Three Kings baking dish leaves a "crown" image on the top of the cake.) These baking dishes must be ordered six months in advance. Any leftover inventory at the end of the promotion will be sold to a discount chain at a reduced price.

Erica has collected some pricing and cost data, listed in the following table, to help her decide how many of the Three Kings baking dishes to order. Erica predicts total demand for the imported baking dish to be normally distributed with mean of 980 and standard deviation of 354. Leftover dishes will be sold to the discount chain for $15.

Three Kings baking dish:	
Selling price	$40.00
Purchase price	$16.00
Shipping cost	$ 3.00
Handling cost *	$ 0.80
Warehouse surcharge **	$ 1.10
Total cost	$20.90

*Estimate of variable cost to uncrate, clean, and transport a dish to the housewares department.

**Allocation of fixed overhead expenses in the shipping and receiving department.

For parts a through c, suppose 1,200 imported Three Kings baking dishes are ordered.

a.   What is the fill rate?

b.   What is the in-stock probability?

c.   How many Three Kings cake dishes should she purchase?

d.   Erica is concerned about customer service. Suppose she feels there is a loss of goodwill of $10 for every customer that wants to purchase the Three Kings dish but is unable to do so due to a stockout. Now how many Three Kings cake dishes should she purchase?

Q 9.9   **(CPG Bagels)** CPG Bagels starts the day with a large production run of bagels. Throughout the morning, additional bagels are produced as needed. The last bake is completed at 3 P.M., and the store closes at 8 P.M. It costs approximately $0.20 in materials and labor to make a bagel. The price of a fresh bagel is $0.60. Bagels not sold by the end of the day are sold the next day as "day old" bagels in bags of six, for $0.99 a bag. About two-thirds of the day-old bagels are sold; the remainder are just thrown away. There are many bagel flavors, but for simplicity, concentrate just on the plain bagels. The store manager predicts that demand for plain bagels from 3 P.M. until closing is normally distributed with mean of 54 and standard deviation of 21.

a. How many bagels should the store have at 3 P.M. to maximize the store's expected profit (from sales between 3 P.M. until closing)? (*Hint:* Assume day-old bagels are sold for $0.99/6 = $0.165 each; i.e., don't worry about the fact that day-old bagels are sold in bags of six.)

b. Suppose the manager would like to ensure at least a 99 percent fill rate on demand that occurs after 3 P.M. How many bagels should the store have at 3 P.M. to ensure that fill rate?

c. Suppose that the store manager is concerned that stockouts might cause a loss of future business. To explore this idea, the store manager feels that it is appropriate to assign a stockout cost of $5 per bagel that is demanded but not filled. (Customers frequently purchase more than one bagel at a time. This cost is per bagel demanded that is not satisfied rather than per customer that does not receive a complete order.) Given the additional stockout cost, how many bagels should the store have at 3 P.M. to maximize the store's expected profit?

d. Suppose the store manager has 101 bagels at 3 P.M. How many bagels should the store manager expect to have at the end of the day?

Q 9.10 **(The Kiosk)** Weekday lunch demand for spicy black bean burritos at the Kiosk, a local snack bar, is approximately Poisson with a mean of 22. The Kiosk charges $4.00 for each burrito, which are all made before the lunch crowd arrives. Virtually all burrito customers also buy a soda that is sold for 60¢. The burritos cost the Kiosk $2.00, while sodas cost the Kiosk 5¢. Kiosk management is very sensitive about the quality of food they serve. Thus, they maintain a strict "No Old Burrito" policy, so any burrito left at the end of the day is disposed of. The distribution function of a Poisson with mean 22 is as follows:

Q	F(Q)	Q	F (Q)	Q	F (Q)	Q	F (Q)
1	0.0000	11	0.0076	21	0.4716	31	0.9735
2	0.0000	12	0.0151	22	0.5564	32	0.9831
3	0.0000	13	0.0278	23	0.6374	33	0.9895
4	0.0000	14	0.0477	24	0.7117	34	0.9936
5	0.0000	15	0.0769	25	0.7771	35	0.9962
6	0.0001	16	0.1170	26	0.8324	36	0.9978
7	0.0002	17	0.1690	27	0.8775	37	0.9988
8	0.0006	18	0.2325	28	0.9129	38	0.9993
9	0.0015	19	0.3060	29	0.9398	39	0.9996
10	0.0035	20	0.3869	30	0.9595	40	0.9998

a. Suppose burrito customers buy their snack somewhere else if the Kiosk is out of stock. How many burritos should the Kiosk make for the lunch crowd?

b. Suppose that any customer unable to purchase a burrito settles for a lunch of Pop-Tarts and a soda. Pop-Tarts sell for 75¢ and cost the Kiosk 25¢. (As Pop-Tarts and soda are easily stored, the Kiosk never runs out of these essentials.) Assuming that the Kiosk management is interested in maximizing profits, how many burritos should they prepare?

10

Assemble-to-Order, Make-to-Order, and Quick Response with Reactive Capacity[1]

A firm facing the newsvendor problem can manage, but not avoid, the possibility of a demand–supply mismatch: order too much and inventory is left over at the end of the season, but order too little and incur the opportunity cost of lost sales. The firm finds itself in this situation because it commits to its entire supply before demand occurs. This mode of operation is often called *make-to-stock* because all items enter finished goods inventory (stock) before they are demanded. In other words, with make-to-stock the identity of an item's eventual owner is not known when production of the item is completed.

To reduce the demand–supply mismatches associated with make-to-stock, a firm could attempt to delay at least some production until better demand information is learned. For example, a firm could choose to begin producing an item only when it receives a firm order from a customer. This mode of operation is often called *make-to-order* or *assemble-to-order*. Dell Computer is probably the most well known and most successful company to have implemented the assemble-to-order model.

Make-to-stock and make-to-order are two extremes in the sense that with one all production begins well before demand is received, whereas with the other production begins only after demand is known. Between any two extremes there also must be an intermediate option. Suppose the lead time to receive an order is short relative to the length of the selling season. A firm then orders some inventory before the selling season starts so that some product is on hand at the beginning of the season. After observing early season sales, the firm then submits a second order that is received well before the end of the season (due to the short lead time). In this situation, the firm should make a conservative initial order and use the second order to strategically respond to initial season sales: Slow-selling products are not replenished mid-season, thereby reducing leftover inventory, while fast-selling products are replenished, thereby reducing lost sales.

---

[1]The data in this chapter have been modified to protect confidentiality.

The capability to place multiple orders during a selling season is an integral part of *Quick Response*. Quick Response is a set of practices designed to reduce the cost of mismatches between supply and demand. It began in the apparel industry as a response to just-in-time practices in the automobile industry and has since migrated to the grocery industry under the label *Efficient Consumer Response.*

The aspect of Quick Response discussed in this chapter is the use of *reactive capacity,* that is, capacity that allows a firm to place one additional order during the season, which retailers often refer to as a "second buy." As in Chapter 9, we use O'Neill Inc. for our case analysis. Furthermore, we assume throughout this chapter that the normal distribution with mean 3,192 and standard deviation 1,181 is our demand forecast for the Hammer 3/2.

The first part of this chapter evaluates and minimizes the demand–supply mismatch cost to a make-to-stock firm, that is, a firm that has only a single ordering opportunity, as in the newsvendor model. Furthermore, we identify situations in which the cost of demand–supply mismatches is large. Those are the situations in which there is the greatest potential to benefit from Quick Response with reactive capacity or make-to-order production. The second part of this chapter discusses make-to-order relative to make-to-stock. The third part studies reactive capacity: How should we choose an initial order quantity when some reactive capacity is available? And, as with the newsvendor model, how do we evaluate several performance measures? The chapter concludes with a summary and managerial implications.

10.1 Evaluating and Minimizing the Newsvendor's Demand–Supply Mismatch Cost

In this section the costs associated in the newsvendor model with demand–supply mismatches are identified, then two approaches are outlined for evaluating the expected demand–supply mismatch cost, and finally we show how to minimize those costs. For ease of exposition, we use the shorthand term *mismatch cost* to refer to the "expected demand–supply mismatch cost."

In the newsvendor model, the mismatch cost is divided into two components: the cost of ordering too much and the cost of ordering too little. Ordering too much means there is leftover inventory at the end of the season. Ordering too little means there are lost sales. The cost for each unit of leftover inventory is the overage cost, which we label C_o. The cost for each lost sale is the underage cost, which we label C_u. (See Chapter 9 for the original discussion of these costs.) Therefore, the mismatch cost in the newsvendor model is the sum of the expected overage cost and the expected underage cost:

$$\text{Mismatch cost} = (C_o \times \text{Expected leftover inventory}) \quad (10.1)$$
$$+ (C_u \times \text{Expected lost sales})$$

Notice that the mismatch cost includes both a tangible cost (leftover inventory) and an intangible opportunity cost (lost sales). The former has a direct impact on the profit and loss statement, but the latter does not. Nevertheless, the opportunity cost of lost sales should not be ignored.

Not only does equation (10.1) provide us with the definition of the mismatch cost, it also provides us with our first method for evaluating the mismatch cost because we already know how to evaluate the expected leftover inventory and the expected lost sales (from Chapter 9). Let's illustrate this method with O'Neill's Hammer 3/2 wetsuit. The Hammer has a selling price of $180 and a purchase cost from the TEC Group of $110. Therefore, the underage cost is $180 − $110 = $70 per lost sale. Leftover inventory is sold at a 50 percent discount, so the overage cost is $110 − $90 = $20 per wetsuit left at the end of the season. The expected profit-maximizing order quantity is 4,101 units. Using the techniques

TABLE 10.1
Summary of Performance Measures for O'Neill's Hammer 3/2 Wetsuit When the Expected Profit-Maximizing Quantity Is Ordered and the Demand Forecast Is Normally Distributed with Mean 3,192 and Standard Deviation 1,181

Order quantity, Q	= 4,101 units
Expected demand, μ	= 3,192 units
Standard deviation of demand, σ	= 1,181
Expected lost sales	= 150 units
Expected sales	= 3,042 units
Expected leftover inventory	= 1,059 units
Expected revenue	= \$642,870
Expected profit	= \$191,760

Expected lost sales = $1,181 \times L(0.77) = 1,181 \times 0.1267 = 150$
Expected sales = $3,192 - 150 = 3,042$
Expected leftover inventory = $4,101 - 3,042 = 1,059$
Expected revenue = Price $\times$ Expected sales + Salvage value $\times$ Expected leftover inventory
= $\$180 \times 3,042 + \$90 \times 1,059 = \$642,870$
Expected profit = $(\$180 - \$110) \times 3,042 - (\$110 - \$90) \times 1,059 = \$191,760$

described in Chapter 9, for that order quantity we can evaluate several performance measures, summarized in Table 10.1. Therefore, the mismatch cost for the Hammer 3/2, despite ordering the expected profit-maximizing quantity, is

$$(\$20 \times 1,059) + (\$70 \times 150) = \$31,680$$

Now let's consider a second approach for evaluating the mismatch cost. Imagine O'Neill had the opportunity to purchase a magic crystal ball. Even before O'Neill needs to submit its order to TEC, this crystal ball reveals to O'Neill the exact demand for the entire season. O'Neill would obviously order from TEC the demand quantity observed with this crystal ball. As a result, O'Neill would be in the pleasant situation of avoiding all mismatch costs (there would be no excess inventory and no lost sales) while still providing immediate product availability to its customers. In fact, the only function of the crystal ball is to eliminate all mismatch costs: for example, the crystal ball does not change demand, increase the selling price, or decrease the production cost. Thus, the difference in O'Neill's expected profit with the crystal ball and without it must equal the mismatch cost: The crystal ball increases profit by eliminating mismatch costs, so the profit increase must equal the mismatch cost. Therefore, we can evaluate the mismatch cost by first evaluating the newsvendor's expected profit, then evaluating the expected profit with the crystal ball, and finally taking the difference between those two figures.

We already know how to evaluate the newsvendor's expected profit (again, see Chapter 9). So let's illustrate how to evaluate the expected profit with the crystal ball. If O'Neill gets to observe demand before deciding how much to order from TEC, then there will not be any leftover inventory at the end of the season. Even better, O'Neill will not stock out, so every unit of demand turns into an actual sale. Hence, O'Neill's expected sales with the crystal ball equals expected demand, which is μ. We already know that O'Neill's profit per sale is the gross margin, the retail price minus the production cost, Price $-$ Cost. Therefore O'Neill's expected profit with this crystal ball is expected demand times the profit per unit of demand, which is (Price $-$ Cost) $\times \mu$. In fact, O'Neill can never earn a higher expected profit than it does with the crystal ball: There is nothing better than having no leftover inventory and earning the full margin on every unit of potential demand. Hence, let's call that profit the *maximum profit:*

$$\text{Maximum profit} = (\text{Price} - \text{Cost}) \times \mu$$

O'Neill's maximum profit with the Hammer 3/2 is $\$70 \times 3,192 = \$223,440$. We already know that the newsvendor expected profit is \$191,760. So the difference between the maximum profit (i.e., crystal ball profit) and the newsvendor expected profit is O'Neill's mismatch costs. That figure is $223,440 − $191,760 = $31,680, which matches our calculation with our first method (as it should). To summarize, our second method for evaluating the mismatch cost uses the following equation:

$$\text{Mismatch cost} = \text{Maximum profit} - \text{Expected profit}$$

Incidentally, you can also think of the mismatch cost as the most O'Neill should be willing to pay to purchase the crystal ball; that is, it is the value of perfect demand information.

The second method for calculating the mismatch cost emphasizes that there exists an easily evaluated maximum profit. As we later see, we might not be able to evaluate expected profit precisely if there is some reactive capacity available to the firm. Nevertheless, we do know that no matter what type of reactive capacity the firm has, that reactive capacity cannot be as good as the crystal ball we just described. Therefore, the expected profit with any form of reactive capacity must be more than the newsvendor's expected profit but less than the maximum profit.

You now may be wondering about how to minimize the mismatch cost and whether that is any different than maximizing the newsvendor's expected profit. The short answer is that these are effectively the same objective, that is, the quantity that maximizes profit also minimizes mismatch costs. One way to see this is to look at the equation above: If expected profit is maximized and the maximum profit does not depend on the order quantity, then the difference between them, which is the mismatch cost, must be minimized.

A second way to think about minimizing mismatch costs is to use the same logic we exploited to obtain the profit-maximizing order quantity (Section 9.4). If we do not order any units, $Q = 0$, then every unit of demand is lost, so our mismatch cost from lost sales is $\mu \times C_u$, our mismatch cost from leftover inventory is zero and our total mismatch cost is $\mu \times C_u$. If we order more units, then our mismatch cost from lost sales decreases (we have fewer lost sales), but our mismatch cost from leftover inventory increases. The Qth unit we could order would decrease our mismatch costs from lost sales by $(1 - F(Q)) \times C_u$ but increase our mismatch costs from leftover inventory by $F(Q) \times C_o$. (Recall that $1 - F(Q)$ is the probability the Qth unit prevents a lost sale and $F(Q)$ is the probability it is left in inventory.) Hence, to minimize mismatch costs we should keep ordering units until the decrease in the lost sales mismatch cost equals the increase in the leftover inventory mismatch cost: $(1 - F(Q)) \times C_u = F(Q) \times C_o$. (If we order more, then the mismatch cost starts to increase again.) Rearrange terms in that equation and you obtain our familiar critical ratio formula:

$$F(Q) = \frac{C_u}{C_o + C_u}$$

Therefore, the quantity that minimizes mismatch costs also maximizes expected profit because the critical ratio provides the solution to either of those objectives.

Now that we know how to evaluate and minimize the mismatch cost, we need to get a sense of its significance. In other words, is $31,680 a big problem or a little problem? To answer that question, we need to compare it with something else. The maximum profit is one reference point: the demand–supply mismatch cost as a percentage of the maximum profit is $31,680/$223,440 = 14.1 percent. You may prefer expected sales as a point of comparison: the demand–supply mismatch cost per unit of expected sales is $31,680/3,042 = $10.40. Alternatively, we can make the comparison with expected revenue, $642,870, or expected profit, $191,760: the demand–supply mismatch cost is approximately 4.9 percent of total revenue ($31,680/$642,870) and 16.5 percent of expected profit ($31,680/$191,760). Companies in the sports apparel industry generally have net profit in the range of 2 to 5 percent of revenue. Therefore, eliminating the mismatch cost from the Hammer 3/2 could potentially double O'Neill's net profit! That is an intriguing possibility.

10.2 When Is the Mismatch Cost High?

No matter which comparison you prefer, the mismatch cost for O'Neill is significant, even if the expected profit-maximizing quantity is ordered. But it is even better to know what causes a large demand–supply mismatch. To answer that question, we could generate many examples, evaluate the mismatch cost for each example, and then attempt to spot consistent patterns. But there is a more precise way.

Let's first choose our point of comparison for the mismatch cost. Of the ones discussed at the end of the previous section, only the maximum profit does not depend on the order quantity chosen: unit sales, revenue, and profit all clearly depend on Q. In addition, the maximum profit is representative of the potential for the product: we cannot do better than earn the maximum profit. Therefore, let's evaluate the mismatch cost as a percentage of the maximum profit.

We next need to make an assumption about how much is ordered before the selling season, that is, clearly the mismatch cost depends on the order quantity Q. Let's adopt the natural assumption that the expected profit-maximizing quantity is ordered, which, as we discussed in the previous section, also happens to minimize the newsvendor's mismatch cost.

If we take the equations for expected lost sales and expected leftover inventory from Chapter 9, plug them into our first mismatch cost equation (10.1), and then do several algebraic manipulations, we arrive at the following equation:

$$\text{Mismatch cost as a percentage of the maximum profit} = \left(\frac{\phi(z)}{\Phi(z)}\right) \times \left(\frac{\sigma}{\mu}\right) \qquad (10.2)$$

where

$$\mu = \text{Expected demand}$$
$$\sigma = \text{Standard deviation of demand}$$
$$Q = \text{Expected profit-maximizing order quantity}$$
$$z = (Q - \mu)/\sigma = \text{Normalized order quantity}$$
$$\phi(z) = \text{Density function of the standard normal distribution}$$
$$\Phi(z) = \text{Distribution function of the standard normal}$$

(If you are curious, see Appendix D for a detailed derivation of equation (10.2).) We can use the Standard Normal Distribution Function Table in Appendix B to evaluate $\Phi(z)$, or we can use the Excel function Normsdist(z). The easiest way to evaluate $\phi(z)$ is to use the Excel function Normdist(z,0,1,0), but it also can be evaluated by hand with the following function:

$$\phi(z) = e^{-(1/2) \times z^2}/\sqrt{2 \times \pi}$$

Before we try to understand equation (10.2), let's first use it for the Hammer 3/2. We already know $\mu = 3{,}192$, $\sigma = 1{,}181$ and $z = 0.77$, so from the Standard Normal Distribution Function Table, $\Phi(z) = 0.7794$. Using Excel we get the last needed piece, $\phi(z) = $ Normdist(0.77,0,1,0) = 0.2966. Plugging those values into equation (10.2) yields

$$\text{Hammer 3/2's mismatch cost/maximum profit} = \left(\frac{0.2966}{0.7794}\right) \times \left(\frac{1{,}181}{3{,}192}\right)$$

$$= 0.141$$

which matches our earlier calculation.

We now want to use equation (10.2) to understand the conditions when the mismatch cost is high.

Equation (10.2) can be divided into two terms, $\phi(z)/\Phi(z)$ and σ/μ, so the mismatch cost is high when the product of those two terms is high. But that is not a satisfying answer, so let's delve deeper into each of those two terms.

The first term in equation (10.2), $\phi(z)/\Phi(z)$, is the ratio of the standard normal density function to the standard normal distribution function evaluated at the normalized order quantity. It is not immediately obvious what that ratio means or how it behaves. But it does appear to depend on z and z depends on the critical ratio (the higher the critical ratio, the higher the optimal z-statistic). So let's plot $\phi(z)/\Phi(z)$ against the critical ratio, as is done in Figure 10.1. We see that as the critical ratio increases, $\phi(z)/\Phi(z)$ decreases. Thus, the mismatch cost becomes smaller as the critical ratio increases. In other words, all else being equal between two products, the product with the lower critical ratio has the higher mismatch cost.

Now look at the second term in the mismatch cost equation, σ/μ. That term is called the *coefficient of variation.* The coefficient of variation is a good measure of the variability of demand, and in particular, it is a better measure than just the standard deviation. You may recall in Chapter 6 we discussed the coefficient of variation with respect to the variability of the activity time (CV_p) or the interarrival time to a queue (CV_a). This coefficient of variation, σ/μ, is conceptually identical to those coefficients of variation: It is the ratio of the standard deviation of a random variable (in this case demand) to its mean.

It is worthwhile to illustrate why the coefficient of variation is the appropriate measure of variability in this setting. Suppose you are informed that the standard deviation of demand for an item is 800. Does that tell you enough information to assess the variability of demand? For example, does it allow you to evaluate the probability actual demand will be less than 75 percent of your forecast? In fact, it does not. Consider two cases, in the first the forecast is for 1,000 units and in the second the forecast is for 10,000 units. Demand is less than 75 percent of the 1,000-unit forecast if demand is less than 750 units. What is the probability that occurs? First, normalize the value 750:

$$z = \frac{Q - \mu}{\sigma} = \frac{750 - 1,000}{800} = -0.31$$

Now use the Standard Normal Distribution Function Table to find the probability demand is less than 750: $\Phi(-0.31) = 0.3783$. With the forecast of 10,000, the comparable event has demand that is less than 7,500 units. Repeating the same process yields

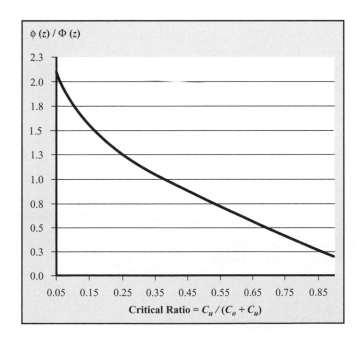

FIGURE 10.1
The Relationship between the Critical Ratio and $\phi(z)/\Phi(z)$

$\phi (z) / \Phi (z)$

Critical Ratio $= C_u / (C_o + C_u)$

TABLE 10.2
Forecast Accuracy
Relative to the
Coefficient of
Variation When
Demand Is Normally
Distributed

Coefficient of Variation	Probability Demand Is Less Than 75% of the Forecast	Probability Demand Is within 25% of the Forecast
0.10	0.6%	98.8%
0.25	15.9	68.3
0.50	30.9	38.3
0.75	36.9	26.1
1.00	40.1	19.7
1.50	43.4	13.2
2.00	45.0	9.9
3.00	46.7	6.6

$z = (7,500 - 10,000)/800 = -3.1$ and $\Phi(-3.1) = 0.0009$. Therefore, with a standard deviation of 800, there is about a 38 percent chance demand is less than 75 percent of the first forecast but much less than a 1 percent chance demand is less than 75 percent of the second forecast. In other words, the standard deviation alone does not capture how much variability there is in demand. Notice that the coefficient of variation with the first product is 0.8 (800/1,000), whereas it is much lower with the second product, 0.08 (800/10,000).

For the Hammer 3/2, the coefficient of variation is $1,181/3,192 = 0.37$. Unfortunately, that might not mean a lot to you because you have not had much experience working with coefficients of variation. While there is no generally accepted standard for what is a "low," "medium," or "high" coefficient of variation, we offer the following guideline: Demand variability is rather low if the coefficient of variation is less than 0.25, medium if it is in the range 0.25 to 0.75, and high with anything above 0.75. A coefficient of variation above 1.5 is extremely high, and anything above 3 would imply that the demand forecast is essentially meaningless.

Table 10.2 provides data to allow you to judge for yourself what is a "low," "medium," and "high" coefficient of variation.

Recall from Chapters 6 and 7 that the coefficient of variation with an exponential distribution is always one. Therefore, if two processes have exponential distributions, they always have the same amount of variability. The same is not true with the normal distribution because with the normal distribution the standard deviation is adjustable relative to the mean.

We are now ready to summarize our conclusions regarding when the newsvendor mismatch cost is high:

• The expected demand–supply mismatch cost becomes larger as the critical ratio $C_u/(C_o + C_u)$ becomes smaller.

• The expected demand–supply mismatch cost becomes larger as demand variability increases, where demand variability is measured with the coefficient of variation σ/μ.

In other words, products with low critical ratios and high demand variability have high mismatch costs and products with high critical ratios and low demand variability have low mismatch costs. Table 10.3 displays data on the mismatch cost for various coefficients of variation and critical ratios.

It is intuitive that the mismatch cost should increase as demand variability increases. The key insight is how to measure demand variability. Furthermore, this result emphasizes that any action that reduces demand variability also reduces the mismatch cost. For example, the coefficient of variation reflects the quality of a firm's forecasting ability, so any improvement in the forecasting process invariably leads to higher profit. The result also can be

TABLE 10.3
The Mismatch Cost (as a Percentage of the Maximum Profit) When Demand Is Normally Distributed and the Newsvendor Expected Profit-Maximizing Quantity Is Ordered

Coefficient of Variation	Critical Ratio					
	0.4	0.5	0.6	0.7	0.8	0.9
0.10	10%	8%	6%	5%	3%	2%
0.25	24%	20%	16%	12%	9%	5%
0.40	39%	32%	26%	20%	14%	8%
0.55	53%	44%	35%	27%	19%	11%
0.70	68%	56%	45%	35%	24%	14%
0.85	82%	68%	55%	42%	30%	17%
1.00	97%	80%	64%	50%	35%	19%

stated in a less optimistic way: Any action that increases demand variability has the negative effect of also increasing the mismatch cost.

The intuition with respect to the critical ratio takes some more thought. A very high critical ratio means there is a large profit margin relative to the loss on each unit of excess inventory. Greeting cards are good examples of products that might have very large critical ratios: the gross margin on each greeting card is large while the production cost is low. With a very large critical ratio the optimal order quantity is quite large, so there are no lost sales. There is also a substantial amount of leftover inventory, but the cost of each unit left over in inventory is not large at all, so the total cost of leftover inventory is relatively small. Therefore, the total mismatch cost is small. Now consider a product with a low critical ratio, that is, the per-unit cost of excess inventory is much higher than the cost of each lost sale. Perishable items often fall into this category as well as items that face obsolescence. (Perishability and obsolescence have the same outcome for different reasons: a perishable product physically decays whereas a product facing obsolescence decays via deterioration in its demand, generally due to the introduction of superior products.) Given that excess inventory is expensive, the optimal order quantity is quite low, possibly lower than expected demand. As a result, excess inventory is not a problem, but lost sales are a big problem, resulting in a high mismatch cost.

10.3 Reducing Mismatch Costs with Make-to-Order

When supply is chosen before demand is observed (make-to-stock), there invariably is either too much or too little supply. A purely hypothetical solution to the problem is to find a crystal ball that reveals demand before it occurs. A more realistic solution is to initiate production of each unit only after demand is observed for that unit, which is often called make-to-order or assemble-to-order. This section discusses the pros and cons of make-to-order with respect to its ability to reduce mismatch costs.

In theory, make-to-order can eliminate the entire mismatch cost associated with make-to-stock (i.e., newsvendor). With make-to-order there is no leftover inventory because production only begins after a firm order is received from a customer. Thus, make-to-order saves on expensive markdown and disposal expenses. Furthermore, there are no lost sales with make-to-order because each customer order is eventually produced. Therefore, products with a high mismatch cost (low critical ratios, high demand variability) would benefit considerably from a switch to make-to-order from make-to-stock.

But there are several reasons to be wary of make-to-order. For instance, make-to-order is never able to satisfy customer demands immediately; that is, customers must wait to have their order filled. If the wait is short, then demand with make-to-order can be nearly as high as with make-to-stock. But there is also some threshold beyond which customers do not wait. That threshold level depends on the product: customers are generally less willing to wait for diapers than they are for custom sofas.

It is helpful to think of queuing theory (Chapters 6 and 7) to understand what determines the waiting time with make-to-order. No matter the number of servers, a key characteristic of a queuing system is that customer service begins only after a customer arrives to the system, just as production does not begin with make-to-order until a customer commits to an order. Another important feature of a queuing system is that customers must wait to be processed if all servers are busy, just as a customer must wait with make-to-order if the production process is working on the backlog of orders from previous customers.

To provide a reference point for this discussion, suppose O'Neill establishes a make-to-order assembly line for wetsuits. O'Neill could keep in inventory the necessary raw materials to fabricate wetsuits in a wide array of colors, styles, and quality levels. Wetsuits would then be produced as orders are received from customers. The assembly line has a maximum production rate, which would correspond to the service rate in a queue. Given that demand is random, the interarrival times between customer orders also would be random, just as in a queuing system.

A key insight from queuing is that a customer's expected waiting time depends nonlinearly (a curve, not a straight line) on the system's utilization (the ratio of the flow rate to capacity): As the utilization approaches 100 percent, the waiting time approaches infinity. (See Figure 6.21.) As a result, if O'Neill wishes to have a reasonably short waiting time for customers, then O'Neill must be willing to operate with less than 100 percent utilization, maybe even considerably less than 100 percent. Less than 100 percent utilization implies idle capacity; for example, if the utilization is 90 percent, then 10 percent of the time the assembly line is idle. Therefore, even with make-to-order production O'Neill experiences demand–supply mismatch costs. Those costs are divided into two types: idle capacity and lost sales from customers who are unwilling to wait to receive their product. When comparing make-to-stock with make-to-order, you could say that make-to-order replaces the cost of leftover inventory with the cost of idle capacity. Whether or not make-to-order is preferable depends on the relative importance of those two costs.

While a customer's expected waiting time may be significant, customers are ultimately concerned with their total waiting time, which includes the processing time. With make-to-order, the processing time has two components: the time in production and the time from production to actual delivery. The delivery time can be considerable, and in many cases it may exceed or nearly exceed the threshold of acceptability. For example, the delivery time of wetsuits from Asia to San Diego via ship could easily destroy the viability of a make-to-order production system based in Asia. One solution is to use a faster shipping mode, but that increases the cost of *every* unit produced. A second solution is to move production closer to demand so as to reduce the delivery time with economical shipping means. But manufacturing in North America implies paying higher labor costs, which also dampens the attractiveness of make-to-order, especially if there is also a considerable amount of idle capacity.

To summarize, make-to-order eliminates some of the demand–supply mismatches associated with make-to-stock, but make-to-order has its own demand–supply mismatch issues. In particular, make-to-order eliminates leftover inventory but introduces idle capacity so that the customer waiting time is acceptable and potentially increases labor and/or delivery costs on every item.

10.4   Quick Response with Reactive Capacity

O'Neill may very well conclude that make-to-order production is not viable either in Asia (due to added shipping expenses) or in North America (due to added labor costs). If pure make-to-order is out of the question, then O'Neill should consider some intermediate solution between make-to-stock (the newsvendor) and make-to-order (a queue). With the newsvendor model, O'Neill commits to its entire supply before *any* demand occurs; whereas with make-to-order, O'Neill commits to supply only after *all* demand occurs. The intermediate solution is to commit to some supply before demand but then maintain the option to produce additional supply after some demand is observed. The capacity associated with that later supply is called **reactive capacity** because it allows O'Neill to react to the demand information it learns before committing to the second order. The ability to make multiple replenishments (even if just one replenishment) is a central goal in Quick Response.

Reactive capacity can take many forms. For example, O'Neill might have access to unlimited capacity with its second order, but units in that second order might cost more than units in the initial order, that is, unlimited but expensive reactive capacity. Alternatively, units in the second order may cost the same as units in the first order, but there may be a capacity limit imposed on the second order. Both types of reactive capacity are discussed in this section.

Unlimited, but Expensive, Reactive Capacity

Suppose O'Neill approaches TEC with the request that TEC reduce its lead time. O'Neill's motivation behind this request is to try to create the opportunity for a replenishment during the selling season. Recall that the Spring season spans six months, starting in February and ending in July. (See Figure 9.2.) It has been O'Neill's experience that a hot product in the first two months of the season (i.e., a product selling above forecast) almost always turns out to be a hot product in the rest of the season. As a result, O'Neill could surely benefit from the opportunity to replenish the hot products midseason. For example, suppose TEC offered a one-month lead time for a midseason order. Then O'Neill could submit to TEC a second order at the end of the second month (March) and receive that replenishment before the end of the third month, thereby allowing that inventory to serve demand in the second half of the season. Figure 10.2 provides a time line in this new situation

While it is clear that O'Neill could benefit from the second order, offering a second order with a one-month lead time can be costly to TEC. For example, TEC might need to reserve some capacity to respond to O'Neill's order. If O'Neill's second order is not as large as TEC anticipated, then some of that reserved capacity might be lost. Or O'Neill's order might be larger than anticipated, forcing TEC to scramble for extra capacity, at TEC's expense. In addition, the one-month lead time may force the use of faster shipping, which again could increase costs. The issue is whether the cost increases associated with the second order justify the mismatch cost savings for O'Neill. To address this issue, let's suppose

FIGURE 10.2
Time Line of Events for O'Neill's Hammer 3/2 Wetsuit with Unlimited, but Expensive, Reactive Capacity

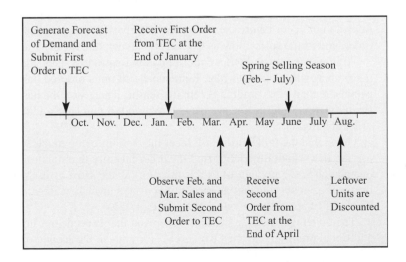

that TEC agrees to satisfy O'Neill's second order but insists on a 20 percent premium for those units to cover TEC's anticipated additional expenses. Given this new opportunity, how should O'Neill adjust its initial order quantity and how much are mismatch costs reduced?

Choosing order quantities with two ordering opportunities is significantly more complex than choosing a single order quantity (i.e., the newsvendor problem). For instance, in addition to our forecast for the entire season's demand, now we need to worry about developing a forecast for demand in the second half of the season given what we observe in the first two months of the season. Furthermore, we do not know what will be our initial sales when we submit our first order, so that order must anticipate all possible outcomes for initial sales and then the appropriate response in the second order for all of those outcomes. In addition, we may stock out within the first half of the season if our first order is not large enough. Finally, even after observing initial sales, some uncertainty remains regarding demand in the second half of the season.

Even though we now face a complex problem, we should not let the complexity overwhelm us. A good strategy when faced with a complex problem is to make it less complex, that is, make some simplifying assumptions that allow for analytical tractability while retaining the key qualitative features of the complex problem. With that strategy in mind, let's assume (1) we do not run out of inventory before the second order arrives; and (2) after we observe initial sales we are able to perfectly predict sales in the remaining portion of the season. Assumption 1 is not bad as long as the first order is reasonably large, that is, large enough to cover demand in the first half of the season with a high probability. Assumption 2 is not bad if initial sales are a very good predictor of subsequent sales, which has been empirically observed in many industries.

Our simplifying assumptions are enough to allow us to evaluate the optimal initial order quantity and then to evaluate expected profit. Let's again consider O'Neill's initial order for the Hammer 3/2. It turns out that O'Neill still faces the "too much–too little" problem associated with the newsvendor problem even though O'Neill has the opportunity to make a second order. To explain, note that if the initial order quantity is too large, then there will be leftover inventory at the end of the season. The second order does not help at all with the risk of excess inventory, so the "too much" problem remains.

We also still face the "too little" issue with our initial order, but it takes a different form than in our original newsvendor problem. Recall, with the original newsvendor problem, ordering too little leads to lost sales. But the second order prevents lost sales: After we observe initial sales, we are able to predict total demand for the remainder of the season. If that total demand exceeds our initial order, we merely choose a second order quantity to ensure that all demand is satisfied. This works because of our simplifying assumptions: Lost sales do not occur before the second order arrives, there is no quantity limit on the second order, and initial sales allow us to predict total demand for the season.

Although the second order opportunity eliminates lost sales, it does not mean we should not bother with an initial order. Remember that units ordered during the season are more expensive than units ordered before the season. Therefore, the penalty for ordering too little in the first order is that we may be required to purchase additional units in the second order at a higher cost.

Given that the initial order still faces the "too little–too much" problem, we can actually use the newsvendor model to find the order quantity that maximizes expected profit. The overage cost, C_o, per unit of excess inventory is the same as in the original model; that is, the overage cost is the loss on each unit of excess inventory. Recall that for the Hammer 3/2 Cost = 110 and Salvage value = 90. So $C_o = 20$.

The underage cost, C_u, per unit of demand that exceeds our initial order quantity is the additional premium we must pay to TEC for units in the second order. That premium is 20 percent, which is $20\% \times 110 = 22$. In other words, if demand exceeds our initial order quantity, then the penalty for ordering too little is the extra amount we must pay TEC for each of those units (i.e., we could have avoided that premium by increasing the initial order). Even though we must pay this premium to TEC, we are still better off having the second ordering opportunity: Paying TEC an extra $22 for each unit of demand that exceeds our initial order quantity is better than losing the $70 margin on each of those units if we did not have the second order. So $C_u = 22$.

We are now ready to calculate our optimal initial order quantity. (See Exhibit 9.4 for an outline of this process.) First evaluate the critical ratio:

$$\frac{C_u}{C_o + C_u} = \frac{22}{20 + 22} = 0.5238$$

Next find the z value in the Standard Normal Distribution Function Table that corresponds to the critical ratio 0.5238: $\Phi(0.05) = 0.5199$ and $\Phi(0.06) = 0.5239$, so let's choose the higher z value, $z = 0.06$. Now convert the z value into an order quantity for the actual demand distribution with $\mu = 3,192$ and $\sigma = 1,181$:

$$Q = \mu + z \times \sigma = 3,192 + 0.06 \times 1,181 = 3,263$$

Therefore, O'Neill should order 3,263 Hammer 3/2s in the first order to maximize expected profit when a second order is possible. Notice that O'Neill should still order a considerable amount in its initial order so as to avoid paying TEC the 20 percent premium on too many units. However, O'Neill's initial order of 3,263 units is considerably less than its optimal order of 4,101 units when the second order is not possible.

Even though O'Neill must pay a premium with the second order, O'Neill's expected profit should increase by this opportunity. (The second order does not prevent O'Neill from ordering 4,101 units in the initial order, so O'Neill cannot be worse off.) Let's evaluate what that expected profit is for any initial order quantity Q. Our maximum profit has not changed. The best we can do is earn the maximum gross margin on every unit of demand,

$$\text{Maximum profit} = (\text{Price} - \text{Cost}) \times \mu = (180 - 110) \times 3,192 = 223,440$$

The expected profit is the maximum profit minus the mismatch costs:

$$\begin{aligned} \text{Expected profit} = \text{Maximum profit} &- (C_o \times \text{Expected leftover inventory}) \\ &- (C_u \times \text{Expected second order quantity}) \end{aligned}$$

The first mismatch cost is the cost of leftover inventory, and the second is the additional premium that O'Neill must pay TEC for all of the units ordered in the second order. We already know how to evaluate expected leftover inventory for any initial order quantity. (See Exhibit 9.6 for a summary.) We now need to figure out the expected second order quantity.

If we order Q units in the first order, then we make a second order only if demand exceeds Q. In fact, our second order equals the difference between demand and Q, which would have been our lost sales if we did not have a second order. This is also known as the *loss function*. Therefore,

$$\text{Expected second order quantity} = \text{Newsvendor's expected lost sales}$$

We already know how to evaluate the newsvendor's expected lost sales. (See Exhibit 9.5 for a summary.) First look up $L(z)$ in the Standard Normal Loss Function Table for the z value that corresponds to our order quantity, $z = 0.06$. We find in that table $L(0.06) = 0.3697$. Next, finish the calculation:

$$\text{Expected lost sales} = \sigma \times L(z) = 1,181 \times 0.3697 = 437$$

Recall that

$$\text{Expected sales} = \mu - \text{Expected lost sales} = 3{,}192 - 437 = 2{,}755$$

where expected sales is the quantity the newsvendor would sell with an order quantity of 3,263. We want to evaluate expected sales for the newsvendor so that we can evaluate the last piece we need:

$$\text{Expected leftover inventory} = Q - \text{Expected sales} = 3{,}263 - 2{,}755 = 508$$

We are now ready to evaluate expected profit for the Hammer 3/2 if there is a second order:

$$\text{Expected profit} = \text{Maximum profit} - (C_o \times \text{Expected leftover inventory})$$
$$- (C_u \times \text{Expected second order quantity})$$

$$= \$223{,}440 - (\$20 \times 508) - (\$22 \times 437)$$

$$= \$203{,}666$$

Recall that O'Neill's expected profit with just one ordering opportunity is $191,760. Therefore, the second order increases profit by ($203,666 − $191,760)/$191,760 = 6.2 percent even though TEC charges a 20 percent premium for units in the second order. We can also think in terms of how much the second order reduces the mismatch cost. Recall that the mismatch cost with only one order is $31,680. Now the mismatch cost is $223,440 − $203,666 = $19,774, which is a 38 percent reduction in the mismatch cost (1 − $19,774/$31,680). In addition, O'Neill's fill rate increases from about 95 percent to essentially 100 percent and the number of leftover units at the end of the season that require markdowns to sell is cut in half (from 1,059 to 508). Therefore, even though reactive capacity in the form of a midseason replenishment does not eliminate all mismatch costs, it provides a feasible strategy for significantly reducing mismatch costs.

Limited Reactive Capacity

One way to ensure that supply is chosen after demand is to postpone supply until after demand occurs, as is done with make-to-order or the midseason replenishment just discussed. An alternative is to accelerate demand so that it occurs before supply is chosen. That is the option considered in this section.

O'Neill's current lead time from TEC is three months. TEC requires the long lead time so that it can plan its capacity and procurement of raw materials to deliver whatever O'Neill orders. However, TEC could probably deliver with a shorter lead time as long as TEC is not obligated to produce whatever O'Neill orders. This insight creates an opportunity for O'Neill to improve upon its current situation of a single order submitted three months before the season starts.

Suppose O'Neill allowed retailers to *prebook* inventory before the season starts. For example, in November a retailer could submit a prebook order to O'Neill for delivery during the actual season that begins in February. To make this attractive for a retailer, O'Neill could allow the retailer to pay for the order only after delivery rather than when the prebook order is submitted. Furthermore, O'Neill can guarantee availability of the retailer's entire prebook order. Finally, O'Neill could give a financial incentive to induce the retailers to prebook, but for now let's assume that the financial incentive is not necessary. (However, the analysis technique in this section could be used to determine whether a financial incentive is justified.)

In an ideal situation, the retailers would prebook their entire demand even before November so that O'Neill would not have to bear any mismatch risk. In effect O'Neill would transfer all of the risk of holding inventory onto the retailers. But it is unlikely that O'Neill can get the retailers to prebook earlier than November and it is also unlikely the retailers will prebook their entire demand. However, an item's prebook quantity probably contains information regarding its total demand, that is, an item that prebooks well probably will have higher-than-expected demand, and an item that prebooks poorly probably will have lower-than-expected demand.

O'Neill's challenge is to exploit the information it learns about demand from prebooks. But if the prebooks arrive in November and O'Neill has already committed to its entire supply, then that prebook information is useless. (Information is only useful if you are willing and able to react to it.) A second order, say in December, would solve that problem for O'Neill. However, because TEC only has two months to deliver a December order, TEC cannot guarantee that it can produce O'Neill's entire December order. In other words, there is a capacity limit on the second order. To ensure that the capacity limit on the second order is not breached, TEC could require that O'Neill submit a certain fraction of its total order in the first order. (The larger the first order, the smaller the second order is likely to be and the less likely the capacity limit will be violated.) Furthermore, TEC is concerned that O'Neill might request in the second order a little bit of every product. Hence, it is also reasonable that TEC impose a minimum order quantity for each item in the December order, for example, a minimum of 1,000 wetsuits. (Many small orders can wreak havoc on an assembly system if there are setup times and setup costs, as discussed in Chapter 5.)

Let's summarize the new situation to analyze. O'Neill will now submit to TEC its first order in October. Given that O'Neill's forecast in October before the season starts is no better or worse than its forecast in November, this benefit for TEC has essentially no cost to O'Neill. To ensure that O'Neill does not abuse the privilege of a second order, TEC requires that O'Neill submit a sufficiently large first order in October. In November O'Neill receives the retailers' prebook orders. Based on the prebook data, O'Neill updates its forecasts and submits a second order in December. TEC produces and delivers the second order before the season begins in February. Kindly, TEC does not charge a premium for the units in the second order. However, TEC does insist on a per-item minimum order quantity. Figure 10.3 summarizes the new time line and constraints.

FIGURE 10.3
Time Line of Events and Constraints for O'Neill with Limited Reactive Capacity

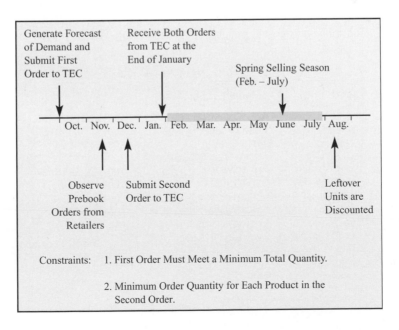

Constraints: 1. First Order Must Meet a Minimum Total Quantity.

2. Minimum Order Quantity for Each Product in the Second Order.

We are again faced with a complex situation: multiple orders, demand forecast updating, and minimum order quantities. As with our unlimited reactive capacity scenario, we need some simplifying assumptions. Again, let's assume the prebook data are extremely informative; that is, O'Neill is able to precisely predict total season sales after observing the prebook data. Fortunately, we do not have to worry about stocking out between the two orders, because the prebook orders do not have to be delivered immediately. However, the minimum order quantity per item is trickier to figure out.

A minimum order quantity reduces O'Neill's ability to respond to demand information. For example, suppose there is a 1,500-unit minimum and O'Neill orders 3,500 Hammer 3/2s in October. After observing prebook demand, O'Neill concludes that it can sell a total of 3,900 Hammer 3/2s, that is, 400 more than it has available with just the initial order. O'Neill has two choices: order no additional Hammers, and probably stock out, or order 1,500 additional Hammers and probably have plenty of leftover wetsuits. Neither option is particularly desirable. However, the minimum does not impose a problem as long as realized demand is substantially greater than the initial order quantity. In particular, if O'Neill did not even order the Hammer 3/2 in the first order, then O'Neill could order precisely 3,900 units in the second order.

This thinking suggests that the minimum forces O'Neill to essentially include an item in either the first order or the second order, but not both orders, especially if the minimum is large relative to expected demand. Therefore, let's approximate the effect of the minimums by imposing on ourselves a different constraint that behaves like the minimum constraint. Specifically, let's adopt the *order-once constraint:* an item is included in either the first order or the second order, but no item has a positive quantity in both orders. Imposing the order-once constraint allows us to ignore the minimum constraint: TEC probably will allow O'Neill to submit any order for each item as long as O'Neill orders each item on only one occasion.

At this point it is useful to consider a specific example. Given that O'Neill sells a large number of different types of wetsuits, it is also useful to consider a condensed version of O'Neill's entire problem. Table 10.4 displays data for a representative sample of 10 wetsuits. Notice that demand variability, margins, and end-of-season discounts differ across categories (sports).

Let's begin the analysis by assuming O'Neill has only a single ordering opportunity. We can use the data in Table 10.4 to evaluate O'Neill's optimal order quantity, expected profit, and mismatch cost for each item. Those results are displayed in Table 10.5. We see that

TABLE 10.4
Data from a Sample of 10 Wetsuits at O'Neill

Sport	Model	μ	σ	σ/μ	Price	Margin	Discount
DIVE	DIVE COMP 3/2 FULL	1,100	660	0.60	120	38%	65%
DIVE	WMS 7000× 7MM FULL	600	360	0.60	275	38	65
SURF	EPIC 5/3 W/HD	800	296	0.37	225	38	50
SURF	HEAT 3/2	1,200	444	0.37	110	38	50
SURF	HEATWAVE 4/3	700	259	0.37	140	38	50
SURF	ZEN-ZIP 4/3	3,100	1,147	0.37	165	38	50
TRIATHLON	TRIATHLON 4/3 FULL	2,600	1,690	0.65	210	45	65
WAKE-BOARD	REACTOR 3/2	1,500	750	0.50	150	45	65
WINDSURF	CYCLONE 4/3	950	665	0.70	325	45	65
WINDSURF	WMS EVOLUTION 4/3	850	595	0.70	275	45	65

μ = Expected demand
σ = Standard deviation of demand
Price = Wholesale price
Margin = Gross margin as a percent of price
Discount = Anticipated end-of-season discount as percent of price to sell leftover inventory

O'Neill would order approximately 17,000 units if only a single order were available and the mismatch cost would be nearly 28 percent of maximum profit (291,794/1,054,105).

For the sake of argument, let's say TEC is willing to offer the second order in December if O'Neill's first replenishment order is for at least 10,200 units, which is about 60 percent of what O'Neill would order if it had only a single ordering opportunity. Which items should O'Neill include in the first order and how much should be ordered?

Any wetsuit included in the first order receives only one opportunity to generate supply; that is, a second order is not allowed for that item in the December order. Therefore, the newsvendor optimal quantity should be ordered for each wetsuit in the first order. So the issue of how much to order is settled, but the issue of which wetsuits to order remains. Unfortunately, there are many possible combinations. In fact, there are $2^{10} = 1,024$ possible initial orders with 10 wetsuits. (Each wetsuit is either in the first order or not, hence, 2^n initial orders can be constructed with n items.) Furthermore, there are 311 possible initial orders that total 10,200 units or more. (Recall that TEC requests the first order include at least 10,200 units in total.) While a computer can sort through these combinations relatively quickly, the number of possible combinations grows rapidly so that even a reasonable scenario with 100 items is intractable if we must fully enumerate ($2^{100} = 1.26 \times 10^{30}$, which is a rather big number).

While there are many possible initial orders, some of them are intuitively not reasonable. If an item is not included in the initial order, then it is in the second order, and the advantage of the second order is that demand is observed before the second order. Hence, the expected profit of any item put into the second order is actually its maximum profit. So each item either earns the newsvendor's expected profit (if it is put into the first order) or the maximum profit (if it is left for the second order). Therefore, our initial intuition suggests that an item with a low mismatch cost, the difference between its maximum profit and its expected profit, should be a good candidate for the initial order, thereby saving room for an item with a high mismatch cost for the second order.

Our initial intuition can be sharpened if we consider the following situation: Suppose two items have the same mismatch cost, but one has a newsvendor order quantity of 3,000 units and the other has a newsvendor quantity of 1,000 units. These items are equally effective at reducing mismatch costs, but they are not the same from the perspective of meeting our initial order quantity obligation of 10,200 units. The first item, with a quantity of 3,000 units, does a better job with that goal. In other words, an item that is attractive for the first order has a low mismatch cost (we would not benefit much by putting it in the second order) and a high newsvendor quantity (it serves to meet our initial order quantity constraint). This suggests a simple algorithm for choosing the items for the initial order

TABLE 10.5
Analysis of Profits and Mismatch Costs If Only a Single Order Is Made for Each Item

Sport	Model	Order Quantity	Expected Profit	Maximum Profit	Mismatch Cost
DIVE	DIVE COMP 3/2 FULL	1,241	$ 30,086	$ 50,160	$ 20,074
DIVE	WMS 7000× 7MM FULL	677	37,608	62,700	25,092
SURF	EPIC 5/3 W/HD	1,009	58,048	68,400	10,352
SURF	HEAT 3/2	1,514	42,568	50,160	7,592
SURF	HEATWAVE 4/3	883	31,604	37,240	5,636
SURF	ZEN-ZIP 4/3	3,910	164,953	194,370	29,417
TRIATHLON	TRIATHLON 4/3 FULL	3,449	164,582	245,700	81,118
WAKE-BOARD	REACTOR 3/2	1,877	75,536	101,250	25,714
WINDSURF	CYCLONE 4/3	1,284	89,538	138,938	49,399
WINDSURF	WMS EVOLUTION 4/3	1,149	67,788	105,188	37,399
Total		16,993	$762,311	$1,054,105	$291,794

TABLE 10.6
An Initial Order
Constructed Using
the Ratios of
Mismatch Costs to
Order Quantities

Model	Order Quantity	Newsvendor Expected Profit	Mismatch Cost	Mismatch Cost–Order Quantity Ratio	First Order Quantity	Profit
HEAT 3/2	1,514	$ 42,568	$ 7,592	5.0	1,514	$ 42,568
HEATWAVE 4/3	883	31,604	5,636	6.4	883	31,604
ZEN-ZIP 4/3	3,910	164,953	29,417	7.5	3,910	164,953
EPIC 5/3 W/HD	1,009	58,048	10,352	10.3	1,009	58,048
REACTOR 3/2	1,877	75,536	25,714	13.7	1,877	75,536
DIVE COMP 3/2 FULL	1,241	30,086	20,074	16.2	1,241	30,086
TRIATHLON 4/3 FULL	3,449	164,582	81,118	23.5	0	245,700
WMS EVOLUTION 4/3	1,149	67,788	37,399	32.6	0	105,188
WMS 7000X 7MM FULL	677	37,608	25,092	37.1	0	62,700
CYCLONE 4/3	1,284	89,538	49,399	38.5	0	138,938
Total	16,993	$762,311	$291,794		10,434	$955,320

quantity. First, evaluate the ratio of each wetsuit's mismatch cost to newsvendor quantity, which we call the *mismatch–quantity ratio:*

$$\text{Mismatch} - \text{quantity ratio} = \frac{\text{Mismatch cost}}{Q}$$

Items with a low value for the mismatch–quantity ratio are good candidates for the initial order. Therefore, sort the items in ascending order by their mismatch–quantity ratios and then choose items to include in the first order in that sequence until the minimum initial order quantity is met.

Let's illustrate this procedure with our data. Table 10.6 displays a table with the items sorted in ascending order according to the mismatch–quantity ratio. The most attractive item for the initial order is the Heat 3/2 because it has a relatively low mismatch cost ($7,592) and an intermediate order quantity (1,514) to yield a ratio of 5.0. The Cyclone 4/3 is the most attractive item to *not* include in the first order because it has a high mismatch cost and a low order quantity.

Items are added to the initial order until the minimum is reached. For example, the total order of the first five items (Heat 3/2 through Reactor 3/2) is 9,193, which does not meet the minimum of 10,200. However, adding the Dive Comp 3/2 Full raises the initial order quantity to 10,434. Therefore, we leave the remaining four wetsuits for the second replenishment.

The performance of our initial order described in Table 10.6 is good: It generates an expected profit of $955,320, which is an increase of $193,009 over the profit that would be earned with only a single order. From another perspective, the second order reduces the total mismatch cost of $291,794 (which occurs when only a single order is allowed) by over 66 percent!

Because we have considered a relatively small problem (only 10 wetsuits), we have the luxury of being able to discover the true optimal initial order. To do that we merely need to enumerate all 1,024 possible initial orders, evaluate their profit, and then choose the one with the highest profit that has at least 10,200 units. Sure enough, the initial order we found is indeed the optimal order. Figure 10.4 displays a scatter plot of all of the possible initial orders.

We see from the figure that the mismatch–quantity ratio technique for choosing an initial order performs extremely well: For any given initial order quantity requirement, the technique generally finds the very best initial order, or at least an initial order that is nearly the best. The point can be emphasized further. There are 54 initial orders with total order

FIGURE 10.4
Expected Profit and Total Initial Order Quantity for All Possible Initial Orders
(Diamonds are the initial orders constructed with the mismatch cost–order quantity ratio).

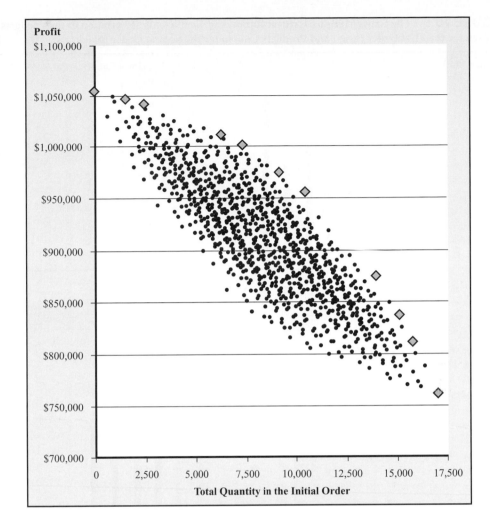

quantities between 10,000 and 10,500 units. Among those initial orders, profit ranges considerably, from a low of $819,394 to a high of $955,320 (with our chosen order).

So we see that we can benefit considerably from some reactive capacity in the form of a second order after learning demand information, even if that reactive capacity is limited. However, we must be smart about which products we order first and which products we leave to the second order if we want to fully exploit the value of that reactive capacity. In particular, products with a low mismatch cost-to-order quantity ratio are prime candidates for early production.

Given the analysis from Sections 10.1 and 10.2, we are even able to say more about which products have a low mismatch–quantity ratio. Recall that the mismatch cost as a percentage of the maximum profit (equation (10.2)) depends on two things: the critical ratio (through the ratio $\phi(z)/\Phi(z)$) and the coefficient of variation. And the maximum profit depends on the gross margin. So the likely candidates for the first order are products with low gross margins (therefore low maximum profit) and products with high critical ratios or low coefficients of variation (therefore high mismatch cost as a percentage of the maximum profit). As we see in Figure 10.5, the products chosen for the first order indeed tend to have those characteristics. The beauty of this simple method is that it provides an easy technique for combining these multiple dimensions into a single score, the mismatch cost–quantity ratio.

FIGURE 10.5 The Gross Margins, Critical Ratios, and Coefficients of Variation of the Products Chosen for the First Order (gray) and Products Chosen for the Second Order (black)

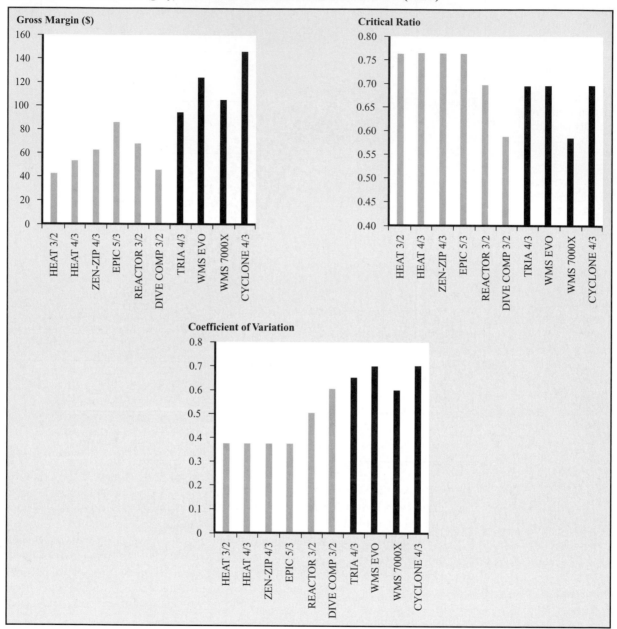

On a final note, recall that TEC imposes the initial order quantity minimum to ensure O'Neill does not ask for more units in the second order than TEC can produce. It is therefore worthwhile to evaluate O'Neill's expected second order quantity given the chosen initial order. For each item not included in the first order, O'Neill's second order for that item equals actual demand (because O'Neill uses the prebook data to determine actual demand before the second order). Therefore, the expected second order quantity for a wetsuit equals its expected demand. The total expected second order quantity then equals the sum of the expected demands of the items in that order.

In the case of the chosen portfolio, there are four items in the second order and their total expected demand is $2,600 + 950 + 850 + 600 = 5,000$ units. Therefore, TEC's requirement that O'Neill order at least 10,200 units in the first order is a sufficient constraint as long as TEC has the ability to produce 5,000 units in the second order. Ideally, TEC should have the ability to produce even more than that because there will be some variation in O'Neill's second order quantity. As a benchmark, recall that TEC needs nearly 17,000 units of capacity if O'Neill submits a single order in November. Given that O'Neill submits its first order one month earlier with this new arrangement, it is plausible that TEC could have 7,000 to 8,000 units of reactive capacity, which should be plenty enough to cover O'Neill's expected second order quantity of 5,000 units.

10.5 Summary

With the newsvendor's make-to-stock system, the firm commits to its entire supply before any updated demand information is learned. As a result, there are demand–supply mismatch costs that manifest themselves in the form of leftover inventory or lost sales. This chapter identifies situations in which the mismatch cost is high and considers several improvements to the newsvendor situation to reduce those mismatch costs.

Mismatch costs are high (as a percentage of a product's maximum profit) when a product has a low critical ratio and/or a high coefficient of variation. A low critical ratio implies that the cost of leftover inventory is high relative to the cost of a lost sale. Perishable products or products that face obsolescence generally have low critical ratios. The coefficient of variation is the ratio of the standard deviation of demand to expected demand. It is high for products that are hard to forecast. Examples include new products, fashionable products, and specialty products with small markets. The important lesson here is that actions that lower the critical ratio or increase the coefficient of variation also increase demand–supply mismatch costs.

Make-to-order is an extreme solution to the newsvendor situation. With make-to-order, the firm begins producing an item only after the firm has an order from a customer. In other words, production begins only when the ultimate owner of an item becomes known. A key advantage with make-to-order is that leftover inventory is eliminated. However, a make-to-order system is not immune to the problems of demand–supply mismatches because it behaves like a queuing system. As a result, customers must wait to be satisfied and the length of their waiting time is sensitive to the amount of idle capacity.

Dell is probably the best example of a company that has used make-to-order to its competitive advantage. Make-to-order is particularly well suited for personal computers for several reasons: inventory is very expensive to hold because of obsolescence and falling component prices; labor is a small portion of the cost of a PC, in part because the modular design of PCs allows for fast and easy assembly; customers are primarily concerned with price and customization and less concerned with how long they must wait for delivery (i.e., they are patient) and unique design features (i.e., it is hard to differentiate one PC from another with respect to design); there is a large pool of educated customers who are willing to purchase without physically seeing the product (i.e., the phone/Internet channels work); and the cost to transport a PC is reasonable (relative to its total value).

While make-to-order is the ideal strategy for PCs, it is not ideal in all situations. Koss Corp., a headphone maker, is an example of a company that discovered that make-to-order is not always a magic bullet (Ramstad, 1999). They experimented with make-to-order and discovered they were unable to provide timely deliveries to their customers (retailers) during their peak season. In other words, demand was variable, but their capacity was not sufficiently flexible. Because they began to lose business due to their slow response time, they switched back to make-to-stock so that they would build up inventory before their peak demand period. For Koss, holding inventory was cheaper than losing sales to impatient customers.

The auto industry also is trying to move toward being more "Dell like," that is, more make-to-order. In fact Toyota sent tremors through the industry in 1999 by announcing it was planning to produce a custom-ordered vehicle in only five days (Simison, 1999). However, due to the challenges of implementing make-to-order with autos, the company quietly backed away from the project.

The intermediate solution between make-to-order and make-to-stock has the firm commit to some production before any demand information is learned, but the firm also has the capability to react to early demand information via a second order, which is called reactive capacity. Reactive capacity can take different forms: there could be unlimited but costly reactive capacity or limited reactive capacity that is no more expensive than initial capacity. Furthermore, reactive capacity can substantially reduce (but not eliminate) the newsvendor's mismatch cost.

Grupo Zara SA of Spain is an excellent example of a company that utilizes reactive capacity in the apparel industry. Their distinctive feature is "fashion on demand": They are constantly introducing new styles to better match their assortment to the trends and tastes of consumers. As a result, Zara is able to produce and deliver a new style to its stores in less than two weeks, while many other apparel retailers take six months to one year or more. They achieve this remarkable lead time because they own their own production within Spain, they hold excess sewing capacity, and, most importantly, they are willing to hold inventory in fabrics that have long lead times: reactive capacity is useless if component inventory is unavailable.

While Zara operates a vertically integrated system, in both of the reactive capacity examples discussed in this chapter, it is clear that O'Neill's access to reactive capacity depends upon the cooperation of its supplier, TEC. It is only through good supplier relations that both firms can restructure their relationship to the benefit of both firms.

If O'Neill were unable to gain the cooperation of TEC, then O'Neill could consider developing its own reactive capacity. For example, O'Neill effectively creates reactive capacity by establishing production in Mexico. Mexican labor is more expensive than Asian labor, so production in Mexico is costlier than in Asia. However, the shipping lead time from Mexico is much faster, thereby allowing O'Neill to replenish midseason, as in our first reactive capacity example (see Figure 10.2). Therefore, a Mexican facility would enable O'Neill to reduce its demand–supply mismatch costs.

Although reactive capacity is useful, some sophistication is required to utilize it to its fullest potential. For example, a limited bit of reactive capacity can reduce mismatch costs, but a firm must be able to prioritize its products accordingly. Roughly speaking, a firm should produce "safe" items first, thereby saving the limited reactive capacity for products that can benefit the most from it.

The following statement summarizes the managerial insights from Chapters 9 and 10: *When managing products with uncertain demand, it is essential that firms quantify uncertainty and, wherever possible, reduce uncertainty.*

Quantifying uncertainty means developing mean and standard deviation forecasts for each item that reflect the true demand variability associated with the item. In other words, all items should not be treated as equally uncertain. Furthermore, *quantifying uncertainty* means understanding each product's underage and overage costs to be able to evaluate each product's critical ratio.

Reducing uncertainty includes collecting and storing data so that good forecasts can be constructed and putting effort into generating forecasts. Switching from make-to-stock to make-to-order also reduces uncertainty, but as we discussed, the cost of that uncertainty reduction does not always justify its benefit. Finding some reactive capacity is also an example of an effort to reduce uncertainty because with reactive capacity at least some production occurs after demand information is learned. In fact, there are a number of other techniques for reducing uncertainty, some of which are discussed in later chapters.

Table 10.7 provides a summary of the key notation and equations presented in this chapter.

TABLE 10.7
A Summary of the Key Notation and Equations in Chapter 10

Q = Order quantity
C_u = Underage cost C_o = Overage cost
μ = Expected demand σ = Standard deviation of demand
$\Phi(Q)$, $\phi(Q)$: Distribution and density functions of the standard normal

Mismatch cost = $(C_o \times$ Expected leftover inventory$)$ + $(C_u \times$ Expected lost sales$)$
          = Maximum profit − Expected profit

Maximum profit = (Price − Cost) $\times \mu$

Mismatch cost as a percentage of the maximum profit = $\left(\dfrac{\phi(z)}{\Phi(z)}\right) \times \left(\dfrac{\sigma}{\mu}\right)$

Coefficient of variation = Standard deviation/Expected demand

Mismatch–quantity ratio = $\dfrac{\text{Mismatch cost}}{Q}$

10.6 Further Reading

More responsive, more flexible, more reactive operations have been the goal over the last 20 years in most industries, in large part due to the success of Dell Inc. in the personal computer business. For an insightful review of Dell's strategy, see Magretta (1998). See McWilliams and White (1999) for an interview with Michael Dell on his views on how the auto industry should change with respect to its sales and production strategy.

For a comprehensive treatment of Quick Response in the apparel industry, see Abernathy, Dunlop, Hammond, and Weil (1999). Vitzthum (1998) describes how Zara, a Spanish fashion retailer, is able to produce "fashion on demand."

Fisher (1997) discusses the pros and cons of flexible supply chains and Zipkin (2001) does the same for mass customization. Karmarkar (1989) discusses the pros and cons of push versus pull production systems.

See Fisher and Raman (1996) or Fisher, Rajaram, and Raman (2001) for technical algorithms to optimize order quantities when early sales information and reactive capacity are available.

10.7 Practice Problems

Q10.1* **(O'Neill)** Consider the case in the relationship between O'Neill and TEC with unlimited, but expensive, reactive capacity, that is, TEC allows O'Neill to submit a second order but charges O'Neill a premium for those units. (See Figure 10.2.) Instead of a 20 percent premium, suppose TEC were to charge O'Neill only a 10 percent premium for units in the second order.

   a. What is O'Neill's optimal first order quantity of Hammer 3/2s?

   b. What is O'Neill's maximum expected profit with the Hammer 3/2?

   c. How many units should TEC expect O'Neill will order in the second order?

   d. What fraction of the mismatch cost is eliminated by this reactive capacity opportunity?

Q10.2* **(Teddy Bower)** Teddy Bower sources a parka from an Asian supplier for $10 each and sells them to customers for $22 each. Leftover parkas at the end of the season have no salvage value. (Recall Q9.5.) The demand forecast is normally distributed with mean 2,100 and standard deviation 1,200. Now suppose Teddy Bower found a reliable vendor in the United States that can produce parkas very quickly but at a higher price than Teddy Bower's Asian supplier. Hence, in addition to parkas from Asia, Teddy Bower can buy an unlimited quantity of additional parkas from this American vendor at $15 each after demand is known.

   a. Suppose Teddy Bower orders 1,500 parkas from the Asian supplier. What is the probability that Teddy Bower will order from the American supplier once demand is known?

(* indicates that the solution is at the end of the book)

b. Again assume that Teddy Bower orders 1,500 parkas from the Asian supplier. What is the American supplier's expected demand; that is, how many parkas should the American supplier expect that Teddy Bower will order?

c. Given the opportunity to order from the American supplier at $15 per parka, what order quantity from its Asian supplier now maximizes Teddy Bower's expected profit?

d. Given the order quantity evaluated in part c, what is Teddy Bower's expected profit?

e. If Teddy Bower didn't order any parkas from the Asian supplier, then what would Teddy Bower's expected profit be?

Q10.3   **(Flextrola)** Flextrola, Inc., an electronics system integrator, is developing a new product. As mentioned in Q9.3, Solectrics can produce a key component for this product. Solectrics sells this component to Flextrola for $72 per unit and Flextrola must submit its order well in advance of the selling season. Flextrola's demand forecast is a normal distribution with mean of 1,000 and standard deviation of 600. Flextrola sells each unit, after integrating some software, for $121. Leftover units at the end of the season are sold for $50.

Xandova Electronics (XE for short) approached Flextrola with the possibility of also supplying Flextrola with this component. XE's main value proposition is that they offer 100 percent fill rate and one-day delivery on all of Flextrola's orders, no matter when the orders are submitted. Flextrola promises its customers a one-week lead time, so the one-day lead time from XE would allow Flextrola to operate with make-to-order production. (The software integration that Flextrola performs can be done within one day.) XE's price is $83.50 per unit.

a. Suppose Flextrola were to procure exclusively from XE. What would be Flextrola's expected profit?

b. Suppose Flextrola plans to procure from both Solectrics and XE; that is, Flextrola will order some amount from Solectrics before the season and then use XE during the selling season to fill demands that exceed that order quantity. How many units should Flextrola order from Solectrics to maximize expected profit?

c. Concerned about the potential loss of business, Solectrics is willing to renegotiate their offer. Solectrics now offers Flextrola an "options contract": Before the season starts, Flextrola purchases Q options and pays Solectrics $25 per option. During the selling season, Flextrola can exercise up to the Q purchased options with a one-day lead time—that is, Solectrics delivers on each exercised option within one day—and the exercise price is $50 per unit. If Flextrola wishes additional units beyond the options purchased, Solectrics will deliver units at XE's price, $83.50. For example, suppose Flextrola purchases 1,500 options but then needs 1,600 units. Flextrola exercises the 1,500 options at $50 each and then orders an additional 100 units at $83.50 each. How many options should Flextrola purchase from Solectrics?

d. Continuing with part c, given the number of options purchased, what is Flextrola's expected profit?

Q10.4   **(Three Kings)** Recall Q9.8. Erica Zhang must decide how many Three Kings baking dishes to purchase for her upcoming promotion. Forecasted demand is normally distributed with mean 980 and standard deviation 354. Leftover cake dishes are sold to a discounter for $15. But now the department store just instituted a new policy regarding stockouts. If a promotion item is out of stock, then a customer can request a comparable item for the same price as the stocked-out item. For example, if the store runs out of Three Kings baking dishes, then a customer can request instead a regular baking dish and pay the Three Kings price. The department store has plenty of regular baking dishes, so there is no risk of running out of them. Furthermore, Erica believes that all of her Three Kings customers would be willing to switch to the regular baking dish should they experience a stockout. Data on the Three Kings baking dish as well as the regular baking dish follow on p. 237:

	Three Kings Baking Dish	Regular Dish
Selling price	$40.00	$55.00
Purchase price	$16.00	$30.00
Shipping cost	$ 3.00	$ 1.20
Handling cost*	$ 0.80	$ 0.80
Warehouse surcharge**	$ 1.10	$ 1.65
Total	$20.90	$33.65

*Estimate of variable cost to uncrate, clean, and transport a dish to the housewares department.
**Allocation of fixed overhead expenses in the shipping and receiving department.

a. How many Three Kings baking dishes should she purchase?

b. Is the department store better off with this new substitution policy?

c. Suppose Erica now believes that only half of her Three Kings customers would be willing to substitute the regular baking dish. Given this new belief, how many Three Kings baking dishes should she purchase?

Q10.5 **(Wildcat Cellular)** Marisol is new to town and is in the market for cellular phone service. She has settled on Wildcat Cellular, which will give her a free phone if she signs a one-year contract. Wildcat offers several calling plans. One plan that she is considering is called "Pick Your Minutes." Under this plan, she would specify a quantity of minutes, say x, per month that she would buy at 5¢ per minute. Thus, her upfront cost would be $0.05x$. If her usage is less than this quantity x in a given month, she loses the minutes. If her usage in a month exceeds this quantity x, she would have to pay 40¢ for each extra minute (that is, each minute used beyond x). For example, if she contracts for $x = 120$ minutes per month and her actual usage is 40 minutes, her total bill is $120 \times 0.05 = \$6.00$. However, if actual usage is 130 minutes, her total bill would be $120 \times 0.05 + (130 - 120) \times 0.40 = \$10.00$.

The same rates apply whether the call is local or long distance. Once she signs the contract, she cannot change the number of minutes specified for a year. Marisol estimates that her monthly needs are best approximated by the normal distribution, with a mean of 250 minutes and a standard deviation of 24 minutes.

a. If Marisol chooses the "Pick Your Minutes" plan described above, how many minutes should she contract for?

b. Instead, Marisol chooses to contract for 240 minutes. Under this contract, how much (in dollars) would she expect to pay at 40 cents per minute?

c. A friend advises Marisol to contract for 280 minutes to ensure limited surcharge payments (i.e., the 40-cents-per-minute payments). Under this contract, how many minutes would she expect to waste (i.e., unused minutes per month)?

d. If Marisol contracts for 260 minutes, what would be her approximate expected monthly cell phone bill?

e. Marisol has decided that she indeed does not like surcharge fees (the 40-cents-per-minute fee for her usage in excess of her monthly contracted minutes). How many minutes should she contract for if she wants only a 5 percent chance of incurring any surcharge fee?

f. Wildcat Cellular offers another plan called "No Minimum" that also has a $5.00 fixed fee per month but requires no commitment in terms of the number of minutes per month. Instead, the user is billed 7¢ per minute for her actual usage. Thus, if her actual usage is 40 minutes in a month, her bill would be $5.00 + 40 \times 0.07 = \$7.80$. Marisol is trying to decide between the "Pick Your Minutes" plan described above and the "No Minimum" plan. Which should she choose?

Q10.6 **(Sarah's Wedding)** Sarah is planning her wedding. She and her fiancé have signed a contract with a caterer that calls for them to tell the caterer the number of guests that will attend the reception a week before the actual event. This "final number" will determine how much they have to pay the caterer; they must pay $60 per guest that they commit to. If, for example, they tell the caterer that they expect 90 guests, they must pay $5,400 ($= 90 \times \$60$) even if only, say, 84 guests show up. The contract calls for a higher rate of $85 per extra guest for the number of guests beyond what the couple commits to. Thus, if Sarah and her fiancé commit to 90 guests but 92 show up, they must pay $5,570 (the original $5,400 plus $2 \times \$85$).

The problem Sarah faces is that she still does not know the exact number of guests to expect. Despite asking that friends and family members reply to their invitations a month ago, some uncertainty remains: her brother may—or may not—bring his new girlfriend; her fiancé's college roommate may—or may not—be able to take a vacation from work; and so forth. Sarah has determined that the expected number of guests (i.e., the mean number) is 100, but the actual number could be anywhere from 84 to 116:

Q	f(Q)	F(Q)	L(Q)	Q	f(Q)	F(Q)	L(Q)
84	0.0303	0.0303	16.00	101	0.0303	0.5455	3.64
85	0.0303	0.0606	15.03	102	0.0303	0.5758	3.18
86	0.0303	0.0909	14.09	103	0.0303	0.6061	2.76
87	0.0303	0.1212	13.18	104	0.0303	0.6364	2.36
88	0.0303	0.1515	12.30	105	0.0303	0.6667	2.00
89	0.0303	0.1818	11.45	106	0.0303	0.6970	1.67
90	0.0303	0.2121	10.64	107	0.0303	0.7273	1.36
91	0.0303	0.2424	9.85	108	0.0303	0.7576	1.09
92	0.0303	0.2727	9.09	109	0.0303	0.7879	0.85
93	0.0303	0.3030	8.36	110	0.0303	0.8182	0.64
94	0.0303	0.3333	7.67	111	0.0303	0.8485	0.45
95	0.0303	0.3636	7.00	112	0.0303	0.8788	0.30
96	0.0303	0.3939	6.36	113	0.0303	0.9091	0.18
97	0.0303	0.4242	5.76	114	0.0303	0.9394	0.09
98	0.0303	0.4545	5.18	115	0.0303	0.9697	0.03
99	0.0303	0.4848	4.64	116	0.0303	1.0000	0.00
100	0.0303	0.5152	4.12				

Q = Number of guests that show up to the wedding
$f(Q)$ = Density function = Prob{Q guests show up}
$F(Q)$ = Distribution function = Prob{Q or fewer guests show up}
$L(Q)$ = Loss function = Expected number of guests above Q

a. How many guests should Sarah commit to with the caterer?

b. Suppose Sarah commits to 105 guests. What is Sarah's expected bill?

c. Suppose that the caterer is willing to alter the contract so that if fewer than the number of guests they commit to show up, they will get a partial refund. In particular, they only have to pay $45 for each "no-show." For example, if they commit to 90 but only 84 show, they will have to pay $84 \times \$60 + 6 \times \$45 = \$5,310$. Now how many guests should she commit to?

d. The caterer offers Sarah another option. She could pay $70 per guest, no matter how many guests show up; that is, she wouldn't have to commit to any number before the wedding. Should Sarah prefer this option or the original option ($60 per committed guest and $85 each guest beyond the commitment)?

Q10.7 **(Lucky Smokes)** Lucky Smokes currently operates a warehouse that serves the Virginia market. Some trucks arrive at the warehouse filled with goods to be stored in the warehouse. Other trucks arrive at the warehouse empty to be loaded with goods. Based on the number of trucks that arrive at the warehouse in a week, the firm is able to accurately estimate the total number of labor hours that are required to finish all of the loading and unloading. The following histogram plots these estimates for each week over the past two

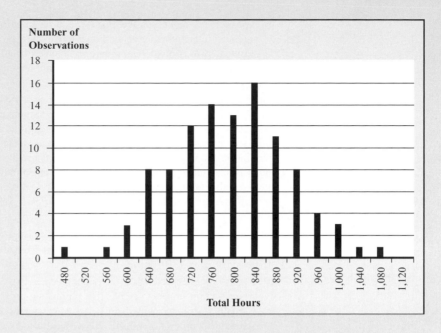

years. (There are a total of 104 weeks recorded in the graph.) For example, there were three weeks in this period that required 600 total labor hours and only one week that recorded 1,080 hours of required labor.

The mean of the data is 793 and the standard deviation is 111. Labor is the primary variable cost in the operation of a warehouse. The Virginia warehouse employed 20 workers, who were guaranteed at least 40 hours of pay per week. Thus, in weeks with less than 800 hours of required labor, the workers either went home early on some days or were idle. On weeks with more than 800 hours of required labor, the extra hours were obtained with overtime. Workers were paid time and a half for each hour of overtime.

You have been placed in charge of a new warehouse scheduled to serve the North Carolina market. Marketing suggests that the volume for this warehouse should be comparable to the Virginia warehouse. Assume that you must pay each worker for at least 40 hours of work per week and time and a half for each hour of overtime. Assume there is no limit on overtime for a given week. Further, assume you approximate your workload requirement with a normal distribution.

a. If you hire 22 workers, how many weeks a year should you expect to use overtime?

b. If you hire 18 workers, how many weeks a year will your workers be underutilized?

c. If you are interested in minimizing your labor cost, how many workers should you hire (again, assuming your workload forecast is normally distributed)?

d. You are now concerned the normal distribution might not be appropriate. For example, you can't hire 20.5 workers. What is the optimal number of workers to hire if you use the empirical distribution function constructed with the data in the above histogram?

Q10.8　(**Shillings**) You are traveling abroad and have only American dollars with you. You are currently in the capital but you will soon be heading out to a small town for an extended stay. In the town, no one takes credit cards and they only accept the domestic currency (shillings). In the capital, you can convert dollars to shillings at a rate of two shillings per dollar. In the town, you learn that one dollar only buys 1.6 shillings. Upon your return to the capital at the end of your trip, you can convert shillings back to dollars at a rate of 2.5 shillings per dollar. You estimate that your expenditures in the town will be normally distributed with mean of 400 shillings and standard deviation of 100 shillings.

a. How many dollars should you convert to shillings before leaving the capital?

b. After some thought, you feel that it might be embarrassing if you run out of shillings and need to ask to convert additional dollars, so you really do not want to run out of shillings. How many dollars should you convert to shillings if you want to ensure there is no more than a 1 in 200 chance you will run out of shillings?

Q10.9 **(TEC)** Consider the relationship between TEC and O'Neill with unlimited, but expensive, reactive capacity. Recall that TEC is willing to give O'Neill a midseason replenishment (see Figure 10.2) but charges O'Neill a 20 percent premium above the regular wholesale price of $110 for those units. Suppose TEC's gross margin is 25 percent of its selling price for units produced in the first production run. However, TEC estimates that its production cost per unit for the second production run (any units produced during the season after receiving O'Neill's second order) is twice as large as units produced for the initial order. Wetsuits produced that O'Neill does not order need to be salvaged at the end of the season. With O'Neill's permission, TEC estimates it can earn $30 per suit by selling the extra suits in Asian markets.

a. What is TEC's expected profit with the traditional arrangement (i.e., a single order by O'Neill well in advance of the selling season)? Recall that O'Neill's optimal newsvendor quantity is 4,101 units.

b. What is TEC's expected profit if it offers the reactive capacity to O'Neill and TEC's first production run equals O'Neill's first production order? Assume the demand forecast is normally distributed with mean 3,192 and standard deviation 1,181. Recall, O'Neill's optimal first order is 3,263 and O'Neill's expected second order is 437 units.

c. What is TEC's optimal first production quantity if its CEO authorizes its production manager to choose a quantity that is greater than O'Neill's first order?

d. Given the order chosen in part c, what is TEC's expected profit? (Warning: this is a hard question.)

Q10.10 **(Parkas)** A firm sells five women's ski parkas. Some data on those parkas is listed below:

Parka	Price	μ	σ	C_o	C_u	Q	Expected Profit
A	$220	1,000	300	35.2	52.8	1,202	$41,740
B	205	2,000	800	28.7	49.2	2,540	73,618
C	190	3,000	1500	22.8	45.6	4,012	98,429
D	175	2,000	1200	17.5	42.0	2,809	59,186
E	160	1,000	700	12.8	38.4	1,472	27,011

Q in the above table is the optimal newsvendor quantity and "Expected Profit" is the newsvendor expected profit if Q is ordered. The firm will produce some parkas well in advance of the selling season. The other parkas are produced after a trade show that occurs shortly before the season starts. After attending the trade show, the firm will basically know demand for each parka. Unfortunately, the firm's capacity is limited after the trade show, so the firm wants to produce at least 5,000 parkas before the trade show. Furthermore, a parka should be produced either before the trade show or after the trade show, but a parka should not be produced in both production opportunities.

a. What is the firm's expected profit if every parka is produced before the trade show?

b. What is the firm's expected profit if every parka is produced after the trade show?

c. What should the production quantities before the trade show be for each parka?

d. What is the expected number of units the firm will produce after the trade show? (Assume that there is sufficient after–trade show capacity given the before–trade show order.)

e. What is the firm's expected profit?

Q10.11 **(Office Supply Company)** Office Supply Company (OSC) has a spare parts warehouse in Alaska to support its office equipment maintenance needs. Once every six months, a major replenishment shipment is received. If the inventory of any given part runs out before the next replenishment, then emergency air shipments are used to resupply the part as needed. Orders are placed on January 15 and June 15, and orders are received on February 15 and July 15, respectively.

OSC must determine replenishment quantities for its spare parts. As an example, historical data show that total demand for part 1AA-66 over a six-month interval is Poisson with mean 6.5. The cost of inventorying the unneeded part for six months is $5 (which includes both physical and financial holding costs and is charged based on inventory at the end of the six-month period). The variable production cost for 1AA-66 is $37 per part. The cost of a regular, semiannual shipment is $32 per part, and the cost of an emergency shipment is $50 per part.

It is January 15, and there are currently three 1AA-66 parts in inventory. How many parts should arrive on February 15?

Chapter 11

Service Levels and Lead Times in Supply Chains: The Order-up-to Inventory Model[1]

Many products are sold over a long time horizon with numerous replenishment opportunities. To draw upon a well-known example, consider the Campbell Soup Company's flagship product, chicken noodle soup. It has a long shelf life and future demand is assured. Hence, if in a particular month Campbell Soup has more chicken noodle soup than it needs, it does not have to dispose of its excess inventory. Instead, Campbell need only wait for its pile of inventory to draw down to a reasonable level. And if Campbell Soup finds itself with less inventory than it desires, its soup factory cooks up another batch. Because obsolescence is not a major concern and Campbell is not limited to a single production run, the newsvendor model (Chapters 9 and 10) is not the right inventory tool for this setting. The right tool for this job is the *order-up-to model.*

Although multiple replenishments are feasible, the order-up-to model still faces the "too little–too much" challenge associated with matching supply and demand. Because soup production takes time (i.e., there is a lead time to complete production), Campbell cannot wait until its inventory draws down to zero to begin production. (You would never let your vehicle's fuel tank go empty before you begin driving to a refueling station!) Hence, production of a batch should begin while there is a sufficient amount of inventory to buffer against uncertain demand while we wait for the batch to finish. Since buffer inventory is not free, the objective with the order-up-to model is to strike a balance between running too lean (which leads to undesirable stockouts, i.e., poor service) and running too fat (which leads to inventory holding costs).

Instead of soup, this chapter applies the order-up-to model to the inventory management of a technologically more sophisticated product: a pacemaker manufactured by Medtronic Inc. We begin with a description of Medtronic's supply chain for pacemakers and then detail the order-up-to model. Next, we consider how to use the model to hit target service levels,

---

[1] Data in this chapter have been modified to protect confidentiality.

discuss what service targets are appropriate, and explore techniques for controlling how frequently we order. We conclude with general managerial insights.

11.1 Medtronic's Supply Chain

Medtronic is a designer and manufacturer of medical technology. They are most well known for their line of cardiac rhythm products, and, in particular, pacemakers (Vice President Dick Cheney is one of their famous clients), but their product line extends into numerous other areas: products for the treatment of cardiovascular diseases and surgery, diabetes, neurological diseases, spinal surgery, and eye/nose/throat diseases.

Medtronic's broad product line is the outcome of relentless innovative activity: Medtronic holds over 3,000 patents and invests more than 10 percent of sales revenue in research and development annually. The reward for this effort has been enviable growth: Over the last decade, Medtronic's revenue and profit have grown 17 percent annually, with fiscal year 2002 revenue of about $6.4 billion and operating income of about $1.5 billion.

Inventory in Medtronic's supply chain is held at three levels: manufacturing facilities, distribution centers (DCs), and field locations. The manufacturing facilities are located throughout the world, and they do not hold much finished goods inventory. In the United States there is a single distribution center, located in Mounds View, Minnesota, responsible for the distribution of cardiac rhythm products. That DC ships to approximately 500 sales representatives, each with his or her own defined territory. All of the Medtronic DCs are responsible for providing very high availability of inventory to the sales representatives they serve in the field, where availability is measured with either the in-stock probability or the fill rate.

The majority of finished goods inventory is held in the field by the sales representatives. In fact, *field inventory* is divided into two categories: *consignment inventory* and *trunk inventory.* Consignment inventory is inventory owned by Medtronic at a customer's location, usually a closet in a hospital. Trunk inventory is literally inventory in the trunk of a sales representative's vehicle. A sales representative has easy access to both of these kinds of field inventory, so they can essentially be considered a single pool of inventory.

Let's now focus on a particular DC, a particular sales representative, and a particular product. The DC is the one located in Mounds View, Minnesota. The sales representative is Susan Magnotto and her territory includes the major medical facilities in Madison, Wisconsin. Finally, the product is the InSync ICD Model 7272 pacemaker, which is displayed in Figure 11.1. (In fact, the InSync ICD Model 7272 is much more sophisticated than a traditional pacemaker because it is capable of dynamically responding to a patient's changing conditions with appropriate interventional actions. Nevertheless, for simplicity, we continue to refer to it as a pacemaker.)

A pacemaker is demanded when it is implanted in a patient via surgery. Even though a surgeon can anticipate the need for a pacemaker for a particular patient, a surgeon may not know the appropriate model for a patient until the actual surgery. For this reason, and for the need to maintain a good relationship with each physician, Susan attends each surgery and always carries the various models that might be needed. Susan can replenish her inventory after an implant by calling an order into Medtronic's Customer Service, which then sends the request to the Mounds View DC. If the model she requests is available in inventory at the DC, then it is sent to her via an overnight carrier. The time between when Susan orders a unit and when she receives the unit is generally one day, and rarely more than two days.

The Mounds View DC requests replenishments from the production facilities on a weekly basis. With the InSync pacemaker, there is currently a three-week lead time to receive each order.

FIGURE 11.1
Medtronic's InSync
ICD Pacemaker

For the InSync pacemaker, Figure 11.2 provides one year's data on monthly shipments and end-of-month inventory at the Mounds View DC. Figure 11.3 provides data on monthly implants (i.e., demand) and inventory for the InSync pacemaker in Susan's territory over the same year. As can be seen from the figures, there is a considerable amount of variation in the number of units demanded at the DC and in particular in Susan's territory. Interestingly, it appears that there is more demand in the summer months in Susan's territory, but the aggregate shipments through the DC do not indicate the same pattern. Therefore, it is reasonable to conclude that the "pattern" observed in Susan's demand data is not real: Just like a splotch of ink might look like something on a piece of paper, random events sometimes appear to form a pattern.

As a sales representative, Susan's primary responsibility is to ensure that Medtronic's products are the choice products of physicians in her territory. To encourage active sales effort, a considerable portion of her yearly income is derived from bonuses to achieve aggressive sales thresholds.

If the decision on inventory investment were left up to Susan, she would err on the side of extra inventory. There are a number of reasons why she would like to hold a considerable amount of inventory:

• Due to the sales incentive system, Susan never wants to miss a sale due to a lack of inventory. Because patients and surgeons do not tolerate waiting for back-ordered inventory, if Susan does not have the right product available, then the sale is almost surely lost to a competitor.

• Medtronic's products are generally quite small, so it is possible to hold a considerable amount of inventory in a relatively small space (e.g., the trunk of a vehicle).

• Medtronic's products have a relatively long shelf life, so spoilage is not a major concern. (However, spoilage can be a concern if a rep fails to stick to a "first-in-first-out" regime, thereby allowing a unit to remain in inventory for a disproportionately long time. Given that spoilage is not a significant issue if first-in-first-out is implemented, we'll not consider this issue further in this discussion.)

• While Susan knows that she can be replenished relatively quickly from the DC (assuming the DC has inventory available), she is not always able to find the time to place an

FIGURE 11.2
Monthly Shipments (bar) and End-of-Month Inventory (line) for the InSync Pacemaker at the Mounds View Distribution Center

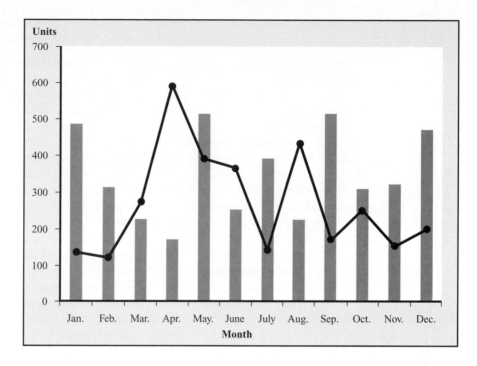

FIGURE 11.3
Monthly Implants (bar) and End-of-Month Inventory (line) for the InSync Pacemaker in Susan's Territory

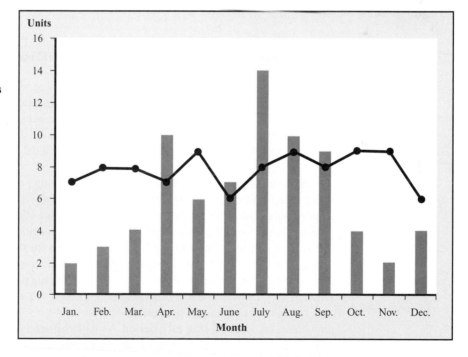

order immediately after an implant. An inventory buffer thereby allows her some flexibility with timing her replenishment requests.

• Although the production facilities are supposed to ensure that the DCs never stock out of product, sometimes a product can become unavailable for several weeks, if not several months. For example, the *production yield* might not be as high as initially planned or a supplier of a key component might be capacity-constrained. Whatever the cause, having a few extra units of inventory helps protect Susan against these shortages.

To ensure that each sales representative holds a reasonable amount of inventory, each sales representative is given a *par level* for each product. The par level specifies the maximum number of units the sales representative can have on-order plus on-hand at any given time. Therefore, once a sales representative's inventory equals her par level, she cannot order an additional unit until one is implanted. The par levels are set quarterly based on previous sales and anticipated demand. If a sales representative feels a higher par level is warranted, he or she can request an adjustment. Even though Medtronic does not wish to give the sales representative full reign over inventory, due to Medtronic's large gross margins, neither does Medtronic want to operate too lean. (Based on their reported income statement, Medtronic's average gross margin is approximately 75 percent.)

An issue for Medtronic is whether its supply chain is supporting its aggressive growth objectives. This chapter first considers the management of field inventory. As of now, the sales representatives are responsible for managing their own inventory (within the limits of set par levels), but maybe a computer-based system should be considered that would choose stocking levels and automatically replenish inventory. This system would relieve Susan Magnotto and other representatives from the task of managing inventory so that they can concentrate on selling product. While that is attractive to Susan, a reduction in product availability is nonnegotiable. After exploring the management of field inventory, attention is turned to the management of the Mounds View distribution center inventory. It is essential that the DC provide excellent availability to the field representatives without holding excessive inventory.

11.2   The Order-up-to Model Design and Implementation

The order-up-to model is designed to manage inventory for a product that has the opportunity for many replenishments over a long time horizon. This section describes the assumptions of the model and how it is implemented in practice. The subsequent sections consider the evaluation of numerous performance measures, how historical data can be used to choose a distribution to represent demand, and how to calibrate the model to achieve one of several possible objectives.

We are working with a single product that is sold over a long period of time. Opportunities to order replenishment inventory occur at regular intervals. The time between two ordering opportunities is called a *period,* and all of the periods are of the same duration. While one day seems like a natural period length for the InSync pacemaker in the field (e.g., in Susan's territory), one week is a more natural period length for the Mounds View DC. In other settings, the appropriate period length could be an hour, a month, or any other interval. See Section 11.8 for additional discussion on the appropriate period length. For the sake of consistency, let's also assume that orders are submitted at the same point in time within the period, say, at the beginning of the period.

Random demand occurs during each period. As with the newsvendor model, among the most critical inputs to the order-up-to model are the parameters of the demand distribution, which is the focus of Section 11.4. However, it is worth mentioning that the model assumes the same demand distribution represents demand in every period. This does not mean that actual demand is the same in every period; it just means that each period's demand is the outcome of a single distribution. The model can be extended to accommodate more complex demand structures, but, as we will see, our simpler structure is adequate for our task.

Receiving a replenishment is the third event within each period. We assume that replenishments are only received at the beginning of a period, before any demand occurs in the period. Hence, if a shipment arrives during a period, then it is available to satisfy demand during that period.

Replenishment orders are received after a fixed amount of time called the *lead time,* which is represented with the variable l. The lead time is measured in periods; if one day is a period, then the lead time to receive an order should be measured in days. Hence, not only should the period length be chosen so that it matches the frequency at which orders can be made and replenishments can be received, it also should be chosen so that the replenishment lead time can be measured in an integer $(0, 1, 2, \ldots)$ number of periods.

There is no limit to the quantity that can be ordered within a period, and no matter the order quantity, the order is always received in the lead time number of periods. Therefore, supply in this model is not capacity-constrained, but delivery of an order does take some time.

Inventory left over at the end of a period is carried over to the next period; there is no obsolescence, theft, or spoilage of inventory.

To summarize, at the start of each period, a replenishment order can be submitted and a replenishment can be received, then random demand occurs. There is no limit imposed on the quantity of any order, but an order is received only after l periods. For example, if the period length is one day and $l = 1$, then a Monday morning order is received Tuesday morning. Each period has the same duration and the same sequence of events occurs in each period (order, receive, demand). Figure 11.4 displays the sequence of events over a sample of three periods when the lead time to receive orders is one period, $l = 1$.

Now let's define several terms we use to describe our inventory system and then we show how the order-up-to level is used to choose an order quantity.

On-order inventory is relatively intuitive: The on-order inventory is the number of units that we ordered in previous periods that we have not yet received. Our on-order inventory should never be negative, but it can be zero. (A negative on-order inventory would imply a return of inventory from the field to the DC, which we are not considering.)

On-hand inventory is also straightforward: It is the number of units of inventory we have on-hand, immediately available to serve demand.

Back order is the number of units on back order, that is, the total amount of demand that has occurred but has not been satisfied. To get the mathematics of the order-up-to model to work precisely, it is necessary to assume that *all* demand is eventually filled, that is, if demand occurs and no units are available in current inventory, then that demand is back-ordered and filled as soon as inventory becomes available. In other words, the order-up-to model assumes there are no lost sales. In some settings, this is not a problem: complete back-ordering is commonplace in the management of inventory between two firms within a supply chain. However, as with the InSync pacemaker in the field, when end consumers generate demand (instead of a firm), the back-order assumption is probably violated (at least to some extent). Nevertheless, if the order-up-to level is chosen so that back orders are

FIGURE 11.4

Sample Sequence of Events in the Order-up-to Model with a One-Period Lead Time, $l = 1$, to Receive Orders

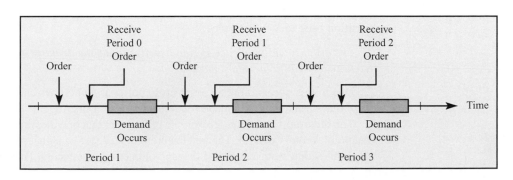

rare, then the order-up-to model is a reasonable approximation. Hence, we use it for the In-Sync pacemaker to manage both the DC inventory as well as Susan's field inventory.

The next measure combines on-hand inventory with the back order:

$$\text{Inventory level} = \text{On-hand inventory} - \text{Back order}$$

Unlike the on-hand inventory and the back order, which are never negative, the inventory level can be negative. It is negative when we have units back-ordered. For example, if the inventory level is -3, then there are three units of demand waiting to be filled.

The following measure combines all of the previous measures:

$$\text{Inventory position} = \text{On-order inventory} + \text{On-hand inventory} - \text{Back order}$$

$$= \text{On-order inventory} + \text{Inventory level}$$

The *order-up-to level* is the maximum inventory position we are willing to have. Let's denote the order-up-to level with the variable S. For example, if $S = 2$, then we are allowed an inventory position up to two units, but no more. Our order-up-to level is essentially equivalent to the par level Medtronic currently uses. It has also been referred to as the *base stock level*. (The order-up-to model is sometimes called the *base stock model*.)

The implementation of our order-up-to policy is relatively straightforward: If we observe at the beginning of any period that our inventory position is less than the order-up-to level S, then we order enough inventory to raise our inventory position to S; that is, in each period we order the difference between S and the inventory position:

$$\text{Each period's order quantity} = S - \text{Inventory position}$$

Because the inventory position includes our on-order inventory, after we submit the order, our inventory position immediately increases to S.

To illustrate an ordering decision, suppose we observe at the beginning of a period that our inventory level is -4 (four units are back-ordered), our on-order inventory is one, and our chosen order-up-to level is $S = 3$. In this situation, we need to order six units: our inventory position is $1 - 4 = -3$ and our order quantity should be S minus the inventory position, $3 - (-3) = 6$.

If we find ourselves in a period with an inventory position that is greater than S, then we should not order anything. Eventually our inventory position will drop below S. After that time we will begin ordering and our inventory position will never again be greater than S as long as we do not change S (because we only order to raise our inventory position to S, never more).

Notice that our inventory position drops below S only when demand occurs. Suppose $S = 3$ and we observe that our inventory position is one at the beginning of the period. If we followed our order-up-to policy in the previous period, then we must have had an inventory position of three after our order in the previous period. The only way that we could then observe an inventory position of one in this period is if two units of demand occurred in the previous period. Thus, we will order two units in this period (to raise our inventory position back to $S = 3$). Hence,

The order quantity in each period exactly equals the demand in the previous period in the order-up-to inventory model.

Due to this observation, an order-up-to policy is sometimes called a *one-for-one ordering policy:* each unit of demand triggers an order for one replenishment unit.

The order-up-to model is an example of a system that operates on the pull principle of production/inventory control. The key feature of a *pull system* is that production-replenishment of a unit is only initiated when a demand of another unit occurs. Therefore, in a pull system, inventory is pulled through the system only by the occurrence of demand. In contrast, with a *push system* production-replenishment occurs in anticipation of demand. The newsvendor model is a push system while a bucket brigade is an example of a pull system. (A literal bucket brigade is a line of people that pass buckets of water to each other in unison to move water from a source, such as a lake, to its destination, such as a burning building.) A kanban system, which is a critical component of any just-in-time system, also operates with pull. Pull systems impose the discipline to prevent the excessive buildup of inventory, but they are not good about anticipating shifts in future demand. Thus, pull systems are most effective when average demand remains steady, as we have assumed in our order-up-to model.

11.3   The End-of-Period Inventory Level

The inventory level (on-hand inventory minus the back order) is an important metric in the order-up-to model: If the inventory level is high, then we incur holding costs on on-hand inventory, but if the inventory level is low, then we may not be providing adequate availability to our customers. Hence, we need to know how to control the inventory level via our decision variable, the order-up-to level. The following result suggests there actually is a relatively simple relationship between them:

> *The inventory level measured at the end of a period equals the order-up-to level S minus demand over l + 1 periods.*

If that result is (magically) intuitive to you, or if you are willing to believe it on faith, then you can now skip ahead to the next section. For the rest of us, the remainder of this section explains and derives that result.

We'll derive our result with the help of a seemingly unrelated example. Suppose at a neighborhood picnic you have a large pot with 30 cups of soup in it. Over the course of the picnic, you add 20 additional cups of soup to the pot and a total of 40 cups are served. How many cups of soup are in the pot at the end of the picnic? Not too hard: start with 30, add 20, and then subtract 40, so you are left with 10 cups of soup in the pot. Does the answer change if you first subtract 40 cups and then add 20 cups? The answer is no as long as people are patient. To explain, if we subtract 40 cups from the original 30 cups, then we will have −10 cups, that is, there will be people waiting in line to receive soup. Once the 20 cups are added, those people in line are served and 10 cups remain. The sequence of adding and subtracting does not matter precisely because everyone is willing to wait in line, that is, there are no lost sales of soup. In other words, the sequence of adding and subtracting does not matter, only the total amount added and the total amount subtracted matter.

Does the answer change in our soup example if the 20 cups are added one cup at a time or in random quantities (e.g., sometimes half a cup, sometime a whole cup, sometimes more than a cup)? Again, the answer is no: the increments by which the soup is added or subtracted do not matter, only the total amount added or subtracted.

Keep the soup example in mind, but let's switch to another example. Suppose a firm uses the order-up-to model, its order-up-to level is $S = 3$, and the lead time is two days, $l = 2$. What is the inventory level at the end of any given day? This seems like a rather hard question to answer, but let's tackle it anyway. To provide a concrete reference, randomly choose a period, say period 10. Let *IL* be the inventory level at the start of period 10. We use a variable for the inventory level because we really do not know the exact inventory level. It turns out, as we will see, that we do not need to know the exact inventory level.

After we submit our order in period 10, we will have a total of $3 − IL$ units on order. When we implement the order-up-to model, we must order so that our inventory level (*IL*) plus our on-order inventory ($3 − IL$) equals our order-up-to level ($3 = IL + 3 − IL$). Some of the on-order inventory may have been ordered in period 10, some of it in period 9. No matter when the on-order inventory was ordered, it will *all* be received by the end of period 12 because the lead time is two periods. For example, the period 10 order is received in period 12, so all of the previously ordered inventory should have been received by period 12 as well.

Now recall the soup example. Think of *IL* as the amount of soup you start with. How much is added to the "pot of inventory" over periods 10 through 12? That is the amount that was on order in period 10, that is, $3 - IL$. So the pot starts with *IL* and then $3 - IL$ is added over periods 10–12. How much is subtracted from the pot of inventory over periods 10 through 12? Demand is what causes subtraction from the pot of inventory. So it is demand over periods 10–12 that is subtracted from inventory; that is, demand over the $l + 1$ periods (10–12 are three periods). So how much is in the pot of inventory at the end of period 12? The answer is simple: just as in the soup example, it is how much we start with (*IL*), plus the amount we add $(3 - IL)$, minus the amount we subtract (demand over periods 10–12):

$$\text{Inventory level at the end of period } 12 = IL + 3 - IL - \text{Demand in periods 10 to 12}$$

$$= 3 - \text{Demand in periods 10 to 12}$$

In other words, our inventory level at the end of a period is the order-up-to level (in this case 3) minus demand over $l + 1$ periods (in this case, periods 10 to 12). Hence, we have derived our result.

Just as in the soup example, it does not matter the sequence by which inventory is added or subtracted; all that matters is the total amount that is added $(3 - IL)$ and the total amount that is subtracted (total demand over periods 10–12). (This is why the back-order assumption is needed.) Nor do the increments by which inventory is added or subtracted matter. In other words, we can add and subtract at constant rates, or we could add and subtract at random rates; either way it is only the totals that matter.

You still may be a bit confused about why it is demand over $l + 1$ periods that is relevant rather than demand over just l periods. Recall that we are interested in the inventory level at the *end* of the period, but we make our ordering decision at the *start* of a period. The time from when an order is placed at the start of a period to the end of the period in which the order arrives is actually $l + 1$ periods' worth of demand.

Now you might wonder why we initiated our analysis at the start of a period, in this case period 10. Why not begin by measuring the inventory position at some other time during a period? The reason is that the inventory position measured at the start of a period is always equal to the order-up-to level, but we cannot be sure about what the inventory position will be at any other point within a period (because of random demand). Hence, we anchor our analysis on something we know for sure, which is that the inventory position equals *S* at the start of every period when an order-up-to policy is implemented.

To summarize, in the order-up-to model, the inventory level at the end of a period equals the order-up-to level *S* minus demand over $l + 1$ periods. Therefore, while we need to know the distribution of demand for a single period, we also need to know the distribution of demand over $l + 1$ periods.

11.4 Choosing Demand Distributions

Every inventory management system must choose a demand distribution to represent demand. In our case, we need a demand distribution for the Mounds View DC and Susan Magnotto's territory. Furthermore, as discussed in the previous section, we need a demand distribution for one period of demand and a demand distribution for $l + 1$ periods of demand. As we will see, the normal distribution works for DC demand, but the Poisson distribution is better for demand in Susan's territory.

The graph in Figure 11.2 indicates that Mounds View's demand is variable, but it appears to have a stable mean throughout the year. This is good sign: as we already mentioned, the order-up-to model assumes average demand is the same across periods. Average demand across the sample is 349 and the standard deviation is 122.38. Seven months of the year have demand less than the mean, so the demand realizations appear to be relatively symmetric about the mean. Finally, there do not appear to be any extreme outliers in the data: the maximum is 1.35 standard deviations from the mean and the minimum is 1.46 standard deviations from the mean. Overall, the normal distribution with a mean of 349 and a standard deviation of 122.38 is a reasonable choice to represent the DC's monthly demand.

However, because the DC orders on a weekly basis and measures its lead time in terms of weeks, the period length for our order-up-to model applied to the DC should be one week. Therefore, we need to pick a distribution to represent weekly demand; that is, we have to chop our monthly demand distribution into a weekly demand distribution. If we are willing to make the assumption that one week's demand is independent of another week's demand, and if we assume that there are 4.33 weeks per month (52 weeks per year/12 months), then we can convert the mean and standard deviation for our monthly demand distribution into a mean and standard deviation for weekly demand:

$$\text{Expected weekly demand} = \frac{\text{Expected monthly demand}}{4.33}$$

$$\text{Standard deviation of weekly demand} = \frac{\text{Standard deviation of monthly demand}}{\sqrt{4.33}}$$

Exhibit 11.1 summarizes the process of converting demand distributions from one period length to another.

In the case of the Mounds View DC, expected weekly demand is $349/4.33 = 80.6$ and the standard deviation of weekly demand is $122.38/\sqrt{4.33} = 58.81$. So we will use a normal distribution with mean 80.6 and standard deviation 58.81 to represent weekly demand at the Mounds View DC.

We also need demand for the InSync pacemaker over $l + 1$ periods, which in this case is demand over $3 + 1 = 4$ weeks. Again using Exhibit 11.1, demand over four weeks has mean $4 \times 80.6 = 322.4$ and standard deviation $\sqrt{4} \times 58.81 = 117.6$.

Now consider demand for the InSync pacemaker in Susan's territory. From the data in Figure 11.3, total demand over the year is 75 units, which translates into average demand of 6.25 (75/12) units per month, 1.44 units per week (75/52), and 0.29 (1.44/5) units per day, assuming a five day week.

Our estimate of 0.29 units per day for expected demand implicitly assumes expected demand in any given day of the year is the same as for any other day of the year. In other words, there is no seasonality in demand across the year, within a month, or within a week. There probably is not too much promotion-related volatility in demand (buy one pacemaker, get one free), nor is there much volatility due to gift giving (what more could a dad want than a new pacemaker under the Christmas tree). There probably is not much variation within the week (the same number of implants on average on Friday as on Monday) or within the month. However, those conjectures could be tested with more refined data. Furthermore, from the data in Figure 11.2, it appears demand is stable throughout the year and there are no upward or downward trends in the data. Hence, our assumption of a constant expected daily demand is reasonable.

Using Exhibit 11.1, if average demand over one day is 0.29 units, then expected demand over $l + 1$ days must be $2 \times 0.29 = 0.58$.

Exhibit 11.1

HOW TO CONVERT A DEMAND DISTRIBUTION FROM ONE PERIOD LENGTH TO ANOTHER

If you wish to divide a demand distribution from a long period length (e.g., a month) into n short periods (e.g., a week), then

$$\text{Expected demand in the short period} = \frac{\text{Expected demand in the long period}}{n}$$

$$\text{Standard deviation of demand in the short period} = \frac{\text{Standard deviation of demand in the long period}}{\sqrt{n}}$$

If you wish to combine demand distributions from n short periods (e.g., a week) into one long period (e.g, a three-week period, $n = 3$), then

$$\text{Expected demand in the long period} = n \times \text{Expected demand in the short period}$$

$$\text{Standard deviation of demand in the long period} = \sqrt{n} \times \text{Standard deviation of demand in the short period}$$

The above equations assume the same demand distribution represents demand in each period and demands across periods are independent of each other.

Unlike the normal distribution, which is defined by two parameters (its mean and its standard deviation), the Poisson distribution is defined by only a single parameter, its mean. For the InSync pacemaker, it is natural to choose the mean equal to the observed mean demand rate: 0.29 for demand over one period and 0.58 for demand over two periods. Even though the Poisson distribution does not allow you to choose any standard deviation while holding the mean fixed, the Poisson distribution does have a standard deviation:

$$\text{Standard deviation of a Poisson distribution} = \sqrt{\text{Mean of the distribution}}$$

For example, with a mean of 0.29, the standard deviation is $\sqrt{0.29} = 0.539$. Table 11.1 provides the distribution and density functions for the chosen Poisson distributions.

Because it can be hard to visualize a distribution from a table, Figure 11.5 displays the graphs of the distribution and density functions of the Poisson distribution with mean 0.29. For comparison, the comparable functions for the normal distribution are also included. (*Note:* The dashed lines with the Poisson distribution are only for visual effect; that is, those functions exist only for integer values.)

The graphs in Figure 11.5 highlight that the Poisson and normal distributions are different in two key respects: (1) the Poisson distribution is discrete (it has integer outcomes), whereas the normal distribution is continuous; and (2) the distribution and density functions for those two distributions have different shapes. The fractional quantity issue is not a major concern if demand is 500 units (or probably even 80 units), but it is a concern when average demand is only 0.29 units. Ideally, we want a discrete demand distribution like the Poisson.

TABLE 11.1
The Distribution and Density Functions for Two Poisson Distributions.
In Excel, $F(S)$ is evaluated with the function POISSON(S, *Expected demand*, 1) and $f(S)$ is evaluated with the function POISSON(S, *Expected demand*, 0).

Mean Demand = 0.29			Mean Demand = 0.58		
S	*F(S)*	*f(S)*	*S*	*F(S)*	*f(S)*
0	0.74826	0.74826	0	0.55990	0.55990
1	0.96526	0.21700	1	0.88464	0.32474
2	0.99672	0.03146	2	0.97881	0.09417
3	0.99977	0.00304	3	0.99702	0.01821
4	0.99999	0.00022	4	0.99966	0.00264
5	1.00000	0.00001	5	0.99997	0.00031

$F(S)$ = Prob{Demand is less than or equal to S}
$f(S)$ = Prob{Demand is exactly equal to S}

Yet another argument can be made in support of the Poisson distribution as our model for demand in Susan's territory. Recall that with the queuing models (Chapters 6 and 7) we use the exponential distribution to describe the time between customer arrivals, which is appropriate if customers arrive independently of each other; that is, the arrival time of one customer does not provide information concerning the arrival time of another customer. This is particularly likely if the arrival rate of customers is quite slow, as it is with the InSync pacemaker. So it is likely that the interarrival time of InSync pacemaker demand has an exponential distribution. And here is the connection to the Poisson distribution: If the interarrival times are exponentially distributed, then the number of arrivals in any fixed interval of time has a Poisson distribution. For example, if the interarrival times between InSync pacemaker demand in Susan's territory are exponentially distributed with a mean of 3.45 days, then the average number of arrivals (demand) per day has a Poisson distribution with a mean of 1/3.45 = 0.29 units.

If we had daily demand data, we would be able to confirm whether or not our chosen Poisson distribution is a good fit to the data. Nevertheless, absent that data, we have probably made the best educated guess.

To summarize, we shall use a normal demand distribution with mean 80.6 and standard deviation 58.81 to represent weekly demand for the InSync pacemaker at the Mounds View DC and a normal demand distribution with mean 322.4 and standard deviation 117.6 to

FIGURE 11.5
The Distribution (left graph) and Density Functions (right graph) of a Poisson Distribution with a Mean of 0.29 (bullets and dashed lines) and a Normal Distribution with a Mean of 0.29 and a Standard Deviation of 0.539 (solid line)

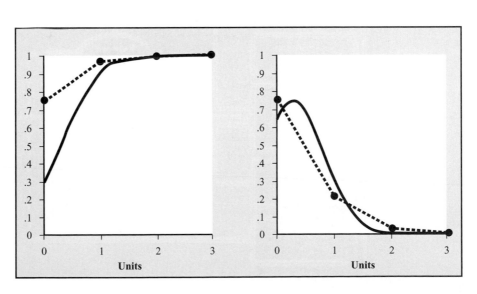

represent demand over $l + 1 = 4$ weeks. We will use a Poisson distribution with mean 0.29 to represent daily demand in Susan Magnotto's territory and a Poisson distribution with mean 0.58 to represent demand over $l + 1 = 2$ days.

11.5 Performance Measures

This section considers the evaluation of several performance measures with the order-up-to method. We consider these measures at two locations in the supply chain: Susan Magnotto's territory and the Mounds View distribution center.

Recall we use a Poisson distribution with mean 0.29 to represent daily demand in Susan's territory and a Poisson distribution with mean 0.58 to represent demand over $l + 1 = 2$ days. We shall evaluate the performance measures assuming Susan uses $S = 3$ as her order-up-to level. The Mounds View weekly demand is normally distributed with mean 80.6 and standard deviation 58.81 and over $l + 1 = 4$ weeks it is normally distributed with mean $\mu = 322.4$ and standard deviation $\sigma = 117.6$. We evaluate the performance measures assuming the order-up-to level $S = 625$ is implemented at Mounds View.

Figure 11.6 summarizes the necessary inputs to evaluate each performance measure.

In-Stock and Stockout Probability

A *stockout* occurs when demand arrives and there is no inventory available to satisfy that demand immediately. *Note:* A stockout is not the same as being *out of stock,* which is the condition of having no inventory on hand. With our definition of a stockout, we must be out of stock *and* a demand must occur. Thus, if we are out of stock and no demand occurs, then a stockout never happened. We are *in stock* in a period if all demand was satisfied in that

FIGURE 11.6
The Relationship between Inputs (boxes) and Performance Measures (ovals) in the Order-up-to Model
μ = Expected demand over $l + 1$ periods and σ = Standard deviation of demand over $l + 1$ periods.

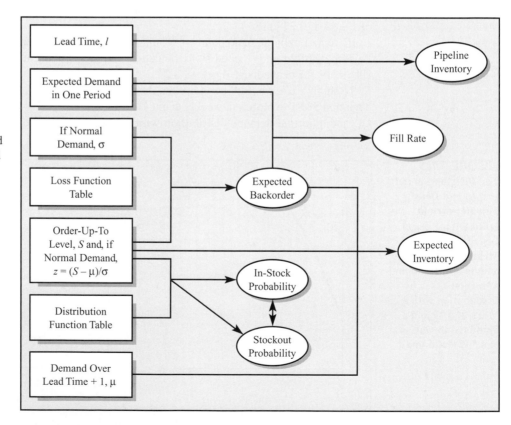

period. *Note:* With this definition, if we start a period with five units and demand is five units, then we are in stock in that period even though we end the period being out of stock.

The *in-stock probability* is the probability we are in stock in a period, and the *stockout probability* is the probability a stockout occurs. (We used these same definitions in the newsvendor model, Chapter 9.)

A stockout causes a back order. Hence, a stockout occurs in a period if there are one or more units back-ordered at the end of the period. If there are back orders at the end of the period, then the inventory level at the end of the period is negative. The main result from Section 11.3 is that the inventory level is related to the order-up-to level and demand over $l + 1$ periods in the following way:

$$\text{Inventory level at the end of the period} = S - \text{Demand over } l + 1 \text{ periods}$$

Therefore, the inventory level at the end of the period is negative if demand over $l + 1$ periods exceeds the order-up-to level. Therefore,

$$\text{Stockout probability} = \text{Prob\{Demand over } l + 1 \text{ periods} > S\}$$

$$= 1 - \text{Prob\{Demand over } l + 1 \text{ periods} \le S\} \quad (11.1)$$

Equation (11.1) is actually an approximation of the stockout probability, but it happens to be an excellent approximation if the chosen service level is high (i.e., if stockouts are rare). See Appendix D for why equation (11.1) is an approximation and for the exact, but more complicated, stockout probability equation.

Because either all demand is satisfied immediately from inventory or not, we know that the

$$\text{In-stock probability} = 1 - \text{Stockout probability}$$

Combining the above equation with equation (11.1), we get

$$\text{In-stock probability} = 1 - \text{Stockout probability}$$

$$= \text{Prob\{Demand over } l + 1 \text{ periods} \le S\}$$

The above probability equations do not depend on which distribution has been chosen to represent demand, but the process for evaluating those probabilities does depend on the particular demand distribution.

When the demand distribution is given in the form of a table, as with the Poisson distribution, then we can obtain the in-stock probability directly from the table. Looking at Table 11.1, for Susan's territory with an order-up-to level $S = 3$,

$$\text{In-stock probability} = \text{Prob\{Demand over } l + 1 \text{ periods} \le 3\}$$

$$= 99.702\%$$

$$\text{Stockout probability} = 1 - \text{Prob\{Demand over } l + 1 \text{ periods} \le 3\}$$

$$= 1 - 0.99702$$

$$= 0.298\%$$

For the Mounds View distribution center, we need to work with the normal distribution. Recall that with the normal you first do the analysis as if demand is a standard normal distribution and then you convert those outcomes into the answers for the actual normal distribution.

Note that the process for evaluating the in-stock and stockout probabilities in the order-up-to model, which is summarized in Exhibit 11.2, is identical to the one described in Table 9.6 for the newsvendor model except the order quantity Q is replaced with the order-up-to

Exhibit 11.2

IN-STOCK PROBABILITY AND STOCKOUT PROBABILITY EVALUATION IN THE ORDER-UP-TO MODEL

If the demand over $l + 1$ periods is a normal distribution with mean μ and standard deviation σ, then follow steps A through D (see Exhibit 11.1 for the process of evaluating μ and σ if you have demand over a single period):

A. Evaluate the z-statistic for the order-up-to level : $z = \dfrac{S - \mu}{\sigma}$.

B. Use the z-statistic to look up in the Standard Normal Distribution Function Table the probability the standard normal demand is z or lower, $\Phi(z)$.

C. In-stock probability = $\Phi(z)$ and Stockout probability = $1 - \Phi(z)$.

D. In Excel, In-stock probability = Normsdist(z) and Stockout probability = 1 − Normsdist(z).

If the demand over $l + 1$ periods is a discrete distribution function, then In-stock probability = $F(S)$ and Stockout probability = $1 - F(S)$, where $F(S)$ is the probability demand over $l + 1$ periods is S or lower.

level S. However, it is critical to use the demand forecast for $l + 1$ periods, not the demand forecast for a single period (unless the lead time happens to be 0).

First, we normalize the order-up-to level, which is $S = 625$, using the parameters for demand over $l + 1$ periods:

$$z = \frac{S - \mu}{\sigma} = \frac{625 - 322.4}{117.6} = 2.57$$

Next, we look up $\Phi(z)$ (the probability the outcome of a standard normal is less than or equal to z) in the Standard Normal Distribution Function Table in Appendix B: $\Phi(2.57) = 0.9949$. Therefore, with $S = 625$, the in-stock probability for the DC is 99.49 percent. The stockout probability is $1 - \Phi(z) = 0.0051$, or 0.51 percent.

Expected Back Order

The *expected back order* is the expected number of back orders at the end of any period. While most managers may not be directly interested in the expected back order, we need the expected back order to evaluate the fill rate and the expected on-hand inventory, which are of direct interest to any manager.

Recall from Section 11.3 that the inventory level at the end of the period is S minus demand over $l + 1$ periods. Hence, if demand over $l + 1$ periods is greater than S, then there will be back orders. The number of back orders equals the difference between demand over $l + 1$ periods and S. Therefore, in the order-up-to model, the expected back order equals the loss function of demand over $l + 1$ periods evaluated at the threshold S. *Note:* This is analogous to the expected lost sales in the newsvendor model. In the order-up-to model, the number of units back-ordered equals the difference between random demand over $l + 1$ periods and S; in the newsvendor model, the expected lost sales is the difference between random demand and Q. So all we need to evaluate the expected back order is the loss function of demand over $l + 1$ periods.

TABLE 11.2
Distribution and Loss Function for Two Poisson Distributions

	Mean Demand = 0.29			Mean Demand = 0.58	
S	F(S)	L(S)	S	F(S)	L(S)
0	0.74826	0.29000	0	0.55990	0.58000
1	0.96526	0.03826	1	0.88464	0.13990
2	0.99672	0.00352	2	0.97881	0.02454
3	0.99977	0.00025	3	0.99702	0.00335
4	0.99999	0.00001	4	0.99966	0.00037
5	1.00000	0.00000	5	0.99997	0.00004

$F(S) =$ Prob{Demand is less than or equal to S}
$L(S) =$ Loss function = Expected back order = Expected amount demand exceeds S

Let's begin with the expected back order in Susan's territory. Recall that with a discrete distribution function table, we need to have a column that has the loss function $L(S)$. Table 11.2 displays the loss function we need. (Appendix C describes how to use the data in Table 11.1 to evaluate $L(S)$.) Appendix B has the loss function table for other Poisson distributions. With $S = 3$ and mean demand over $l + 1$ periods equal to 0.58, we see that $L(3) = 0.00335$. Therefore, the expected back order in Susan's territory is 0.00335 units if she operates with $S = 3$.

With the Mounds View DC we follow the process of evaluating expected lost sales with a normal distribution. (See Exhibit 9.5.) First, find the z-statistic that corresponds to the order-up-to level:

$$z = \frac{S - \mu}{\sigma} = \frac{625 - 322.4}{117.6} - 2.57$$

Note again that we are using the mean and standard deviation of the normal distribution that represents demand over $l + 1$ periods. Now look up in the Standard Normal Distribution Loss Function Table the loss function with the standard normal distribution and a z-statistic of 2.57: $L(2.57) = 0.0016$. Next, convert that expected loss with the standard normal distribution into the expected back order:

$$\text{Expected back order} = \sigma \times L(z) = 117.6 \times 0.0016 = 0.19$$

Exhibit 11.3 summarizes the process.

Fill Rate

The fill rate is the expected fraction of demand served immediately from stock and can be evaluated with the following equation:

$$\text{Fill rate} = 1 - \frac{\text{Expected back order}}{\text{Expected demand in one period}}$$

The logic behind the above equation is as follows: The number of customers in a period is the expected demand in one period and the number of customers that are not served in a period is the expected back order, so the ratio of the expected back order to the expected demand is the fraction of customers that are not served. One minus the fraction of customers that are not served is the fraction of customers that are served, which is the fill rate. Note that this logic does not depend on the particular demand distribution (but the evaluation of the expected back order does depend on the demand distribution).

The above equation for the fill rate is actually an approximation of the fill rate, but it happens to be an excellent approximation if the fill rate is reasonably high (say 90 percent or higher). If needed, see Appendix D for the exact (but more complex) formula for the fill rate.

Exhibit 11.3

You also might wonder why the denominator of the fraction in the fill rate equation is the expected demand over a single period and not the expected demand over $l + 1$ periods. For example, we are careful to emphasize that the evaluations of the stockout probability and the expected back order use the expected demand over $l + 1$ periods. What we are interested in is the fraction of customers that are not served immediately from stock (one minus that fraction is the expected fill rate). The lead time influences the fraction of customers in a period that are not served (the expected back order), but it does not influence the number of customers we have. Therefore, the lead time influences the numerator of that ratio (the number of customers that are not served) but not the denominator (the number of customers that arrive).

In Susan's territory, the expected back order with $S = 3$ is 0.00335 unit, so the fill rate is $1 - 0.00335/0.29 = 98.84$ percent.

For the Mounds View DC, the expected back order with $S = 625$ is 0.19, so the fill rate is $1 - 0.19/80.6 = 99.76$ percent.

Expected On-Hand Inventory

Expected on-hand inventory, or just *expected inventory* for short, is the expected number of units of inventory at the end of a period. We choose to measure inventory at the end of the period because that is when inventory is at its lowest point in the period. (Most managers like to indicate that they operate "lean," so they tend to prefer to measure inventory at its lowest point.)

Recall that the inventory level at the end of a period is equal to the order-up-to level S minus demand over $l + 1$ periods. Hence, inventory at the end of a period is the difference between S and demand over $l + 1$ periods: if $S = 5$ and demand over $l + 1$ periods is three, then there are two units left in inventory. In other words, expected inventory is the expected amount by which S exceeds demand over $l + 1$ periods. Referring to the insights from the newsvendor model, if we think of S in terms of the order quantity and demand over $l + 1$

periods in terms of "sales," then inventory is analogous to "leftover inventory." Recall that in the newsvendor model

$$\text{Expected leftover inventory} = Q - \text{Expected sales}$$

$$= Q - \mu + \text{Expected lost sales}$$

As a result, in the order-up-to model

$$\text{Expected inventory} = S - \text{Expected demand over } l + 1 \text{ periods} + \text{Expected back order}$$

In Susan's territory with $S = 3$, the expected inventory is $3 - 0.58 + 0.00335 = 2.42$. At the Mounds View DC with $S = 625$, the expected inventory is $625 - 322.4 + 0.19 = 302.8$.

Pipeline Inventory/Expected On-Order Inventory

Pipeline inventory, which also will be called *expected on-order inventory,* is the average amount of inventory on order at any given time. It is relevant because Medtronic owns the inventory between the Mounds View distribution center and Susan Magnotto's territory. To evaluate pipeline inventory, we refer to Little's Law, described in Chapter 2,

$$\text{Inventory} = \text{Flow rate} \times \text{Flow time}$$

Now let's translate the terms in the Little's Law equation into the comparable terms in this setting: inventory is the number of units on order; flow rate is the expected demand in one period (the expected order in a period equals expected demand in one period, so on-order inventory is being created at a rate equal to expected demand in one period); and flow time is the lead time, since every unit spends l periods on order. Therefore,

$$\text{Expected on-order inventory} = \text{Expected demand in one period} \times \text{Lead time}$$

In the case of the InSync pacemaker, Susan's territory has $0.29 \times 1 = 0.29$ units on order on average, and the Mounds View DC has $80.6 \times 3 = 241.8$ units on order.

Note: The expected on-order inventory is based on demand over l periods of time, and not $l + 1$ periods of time. Furthermore, the above equation for the expected on-order inventory holds for any demand distribution because Little's Law depends only on average rates, and not on the variability of those rates.

11.6   Choosing an Order-up-to Level to Meet a Service Target

This section discusses the actual choice of InSync order up-to levels for Susan Magnotto's territory and the Mounds View DC. To refer to a previously mentioned analogy, the order up-to level is somewhat like the point in the fuel gauge of your car at which you decide to head to a refueling station. The more you are willing to let the dial fall below the "E," the higher the chance you will run out of fuel. However, while increasing that trigger point in the fuel gauge makes you feel safer, it also increases the average amount of fuel you drive around with. With that trade-off in mind, this section considers two objectives for choosing an order-up-to level: minimize inventory while achieving an in-stock probability no lower than an in-stock target level and minimize inventory while achieving an expected fill rate no lower than a fill rate target level. The in-stock probability objective is equivalent to the objective of minimizing inventory while yielding a stockout probability no greater than one minus the in-stock target level.

Exhibit 11.4

An In-Stock Probability Target

Given Medtronic's large gross margin, let's say we want the in-stock probability to be at least 99.9 percent for the InSync pacemaker in Susan's territory as well as at the Mounds View DC. With a 99.9 percent in-stock probability, a stockout should occur no more than 1 in 1,000 days on average. Section 11.7 discusses whether we have chosen a reasonable target.

From Section 11.5 we know that the in-stock probability is the probability demand over $l + 1$ periods is S or lower. Hence, when demand is modeled with a discrete distribution function, we find the appropriate order-up-to level by looking directly into that table. From Table 11.2, we see that in Susan's territory, $S = 0$ clearly does not meet our objective with an in-stock probability of about 56 percent, that is, $F(0) = 0.5599$. Neither is $S = 3$ sufficient because it has an in-stock probability of about 99.7 percent. However, with $S = 4$ our target is met: the in-stock probability is 99.97 percent. In fact, $S = 4$ exceeds our target by a considerable amount: that translates into one stockout every $1/0.00034 = 2,941$ days, or one stockout every 11.31 years, if we assume 260 days per year.

With the Mounds View DC, we must work with the normal distribution. We first find the order-up-to level that meets our in-stock probability service requirement with the standard normal distribution and then convert that standard normal order-up-to level to the order-up-to level that corresponds to the actual demand distribution. In the Standard Normal Distribution Function Table, we see that $\Phi(3.08) = 0.9990$, so an order-up-to level of 3.08 would generate our desired in-stock probability if demand over $l + 1$ periods followed a standard normal. It remains to convert that z-statistic into an order-up-to level: $S = \mu + z \times \sigma$. Remember that the mean and standard deviation should be from the normal distribution of demand over $l + 1$ periods. Therefore,

$$S = 322.4 + 3.08 \times 117.62 = 685$$

See Exhibit 11.5 for a summary of the process to choose an order-up-to level to achieve a target in-stock probability.

Exhibit 11.5

HOW TO CHOOSE AN ORDER-UP-TO LEVEL *S* TO ACHIEVE AN IN-STOCK PROBABILITY TARGET IN THE ORDER-UP-TO MODEL

If the demand over $l + 1$ periods is a normal distribution with mean μ and standard deviation σ, then follow steps A and B (see Exhibit 11.1 for the process of evaluating μ and σ if you have demand over a single period):

A. In the Standard Normal Distribution Function Table, find the probability that corresponds to the target in-stock probability. Then find the *z*-statistic that corresponds to that probability. If the target in-stock probability falls between two entries in the table, choose the entry with the larger *z*-statistic.

   In Excel the appropriate *z*-statistic can be found with the following equation:

$$z = \text{Normsinv (Target in-stock probability)}$$

B. Convert the *z*-statistic chosen in part A to an order-up-to level: $S = \mu + z \times \sigma$. Recall that you are using the mean and standard deviation of demand over $l + 1$ periods.

If the demand forecast for $l + 1$ periods is a discrete distribution function table, then find the *S* in the table such that $F(S)$ equals the target in-stock probability, where $F(S)$ is the probability demand is less than or equal to *S* over $l + 1$ periods. If the target in-stock probability falls between two entries in the table, choose the larger *S*.

A Fill Rate Target

Now consider our second objective: Minimize inventory while achieving at least a fill rate target. Let's choose a 99.9 percent fill rate target to match our in-stock target.

In the newsvendor model, we were able to choose an order quantity Q to meet a target fill rate with the following steps: Find the target expected lost sales that corresponds to the target fill rate and then find the order quantity that yields the target expected lost sales. The process here is essentially the same.

Recall that the fill rate depends on the expected back order:

$$\text{Fill rate target} = 1 - \frac{\text{Expected back order}}{\text{Expected demand in one period}}$$

Now rearrange terms in the above equation:

$$\text{Expected back order} = (\text{Expected demand in one period}) \times (1 - \text{Fill rate target})$$

Thus, to hit our target fill rate, we need to find the order up-to level that satisfies the above equation.

In Susan's territory, we can evaluate the above equation:

$$\text{Expected back order} = (0.29) \times (1 - 0.999) = 0.00029$$

Hence, we need to find the order-up-to level such that the expected back order is 0.00029 unit. Looking at Table 11.2, with a mean of 0.58 we see that $L(4) = 0.00037$ and $L(5) = 0.00004$. Remember, the expected back order depends on demand over $l + 1$ periods, so we are looking at the Poisson table with mean 0.58. It appears that $S = 4$ generates an expected back order that is above the target of 0.00029 and $S = 5$ generates an expected back order that is below the target. As before, rely on the round-up rule: choose $S = 5$.

With the Mounds View DC, we are working with the normal distribution. As usual, we find the z-statistic that hits our target fill rate if demand over $l + 1$ periods followed a standard normal distribution, and then we convert that z-statistic into an order-up-to level for the actual distribution. Recall that with the normal distribution,

$$\text{Expected back order} = (\text{Standard deviation of demand over } l + 1 \text{ periods}) \times L(z)$$

Therefore, with the standard normal distribution, our target expected back order is

$$L(z) = \left(\frac{\text{Expected demand in one period}}{\text{Standard deviation of demand over } l + 1 \text{ periods}} \right) \times (1 - \text{Fill rate target})$$

You may recall a similar expression when we were looking for an order quantity in the newsvendor model to achieve a target expected fill rate. (See Exhibit 9.8.) But those expressions are slightly different. In particular, the above expression is the ratio of the mean demand over *one* period to the standard deviation of demand over $l + 1$ periods.

Using the above equation, our target back order is

$$L(z) = \left(\frac{80.6}{117.62} \right)(1 - 0.999) = 0.0007$$

From the *Standard Normal Loss Function Table,* we see

$$L(2.81) = L(2.82) = L(2.83) = L(2.84) = 0.0007$$

To be conservative, choose the highest z-statistic, 2.84. Now convert that z-statistic into an order-up-to level:

$$S = 322.4 + 2.84 \times 117.6 = 656$$

Remember to use the mean (322.4) and standard deviation (117.6) for demand over $l + 1$ periods.

Exhibit 11.6 summarizes the process of choosing an order-up-to level to meet a target fill rate.

11.7   Choosing an Appropriate Service Level

So far in our discussion we have chosen high service levels because we suspect that a high service level is appropriate. This section puts more rigor behind our hunch. For the sake of brevity, we'll explicitly consider only the in-stock probability measure of service and the management of field inventory. At the end of the section, we briefly discuss the fill rate measure of service and the management of distribution center inventory.

The appropriate service level minimizes the cost of holding inventory plus the cost of poor service. The holding cost of inventory is usually expressed as a *holding cost rate,* which is the cost of holding one unit in inventory for one year, expressed as a percentage of the item's cost. For example, if a firm assigns its holding cost rate to be 20 percent, then it believes the cost of holding a unit in inventory for one year equals 20 percent of the item's cost. The holding cost includes the opportunity cost of capital, the cost of spoilage, obsolescence, insurance, storage, and so forth, all variable costs associated with holding inventory. Because Medtronic is a growing company, with a high internal opportunity cost of capital, let's say their holding cost rate is 35 percent for field inventory. We'll use the variable h to represent the holding cost. See Chapter 2 for additional discussion on the holding cost rate.

Exhibit 11.6

HOW TO CHOOSE AN ORDER-UP-TO LEVEL *S* TO ACHIEVE A FILL RATE TARGET IN THE ORDER-UP-TO MODEL

If the demand over $l + 1$ periods is a normal distribution with mean μ and standard deviation σ, then follow steps A through C (see Exhibit 11.1 for the process of evaluating μ and σ if you have demand over a single period):

A. Evaluate the target backorder $L(z)$:

$$L(z) = \left(\frac{\text{Expected demand in one period}}{\text{Standard deviation of demand over } l + 1 \text{ periods}} \right) \times (1 - \text{Fill rate target})$$

Note that the numerator is expected demand over *one* period while the denominator is the standard deviation of demand over $l + 1$ periods.

B. In the Standard Normal Loss Function Table, find the *z* such that $L(z)$ matches the target back order evaluated in part A. If the target back order falls between two entries in the table, choose the entry with the larger *z*-statistic.

C. Convert the *z*-statistic chosen in part B to an order-up-to level: $S = \mu + z \times \sigma$. Recall that you are using the mean and standard deviation of demand over $l + 1$ periods.

If the demand forecast for $l + 1$ periods is a discrete distribution function table that includes the loss function $L(S)$, then follow steps D and E. (If the table does not include the loss function, see Appendix C for a procedure to evaluate it.)

D. Evaluate the target expected back order:

Expected back order = (Expected demand in one period) $\times$ (1 − Fill rate target)

E. Find the *S* in the table such that $L(S)$ equals the target expected back order from part D, where $L(S)$ is the loss function. If the target expected back order falls between two entries in the table, choose the entry with the larger *S*.

If we assume the InSync pacemaker has a 75 percent gross margin, then the cost of an InSync pacemaker is $(1 - 0.75) \times \text{Price} = 0.25 \times \text{Price}$, where Price is the selling price.[2] Therefore, the annual holding cost is $0.35 \times 0.25 \times \text{Price} = 0.0875 \times \text{Price}$ and the daily holding cost, assuming 260 days per year, is $0.875 \times \text{Price}/260 = 0.000337 \times \text{Price}$.

The cost of poor service requires some thought. We first need to decide how we will measure poor service and then decide on a cost for poor service. In the order-up-to model, a natural measure of poor service is the occurrence of a back order. Therefore, we say that we incur a cost for each unit back-ordered and we'll let the variable *b* represent that cost. We'll also refer to the variable *b* as the *back-order penalty cost*. Now we must decide on an appropriate value for *b*. A natural focal point with field inventory (i.e., inventory for serving final customers) is to assume each back order causes a lost sale and the cost of a lost sale equals the product's gross margin. However, if you believe there are substantial long-run implications of a lost sale (e.g., the customer will switch his or her future business to a competitor), then maybe the cost of a lost sale is even higher than the gross margin. On the

---

[2] Recall that Medtronic's gross margin across all products, as reported on their income statement, is approximately 75 percent. The actual gross margin of the InSync pacemaker may deviate from this.

other hand, if customers are somewhat patient, that is, a back order does not automatically lead to a lost sale, then maybe the cost of a back order is lower than the gross margin. In the case of Medtronic, the former story is more likely. Let's suppose each back order leads to a lost sale and, to be conservative, the cost of a back order is just the gross margin; that is, $b = 0.75 \times \text{Price}$.

Now let's minimizes Medtronic's holding and back-order costs. The holding cost in a period is h times the number of units in inventory (which we measure at the end of the period). The back-order cost in a period is b times the number of units back-ordered.[3] As a result, we face the "too little–too much" challenge: Choose S too high and incur excessive inventory holding costs; but if S is too low, then we incur excessive back-order costs. We can actually use the newsvendor logic to strike the correct balance.

Our overage cost is $C_o = h$: the consequence of setting S too high is inventory, and the cost per unit of inventory per period is h. Our underage cost is $C_u = b$: back orders are the consequence of setting S too low, and the cost per back order is b. In the newsvendor model, we chose an order quantity Q such that the critical ratio equals the probability demand is Q or lower, which is the same as the probability that a stockout does not occur. In the order-up-to model, the probability a stockout does not occur in a period is

$$\text{Prob}\{\text{Demand over } l + 1 \text{ periods} \leq S\}$$

Hence, the order-up-to level that minimizes costs in a period satisfies the following newsvendor equation:

$$\text{Prob}\{\text{Demand over } l + 1 \text{ periods} \leq S\} = \frac{C_u}{C_o + C_u} = \frac{b}{h + b} \tag{11.2}$$

For Medtronic, the critical ratio is

$$\frac{b}{h + b} = \frac{(0.75 \times \text{Price})}{(0.000337 \times \text{Price}) + (0.75 \times \text{Price})} = 0.9996$$

Notice the following with respect to equation (11.2):

• We do not need to know the product's actual price, Price, because it cancels out of both the numerator and the denominator of the critical ratio.

• It is important that we use the holding cost per unit per period to evaluate the critical ratio, because the order-up-to level determines the expected inventory in a period. In other words, h should be the holding cost for a single unit for a single period.

Now we are ready to justify our service level based on costs. Recall that

$$\text{In-stock probability} = \text{Prob}\{\text{Demand over } l + 1 \text{ periods} \leq S\}$$

If we combine the above equation with equation (11.2), then the in-stock probability that is consistent with cost minimization is

$$\text{In-stock probability} = \text{Critical ratio} = \frac{b}{h + b} \tag{11.3}$$

[3] If you have been reading carefully, you might realize that this is not entirely correct. The back-order cost in a period is b times the number of demands *in that period* that are back-ordered, that is, we do not incur the cost b per unit that became back-ordered in a previous period and still is on back order. However, with a high in-stock probability, it should be the case that units are rarely back-ordered, and if they are back-ordered, then they are back-ordered for no more than one period. Hence, with a high in-stock probability, assuming the back-order cost is b times the number of units back-ordered is an excellent approximation.

TABLE 11.3
The Optimal Target In-Stock Probability for Various Gross Margins
The annual holding cost rate is 35 percent, the back order penalty cost equals the gross margin, and inventory is reviewed daily.

Gross Margin	Optimal Target In-Stock Probability	Gross Margin	Optimal Target In-Stock Probability
1%	90.00%	35%	99.75%
2	95.00	57	99.90
3	96.00	73	99.95
4	97.00	77	99.96
6	98.00	82	99.97
12	99.00	87	99.98
21	99.50	93	99.99

In other words, the appropriate in-stock probability equals the critical ratio. Recall that we chose 99.9 percent as our target in-stock probability. Even though that might seem high, our calculations above suggest that an in-stock probability of up to 99.96 percent is consistent with cost minimization.

Holding inventory is not cheap for Medtronic (35 percent holding cost rate), but due to Medtronic's large gross margins, the underage cost ($0.75 \times$ Price) is still about 2,200 times greater than the overage cost ($0.000337 \times$ Price)! With such a lopsided allocation of costs, it is no surprise that the appropriate in-stock probability is so high.

Table 11.3 indicates for various gross margins the optimal target in-stock probability. We can see that an obscene gross margin is needed (93 percent) to justify a 99.99 percent in-stock probability, but a modest gross margin (12 percent) is needed to justify a 99 percent in-stock probability.

To extend our discussion to include the fill rate measure of service, recall that while the fill rate and the in-stock probability are not exactly the same, their behaviors are qualitatively similar: They both increase nonlinearly as the order-up-to level is increased (see Figure 9.5). Thus, for any holding and back-order cost, we can find the implied fill rate, and that fill rate would increase as back orders become more expensive relative to holding inventory. The mechanics of that process are slightly different (and are beyond of the scope of this discussion), but the general idea is the same.

Now consider the appropriate service level at the distribution center. While the opportunity cost of capital remains the same whether it is tied up in inventory in the field or at the distribution center, all other inventory holding costs are likely to be lower at the distribution center (e.g., physical space, theft, spoilage, insurance, etc.). But even with a lower holding cost, the appropriate service level at the distribution center is unlikely to be as high as it is in the field because the distribution center's back-order cost should be lower. Why? A back order in the field is likely to lead to a lost sale, but a back order at the distribution center does not necessarily lead to a lost sale. Each field representative has a buffer of inventory, and that buffer might prevent a lost sale as long as the back order at the distribution center does not persist for too long. This is not to suggest that the appropriate in-stock probability at the distribution center is low. Rather, it suggests that the appropriate in-stock probability might not be 99.9 percent.[4]

The main insight from this section is that the optimal target in-stock probability in the order up-to model is likely to be quite high (99 percent and above), even with a relatively modest gross margin and high annual holding cost rate. However, that result depends on two

---

[4] Evaluation of the appropriate in-stock probability for the distribution center is beyond the scope of this discussion. However, simulation can be a useful tool to begin to understand the true back-order cost at the distribution center. Via simulation it is possible to estimate the likelihood that a back order at the distribution center causes a lost sale in the field.

key assumptions: back orders lead to lost sales and inventory does not become obsolete. The latter assumption highlights a connection and a useful contrast between the order-up-to model and the newsvendor model. In the newsvendor model, obsolescence is the primary concern; that is, demand is not expected to continue into the future, so leftover inventory is expensive. As a result, optimal service levels in the newsvendor model are rarely as high as in the order-up-to model. Furthermore, the appropriate model to employ depends on where a *product* is in its *life cycle.* Up to and including the mature stage of a product's life cycle, the order-up-to model is more appropriate. As a product's end of life approaches, the newsvendor model is needed. Some products have very long life cycles—for example, chicken noodle soup—so the newsvendor model is never needed. Others have very short life cycles—for example, O'Neill's Hammer 3/2—so a firm is relegated to the newsvendor model almost immediately. It is the products with an intermediate life cycle (one to two years)—for example, the InSync pacemaker—that can be very tricky to manage. A firm should start thinking in terms of the order-up-to model and then switch to the newsvendor model shortly before the product dies. Many firms botch this "end-of-life" transition: by holding on to high service levels too long, they find themselves with far too much inventory when the product becomes obsolete.

11.8   Controlling Ordering Costs

In our analysis of Medtronic's supply chain, the focus has been on service levels (fill rate or in-stock) and the expected amount of inventory on hand at the end of each period. Although we have not addressed the issue of *order frequency* (i.e., how many shipments are made each year to the DC or to each sales territory), there are other settings for which it is important to control the order frequency. For example, most online book shoppers realize, due to how online retailers charge for shipping, that five separate orders with one book in each order is generally more expensive than one book order containing the same five books. In other words, when there is a significant cost incurred with each order that is independent of the amount ordered (i.e., a fixed cost), it is necessary to be smart about how often orders are made. The focus of this section is on how we can account for fixed ordering costs in the order-up-to model.

As we have already seen, in the order-up-to model, the order quantity in a period equals the demand in the previous period. Hence, an order is submitted in a period whenever demand in the previous period is not zero. Therefore, the probability we submit an order in a period is $1 -$ Prob{Demand in one period $= 0$} and the frequency at which we submit orders is

$$\frac{1 - \text{Prob\{Demand in one period} = 0\}}{\text{Length of period}}$$

For example, if there is a 90 percent probability we order in a period, and a period is two weeks, then our order frequency is 0.9/2 weeks = 0.45 orders per week. If demand occurs frequently, so the probability of zero demand is very small no matter the length of the period, then it follows that we can reduce our ordering frequency by increasing the length of our period; that is, we are likely to submit nearly twice as many orders with a one-week period than with a two-week period. But increasing the length of the period is costly from the perspective of inventory holding costs. We illustrate that point via an example.

Suppose all orders are received precisely eight weeks after they are submitted to a supplier, weekly demand is normally distributed with mean 100 and standard deviation 75, the target in-stock probability is 99.25 percent, and demands across weeks are independent. We can choose a period length of one, two, four, or eight weeks. If the period is one week, then

TABLE 11.4
Analysis of Ending Inventory for Different Period Lengths
In each case, the delivery time is eight weeks and demand is normally distributed and independent across weeks.

	Period Length (in weeks)			
	1	2	4	8
One period expected demand	100	200	400	800
One period standard deviation	75.0	106.1	150.0	212.1
Lead time (in periods)	8	4	2	1
Target in-stock probability	99.25%	99.25%	99.25%	99.25%
z	2.43	2.43	2.43	2.43
S	1,447	1,576	1,831	2,329
Average back order	0.56	0.59	0.65	0.75
Average ending inventory	548	577	632	730

the lead time is eight periods, whereas if the period length is four weeks, then the lead time is two periods. Using the methods developed in the previous sections, we can determine the end-of-period average inventory for each period length. Those results are summarized in Table 11.4. The table reveals that our end-of-period inventory is indeed higher as we lengthen the period. But that is not really a fair comparison across our different options.

As we have already stated, the average order quantity equals average demand in the previous period. Thus, our average order quantity with a period length of one week is 100 units, whereas our average order quantity with an eight-week period is 800 units. Figure 11.7 plots the average inventory level over time for our four options; on average, inventory increases at the start of the period by the average order quantity and then decreases at the rate of 100 units per week, that is, average inventory follows a "saw-toothed" pattern. (Due to randomness in demand, the actual inventory pattern varies around those patterns, but those saw toothed patterns capture the average behavior of inventory.) The average inventory over time is the average end-of-period inventory plus half of the average order quantity, which for our four options is 598, 677, 832, and 1,130 respectively. Hence, longer periods mean less frequent ordering but more inventory.

Incidentally, you may recall that the graphs in Figure 11.7 resemble Figure 2.11 in Chapter 2. Back in Chapter 2 we used the term *cycle inventory* to refer to the inventory held due to lumpy ordering. In this case, the average cycle inventory would be half of the average order quantity: with four-week periods, the average cycle inventory is 400/2 = 200 units. The average end-of-period inventory is often referred to as *safety inventory* because that is the inventory that is needed to buffer demand variability. The average inventory over time is then safety inventory plus cycle inventory.

To balance the cost of more inventory with the benefit of fewer orders, we need information about holding and ordering costs. Let's say this item costs $50, annual holding costs are 25 percent, and we incur a fixed cost of $275 per shipment (e.g., we could be talking about a truck delivery). If the period length is one week, then the average inventory is 598 units, which has value 598 × $50 = $29,900 and costs us 25% × $29,900 = $7,475 per year. With mean demand of 100 and a standard deviation of 75, the z-statistic for 0 is $(0 - 100)/75 = -1.33$. Hence, the probability we order in any given week is $1 - \Phi(-1.33) = 0.91$.[5] With 52 weeks per year, we can expect to make 0.91 × 52 = 47.32 orders per year for a total ordering cost of 47.32 × $275 = $13,013. Total cost is then $7,475 + $13,013 = $20,488. Repeating those calculations for the remaining three period-length options reveals their annual costs to be $15,398, $13,975, and $15,913. Figure 11.8 plots those costs as well as the inventory holding and ordering costs of the four options.

---

[5] We actually just evaluated that the probability demand is *less* than or equal to zero because the normal distribution allows for negative demand. We are implicitly assuming that all negative realizations of demand are really zero demand outcomes.

FIGURE 11.7
Average Inventory Pattern over Time for Four Different Period Lengths
Upper left, one week; upper right, two weeks; lower left, four weeks; and lower right, eight weeks.

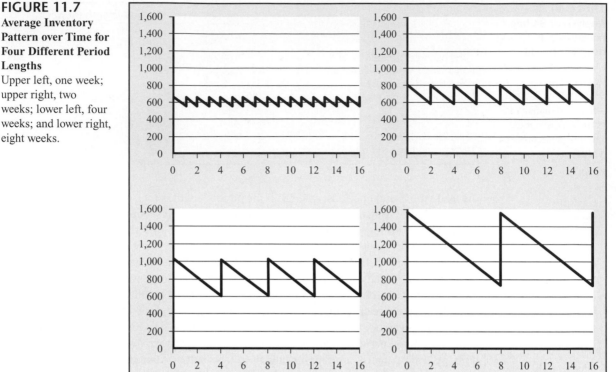

Figure 11.8 reveals that out best option is to set the period length to four weeks (which implies the lead time is then two periods). A shorter period length results in too many orders so the extra ordering costs dominate the reduced holding costs. A longer period suffers from too much inventory.

Although this analysis has been done in the context of the order-up-to model, it may very well remind you of another model, the *Economic Order Quantity (EOQ)* model discussed in Chapter 5. Recall that in the EOQ model there is a fixed cost per order/batch K, a holding cost per unit per unit of time h, and demand occurs at a constant flow rate R; in this case, $R = 100$ per week or $R = 5,200$ per year. The key difference between our model and the EOQ model is that here we have random demand whereas the EOQ model assumes demand occurs at a constant rate. Nevertheless, it is interesting to evaluate the EOQ model in this setting. We already know that the fixed ordering cost is $K = \$275$. The holding cost per unit per year is $25\% \times \$50 = \$12.5$. So the EOQ quantity (see Chapter 5) is

$$Q = \sqrt{\frac{2 \times K \times R}{h}} = \sqrt{\frac{2 \times 275 \times 5200}{12.5}} = 478$$

(Note that we need to use the yearly flow rate because the holding cost is per unit per year.) Hence, the EOQ model suggests that each order should be for 478 units, which implies submitting an order every $478/100 = 4.78$ weeks. (This follows from Little's Law.) Hence, even though the order-up-to and the EOQ models are different, the EOQ model's recommendation is quite similar (order every 4.78 weeks versus order every 4 weeks). Although we have only demonstrated this for one example, it can be shown that the EOQ model generally gives a very good recommendation for the period length (note that the EOQ actually recommends an order quantity that can then be converted to a period length).

FIGURE 11.8
Annual Ordering Costs (squares), Inventory Costs (diamonds), and Total Costs (circles) for Periods of Length One, Two, Four, and Eight Weeks

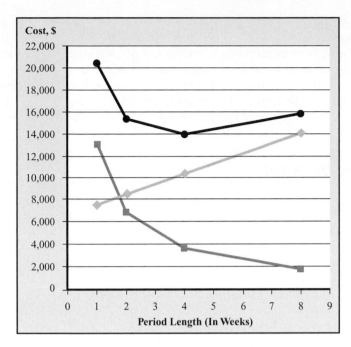

One limitation of our order-up-to model is that the lead time must equal an integer number of periods. In our example, because the delivery time is eight weeks, this allows us to choose period lengths of one, two, four, or eight, but we cannot choose a period length of 3 or 5 or 4.78 weeks (because with a period length of 3 weeks the lead time is 2.67 periods, i.e., deliveries would be received two-thirds of the way into a period instead of at the beginning of the period). If the delivery time were three weeks, then we would be even more restricted in our period length options. Fortunately, the order-up-to model can be extended to handle situations in which the lead time is a fraction of the period length. But that extension is beyond the scope of this text, and, rest assured, the qualitative insights from our model carry over to that more complex setting.

So we have shown that we can adjust our period length in the order-up-to model to control our ordering costs. Furthermore, the average order quantity with the optimal period length will approximately equal the EOQ quantity. (Hence, the EOQ formula gives us an easy way to check if our period length is reasonable.) One advantage of this approach is that we submit orders on a regular schedule. This is a useful feature if we need to coordinate the orders across multiple items. For example, since we incur a fixed cost per truck shipment, we generally deliver many different products on each truck because no single product's demand is large enough to fill a truck (imagine sending a tractor trailer load of spices to a grocery store). In that situation, it is quite useful to order items at the same time so that the truck can be loaded quickly and we can ensure a reasonably full shipment (given that there is a fixed cost per shipment, it makes sense to utilize the cargo capacity as much as possible). Therefore, we need only ensure that the order times of different products align.

Instead of using fixed order intervals, as in the order-up-to model, we could control ordering costs by imposing a minimum order quantity. For example, we could wait for Q units of demand to occur and then order exactly Q units. With such a policy, we would order on average every Q/R units of time, but due to the randomness in demand, the time between orders would vary. Not surprisingly, the EOQ quantity provides an excellent recommendation for that minimum order quantity, but we omit the analytical details as they are beyond the scope of this text. The important insight from this discussion is that it is possible to control ordering costs by restricting ourselves to a periodic schedule of orders (as in the order-up-to model) or we could restrict ourselves to a minimum order quantity. With the first option, there is little variability in the timing of orders, which facilitates the coordination of orders across multiple items, but the order quantities are variable (which may increase handling costs). With the second option, the order quantities are not variable (we always order Q), but the timing of those orders varies.

11.9   Medtronic Wrap-up

This section concludes our analysis of Medtronic's inventory management. We begin with the Mounds View DC and then discuss field inventory in Susan Magnotto's territory.

According to our analysis, to achieve a 99.9 percent in-stock probability requires the Mounds View distribution center to operate with an order-up-to level of 685 units, $S = 685$. With that order-up-to level, the expected inventory is about 363 units (measured at the end of each day). From Figure 11.2, Medtronic's current average end-of-month inventory is 270 units, which is considerably less than the 363 units predicted with the 99.9 percent in-stock probability requirement. (We are assuming that the end-of-month inventory is comparable to the end-of-week inventory, which is a valid assumption if the end of the month always coincides with the end of some week. Unfortunately, that is not always the case, so our comparison between the inventory data in Figure 11.2 and our end-of-the week expected inventory is not entirely fair. Nevertheless, it is a good starting point.)

With a little bit of leg work, we can discover that our model predicts the DC would carry 270 units of inventory on average if it implemented $S = 592$. The resulting in-stock probability would be 98.4 percent. We can conclude that the Mounds View DC indeed operates with a very high in-stock probability. Increasing the in-stock probability from 98.4 percent to 99.9 percent requires about a 34 percent increase in inventory investment [(363 − 270)/270]. (However, based on the discussion at the end of Section 11.7, maybe such a high in-stock probability is not desirable.)

The application of the order-up-to model to Susan's inventory results in a more dramatic discrepancy between the inventory actually held and the amount theoretically needed. We found that an order-up-to level of four units is required to achieve an in-stock probability of 99.9 percent in Susan's territory. With that order-up-to level Susan should have about 3.42 units on average at the end of each day, but Figure 11.3 indicates that her average inventory at the end of the month is about 7.8 units. (Because the end of the month always coincides with the end of a day, there are no issues regarding the validity of this comparison.) In other words, the model suggests that the extremely high target of a 99.9 percent in-stock probability is achievable with less than half the amount of inventory Susan currently holds!

This is an intriguing finding, but it does require some qualification. Because the order-up-to model is only a representation of reality, it is possible that one or more of its assumptions are violated, thereby calling the finding into question, at least to some degree. For example, maybe a Poisson distribution with mean 0.29 is not the best representation of daily demand, or maybe daily demand varies throughout the week or throughout the month. Regular spikes in demand at the end of the month could explain Susan's higher inventory level. In addition, maybe true demand has "fatter tails" than the Poisson distribution suggests; that is, the Poisson distribution underestimates the probability of low demand (0 units) and very high demand (3+ units). If Susan recognizes that days with three or more units of demand are more likely than the Poisson model predicts, then she could be justified in holding more inventory. Fortunately, it is not too hard to investigate this possibility: Medtronic should collect daily demand data throughout the year to see if the demand distribution has been chosen correctly.

The demand distribution is only one of the inputs to the order-up-to model. The other key input is the lead time, which we took to be one day. If Susan believes, or correctly realizes, that the lead time is longer, then she could again be justified in holding more inventory. For example, with a lead time of five days, the needed order-up-to level is six units to achieve a 99.9 percent in-stock probability and that results in about 4.55 units of inventory on average. With a lead time of 12 days, the 99.9 percent in-stock target requires about 7.23 units of inventory, which is close to what Susan actually carries. In other words, she seems to order inventory as if the lead time is 12 days rather than one day.

Why does Susan operate as if the lead time is so long? There are a number of possible explanations. Maybe factory shortages have caused the Mounds View DC to be out of inventory for a considerable amount of time; therefore, she is protecting herself from those shortages. If that is the case, then maybe blame should be put on the Mounds View DC: one can argue that it is the DC's job to carry enough inventory to buffer the sales representatives from the uncertainty of supply shortages at the manufacturing facilities. Alternatively, maybe Susan does not like the phone calls, faxes, and paper work to submit orders. Hence, maybe she batches her orders, that is, she does not order every day. Our definition of the lead time states that it is the time between when an order is submitted and when it is received, *assuming* an order for a unit is submitted at the first ordering opportunity. If there is a gap between when an implant occurs and when it triggers an order, then that extra time should be included in the lead time.

A third explanation for Susan's considerable inventory investment is that the extra inventory has very little consequence to her. As a result, she carries enough inventory to give her plenty of buffer without having to worry about calculating how much less inventory she could safely operate with. Remember, Susan is managing the inventory for hundreds of products, not just the InSync pacemaker. It is quite unlikely that she has the time, desire, or skill to fit a Poisson demand distribution to each product; determine the appropriate order-up-to level; and then implement those order-up-to levels on a daily basis for each of her products.

To conclude, if Medtronic were to replenish field inventory with an automatic replenishment system based on the order-up-to model, then it is possible that field inventory can be reduced without degrading service. While the sales representatives would lose control over their inventory, they would be relieved of the burden of tracking, adjusting, and implementing inventory control parameters for a wide array of products. Without having to worry about the gritty details of inventory management, sales representatives could spend more time working on sales.

11.10   Managerial Insights

This section discusses general managerial insights from the order-up-to model.

One of the key lessons from the queuing and newsvendor chapters is that variability in demand is costly. (Recall that the mismatch cost in the newsvendor model is increasing with the coefficient of variation, which is the ratio of the standard deviation of demand to expected demand.) That result continues to hold in the order-up-to model. Figure 11.9 illustrates the result graphically. The figure presents the trade-off curve between the fill rate and the expected inventory: as the desired fill rate increases, so does the required amount of inventory. Furthermore, we see that for any given fill rate the expected inventory increases in the standard deviation of demand over $l + 1$ periods: increased variability means more inventory is needed on average to achieve a fixed service level.

FIGURE 11.9
The Trade-off between Inventory and Fill Rate with Normally Distributed Demand and Mean 100 over *l* + 1 Periods
The curves differ in the standard deviation of demand over *l* + 1 periods: 60, 50, 40, 30, 20, 10 from top to bottom.

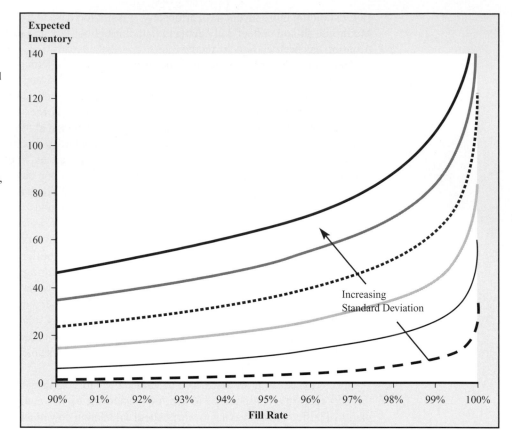

In addition to the variability in demand, the expected inventory in the order-up-to model is sensitive to the lead time, as illustrated by Figure 11.10: as the lead time is reduced, so is the required inventory for any service target.

While expected inventory depends on the variability of demand and the lead time, the expected on-order inventory, or pipeline inventory, depends only on the lead time. Therefore, while reducing the uncertainty in demand reduces expected inventory, pipeline inventory can only be reduced with a faster lead time. (Actually, reducing demand also reduces pipeline inventory, but that is rarely an attractive option, and reducing demand does not even reduce pipeline inventory when it is measured relative to the demand rate, e.g., with inventory turns or days of demand.) Furthermore, the amount of pipeline inventory can be considerable, especially for long lead times, as demonstrated in Figure 11.11, where the distance between the two curves is the pipeline inventory, which is clearly growing as the lead time increases.

Wal-Mart is a company that clearly understands the importance of lead times. As shown in Figure 11.12, Wal-Mart has consistently improved its annual inventory turns over (approximately) the last two decades. While a number of factors could explain this dramatic improvement, reductions in its lead time is surely a significant factor. These reductions were achieved through numerous initiatives. To improve the lead time Wal-Mart receives from its suppliers to its distribution centers, Wal-Mart built electronic linkages with its suppliers. These linkages ensure that no time is wasted in order transmission and order processing. Furthermore, they allow Wal-Mart to share demand data with suppliers so that suppliers can ensure they have enough capacity to meet Wal-Mart's needs on a timely basis. (Lead times can become quite long if a supplier runs out of critical components or if

FIGURE 11.10
The Impact of Lead Time on Expected Inventory for Four Fill Rate Targets
Fill rate targets are 99.9, 99.5, 99.0, and 98 percent, top curve to bottom curve, respectively. Demand in one period is normally distributed with mean 100 and standard deviation 60.

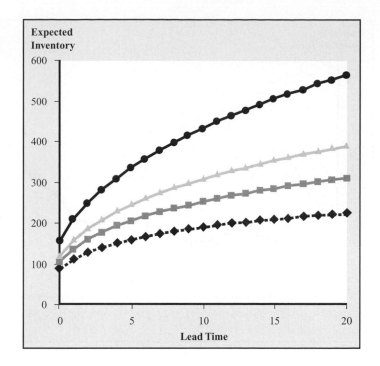

the supplier runs out of capacity.) Next, Wal-Mart designed its distribution centers and logistics so that inventory spends very little time in the distribution centers. For example, a popular product such as Crest toothpaste generally spends less than eight hours in a Wal-Mart distribution center: Through a process called *cross-docking,* inventory is moved from in-bound trucks directly to out-bound trucks, that is, it is never actually put on a shelf in the warehouse (Nelson, 1999). Finally, via computerized replenishment and control of its

FIGURE 11.11
Expected Inventory (circles) and Total Inventory (squares), Which Is Expected Inventory Plus Pipeline Inventory, with a 99.9 Percent Fill Rate Requirement
Demand in one period is normally distributed with mean 100 and standard deviation 60.

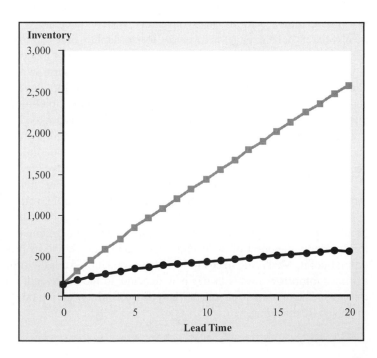

FIGURE 11.12
Annual Inventory Turns for Wal-Mart

Source: 10-K filings.

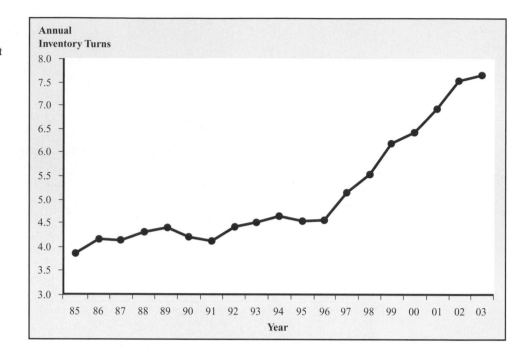

own delivery fleet of vehicles, Wal-Mart's lead time from its distribution centers to its stores is as fast as can be. As a result of the combined impact of these initiatives, Wal-Mart is able to sell much of its inventory even before it must pay for that inventory, a rather enviable situation for any retailer.

Now that we have illustrated the key insights from the order-up-to model (reduce demand variability and lead times wherever possible), it is useful to consider the relationship between the order-up-to inventory model and the newsvendor model. Both models face the "too much–too little" challenge associated with matching supply to demand. In each model the "too much" cost results in excess inventory, which either needs to be disposed at a loss (newsvendor) or held longer in inventory than desirable (order-up-to). The "too little" cost results in the opportunity cost of lost sales with the newsvendor model and poor service, which is believed to lead to lost sales either in the short or long term, with the order-up-to model. However, because the newsvendor model is appropriate for situations of product obsolescence, the "too much" cost is generally high relative to the "too little" cost, thereby implying that the optimal in-stock probability or expected fill rate is not too high, surely not 99.9 percent. In contrast, because the order-up-to model is designed for a product with stable demand and no imminent threat of obsolescence, the concern with "too little" far outweighs the concern with "too much," thereby leading to justifiably aggressive service objectives.

This discussion is particularly relevant for a firm that must manage products that move through the product life cycle relatively quickly. For example, while the InSync pacemaker appears to be in a stable stage of its life cycle, the introduction of new technology, either by Medtronic or by a competitor, can easily push the InSync pacemaker into its decline stage. Furthermore, the onset of the decline stage can be quick and its progression can be rapid. At that point, Medtronic needs to be able to transition from the order-up-to model, which assumes tomorrow always brings new demand, to the newsvendor model, which assumes tomorrow the product is obsolete. Many firms find navigating this "end-of-life" transition to be very challenging.

11.11 Summary

This chapter illustrates the application of the order-up-to model to one product, the InSync pacemaker, at two different levels in Medtronic's supply chain: the Mounds View distribution center and Susan Magnotto's Madison, Wisconsin, territory. The order-up-to model periodically reviews (weekly at Mounds View, daily for Susan) the inventory position at a location and submits an order, which is received after a fixed lead time, to raise the inventory position to an order-up-to level. The order-up-to level is chosen, based on the demand distribution, to minimize inventory while maintaining a service standard measured either with the in-stock probability or the expected fill rate.

The analysis of the order-up-to model reveals that raising the desired service level increases the required inventory investment, and the amount of inventory needed increases nonlinearly as the target service level increases. In other words, as high service levels are desired, proportionally more inventory is needed.

There are two other key factors that determine the amount of inventory that is needed: the variability of demand, measured by the coefficient of variation, and the length of the lead time. Just as we saw in the newsvendor model, an increase in the coefficient of variation leads to an increase in the amount of inventory needed for any fixed service level.

The length of the lead time is critical for two reasons. First, a reduction in the lead time reduces the amount of inventory needed at any location. Second, and maybe even more importantly, a reduction in the lead time reduces the amount of inventory in transit between locations, that is, the pipeline inventory. In fact, reducing the lead time is the only way to reduce the pipeline inventory: While reducing the variability of demand reduces the expected inventory at a location, it has no effect on pipeline inventory because of Little's Law.

Table 11.5 provides a summary of the key notation and equations presented in this chapter.

TABLE 11.5
Summary of Key Notation and Equations in Chapter 11

l = Lead time
S = Order-up-to level
Inventory level = On-hand inventory − Back order
Inventory position = On-order inventory + Inventory level
In-stock probability = 1 − Stockout probability
= Prob{Demand over l + 1 periods ≤ S}

Expected back order:
If demand over l + 1 periods is normally distributed with mean μ and standard deviation σ:
Expected back order = $\sigma \times L(z)$, where $z = (S - \mu)/\sigma$

In Excel:
Expected back order = σ*(Normdist (z, 0, 1, 0) − z*(1 − Normsdist (z)))
  If demand over l + 1 periods is a discrete distribution function table, then
  Expected back order = $L(S)$

Fill rate = $1 - \dfrac{\text{Expected back order}}{\text{Expected demand in one period}}$

Expected inventory = S − Expected demand over l + 1 periods + Expected back order
Expected on-order inventory = Expected demand in one period × Lead time
To achieve a fill rate with normally distributed demand,
$L(z) = \left(\dfrac{\text{Expected demand in one period}}{\text{Standard deviation of demand over } l + 1 \text{ periods}} \right) \times (1 - \text{Fill rate})$,
otherwise,
Expected back order = (Expected demand in one period) × (1 − Fill rate)

11.12
Further
Reading

The order-up-to model is just one of many possible inventory policies that could be implemented in practice. For example, there are policies that account for stochastic lead times, lost sales, and/or batch ordering (ordering in integer multiples of a fixed batch quantity). However, no matter what extensions are included, the key insights remain: Inventory increases as demand variability increases or as the lead time increases.

See Zipkin (2000) for an extensive treatment of the theory of inventory management. For less technical, but still sophisticated, treatments, see Nahmias (2005) or Silver, Pyke, and Peterson (1998). Those texts cover the additional polices we discussed in the chapter (for example, a minimum order quantity with a fixed lead time and stochastic demand). In addition, they discuss the issue of the appropriate service level for upstream stages in a supply chain.

See Simchi-Levi, Kaminsky, and Simchi-Levi (2003) and Chopra and Meindl (2004) for managerial discussions of supply-chain management.

11.13
Practice
Problems

Q11.1* **(Furniture Store)** You are the store manager at a large furniture store. One of your products is a study desk. Weekly demand for the desk is normally distributed with mean 40 and standard deviation 20. The lead time from the assembly plant to your store is two weeks and you order inventory replenishments weekly. You use the order-up-to model to control inventory.

  a. Suppose your order-up-to level is $S = 220$. You are about to place an order and note that your inventory level is 100 and you have 85 desks on order. How many desks will you order?

  b. Suppose your order-up-to level is $S = 220$. You are about to place an order and note that your inventory level is 160 and you have 65 desks on order. How many desks will you order?

  c. What is the optimal order-up-to level if you want to target a 98 percent in-stock probability?

  d. What is the optimal order-up-to level if you want to target a 98 percent fill rate?

  e. Suppose your order-up-to level is $S = 120$. What is your expected on-hand inventory?

  f. Suppose your order-up-to level is $S = 200$. What is your fill rate?

  g. Suppose you now decide to maintain a 95 percent in-stock probability for the desk. What is the expected fill rate in this case?

  h. Suppose your order-up-to level is $S = 120$. Your internal cost of capital is 15 percent and each desk costs $200. What is your total cost of capital for the year for inventory in the store?

Q11.2* **(Campus Bookstore)** A campus bookstore sells the Palm m505 handheld for $399. The wholesale price is $250 per unit. The store estimates that weekly demand averages 0.5 unit and has a Poisson distribution. The bookstore's annual inventory holding cost is 20 percent of the cost of inventory. Assume orders are made weekly and the lead time to receive an order from the distributor is four weeks.

  a. What base stock level minimizes inventory while achieving a 99 percent in-stock probability?

  b. What base stock level minimizes inventory while achieving a 99 percent fill rate?

  c. Suppose the base stock level is $S = 4$. What is the average pipeline inventory?

  d. Suppose the base stock level is $S = 5$. What is the average inventory held at the end of the week in the store?

  e. Suppose the base stock level is $S = 5$. What is the store's fill rate?

  f. Suppose the base stock level is $S = 6$. What is the probability a stockout occurs during a week (i.e., some customer is back-ordered)?

(* indicates that the solution is at the end of the book)

g. Suppose the base stock level is $S = 6$. What is the probability the store is out of stock (i.e., has no inventory) at the end of a week?

h. Suppose the base stock level is $S = 6$. What is the probability the store has one or more units of inventory at the end of a week?

The bookstore is concerned that it is incurring excessive ordering costs by ordering weekly. For parts i and j, suppose the bookstore now submits orders every two weeks. The demand forecast remains the same and the lead time is still four weeks.

i. What base stock level yields at least a 99 percent in-stock probability while minimizing inventory?

j. What is the average pipeline stock?

Q11.3* **(Quick Print)** Quick Print Inc. uses plain and three-hole-punched paper for copying needs. Demand for each paper type is highly variable. Weekly demand for the plain paper is estimated to be normally distributed with mean 100 and standard deviation 65 (measured in boxes). Each week, a replenishment order is placed to the paper factory and the order arrives five weeks later. All copying orders that cannot be satisfied immediately due to the lack of paper are back-ordered. The inventory holding cost is about $1 per box per year.

a. Suppose that Quick Print decides to establish an order-up-to level of 700 for plain paper. At the start of this week, there are 523 boxes in inventory and 180 boxes on order. How much will Quick Print order this week?

b. Again, assume that Quick Print uses an order-up-to level of 700. What is Quick Print's fill rate?

c. What is Quick Print's optimal order-up-to level for plain paper if Quick Print operates with a 99 percent in-stock probability?

d. Now evaluate Quick Print's optimal order-up-to level for plain paper if Quick Print operates with a 99 percent fill rate requirement.

Q11.4 **(Main Line Auto Distributor)** Main Line Auto Distributor is an auto parts supplier to local garage shops. None of its customers have the space or capital to store all of the possible parts they might need so they order parts from Main Line several times a day. To provide fast service, Main Line uses three pickup trucks to make its own deliveries. Each Friday evening Main Line orders additional inventory from its supplier. The supplier delivers early Monday morning. Delivery costs are significant, so Main Line only orders on Fridays. Consider part A153QR, or part A for short. Part A costs Main Line $175 and Main Line sells it to garages for $200. If a garage orders part A and Main Line is out of stock, then the garage finds the part from some other distributor. Main Line has its own capital and space constraints and estimates that each unit of part A costs $0.50 to hold in inventory per week. (Assume you incur the $0.50 cost for units left in inventory at the end of the week, not $0.50 for your average inventory during the week or $0.50 for your inventory at the start of the week.) Average weekly demand for this part follows a Poisson distribution with mean 1.5 units. Suppose it is Friday evening and Main Line currently doesn't have any part A's in stock. The distribution and loss functions for a Poisson distribution with mean 1.5 can be found in Appendix B.

a. How many part A's should Main Line order from the supplier?

b. Suppose Main Line orders three units. What is the probability Main Line is able to satisfy all demand during the week?

c. Suppose Main Line orders four units. What is the probability Main Line is *not* able to satisfy all demand during the week?

d. If Main Line seeks to hit a target fill rate of 99.5 percent, then how many units should Main Line order?

e. If Main Line seeks to hit a target in-stock probability of 99.5 percent, then how many units should Main Line order?

f. Suppose Main Line orders five units. What is Main Line's expected holding cost for the upcoming week?

Q11.5   (**Hotspices.com**) You are the owner of Hotspices.com, an online retailer of hip, exotic, and hard-to-find spices. Consider your inventory of saffron, a spice (generally) worth more by weight than gold. You order saffron from an overseas supplier with a shipping lead time of four weeks and you order weekly. Average quarterly demand is normally distributed with a mean of 415 ounces and a standard deviation of 154 ounces. The holding cost per ounce per week is $0.75. You estimate that your back-order penalty cost is $50 per ounce. Assume there are 4.33 weeks per month.

     a. If you wish to minimize inventory holding costs while maintaining a 99.25 percent fill rate, then what should your order-up-to level be?

     b. If you wish to minimize inventory holding costs while maintaining a 99.25 percent in-stock probability, then what should your order-up-to level be?

     c. If you wish to minimize holding and back-order penalty costs, then what should your order-up-to level be?

     d. Now consider your inventory of pepperoncini (Italian hot red peppers). You can order this item daily and your local supplier delivers with a two-day lead time. While not your most popular item, you do have enough demand to sell the five kilogram bag. Average demand per day has a Poisson distribution with mean 1.0. The holding cost per bag per day is $0.05 and the back-order penalty cost is about $5 per bag. What is your optimal order-up-to level?

Q11.6   (**ACold**) ACold Inc. is a frozen food distributor with 10 warehouses across the country. Iven Tory, one of the warehouse managers, wants to make sure that the inventory policies used by the warehouse are minimizing inventory while still maintaining quick delivery to ACold's customers. Since the warehouse carries hundreds of different products, Iven decided to study one. He picked Caruso's Frozen Pizza. Demand for CFPs averages 400 per day with a standard deviation of 200. Weekly demand (five days) averages 2,000 units with a standard deviation of 555. Since ACold orders at least one truck from General Foods each day (General Foods owns Caruso's Pizza), ACold can essentially order any quantity of CFP it wants each day. In fact, ACold's computer system is designed to implement a base stock policy for each product. Iven notes that any order for CFPs arrives four days after the order. Further, it costs ACold $0.01 per day to keep a CFP in inventory, while a back order is estimated to cost ACold $0.45.

     a. What base stock level should Iven choose for CFPs if his goal is to minimize holding and back-order costs?

     b. Suppose the base stock level 2,800 is chosen. What fraction of customer demands are met immediately from stock?

     c. Suppose the base stock level 2,800 is chosen. What is the average amount of inventory on order?

     d. Suppose the base stock level 2,800 is chosen. What is the annual holding cost? (Assume 260 days per year.)

     e. What base stock level minimizes inventory while maintaining a 97 percent in-stock probability?

Q11.7   (**Cyber Chemicals**) Cyber Chemicals uses liquid nitrogen on a regular basis. Average daily demand is 178 gallons with a standard deviation of 45. Due to a substantial ordering cost, which is estimated to be $58 per order (no matter the quantity in the order), Cyber currently orders from its supplier on a weekly basis. Cyber also incurs holding costs on its inventory. Cyber recognizes that its inventory is lowest at the end of the week but prefers a more realistic estimate of its average inventory. In particular, Cyber estimates its average inventory to be its average end-of-week inventory plus half of its average order quantity. The holding cost Cyber incurs on that average inventory is $0.08 per gallon per week. Cyber's supplier delivers in less than a day. Assume 52 weeks per year, five days per week.

     a. Cyber wishes to maintain a 99.9 percent in-stock probability. If it does so, what is Cyber's annual inventory holding cost?

     b. What is Cyber's annual ordering cost?

     c. Should Cyber consider ordering every two weeks?

Q11.8   (**Southern Fresh**) Shelf space in the grocery business is a valuable asset. Every good supermarket spends a significant amount of effort attempting to determine the optimal shelf space allocation across products. Many factors are relevant to this decision: the profitability of each product, the size of each product, the demand characteristics of each product, and so forth. Southern Fresh has decided to make a policy that every product will receive enough shelf space to ensure that 98.75 percent of customers will find that their first choice is available. Consider Hot Bull corn chips, a local favorite. Average daily demand for this product is 55, with a standard deviation of 30. Bags of Hot Bull can be stacked 20 deep per facing. (A facing is the width on a shelf required to display one item of a product.) Deliveries from Southern Fresh's central warehouse occur two days after a store manager submits an order. (Actually, in most stores, orders are generated by a centralized computer system that is linked to its point-of-sales data. But even these orders are received two days after they are transmitted.)

a. How many facings should Southern Fresh allocate to Hot Bull corn chips?

b. How many facings are needed to achieve a 98.75 percent in-stock probability?

c. Suppose Southern Fresh allocates 11 facings to Hot Bull corn chips. On average, how many bags of Hot Bull are on the shelf at the end of the day?

d. Although Southern Fresh does not want to incur the cost of holding inventory, it does want to leave customers with the impression that it is well stocked. Hence, Southern Fresh employees continually roam the aisles of the store to adjust the presentation of the product. In particular, they shift product around so that there is an item in each facing whenever possible. Suppose Southern Fresh allocates 11 facings to Hot Bull corn chips. What is the probability that at the end of the day there will be an empty facing, that is, a facing without any product?

Chapter **12**

Risk-Pooling Strategies to Reduce and Hedge Uncertainty[1]

Uncertainty is the bane of operations. No matter in what form—for example, uncertain demand, uncertain supply, or uncertain quality—operational performance never benefits from the presence of uncertainty. Previous chapters have discussed models for coping with uncertainty (e.g., queuing, newsvendor, and order-up-to) and have emphasized the need to quantify uncertainty. Some strategies for reducing and hedging uncertainty have already been suggested: combine servers in a queuing system (Chapter 7); reduce uncertainty by collecting data to ensure that the best demand forecast is always implemented (Chapter 9); establish make-to-order production and invest in reactive capacity to better respond to demand (Chapter 10).

This chapter explores several additional strategies based on the concept of risk pooling. The idea behind risk pooling is to redesign the supply chain, the production process, or the product to either reduce the uncertainty the firm faces or to hedge uncertainty so that the firm is in a better position to mitigate the consequence of uncertainty. Several types of risk pooling are presented (location pooling, virtual pooling, product pooling, lead time pooling, and capacity pooling), but these are just different names to describe the same basic phenomenon. With each strategy, we work through a numerical example to illustrate its effectiveness and to highlight the situations in which the strategy is most appropriate.

12.1 Location Pooling

The newsvendor and the order-up-to inventory models are tools for deciding how much inventory to put at a single location to serve demand. An equally important decision, and one that we have ignored so far, is in how many different locations should the firm store inventory to serve demand. To explain, consider the Medtronic supply chain discussed in Chapter 11. In that supply chain, each sales representative in the field manages a cache of inventory to serve the rep's territory and there is a single distribution center to serve the en-

---

[1]Data in this chapter have been disguised to protect confidentiality.

tire U.S. market. Should there be one stockpile of inventory per sales representative, or should the demands from multiple territories be served from a single location? Should there be a single distribution center, or should the U.S. market demand be divided among multiple distribution centers? We explore those questions in this section.

Pooling Medtronic's Field Inventory

Let's begin with where to locate Medtronic's field inventory. Instead of the current system in which each sales representative manages his or her own inventory, maybe the representatives in adjacent territories could share inventory. For example, Medtronic could rent a small space in a centrally located and easily accessible location (e.g., a back room in a strip mall off the interchange of two major highways) and two to five representatives could pool their inventory at that location. Sharing inventory means that each representative would only carry inventory needed for immediate use; that is, each representative's trunk and consignment inventory would be moved to this shared location. Control of the pooled inventory would be guided by an automatic replenishment system based on the order-up-to model. What impact would this new strategy have on inventory performance?

Recall that average daily demand for Medtronic's InSync pacemaker in Susan Magnotto's Madison, Wisconsin, territory is represented with a Poisson distribution with mean 0.29 units per day. For the sake of argument, let's suppose there are several other territories adjacent to Susan's, each with a single sales representative, and each with average daily demand of 0.29 units for the InSync pacemaker. Instead of each representative carrying his or her own inventory, now they share a common pool of inventory. We refer to the combined territories in this new system as the *pooled territory* and the inventory there as the *pooled inventory*. In contrast, we refer to the territories in the current system as the *individual territories* and the inventory in one of those territories as the *individual inventory*. We refer to the strategy of combining the inventory from multiple territories/locations into a single location as *location pooling*. We have already evaluated the expected inventory with the current individual territory system, so now we need to evaluate the performance of the system with pooled territories, that is, the impact of location pooling.

The order-up-to model is used to manage the inventory at the pooled territory. The same aggressive target in-stock probability is used for the pooled territory as is used at the individual territories, 99.9 percent. Furthermore, the lead time to replenish the pooled territory is also one day. (There is no reason to believe the lead time to the pooled territory should be different than to the individual territories.)

As discussed in Chapter 11, if the Poisson distribution represents demand at two different territories, then their combined demand has a Poisson distribution with a mean that equals the sum of their means. (See Exhibit 11.1.) For example, suppose Susan shares inventory with two nearby sales representatives and they all have mean demand for the InSync pacemaker of 0.29 units per day. Then total demand across the three territories is Poisson with mean $3 \times 0.29 = 0.87$ units per day. We then can apply the order-up-to model to that pooled territory assuming a lead time of one day and a mean demand of 0.87 units.

Table 12.1 presents data on the impact of pooling the sales representatives' territories. To achieve the 99.9 percent in-stock probability for three sales representatives requires $S = 7$, where S is the order-up-to level. If Susan's inventory is not combined with another representative's, then (as we evaluated in Chapter 11) $S = 4$ is needed to hit the target in-stock probability. The expected inventory at the pooled location is 5.3 units, in contrast to 3.4 units for each individual location. However, the total inventory for three individual locations is $3 \times 3.4 = 10.2$ units. Hence, pooling three locations reduces expected inventory by about 48 percent $[(10.2 - 5.3)/10.2]$, without any degradation in service!

Number of Territories Pooled	Pooled Territory's Expected Demand per Day (a)	S	Expected Inventory		Pipeline Inventory	
			Units (b)	Days-of-Demand (b/a)	Units (c)	Days-of-Demand (c/a)
1	0.29	4	3.4	11.7	0.29	1.0
2	0.58	6	4.8	8.3	0.58	1.0
3	0.87	7	5.3	6.1	0.87	1.0
4	1.16	8	5.7	4.9	1.16	1.0
5	1.45	9	6.1	4.2	1.45	1.0
6	1.74	10	6.5	3.7	1.74	1.0
7	2.03	12	7.9	3.9	2.03	1.0
8	2.32	13	8.4	3.6	2.32	1.0

There is another approach to make the comparison between pooled territories and individual territories: Evaluate each inventory quantity relative to the demand it serves, that is, calculate expected inventory measured in days-of-demand rather than units:

$$\text{Expected inventory in days-of-demand} = \frac{\text{Expected inventory in units}}{\text{Expected daily demand}}$$

Table 12.1 also provides that measure of expected inventory. We see that inventory at each individual territory equals 3.4/0.29 = 11.7 days-of-demand whereas inventory at three pooled territories equals only 5.3/0.87 = 6.1 days-of-demand. Using our days-of-demand measure, we see that pooling three territories results in a 48 percent [(11.7 − 6.1)/11.7] reduction in inventory investment. We obtain the same inventory reduction (48 percent) because the two measures of inventory, units and days-of-demand, only differ by a constant factor (the expected daily demand). Hence, we can work with either measure.

While pooling two or three territories has a dramatic impact on inventory, Table 12.1 indicates that there are decreasing marginal returns to pooling territories; that is, each new territory added to the pool brings a smaller reduction in inventory than the previous territory added to the pool. For example, adding two more territories to a pool of six (to make a total of eight combined territories) has very little impact on the inventory investment (3.6 days-of-demand versus 3.7 days-of-demand), whereas adding two more territories to a pool of one (to make a total of three combined territories) has a dramatic impact in inventory (6.1 days-of-demand versus 11.7 days-of-demand). This is good news: the majority of the benefit of pooling territories comes from the first couple of territories combined, so there is little value in trying to combine many territories together.

Although location pooling generally reduces inventory, a careful observer of the data in Table 12.1 would discover that this is not always so: adding the seventh location to the pool slightly increases inventory (3.9 days-of-demand versus 3.7 days-of-demand). This is due to the restriction that the order-up-to level must be an integer (0, 1, 2, . . .) quantity. As a result, the in-stock probability might be even higher than the target: the in-stock probability with six pooled territories is 99.90 percent, whereas it is 99.97 percent with seven pooled territories. Overall, this issue does not invalidate the general trend that location pooling reduces inventory.

This discussion obviously leads to the question of why does location pooling reduce the required inventory investment? We'll find a good answer by looking at how demand variability changes as locations are added to the pooled location. And, as we have already discussed, the coefficient of variation (the ratio of the standard deviation to the mean) is our choice for measuring demand variability.

FIGURE 12.1

The Relationship between Expected Inventory (circles) and the Coefficient of Variation (squares) as Territories Are Pooled

Demand in each territory is Poisson with mean 0.29 units per day, the target in-stock probability is 99.9 percent, and the lead time is one day.

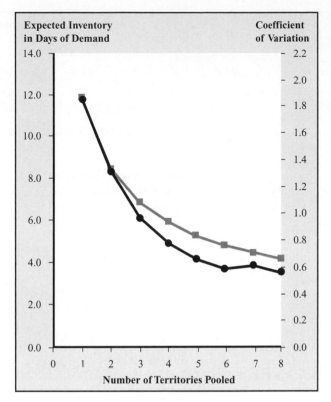

Recall that the standard deviation of a Poisson distribution equals the square root of its mean. Therefore,

$$\text{Coefficient of variation of a Poisson distribution} =$$
$$\frac{\text{Standard deviation}}{\text{Mean}} = \frac{\sqrt{\text{Mean}}}{\text{Mean}} = \frac{1}{\sqrt{\text{Mean}}} \tag{12.1}$$

As the mean of a Poisson distribution increases, its coefficient of variation decreases, that is, the Poisson distribution becomes less variable. Less variable demand leads to less inventory for any given service level. Hence, combining locations with Poisson demand reduces the required inventory investment because a higher demand rate implies less variable demand. However, because the coefficient of variation decreases with the square root of the mean, it decreases at a decreasing rate. In other words, each incremental increase in the mean has a proportionally smaller impact on the coefficient of variation, and hence on the expected inventory investment.

Figure 12.1 displays the relationship between inventory and the coefficient of variation for the data in Table 12.1. Notice that the decreasing pattern in inventory closely mimics the decreasing pattern in the coefficient of variation.

In addition to the total expected inventory in the field, we are also interested in the total pipeline inventory (inventory on order between the distribution center and the field). Table 12.1 provides the pipeline inventory in terms of units and in terms of days-of-demand. While location pooling decreases the expected inventory in days-of-demand, it has absolutely no impact on the pipeline inventory in terms of days-of-demand! Why? Little's Law governs pipeline inventory, and Little's Law depends on averages, not variability. Hence, because pooling territories reduces the variability of demand, it reduces expected inventory in the field but

Number of Territories Pooled	Pooled Territory's Expected Demand per Day	S	Expected Inventory		
			Units	Days-of-Demand	In-Stock Probability
1	0.29	4	3.4	11.7	99.96615%
2	0.58	8	6.8	11.7	99.99963
3	0.87	12	10.3	11.8	100.00000

it has no impact on the pipeline inventory. As we mentioned before, the only way to reduce pipeline inventory is to get a faster lead time. (Reducing demand reduces pipeline inventory in terms of units but does not change pipeline inventory measured in days-of-demand.)

While we can exploit location pooling to reduce inventory while maintaining a service level, we also can use location pooling to increase our service level. For example, we could choose an order-up-to level in the pooled territory that generates the same inventory investment as the individual territories (measured in days-of-demand) and see how much higher our in-stock could be. Table 12.2 presents those data for pooling up to three territories; beyond three territories we can raise the in-stock to essentially 100 percent with the same inventory investment as the individual territories.

Because the in-stock probability target with individual territories is so high (99.9 percent), it probably makes better sense to use location pooling to reduce the inventory investment rather than to increase the service level. However, in other settings it may be more desirable to increase the service level, especially if the target service level is deemed to be too low.

Figure 12.2 provides another perspective on this issue. It displays the inventory–service trade-off curves with four different degrees of location pooling: individual territories, two territories pooled, four territories pooled, and eight territories pooled. As displayed in the figure, pooling territories shifts the inventory–service trade-off curve down and to the right. Hence, location pooling gives us many options: we can choose to (1) maintain the same service with less inventory, (2) maintain the same inventory with a higher service, or (3) reduce inventory and increase service simultaneously (i.e., "we can have our cake and eat it too"). We saw a similar effect when pooling servers in a queuing environment. There you can use pooling to reduce waiting time without having to staff extra workers, or you can reduce workers while maintaining the same responsiveness, or a combination of both.

Although our analysis highlights the potential dramatic benefit of location pooling, this does not imply that Medtronic should pool territories without further thought. There will be an explicit storage cost for the space to house the pooled inventory, whereas the current system does not have a storage cost for trunk and consignment inventory. However, location pooling might reduce theft and spoilage costs because inventory is stored in fewer locations. Furthermore, location pooling probably would reduce shipping costs because the number of items per delivery is likely to increase.

The greatest concern with location pooling is the impact on the efficiency of the sales representatives. Even if only a few territories are pooled, it is likely that the pooled location would not be as convenient to each sales representative as their own individual inventory. As a result, the savings in inventory is offset by the extra time sales representatives spend pulling inventory from the pooled location instead of their own trunk or consignment closet. If that time penalty is sufficient, then the sales representatives might choose to still maintain their own trunk inventory. In a worst-case scenario, the sale's representatives continue to hold the same amount of inventory in their individual territories in addition to the inventory at the pooled location. To avoid this worst-case scenario,

FIGURE 12.2

The Inventory–Service Trade-off Curve for Different Levels of Location Pooling

The curves represent, from highest to lowest, individual territories, two pooled territories, four pooled territories, and eight pooled territories. Demand in each territory is Poisson with mean 0.29 units per day, and the lead time is one day.

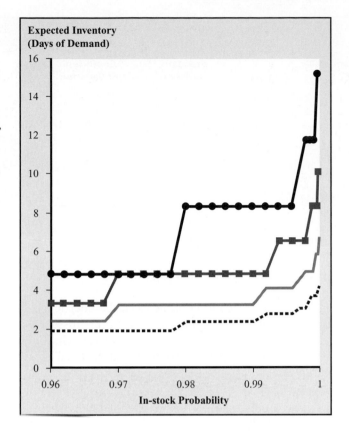

Medtronic should involve the sales representatives in the design of the pooled territories to ensure that they have "bought into the idea." Imposing a new supply chain structure without the cooperation of all interested parties can lead to unintended consequences, especially when human behavior is at work.

The physical separation between user and inventory can be mitigated via *virtual pooling:* Representatives maintain control of their inventory, but inventory information is shared among all representatives so that each rep can obtain inventory from the central distribution center and any other rep that has excess inventory. Although virtual pooling has its own challenges (e.g., the additional cost of maintaining the necessary information systems, the added expense of transshipping inventory among territories, and the sticky design issue of how to decide when inventory can be taken from one rep to be given to another rep), it can still be better than the current system that has isolated pockets of inventory.

Medtronic's Distribution Center(s)

Now let's turn our attention to the distribution center. For the U.S. market, Medtronic currently operates a single distribution center in Mounds View, Minnesota. Suppose Medtronic were to subdivide the United States into two or more regions, with each region assigned a single distribution center. This idea is location pooling in reverse. Hence, the total inventory investment is likely to increase. Let's see by how much.

Recall that weekly demand of the InSync Pacemaker at the Mounds View DC is normally distributed with mean 80.6 and standard deviation 58.81. There is a three-week lead time and the target in-stock probability is 99.9 percent. Table 12.3 provides data on the expected inventory required given the number of DCs Medtronic operates.

TABLE 12.3 The Increase in Inventory Investment as More Distribution Centers Are Operated
Assume demand is equally divided among the DCs, demands across DCs are independent, total demand is normally distributed with mean 80.6 and standard deviation 58.8, and the lead time is three weeks in all situations.

Number of DCs	Weekly Demand Parameters at Each DC			Expected Inventory at Each DC	
	Mean	Standard Deviation	Coefficient of Variation	Units	Weeks-of-Demand
1	80.6	58.8	0.73	257	3.2
2	40.3	41.6	1.03	182	4.5
3	26.9	34.0	1.26	148	5.5
4	20.2	29.4	1.46	129	6.4
5	16.1	26.3	1.63	115	7.1
6	13.4	24.0	1.79	105	7.8
7	11.5	22.2	1.93	97	8.4
8	10.1	20.8	2.06	91	9.0

Table 12.3 reveals that it is indeed costly to subdivide the U.S. market among multiple distribution centers: eight DCs require nearly three times more inventory to achieve the same service level as a single DC! (To be precise, it requires 9.0/3.2 = 2.83 times more inventory.)

In this situation, the connection between the coefficient of variation and the expected inventory savings from location pooling (or "dissavings" from location disintegration, as in this case) is even stronger than we saw with field inventory, as displayed in Figure 12.3. In fact, expected inventory and the coefficient of variation in this setting are proportional to one another (i.e., their ratio is a constant no matter the number of distribution centers).

To summarize, we have seen that location pooling dramatically reduces demand variability (measured with the coefficient of variation), and, in turn, dramatically reduces the

FIGURE 12.3
The Expected Inventory in Units (circles) and the Coefficient of Variation (squares) Depending on the Number of Distribution Centers Medtronic Operates
Demand is assumed to be equally divided and independent across distribution centers. The target in-stock probability is 99.9 percent and the lead time is three weeks in all cases.

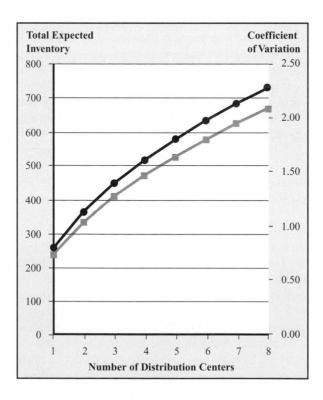

expected inventory investment needed to achieve a target service level. By storing inventory in fewer locations, location pooling is also likely to lead to lower storage costs. However, there are drawbacks to location pooling as well.

The key drawback with location pooling is that inventory moves further away from demand. For example, Medtronic could really reduce the needed inventory investment of In-Sync pacemakers if it were to require that inventory be stored only in one location per state. That might work for the Delaware representatives, but it is silly even for Wisconsin for two reasons. First, we saw that there are declining returns from location pooling, that is, pooling two to three locations gives most of the "bang for the buck," so there is no need to pool many locations. Second, Medtronic does not want to save on inventory at the expense of sales representatives spending too much time driving to and from the pooled inventory location. Thus, Medtronic may be able to use some location pooling of field inventory, but they should not get carried away with this idea.

The physical separation between inventory and customer is also a relevant issue at the distribution-center level of the supply chain. For example, we investigated the consequence of dividing the U.S. market into multiple regions, each served with a single distribution center. This "reverse location pooling" increases inventory investment, but it does put inventory closer to customers (i.e., sales representatives). The question is whether there is any value in having DC inventory closer to the field. Given that Medtronic uses an overnight carrier for all of its shipments, it is unlikely that the lead time to the field representatives would decrease (which would reduce field inventory). Furthermore, it is unlikely that the overnight carriers would charge Medtronic less per shipment, so Medtronic's shipping costs probably would not decrease. Finally, Medtronic's storage facility cost would increase with more DCs, so there really does not appear to be any justification for Medtronic to operate more than its one DC. Nevertheless, the outcome of this analysis could be different for other firms.

While we have concluded that Medtronic should operate with no more than one distribution center in the United States, we can now speculate on whether Medtronic should operate with only one distribution center worldwide. While consolidating down to one worldwide distribution center would further reduce the required inventory investment, it is unlikely that a single distribution center for the entire world market could provide a one-day lead time to replenish field inventory in all regions of the world. Therefore, while consolidating DCs would reduce inventory at the distribution-center level of the supply chain, it would also increase field inventory. While we have not done the analysis formally, the extra field inventory needed to compensate for the longer lead time almost surely would be greater than the inventory savings at the DCs. This idea is probably a "nonstarter."

We cannot finish our discussion on location pooling without mentioning electronic commerce. One of the well-known advantages to the e-commerce model, especially with respect to e-tailers, is the ability to operate with substantially lower inventory. As our analysis suggests, keeping inventory in fewer locations should allow an e-tailer to turn inventory much faster than a comparable brick-and-mortar retailer. However, there are extra costs to position inventory in a warehouse rather than in a neighborhood store: shipping individual items to consumers is far more expensive than shipping in bulk to retail stores, and while physical stores need not be constructed, an e-tailer needs to invest in the technology to create an electronic store (i.e., user interface).

We also saw that there are declining returns to location pooling. Not surprisingly, while many e-tailers, such as Amazon.com, started with a single distribution center, they now operate several distribution centers in the United States. This requires that some products are stored in multiple locations, but it also means that the average customer is located closer to a distribution center, which accelerates the average delivery time and reduces shipping costs.

The ability to offer customers a huge product selection is another claimed advantage of the e-commerce model. While we have focused on using location pooling to reduce inventory, location pooling also can enable a broad product assortment. Consider an item that sells but is a rather slow seller. Unfortunately for most businesses, the majority of products fall into that category. To include this item in the product assortment requires at least one unit. Placing one unit in thousands of locations may not be economical, but it may be economical to place a few units in a single location. This is related to our brief discussion on another use for location pooling: Instead of reducing inventory while maintaining the same service level, location pooling can be used to increase the service level while maintaining the same or lower inventory. An item's service level is 0 if it is not in the assortment, and if a slow-moving item is in the assortment at many locations, then its inventory level is quite high. Neither extreme is desirable. Location pooling allows a firm to achieve the intermediate situation with good service and a reasonable amount of inventory.

If a firm does not want to establish a central warehouse to use location pooling to broaden its product assortment, then it can hire another firm to do that job. That practice is called *drop shipping.* For example, Circuit City hired Alliance Entertainment to hold the inventory of the approximately 55,000 video and DVD titles Circuit City wanted to offer online (Sechler, 2002). Customers would browse and purchase items on Circuit City's Web site, but then the order would be transmitted to Alliance Entertainment to be shipped to the customer. Circuit City surely would not be able to provide economically that assortment at its physical stores, which currently carry 500 to 3,000 titles, and it may not have been economical to carry that many titles even if Circuit City operated a single warehouse. Alliance Entertainment makes it feasible by applying location pooling across many different retailers.

12.2   Product Pooling

The previous section considered serving demand with fewer inventory locations. A closely related idea is to serve demand with fewer products. To explain, consider O'Neill's Hammer 3/2 wetsuit discussed in Chapters 9 and 10. The Hammer 3/2 we studied is targeted to the market for surfers, but O'Neill sells another Hammer 3/2 that serves the market for recreational divers. The two wetsuits are identical with the exception that the surf Hammer has the "wave" logo (see Figure 9.1) silk screened on the chest, while the dive Hammer has O'Neill's dive logo, displayed in Figure 12.4. O'Neill's current product line has two products to serve demand for a Hammer 3/2 wetsuit, some of it from surfers, the other portion from divers. An alternative is to combine these products into a single product to serve all Hammer 3/2 wetsuit demand, that is, a *universal design.* The strategy of using a universal design is called *product pooling.* This section focuses on the merits of the product-pooling strategy with a universal design.

Recall that demand for the surf Hammer is normally distributed with mean 3,192 and standard deviation 1,181. For the sake of simplicity, let's assume demand for the dive Hammer is also normally distributed with the same mean and standard deviation. Both wetsuits sell for $180, are purchased from O'Neill's supplier for $110, and are liquidated at the end of the season for $90.

We have already evaluated the optimal order quantity and expected profit for the surf Hammer: ordering 4,101 units earns an expected profit of $191,760 (see Table 10.1). Because the dive Hammer is identical to the surf Hammer, it has the same optimal order quantity and expected profit. Therefore, the total profit from both Hammer wetsuits is $383,520 (2 × $191,760).

Now let's consider what O'Neill should do if it sold a single Hammer wetsuit, which we call the universal Hammer. We need a distribution to represent demand for the universal

Hammer and then we need an order quantity. Expected demand for the universal Hammer is $3,192 \times 2 = 6,384$ units. If demand in the dive market is independent of demand in the surf market, then the standard deviation for the universal Hammer is $1,181 \times \sqrt{2} = 1,670$ (see Exhibit 11.1). The underage cost for the universal Hammer is still $C_u = 180 - 110 = 70$ and the overage cost is still $C_o = 110 - 90 = 20$. Hence, the critical ratio has not changed:

$$\frac{C_u}{C_o + C_u} = \frac{70}{20 + 70} = 0.7778$$

The corresponding z-statistic is still 0.77, and so the optimal order quantity is

$$Q = \mu + \sigma \times z = 6,384 + 1,670 \times 0.77 = 7,670$$

The expected profit with the universal Hammer is

$$\text{Expected profit} = (C_u \times \text{Expected sales}) - (C_o \times \text{Expected leftover inventory})$$

$$= (70 \times 6,172.4) - (20 \times 1,497.6)$$

$$= \$402,116$$

Therefore, pooling the surf and dive Hammers together can potentially increase profit by 4.85 percent $[(402,116 - 383,520)/383,520]$. This profit increase is 1.45 percent of the expected revenue when O'Neill sells two wetsuits. Given that net profit in this industry ranges from 2 to 5 percent of revenue, this potential improvement is not trivial.

As with the location pooling examples at Medtronic, the potential benefit O'Neill receives from product pooling occurs because of a reduction in the variability of demand. With two Hammer wetsuits, O'Neill faces a coefficient of variation of about 0.37 with each suit. With a universal Hammer, the coefficient of variation is about $1,670/6,384 = 0.26$. Recall from Chapter 10 that the mismatch cost in the newsvendor model is directly proportional to the coefficient of variation, hence the connection between a lower coefficient of variation and higher expected profit.

Given this link between the coefficient of variation and the benefit of product pooling, it is important for us to understand how product pooling influences the coefficient of variation. In this example, as well as the Medtronic examples in the previous two sections, we make a key assumption that the demands we are combining are independent. Recall that independence means that the outcome of one demand provides no information about the outcome of the other demand. There are many settings in which demands are indeed independent. But there are also situations in which demands are not independent.

The link between two random events can be measured by their correlation, which ranges from -1 to 1. Independent random events have zero correlation. Positive correlation means two random events tend to move in lock step; that is, when one is high, the other tends to be high as well, and when one is low, the other tends to be low as well. In contrast, negative correlation means two random events tend to move in opposite directions; that is, when one is high, the other tends to be low, and when one is low, the other tends to be high.

We can illustrate the effect of correlation graphically with two products. Figure 12.5 displays the outcome of 100 random demand realizations for two products in three scenarios. (For example, if the random demands of the two products are five and seven respectively, then a point is plotted at {5,7}.) In the first scenario, the product's demands are negatively correlated, in the second they are independent, and in the third they are positively correlated. In the independent scenario (scenario two), we see that the outcomes form a "cloud" that roughly fits into a circle; that is, the outcome of one demand says nothing about the outcome of the other demand. In the negative correlation scenario (scenario one), the outcome cloud is a downward-sloping ellipse: high demand with one product suggests low demand with the other product. The positive correlation scenario (scenario three) also has an outcome cloud shaped like an ellipse, but now it is upward sloping: high demand with one product suggests high demand with the other product.

Many different demand outcomes lead to the same total demand. For example, in the graphs in Figure 12.5, the total demand is 20 units if the products' demands are {0,20},

FIGURE 12.5
Random Demand for Two Products
In the graphs, x-axis is product 1 and y-axis is product 2. In scenario 1 (upper-left graph), the correlation is −0.90; in scenario 2 (upper-right graph), the correlation is 0; and in scenario 3 (the lower graph), the correlation is 0.90. In all scenarios, demand is normally distributed for each product with mean 10 and standard deviation 3.

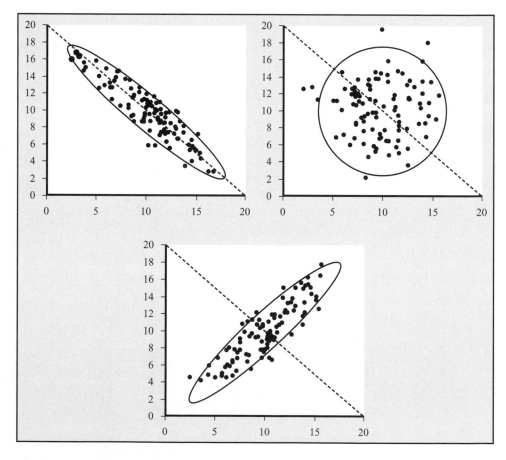

{1,19}, . . ., {19,1}, {20,0}. In other words, all of the points along the dashed line in each graph have total demand of 20 units. In general, all points along the same downward-sloping 45° line have the same total demand. Because the outcome ellipse in the negative correlation scenario is downward sloping along a 45° line, the total demands of those outcomes are nearly the same. In contrast, because the outcome ellipse in the positive correlation scenario is *upward* sloping, those outcomes generally sum to different total demands. In other words, we expect to see more variability in the total demand with positive correlation than with negative correlation.

We can now be more precise about the impact of correlation. If we combine two demands with the same mean μ and standard deviation σ, then the pooled demand has the following parameters:

$$\text{Expected pooled demand} = 2 \times \mu$$

$$\text{Standard deviation of pooled demand} = \sqrt{2 \times (1 + \text{Correlation})} \times \sigma$$

Notice that the correlation has no impact on the expected demand, but it does influence the standard deviation. Furthermore, the above equations are equivalent to the ones we have been using (e.g., Exhibit 11.1) when the correlation is zero, that is, when the two demands are independent.

The coefficient of variation for the pooled demand is then

$$\text{Coefficient of variation of pooled demand} = \sqrt{\frac{1}{2}(1 + \text{Correlation})} \times \left(\frac{\sigma}{\mu}\right)$$

As the correlation increases, the coefficient of variation of pooled demand increases as well, just as the graphs in Figure 12.5 suggest.

Now let's visualize what happens when we choose quantities for both the dive and the surf suits. Figure 12.6 displays the result of our quantity choices for different demand outcomes. For example, if the demand outcome is in the lower-left-hand "square" of the graph, then we have leftover surf and dive suits. The ideal outcome is if demand for each

FIGURE 12.6
The Inventory/ Stockout Outcome Given the Order Quantities for Surf and Dive Suits, Q_{surf} **and** Q_{dive}

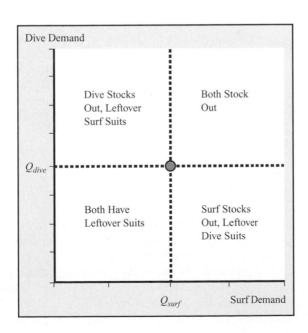

FIGURE 12.7
Outcomes for the Universal Hammer Given *Q* Units Purchased
Outcomes on the diagonal line with circles are ideal; there is no leftover inventory and no stockouts. Outcomes below and to the left of that line have leftover suits; outcomes to the right and above that line result in stockouts. Ellipses identify likely outcomes under different correlations.

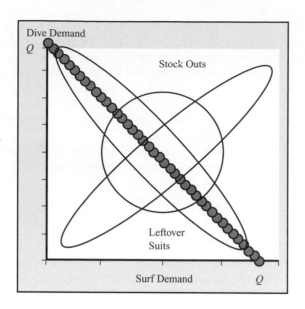

suit happens to equal its order quantity, an outcome labeled with a circle in the graph. The demand–supply mismatch penalty increases as the demand outcome moves further away from that ideal point in any direction.

The comparable graph for the universal Hammer is different, as is shown in Figure 12.7. Now any demand outcome along the downward-sloping 45° line (circles) is an ideal outcome because total demand equals the quantity of universal suits. In other words, the number of ideal demand outcomes with the universal suit has expanded considerably relative to the single ideal demand outcome with two suits. How likely are we to be close to one of those ideal points? Figure 12.7 also superimposes the three "outcome clouds" from Figure 12.5. Clearly, with negative correlation we are more likely to be close to an ideal point (the downward-sloping ellipse), and with positive correlation we are least likely to be near an ideal point.

We can confirm the intuition developed with the graph in Figure 12.7 by actually evaluating O'Neill's optimal order quantity for the universal Hammer 3/2 and its expected profit for the entire range of correlations. We first notice that the optimal order quantity for the Hammer 3/2 is generally *not* the sum of the optimal order quantities of the two suits. For example, O'Neill's total order with two wetsuits is $4,101 \times 2 = 8,202$ units, but with correlation 0.2 the optimal order for the universal Hammer is 7,793 units, and with correlation -0.7 the optimal order is 7,088.

The results with respect to expected profit are displayed in Figure 12.8: We indeed see that the expected profit of the universal Hammer declines as surf and dive demand become more positively correlated.

The extreme ends in Figure 12.8 are interesting. With perfectly positive correlation (i.e., correlation = 1), there is absolutely no benefit from inventory pooling: The expected profit with the universal Hammer is $383,520, and that is also the profit with two Hammer wetsuits! At the other end of the spectrum, correlation = -1, the coefficient of variation of total Hammer demand is 0, and so the maximum profit is achieved, $446,880! In fact, in that situation, the optimal order quantity for universal suits is just 6,384 units, which also happens to be the expected demand for universal suits. (This makes sense; we only earn the maximum profit if we sell on average the expected demand and we never have leftover inventory.)

FIGURE 12.8
The Correlation between Surf and Dive Demand for the Hammer 3/2 and the Expected Profit of the Universal Hammer Wetsuit (decreasing curve) and the Coefficient of Variation of Total Demand (increasing curve)

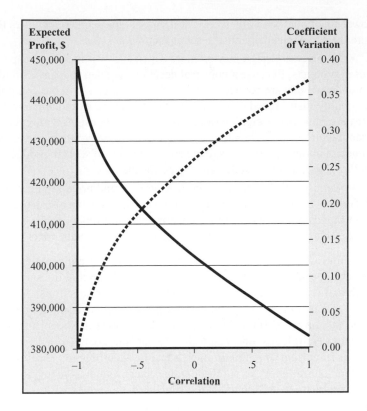

While we have been discussing the impact of demand correlation on the efficacy of product pooling, this issue applies even with location pooling. If the demands at two locations are negatively correlated, then location pooling is even more effective than if the demands were merely independent. And if demands are positively correlated across locations, then location pooling is less effective than we evaluated, given our assumption of independence.

We also should discuss the conditions that we can expect when demand has a particular type of correlation. Positive correlation can occur if the products are linked to some common source of uncertainty, for example, general economic conditions. For example, positive correlation is likely to be present if all of a firm's products tend to perform poorly in a depressed economy and perform well in a robust economy. Negative correlation is present when there is relatively little uncertainty with respect to total category sales but substantial uncertainty with respect to the allocation of those sales across the product line. For example, a firm selling fashionable jackets may know pretty well how many jackets will sell in total but have considerable uncertainty over which colors will be hot this season.

To summarize, a key benefit of a universal design is the reduction in demand variability, which leads to better performance in terms of matching supply and demand (e.g., higher profit or lower inventory for a targeted service level). But there are drawbacks to a universal design strategy as well:

• A universal design may not provide the needed functionality to consumers with special needs. For example, most bicycle manufacturers produce road bikes designed for fast touring on well-paved roads and mountain bikes for tearing through rugged trails. They even sell hybrid bikes that have some of the features of a road bike as well as some of the features of a mountain bike. But it is not sufficient to just sell a hybrid bike because it would not satisfy the high-performance portions of the road and mountain bike segments. The lower functionality of a universal design for some segments implies that it might not capture the same total demand as a set of focused designs.

• A universal design may be more expensive or it may be cheaper to produce than focused products. Because a universal design is targeted to many different uses, it either has components that are not necessary to some consumers or it has components that are of better quality than needed by certain consumers. These extra components or extra quality increase a universal design's cost relative to focused designs. However, it is often cheaper to manufacture or procure a large quantity of a single component than small quantities of a bunch of components; that is, there are economies of scale in production and procurement. In that sense, a universal design may be cheaper.

• A universal design may eliminate some brand/price segmentation opportunities. By definition, a universal design has a single brand/price, but a firm may wish to maintain distinct brands/prices. As with the concern regarding functionality, a single brand/price may not be able to capture the same demand as multiple brands/prices.

With respect to O'Neill's Hammer 3/2 wetsuit, it appears that the first two concerns regarding a universal design are not relevant: Given that the surf and dive Hammers are identical with the exception of the logo, their functionality should be identical as well, and there is no reason to believe their production costs should be much different. However, the universal Hammer wetsuit does eliminate the opportunity to maintain two different O'Neill logos, one geared for the surf market and one geared for the dive market. If it is important to maintain these separate identities (e.g., you might not want serious surfers to think they are purchasing the same product as recreational divers), then maybe two suits are needed. On the other hand, if you wish to portray a single image for O'Neill, then maybe it is even better to have a single logo, in which case two different wetsuits make absolutely no sense.

While we have concentrated on the benefits of serving demand with a universal design, this discussion provides a warning for firms that may be engaging in excessive product proliferation. Every firm wishes to be "customer focused" or "customer oriented," which suggests that a firm should develop products to meet all of the needs of its potential customers. Truly innovative new products that add to a firm's customer base should be incorporated into a firm's product assortment. But if extra product variety merely divides a fixed customer base into smaller pieces, then the demand–supply mismatch cost for each product will increase. Given that some of the demand–supply mismatch costs are indirect (e.g., loss of goodwill due to poor service), a firm might not even realize the additional costs it bears due to product proliferation. Every once in a while a firm realizes that its product assortment has gone amok and *product line rationalization* is sorely needed. The trick to assortment reductions is to "cut the fat, but leave the meat (and surely the bones)"; that is, products should only be dropped if they merely cannibalize demand from other products.

12.3   Lead Time Pooling: Consolidated Distribution and Delayed Differentiation

Location and product pooling, discussed in the previous two sections, have limitations: location pooling creates distance between inventory and customers and product pooling potentially degrades product functionality. This section studies two strategies that address those limitations: consolidated distribution and delayed differentiation. Both of those strategies use a form of risk pooling that we call lead time pooling.

Consolidated Distribution

The key weakness of location pooling is that inventory is moved away from customers, thereby preventing customers from physically seeing a product before purchase, thus increasing the time a customer must wait to receive a product and generally increasing the delivery cost. However, as we have learned, it also can be costly to position inventory near every customer. A major reason for this cost is the problem of having product in the wrong place. For example, with Medtronic's approximately 500 sales territories, it is highly unlikely that all 500 territories will stock out at the same time. If a stockout occurs in one territory, it is quite likely that there is some other territory that has inventory to spare, even maybe a nearby territory. This imbalance of inventory occurs because a firm faces two different kinds of uncertainty, even with a single product: uncertainty with respect to total demand (e.g., how many InSync pacemakers are demanded in the United States on a particular day) and uncertainty with respect to the allocation of that demand (e.g., how many InSync pacemakers are demanded in each territory in the United States on a particular day). The consolidated-distribution strategy attempts to keep inventory close to customers while hedging against the second form of uncertainty.

We'll demonstrate the consolidated-distribution strategy via a retail example. Imagine demand for a single product occurs in 100 stores and average weekly demand per store follows a Poisson distribution with a mean of 0.5 units per week. Each store is replenished directly from a supplier with an eight-week lead time. To provide good customer service, the retailer uses the order-up-to model and targets a 99.5 percent in-stock probability. The top panel of Figure 12.9 displays a schematic of this supply chain. Let's evaluate the amount of inventory the retailer needs.

With an eight-week lead time and a mean demand of 0.5 units per week, the expected demand over $l + 1$ periods is $(8 + 1) \times 0.5 = 4.5$. From the Poisson Distribution Function Table in Appendix B we see that with a mean of 4.5, the order-up-to level $S = 10$ yields an in-stock probability of 99.33 percent and $S = 11$ yields an in-stock probability of 99.76 percent, so we need to choose $S = 11$ for each store. According to the Poisson Loss Function Table in Appendix B, with mean demand of 4.5 units over $l + 1$ periods and an order-up-to

FIGURE 12.9
Two Retail Supply Chains, One with Direct Shipments from the Supplier, the Other with Consolidated Distribution in a Distribution Center
Expected weekly demand at each store is 0.5 units and the target in-stock probability is 99.5 percent.

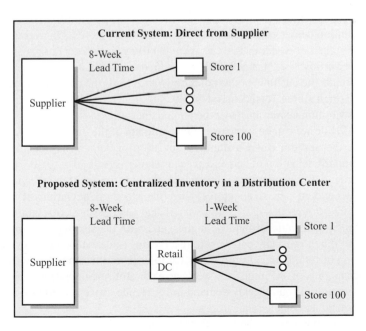

level $S = 11$, the expected back order is 0.00356 units per week. Hence, each of the 100 stores will have the following expected inventory:

$$\text{Expected inventory} = S - \text{Expected demand over } l + 1 \text{ periods}$$

$$+ \text{ Expected back order}$$

$$= 11 - 4.5 + 0.00356$$

$$= 6.50356$$

The total inventory among the 100 stores is then $6.504 \times 100 = 650.4$ units.

Now suppose the retailer builds a distribution center to provide consolidated distribution. The distribution center receives all shipments from the supplier and then replenishes each of the retail stores; it allows for consolidated distribution. The lead time for the distribution center remains eight weeks from the supplier. The lead time to replenish each of the retail stores is one week. To ensure a reliable delivery to the retail stores, the distribution center operates with a high in-stock probability, 99.5 percent. The bottom panel in Figure 12.9 displays the proposed supply chain with a distribution center.

The distribution center provides the retailer with a centralized location for inventory while still allowing the retailer to position inventory close to the customer. In contrast, the location pooling strategy would just create the centralized inventory location, eliminating the 100 stores close to customers. Therefore, this centralized-inventory strategy resembles location pooling without the major drawback of location pooling. But what does it do for the total inventory investment?

We can repeat the evaluation of the inventory investment for each store, assuming a 99.95 percent in-stock probability target and now a one-week lead time. From the Poisson Distribution Function Table, given expected demand over $l + 1$ periods is 1.0 unit, the order-up-to level $S = 4$ generates an in-stock probability of 99.63 percent. The resulting expected inventory per store is 3.00 units, nearly a 54 percent reduction in inventory from the direct-supply model (3.00 versus 6.5 units)! Because each store now receives a one-week lead time instead of an eight-week lead time, the inventory at the retail stores is dramatically reduced.

Now we need to evaluate the inventory at the distribution center. The demand at the distribution center equals the orders from the retail stores. On average, the retail stores order 0.5 units per week; that is, the average inflow (i.e., order) into a store must equal the average outflow (i.e., demand), otherwise inventory either builds up continuously (if the inflow exceeds the outflow) or dwindles down to zero (if the outflow exceeds the inflow). Because the retail stores' total demand is $100 \times 0.5 = 50$ units per week, the average demand at the distribution center must also be 50 units per week.

While we can be very sure of our estimate of the distribution center's expected demand, the distribution center's standard deviation of demand is not immediately apparent. The standard deviation of demand at each retailer is $\sqrt{0.50} = 0.707$. (Recall that with Poisson demand, the standard deviation equals the square root of the mean.) Hence, if demand were independent across all stores, then the standard deviation of total demand would be $0.707 \times \sqrt{100} = 7.07$. However, if there is positive correlation across stores, then the standard deviation would be higher, and with negative correlation the standard deviation would be lower. The only way to resolve this issue is to actually evaluate the standard deviation of total demand from historical sales data (the same data we used to estimate the demand rate of 0.5 units per week at each store). Suppose we observe that the standard deviation of total weekly demand is 15. Hence, there is evidence of positive correlation in demand across the retail stores.

We now need to choose a distribution to represent demand at the distribution center. In this case the Poisson is not the best choice. The standard deviation of a Poisson distribution is the square root of its mean, which in this case would be $\sqrt{50} = 7.07$. Because we have observed the standard deviation to be significantly higher, the Poisson distribution would not provide a good fit with the data. Our alternative, and a reasonable choice, is the normal distribution with mean 50 and standard deviation 15. Using the techniques from Chapter 11, we can determine that the distribution center's expected inventory is about 116 units if its target in-stock is 99.5 percent, the lead time is eight weeks, and weekly demand is normally distributed with mean 50 and standard deviation 15.

The only inventory that we have not counted so far is the pipeline inventory. In the direct-delivery model, there is pipeline inventory between the supplier and the retail stores. Using Little's Law, that pipeline inventory equals $0.5 \times 100 \times 8 = 400$ units. The consolidated-distribution model has the same amount of inventory between the supplier and the distribution center. However, with both models let's assume that pipeline inventory is actually owned by the supplier (e.g., the retailer does not start to pay for inventory until it is received). Hence, from the retailer's perspective, that inventory is not a concern. On the other hand, the retailer does own the inventory between the distribution center and the retail stores in the consolidated-distribution model. Again using Little's Law, there are $0.5 \times 100 \times 1 = 50$ units in that pipeline.

Table 12.4 summarizes the retailer's inventory in both supply chain structures. For comparison, the location pooling strategy is also included. With location pooling, all of the stores are eliminated and the retailer ships to customers from a central distribution center. Because that distribution center has an eight-week lead time and faces the same demand distribution as the DC in the consolidated-distribution strategy, its expected inventory is also 116 units.

We see from Table 12.4 that the consolidated-distribution strategy is able to reduce the expected inventory investment 28 percent $[(650 - 466)/650]$ relative to the original direct-delivery structure. In fact, the advantage of the consolidated-distribution strategy is even better than this analysis suggests. The cost of holding one unit of inventory at a retail store is surely substantially higher than the cost of holding one unit in a distribution center: retail shelf space is more expensive than DC space, shrinkage is a greater concern, and so forth. Because the consolidated-distribution model reduces retail inventory by more than 50 percent, merely adding up the total inventory in the system underestimates the value of the consolidated-distribution model.

Interestingly, the consolidated-distribution model outperforms direct delivery even though the total lead time from the supplier to the retail stores is increased by one week due to the routing of all inventory through the DC. Why is inventory reduced despite the longer total lead time? As mentioned earlier, in this system there are two types of uncertainty: uncertainty with total demand in a given week and uncertainty with the allocation of that demand over the retail stores. When inventory leaves the supplier, the retailer is essentially betting on how much inventory will be needed eight weeks later. However, in the direct-delivery model, the retailer also must predict *where* that inventory is needed; that is, the retailer must gamble on a total quantity and an allocation of that quantity across the retail

TABLE 12.4
Retail Inventory with Three Supply Chain Structures

	Direct Delivery Supply Chain	Consolidated-Distribution Supply Chain	Location Pooling
Expected total inventory at the stores	650	300	0
Expected inventory at the DC	0	116	116
Pipeline inventory between the DC and the stores	0	50	0
Total	650	466	116

stores. There is uncertainty with the total inventory needed, but even more uncertainty with where that inventory is needed. The consolidated-distribution model allows the retailer to avoid that second gamble: The retailer only needs to bet on the amount of inventory needed for the central distribution center. In other words, while the retailer must commit to a unit's final destination in the direct-delivery model, in the consolidated-distribution model the retailer delays that commitment until the unit arrives at the distribution center. It is precisely because the DC allows the retailer to avoid that second source of uncertainty that the consolidated-distribution model can outperform the direct-delivery model.

The consolidated-distribution model exploits what is often called *lead time pooling*. Lead time pooling can be thought of as combining the lead times for multiple inventory locations. Actually, it is easier to explain graphically: in Figure 12.9 we see that the 100 connections between the supplier and the retail stores in the direct-delivery model (four of which are actually drawn) are pooled into a single connection between the supplier and the DC in the consolidated-distribution model.

We saw that demand correlation influenced the effectiveness of product pooling and location pooling. Not surprisingly, demand correlation has the same effect here. The greater the correlation, the higher the standard deviation of demand at the distribution center. Figure 12.10 displays supply chain inventory with the consolidated-distribution model over a range of demand variability for the distribution center. As retail demand becomes more negatively correlated, the inventory in the consolidated-distribution model declines. However, we have seen that inventory can be reduced even with some positive correlation: The consolidated-distribution model outperforms direct delivery if the DC's standard deviation is about 40 or lower.

Another factor that determines the attractiveness of the consolidated-distribution model relative to the direct-delivery model is the lead time from the supplier. Figure 12.11 displays total supply chain inventory with both models for various supplier lead times. The direct-delivery model performs better than the consolidated-distribution model if the supplier's lead time is three weeks or fewer, otherwise the consolidated-distribution model does better. This occurs because lead time pooling is most effective as the lead time in-

FIGURE 12.10
Inventory with the Consolidated-Distribution Supply Chain
Diamonds = total retail store inventory, squares = retail + pipeline inventory, circles = retail + pipeline + DC inventory.

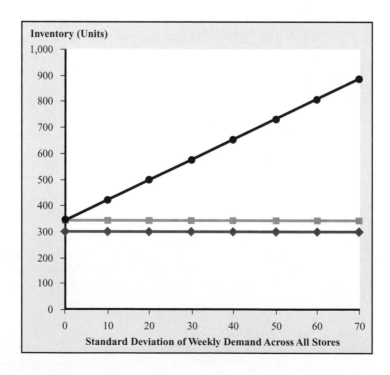

creases. In particular, the lead time before the distribution center (i.e., from the supplier) should be longer than the lead time after the distribution center (i.e., to the stores).

To summarize, a central inventory location (i.e., a distribution center) within a supply chain can exploit lead time pooling to reduce the supply chain's inventory investment while still keeping inventory close to customers. This strategy is most effective if total demand is less variable than demand at the individual stores and if the lead time before the distribution center is much longer than the lead time after the distribution center.

While we have concentrated on the inventory impact of the consolidated distribution strategy, that strategy has other effects on the supply chain. We have not included the extra cost of operating the distribution center, even though we did mention that the holding cost for each unit of inventory at the distribution center is likely to be lower than at the retail stores. Furthermore, we have not included the extra transportation cost from the DC to the retailer. A common critique of this kind of supply chain is that it clearly increases the distance a unit must travel from the supplier to the retailer. However, there are some additional benefits of a distribution center that we also have not included.

A DC enables a retailer to take better advantage of temporary price discounts from the supplier; that is, it is easier to store a large buy at the DC than at the retail stores. (See the Trade Promotions and Forward Buying Part of Section 14.1 for an analytical model of this issue.) The DC also will facilitate more frequent deliveries to the retail stores. With the direct-delivery model, each store receives a shipment from each supplier. It is generally not economical to make partial truckload shipments, what is referred to as a "less-than-load" or LTL shipment. Therefore, in our example, the retailer receives weekly shipments from the supplier because the retailer would not be able to order a full truckload for each store on a more frequent basis.

But with a DC, more frequent shipments are economical. The DC allows the retailer to put products from multiple suppliers into a truck bound for a store. Because now a truck is filled with products from multiple suppliers, it can be filled more frequently. As a result, with the DC in the supply chain, each store might be able to receive a full truckload per day, whereas without the DC each store can only receive a shipment every week. (This argument

FIGURE 12.11
Inventory with the Consolidated-Distribution Supply Chain (squares) and the Direct-Delivery Supply Chain (circles) with Different Supplier Lead Times

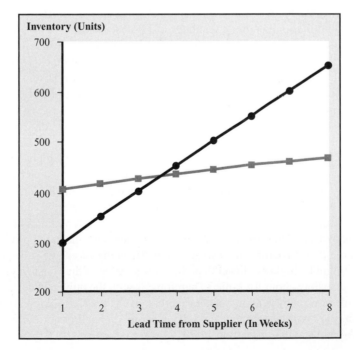

also is used to justify the airlines' "hub-and-spoke" systems: It may be difficult to consistently fill a plane from Gainesville to Los Angeles on a daily basis, but Delta Airlines offers service between those two cities via its Atlanta hub because the Atlanta–Los Angeles leg can be filled with passengers flying from other southeast cities.) More frequent deliveries reduce inventory even further than our analysis suggests. (See Section 11.8 for more discussion.) Even the DC may be able to order more frequently from the supplier than weekly because the DC consolidates the orders from all of the retailers. In fact, while the lead time pooling benefit of a DC in this example is significant, it is quite possible that some of these other reasons for operating a DC are even more important.

Delayed Differentiation

Consolidated distribution is a strategy that uses lead time pooling to provide some of the benefits of location pooling without moving inventory far away from customers. Delayed differentiation is the analogous strategy with respect to product pooling; that is, delayed differentiation hedges the uncertainty associated with product variety without taking the variety away from customers. We'll illustrate delayed differentiation with our Hammer 3/2 example from O'Neill.

Recall that the Hammer 3/2 is sold by O'Neill in two versions: a surf wetsuit with the traditional wave logo silk-screened on the chest and a dive wetsuit with O'Neill's dive logo put in the same place. The product-pooling approach to this variety is to eliminate it: sell only one Hammer 3/2 suit with a single logo. However, that is an extreme solution and there may be reasons to maintain two different products.

The problem with two different products is that we might run out of surf Hammers while we have extra dive Hammers. In that situation, it would be great if we could just erase the dive logo and put on the surf logo, since the rest of the wetsuit is identical. Better yet, if we just stocked "logo-less" or generic wetsuits, then we could add the appropriate logo as demand arrives. That strategy is called *delayed differentiation* because we are delaying the differentiation of the wetsuit into its final form until after we observe demand.

Several things are necessary to make this delayed-differentiation strategy work. First, we need to be able to silk-screen the logo onto the generic wetsuit. This is a nontrivial issue. Currently the logo is silk-screened onto the chest piece before it is sewn into the suit. Silk-screening the logo onto a complete suit is substantially harder and may require some re-designing of the silk-screening process. Assuming we can overcome that technical difficulty, we still need to be able to add the silk screen quickly so that there is not much delay between the time a wetsuit is requested and when it is shipped. Hence, we'll need a sufficient amount of idle capacity in that process to ensure fast delivery even though demand may fluctuate throughout the season.

If these challenges are resolved, then we are left with deciding how many of the generic wetsuits to order and evaluating the resulting profit savings. In fact, we have already completed those steps. If we assume that we only silk-screen the logo onto wetsuits when we receive a firm demand for a surf or dive wetsuit, then we never keep finished goods inventory; that is, we only have to worry about our generic wetsuit inventory. The demand for the generic wetsuit is identical to the demand for the universal wetsuit; that is, it is the sum of surf Hammer demand and dive Hammer demand. The economics of the generic suit are the same as well: They sell for the same price, they have the same production cost, and we'll assume they have the same salvage value. (In some cases, the salvage value of the generic suit might be higher or lower than the salvage value of the finished product, but in this case it is plausibly about the same.) Therefore, as with the universal design analysis, we need to decide how many generic wetsuits to order given they are sold for $180 each, they cost $110 each, they will be salvaged for $90 each, and demand is normally distributed with mean 6,384 and standard deviation 1,670.

Using our analysis from the section on product pooling, the optimal order quantity is 7,670 units with the delayed differentiation strategy and expected profit increases to $402,116. Although product pooling and delayed differentiation result in the same numerical analysis, the two strategies are different. Delayed differentiation still offers multiple wetsuits to consumers, so their demands are not pooled together as with a universal design. Instead, delayed differentiation works like lead time pooling with consolidated distribution: a key differentiating feature of the product is delayed until after better demand information is observed; with location pooling that feature is the product's final destination (i.e., store) and with delayed differentiation that feature is the product's logo. Furthermore, product pooling does not require a significant modification to the production process, whereas delayed differentiation does require a change to the silk-screening process. In other applications, delayed differentiation may require a more dramatic change to the process and/or the product design.

In general, delayed differentiation is an ideal strategy when

1. Customers demand many versions, that is, variety is important.
2. There is less uncertainty with respect to total demand than there is for individual versions.
3. Variety is created late in the production process.
4. Variety can be added quickly and cheaply.
5. The components needed to create variety are inexpensive relative to the generic component (i.e., the main body of the product).

Let's explain further each of the five points just mentioned. (1) If variety isn't important, then the firm should offer fewer variants or just a universal design. (2) There should be less uncertainty with total demand so there will be few demand–supply mismatches with the generic component. In general, the more negative correlation across product variants the better, since negative correlation reduces uncertainty in the total demand. (3) Just as we saw that consolidated distribution works best if the supplier lead time to the distribution center is long relative to the lead time from the distribution center to the retail stores, delayed differentiation is most valuable if there is a long lead time to produce the generic component and a short lead time to convert the generic component into a finished product. (4) If adding variety to the generic component is too slow, then the waiting time for customers may be unacceptable, thereby rendering delayed differentiation unacceptable. In addition, if adding variety at the end of the process is costly, then the inventory savings from delayed differentiation may not be worth the extra production cost. (5) Finally, delayed differentiation saves inventory of the generic component (e.g., the generic wetsuit) but does not save inventory of the differentiating components. Hence, delayed differentiation is most useful if the majority of the product's value is in the generic component.

Delayed differentiation is particularly appropriate when variety is associated with the cosmetic features of a product, for example, color, labels, and packaging. For example, suppose a company such as Black and Decker sells power drills to both Home Depot and Wal-Mart. Those are two influential retailers; as a result, they may wish to have slightly different packaging, and, in particular, they might wish to have different product codes on their packages so that consumers cannot make direct price comparisons. The power drill company could store drills in the two different packages, but that creates the possibility of having Home Depot drills available while Wal-Mart drills are stocked out. Because it is relatively easy to complete the final packaging, the delayed-differentiation strategy only completes the packaging of drills after it receives firm orders from the retailers. Furthermore, packaging material is cheap compared to the drill, so while the firm doesn't want to have excessive inventory of drills, it isn't too costly to have plenty of packages available.

Retail paints provide another good example for the application of delayed differentiation. Consumers surely do not want a universal design when it comes to paint color, despite Henry Ford's famous theory of product assortment.[2] But at the same time, a store cannot afford to keep paint available in every possible shade, hue, tone, sheen, and color. One alternative is for paint to be held in a central warehouse and then shipped to customers as needed, that is, a location pooling strategy. Given the vast variety of colors, it is not clear that even a location pooling strategy can be economical. Furthermore, paint is very costly to ship directly to consumers, so that pretty much kills that idea. Instead, the paint industry has developed equipment so that a retailer can use generic materials to mix any color in their vast catalog. The final production process takes some time, but an acceptable amount of time for consumers (5 to 15 minutes). The in-store production equipment is probably more expensive than mixing paints at a factory, but again, the extra cost here is worth it. Hence, by redesigning the product to add variety at the very end of the production process (i.e., even after delivery to the retail store), paint companies are able to economically provide consumers with extensive variety.

Delayed differentiation can even be used if the "generic component" can be sold to some customers without additional processing. To explain, suppose a company sells two different quality levels of a product, for example, a fast and a slow printer or a fast and a slow microprocessor. These quality differences might allow a firm to price discriminate and thereby increase its overall margins. However, the quality difference might not imply radically different costs or designs. For example, it might by possible to design the fast and the slow printer such that a fast printer could be converted into a slow printer merely by adding a single chip or by flipping a single switch. Hence, the firm might hold only fast printers so they can serve demand for fast printers immediately. When demand for a slow printer occurs, then a fast printer is taken from inventory, the switch is flipped to make it a slow printer, and then it is shipped as a slow printer.

Delayed differentiation is indeed a powerful strategy. In fact, it bears a remarkable resemblance to another powerful strategy, make-to-order production (Chapter 10). With make-to-order production, a firm only begins making a product after it receives a firm order from a customer. Dell Inc. has used the make-to-order strategy with remarkable effectiveness in the personal computer industry. With delayed differentiation, a generic component is differentiated into a final product only after demand is received for that final product. So what is the difference between these two ideas? In fact, they are conceptually quite similar. Their difference is one of degree. Delayed differentiation is thought of as a strategy that stores nearly finished product and completes the remaining few production steps with essentially no delay. Make-to-order is generally thought to apply to a situation in which the remaining production steps from components to a finished unit are more substantial, therefore involving more than a trivial delay. Hence, delayed differentiation and make-to-order occupy two ends of the same spectrum with no clear boundary between them.

12.4   Capacity Pooling with Flexible Manufacturing[3]

Delayed differentiation takes advantage of completely flexible capacity at the end of the manufacturing process; that is, the final production step is capable of taking a generic component and converting it into any final product. Unfortunately, the luxury of complete flexibility is not always available or affordable to a firm, especially if one considers a larger

[2]Consumers can have any Model T they want, as long as it is black.
[3]This section is based on the research reported in Jordon and Graves (1995).

portion of the manufacturing process. This section studies how a firm can use risk pooling with flexible capacity, but not necessarily completely flexible capacity.

To provide a context, consider the manufacturing challenge of an auto manufacturer such as General Motors. GM operates many different assembly plants and produces many different vehicles. Assembly capacity is essentially fixed in this industry over a substantial time horizon due to rigid labor contracts and the extensive capital requirements of an assembly plant. However, demand for individual vehicles can be quite variable: some products are perennially short on capacity, while others seem to always have too much capacity. To alleviate the resulting demand–supply mismatches, auto manufacturers continually strive for more manufacturing flexibility, that is, the ability to produce more than one vehicle type with the same capacity. GM could use flexible manufacturing to move capacity from slow-selling products to fast-selling products, thereby achieving higher sales and higher capacity utilization. But flexibility is not free: Tooling and assembly equipment capable of making more than one vehicle is more expensive than dedicated equipment, and equipment capable of making any vehicle (complete flexibility) is extremely expensive. So how much flexibility does GM need and where should that flexibility be installed?

Let's define a specific problem that is representative of the challenge GM faces. There are 10 manufacturing plants and 10 vehicles (e.g., Chevy Malibu, GMC Yukon XL, etc.). For now each plant is assigned to produce just one vehicle, that is, there is no flexibility in the network. Capacity for each vehicle is installed before GM observes the vehicle's demand in the market. Demand is uncertain: a normal distribution represents each vehicle's demand with mean 100 and standard deviation 40. For a slight twist on the distribution, let's assume the minimum demand is 20 and the maximum demand is 180; that is, the normal distribution is truncated so that excessively extreme outcomes are not possible.[4] Even though we impose upper and lower bounds on demand, demand is still quite uncertain, a level of uncertainty that is typical in the auto industry. One last point with respect to demand: We assume the demands for each vehicle are independent; therefore, the correlation between the demands for any two vehicles is zero.

Each plant has a capacity to produce 100 units. If demand exceeds capacity for a vehicle, then the excess is lost. If demand is less than capacity, then demand is satisfied but capacity is idle. Figure 12.12 displays this situation graphically: The left-hand side of the figure represents the 10 production plants; the right-hand side represents the 10 vehicle types; and the lines are "links" that indicate which plant is capable of producing which vehicles. In the "no flexibility" situation, each plant is capable of producing only one vehicle, so there is a total of 10 links. The configuration with the smallest amount of flexibility has 11 links, an example of which is displayed on the right-hand side of Figure 12.12. With 11 links, one plant is capable of producing two different vehicles. As we add more links, we add more flexibility. Total flexibility is achieved when we have 100 links, that is, every plant is able to produce every product. Figure 12.13 displays the full flexibility configuration as well as one of the possible configurations with 20 links.

With each configuration we are interested in evaluating the expected unit sales and expected capacity utilization. Unfortunately, for most configurations, it is quite challenging to evaluate those performance measures analytically. However, we can obtain accurate estimates of those performance measures via simulation. Each iteration of the simulation draws random demand for each product and then allocates the capacity to maximize unit sales within the constraints of the feasible links. For example, in the configuration with 11

---

[4]In other words, any outcome of the normal distribution that is either lower than 20 or higher than 180 is ignored and additional random draws are made until an outcome is received between 20 and 180. There is only a 4.6 percent chance that an outcome of a normal distribution is greater than two standard deviations from the mean (as in this case).

FIGURE 12.12
Two Configurations, One with No Flexibility (10 links) and One with Limited Flexibility (11 links)

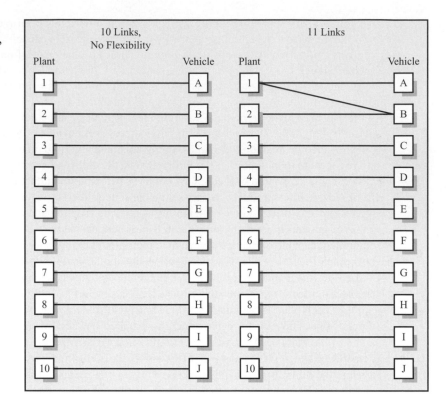

FIGURE 12.13
Flexibility Configurations with Approximately Equal Capability to Respond to Demand Uncertainty

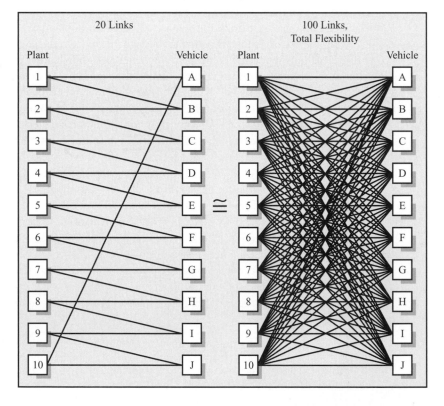

links displayed in Figure 12.12, suppose in one of the iterations that demand for vehicle A is 85 units and vehicle B is 125 units. In that case, plant 2 uses its entire 100 units of capacity to produce vehicle B and plant 1 uses its entire 100 units of capacity to produce 85 units of vehicle A and 15 units of vehicle B, thereby only losing 10 units of potential vehicle B sales. Our estimate of each performance measure is just its average across the iterations. After many iterations, our estimates will be quite accurate.

Via simulation we find that with no flexibility, expected unit sales are 853 units and expected capacity utilization is 85.3 percent. With 11 links, the expected unit sales increase to 858 units and capacity utilization increases to 85.8 percent. We do slightly better with this additional flexibility when demand for vehicle B exceeds plant 2's capacity and demand for vehicle A is below plant 1's capacity, because then plant 1 can use its capacity to produce both vehicles A and B (as in our previous example). Figure 12.14 provides data on the performance of configurations with 10 to 20 links and the full flexibility configuration.

Figure 12.14 reveals that total flexibility is able to increase our performance measures considerably: Capacity utilization jumps to 95.4 percent and expected sales increase to 954 units. But what is more remarkable is that adding only 10 additional links produces nearly the same outcome as full flexibility, which has an additional 90 links: capacity utilization is 94.9 percent with 20 links and expected sales are 949 units. Apparently, there is very little incremental value to the additional flexibility achieved by adding the 11th through the 90th additional links to the no-flexibility configuration. In other words, given that installing flexibility is costly, it is unlikely that total flexibility will be economically rational. This result has a similar feel to our finding that with location pooling, the majority of the benefit is captured by pooling only a few locations.

It may seem surprising that capacity pooling increases utilization, given that pooling server capacity in a queuing system has no impact on utilization, as discussed in Chapter 7. The key difference is that in a queuing system, demand is never lost; it just has to wait longer than it might want to be served. Hence, the amount of demand served is independent

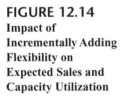

FIGURE 12.14
Impact of Incrementally Adding Flexibility on Expected Sales and Capacity Utilization

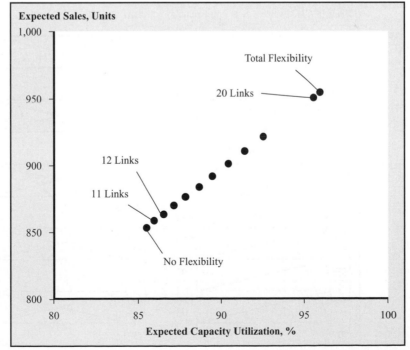

of how the capacity is structured. Here, demand is lost if there isn't a sufficient amount of capacity. Therefore, more flexibility increases the demand served, which increases the utilization of the capacity.

Although flexibility with 20 links can perform nearly as well as total flexibility with 100 links, not every configuration with 20 links performs that well. Figure 12.13 displays the particular 20-link configuration that nearly equals total flexibility. The effectiveness of that configuration can be explained by the concept of *chaining*. A chain is a group of plants and vehicles that are connected via links. For example, in the 11-link configuration displayed in Figure 12.12, the first two plants and vehicles form a single chain and the remaining plant–vehicle pairs form eight additional chains. With the 20-link configuration displayed in Figure 12.13, there is a single chain, as there is with the total flexibility configuration.

In general, flexibility configurations with the longest and fewest chains for a given number of links perform the best. Figure 12.15 displays two 20-link configurations, one with a single chain (the same one as displayed in Figure 12.13) and the other with five chains. We already know that the single chain configuration has expected sales of 949 units. Again via simulation, we discover that the 20-link configuration with five chains generates expected sales of only 896 units, which compares to the 853 expected unit sales with no-flexibility.

Long chains are beneficial because they facilitate the reallocation of capacity to respond to demand. For example, suppose demand for vehicle A is less than expected, but demand for vehicle G is very strong. If both vehicles are in the same chain, then plant 1's idle capacity can be shifted along the chain to help fill vehicle G's demand: plant 1 produces some vehicle B, plant 2 produces some of both vehicles B and C, and so forth so that both plants 6 and 7 can produce some vehicle G. If both of those vehicles are not part of the same chain (as in our five-chain configuration), then this swapping of capacity is not possible.

FIGURE 12.15
Flexibility Configurations with the Same Number of Links but Different Number of Chains

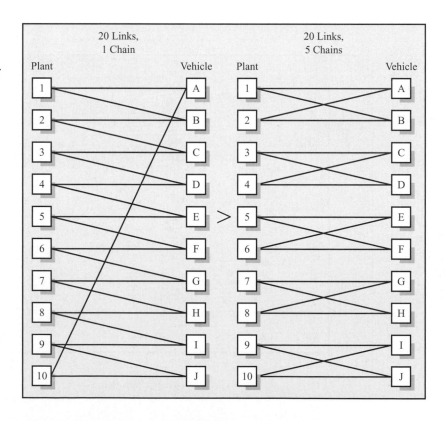

In addition to how flexibility is configured, there are two additional issues worth mentioning that influence the value of flexibility: correlation and total capacity. So far we have assumed that demands across vehicles are independent. We learned with the other risk-pooling strategies that risk pooling becomes more effective as demand becomes more negatively correlated. The same holds here: With pooled capacity, the uncertainty in total demand is more important than the uncertainty with individual products; hence, negative correlation is preferred. However, this does not mean that two negatively correlated products must be produced in the same plant. Instead, it is sufficient that two negatively correlated products are produced in the same chain. This is a valuable insight if the negatively correlated products are physically quite different (e.g., a full-size truck and a compact sedan) because producing them in the same chain might be far cheaper than producing them in the same plant.

The total available capacity also influences the effectiveness of flexibility. Suppose capacity for each plant were only 20 units. In that case, each plant would always operate at 100 percent utilization, so flexibility has no value. The end result is the same with the other extreme situation. If each plant could produce 180 units, then flexibility is again not needed because every plant is sure to have idle capacity. In other words, flexibility is more valuable when capacity and demand are approximately equal, as in our numerical examples.

Figure 12.16 further emphasizes that flexibility is most valuable with intermediate amounts of capacity: The biggest gap between the no-flexibility trade-off curve and the 20-link trade-off curve occurs when total capacity equals expected total demand, 1,000 units.

Figure 12.16 illustrates another observation: flexibility and capacity are substitutes. For example, to achieve expected sales of 950 units, GM can either install total capacity of 1,250

FIGURE 12.16
Expected Sales and Capacity Utilization
Shown are seven different capacities (*C*) and two configurations, one with no flexibility (10 links) and one with 20 links and one chain (displayed in Figure 12.15). In each case, the total capacity is equally divided among the 10 products and expected total demand is 1,000 units.

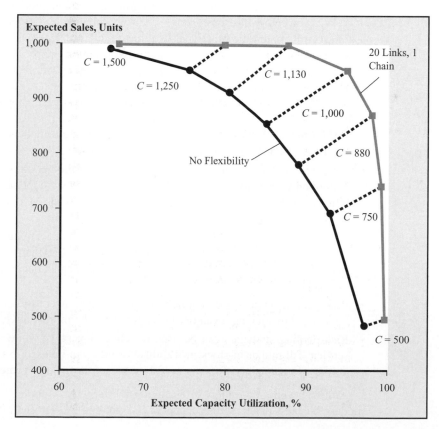

units with no flexibility or 1,000 units of capacity with 20-link flexibility. If capacity is cheap relative to flexibility, then the high-capacity–no-flexibility option may be preferable. But if capacity is expensive relative to flexibility (especially given that we only need 10 additional links of flexibility), then the low-capacity–some-flexibility option may be better.

To summarize, this section considers the pooling of capacity via manufacturing flexibility. The main insights are

- A limited amount of flexibility can accommodate demand uncertainty nearly as well as total flexibility as long as the flexibility is configured to generate long chains.
- Flexibility should be configured so that negatively correlated products are part of the same chain but need not be produced in the same plant.
- Flexibility is most valuable when total capacity roughly equals expected demand.

Therefore, it is generally neither necessary nor economically rational for a firm to sink the huge investment needed to achieve total flexibility. Flexibility is surely valuable, but it should not be installed haphazardly. Finally, while we have used the context of automobile manufacturing to illustrate these insights, they nevertheless apply to workers in service environments. For example, it is not necessary to cross-train workers so that they can handle every task (full flexibility). Instead, it is sufficient to train workers so that long chains of skills are present in the organization.

12.5 Summary

This chapter describes and explores several different strategies that exploit risk pooling to better match supply and demand. Each has its strengths and limitations. For example, location pooling is very effective at reducing inventory but moves inventory away from customers. Consolidated distribution is not as good as location pooling at reducing inventory, but it keeps inventory near customers. Product pooling with a universal design is also quite useful but might limit the functionality of the products offered. Delayed differentiation addresses that limitation but probably requires redesigning the product/process and may introduce a slight delay to fulfill demand. Capacity pooling can increase sales and capacity utilization but requires flexible capacity, which is probably not free and may be quite expensive. Hence, these are effective strategies as long as they are applied in the appropriate settings.

Even though we considered a variety of situations and models (e.g., order-up-to and newsvendor), we have developed some consistent observations:

- A little bit of risk pooling goes a long way. With location pooling it is usually necessary to pool only a few locations, not all of them. With capacity pooling, a little bit of flexibility, as long as it is properly designed (i.e., long chains), yields nearly the same outcome as full flexibility.
- Risk-pooling strategies are most effective when demands are negatively correlated because then the uncertainty with total demand is much less than the uncertainty with any individual item/location. It follows that theses strategies become less effective as demands become more positively correlated.
- Risk-pooling strategies do not help reduce pipeline inventory. That inventory can only be reduced by moving inventory through the system more quickly.
- Risk-pooling strategies can be used to reduce inventory while maintaining the same service (fill rate or in-stock probability) or they can be used to increase service while holding the same inventory, or a combination of those improvements.

Although you are unlikely to encounter the term "risk pooling" in any discussion of modern business practice, the concept of risk pooling is often central to many recent operational innovations and strategies. The remainder of this section illustrates this point with several examples.

In the auto industry, it is estimated that 20 to 30 percent of a vehicle's cost is incurred after a vehicle leaves the factory (Simison, 1998), an amount that is unacceptably high to most manufacturers. Ford attempted to improve the efficiency of distribution by consolidating dealerships in major markets. For example, Ford consolidated the eight competing dealerships in the Salt Lake City area into a single organization (Warner, 1998). In addition to eliminating redundant advertising and back-office administration, this move was meant to provide consumers with a broader assortment for two reasons: the total number of retail locations would be reduced and inventory would be better shared across locations. In other words, by aggregating demand in fewer locations, the Salt Lake City dealer would use location pooling to reduce demand variability, thereby allowing fewer vehicles for the same service level or a broader assortment with the same inventory investment. The same consolidation strategy is being used by independent firms that have been acquiring dealerships, such as Republic Industries Inc. (Simison, 1998). However, Ford's efforts were not too successful, not due to a flaw in the theory of risk pooling, but instead because the initiative ran afoul of state franchise laws.

Cadillac also attempted to carry less inventory yet provide customers with greater variety via their XPress Delivery initiative in Florida: Instead of just holding vehicles in dealer lots, popularly configured vehicles would be kept in a central location near Orlando (Popely, 1998). Any vehicle in the central depot could be delivered to any Florida dealer within one day, thereby effectively allowing each dealer to offer customers a greater inventory than what was held on the dealers' lots. However, like most examples of location pooling, there are limitations: it moves inventory away from customers.

Chrysler uses a virtual pooling to reduce the amount of spare parts inventory needed among dealerships: Instead of physically pooling inventory in fewer locations (location pooling), Chrysler developed a system to share spare parts inventory data among dealerships (Simison, 1998). In other words, through this system, a dealer can find and quickly obtain a needed spare part at another dealership, so each dealership can improve its reliability with the same inventory investment, or can maintain its reliability with lower inventory.

Several firms in the PC industry are using a form of delayed differentiation, called *channel assembly,* to try to compete against Dell (Hansell, 1998). With channel assembly a PC manufacturer such as IBM provides its distributor, such as Ingram Micron, with PC parts instead of assembled PCs. As demand occurs, the channel (Ingram), rather than the manufacturer (IBM), assembles the PCs from its parts. Relative to the traditional system in which PCs are assembled at the manufacturer and shipped to the distributor, channel assembly delays the assembly decision; hence it is a version of delayed differentiation.

In the cell phone industry, Nokia Corp. has been quite successful, and one reason for its success has been the use of *capacity pooling* (Pringle, 2003). Unlike most of its leading competitors, Nokia owns and operates its own manufacturing facilities, some in rather high-labor-cost locations such as Finland. But that has not resulted in a competitive disadvantage because Nokia designs its handsets for manufacturing flexibility: components are shared across different models and even different components have similar geometries so that different models can be produced on the same production line without wasting setup times to switch among different models. In other words, the flexibility to switch production quickly and easily between different handsets effectively pools Nokia's capacity across the different models. This capability was particularly useful in the summer of 2002 when demand moved rapidly into color-screen models: Nokia took capacity that was planned for other models and reassigned it to produce the faster-selling color-screen models.

The concept of capacity pooling is a primary component of the contract manufacturing industry's value added. While certainly not household names (e.g., Solectron and

FIGURE 12.17
Total Revenue of Six Leading Contract Manufacturers by Fiscal Year: Solectron Corp., Flextronics International Ltd., Sanmina-SCI, Jabil Circuit Inc., Celestica Inc., and Plexus Corp.
Note: The fiscal years of these firms vary somewhat, so total revenue in a calendar year will be slightly different.

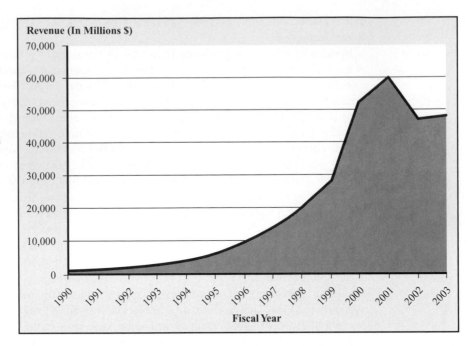

Flextronics), the global contract manufacturing market has grown from almost nothing 15 years ago to an over $90 billion global industry (Thurm, 1998). Figure 12.17 displays the revenue growth from six leading firms; the sharp dip in revenue for fiscal 2002 was due to the bursting of the "tech bubble," in particular in telecommunications, from which these firms have not yet fully recovered.

Contract manufacturers produce closely related products for multiple customers. For example, in the same facility Solectron could be assembling circuit boards for IBM, Hewlett-Packard, and Cisco Systems. The same equipment and often the same components are used by these multiple manufacturers, so, instead of each one investing in its own capacity and component inventory, Solectron pools their needs. In other words, while any of these companies could produce its own circuit boards, due to capacity pooling Solectron is able to produce them with higher utilization and therefore lower cost. This added efficiency allows Solectron to charge a margin, albeit a rather thin margin, as indicated in Table 12.5.

Table 12.6 provides a summary of the key notation and equations presented in this chapter.

TABLE 12.5
Fiscal Year 2003 Results for Several Contract Manufacturers

Firm	Revenue*	Cost of Goods*	Gross Margin
Flextronics	14,530	13,705	5.7%
Solectron	11,014	10,432	5.3%
Sanmina-SCI	10,361	9,899	4.5%
Celestica	6,735	6,474	3.9%
Jabil Circuit	4,729	4,294	9.2%
Plexus	807	755	6.4%

* In millions of dollars.

TABLE 12.6
Summary of Notation and Key Equations in Chapter 12

The combination of two demands with the same mean μ and standard deviation σ yields

$$\text{Expected pooled demand} = 2 \times \mu$$

$$\text{Standard deviation of pooled demand} = \sqrt{2 \times (1 + \text{Correlation})} \times \sigma$$

$$\text{Coefficient of variation of pooled demand} = \sqrt{\frac{1}{2}(1 + \text{Correlation})} \times \left(\frac{\sigma}{\mu}\right)$$

12.6 Further Reading

In recent years, risk-pooling strategies have received considerable attention in the academic community as well as in practice.

Lee (1996) provides a technical treatment of the delayed-differentiation strategy. A more managerial description of delay differentiation can be found in Feitzinger and Lee (1997). Brown, Lee, and Petrakian (2000) describe the application of delayed differentiation at a semiconductor firm. Simchi-Levi, Kaminsky, and Simchi-Levi (2003) and Chopra and Meindl (2004) cover risk-pooling strategies in the context of supply chain management.

Ulrich and Eppinger (2004) discuss the issues of delayed differentiation and product architecture from the perspective of a product development team.

Upton (1994, 1995) provides broad discussions on the issue of manufacturing flexibility.

12.7 Practice Problems

Q12.1*   **(Fancy Paints)** Fancy Paints is a small paint store. Fancy Paints stocks 200 different SKUs (stocking-keeping units) and places replenishment orders weekly. The order arrives one month (let's say four weeks) later. For the sake of simplicity, let's assume weekly demand for each SKU is Poisson distributed with mean 1.25. Fancy Paints maintains a 95 percent fill rate.

a. What is the average inventory at the store at the end of the week?

b. Now suppose Fancy Paints purchases a color-mixing machine. This machine is expensive, but instead of stocking 200 different SKU colors, it allows Fancy Paints to stock only five basic SKUs and to obtain all the other SKUs by mixing. Weekly demand for each SKU is normally distributed with mean 50 and standard deviation 8. Suppose Fancy Paints maintains a 95 percent fill rate for each of the five colors. How much inventory on average is at the store at the end of the week?

c. After testing the color-mixing machine for a while, the manager realizes that a 95 percent fill rate for each of the basic colors is not sufficient: Since mixing requires the presence of multiple mixing components, a higher fill rate for components is needed to maintain a 95 percent fill rate for the individual SKUs. The manager decides that a 98 percent fill rate for each of the five basic SKUs should be adequate. Suppose that each can costs $14 and 20 percent per year is charged for holding inventory (assume 50 weeks per year). What is the change in the store's holding cost relative to the original situation in which all paints are stocked individually?

Q12.2*   **(Burger King)** Consider the following excerpts from a *Wall Street Journal* article on Burger King (Beatty, 1996):

Burger King intends to bring smiles to the faces of millions of parents and children this holiday season with its "Toy Story" promotion. But it has some of them up in arms because local restaurants are running out of the popular toys . . . Every Kids Meal sold every day of the year comes with a giveaway, a program that has been in place for about six years and has helped Grand Metropolitan PLC's Burger King increase its market share. Nearly all of Burger King's 7,000 U.S. stores are participating in the "Toy Story" promotion . . . Nevertheless, meeting consumer demand still remains a conundrum for the

(* indicates that the solution is at the end of the book)

giants. That is partly because individual Burger King restaurant owners make their tricky forecasts six months before such promotions begin. "It's asking you to pull out a crystal ball and predict exactly what consumer demand is going to be," says Richard Taylor, Burger King's director of youth and family marketing. "This is simply a case of consumer demand outstripping supply." The long lead times are necessary because the toys are produced overseas to take advantage of lower costs . . . Burger King managers in Houston and Atlanta say the freebies are running out there, too, . . . But Burger King, which ordered nearly 50 million of the small plastic dolls, is "nowhere near running out of toys on a national level."

Let's consider a simplified analysis of Burger King's situation. Consider a region with 200 restaurants served by a single distribution center. At the time the order must be placed with the factories in Asia, demand (units of toys) for the promotion at each restaurant is fore-casted to be gamma distributed with mean 2,251 and standard deviation 1,600. A discrete version of that gamma distribution is provided in the following table, along with a graph of the density function:

Q	F(Q)	L(Q)		Q	F(Q)	L(Q)
0	0.0000	2,251.3		6,500	0.9807	31.4
500	0.1312	1,751.3		7,000	0.9865	21.7
1,000	0.3101	1,316.9		7,500	0.9906	15.0
1,500	0.4728	972.0		8,000	0.9934	10.2
2,000	0.6062	708.4		8,500	0.9954	6.9
2,500	0.7104	511.5		9,000	0.9968	4.6
3,000	0.7893	366.6		9,500	0.9978	3.0
3,500	0.8480	261.3		10,000	0.9985	1.9
4,000	0.8911	185.3		10,500	0.9989	1.2
4,500	0.9224	130.9		11,000	0.9993	0.6
5,000	0.9449	92.1		11,500	0.9995	0.3
5,500	0.9611	64.5		12,000	1.0000	0.0
6,000	0.9726	45.1				

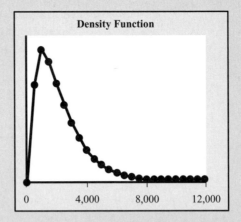

Density Function

Suppose, six months in advance of the promotion, Burger King must make a single order for each restaurant. Furthermore, Burger King wants to have an in-stock probability of at least 85 percent.

a. Given those requirements, how many toys must each restaurant order?

b. How many toys should Burger King expect to have at the end of the promotion?

Now suppose Burger King makes a single order for all 200 restaurants. The order will be delivered to the distribution center and each restaurant will receive deliveries from that stockpile as needed. If demands were independent across all restaurants, total demand would be $200 \times 2{,}251 = 450{,}200$ with a standard deviation of $\sqrt{200} \times 1{,}600 = 22{,}627$. But it is unlikely that demands will be independent across restaurants. In other words, it is likely that there is positive correlation. Nevertheless, based on historical data, Burger King estimates the coefficient of variation for the total will be half of what it is for individual stores. As a result, a normal distribution will work for the total demand forecast.

c. How many toys must Burger King order for the distribution center to have an 85 percent in-stock probability?

d. If the quantity in part c is ordered, then how many units should Burger King expect to have at the end of the promotion?

e. If Burger King ordered the quantity evaluated in part a (i.e., the amount such that each restaurant would have its own inventory and generate an 85 percent in-stock probability) but kept that entire quantity at the distribution center and delivered to each restaurant only as needed, then what would the DC's in-stock probability be?

Q12.3 (**Livingston Tools**) Livingston Tools, a manufacturer of battery-operated, hand-held power tools for the consumer market (such as screwdrivers and drills), has a problem. Its two biggest customers are "big box" discounters. Because these customers are fiercely price competitive, each wants exclusive products, thereby preventing consumers from making price comparisons. For example, Livingston will sell the exact same power screwdriver to each retailer, but Livingston will use packing customized to each retailer (including two different product identification numbers). Suppose weekly demand of each product to each retailer is normally distributed with mean 5,200 and standard deviation 3,800. Livingston makes production decisions on a weekly basis and has a three-week replenishment lead time. Because these two retailers are quite important to Livingston, Livingston sets a target fill rate of 99.9 percent.

a. Based on the order-up-to model, what is Livingston's average inventory of each of the two versions of this power screwdriver?

b. Someone at Livingston suggests that Livingston stock power screwdrivers without putting them into their specialized packaging. As orders are received from the two retailers, Livingston would fulfill those orders from the same stockpile of inventory, since it doesn't take much time to actually package each tool. Interestingly, demands at the two retailers have a slight negative correlation, -0.20. By approximately how much would this new system reduce Livingston's inventory investment?

Q12.4 (**Restoration Hardware**) Consider the following excerpts from a *New York Times* article (Kaufman, 2000):

Despite its early promise . . . Restoration has had trouble becoming a mass-market player. . . . What went wrong? High on its own buzz, the company expanded at breakneck speed, more than doubling the number of stores, to 94, in the year and a half after the stock offering . . . Company managers agree, for example, that Restoration's original inventory system, which called for all furniture to be kept at stores instead of at a central warehouse, was a disaster.

Let's look at one Restoration Hardware product, a leather chair. Average weekly sales of this chair in each store is Poisson with mean 1.25 units. The replenishment lead time is 12 weeks. (This question requires using Excel to create Poisson distribution and loss function tables that are not included in the appendix. See Appendix C for the procedure to evaluate a loss function table.)

a. If each store holds its own inventory, then what is the company's annual inventory turns if the company policy is to target a 99.25 percent in-stock probability?

b. Suppose Restoration Hardware builds a central warehouse to serve the 94 stores. The lead time from the supplier to the central warehouse is 12 weeks. The lead time from the central warehouse to each store is one week. Suppose the warehouse operates with a 99 percent in-stock probability, but the stores maintain a 99.25 percent in-stock probability. If only inventory at the retail stores is considered, what is Restoration's annual inventory turns?

Q12.5   **(Study Desk)** You are in charge of designing a supply chain for furniture distribution. One of your products is a study desk. This desk comes in two colors: black and cherry. Weekly demand for each desk type is normal with mean 100 and standard deviation 65 (demands for the two colors are independent). The lead time from the assembly plant to the retail store is two weeks and you order inventory replenishments weekly. There is no finished goods inventory at the plant (desks are assembled to order for delivery to the store).

a. What is the expected on-hand inventory of desks at the store (black and cherry together) if you maintain a 97 percent in-stock probability for each desk color?

You notice that only the top part of the desk is black or cherry; the remainder (base) is made of the standard gray metal. Hence, you suggest that the store stock black and cherry tops separately from gray bases and assemble them when demand occurs. The replenishment lead time for components is still two weeks. Furthermore, you still choose an order-up-to level for each top to generate a 97 percent in-stock probability.

b. What is the expected on-hand inventory of black tops?

c. How much less inventory of gray bases do you have on average at the store with the new in-store assembly scheme relative to the original system in which desks are delivered fully assembled? (*Hint:* Remember that each assembled desk requires one top and one base.)

Q12.6   **(O'Neill)** One of O'Neill's high-end wetsuits is called the Animal. Total demand for this wetsuit is normally distributed with a mean of 200 and a standard deviation of 130. In order to ensure an excellent fit, the Animal comes in 16 sizes. Furthermore, it comes in four colors, so there are actually 64 different Animal SKUs (stock-keeping units). O'Neill sells the Animal for $350 and its production cost is $269. The Animal will be redesigned this season, so at the end of the season leftover inventory will be sold off at a steep markdown. Because this is such a niche product, O'Neill expects to receive only $100 for each leftover wetsuit. Finally, to control manufacturing costs, O'Neill has a policy that at least five wetsuits of any size/color combo must be produced at a time. Total demand for the smallest size (extra small-tall) is forecasted to be Poisson with mean 2.00. Mean demand for the four colors are black = 0.90, blue = 0.50, green = 0.40, and yellow = 0.20.

a. Suppose O'Neill already has no extra small-tall Animals in stock. What is O'Neill's expected profit if it produces one batch (five units) of extra small-tall black Animals?

b. Suppose O'Neill announces that it will only sell the Animal in one color, black. If O'Neill suspects this move will reduce total demand by 12.5 percent, then what now is its expected profit from the black Animal?

Chapter

13

Revenue Management with Capacity Controls

The operations manager constantly struggles with a firm's supply process to better match it to demand. In fact, most of our discussion in this text has concentrated on how the supply process can be better organized, structured, and managed to make it more productive and responsive. But if supply is so inflexible that it cannot be adjusted to meet demand, then another approach is needed. In particular, this chapter takes the opposite approach: Instead of matching supply to demand, we explore how demand can be adjusted to match supply. The various techniques for achieving this objective are collected under the umbrella term *revenue management,* which is also referred to as *yield management.* Broadly speaking, revenue management is the science of maximizing the revenue earned from a fixed supply.

This chapter discusses two specific techniques within revenue management: *protection levels/booking limits* and *overbooking.* (We will see that protection levels and booking limits are really two different concepts that implement the same technique.) Those techniques perform revenue management via capacity controls; that is, they adjust over time the availability of capacity. Prices are taken as fixed, so protection levels and overbooking attempt to maximize revenue without changing prices.

We begin the chapter with a brief introduction to revenue management: its history, its success stories, and some "margin arithmetic" to explain why it can be so powerful. We next illustrate the application of protection levels and overbooking to an example from the hotel industry. The final sections discuss the implementation of these techniques in practice and summarize insights.

13.1 Revenue Management and Margin Arithmetic

Revenue management techniques were first developed in the airline industry in the early 1980s. Because each flown segment is a perishable asset (once a plane leaves the gate, there are no additional opportunities to earn additional revenue on that particular flight), the airlines wanted to maximize the revenue they earned on each flight, which is all the more important given the razor-thin profit margins in the industry. For example, the average airline operates with about 73 percent of its seats filled but needs to fill about 70 percent of its seats to break even: on a 100-seat aircraft, the difference between making and losing money is measured by a handful of passengers.

Despite the airline industry's lack of profitability, revenue management is considered a success: American Airlines credits revenue management techniques for increasing revenue by $500 million per year and Delta airlines has attributed a $300 million gain (Boyd, 1998). As a result of this success, these techniques have spread to other service industries such as hotels, car rentals, freight shipping, and advertising. For example, National Car Rental used revenue management to rescue itself from the brink of bankruptcy (Geraghty and Johnson, 1997) and Marriott Hotel attributes $100 million in additional annual revenue to revenue management (Cross, 1997).

Firms that implement revenue management techniques generally report revenue increases in the range of 3 to 7 percent with relatively little additional capital investment. The importance of that incremental revenue can be understood with the use of "margin arithmetic." A firm's net profit equation is straightforward:

$$\text{Profit} = R \times M - F = \text{Net profit \%} \times R$$

where

$$R = \text{Revenue}$$
$$M = \text{Gross margin as a percentage of revenue}$$
$$F = \text{Fixed costs}$$

$$\text{Net profit \%} = \text{Net profit as a percentage of revenue}$$

A firm's net profit as a percentage of its revenue (Net profit %) is generally in the range of 1 to 10 percent.

Now let's suppose we implement revenue management and increase revenue. Let Revenue increase be the percentage increase in revenue we experience, which, as has already been mentioned, is typically in the 3 to 7 percent range. Our percentage change in profit is then

$$\text{\% change in profit} = \frac{[(100\% + \text{Revenue increase}) \times R \times M - F] - [R \times M - F]}{R \times M - F}$$

$$= \frac{\text{Revenue increase} \times R \times M}{R \times M - F}$$

$$= \frac{\text{Revenue increase} \times M}{\text{Net profit \%}}$$

(The second line above cancels out terms in the numerator such as the fixed costs. The third line replaces the denominator with Net profit % $\times R$ and then cancels R from both the numerator and denominator.) Table 13.1 presents data evaluated with the above equation for various gross margins, revenue increases, and net profits as a percentage of revenues. The table dramatically illustrates that a seemingly small increase in revenue can have a significant impact on profit, especially when the gross margin is large. Thus, a 3 to 7 percent increase in revenue can easily generate a 50 to 100 percent increase in profit, es-

TABLE 13.1
Percentage Change in Profit for Different Gross Margins, Revenue Increases, and Net Profits as a Percentage of Revenue

Net Profit % = 2%					Net Profit % = 6%				
Revenue increase					Revenue increase				
Gross Margin	1%	2%	5%	8%	Gross Margin	1%	2%	5%	8%
100%	50%	100%	250%	400%	100%	17%	33%	83%	133%
90	45	90	225	360	90	15	30	75	120
75	38	75	188	300	75	13	25	63	100
50	25	50	125	200	50	8	17	42	67
25	13	25	63	100	25	4	8	21	33
15	8	15	38	60	15	3	5	13	20

pecially in a high-gross-margin setting; revenue management indeed can be an important set of tools. We next illustrate in detail two of the tools in that set with an example from the hotel industry.

13.2 Protection Levels and Booking Limits

The Park Hyatt Philadelphia at the Bellevue, located at Walnut and Broad in downtown Philadelphia, has 118 king/queen rooms that it offers to both leisure and business travelers.[1] Leisure travelers are more price sensitive and tend to reserve rooms well in advance of their stay. Business travelers are generally willing to pay more for a room, in part because they tend to book much closer to the time of their trip, and in part because they wish to avoid the additional restrictions associated with the discount fare (e.g., advance purchase requirements and more restrictive cancellation policies). With leisure travelers in mind, the Hyatt offers a $159 discount fare for a midweek stay, which contrasts with the regular fare of $225. We'll refer to these as the low and high fares and use the notation $r_l = 159$ and $r_h = 225$ (r stands for revenue and the subscript indicates l for low fare or h for high fare).

Suppose today is April 1, but we are interested in the Hyatt's bookings on May 29th, which is a midweek night. The Hyatt knows that there will be plenty of travelers willing to pay the low fare, so selling all 118 rooms by May 29th is not a problem. However, all else being equal, the Hyatt would like those rooms to be filled with high-fare travelers rather than low-fare travelers. Unfortunately, there is little chance that there will be enough demand at the high fare to fill the hotel, and the lost revenue from an empty room is significant: Once May 29th passes, the Hyatt can never again earn revenue from that capacity. So the Hyatt's challenge is to extract as much revenue as possible from these two customer segments for its May 29th rooms, that is, we wish to maximize revenue.

The objective to maximize revenue implicitly assumes that the variable cost of an occupied room is inconsequential. The zero-variable cost assumption is quite reasonable for an airline: the variable cost of a passenger includes a beverage, maybe some inexpensive food, and the incremental labor of baggage and ticketing. It is probably less appropriate for a hotel, given that an occupied room requires additional utilities and cleaning staff labor. Nevertheless, we stick with the traditional maximize-revenue objective in this chapter. If the variable cost of a customer is significant, then the techniques we present can be easily modified to implement a maximize-profit objective. (For example, see Practice Problems Q13.7, and Q13.9.)

Returning to our example, the Hyatt could just accept bookings in both fare classes as they occur until either it has 118 reservations or May 29th arrives; the first-come, first-served regime is surely equitable. With that process, it is possible the Hyatt has all 118 rooms reserved one week before May 29th. Unfortunately, because business travelers tend to book late, in that situation it is likely some high-fare travelers will be turned away in that last week; the Hyatt is not allowed to cancel a low-fare reservation to make room for a high-fare traveler. Turning away a high-fare reservation is surely a lost revenue opportunity.

There is a better way than just accepting reservations on a first-come, first-served basis. Instead, the Hyatt could reserve a certain number of rooms just for the high-fare travelers, that is, to protect some rooms for last-minute bookings. This is formalized with the concept of protection levels and booking limits.

---

[1] The Park Hyatt in Philadelphia does have 118 king/queen rooms, but the demand and fare data in this case are disguised. Furthermore, the revenue management techniques described in the chapter are meant to be representative of how the Park Hyatt could do revenue management, but should not be taken to represent the Park Hyatt's actual operating procedures.

The *protection level* for a fare is the number of rooms that are reserved for that fare or higher. We let Q represent our protection level for the high fare. If $Q = 35$, then we protect 35 rooms for the high fare. What does it mean to "protect" 35 rooms? It means that at all times there must always be *at least* 35 rooms that could be reserved with the high fare. For example, suppose there were 83 rooms reserved at the low fare, 30 rooms reserved at the high fare, and 5 unreserved rooms. Because there are enough unreserved rooms to allow us to possibly have 35 high-fare rooms, we have not violated our protection level.

But now suppose the next traveler requests a low-fare reservation. If we were to allow that reservation, then we would no longer have enough unreserved rooms to allow at least 35 high-fare rooms. Therefore, according to our protection level rule, we would not allow that low-fare reservation. In fact, the limit of 83 has a name; it is called a booking limit: The *booking limit* for a fare is the maximum number of reservations allowed at that fare or lower. There is a relationship between the high-fare protection level and the low-fare booking limit:

$$\text{High-fare protection level} = \text{Capacity} - \text{low-fare booking limit} \qquad (13.1)$$

In order to have at least 35 rooms available for the high fare (its protection level), the Hyatt cannot allow any more than 83 reservations at the low fare (its booking limit) as long as the total number of allowed reservations (capacity) is 118.

You might now wonder about the protection level for the low fare and the booking limit for the high fare. There is no need to protect any rooms at the low fare because the next best alternative is for the room to go empty. So the protection level for the low fare is 0. Analogously, we are willing to book as many rooms as possible at the high fare, because there is no better alternative, so the booking limit on the high fare should be set to at least 118. (As we will see in the next section, we may even wish to allow more than 118 bookings.)

Given that we have defined a booking limit to be the maximum number of reservations allowed for a fare class *or lower,* we have implicitly assumed that our booking limits are *nested.* With *nested booking limits,* it is always true that if a particular fare class is open (i.e., we are willing to accept reservations at that fare class), then we are willing to accept all higher fare classes as well. It is also true that if a particular fare class is closed, then all lower fare classes are closed as well.

Nested booking limits make intuitive sense: If we are willing to sell a discount fare, why wouldn't we be willing to sell a full fare? if we are not willing to sell a high fare, why would we be willing to sell a lower fare? But it is worth mentioning that booking limits need not always be nested. For example, suppose we were to define a booking limit as the number of reservations that are allowed just for a single fare. For example, suppose we have three fare classes on a flight with 100 seats, Y, M, Q, from highest fare to lowest fare, with booking limits Y = 50, M = 30, Q = 20. (Airlines generally use single letters to denote fare classes, and *Y* is generally used for the full fare coach class, i.e., the highest coach cabin fare.) With these nonnested booking limits, it is possible that the highest fare is closed, that is, we already have 50 Y reservations so we do not accept any more, while the lowest fare is open, that is, we have fewer than 20 Q reservations, so we are accepting more low-fare reservations. But because nested booking limits make intuitive sense, most revenue management systems operate with nested booking limits. As a result, throughout our discussion, we shall assume nested booking limits.[2]

---

[2]You might be tempted to believe that nested booking limits are always optimal. If they are always optimal, then there is never a need to use nonnested booking limits. While this intuition is generally true, it is not always true. Take the example of three fare classes. You may wish to have the lowest and highest fare classes open while closing the middle fare class if closing the middle fare class gets enough of those customers to trade up to the higher fare.

So now let's turn to the issue of choosing a booking limit for the low fare or, equivalently, a protection level for the high fare. As in many operational decisions, we again face the "too much–too little" problem. If we protect too many rooms for the high-fare class, then some rooms might remain empty on May 29th. To explain, suppose one week before May 29th we have 83 low-fare bookings but only 10 high-fare bookings. Because we have reached the low-fare booking limit, we "close down" that fare and only accept high-fare bookings in the last week. If only 20 additional high-fare bookings arrive, then on May 29th we have five unreserved rooms, which we might have been able to sell at the low fare. Nevertheless, those five rooms go empty. So protecting too many rooms for a fare class can lead to empty rooms.

But the Hyatt can also protect too few rooms. Suppose one week before May 29th we have 80 low-fare bookings and 35 high-fare bookings. Because only 35 rooms are protected for the high fare, the remaining three unreserved rooms could be taken at the low fare. If they are reserved at the low fare, then some high-fare travelers might be turned away; that is, the Hyatt might end up selling a room at the low fare that could have been sold at a high fare. If the protection level were three rooms higher, then those three unreserved rooms could only go at the high fare. Therefore, because the low-fare bookings tend to come before the high-fare bookings, it is possible to protect too few rooms for the high fare.

Our discussion so far suggests the Hyatt could use the newsvendor model logic to choose a protection level. (Peter Belobaba of MIT first developed this approach and labeled it the "Expected Marginal Seat Revenue" analysis. See Belobaba, 1989) To implement the model, we need a forecast of high-fare demand and an assessment of the underage and overage costs. Let's say the Hyatt believes a Poisson distribution with mean 27.3 represents the number of high-fare travelers on May 29th. (This forecast could be constructed using booking data from similar nights, similar times of the year, and managerial intuition.) Table 13.2 provides a portion of the distribution function for that Poisson distribution.

Now we need an overage cost C_o and an underage cost C_u. The underage cost is the cost per unit of setting the protection level too low (i.e., "under" protecting). If we do not protect enough rooms for the high fare, then we sell a room at the low fare that could have been sold at the high fare. The lost revenue is the difference between the two fares, that is, $C_u = r_h - r_l$.

The overage cost is the cost per unit of setting the protection level too high (i.e., "over" protecting). If we set the protection level too high, it means that we did not need to protect so many rooms for the high-fare passengers. In other words, demand at the high fare is less than Q, our protection level. If Q were lower, then we could have sold another room at the low fare. Hence, the overage cost is the incremental revenue of selling a room at the low fare: $C_o = r_l$. According to the newsvendor model, the optimal protection level (i.e., the one that maximizes revenue, which is also the one that minimizes the overage and underage

TABLE 13.2
The Distribution and Loss Function for a Poisson with Mean 27.3

Q	F(Q)	L(Q)	Q	F(Q)	L(Q)	Q	F(Q)	L(Q)
10	0.0001	17.30	20	0.0920	7.45	30	0.7365	1.03
11	0.0004	16.30	21	0.1314	6.55	31	0.7927	0.77
12	0.0009	15.30	22	0.1802	5.68	32	0.8406	0.56
13	0.0019	14.30	23	0.2381	4.86	33	0.8803	0.40
14	0.0039	13.30	24	0.3040	4.10	34	0.9121	0.28
15	0.0077	12.31	25	0.3760	3.40	35	0.9370	0.19
16	0.0140	11.31	26	0.4516	2.78	36	0.9558	0.13
17	0.0242	10.33	27	0.5280	2.23	37	0.9697	0.09
18	0.0396	9.35	28	0.6025	1.76	38	0.9797	0.06
19	0.0618	8.39	29	0.6726	1.36	39	0.9867	0.04

costs) is the Q such that the probability the high-fare demand is less than or equal to Q equals the critical ratio, which is

$$\frac{C_u}{C_o + C_u} = \frac{r_h - r_l}{r_l + (r_h - r_l)} = \frac{r_h - r_l}{r_h} = \frac{225 - 159}{225} = 0.2933$$

In words, we want to find the Q such that there is a 29.33 percent probability high-fare demand is Q or lower. From Table 13.2, we see that $F(23) = 0.2381$ and $F(24) = 0.3040$, so the optimal protection level is $Q = 24$ rooms. (Recall the round-up rule: When the critical ratio falls between two values in the distribution function table, choose the entry that leads to the higher decision variable.) The corresponding booking limit for the low fare is $118 - 24 = 94$ rooms.

In some situations, it is more convenient to express a booking limit as an *authorization level:* The authorization level for a fare class is the percentage of available capacity that can be reserved at that fare or lower. For example, a booking limit of 94 rooms corresponds to an authorization level of 80 percent (94/118) because 80 percent of the Hyatt's rooms can be reserved at the low fare. The process of evaluating protection levels and booking limits is summarized in Exhibit 13.1.

If the Hyatt uses a protection level of 24 rooms, then the Hyatt's expected revenue is higher than if no protection level is used. How much higher? To provide some answer to that question, we need to make a few more assumptions. First, let's assume that there is ample low-fare demand. In other words, we could easily book all 118 rooms at the low fare. Second, let's assume the low-fare demand arrives before any high-fare bookings. Hence, if we do not protect any rooms for the high fare, then the low-fare customers will reserve all 118 rooms before any high-fare customer requests a reservation.

Given our assumptions, the Hyatt's revenue without any protection level would be 118 $\times$ \$159 = \$18,762: all 118 rooms are filled at the low fare. If we protect 24 rooms, then we surely fill 94 rooms at the low fare, for an expected revenue of 94 $\times$ \$159 = \$14,946. What is the expected revenue from the 24 protected rooms? Given that high-fare demand is Poisson with mean 27.3, from Table 13.2 we see that we can expect to turn away 4.1 high-fare bookings, that is, the loss function is $L(24) = 4.1$. In other words, we can expect to lose 4.1 high-fare bookings. Our expected high-fare bookings is analogous to expected sales in the newsvendor model, so

Expected high-fare bookings = Expected high-fare demand − Expected lost sales

$$= 27.3 - 4.1$$

$$= 23.2$$

In other words, we expect to have 23.2 high-fare reservations if we protect 24 rooms and high-fare demand is Poisson with mean 27.3. Therefore, because the Hyatt protects fewer rooms than expected demand, the Hyatt can expect to sell most of the rooms it protects with very few empty rooms. To be precise, of the 24 protected rooms, only 0.8 of them is expected to be empty:

Expected number of empty rooms = Q − Expected high-fare bookings

$$= 24 - 23.2$$

$$= 0.8$$

This makes sense. The incremental revenue of selling a high fare is only \$66, but the cost of an empty room is \$159, so a conservative protection level is prudent.

If the Hyatt expects to sell 23.2 rooms at the high fare, then the revenue from those rooms is 23.2 $\times$ \$225 = \$5,220. Total revenue when protecting 24 rooms is then \$14,946 +

Exhibit 13.1

Exhibit 13.1

EVALUATING THE OPTIMAL PROTECTION LEVEL FOR THE HIGH FARE OR THE OPTIMAL BOOKING LIMIT FOR THE LOW FARE WHEN THERE ARE TWO FARES AND REVENUE MAXIMIZATION IS THE OBJECTIVE

Step 1. Evaluate the critical ratio:

$$\text{Critical ratio} = \frac{C_u}{C_o + C_u} = \frac{r_h - r_l}{r_h}$$

Step 2. Find the Q such that $F(Q)$ = Critical ratio, where $F(Q)$ is the distribution function of high-fare demand:

    a. If $F(Q)$ is given in table form, then find the Q in the table such that $F(Q)$ equals the critical ratio. If the critical ratio falls between two entries in the table, choose the entry with the higher Q.

    b. If high-fare demand is normally distributed with mean μ and standard deviation σ, then find the z-statistic in the Standard Normal Distribution Function Table such that $\Phi(z)$ = Critical ratio. If the critical ratio falls between two entries in the table, choose the entry with the higher z. Finally, convert the chosen z into Q: $Q = \mu + z \times \sigma$.

Step 3. The optimal high-fare protection level is Q evaluated in Step 2. The optimal low-fare booking limit is Capacity – Q, where Capacity is the number of allowed reservations.

$5,220 = \$20,166$. Hence, our expected revenue increases by $(20,166 - 18,762) / 18,762 = 7.5$ percent. As a point of reference, we can evaluate the *maximum expected revenue,* which is achieved if we sell to every high-fare customer and sell all remaining rooms at the low fare:

$$\text{Maximum expected revenue} = 27.3 \times \$225 + (118 - 27.3) \times \$159$$

$$= \$20,564$$

Thus, the difference between the maximum expected revenue and the revenue earned by just selling at the low fare is $\$20,564 - \$18,762 = \$1,802$. The Hyatt's revenue with a protection level falls short of the maximum expected revenue by only $\$20,564 - \$20,166 = \$398$. Hence, a protection level for the high fare allows the Hyatt to capture about 78 percent $(1 - \$397/\$1,802)$ of its potential revenue improvement.

A revenue increase of 7.5 percent is surely substantial given that it is achieved without the addition of capacity and without a change in the fare structure. Nevertheless, we must be reminded of the assumptions that were made. We assumed there is ample demand for the low fare. If low-fare demand is limited, then a protection level for the high fare is less valuable and the incremental revenue gain is smaller. For example, if the sum of low- and high-fare demand is essentially always lower than 118 rooms, then there is no need to protect the high fare. More broadly, revenue management with protection levels is most valuable when operating in a capacity-constrained situation.

The second key assumption is that low-fare demand arrives before high-fare demand. If some high-fare demand "slips in" before the low-fare demand snatches up all 118 rooms, then the revenue estimate without a protection level, $\$18,762$, is too low. In other words, even if we do not protect any rooms for the high fare, it is possible that we would still obtain some high-fare bookings.

Although we would need to look at actual data to get a more accurate sense of the potential revenue improvement by using protection levels, our estimate is in line with the typical revenue increases reported in practice due to revenue management, 3 to 8 percent.

Now that we have considered a specific example of booking limits at a hotel, it is worth enumerating the characteristics of a business that are conducive to the application of booking limits.

- *The same unit of capacity can be used to sell to different customer segments.* It is easy for an airline to price discriminate between leisure and business travelers when the capacity that is being sold is different, for example, a coach cabin seat and a first-class seat. Those are clearly distinguishable products/services. Booking limits are applied when the capacity sold to different segments is identical; for example, a coach seat on an aircraft or a king/queen room in the Hyatt sold at two different fares.

- *There are distinguishable customer segments and the segments have different price sensitivity.* There is no need for protection levels when the revenue earned from all customers is the same, for example, if there is a single fare. Booking limits are worthwhile if the firm can earn different revenue from different customer segments with the same type of capacity. Because the same unit of capacity is being sold, it is necessary to discriminate between the customer segments. This is achieved with *fences:* additional restrictions that are imposed on the low fare that prevent high-fare customers from purchasing with the low fare. Typical fences include advanced purchase requirements, Saturday night stay requirements, cancellation fees, change fees, and so forth. Of course, one could argue that these fences make the low and high fares different products; for example, a full-fare coach ticket is not the same product as a supersaver coach ticket even if they both offer a seat in the coach cabin. True, these are different products in the broad sense, but they are identical products with respect to the capacity they utilize.

- *Capacity is perishable.* An unused room on May 29th is lost forever, just as an unused seat on a flight cannot be stored until the next flight. In contrast, capacity in a production facility can be used to make inventory, which can be sold later whenever capacity exceeds current demand.

- *Capacity is restrictive.* If the total demand at the leisure and business fares is rarely greater than 118 rooms, then the Hyatt has no need to establish protection levels or booking limits. Because capacity is expensive to install and expensive to change over time, it is impossible for a service provider to always have plenty of capacity. (Utilization would be so low that the firm would surely not be competitive and probably not viable.) But due to seasonality effects, it is possible that the Hyatt has plenty of capacity at some times of the year and not enough capacity at other times. Booking limits are not needed during those lull times but are quite useful during the peak demand periods.

- *Capacity is sold in advance.* If we were allowed to cancel a low-fare reservation whenever someone requested a high-fare reservation (i.e., bump a low-fare passenger off the plane without penalty), then we would not need to protect seats for the high fare: We would accept as many low-fare bookings as they arrive and then cancel as many as needed to accommodate the high-fare travelers. Similarly, we do not need protection levels if we were to conduct an auction just before the flight departs. For example, imagine a situation in which all potential demand would arrive at the airport an hour or so before the flight departs and then an auction is conducted to determine who would earn a seat on that flight. This is a rather silly way to sell airline seats, but in other contexts there is clearly a movement toward more auction-like selling mechanisms. Because the auction ensures that capacity is sold to the highest bidders, there is no need for protection levels.

- *A firm wishes to maximize revenue, has the flexibility to charge different prices, and may withhold capacity from certain segments.* A hotel is able to offer multiple fares and withhold fares. In other words, even though the practice of closing a discount fare means the principle of first-come, first-served is violated, this practice is generally not viewed as unethical or scrupulous. However, there are settings in which the violation of first-come, first-served, or the charging of different prices, or the use of certain fences is not acceptable to consumers, for example, organ transplants.

- *A firm faces competition from a "discount competitor."* The low fares charged by People Express, a low-frills airline started after deregulation, were a major motivation for the development of revenue management at America Airlines. In order to compete in the low-fare segment, American was forced to match People Express's fares. But American did not want to have its high fare customers paying the low fare. Booking limits and low-fare fences were the solution to the problem: American could compete at the low-fare segment without destroying the revenue from its profitable high-fare customers. People Express did not install a revenue management system and quickly went bankrupt after American's response.

13.3 Overbooking

In many service settings, customers are allowed to make reservations and then to cancel their reservations with relatively short notice. In some cases there is a cancellation penalty, but in many situations there is no penalty. For example, on May 28th, the Hyatt might have all of its 118 rooms reserved for May 29th but then only 110 customers might actually show up, leaving eight rooms empty and not generating any revenue. Overbooking, described in this section, is one solution to the no-show problem. If the Hyatt chooses to overbook, then that means the Hyatt accepts more than 118 reservations even though a maximum of 118 guests can be accommodated.

Let the variable Y represent the number of additional reservations beyond capacity that the Hyatt is willing to accept, that is, up to $118 + Y$ reservations are accepted. Overbooking can lead to two kinds of outcomes. On a positive note, the number of no-shows can be greater than the number of overbooked reservations, so all the actual customers can be accommodated and more customers are accommodated than would have been without overbooking. For example, suppose the Hyatt accepts 122 reservations and there are six no-shows. As a result, 116 rooms are occupied, leaving only two empty rooms, which is almost surely fewer empty rooms than if the Hyatt had only accepted 118 reservations.

On the negative side, the Hyatt can get caught overbooking. For example, if 122 reservations are accepted, but there arc only two no-shows, then 120 guests hold reservations for 118 rooms. In that situation, two guests need to be accommodated at some other hotel and the Hyatt probably must give some additional compensation (e.g., cash or free future stay) to mitigate the loss of goodwill with the customer. In the case of airlines, there are regulated minimum compensation levels, but airlines often exceed those minimums.[3] In fact, the airlines have a considerable amount of experience dealing with bumped passengers: in the United States, airlines deny boarding to about one million passengers annually (Stringer, 2002). In fact, if the practice of overbooking were not allowed, then it is estimated the world's airlines would lose over $3 billion annually due to no-shows (Cross, 1995).

In deciding the proper amount of overbooking, there is a "too much–too little" trade-off: Overbook too much and the hotel angers some customers, but overbook too little and the hotel has the lost revenue associated with empty rooms. Hence, we can apply the newsvendor model to choose the appropriate Y. We first need a forecast of the number of customers

[3]The Department of Transportation requires airlines to pay up to $400 in cash to involuntary bumpees.

TABLE 13.3
Poisson Distribution
Function with
Mean 8.5

Q	F(Q)	Q	F(Q)
0	0.0002	10	0.7634
1	0.0019	11	0.8487
2	0.0093	12	0.9091
3	0.0301	13	0.9486
4	0.0744	14	0.9726
5	0.1496	15	0.9862
6	0.2562	16	0.9934
7	0.3856	17	0.9970
8	0.5231	18	0.9987
9	0.6530	19	0.9995

that will not show up based on historical data. Let's say the Hyatt believes for the May 29th night that the no-show distribution is Poisson with mean 8.5. Table 13.3 provides the distribution function.[4]

Next, we need underage and overage costs. If the Hyatt chooses Y to be too low, then there will be empty rooms on May 29th (i.e., the Hyatt "under" overbooked). If the Hyatt indeed has plenty of low-fare demand, then those empty rooms could have at least been sold for $r_l = \$159$, so the underage cost is $C_u = r_l = 159$.

If the Hyatt chooses Y to be too high, then there will be more guests than rooms. The bumped guests need to be accommodated at some other hotel and Hyatt offers other compensation. The total cost to Hyatt for each of those guests is estimated to be about $350 after refunding the fare paid, so the overage cost is $C_o = 350$.

The critical ratio is

$$\frac{C_u}{C_o + C_u} = \frac{159}{350 + 159} = 0.3124$$

Looking in Table 13.3 we see that $F(6) = 0.2562$ and $F(7) = 0.3856$, so the optimal quantity to overbook is $Y = 7$. In other words, the Hyatt should allow up to $118 + 7 = 125$ reservations for May 29th. Exhibit 13.2 summarizes the process of evaluating the optimal quantity to overbook.

If the Hyatt chooses to overbook by seven reservations and if the Hyatt indeed receives 125 reservations, then there is about a 26 percent chance ($F(6) = 0.2562$) that the Hyatt will find itself overbooked on May 29th. Because it is not assured that the Hyatt will receive that many reservations, the actual frequency of being overbooked would be lower. Indeed, the Hyatt might plan to allow up to seven additional reservations over its capacity, but that does not mean that the Hyatt will even receive 118 reservations. Nevertheless, overbooking is a useful tool to enable the Hyatt to better utilize its fixed capacity.

A natural question is how should the Hyatt integrate its protection-level/booking-limit decision with its overbooking decision. The following describes a reasonable heuristic. If the Hyatt is willing to overbook by seven rooms, that is, $Y = 7$, then its effective capacity

---

[4]A careful reader will notice that our distribution function for no-shows is independent of the number of reservations made. In other words, we have assumed the average number of no-shows is 8.5 whether we make 118 reservations or 150 reservations. Hence, a more sophisticated method for choosing the overbooking quantity would account for the relationship between the number of reservations allowed and the distribution function of no-shows. While that more sophisticated method is conceptually similar to our procedure, it is also computationally cumbersome. Therefore, we shall stick with our heuristic method. Fortunately, our heuristic method performs well when compared against the more sophisticated algorithm.

Exhibit 13.2

THE PROCESS TO EVALUATE THE OPTIMAL QUANTITY TO OVERBOOK

Step 1.   Evaluate the critical ratio:

$$\text{Critical ratio} = \frac{C_u}{C_o + C_u} = \frac{r_l}{\text{Cost per bumped customer} + r_l}$$

Step 2.   Find the Y such that $F(Y) =$ Critical ratio, where $F(Y)$ is the distribution function of no-shows:

   a. If $F(Y)$ is given in table form, then find the Y in the table such that $F(Y)$ equals the critical ratio. If the critical ratio falls between two entries in the table, choose the entry with the higher Y.

   b. If no-shows are normally distributed with mean μ and standard deviation σ, then find the z-statistic in the Standard Normal Distribution Function Table such that $\Phi(z) =$ Critical ratio. If the critical ratio falls between two entries in the table, choose the entry with the higher z. Finally, convert the chosen z into Y: $Y = \mu + z \times \sigma$.

Step 3. Y is the optimal amount to overbook; that is, the number of allowed reservations is $Y +$ Capacity, where Capacity is the maximum number of customers that can actually be served.

is $118 + 7 = 125$ rooms. Based on the forecast of high-fare demand and the underage and overage costs associated with protecting rooms for the high-fare travelers, we determined that the Hyatt should protect 24 rooms for the high fare. Using equation (13.1), that suggests the booking limit for the low fare should be

$$\text{Low-fare booking limit} = \text{Capacity} - \text{High-fare protection level}$$

$$= 125 - 24$$

$$= 101$$

The high-fare booking limit would then be 125, that is, the Hyatt accepts up to 101 low-fare reservations and up to 125 reservations in total.

From our preceding analysis, it is clear that the optimal amount of overbooking depends on the cost of bumping a passenger with a confirmed reservation. But firms long ago realized that the cost of bumping a customer depends on how the process is handled. For example, it can be quite expensive to bump a passenger off a flight if the customer is randomly chosen or if the chosen customer is the last one to arrive at the airport. That particular customer might be extremely hesitant to relinquish his or her seat: the passenger could be traveling with a group or the passenger could have set appointments. So one solution is to ask for volunteers in the hope of finding the passengers that are least costly to bump. In some sense, this is like conducting an auction: "We are giving away the following amenities; who is willing to wait until the next flight?" While asking for volunteers seems like an obvious idea, interestingly, it took the industry quite some time to accept that approach (Cross, 1995). But it might not be the best possible approach. For example, a passenger might be willing to accept a bump if the passenger is given enough notice, for instance, if the passenger is phoned the day before, that is, contacted before taking the time to arrive at the airport. By constructing a database of customers that are most likely to accept a bump the day before their departure, an airline might be able to further reduce the cost of overbooking, thereby making overbooking even more attractive.

To summarize, overbooking is a useful tool when customers might be no-shows or are allowed to cancel their reservations and if bumping customers is not too costly.

13.4   Implementation of Revenue Management

Although the applications of revenue management described in this chapter present a reasonably straightforward analysis, in practice there are many additional complications encountered in the implementation of revenue management. A few of the more significant complications are discussed below.

Demand Forecasting

We saw that forecasts are a necessary input to the choice of both protection levels and overbooking quantities. As a result, the choices made are only as good as the inputted forecasts; as the old adage says, "garbage in, garbage out." Fortunately, reservation systems generally provide a wealth of information to formulate these forecasts. Nevertheless, the forecasting task is complicated by the presence of seasonality, special events (e.g., a convention in town), changing fares (both the firm's own fares as well as the competitors' fares), and truncation (once a booking limit is reached, most systems do not capture the lost demand at that fare level), among others. Furthermore, it is possible that the revenue management decisions themselves might influence demand and, hence, the forecasts used to make those decisions. As a result, with any successful revenue management system, a considerable amount of care and effort is put into the demand forecasting task.

Dynamic Decisions

Our analysis provided a decision for a single moment in time. However, fares and forecasts change with time and, as a result, booking limits need to be reviewed frequently (generally daily). In fact, sophisticated systems take future adjustments into consideration when setting current booking limits.

Variability in Available Capacity

A hotel is a good example of a service firm that generally does not have much variation in its capacity: it is surely difficult to add a room to a hotel and the number of rooms that cannot be occupied is generally small. The capacity of an airline's flight is also rigid but maybe less so than a hotel's capacity because the airline can choose to switch the type of aircraft used on a route. However, a car rental company's capacity at any given location is surely variable and not even fully controllable by the firm. Hence, those firms also must forecast the amount of capacity they think will be available at any given time.

Reservations Coming in Groups

If there is a convention in town for May 29th, then the Hyatt may receive a single request for 110 rooms at the low fare. Although this request violates the booking limit, the booking limit was established assuming reservations come one at a time. It is clearly more costly to turn away a single block of 110 reservations than it is to turn away one leisure traveler.

Effective Segmenting of Customers

We assumed there are two types of customers: a low-fare customer and a high-fare customer. In reality, this is too simplistic. There surely exist customers that are willing to pay the high fare, but they are also more than willing to book at the low fare if given the opportunity. Hence, fences are used to separate out customers by their willingness to pay. Well-known fences include advance purchase requirements, cancellation fees, change fees, Saturday night stay requirements, and so on. But these fences are not perfect, that is, they do not perfectly segment out customers. As a result, there is often spillover demand from one fare class to another. It is possible that more effective fences exist, but some fences might generate stiff resistance from customers. For example, a firm could regulate a customer's access to various fare classes based on their annual income, or the average price the customer paid in past service encounters, but those schemes will surely not receive a warm reception.

Multiple Fare Classes

In our application of revenue management, we have two fare classes: a low fare and a high fare. In reality there can be many more fare classes. With multiple fare classes it becomes necessary to forecast demand for each fare class and to establish multiple booking limits.

Software Implementation

While the investment in revenue management software is often reasonable relative to the potential revenue gain, it is nevertheless not zero. Furthermore, revenue management systems have often been constrained by the capabilities of the reservation systems they must work with. In other words, while the revenue management software might be able to make a decision as to whether a fare class should be open or closed (i.e., whether to accept a request for a reservation at a particular fare), it also must be able to communicate that decision to the travel agent or customer via the reservation system. Finally, there can even be glitches in the revenue management software, as was painfully discovered by American Airlines. Their initial software had an error that prematurely closed down the low-fare class on flights with many empty seats (i.e., it set the low-fare class booking limit too low). American Airlines discovered the error only when they realized that the load on those flights was too low (the load is the percent of seats occupied; it is the utilization of the aircraft). By that time it was estimated $50 million in revenue had been lost. Hence, properly chosen booking limits can increase revenue, but poorly chosen booking limits can decrease revenue. As a result, careful observation of a revenue management system is always necessary.

Variation in Capacity Purchase: Not All Customers Purchase One Unit of Capacity

Even if two customers pay the same fare, they might be different from the firm's perspective. For example, suppose one leisure traveler requests one night at the low fare whereas another requests five nights at the low fare. While these customers pay the same amount for a given night, it is intuitive that turning away the second customer is more costly. In fact, it may even be costlier than turning away a single high-fare reservation.

Airlines experience a challenge similar to a hotel's multinight customer. Consider two passengers traveling from Chicago (O'Hare) to New York (JFK) paying the discount fare. For one passenger JFK is the final destination, whereas the other passenger will fly from JFK to London (Heathrow) on another flight with the same airline. The revenue management system should recognize that a multileg passenger is more valuable than a single-leg customer. But booking limits just defined for each fare class on the O'Hare–JFK segment do not differentiate between these two customers. In other words, the simplest version of revenue management does *single-leg* or *single-segment control* because the decision rules are focused on the fares of a particular segment in the airline's network. Our example from the Hyatt could be described as *single-night control* because the focus is on a room for one evening.

One solution to the multileg issue is to create a booking limit for each fare class–itinerary combination, not just a booking limit for each fare class on each segment. This is called *origin-destination control,* or *O-D control* for short. For example, suppose there are three fare classes, Y, M, Q (from highest to lowest), on two itineraries, O'Hare–JFK and O'Hare–Heathrow (via JFK):

Fare Class	O'Hare to JFK	O'Hare to Heathrow
Y	$724	$1,610
M	475	829
Q	275	525

Six booking limits could be constructed to manage the inventory on the O'Hare–JFK leg. For example:

Fare Class	O'Hare to JFK	O'Hare to Heathrow
Y		100
M		68
Y	60	
Q		40
M	35	
Q	20	

Hence, it would be possible to deny a Q fare request to an O'Hare–JFK passenger while accepting a Q fare request to an O'Hare–Heathrow passenger: There could be 20 Q fare reservations on the O'Hare–JFK itinerary but fewer than 40 reservations between the M and Q fares on the O'Hare–JFK itinerary and the Q fare on the O'Hare–Heathrow itinerary. If there were only three booking limits on that leg, then all Q fare requests are either accepted or rejected, but it is not possible to accept some Q fare requests while denying others.

While creating a booking limit for each fare class–itinerary combination sounds like a good idea, unfortunately, it is not a practical idea for most revenue management applications. For example, there could be thousands of possible itineraries that use the O'Hare–JFK leg. It would be a computational nightmare to derive booking limits for such a number of itineraries on each possible flight leg, not to mention an implementation challenge. One solution to this problem is *virtual nesting*. With virtual nesting, a limited number of *buckets* are created, each with its own booking limit, each with its own set of fare class–itinerary combinations. Fare class–itinerary combinations are assigned to buckets in such a way that the fare class–itinerary combinations within the same bucket have similar value to the firm, while fare class–itinerary combinations in different buckets have significantly different values.

For example, four buckets could be created for our example, labeled 0 to 3:

Bucket	Itinerary	Fare class
0	O'Hare to Heathrow	Y
1	O'Hare to Heathrow	M
	O'Hare to JFK	Y
2	O'Hare to Heathrow	Q
	O'Hare to JFK	M
3	O'Hare to JFK	Q

The O'Hare–JFK Y fare is combined into one bucket with the O'Hare–Heathrow M fare because they generate similar revenue ($724 and $829), whereas the O'Hare–Heathrow Y fare is given its own bucket due to its much higher revenue ($1,610). Thus, with virtual nesting, it is possible to differentiate among the customers on the same leg willing to pay the same fare. Furthermore, virtual nesting provides a manageable solution if there are many different fare classes and many different types of customers (e.g., customers flying different itineraries or customers staying a different number of nights in a hotel)

While virtual nesting was the first solution implemented for this issue, it is not the only solution. A more recent, and more sophisticated, solution is called *bid-price control*. Let's explain bid-price controls in the context of our airline example. The many different itineraries that use the O'Hare–JFK segment generate different revenue to the airline, but they all use the same unit of capacity, a coach seat on the O'Hare to JFK flight. With bid-price control, each type of capacity on each flight segment is assigned a *bid price*. Then, a fare class–itinerary combination is accepted as long as its fare exceeds the sum of the bid prices of the flight legs in its itinerary. For example, the bid prices could be

	O'Hare to JFK	JFK to Heathrow
Bid price	$290	$170

Hence, an O'Hare–JFK itinerary is available as long as its fare exceeds $290 and an O'Hare–Heathrow itinerary (via JFK) is available as long as its fare exceeds $290 + $170 = $460. Therefore, on the O'Hare–JFK itinerary, the Y and M fare classes would be open (fares $724 and $475 respectively); while on the O'Hare–Heathrow itinerary, all fares would be available (because the lowest Q fare, $525, exceeds the total bid price of $460).

With bid-price control, there is a single bid price on each flight segment, so it is a relatively intuitive and straightforward technique to implement. The challenge with bid-price control is to find the correct bid prices. That challenge requires the use of sophisticated optimization techniques.

13.5 Summary

Revenue management is the science of using pricing and capacity controls to maximize revenue given a relatively fixed supply/capacity. This chapter focuses on the capacity control tools of revenue management: protection levels/booking limits and overbooking. Protection levels/booking limits take advantage of the price differences between fares and the generally staggered nature of demand arrivals; that is, low-fare reservations made by leisure travelers usually occur before high fare reservations made by business travelers. By establishing a booking limit for low fares, it is possible to protect enough capacity for the later-arriving high fares. Overbooking is useful when customer reservations are not firm; if a portion of the customers can be expected to not use the capacity they reserved, then it is wise to accept more reservations than available capacity.

The science of revenue management is indeed quite complex and continues to be an extremely active area of research. Despite these challenges, revenue management has been proven to be a robust and profitable tool, as reflected in the following quote by Robert Crandall, former CEO of AMR and American Airlines (Smith, Leimkuhler, and Darrow, 1992):

> I believe that revenue management is the single most important technical development in transportation management since we entered the era of airline deregulation in 1979 . . . The development of revenue management models was a key to American Airlines' survival in the post-deregulation environment. Without revenue management we were often faced with two unsatisfactory responses in a price competitive marketplace. We could match deeply discounted fares and risk diluting our entire inventory, or we could not match and certainly lose market share. Revenue management gave us a third alternative—match deeply discounted fares on a portion of our inventory and close deeply discounted inventory when it is profitable to

TABLE 13.4
Summary of Key Notation and Equations in Chapter 13

Choosing protection levels and booking limits:
  With two fares, r_h = high fare and r_l = low fare, the high-fare protection level Q has the following critical ratio:

$$\text{Critical ratio} = \frac{C_u}{C_o + C_u} = \frac{r_h - r_l}{r_h}$$

(Find the Q such that the critical ratio is the probability high-fare demand is less than or equal to Q.)
  Low-fare booking limit = Capacity − Q
Choosing an overbooking quantity Y:
  Let r_l be the low fare. The optimal overbooking quantity Y has the following critical ratio:

$$\text{Critical ratio} = \frac{C_u}{C_o + C_u} = \frac{r_e}{\text{Cost per bumped customer} + r_e}$$

save space for later-booking higher value customers. By adjusting the number of reservations which are available at these discounts, we can adjust our minimum available fare to account for differences in demand. This creates a pricing structure which responds to demand on a flight-by-flight basis. As a result, we can more effectively match our demand to supply.

Table 13.4 provides a summary of the key notation and equations presented in this chapter.

13.6 Further Reading

For a brief history of the development of revenue management, see Cross (1995). For a more extensive history, see Cross (1997). Cross (1997) also provides a detailed overview of revenue management techniques.

See Talluri and van Ryzin (forthcoming) for an extensive treatment of the state of the art in revenue management for both theory and practice. Two already-published reviews on the theory of revenue management are McGill and van Ryzin (1999) and Weatherford and Bodily (1992).

For a good introduction to virtual nesting and bid-price controls along with several examples, see Vinod (1995).

Applications of revenue management to car rentals, golf courses, and restaurants can be found in Geraghty and Johnson (1997), Kimes (2000) and Kimes, Chase, Choi, Lee, and Ngonzi (1998).

13.7 Practice Problems

Q13.1* **(The Inn at Penn)** The Inn at Penn hotel has 150 rooms with standard queen-size beds and two rates: a full price of $200 and a discount price of $120. To receive the discount price, a customer must purchase the room at least two weeks in advance (this helps to distinguish between leisure travelers, who tend to book early, and business travelers, who value the flexibility of booking late). For a particular Tuesday night, the hotel estimates that the demand from leisure travelers could fill the whole hotel while the demand from business travelers is distributed normally with a mean of 70 rooms and a standard deviation of 29.

  a. Suppose 50 rooms are protected for full-price rooms. What is the booking limit for the discount rooms?

  b. Find the optimal protection level for full-price rooms (the number of rooms to be protected from sale at a discount price).

  c. The Sheraton declared a fare war by slashing business travelers' prices down to $150. The Inn at Penn had to match that fare to keep demand at the same level. Does the optimal protection level increase, decrease, or remain the same? Explain your answer.

(* indicates that the solution is at the end of the book)

d. What number of rooms (on average) remain unfilled if we establish a protection level of 61 for the full-priced rooms?

e. If The Inn were able to ensure that every full-price customer would receive a room, what would The Inn's expected revenue be?

f. If The Inn did not choose to protect any rooms for the full price and leisure travelers book before business travelers, then what would The Inn's expected revenue be?

g. Taking the assumptions in part f and assuming now that The Inn protects 50 rooms for the full price, what is The Inn's expected revenue?

Q13.2* **(Overbooking The Inn at Penn)** Due to customer no-shows, The Inn at Penn hotel is considering implementing overbooking. Recall from Q13.1 that The Inn at Penn has 150 rooms, the full fare is $200, and the discount fare is $120. The forecast of no-shows is Poisson with a mean of 15.5. The distribution and loss function of that distribution are as follows:

Y	F(Y)	L(Y)	Y	F(Y)	L(Y)	Y	F(Y)	L(Y)
8	0.0288	7.52	14	0.4154	2.40	20	0.8944	0.28
9	0.0552	6.55	15	0.5170	1.82	21	0.9304	0.18
10	0.0961	5.61	16	0.6154	1.33	22	0.9558	0.11
11	0.1538	4.70	17	0.7052	0.95	23	0.9730	0.06
12	0.2283	3.86	18	0.7825	0.65	24	0.9840	0.04
13	0.3171	3.08	19	0.8455	0.44	25	0.9909	0.02

The Inn is sensitive about the quality of service it provides alumni, so it estimates the cost of failing to honor a reservation is $325 in lost goodwill and explicit expenses.

a. What is the optimal overbooking limit, that is, the maximum reservations above the available 150 rooms that The Inn should accept?

b. If The Inn accepts 160 reservations, what is the probability The Inn will not be able to honor a reservation?

c. If the Inn accepts 165 reservations, what is the probability The Inn will be fully occupied?

d. If the Inn accepts 170 reservations, what is the expected total cost incurred due to bumped customers?

Q13.3* **(WAMB)** WAMB is a television station that has 25 thirty-second advertising slots during each evening. It is early January and the station is selling advertising for Sunday, March 24. They could sell all of the slots right now for $4,000 each, but, because on this particular Sunday the station is televising the Oscar ceremonies, there will be an opportunity to sell slots during the week right before March 24 for a price of $10,000. For now, assume that a slot not sold in advance *and* not sold during the last week is worthless to WAMB. To help make this decision, the salesforce has created the following probability distribution for last-minute sales:

Number of Slots, x	Probability Exactly x Slots Are Sold
8	0.00
9	0.05
10	0.10
11	0.15
12	0.20
13	0.10
14	0.10
15	0.10
16	0.10
17	0.05
18	0.05
19	0.00

a. How many slots should WAMB sell in advance?

b. In practice, there are companies willing to place standby advertising messages: if there is an empty slot available (i.e., this slot was not sold either in advance or during the last week), the standby message is placed into this slot. Since there is no guarantee that such a slot will be available, standby messages can be placed at a much lower cost. Now suppose that if a slot is not sold in advance *and* not sold during the last week, it will be used for a standby promotional message that costs advertisers $2,500. Now how many slots should WAMB sell in advance?

c. Suppose WAMB chooses a booking limit of 10 slots on advanced sales. In this case, what is the probability there will be slots left over for stand-by messages?

d. One problem with booking for March 24 in early January is that advertisers often withdraw their commitment to place the ad (typically this is a result of changes in promotional strategies; for example, a product may be found to be inferior or an ad may turn out to be ineffective). Because of such opportunistic behavior by advertisers, media companies often overbook advertising slots. WAMB estimates that in the past the number of withdrawn ads has a Poisson distribution with mean 9. Assume each withdrawn ad slot can still be sold at a standby price of $2,500 although the company misses an opportunity to sell these slots at $4,000 a piece. Any ad that was accepted by WAMB but cannot be accommodated (because there isn't a free slot) costs the company $10,000 in penalties. How many slots (at most) should be sold?

e. Over time, WAMB saw a steady increase in the number of withdrawn ads and decided to institute a penalty of $1,000 for withdrawals. (Actually, the company now requires a $1,000 deposit on any slot that is refunded only if WAMB is unable to provide a slot due to overbooking.) The expected number of withdrawn ads is expected to be cut in half (to only 4.5 slots). Now how many slots (at most) should be sold?

Q13.4 (**Designer Dress**) A fashion retailer in Santa Barbara, California, presents a new designer dress at one of the "by invitation only" fashion shows. After the show, the dress will be sold at the company's boutique store for $10,000 a piece. Demand at the boutique is limited due to the short time the dress remains fashionable and is estimated to be normal with mean 70 and standard deviation 40. There were only 100 dresses produced to maintain exclusivity and high price. It is the company's policy that all unsold merchandise is destroyed.

a. How many dresses remain unsold on average at the end of the season?

b. What is the retailer's expected revenue?

c. Fashion companies often sell a portion of new merchandise at exhibitions for a discount while the product is still "fresh" in the minds of the viewers. The company decides to increase revenues by selling a certain number of dresses at a greatly discounted price of $6,000 during the show. Later, remaining dresses will be available at the boutique store for a normal price of $10,000. Typically, all dresses offered at the show get sold, which, of course, decreases demand at the store: it is now normal with mean 40 and standard deviation 25. How many dresses should be sold at the show?

d. Given your decision in part c, what is expected revenue?

e. Given your decision in part c, how many dresses are expected to remain unsold?

Q13.5 (**Overbooking PHL-LAX**) On a given Philadelphia–Los Angeles flight, there are 200 seats. Suppose the ticket price is $475 on average and the number of passengers who reserve a seat but do not show up for departure is normally distributed with mean 30 and standard deviation 15. You decide to overbook the flight and estimate that the average loss from a passenger who will have to be bumped (if the number of passengers exceeds the number of seats) is $800.

a. What is the maximum number of reservations that should be accepted?

b. Suppose you allow 220 reservations. How much money do you expect to pay out in compensation to bumped passengers?

c. Suppose you allow 220 reservations. What is the probability that you will have to deal with bumped passengers?

Q13.6   (**PHL-LAX**) Consider the Philadelphia–Los Angeles flight discussed in Q13.5. Assume the available capacity is 200 seats and there is no overbooking. The high fare is $675 and the low fare is $375. Demand for the low fare is abundant while demand for the high fare is normally distributed with a mean of 80 and standard deviation 35.

    a. What is the probability of selling 200 reservations if you set an optimal protection level for the full fare?

    b. Suppose a protection level of 85 is established. What is the average number of lost high-fare passengers?

    c. Continue to assume a protection level of 85 is established. What is the expected number of unoccupied seats?

    d. Again assume a protection level of 85 is established. What is the expected revenue from the flight?

Q13.7   (**Park Hyatt**) Consider the example of the Park Hyatt Philadelphia discussed in the text. Recall that the full fare is $225, the expected full-fare demand is Poisson with mean 27.3, the discount fare is $159, and there are 118 king/queen rooms. Now suppose the cost of an occupied room is $45 per night. That cost includes the labor associated with prepping and cleaning a room, the additional utilities used and the wear and tear on the furniture and fixtures. Suppose the Park Hyatt wishes to maximize expected profit rather than expected revenue. What is the optimal protection level for the full fare?

Q13.8   (**The Wharton School**) Each year the admissions committee at The Wharton School receives a large number of applications for admission to the MBA program and they have to decide on the number of offers to make. Since some of the admitted students may decide to pursue opportunities other than the Wharton MBA program, the committee typically admits more students than the ideal class size of 720 students. You were asked to help the admissions committee estimate the appropriate number of people who should be offered admission. It is estimated that in the coming year the number of people who will not accept the offer from The Wharton School is normally distributed with mean 50 and standard deviation 21. Suppose for now that The Wharton School does not maintain a waiting list, that is all students are accepted or rejected.

    a. Suppose 750 students are admitted. What is the probability that the class size will be at least 720 students?

    b. It is hard to associate a monetary value with admitting too many students or admitting too few. However, there is a mutual agreement that it is about two times more expensive to have a student in excess of the ideal 720 than to have fewer students in the class. What is the appropriate number of students to admit?

    c. A waiting list mitigates the problem of having too few students since at the very last moment there is an opportunity to admit some students from the waiting list. Hence, the admissions committee revises its estimate: It claims that it is five times more expensive to have a student in excess of 720 than to have fewer students accept among the initial group of admitted students. What is your revised suggestion?

Q13.9   (**Air Cargo**) An air cargo company must decide how to sell its capacity. It could sell a portion of its capacity with long-term contracts. A long-term contract specifies that the buyer (the air cargo company's customer) will purchase a certain amount of cargo space at a certain price. The long-term contract rate is currently $1,875 per standard unit of space. If long-term contracts are not signed, then the company can sell its space on the spot market. The spot market price is volatile, but the expected future spot price is around $2,100. In addition, spot market demand is volatile: sometimes the company can find customers; other times it cannot on a short-term basis. Let's consider a specific flight on a specific date. The company's capacity is 58 units. Furthermore, the company expects that spot market demand is normally distributed with mean 65 and standard deviation 45. On average it costs the company $330 in fuel, handling, and maintenance to fly a unit of cargo.

    a. Suppose the company relied exclusively on the spot market, that is, it signed no long-term contracts. What would be the company's expected profit?

b. Suppose the company relied exclusively on long-term contracts. What would be the company's expected profit?

c. Suppose the company is willing to use both the long-term and the spot markets. How many units of capacity should the company sell with long-term contracts to maximize *revenue?*

d. Suppose the company is willing to use both the long-term and the spot markets. How many units of capacity should the company sell with long-term contracts to maximize *profit?*

Chapter 14

Supply Chain Coordination

Supply chain performance depends on the actions taken by all of the members in the supply chain; one weak link can negatively affect every other location in the chain. While everyone supports in principle the objective of optimizing the supply chain's performance, each firm's primary objective is the optimization of its own performance. And unfortunately, as shown in this chapter, self-serving behavior by each member of the supply chain can lead to less than optimal supply chain performance. In those situations, the firms in the supply chain can benefit from better operational coordination.

In this chapter we explore several challenges to supply chain coordination. The first challenge is the *bullwhip effect:* the tendency for demand variability to increase, often considerably, as you move up the supply chain (from retailer, to distributor, to factory, to raw material suppliers, etc.). Given that variability in any form is problematic for effective operations, it is clear the bullwhip effect is not a desirable phenomenon. We identify the causes of the bullwhip effect and propose several techniques to combat it.

A second challenge to supply chain coordination comes from the *incentive conflicts* among the supply chain's independent firms: An action that maximizes one firm's profit might not maximize another firm's profit. For example, one firm's incentive to stock more inventory, or to install more capacity, or to provide faster customer service, might not be the same as another firm's incentive, thereby creating some conflict between them. We use a stylized example of a supply chain selling sunglasses to illustrate the presence and consequences of incentive conflicts. Furthermore, we offer several remedies to this problem.

14.1 The Bullwhip Effect: Causes and Consequences

Figure 14.1 displays the percentage change in activity at three levels along a supply chain: the machine tool industry, the auto industry (which is a major customer for the machine tool industry), and the entire economy. The figure illustrates that automotive production is more volatile than the overall economy (which presumably matches well with automotive demand) and machine tool orders are even more volatile that automotive production.

Figure 14.2 displays a similar pattern, except these data are the percentage change in demand (in dollars) at three levels in the semiconductor supply chain: demand for personal computers is least volatile, demand for semiconductors has intermediate volatility, and demand for semiconductor manufacturing equipment is the most volatile.

FIGURE 14.1
Percentage Changes in Activity from 1961 to 1991 at Three Levels of the Machine Tool Supply Chain: GDP (solid line), Auto Industry Production Index (diamonds), and New Orders in the Machine Tool Industry (circles)

Source: Anderson, Fine, and Parker (1996).

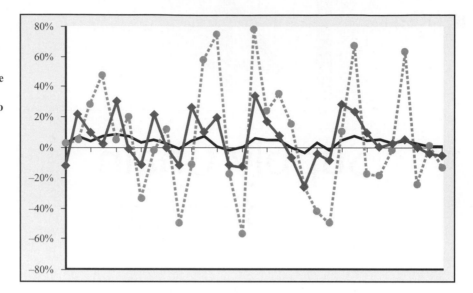

This increasing volatility pattern as you move up a supply chain (from retail, to distribution, to production, etc.) is called the *bullwhip effect* because it resembles the increased amplitude one observes as a whip is cracked. The term was coined by Procter & Gamble to describe what they observed in their diaper supply chain: They knew that final demand for diapers was reasonably stable (consumption by babies), but the demands requested on their diaper factories were extremely variable. Somehow variability was propagating up their supply chain.

The bullwhip effect does not enhance the performance of a supply chain: Increased volatility at any point in the supply chain can lead to product shortages, excess inventory (which leads to markdown expenses), low utilization of capacity, and/or poor quality. It impacts upstream stages in the supply chain, which must directly face the impact of variable demand, but it also indirectly affects downstream stages in the supply chain, which must cope with less reliable replenishments from upstream stages. In addition, as we see in Figures 14.1 and 14.2, the bullwhip effect is common. Hence, it is extremely important that its causes be identified so that cures, or at least mitigating strategies, can be developed.

Figures 14.1 and 14.2 provide real-world evidence of the bullwhip effect, but to understand the causes of the bullwhip effect it is helpful to bring it into the laboratory, that is, to study it in a controlled environment. Our controlled environment is a simple supply chain with two levels. The top level has a single supplier and the next level has 20 retailers, each with one store. Let's focus on a single product, a product in which daily demand has a Poisson distribution with mean 1.0 unit at each retailer. Hence, total consumer demand follows a Poisson distribution with mean 20.0 units. (Recall that the sum of Poisson distributions is also a Poisson distribution.) Figure 14.3 displays this supply chain.

Before we can identify the causes of the bullwhip effect, we must agree on how we will measure and identify it. We use the following definition:

The bullwhip effect is present in a supply chain if the variability of demand at one level of the supply chain is greater than the variability of demand at the next lower level in the supply chain, where variability is measured with the coefficient of variation.

For example, if the coefficient of variation in the supplier's demand (which is the sum of the retailer's orders) is greater than the coefficient of variation of the retailers' total demand, then the bullwhip effect is present in our supply chain.

FIGURE 14.2
Annual Percentage Changes in Demand (in dollars) at Three Levels of the Semiconductor Supply Chain: Personal Computers, Semiconductors, and Semiconductor Manufacturing Equipment

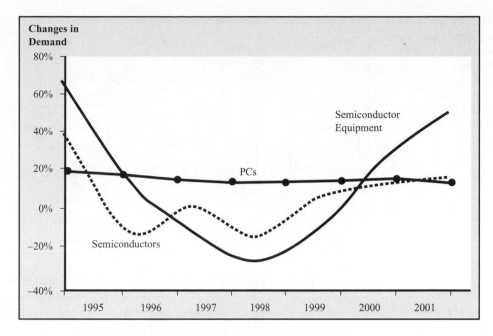

We already know how to evaluate the coefficient of variation in the retailers' total demand: Total demand is Poisson with mean 20, so the standard deviation of demand is $\sqrt{20} = 4.47$ and the coefficient of variation is $4.47/20 = 0.22$. The coefficient of variation of the supplier's demand (i.e., the coefficient of variation of the retailer's orders) depends on how the retailers place orders with the supplier.

Interestingly, while the way in which the retailers submit orders to the supplier can influence the standard deviation of the retailers' orders, it cannot influence the mean of the retailers' orders. To explain, due to the law of the conservation of matter, what goes into a retailer must equal what goes out of the retailer on average, otherwise the amount inside the retailer will not be stable: If more goes in than goes out, then the inventory at the retailer continues to grow, whereas if less goes in than goes out, then inventory at the retailer continues to fall. Hence, no matter how the retailers choose to order inventory from the supplier, the mean of the supplier's demand (i.e., the retailers' total order) equals the mean of the retailers' total demand. In this case the supplier's mean demand is 20 units per day, just as the mean of consumer demand is 20 units per day.

To evaluate the coefficient of variation in the supplier's demand, we still need to evaluate the standard deviation of the supplier's demand, which does depend on how the retailers submit orders. Let's first suppose that the retailers use an order-up-to policy to order replenishments from the supplier.

A key characteristic of an order-up-to policy is that the amount ordered in any period equals the amount demanded in the previous period (see Chapter 11). As a result, if all of the retailers use order-up-to policies with daily review, then their daily orders will match their daily demands. In other words, there is no bullwhip effect!

If all retailers use an order-up-to policy (with a constant order-up-to level S), then the standard deviation of the retailer's orders in one period equals the standard deviation of consumer demand in one period; that is, there is no bullwhip effect.

So we started our experiment with the intention of finding a cause of the bullwhip effect and discovered that the bullwhip effect need not occur in practice. It does not occur when every member at the same level of the supply chain implements a *"demand-pull"* inventory

FIGURE 14.3
**A Supply Chain with
One Supplier and 20
Retailers**
Daily demand at each
retailer follows a
Poisson distribution
with mean 1.0 unit.

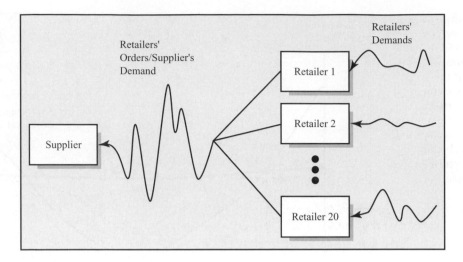

policy each period, that is, their orders each period exactly match their demands. Unfortunately, firms do not always adopt such "distortion free" inventory management. In fact, they may have good individual reasons to deviate from such behavior. It is those deviations that cause the bullwhip effect. We next identify five of them.

Order Synchronization

Suppose the retailers use order-up-to policies, but they order only once per week. They may choose to order weekly rather than daily because they incur a fixed cost per order, and therefore wish to reduce the number of orders they make. (See section 11.8.) Hence, at the start of each week, a retailer submits to the supplier an order that equals the retailer's demand from the previous week. But because we are interested in the supplier's *daily* demand, we need to know on which day of the week each retailer's week begins. For simplicity let's assume there are five days per week and the retailers are evenly spaced out throughout the week; that is, four of the 20 retailers submit orders on Monday, four submit orders on Tuesday, and so forth. Figure 14.4 displays a simulation outcome of this scenario. From the figure it appears that the variability in consumer demand is about the same as the variability in the supplier's demand. In fact, if we were to simulate many more periods and evaluate the standard deviations of those two data series, we would in fact discover that the standard deviation of consumer demand *exactly* equals the standard deviation of the supplier's demand. In other words, we still have not found the bullwhip effect.

But we made a critical assumption in our simulation. We assumed the retailers' order cycles were evenly spaced throughout the week: the same number of retailers order on Monday as on Wednesday as on Friday. But that is unlikely to be the case in practice: firms tend to prefer to submit their orders on a particular day of the week or a particular day of the month. To illustrate the consequence of this preference, let's suppose the retailers tend to favor the beginning and the end of the week: nine retailers order on Monday, five on Tuesday, one on Wednesday, two on Thursday, and three on Friday. Figure 14.5 displays the simulation outcome with that scenario.

We have discovered the bullwhip effect! The supplier's daily demand is clearly much more variable than consumer demand. For this particular sample, the coefficient of variation of the supplier's demand is 0.78 even though the coefficient of variation of consumer demand is only 0.19: the supplier's demand is about four times more variable than consumer demand! And this is not the result of a particularly strange demand pattern; that is, the same qualitative result is obtained if a very long interval of time is simulated. In fact, for comparison, you can note that the consumer demand in Figure 14.5 is identical to consumer demand in Figure 14.4.

FIGURE 14.4
Simulated Daily Consumer Demand (solid line) and Daily Supplier Demand (circles)
Supplier demand equals the sum of the retailers' orders.

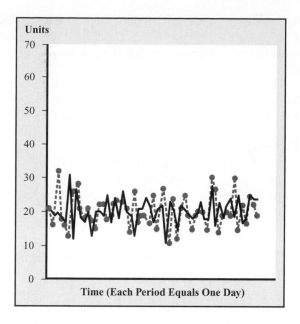

Not only do we now observe the bullwhip effect, we have just identified one of its causes, *order synchronization:* If the retailers' order cycles become even a little bit synchronized, that is, they tend to cluster around the same time period, then the bullwhip effect emerges. While the retailers order on average to match average consumer demand, due to their order synchronization there will be periods in which they order considerably more than the average and periods in which they order considerably less than the average, thereby imposing additional demand volatility on the poor supplier.

Order synchronization also can be observed higher up in the supply chain. For example, suppose the supplier implements a materials requirement planning (MRP) system to manage the replenishment of component inventory. (This is a computer system that determines

FIGURE 14.5
Simulated Daily Consumer Demand (solid line) and Supplier Demand (circles) When Retailers Order Weekly
Nine retailers order on Monday, five on Tuesday, one on Wednesday, two on Thursday, and three on Friday.

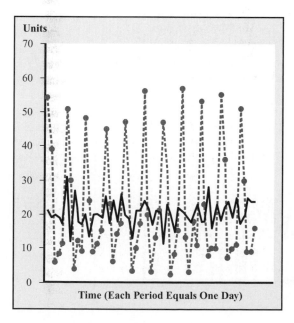

the quantity and timing of component inventory replenishments based on future demand forecasts and production schedules.) Many firms implement their MRP systems on a monthly basis. Furthermore, many implement their systems to generate replenishment orders in the first week of the month. So a supplier's supplier may receive a flood of orders for its product during the first week of the month and relatively little demand later in the month. This has been called *MRP jitters* or the *hockey stick phenomenon* (the graph of demand over the month looks like a series of hockey sticks, a flat portion and then a spike up).

Order Batching

We argued that the retailers might wish to order weekly rather than daily to avoid incurring excessive ordering costs. This economizing on ordering costs can also be achieved by *order batching:* each retailer orders so that each order is an integer multiple of some batch size. For example, now let's consider a scenario in which each retailer uses a batch size of 15 units. This batch size could represent a case or a pallet or a full truckload. Let's call it a pallet. By ordering only in increments of 15 units, that is, in pallet quantities, the retailer can facilitate the movement of product around the warehouse and the loading of product onto trucks. How does the retailer decide when to order a pallet? A natural rule is to order a batch whenever the accumulated demand since the last order exceeds the batch size. Therefore, in this example, every 15th demand triggers an order for a pallet. Naturally, ordering in batches economizes on the number of orders the retailer must make:

$$\text{Average number of periods between orders} = \frac{\text{Batch size}}{\text{Mean demand per period}}$$

In this situation the retailer orders on average every $15/1 = 15$ periods.

Figure 14.6 displays a simulation outcome with batch ordering. Because the retailers only order in pallet quantities, the supplier's demand equals a multiple of 15: on some days there are no orders, on most days one pallet is ordered by some retailer, on a few days there are up to five pallets ordered.

We again observe the bullwhip effect: The variability of the supplier's demand is considerably greater than the variability of consumer demand. To be specific, the supplier's demand has a coefficient of variation equal to 0.87 in this example, which contrasts with the

FIGURE 14.6
Simulated Daily Consumer Demand (solid line) and Supplier Demand (circles) When Retailers Order in Batches of 15 Units
Every 15th demand, a retailer orders one batch from the supplier that contains 15 units.

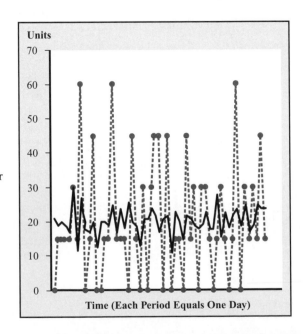

0.19 coefficient of variation for consumer demand. Thus, we have identified a second cause of the bullwhip effect, *order batching:* The bullwhip effect emerges when retailers order in batches that contain more than one unit (e.g., pallet quantities or full truckload quantities). Again, the retailers' total order on average equals average consumer demand, but not the variability of their orders. This occurs because, due to the batch quantity requirement, the retailer's order quantity in a period generally does not match the retailer's demand in that period: it tends to be either greater than or less than consumer demand. In other words, the batch quantity requirement forces the retailer to order in a way that is more variable than consumer demand even though on average it equals consumer demand.

Trade Promotions and Forward Buying

Suppliers in some industries offer their retailers *trade promotions:* a discount off the wholesale price that is available only for a short period of time. Trade promotions cause retailers to buy on-deal, also referred to as a *forward buy,* which means they purchase much more than they need to meet short-term needs. Trade promotions are a key tool for a supplier when the supplier wants to engage in the practice of *channel stuffing:* providing incentives to induce retailers (the channel) to hold more inventory than needed for the short term. Because with trade promotions many retailers purchase at the same time (order synchronization) and because they order in large quantities (order batching), trade promotions are capable of creating an enormous bullwhip. Let's illustrate this with another simple scenario.

Suppose a supplier sells chicken noodle soup; let's consider one of the supplier's retailers. The supplier's regular price of chicken noodle soup is $20 per case, but twice a year the supplier offers an 8 percent discount for cases purchased during a one week period, for example, the first week in January and the first week in July. The retailer sells on average 100 cases of soup per week and likes to carry a one-week safety stock, that is, the retailer does not let its inventory fall below 100 cases. To avoid unnecessary complications, let's further assume that the retailer's order at the beginning of a week is delivered immediately and demand essentially occurs at a constant rate. The retailer's annual holding cost rate is 24 percent of the dollar value of its inventory.

We now compare the retailer's profit with two different ordering strategies. With the first strategy, the retailer orders every week throughout the year; with the second strategy, the retailer orders only twice per year during the trade promotion. We call the first strategy *demand-pull* because the retailer matches orders to current demand. The second strategy is called *forward buying* because each order covers a substantial portion of future demand. Figure 14.7 displays the retailer's on-hand inventory over the period of one year with both ordering strategies.

With demand-pull, the retailer's inventory "saw-tooths" between 200 and 100 units, with an average of 150 units. With forward buying, the retailer's inventory also "saw-tooths" but now between 2,700 and 100, with an average of 1,400 units.

Let's now evaluate the retailer's total cost with each strategy. With demand-pull, the retailer's average inventory is 150 units. During the two promotion weeks, the average inventory in dollars is $150 \times \$18.4 = \$2,760$ because the promotion price is $\$20 \times (1 - 0.08) = \$18.40$. During the remaining 50 weeks of the year, the average inventory in dollars is $150 \times \$20 = \$3,000$. The weighted average inventory in dollars is

$$\frac{(\$2,760 \times 2) + (\$3,000 \times 50)}{52} = \$2,991$$

The purchased cost during the year is

$$(\$20 \times 100 \times 50) + (\$18.40 \times 100 \times 2) = \$103,680$$

FIGURE 14.7

On-Hand Inventory of Chicken Noodle Soup at a Retailer under Two Procurement Strategies

The first strategy, called demand-pull (lower sawtooth), has the retailer ordering 100 cases each week. The second strategy, called forward buying (upper sawtooth), has the retailer ordering 2,600 cases twice per year.

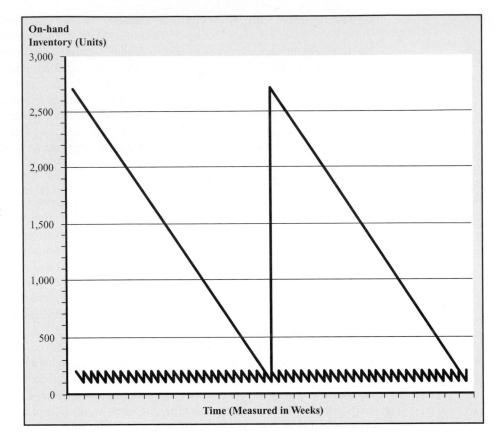

because 100 units are purchased at the regular price over 50 weeks of the year and 100 units are purchased at the discount price during the two promotion weeks of the year. The demand-pull strategy's total cost is $2,991 + $103,680 = $104,398.

The analysis of the forward buying strategy is analogous to the demand-pull strategy. A summary is provided in Table 14.1.

From Table 14.1 we see that forward buying is more profitable to the retailer than weekly ordering with demand-pull: the forward buying total cost is 2.4 percent less than the demand-pull strategy, which is a considerable amount in the grocery industry. We can conclude that a relatively small trade promotion can rationally cause a retailer to purchase a significant volume of product. In fact, the retailer may wish to purchase enough product to cover its demand until the supplier's next promotion. In contrast, it is highly unlikely that an 8 percent discount would induce consumers to purchase a six-month supply of chicken noodle soup; rational retailers are more price sensitive than consumers.

The impact of the trade promotion on the supplier is not good. Imagine the supplier sells to many retailers, all taking advantage of the supplier's trade promotion. Hence, the retailers' orders become synchronized (they order during the same trade promotion weeks of the year) and they order in very large batch quantities (much more than is needed to cover their immediate needs). In other words, trade promotions combine order synchronization and order batching to generate a significant bullwhip effect.

Interestingly, with the forward buying strategy, the retailer does not ever purchase at the regular price. Hence, if the supplier were to offer the retailer the $18.40 price through-

TABLE 14.1
Analysis of Total Holding and Procurement Costs for Two Ordering Strategies
In demand-pull the retailer orders every week; in forward buying, the retailer orders twice per year during the supplier's trade promotions.

	Demand-Pull	Forward Buying
Annual purchase (units)	5,200	5,200
Average inventory (units)	150	1,400
Average inventory	$2,991	$25,760
Holding cost	$718	$6,182
Units purchased at regular price	5,000	0
Units purchased at discount price	200	5,200
Total puchase cost	$103,680	$95,680
Total holding plus procurement cost	$104,398	$101,862

out the year (instead of just during the two trade promotion weeks), then the supplier's revenue would be the same. However, the retailer could then order on a weekly basis, thereby reducing the retailer's holding cost. It is not too difficult to calculate that the retailer's total cost in this constant-price scenario is $96,342, which is 5.4 percent less than the forward buying cost and 7.7 percent less than the original demand-pull strategy. Thus, due to forward buying, the supply chain's costs are about 5 percent higher than they need be without providing any benefit to the firms in the supply chain (the retailer surely does not benefit from holding extra inventory and the supplier does not benefit from higher revenue).

While our analysis has been with a theoretical supply chain of chicken noodle soup, Campbell Soup would concur that this analysis is consistent with their experience. For example, Figure 14.8 presents data on one retailer's purchases of Campbell's Chicken Noodle Soup over the course of the year. This product is traditionally promoted in January and June even though consumers primarily eat soup during the winter months.[1] As a result, this retailer requires substantial storage space to hold its forward buys. Other retailers may lack the financial and physical capabilities to be so aggressive with forward buying, but they nevertheless will take advantage of trade promotions to some extent. This is confirmed by Figure 14.9, which shows total consumption and shipments of Campbell's Chicken Noodle Soup over a one-year period: Shipments are clearly more volatile than consumption, thereby indicating the presence of the bullwhip effect.

Due to the trade promotion spike in demand in January of every year, Campbell Soup must put its chicken deboning plants on overtime from September through October, its canning plant works overtime November through December, and its shipping facility works overtime throughout January. All of these activities add to production costs, and all because of a spike in demand caused by the company's own pricing.

The negative effects of forward buying also are not limited to the supplier's operational efficiency. Some retailers purchase on-deal with no intention of selling those units to consumers. Instead, they intend on selling to other retailers that cannot take advantage of the deal either due to physical or capital constraints. Those retailers that sell to other retailers are called *diverters* and that practice is called *diversion*. In addition to extra handling (which reduces quality and leads to spoilage), diversion needlessly adds to transportation costs. It also should be mentioned that diversion occurs when a supplier attempts to lower its price in one region of the country while maintaining a higher price in another region, possibly because the supplier faces a regional competitor in the former region. That form

[1]Campbell's traditionally raises the price of its Chicken Noodle Soup during the summer, so the June buy avoids the imminent price increase. While this is technically not a promotion, the analysis is quite similar and the effect is essentially the same as a trade promotion.

FIGURE 14.8
One Retailer's
Purchases of
Campbell's Chicken
Noodle Soup over
One Year

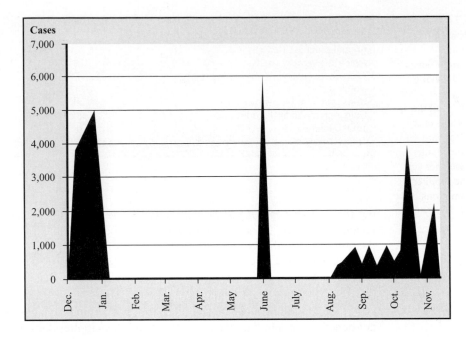

of diversion was greatly reduced in the grocery industry when several national grocery chains emerged (Kroger, Safeway, etc.) in the late 80s and early 90s. Those national chains insisted that they would receive a single low price from their suppliers, thereby preventing regional price discrimination.

Reactive and Overreactive Ordering

So far in our experimental supply chains we have assumed the retailer knows what expected demand is in each period even though demand could be stochastic. This is a reasonable assumption for well-established products, such as chicken noodle soup. But for many other products, a retailer might not know expected demand with certainty. And this uncertainty creates a complication for the retailer's inventory management.

Suppose the retailer observes higher than usual demand in one period. How should the retailer react to this observation? One explanation for this outlier is that it occurred merely due to random fluctuation. In that case the retailer probably should not change her expectation of future demand and so not change how she manages inventory. But there is another explanation for the outlier: It could signal that demand has shifted, suggesting the product's actual expected demand is higher than previously thought. If that explanation is believed, then the retailer should increase her order quantity to cover the additional future demand, otherwise she will quickly stock out. In other words, it is rational for a retailer to increase her order quantity when faced with an unusually high demand observation. Analogously, the retailer should decrease her order quantity when faced with an unusually low demand observation because future demand may be weaker than previously thought. Hence, when a retailer cannot be sure that demand is stable over time, a retailer should rationally react aggressively to possible shifts in demand.

These reactions by the retailer contribute to the bullwhip effect. Suppose the retailer's high-demand observation is really due to random fluctuation. As a result, future demand will not be higher than expected even though the retailer reacted to this information by ordering more inventory. Hence, the retailer will need to reduce future orders so that the excess inventory just purchased can be drawn down. Ordering more than needed now and less

FIGURE 14.9
Total Shipments to Retailers and Consumption by Consumers of Campbell's Chicken Noodle Soup over a One-Year Period (roughly July to July)

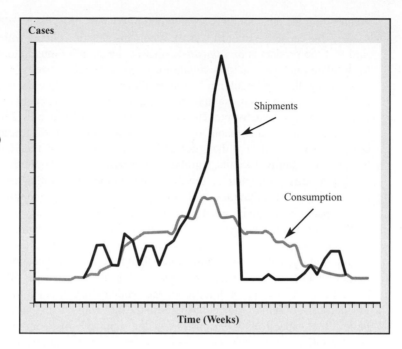

than needed later implies the retailer's orders are more volatile than the retailer's demand, which is the bullwhip effect.

While it can be rational to react to extreme demand observations, it is also human nature to *over*react to such information, that is, to act too aggressively. For example, a high-demand signal may rationally warrant a 125 percent increase in a retailer's order quantity, but a retailer may "play it safe" and order 150 percent more just in case. Unfortunately, the retailer might not realize the consequence of this action. Suppose the retailer is replenished by a wholesaler, who is replenished by a distributor, who is replenished by a supplier. The retailer sees a blip in demand and so reacts with a larger order. The retailer's order is the wholesaler's demand, and so the wholesaler sees an even larger blip in demand. The wholesaler reacts and increases his order, which surprises the distributor. So the distributor reacts with an increased order, so large that the supplier only concludes that demand has accelerated substantially. In other words, overreactions can propagate up the supply chain, thereby generating a bullwhip effect.

Shortage Gaming

Under normal circumstances, a retailer will only order as much inventory as needed to cover short-term needs, in particular, the inventory needed to cover demand until the next possible replenishment. But it is not always known when the next possible replenishment will occur. If demand is increasing and capacity is constrained, then a retailer may anticipate a long wait for the next possible replenishment. A rational response is to order plenty of inventory, while inventory is potentially available, in case future replenishment opportunities do not materialize.

Imagine a supply chain with one supplier, a hot-selling product, limited capacity, and multiple retailers. Each retailer knows capacity is tight: While it is possible the supplier will have enough capacity to fill all of the retailers' orders, it is quite likely the supplier will not have enough capacity. The retailers also know that if the supplier runs out of capacity, then the supplier will allocate that scarce capacity to the retailers. The supplier may very well use a proportional allocation scheme: a retailer's share of the capacity is proportional to the retailer's order quantity relative to the total order quantity. For example, if a retailer orders

10 units and the other retailers order a total of 40 units, then the retailer will get a one-fifth share of the capacity $(10 / (10 + 40))$. When this situation occurs with a product, it is often said that the product is *on allocation;* that is, the supplier must allocate capacity because the total amount demanded by retailers exceeds available capacity.

Knowing that a product may be put on allocation, what should a retailer's ordering strategy be? Returning to our example, the retailer wants 10 units but anticipates only one-fifth of that order will be delivered. Hence, if 10 units are ordered, only 2 units will be received, far less than the retailer wants. An obvious solution is to instead order 50 units: if the retailer receives one-fifth of the order, and 50 units are ordered, then the retailer will receive the desired quantity, 10 units. But the other retailers are probably thinking the same thing. So they too may order much more than needed in anticipation of receiving only a fraction of their order. This behavior of ordering more than needed due to the anticipation of a possible capacity shortage is called *shortage gaming* or *order inflation.*

Shortage gaming can result in quite a mess for the supply chain. Some retailers may receive far less than they could sell (because they did not inflate their order enough) while others might actually receive much more than they can sell (because they inflated their order too much). For instance, the retailer in our example can order 50 units and actually receive 12 units, still only a fraction of the retailer's order, but 2 units more than wanted. Furthermore, order inflation contributes to the bullwhip effect: Once a supplier's customers believe that capacity may be constrained, the supplier's customers may inflate their orders substantially, thereby creating excessive volatility in the supplier's demand. Interestingly, this may occur even if there is enough capacity to satisfy the retailers' desired quantity; all that is needed to create order inflation is the belief among the retailers that they may not get their full order.

A supplier also can exacerbate the bullwhip effect with her own actions via shortage gaming. For example, suppose a supplier allows retailers to return unsold inventory. This was a common practice in the PC industry: Suppliers such as IBM would allow distributors to return any PC at any time for a full refund and IBM would even pay for shipping costs. With little risk associated with having too much inventory, distributors focused on the risk of having too little inventory, especially if they had less inventory than they wanted due to a capacity shortage (which was common). Hence, distributors actively participated in shortage gaming.

In the PC industry it was also common to allow distributors to submit orders that could be canceled without penalty before the order was delivered. In effect, the distributor would be allowed to return an order even before receiving the order. Again, this practice mitigated the distributors' risk of excess ordering, so the focus turned to the risk of not receiving enough product. Distributors would submit excessively large orders knowing full well that they would later cancel a portion of their order. The amount that they would later cancel would depend on how well the product was selling and the available capacity. Not surprisingly, these *phantom orders,* as they are called in the industry (orders that are submitted even though a larger portion of them will disappear, like a phantom), create a bullwhip effect and substantial headaches for the supplier: the supplier receives plenty of orders but does not know what fraction of them will materialize into actual accepted deliveries.

14.2 Bullwhip Effect: Mitigating Strategies

This section discusses how firms have changed their business practices to combat the bullwhip effect. In the grocery industry, many of these changes came with the *Efficient Consumer Response* initiative that was initiated in the early 1990s. The claim was that this set of business practices, if fully implemented, could reduce U.S. grocery industry costs by $30 billion.

Not surprisingly, effective change begins with an understanding of root causes. In the case of the bullwhip effect, we identified five causes in the previous section: order synchronization, order batching, trade promotions, overreactive ordering, and shortage gaming.

Sharing Information

Greater information sharing about actual demand between the stages of the supply chain is an intuitive step toward reducing the bullwhip effect. As we saw in the simulations reported in the previous section, the pattern of retail orders may have very little resemblance to the pattern of retail demand. As a result, when retail orders are fluctuating wildly, it can be extremely difficult for a supplier to correctly forecast demand trends and it is not surprising at all if the supplier overreacts to those data. By giving the supplier frequent access to actual consumer demand data, the supplier can better assess trends in demand and plan accordingly.

But sharing current demand data is often not enough to mitigate the bullwhip effect. Demand also can be influenced by retailer actions on pricing, merchandizing, promotion, advertising, and assortment planning. As a result, a supplier cannot accurately forecast sales for a product unless the supplier knows what kind of treatment that product will receive from its retailers. Without that information, the supplier may not build sufficient capacity for a product that the retailers want to support, or the supplier may build too much capacity of a product that generates little interest among the retailers. Both errors may be prevented if the supplier and retailers share with each other their intentions. This sharing process is often labeled *Collaborative Planning, Forecasting, and Replenishment,* or CPFR for short.

While it is quite useful for a retailer to share information with its upstream suppliers, it also can be useful for a supplier to share information on availability with its downstream retailers. For example, a supplier may be aware of a component shortage that will lead to a shortage in a product that a retailer intends to promote. By sharing that information, the retailer could better allocate its promotional effort. It also can be useful to share information when the supplier knows that a capacity shortage will not occur, thereby preventing some shortage gaming.

Smoothing the Flow of Product

It is important to recognize that information sharing is quite helpful for reducing the bullwhip effect, but it is unlikely to eliminate it. The bullwhip effect is also a result of physical limitations in the supply chain like order synchronization and order batching.

Order synchronization can be reduced by eliminating reasons why retailers may wish to order at the same time (such as trade promotions). Coordinating with retailers to schedule them on different order cycles also helps.

Reducing order batching means smaller and more frequent replenishments. Unfortunately, this objective conflicts with the desire to control ordering, transportation, and handling costs. The fixed cost associated with each order submitted to the supplier can be reduced with the use of computerized automatic replenishment systems for deciding when and how much to order. In addition, some kind of standards technology, like *electronic data interchange* (EDI), is needed so that orders can be transmitted in an electronic format that can be received by the supplier.

Transportation costs can conflict with small batches because the cost of a truck shipment depends little on the amount that is shipped. Hence, there are strong incentives to ship in full truckloads. (In transportation, the main costs include the capital expenditure for equipment, labor, and maintenance, the latter is highly correlated with distanced traveled.) There are also economies of scale in handling inventory, which is why it is cheaper to ship in cases than in individual units, and cheaper to move pallets rather than individual cases. So the trick is to find a way to have more frequent replenishments while still controlling handling and transportation costs.

One solution is for multiple retailers to consolidate their orders with a supplier through a distributor. By ordering from a distributor rather than directly from a supplier, a retailer can receive the supplier's products on a more frequent basis and still order in full truckloads. The difference is that with direct ordering the retailer is required to fill a truck with the supplier's products whereas by going through a distributor the retailer can fill a truck with product from multiple suppliers that sell through that distributor.

Eliminating Pathological Incentives

As we saw in the previous section, trade promotions provide an extremely strong incentive for a retailer to forward buy and forward buying creates a substantial bullwhip effect. A constant wholesale price completely eliminates this incentive. Furthermore, a constant wholesale price might not even cost the supplier too much in revenue, especially if the majority of the retailers never purchased at the regular price.

However, there are perceived negatives associated with eliminating trade promotions. Suppliers began using trade promotions to induce retailers to offer consumer promotions with the objective of using these consumer promotions to increase final consumer demand. And, in fact, trade promotion did succeed somewhat along these lines: Most retailers would cut the retail price during a trade promotion, thereby passing on at least a portion of the deal to consumers. Hence, if trade promotions can no longer be used to induce retailers to conduct consumer promotions, and if consumer promotions are deemed to be necessary, then suppliers must develop some other tool to generate the desired consumer promotions.

Generous returns and order cancellation policies are the other self-inflicted pathological incentives because they lead to shortage gaming and phantom ordering. One solution is to either eliminate these policies or at least make them less generous. For example, the supplier could agree to only partially refund returned units or the supplier could limit the number of units that can be returned or the supplier could limit the time in which they can be returned. The supplier also could impose an order cancellation penalty or require a nonrefundable deposit when orders are submitted.

Shortage gaming also can be eliminated by forgoing retailer orders altogether. To explain how this could work, suppose a supplier knows that a product will be on allocation, which means that each retailer will want more than they can receive. So the supplier does not even bother collecting retailer orders. Instead, the supplier could announce an allocation to each retailer proportional to the retailer's past sales. In the auto industry this scheme is often called *turn-and-earn:* if a dealer turns a vehicle (i.e., sells a vehicle), then the dealer earns the right to another vehicle. Turn-and-earn allocation achieves several objectives: it ensures the supplier's entire capacity is allocated; it allocates more capacity to the higher selling retailers, which makes intuitive sense; and it motivates retailers to sell more of the supplier's product. For example, in the auto industry, a supplier can use the allocation of a hot-selling vehicle to encourage a dealer to increase its sales effort for all vehicles so that the dealer can defend its allocation. While this extra motivation imposed on dealers is probably beneficial to the auto manufacturers, it is debatable whether it benefits dealers.

Using Vendor-Managed Inventory

Proctor & Gamble and Wal-Mart were among the first companies to identify the bullwhip effect and to take multiple significant steps to mitigate it. (Campbell's Soup was another early innovator in North America.) The set of changes they initiated are often collected under the label *Vendor-Managed Inventory,* or VMI for short. While many firms have now implemented their own version of VMI, VMI generally includes the following features:

- The retailer no longer decides when and how much inventory to order. Instead, the supplier decides the timing and quantity of shipments to the retailer. The firms mutually agree on an objective that the supplier will use to guide replenishment decisions (e.g., a fill rate target). The supplier's "reach" into the retailer can vary: In some applications, the supplier merely manages product in the retailer's distribution center and the retailer retains responsibility of replenishments from the distribution center to the stores. In other applications, the supplier manages inventory all the way down to the retailer's shelves. The scope of the supplier's reach also can vary by application: Generally, the supplier only controls decisions for its own products, but in some cases the supplier assumes responsibility for an entire category, which generally includes making replenishment decisions for the supplier's competitor's products on behalf of the retailer.

- If the supplier is going to be responsible for replenishment decisions, the supplier also needs information. Hence, with VMI the retailer shares with the supplier demand data (e.g., distribution center withdrawals and/or retail store point-of-sale data, POS data for short). The supplier uses those data as input to an automatic replenishment system; that is, a computer program that decides the timing and quantity of replenishments for each product and at each location managed. In addition to normal demand movements, the supplier must be made aware of potential demand shifts that can be anticipated. For example, if the retailer is about to conduct a consumer promotion that will raise the base level of demand by a factor of 20, then the supplier needs to be aware of when that promotion will occur. These computer-guided replenishment systems are often referred to as *continuous replenishment* or *continuous product replenishment.* However, these are somewhat misnomers since product tends to be replenished more frequently but not continuously.

- The supplier and the retailer eliminate trade promotions. This is surely necessary if the retailer is going to give the supplier control over replenishment decisions because a retailer will not wish to forgo potential forward-buying profits. Hence, the adoption of VMI usually includes some agreement that the supplier will maintain a stable price and that price will be lower than the regular price to compensate the retailer for not purchasing on deal.

The innovations included in VMI are complementary and are effective at reducing the bullwhip effect. For example, transferring replenishment control from the retailer to the supplier allows the supplier to control the timing of deliveries, thereby reducing, if not eliminating, any order synchronization effects. VMI also allows a supplier to ship in smaller lots than the retailer would order, thereby combating the order-batching cause of the bullwhip. For example, prior to the adoption of VMI, many of Campbell Soup's customers would order three to five pallets of each soup type at a time, where a pallet typically contains about 200 cases. They would order in multiple pallets to avoid the cost of frequent ordering. With VMI Campbell Soup decided to ship fast-moving soups in pallet quantities and slower moving varieties in mixed pallet quantities (e.g., in one-half- or one-quarter-pallet quantities). Frequent ordering was not an issue for Campbell Soup because they implemented an automatic replenishment system. But Campbell Soup was still concerned about handling and transportation costs. As a result, with VMI Campbell Soup continued to ship in full truckloads, which are about 20 pallets each. However, with VMI each of the 20 pallets could be a different product, whereas before VMI there would be fewer than 20 products loaded onto each truck (because more than one pallet would be ordered for each product). Hence, with VMI it was possible to maintain full truckloads while ordering each product more frequently because each product was ordered in smaller quantities.

In some cases VMI also assists with order batching because it allows the supplier to combine shipments to multiple retailers. Before VMI it would be essentially impossible for two retailers to combine their order to construct a full truckload. But if the supplier has a VMI relationship with both retailers, then the supplier can combine their orders onto a truck as long as the retailers are located close to each other. By replenishing each retailer in smaller than full truckload batches, the supplier reduces the bullwhip effect while still maintaining transportation efficiency.

VMI also can combat the overreaction cause of the bullwhip effect. Because demand information is shared, the supplier is less likely to overreact to changes in the demand. In addition, because VMI is implemented with computer algorithms that codify replenishment strategies, a VMI system is not as emotionally fickle as a human buyer.

While VMI changes many aspects of the supply chain relationship between a supplier and retailer, some aspects of that relationship are generally not disturbed. For example, VMI eliminates trade promotions, but it does not necessarily seek to eliminate consumer promotions. Consumer promotions also can contribute to the bullwhip effect, but there are several reasons why they do not tend to increase volatility as much as trade promotions: Not every retailer runs a consumer promotion at the same time, so order synchronization is not as bad as with a trade promotion, and consumers do not forward buy as much as retailers. In addition, while some companies are willing to forgo trade promotions, only a few are willing to forgo consumer promotions as well: Consumer promotions are viewed as a competitive necessity.

14.3   Incentive Conflicts in a Sunglass Supply Chain

The bullwhip effect deteriorates supply chain performance by propagating demand variability up the supply chain. But optimal supply chain performance is also not guaranteed in the absence of the bullwhip effect. This section considers the incentive conflicts that can occur between two firms in a supply chain even without the presence of the bullwhip effect. We illustrate these conflicts with a detailed example based on a supply chain for sunglasses.

Zamatia Ltd. (pronounced zah-MAH-tee-ah, to the cognoscenti) is an Italian upscale maker of eyewear. UV Inc., short for Umbra Visage, is one of their retailers in the United States. To match UV's stylish assortment, UV only operates small boutique stores located in trendy locations. We focus on one of their stores located in Miami Beach, Florida. Zamatia manufactures its sunglasses in Europe and Asia, so the replenishment lead time to the United States is long. Furthermore, the selling season for sunglasses is short and styles change significantly from year to year. As a result, UV receives only one delivery of Zamatia glasses before each season. As with any fashion product, some styles sell out quickly while others are left over at the end of the season.

Consider Zamatia's entry level sunglass for the coming season, the Bassano. UV purchases each one of those pairs of sunglasses from Zamatia for $75 and retails them for $115. Zamatia's production and shipping costs per pair is $35. At the end of the season, UV generally needs to offer deep discounts to sell remaining inventory; UV estimates that it will only be able to fetch $25 per leftover Bassano at the Miami Beach store. UV's Miami Beach store believes this season's demand for the Bassano can be represented by a normal distribution with a mean of 250 and a standard deviation of 125.

UV's procurement quantity decision can be made with the use of the newsvendor model (Chapter 9). Let Q be UV's order quantity. UV's underage cost per unit is $C_u = \$115 - \$75 = \$40$, that is, each lost sale due to underordering costs UV the opportunity cost of $40. UV's overage cost per unit is $C_o = \$75 - \$25 = \$50$; the consequence of leftover inventory is substantial. UV's critical ratio is

$$\frac{C_u}{C_o + C_u} = \frac{40}{50 + 40} = \frac{4}{9} = 0.4444$$

Hence, to maximize expected profit, UV should choose an order quantity such that 44.4 percent is the probability there is some leftover inventory and 55.6 percent is the probability there is a stockout.

From the Standard Normal Distribution Function Table, we find $\Phi(-0.14) = 0.4433$ and $\Phi(-0.13) = 0.4483$, so the optimal z-statistic is -0.13 and the optimal order quantity is

$$Q = \mu + z \times \sigma = 250 - 0.13 \times 125 = 234$$

Using the equations and procedures described in Chapter 9, we also are able to evaluate several performance measures for UV's store:

Expected sales (units) = 192

Expected leftover inventory = 42

Expected profit = $5,580

Zamatia's profit from selling the Bassano at UV's Miami Beach store is $234 \times \$40 = \$9,360$, where 234 is the number of Bassano sunglasses that UV purchases and $40 is Zamatia's gross margin ($75 − $35 = $40).

While Zamatia might be quite pleased with this situation (it does earn $9,360 relative to UV's $5,580), it should not be. The total supply chain's profit is $14,940, but it could be higher. To explain, suppose we choose an order quantity to maximize the supply chain's profit, that is, the combined expected profits of Zamatia and UV. In other words, what order quantity would a firm choose if the firm owned both Zamatia and UV? We call this the *supply chain optimal quantity* because it is the quantity that maximizes the *integrated supply chain.*

We can still use the newsvendor model to evaluate the supply chain's order quantity decision and performance measures. Each lost sale costs the supply chain the difference between the retail price and the production cost, $115 − $35 = $80; that is, the supply chain's underage cost is $C_u = 80$. Each leftover Bassano costs the supply chain the difference between the production cost and the salvage value, $35 − $25 = $10; that is, the supply chain's overage cost is $C_o = 10$. The supply chain's critical ratio is

$$\frac{C_u}{C_o + C_u} = \frac{80}{10 + 80} = 0.8889$$

The appropriate z-statistic for that critical ratio is 1.23 because $\Phi(1.22) = 0.8888$ and $\Phi(1.23) = 0.8907$. The supply chain's expected profit-maximizing order quantity is then

$$Q = \mu + z \times \sigma = 250 + 1.23 \times 125 = 404$$

which is considerably higher than UV's order of 234 units. The supply chain's performance measures can then be evaluated assuming the supply chain optimal order quantity, 404 units:

Expected sales (units) = 243

Expected leftover inventory = 161

Expected profit = $17,830

Thus, while Zamatia and UV currently earn an expected profit of $14,940, their supply chain could enjoy an expected profit that is about 19 percent higher, $17,830.

Why does the current supply chain perform significantly worse than it could? The obvious answer is that UV does not order enough Bassanos: UV orders 234 of them, but the supply chain's optimal order quantity is 404 units. But why doesn't UV order enough? Because UV is acting in its own self interest to maximize its own profit. To explain further, UV must pay Zamatia $75 per sunglass and so UV acts as if the cost to produce each Bassano is $75, not the actual $35. From UV's perspective, it does not matter if the actual production cost is $35, $55, or even $0; its "production cost" is $75. UV correctly recognizes that it only makes $40 on each sale but loses $50 on each leftover sunglass. Hence, UV is prudent to order cautiously.

UV's trepidation with respect to ordering is due to a phenomenon called *double marginalization*. Because UV's profit margin ($40) is one of two profit margins in the supply chain, and necessarily less than the supply chain's total profit margin ($80), UV orders less than the supply chain optimal quantity. In other words, because UV only earns a portion ($40) of the total benefit of each sale ($80), UV is not willing to purchase as much inventory as would be optimal for the supply chain.

This example illustrates an important finding:

> *Even if every firm in a supply chain chooses actions to maximize its own expected profit, the total profit earned in the supply chain may be less than the entire supply chain's maximum profit.*

In other words, rational and self-optimizing behavior by each member of the supply chain does not necessarily lead to optimal supply chain performance. So what can be done about this? That is the question we explore next.

There is an obvious solution to get UV to order more Bassanos: Zamatia could reduce the wholesale price. A lower wholesale price increases UV's underage cost (gross margin) and decreases the overage cost (loss on leftover inventory), thereby making stockouts costlier and leftover inventory less consequential. More technically, reducing the wholesale price increases UV's critical ratio, which leads UV to order more. Table 14.2 provides some data on supply chain performance with various wholesale prices.

We indeed see that if Zamatia were to reduce its wholesale price from $75 to $65, then UV would increase its Bassano order from 234 to 268 units. UV is quite happy: Its profit increases from $5,580 to $8,090. Furthermore, the supply chain's profit increases from $14,905 to $16,130. In fact, why stop with a $10 wholesale price reduction? If Zamatia were to reduce the wholesale price down to the production cost, $35, then (1) UV orders the supply chain optimal quantity, 404 units, and (2) the supply chain's profit is optimal, $17,830! That strategy is called *marginal cost pricing* because the supplier only charges the retailer the marginal cost of production.

TABLE 14.2
UV's Order Quantity Q and Performance Measures for Several Possible Wholesale Price Contracts

	Wholesale Price			
	$35	$65	$75	$85
C_u	$80	$50	$40	$30
C_o	$10	$40	$50	$60
Critical ratio	0.8889	0.5556	0.4444	0.3333
z	1.23	0.14	−0.13	−0.43
Q	404	268	234	196
Expected sales	243	209	192	169
Expected leftover inventory	161	59	42	27
Umbra's expected profit	$17,830	$8,090	$5,580	$3,450
Zamatia's expected profit	$0	$8,040	$9,360	$9,800
Supply chain's profit	$17,830	$16,130	$14,940	$13,250

But while marginal cost pricing is terrific for UV and the supply chain, it is disastrous for Zamatia: by definition, Zamatia's profit plunges to zero with marginal cost pricing.

We now see a classic tension within a supply chain: An increase in one firm's profit might come at the expense of a decrease in the other firm's profit. Some might refer to this distributive situation as a *zero-sum game,* but in fact it is even worse! In a zero-sum game, two parties negotiate over how to split a fixed reward (in this case the total profit), but in this situation the total amount to be allocated between Zamatia and UV is not even fixed: Increasing Zamatia's profit may result in a smaller total profit to be shared.

With respect to the allocation of supply chain profit, firms should care about two things:

1. The size of a firm's piece of the "pie," where the pie refers to the supply chain's total profit.
2. The size of the total "pie," that is, the supply chain's total profit.

Number 1 is obvious: every firm always wants a larger piece of the pie. Number 2 is less obvious. For a fixed piece of the pie, why should a firm care about the size of the pie, that is, the size of the other firm's piece? "Petty jealousy" is not the answer. The answer is that it is always easier to divide a bigger pie: If a pie gets bigger, then it is possible to give everyone a bigger piece, that is, everyone can be better off if the pie is made bigger. In practice this is often referred to as a *win-win* deal, that is, both parties are better off.

Turning back to our discussion of the wholesale price for Zamatia and UV, we see that arguing over the wholesale price is akin to arguing over each firm's piece of the pie. And in the process of arguing over how to divide the pie, the firms may very well end up destroying part of the pie, thereby serving no one. What these firms need is a tool that first maximizes the size of the pie ($17,830) and then allows them to decide how to divide it between them without damaging any part of it. Such a tool is discussed in the next section.

14.4 Buy-Back Contracts

Without changing the wholesale price, Zamatia would get UV to order more Bassano sunglasses if Zamatia could mitigate UV's downside risk of leftover inventory: UV loses a considerable amount ($50) on each unit it is stuck with at the end of the season. One solution is for Zamatia to buy back from UV all leftover sunglasses for a full refund of $75 per sunglass; that is, Zamatia could offer UV a *buy-back contract,* also called a *returns policy.*

Unfortunately, buy-back contracts introduce new costs to the supply chain. In particular, UV must ship leftover inventory back to Zamatia, which it estimates costs about $1.50 per sunglass. And then there is the issue of what Zamatia will do with these leftover Bassano sunglasses when it receives them. One possibility is that Zamatia just throws them out, thereby "earning" a zero salvage value on each leftover Bassano. However, Zamatia may be able to sell a portion of its leftover inventory to a European retailer that may be experiencing higher sales or Zamatia may be able to collect some revenue via an outlet store. It is even possible that Zamatia has higher salvage revenue from each Bassano at the end of the season than UV. But let's suppose Zamatia is able to earn $26.50 per Bassano at the end of the season. Hence, from the perspective of the supply chain, it does not matter whether UV salvages these sunglasses at the end of the season (which earns $25) or if Zamatia salvages these sunglasses at the end of the season (which also earns $25, net of the shipping cost). In contrast, Zamatia and UV might care which firm does the salvaging of leftover inventory. We later expand upon this issue.

Let's begin the analysis of UV's optimal order quantity given the buy-back contract. UV's underage cost with this buy-back contract is still the opportunity cost of a lost sale, which is $C_u = \$115 - \$75 = \$40$. However, UV's overage cost has changed. Now UV only loses $1.50 per leftover sunglass due to Zamatia's generous full refund returns policy, $C_o = 1.50. UV's critical ratio is

$$\frac{C_u}{C_o + C_u} = \frac{40}{1.5 + 40} = 0.9639$$

With a critical ratio of 0.9639, the optimal z-statistic is 1.8 (i.e., $\Phi(1.79) = 0.9633$ and $\Phi(1.8) = 0.9641$), so UV's optimal order quantity is now

$$Q = \mu + z \times \sigma = 250 + 1.8 \times 125 = 475$$

We can evaluate UV's expected profit and discover that it has increased from $5,580 (with no refund on returns) to $9,580 with the returns policy. Furthermore, with an order quantity of 475 units, UV's expected leftover inventory is 227 units.

Zamatia has surely provided an incentive to UV to increase its order quantity, but is this offer also good for Zamatia? Zamatia's expected profit has several components: It sells 475 units to UV at the beginning of the season, which generates $475 \times $75 = $35,625$ in revenue; its production cost is $475 \times $35 = $16,625$; it expects to pay UV $227 \times $75 = $17,009$ to buy back the expected 227 units of leftover inventory; and it collects $227 \times $26.5 = $6,016$ in salvage revenue. Combining those components together yields an expected profit of $7,991 for Zamatia, which is *lower* than Zamatia's profit without the returns policy, $9,350.

How did Zamatia go wrong with this buy-back contract? Zamatia did encourage UV to order more Bassano sunglasses by reducing UV's exposure to leftover inventory risk. But Zamatia reduced that risk so much that UV actually ordered more than the supply chain optimal quantity, thereby setting Zamatia up for a large bill when leftover inventory gets shipped back. Is there a compromise between the wholesale price contract with too little inventory and the full refund buy-back contract with too much inventory? (Of course there is.)

Instead of giving a full refund on returned inventory, Zamatia could give a partial refund. For example, suppose Zamatia offers to buy back inventory from UV for $65 per sunglass. This is still not a bad deal for UV. Its underage cost remains $C_u = 40$, but now its overage cost is $C_o = $1.50 + $75 - $65 = 11.50: each unit left over costs UV the $1.50 to ship back and due to the partial credit, it loses an additional $10 per unit. Table 14.3 provides data on UV's optimal order quantity, expected sales, expected leftover inventory, and expected profit. The table also indicates Zamatia's profit with this partial refund is $9,528, which is slightly better than its profit without a buy-back at all. Furthermore, the supply chain's total profit has jumped to $17,600, which is reasonably close to the maximum profit, $17,830. One way to evaluate the quality of a contract is by its *supply chain efficiency,* which is the fraction of the optimal profit the supply chain achieves. In this case efficiency is $17,600 / 18,830 = 99$ percent; that is, the supply chain earns 99 percent of its potential profit.

Instead of holding the wholesale price fixed and reducing the buy-back price, Zamatia could hold the buy-back price fixed and increase the wholesale price. For example, it could increase the wholesale price to $85 and still agree to buy back inventory for $75. That contract indeed works well for Zamatia: it earns a whopping $11,594. It even is not a bad deal for UV: its profit is $5,766, which is still better than the original situation without any refund on returned inventory. But overall supply chain performance has slipped a bit: efficiency is now only $17,360 / 18,830 = 97$ percent.

While we seem to be making some progress, we also seem to be fishing around without much guidance. There are many possible combinations of wholesale prices and buy-back prices, so what combinations should we be considering? Recall from the previous section that our objective should be to maximize the size of the pie and then worry about how to divide it. Every firm can be given a bigger piece if the pie is made bigger. So let's first look

TABLE 14.3 UV's Order Quantity Q and Performance Measures for Several Possible Wholesale Price Contracts

Wholesale price	$75	$75	$75	$85
Buy-back price	$55	$65	$75	$75
C_u	$40	$40	$40	$30
C_o	$21.50	$11.50	$1.50	$11.50
Critical ratio	0.6504	0.7767	0.9639	0.7229
z	0.39	0.77	1.80	0.60
Q	299	346	475	325
Expected sales	221	234	248	229
Expected leftover inventory	78	112	227	96
Expected profits:				
Umbra	$7,163	$8,072	$9,580	$5,766
Zamatia	$9,737	$9,528	$7,991	$11,594
Supply chain	$16,900	$17,600	$17,570	$17,360

for wholesale/buy-back price combinations that maximize supply chain profit. In other words, we are looking for a wholesale price and a buy-back price such that UV's expected profit-maximizing order quantity given those terms is the supply chain optimal order quantity, 404 Bassanos. If we find such a contract, then we say that contract "coordinates the supply chain" because the supply chain achieves 100 percent efficiency, that is, it earns the maximum supply chain profit.

We could hunt for our desired wholesale/buy-back price combinations in Excel (for every wholesale price, slowly adjust the buy-back price until we find the one that makes UV order 404 Bassanos), or we could take a more direct route by using the following equation:

$$\text{Buy-back price} = \text{Shipping cost} + \text{Price} - (\text{Price} - \text{Wholesale price})$$

$$\times \left(\frac{\text{Price} - \text{Salvage value}}{\text{Price} - \text{Cost}} \right) \qquad (14.1)$$

In other words, if we have chosen a wholesale price, then equation (14.1) gives us the buy-back price that would cause UV to choose the supply chain optimal order quantity. In that case, the pie would be maximized; that is, we coordinate the supply chain and supply chain efficiency is 100 percent! (If you are curious about how to derive equation (14.1), see Appendix D.)

Let's evaluate equation (14.1) with the wholesale price of $75:

$$\text{Buy-back price} = \$1.50 + \$115 - (\$115 - \$75) \times \left(\frac{\$115 - \$25}{\$115 - \$35} \right) = \$71.50$$

Hence, if the wholesale price is $75 and Zamatia agrees to buy back leftover inventory for $71.50 per sunglass, then UV orders 404 Bassano sunglasses and the supply chain earns the maximum profit, $17,830.

Table 14.4 provides performance data for several different wholesale prices assuming equation (14.1) is used to choose the buy-back price.

Interestingly, with a wholesale price of $75, the firms split the supply chain's profit, that is, each earns $8,915. In that case, UV does much better than just a wholesale price contract, but Zamatia does worse. However, both firms do significantly better with the wholesale price of $85 and the buy-back price of $82.75 than they do with the original contract we considered (just a $75 wholesale price and no buy-back).

Table 14.4 reveals some remarkable observations:

- There are many different wholesale price/buy-back price pairs that maximize the supply chain's profit. In other words, there are many different contracts that achieve 100 percent supply chain efficiency.

TABLE 14.4
Performance Measures When the Buy-Back Price Is Chosen to Coordinate the Supply Chain—to Ensure 100 percent Supply Chain Efficiency

Wholesale price	$35	$45	$55	$65	$75	$85	$95	$105
Buy back price	$26.50	$37.75	$49.00	$60.25	$71.50	$82.75	$94.00	$105.25
C_u	$80	$70	$60	$50	$40	$30	$20	$10
C_o	$10.00	$8.75	$7.50	$6.25	$5.00	$3.75	$2.50	$1.25
Critical ratio	0.8889	0.8889	0.8889	0.8889	0.8889	0.8889	0.8889	0.8889
z	1.23	1.23	1.23	1.23	1.23	1.23	1.23	1.23
Q	404	404	404	404	404	404	404	404
Expected sales	243	243	243	243	243	243	243	243
Expected leftover inventory	161	161	161	161	161	161	161	161
Expected profits:								
Umbra	$17,830	$15,601	$13,373	$11,144	$8,915	$6,686	$4,458	$2,229
Zamatia	$0	$2,229	$4,458	$6,686	$8,915	$11,144	$13,373	$15,601
Supply chain	$17,830	$17,830	$17,830	$17,830	$17,830	$17,830	$17,830	$17,830

• Virtually any allocation of the supply chain's profit between the two firms is feasible; that is, there exist contracts that give the lion's share of the profit to the supplier, contracts that equally divide the profit, and contracts that give the lion's share to the retailer.

• The firms now truly do face a zero-sum game; that is, increasing one firm's profit means the other firm's profit decreases. However, at least now the sum that they can fight over is the maximum possible.

Which contracts will the firms ultimately agree upon? We cannot really say. If Zamatia is the better negotiator or if it is perceived to have more bargaining power than UV, then we would expect Zamatia might get UV to agree to a buy-back contract with a high wholesale price. Even though Zamatia's profit can increase substantially, it is important to note that UV's profit also may increase relative to the status quo because buy-back contracts increase the size of the pie. However, if UV has the stronger negotiating skills, then it is possible UV will secure a contract that it favors (a buy-back contract with a low wholesale price).

So far our analysis of buy-back contracts has focused on how the firms can use these contracts to coordinate the supply chain from the perspective of inventory control. But there are other reasons why a supplier may wish to offer to accept returns for a partial credit:

• Zamatia may wish to accept returns to protect its brand image. Being a provider of high-end fashion means that Zamatia must convince consumers that their products are popular. Otherwise, why would consumers pay so much for their sunglasses? It can be rather hard to convince consumers that your products are hip if they see many of them with steeply marked down prices at the end of the season. Accepting returns allows Zamatia to prevent public markdowns that detract from Zamatia's brand-building effort.

• End-of-season markdowns also can be problematic because they create strategic shoppers; that is, shoppers that are willing to pay full price during the season but nevertheless wait to the end-of-season sale to buy at the discount price. If UV does not mark down inventory because Zamatia accepts returns, then these strategic shoppers are forced to purchase at the full price.

• For some products, it can be important for a supplier to accept returns to ensure the quality of the product. For example, a retailer may be willing to try to sell a perishable item that is still legally acceptable but nevertheless close to the end of its life. As a result, some consumers might end up with a poor-quality product (e.g., sour milk, depleted batteries, inactive chemicals, etc.). Again, to protect the supplier's reputation for quality, the supplier may wish to accept returns from the retailer so that old products are not sold to consumers.

- Accepting returns facilitates the redistribution of inventory among retailers. In our example, there is only one retailer, but in practice there are generally many retailers, some of which experience higher demand than others. To achieve high supply chain efficiency, it may be necessary to move product from slow selling retailers to higher-selling retailers. The retailers could accomplish this redistribution on their own, but it generally is more efficient to coordinate the redistribution through the supplier.

- The supplier may wish to accept returns to signal to retailers that it is not about to introduce a new product that makes the current product obsolete. This is often a concern in the high technology industry, but it can even be a concern in "low tech" industries like cosmetics. If the retailer is concerned that a new innovation could be introduced (either by the supplier or some other firm), then the retailer may be excessively cautious in its inventory investment. The supplier emboldens the retailer by taking on a portion of this obsolescence risk via its returns policy.

- The supplier may wish to accept returns to signal that it will commit significant marketing effort to the product. A retailer may be reluctant to carry a product unless it knows the supplier will expend the necessary advertising dollars to generate demand. If the supplier does not accept returns, then the supplier does not have a direct stake in the product once the retailer has made its procurement decision. However, the supplier is directly interested in the demand for the product during the season if the supplier is accepting returns at the end of the season. In that case, the supplier is more willing to expend advertising money to ensure that returns are not numerous.

We also should mention potential limitations or concerns that have not been explicitly addressed so far in our discussion of buy-back contracts:

- Returns are less effective if the retailer's salvage value is higher than the supplier's salvage value. In our example, the supplier's salvage value net of the transportation cost is the same as the retailer's salvage value. Hence, it does not matter (from the perspective of supply chain efficiency) whether the leftover Bassano sunglasses are salvaged by Zamatia or by UV. But what if Zamatia were unable to sell these leftover sunglasses to other retailers or to an outlet store. Then accepting returns is costly, especially if there are significant transportation and handling costs to ship leftover inventory back to the supplier. On the other hand, it is possible that Zamatia's salvage value could be considerably higher than UV's salvage value. Then returns clearly make sense: The supply chain should salvage inventory at the most profitable location, and if that is with the supplier, then the supplier should accept returns. For instance, the supplier may have a higher salvage value because the supplier can redistribute leftover product from a slow-selling retailer to a high-selling retailer.

- As already mentioned, without returns the supplier faces little uncertainty: the retailer orders product, the supplier delivers, and then their interactions are done for that season. But with returns the supplier faces the uncertainty over how many units will be returned at the end of the season. This added risk might make the supplier nervous. However, there is an even greater concern: What happens if the supplier is dealing with an irrational or an excessively optimistic retailer? For example, if the retailer has an overly rosy forecast of demand, then the retailer is likely to order too many units of inventory. The consequence of that excessive buy falls on the supplier in the form of excessive returns. Hence, a supplier might be willing to offer a responsible and well-managed retailer a buy-back contract, but can the supplier be sure that every one of its retailers is responsible and well managed?

- Accepting returns is likely to dampen a retailer's incentive to sell. If demand depends on how much selling effort a retailer exerts (e.g., salesperson time and helpfulness with customers, cleanliness of stores, etc.), then will a retailer exert that effort if the retailer can return inventory at the end of the season? This is particularly relevant if the buy-back price is high relative to the wholesale price. A related concern is that the retailer may exert effort for the wrong product. Suppose a retailer carries product from two different suppliers, one that offers a generous return while the other does not. If the retailer can push demand toward one product or the other (e.g., giving the desired product a better shelf allocation or a more prominent location within the store), then the retailer may be tempted to push the product for which it cannot return inventory.

- In our sunglass supply chain, there is no supplier capacity constraint. But if the supplier's capacity is constrained, then shortage gaming can occur when retailers are offered generous returns policies. And shortage gaming leads to the bullwhip effect and its associated inefficiencies. Therefore, while a supplier may wish to use a returns policy to induce retailers to order more inventory, the supplier must be careful to not induce retailers to order too much inventory.

So while the simple and traditional wholesale price contract generally does not coordinate the supply chain, we have shown that buy-back contracts can maximize the supply chain's profit and arbitrarily allocate the supply chain's profit between the two firms. And there are other virtues to buy-back contracts; for example, they can protect the supplier's brand image or reputation for quality. But there are also potential complications with offering a returns policy: returning inventory to the supplier may create a needless shipping and handling expense, an irrational retailer can overbuy, and/or a retailer's incentive to push the supplier's product is dampened by the opportunity to return inventory for a partial credit. Nevertheless, there are industries in which the positives associated with returns policies appear to outweigh the negatives.

The book industry is probably the most well-known example of an industry in which the use of returns policies is widespread. Furthermore, retailers surely take advantage of these policies: it is estimated that between 30 and 35 percent of new hardcover books produced are returned to the publisher. In our example, we see that UV returns about 40 percent (161/404) of the Bassano sunglasses it purchases from Zamatia.

While we have concentrated on buy-back contracts with partial return credits, the typical contract in the book industry has the publisher offering 100 percent return credit. However, retailers pay the cost of packaging and shipping books back to the publisher. It is possible that publishers must offer this generous policy to induce retailers to order the supply chain optimal quantity. But it is also possible that this full refund policy is too generous. A careful analysis along the lines of the one in this chapter (with realistic prices, costs, and demand distributions for the book industry) might reveal the answer. Interestingly, up until relatively recently, the music industry offered 100 percent credit as well but has since shifted to partial return credits in the range of 95 percent (e.g., $b = 0.95 \times w$).

It is also interesting to note that publishers generally complain about returns policies. Many publishers refer to them as a necessary evil or a competitive necessity but surely not as a tool for supply chain coordination. This impression is probably derived from a focus on the explicit costs of a returns policy; that is, the costs, aggravation, and frustration of receiving returned books from retailers. It is easy to miss the less explicit benefit of returns policies: with a returns policy, the publisher would either have to cut the wholesale price to get the retailers to hold inventory or the publisher would have to accept that retailers carry less than the optimal amount of inventory. Our analysis demonstrates that with a well-designed returns policy (e.g., with the use of equation (14.1)), the benefits of these policies to the publishers can outweigh the costs.

Another peculiar feature of the book publishing industry is the practice of returning just the cover of the book and not the entire book to the publisher. This makes sense if the publisher plans on just dumping the book (i.e., it does not plan to resell the book to another retailer or to other consumers) because then the shipping cost is reduced.

14.5   More Supply Chain Contracts

The previous section focused on buy-back contracts, but those are not the only type of contracts that are implemented in supply chains. This section briefly describes several other types of contracts and how they may alleviate supply chain incentive conflicts. This is by no means an exhaustive list of the types of contracts that are observed in practice.

Quantity Discounts

Quantity discounts are quite common, but they come in many different forms. For example, with an all-unit quantity discount, a buyer receives a discount on all units if the quantity ordered exceeds a threshold; whereas with an incremental quantity discount, a buyer receives a discount on all units purchased above a threshold. No matter the form, quantity discounts encourage buyers to order additional inventory because the purchase price of the last unit purchased is decreasing with the amount purchased. In the context of the newsvendor model, a quantity discount increases the underage cost, thereby increasing the critical ratio. In contrast, recall that the buy-back contract increases the critical ratio by decreasing the overage cost.

Options Contracts

With an options contract, a buyer pays one price to purchase options, say w_o, and another price to exercise the purchased options, w_e. These contracts are often used when a buyer wants a supplier to build capacity well in advance of the selling season. At that time the buyer has only an uncertain forecast of demand. As the selling season approaches the buyer anticipates that she will have a much better demand forecast, but by then it is too late to build additional capacity if demand is quite high. Without the options contract, the supplier bears all of the supply chain's risk, so the supplier is likely to build too little capacity. The options contract allows the firms to share the risk of demand–supply mismatches: The supplier earns at least something up front (the option's price) while the buyer doesn't have to pay for all of the unused capacity (the exercise price is paid only on capacity actually exercised). Hence, just as with buy-back contracts, options contracts are able in some settings to achieve 100 percent supply chain efficiency (i.e., the supplier builds the right amount of capacity) and arbitrarily divide the supply chain's profit between the two firms (i.e., there is more than one options contract that achieves supply chain coordination).

Revenue Sharing

With revenue sharing, a retailer pays a wholesale price per unit purchased to a supplier but then also pays a portion of the revenue earned on that unit to the supplier. As with buy-back contracts, revenue sharing allows the firms in the supply chain to share the risk of demand–supply mismatches: The retailer pays something to the supplier upfront (the wholesale price) but only pays an additional amount if the unit actually generates revenue (the revenue share).

The most notable application of revenue sharing occurred in the video-rental industry. Back around 1998, the standard wholesale price contract was predominant in the industry: studios would sell videocassettes to video rental retailers for about $60 to $75 per tape and retailers would keep all rental revenue. At a rental price of about $3, retailers could only break even on a tape if it rented more than 20 times. But because demand for tapes generally starts high upon its release and fades quickly, retailers could not afford to purchase too many tapes. As a result, availability of newly released movies was quite low, driving many consumers to consider other entertainment forms (cable TV, pay-per-view, etc.). Considering that the manufacturing cost of a tape is quite low, it is clear that maximizing supply chain profit requires additional tapes at the retailer.

Around 1998 the industry's biggest player, Blockbuster, negotiated revenue sharing deals with the major studios. With revenue sharing, the retailer pays a far lower wholesale price (about $8) but shares a portion of the rental revenue (about 50 percent). With those terms, the breakeven on a tape reduces to fewer than six rentals, thereby allowing Blockbuster to justify purchasing many more tapes. They used their additional availability to launch their "Guaranteed to be there" and "Go home happy" marketing campaigns.

Quantity Flexibility Contracts

Consider an ongoing relationship between a buyer and a supplier. For example, the buyer is Sun Microsystems, the supplier is Sony, and the product is a monitor. Sun's demand fluctuates over time, but Sun nevertheless wants Sony to build enough capacity to satisfy all of Sun's needs, which could be either higher or lower than forecasted. But since Sun probably doesn't incur the cost of idle capacity, Sun is biased toward giving Sony overly rosy forecasts in the hope that Sony will respond to the forecast by building extra capacity. But Sony is no fool; that is, Sony knows that Sun is biased toward optimistic forecasts and so Sony may view Sun's forecasts with a skeptical eye. Unfortunately, Sun may actually have an optimistic forecast, but due to its lack of credibility with Sony, Sony may not respond with additional capacity.

The problem in this relationship is that Sony bears the entire risk of excess capacity; hence, Sun is biased toward rosy forecasts. One solution is to implement *quantity flexibility (QF) contracts:* with a QF contract, Sun provides an initial forecast but then must purchase some quantity within a certain percentage of that forecast. For example, suppose the firms agree to a 25 percent QF contract. Furthermore, it is the first quarter of the year and Sun forecasts its demand for the fourth quarter will be 2,000 units. By the time the fourth quarter rolls around, Sun is committed to purchasing from Sony at least 1,500 units (75 percent of the forecast) and Sony is committed to delivering up to 2,500 units (125 percent of the forecast) should Sun need more than the forecast. If demand turns out to be low, Sony is somewhat protected by the lower collar, whereas if demand turns out to be high, Sun can take advantage of that upside by knowing that Sony has some additional capacity (up to the upper collar). Hence, via quantity flexibility contracts, it can be shown that both firms are better off; that is, the supply chain pie gets bigger and each firm gets a bigger share.

Price Protection

In the PC industry, distributors are concerned with holding too much inventory because that inventory could become obsolete; that is, they must sell that inventory at deeply discounted prices. But there is another concern with holding too much inventory. Suppose a distributor purchases 1,000 computers today at $2,000 each, but one week later the supplier cuts the price to $1,800. Unless the distributor sells the entire batch of 1,000 computers in the next week, the distributor would be better off to purchase fewer computers at $2,000 and to purchase the remainder one week later at $1,800. In other words, the tendency of suppliers to cut their wholesale prices frequently and without notice creates an incentive among distributors to be cautious in the purchase quantities. If distributors then curtail their purchases below the supply chain optimal amount, it can be beneficial to provide them with an incentive to increase their order quantities.

Allowing distributors to return inventory helps to encourage distributors to order more inventory, but it is not the only way. *Price protection* is another way: with price protection, a supplier compensates the distributor on remaining inventory for any price reductions. For example, suppose at the end of the week the distributor sold 700 computers purchased at $2,000, but has 300 computers remaining. With price protection, the supplier would then send the distributor a check for $300 \times (\$2,000 - \$1,800) = \$60,000$. In other words, the distributor becomes indifferent between purchasing 1,000 computers for $2,000 now and purchasing 700 computers for $2,000 now and 300 computers for $1,800 in one week.

14.6 Summary

Optimal supply chain performance is not guaranteed even if every firm in the supply chain optimizes its own performance. Self-interest and decentralized decision making do not naturally lead to 100 percent supply chain efficiency. As a result, firms in a supply chain can benefit from better coordination of their actions.

The bullwhip effect (the propagation of demand variability up the supply chain) provides a serious challenge to supply chain operations. There are many causes of the bullwhip effect (order synchronization, order batching, trade promotions, overreactive ordering, and shortage gaming) and more than one of them can be present at the same time. The solutions to the bullwhip effect, such as sharing demand information, removing pathological incentives, and Vendor-Managed Inventory, are designed to combat those root causes.

The bullwhip effect is not the only challenge posed upon supply chains. Given the terms of trade between supply chain members, it is quite possible that supply chain actions will not be taken because of conflicting incentives. For example, with a simple wholesale price contract, it is generally found that the retailer's incentive to order inventory leads it to order less than the supply chain optimal amount of inventory, a phenomenon called double marginalization. Fortunately, incentive conflicts can be alleviated or even eliminated with the use of carefully designed contractual terms, such as buy-back contracts.

14.7 Further Reading

For a description of the causes, consequences, and solutions to the bullwhip effect, see Lee, Padmanabhan, and Whang (1997).

Buzzell, Quelch and Salmon (1990) provide a history of trade promotions and discuss their pros and cons.

For the original research on buy-back contracts, see Pasternack (1985). For a more managerial description of the application of buy-back contracts, see Padmanabhan and Png (1995). For a review of the theoretical literature on supply chain contracting, see Cachon (2003).

14.8 Practice Problems

Q14.1* **(Buying tissues)** P&G, the maker of Puffs tissues, traditionally sells these tissues for $9.40 per case, where a case contains eight boxes. A retailer's average weekly demand is 25 cases of a particular Puffs SKU (color, scent, etc.). P&G has decided to change its pricing strategy by offering two different plans. With one plan the retailer can purchase that SKU for the everyday-low-wholesale price of $9.25 per case. With the other plan, P&G charges the regular price of $9.40 per case throughout most of the year, but purchases made for a single delivery at the start of each quarter are given a 5% discount. The retailer receives weekly shipments with a one week lead time between ordering and delivery. Suppose with either plan the retailer manages inventory so that at the end of each week there is on average a one week supply of inventory. Holding costs are incurred at the rate of 0.4% of the value of inventory at the end of each week. Assume 52 weeks per year.

a. Suppose the retailer chose the first plan ($9.25 per case throughout the year). What is the retailer's expected annual purchasing and inventory holding cost?

b. Suppose the retailer chooses the second plan and only buys at the discount price ($9.40 is the regular price and a 5% discount for delivery at the start of each quarter). What is the retailer's expected annual purchasing and inventory holding cost?

c. Consider the first plan and propose a new every-day-low wholesale price. Call this the third plan. Design your plan so that both P&G and the retailer prefer it relative to the second plan.

(* indicates that the solution is at the end of the book)

Q14.2*   **(Returning books)** Dan McClure is trying to decide on how many copies of a book to purchase at the start of the upcoming selling season for his bookstore. The book retails at $28.00. The publisher sells the book to Dan for $20.00. Dan will dispose of all of the unsold copies of the book at 75% off the retail price, at the end of the season. Dan estimates that demand for this book during the season is Normal with a mean of 100 and a standard deviation of 42.

   a. How many books should Dan order to maximize his expected profit?

   b. Given the order quantity in part *a* what is Dan's expected profit?

   c. The publisher's variable cost per book is $7.5. Given the order quantity in part *a*, what is the publisher's expected profit?

   The publisher is thinking of offering the following deal to Dan. At the end of the season, the publisher will buy back unsold copies at a pre-determined price of $15.00. However, Dan would have to bear the costs of shipping unsold copies back to the publisher at $1.00 per copy.

   d. How many books should Dan order to maximize his expected profits given the buy back offer?

   e. Given the order quantity in part *d*, what is Dan's expected profit?

   f. Assume the publisher is able on average to earn $6 on each returned book net the publisher's handling costs (some books are destroyed while others are sold at a discount and others are sold at full price). Given the order quantity in part *d* what is the publisher's expected profit?

   g. Suppose the publisher continues to charge $20 per book and Dan still incurs a $1 cost to ship each book back to the publisher. What price should the publisher pay Dan for returned books to maximize the supply chain's profit (the sum of the publisher's profit and Dan's profit)?

Q14.3   **(Component options)** Handi Inc., a cell phone manufacturer, procures a standard display from LCD Inc. via an options contract. At the start of quarter 1 (Q1) Handi pays LCD $4.5 per option. At that time Handi's forecast of demand in Q2 is Normally distributed with mean 24000 and standard deviation 8000. At the start of Q2 Handi learns exact demand for Q2 and then exercises options at the fee of $3.5 per option (for every exercised option LCD delivers one display to Handi). Assume Handi starts Q2 with no display inventory and displays owned at the end of Q2 are worthless. Should Handi's demand in Q2 be larger than the number of options held, Handi purchases additional displays on the spot market for $9 per unit.

   For example, suppose Handi purchases 30,000 options at the start of Q1 but at the start of Q2 Handi realizes that demand will be 35,000 units. Then Handi exercises all of its options and purchases 5,000 additional units on the spot market. If, on the other hand, Handi realizes demand is only 27,000 units, then Handi merely exercises 27000 options.

   a. Suppose Handi purchases 30,000 options. What is the expected number of options that Handi will exercise?

   b. Suppose Handi purchases 30,000 options. What is the expected number of displays Handi will buy on the spot market?

   c. Suppose Handi purchases 30,000 options. What is Handi's expected total procurement cost?

   d. How many options should Handi purchase from LCD?

   e. What is Handi's expected total procurement cost given the number of purchased options from part *d*?

Q14.4   **(Selling grills)** Smith and Jackson Inc. (SJ) sells an outdoors grill to Cusano's Hardware Store. SJ's wholesale price for the grill is $185. (The wholesale price includes the cost of shipping the grill to Cusano). Cusano sells the grill for $250 and SJ's variable cost per grill $100. Suppose Cusano's forecast for season sales can be described with a Poisson distribution with mean 8.75. Furthermore, Cusano plans to make only one grill buy for the season. Grills left over at the end of the season are sold at a 75% discount.

   a. How many grills should Cusano order?

b. What is Cusano's expected profit given Cusano's order in part *a*?

c. What is SJ's expected profit given Cusano's order in part *a*?

d. To maximize the supply chain's total profit (SJ's profit plus Cusano's profit), how many grills should be shipped to Cusano's Hardware?

Suppose SJ were to accept unsold grills at the end of the season. Cusano would incur a $15 shipping cost per grill returned to SJ. Among the returned grills, 45% of them are damaged and SJ cannot resell them the following season, but the remaining 55% can be resold to some retailer for the full wholesale price of $185.

e. Given the possibility of returning grills to SJ, how many grills should be sent to Cusano's to maximize the supply chain's total profit?

Suppose SJ gives Cusano a 90% credit for each returned grill, that is, SJ pays Cusano $166.5 for each returned grill. Cusano still incurs a $15 cost to ship each grill back to SJ.

f. How many grills should Cusano order to maximize his profit?

g. What is Cusano's expected profit given Cusano's order in part *f*?

h. What is SJ's expected profit given Cusano's order in part *f*?

i. To maximize the supply chain's total profit, what should SJ's credit percentage be? (The current credit is 90%.)

Dave Luna, the director of marketing and sales at SJ, suggests yet another arrangement. He suggests that SJ offer an advanced purchase discount. His plan works as follows: there is a 10% discount on any grill purchased before the season starts (the pre-book order) but then retailers are able to purchase additional grills as needed during the season at the regular wholesale price (at-once orders). With this plan retailers are responsible for selling any excess grills at the end of the season, i.e., SJ will not accept returns. Assume SJ makes enough grills to satisfy Cusano's demand during the season and any leftover grills can be sold the next season at full price.

j. Given this advanced purchase discount plan, how many grills should Cusano pre-book to maximize his profit?

k. What is Cusano's expected profit given Cusano's pre-book order quantity in part *j*?

l. What is SJ's expected profit from sales to Cusano this season given Cusano's pre-book order quantity in part *j*?

m. As a thought experiment, which one of these contractual arrangements would you recommend to SJ?

Appendix A

Statistics Tutorial

This appendix provides a brief tutorial to the statistics needed for the material in this book.

Statistics is about understanding and quantifying uncertainty (or, if you prefer, variability). So suppose we are interested in an event that is stochastic, that is, it has an uncertain outcome. For example, it could be the demand for a product, the number of people that call us between 10:00 A.M. and 10:15 A.M., the amount of time until the arrival of the next patient to the emergency room, and so forth. In each case the outcome of this stochastic event is some number (units of demand, minutes between arrival, etc.). This stochastic event can also be called a *random variable.* Because our random variable could represent a wide variety of situations, for the purpose of this tutorial, let's give our random variable a generic name, X.

All random variables have an *expected value,* which is also called the *mean.* Depending on the context, we use different symbols to represent the mean. For example, we generally use the Greek symbol μ to represent the mean of our stochastic demand whereas we use a to represent the mean of the interarrival time of customers to a queuing system. A random variable is also characterized by its *standard deviation,* which roughly describes the amount of uncertainty in the distribution, or how "spread out" the distribution is. The Greek symbol σ is often used to describe the standard deviation of a random variable. Uncertainty also can be measured with the *variance* of a random variable. The variance of a random variable is closely related to its standard deviation: it is the square of the standard deviation:

$$\text{Variance} = (\text{Standard deviation})^2 = \sigma^2$$

Hence, it is sufficient to just work with the standard deviation because the variance can always be evaluated quickly once you know the standard deviation.

The standard deviation measures the absolute amount of uncertainty in a distribution, but it is often useful to think about the relative amount of uncertainty. For example, suppose we have two random variables, one with mean 20 and the other with mean 200. Suppose further they both have standard deviations equal to 10, that is, they have the same absolute amount of uncertainty. A standard deviation of 10 means there is about a two-thirds chance the outcome of the random variable will be with 10 units of the mean. Being within 10 units of a mean of 20 is much more variable in a relative sense than being within 10 units of a mean of 200: in the first case we have a two-thirds chance of being within 50 percent of the mean, whereas in the second case we have a two-thirds chance of being within 5 percent of the mean. Hence, we need a relative measure of uncertainty. We'll use the *coefficient of variation,* which is the standard deviation of a distribution divided by its mean, for example, σ/μ. In some cases we will use explicit variables to represent the coefficient of variation. For example, in our work with queuing systems, we will let CV_a be the coefficient of variation of the arrival times to the queue and CV_p be the coefficient of variation of the service times in the queue.

Every random variable is defined by its *distribution function* and its *density function*. (Actually, only one of those functions is sufficient to define the random variable, but that is a picky point.) Let's say $F(Q)$ is the distribution function of X and $f(Q)$ is the density function. The density function returns the probability our stochastic event will be exactly Q, while the distribution function returns the probability our stochastic event will be Q or lower:

$$F(Q) = \text{Prob}\{X \text{ will be less than or equal to } Q\}$$

$$f(q) = \text{Prob}\{X \text{ will be exactly } Q\}$$

There are an infinite number of possible distribution and density functions, but a few of the more useful ones have been given names. The *normal distribution* is probably the most well-known distribution: the density function of the normal distribution is shaped like a bell. The normal distribution is defined with two parameters, its mean and its standard deviation, that is, a μ and a σ. The distribution and density functions of a normal distribution with mean 1,000 and standard deviation 300 are displayed in Figure A.1.

Distribution functions are always increasing from 0 to 1, and often have an S shape. Density functions do not have a typical pattern: some have the bell shape like the normal, others are downward curving.

While there are an infinite number of normal distributions (essentially any mean and standard deviation combination), there is one normal distribution that is particularly useful, the *standard normal*. The standard normal distribution has mean 0 and standard deviation 1. Because the standard normal is a special distribution, its distribution function is given special notation: the distribution function of the standard normal is $\Phi(z)$; that is, $\Phi(z)$ is the probability the outcome of a standard normal distribution is z or lower. The density function

FIGURE A.1

Distribution (solid line) and Density (circles) Functions of a Normal Distribution with Mean 1,000 and Standard Deviation 300

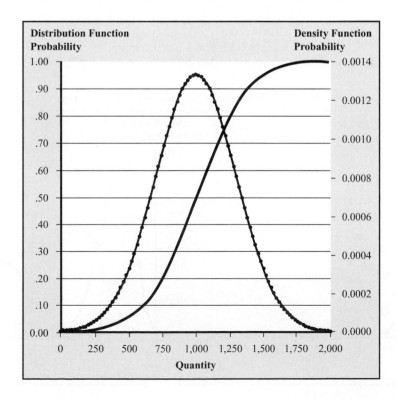

TABLE A.1

The Density Function
$f(Q)$ **and Distribution**
Function $F(Q)$ **of a**
Poisson Distribution
with Mean 1.25

Q	f(Q)	F(Q)
0	0.28650	0.28650
1	0.35813	0.64464
2	0.22383	0.86847
3	0.09326	0.96173
4	0.02914	0.99088
5	0.00729	0.99816
6	0.00152	0.99968
7	0.00027	0.99995
8	0.00004	0.99999
9	0.00001	1.00000

of the standard normal is $\phi(z)$. (Φ and ϕ are the upper- and lowercase, respectively, of the Greek letter phi.)

The normal distribution is a *continuous distribution* because all outcomes are possible, even fractional quantities such as 989.56. The *Poisson distribution* is also common, but it is a *discrete distribution* because the outcome of a Poisson random variable is always an integer value (i.e., 0, 1, 2, . . .). The Poisson distribution is characterized by a single parameter, its mean. The standard deviation of a Poisson distribution equals the square root of its mean:

$$\text{Standard deviation of a Poisson distribution} = \sqrt{\text{Mean of the Poisson distribution}}$$

While the outcome of a Poisson distribution is always an integer, the mean of the Poisson does not need to be an integer. The distribution and density functions of a Poisson distribution with mean 1.25 are displayed in Table A.1. Figure A.2 displays the density function of six different Poisson distributions. Unlike the familiar bell shape of the normal distribution, we can see that there is no standard shape for the Poisson: with a very low mean, the Poisson is a downward-sloping curve, but then as the mean increases, the Poisson begins to adopt a bell-like shape.

Because the outcome of a Poisson distribution is never negative and always integer, the Poisson generally better fits data with a low mean, say less than 20. For large means (say

FIGURE A.2   **The Density Function of Six Different Poisson Distributions with Means 0.625, 1.25, 2.5, 5, 10, and 20**

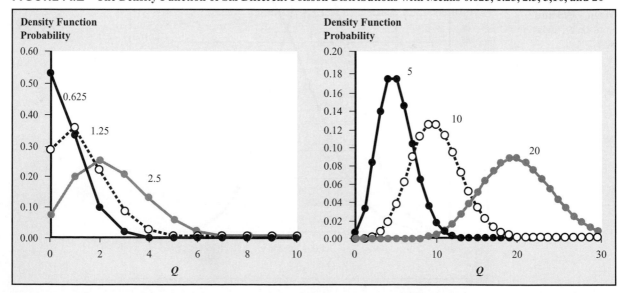

more than 20), the Poisson generally does not fit data as well as the normal for two reasons: (1) the Poisson adopts a bell-like shape, so it does not provide a shape advantage, and (2) the Poisson's standard deviation *must* equal the square root of the mean, so it does not allow the flexibility to expand or contract the width of the bell like the normal does (i.e., the normal allows for mean bell shapes with the same mean but the Poisson only allows one bell shape for a given mean).

We also make extensive use of the exponential distribution in this text because it provides a good representation of the interarrival time of customers (i.e., the time between customer arrivals). The exponential distribution is characterized by a single parameter, its mean. We'll use a as the mean of the interarrival time. So if X is the interarrival time of customers and it is exponentially distributed with mean a, then the distribution function of X is

$$\text{Prob}\{X \text{ is less than or equal to } t\} = F(X) = 1 - e^{-t/a}$$

where e in the above equation is the natural constant that approximately equals 2.718282. In Excel you would write the exponential distribution function with the Exp function: $1 - \text{Exp}(-t/a)$. Notice that the exponential distribution function is a continuous distribution, which makes sense given that we are talking about time. Figure A.3 displays the distribution and density functions of an exponential distribution with mean 0.8.

The exponential distribution and the Poisson distribution are actually closely related. If the interarrival time of customers is exponentially distributed with mean a, then the number of customers that arrive over an interval of a unit of time is Poisson distributed with mean $1/a$. For example, if the interarrival time of customers is exponentially distributed with a mean of 0.8 (as in Figure A.3), then the number of customers that arrive in one unit of time has a Poisson distribution with mean $1/0.8 = 1.25$ (as in Table A.1).

FIGURE A.3
Distribution (solid line) and Density (circles) Functions of an Exponential Distribution with Mean 0.8

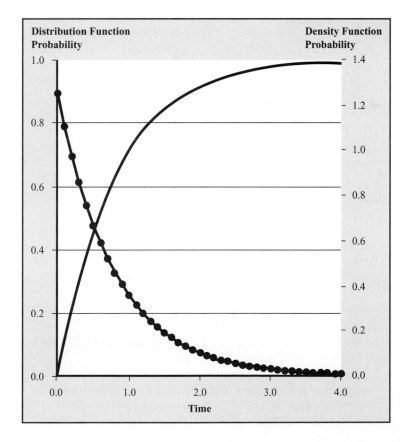

Other commonly used distributions include the negative binomial and the gamma, but we will not make much use of them in this text.

Finding the Probability *X* Will Be Less Than *Q* or Greater Than *Q*

When working with a random variable, we often need to find the probability the outcome of the random variable will be less than a particular quantity or more than the particular quantity. For example, suppose *X* has a Poisson distribution with mean 1.25. What is the probability *X* will be four units or fewer? That can be answered with the distribution function: from Table A.1, $F(4) = 99.088$ percent. What is the probability *X* will be greater than four units, that is, that it is five or more units? *X* is either *Q* or fewer units or it is more than *Q* units, so

$$\text{Prob}\{X \text{ is } Q \text{ or fewer units}\} + \text{Prob}\{X \text{ is more than } Q \text{ units}\} = 1$$

If we rearrange terms in the above equation, we get

$$\text{Prob}\{X \text{ is more than } Q \text{ units}) = 1 - \text{Prob}\{X \text{ is } Q \text{ or fewer units}\} = 1 - F(Q)$$

Hence, *X* will be greater than four units with probability $1 - F(4) = 0.00912$.

A tricky issue in these evaluations is the difference between the "probability *X* is fewer than *Q*" and the "probability *X* is *Q* or fewer". The first case does not include the outcome that *X* exactly equals *Q*, whereas the second case does. For example, when we evaluate the "probability *X* is more than *Q* units," we are not including the outcome that *X* equals *Q* units. Therefore, be aware of this issue and remember that $F(Q)$ is the probability *X* is *Q* or fewer, that is, it includes the probability that *X* exactly equals *Q* units.

We also need to find the probability *X* is more or less than *Q* when *X* is normally distributed. Working with the normal distribution is not too hard because all normal distributions, no matter their mean or standard deviation, are related to the standard normal distribution, which is why the standard normal is special and important. Hence, we can find out the probability *X* will be more or less than *Q* by working with the standard normal distribution.

Suppose *X* is normally distributed with mean 1,000 and standard deviation 300 ($\mu = 1{,}000$, $\sigma = 300$) and we want to find the probability *X* will be less than $Q = 1{,}600$ units. First convert *Q* into the equivalent order quantity if *X* followed the standard normal distribution. That equivalent order quantity is *z*, which is called the *z-statistic:*

$$z = \frac{Q - \mu}{\sigma} = \frac{1{,}600 - 1{,}000}{300} = 2.0$$

Hence, the quantity 1,600 relative to a normal distribution with mean 1,000 and standard deviation 300 is equivalent to the quantity 2.0 relative to a standard normal distribution. The probability we are looking for is then $\Phi(2.0)$, which we can find in the Standard Normal Distribution Function Table in Appendix B: $\Phi(2.0) = 0.9772$. In other words, there is a 97.72 percent chance *X* is less than 1,600 units if *X* follows a normal distribution with mean 1,000 and standard deviation 300.

What is the probability *X* will be greater than 1,600 units? That is just $1 - \Phi(2.0) = 0.0228$, that is, the probability *X* will be greater than 1,600 units is just 1 minus the probability *X* will be less than 1,600 units.

With the normal distribution, unlike the Poisson distribution, we do not need to worry too much about the distinction between the "probability *X* is fewer than *Q*" and the "probability *X* is *Q* or fewer." With the Poisson distribution, there can be a significant probability that the outcome is exactly *Q* units because the Poisson distribution is a discrete distribution and usually has a low mean, which implies that there are relatively few possible outcomes. The normal distribution is continuous, so there essentially is no distinction between "X being exactly Q units" and "X being just a tiny fraction below Q units."

Expected Value

We often need to know the expected value of something happening. For example, suppose we make a decision and there are two possible outcomes, G for good and B for bad, that is, $X = $ G or $X = $ B. If the outcome is G, then we earn \$100, but if the outcome is B, we lose \$40. Furthermore, we know the following probabilities: Prob$\{X = $ G$\} = 0.25$ and Prob$\{X = $ B$\} = 0.75$. (Note, these probabilities must sum to 1 because they are the only two possible outcomes.) The expected value of this decision is

$$\$100 \times \text{Prob}\{X = \text{G}\} + (-\$40 \times \text{Prob}\{X = \text{B}\})$$

$$= \$100 \times 0.25 + (-\$40 \times 0.75)$$

$$= -\$5$$

In words, to evaluate the expected value, we multiply the probability of each outcome with the value of each outcome and then sum up all of those calculations

The Loss Function

In statistics the distribution and density functions are well known and used often. Less well known in statistics is the *loss function,* but we make extensive use of it in this text. The loss function $L(Q)$ is the expected amount X is greater than Q. In other words, the expected loss is the expected amount a random variable X exceeds a chosen threshold Q.

To explain further, let X be a Poisson distribution with mean 1.25 and say our chosen threshold is $Q = 2$. (Table A.1 has the distribution function.) If $X = 3$, then X exceeds Q by one unit. If $X = 4$, then X exceeds Q by two units and if $X = 5$, then X exceeds Q by three units, and so on. Furthermore, if X is 2 or fewer, then X exceeds Q by 0 units. The loss function is the expected value of all of those events; that is, $L(2)$ is the expected amount by which X exceeds Q. Table A.2 provides those calculations for $L(2)$.

Figure A.4 gives a graphical perspective on the loss function. Depicted is a density function of a random variable X that has a bell shape like a normal distribution, but the

TABLE A.2
Calculation of the Loss Function for $Q = 2$ and a Poisson Distribution with Mean 1.25

Q	f(Q)(a)	Amount X Exceeds 2 (b)	(a*b)
0	0.286505	0	0.00000
1	0.358131	0	0.00000
2	0.223832	0	0.00000
3	0.093263	1	0.09326
4	0.029145	2	0.05829
5	0.007286	3	0.02186
6	0.001518	4	0.00607
7	0.000271	5	0.00136
8	0.000042	6	0.00025
9	0.000006	7	0.00004
10	0.000001	8	0.00001
$L(2) = $ Total of last column $=$			0.18114

FIGURE A.4   **Calculation of the Loss Function for a Bell-like Distribution Function That Has Discrete Outcomes 0, 10, . . ., 200.**

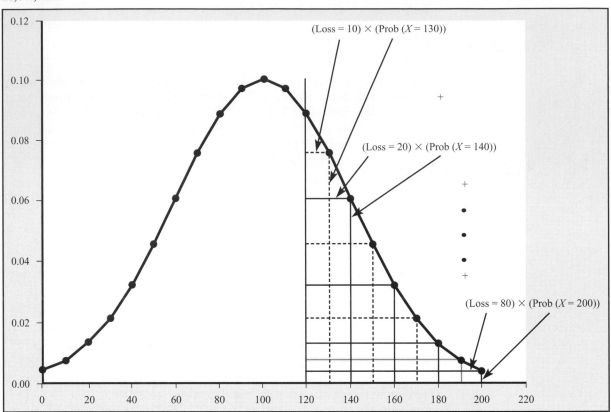

only possible outcomes are 0, 10, 20, . . ., 190, and 200. Suppose we are interested in $L(120)$, the expected loss function evaluated at the threshold of $Q = 120$. If $X <= 120$, there is no loss; that is, the random variable does not exceed the threshold Q. If $X = 130$, then the loss is $130 - 120 = 10$, so we take that loss and multiply it by the probability it occurs. We repeat that procedure for the remaining possible outcomes that generate a loss (140 through 200) and sum those values to yield $L(120) = 7.486$. In other words, the random variable X exceeds the fixed threshold $Q = 120$ on average by 7.486. This might strike you as too low given that the losses ranged in our calculations from 10 to 80, but remember that for most outcomes there is actually no loss, that is, X is less than or equal to Q.

We displayed the calculation of the loss function with a discrete random variable in Figure A.4, but conceptually we can do the same calculation with a continuous random variable such as the normal. The only difference is that there is a lot more work to do with a continuous random variable because we need to multiply every possible loss by its probability and sum all of those calculations.

At this point you (hopefully) understand that the loss function is not conceptually difficult, but it is a "pain in the neck" to evaluate. Fortunately, Appendix C provides an easier way to evaluate the loss function of a discrete random variable. But even that easier way requires a decent amount of work, more work than should be done by hand. In other words, either you have a spreadsheet to help you evaluate the loss function, or you should have a table that has already been evaluated for you, as in the following for the Poisson with mean 1.25:

Q	f(Q)	F(Q)	L(Q)
0	0.286505	0.286505	1.25000
1	0.358131	0.644636	0.53650
2	0.223832	0.868468	0.18114
3	0.093263	0.961731	0.04961
4	0.029145	0.990876	0.01134
5	0.007286	0.998162	0.00221
6	0.001518	0.999680	0.00038
7	0.000271	0.999951	0.00006
8	0.000042	0.999993	0.00001
9	0.000006	0.999999	0.00000
10	0.000001	1.000000	0.00000

If X is normally distributed, then our loss function is already provided to us in Appendix B. Actually, the loss function of the standard normal distribution is provided, that is, the Standard Normal Loss Function Table gives us $L(z)$, the expected loss function if X is a standard normal distribution. Because we often work with a different normal distribution, we need to learn how to convert the answer we get from that table into the answer that is appropriate for the normal distribution we are working with.

Suppose X is normally distributed with mean 1,000 and standard deviation 300. We are interested in the loss function with $Q = 1,600$. Just as we did when we were looking for the probability X will be greater than Q, first convert Q into the corresponding z value for the standard normal distribution:

$$z = \frac{Q - \mu}{\sigma} = \frac{1,600 - 1,000}{300} = 2.0$$

In other words, $Q = 1,600$ and a normal distribution with mean 1,000 and standard deviation 300 is equivalent to $z = 2.0$ and a standard normal distribution. Next, look up $L(z)$ in the Standard Normal Loss Function Table: $L(z) = 0.0085$. In other words, 0.0085 unit is the expected amount a standard normal will exceed the threshold of $z = 2.0$. Finally, we need to convert that value in the loss function to the value for the actual normal distribution. We use the following equation to do that:

$$L(Q) = \sigma \times L(z)$$

which in this case means

$$L(1,600) = 300 \times 0.0085 = 2.55$$

Hence, if $Q = 1,600$ and X is normally distributed with mean 1,000 and standard deviation 300, then the expected amount X will exceed Q is only 2.55 units. Why is the loss function so small? We evaluated the probability X exceeds Q to be only 2.28 percent, so most of the time X exceeds Q by 0 units.

Independence, Correlation, and Combining (or Dividing) Random Variables

We often need to combine several random variables or to divide a random variable. For example, if we have five random variables, each one representing demand on a particular day of the week, we might want to combine them into a single random variable that represents weekly demand. Or we might have a random variable that represents monthly demand and we might want to divide it into random variables that represent weekly demand. In addition to combining and dividing random variables across time, we may wish to combine or divide random variables across products or categories.

Suppose you wish to combine n random variables, labeled $X_1, X_2, \ldots, X_n$, into a single random variable X; that is, you want $X = X_1 + X_2 + \ldots + X_n$. Furthermore, we assume each of the n original random variables comes from the same "family," for example, they are all normal or all Poisson. Hence, the combined random variable X is also part of the same family: the sum of two normally random variables is normally distributed; the sum of two Poisson random variables is Poisson; and so forth. So we need a mean to describe X and maybe a standard deviation. The mean of X is easy to evaluate:

$$\mu = \mu_1 + \mu_2 + \ldots + \mu_n$$

In other words, the mean of X is just the sum of the means of the n individual random variables.

If we need a standard deviation for X and the n random variables are independent, then the standard deviation of X is

$$\sigma = \sqrt{\sigma_1^2 + \sigma_2^2 + \cdots + \sigma_n^2}$$

In words, the standard deviation of X is the square root of the sum of the variances of the n random variables. If the n random variables have the same standard deviation (i.e., $\sigma_1 = \sigma_2 = \ldots = \sigma_n$), then the above simplifies to $\sigma = \sqrt{n} \times \sigma_1$.

The key condition in our evaluation of the standard deviation of X is that the n individual random variables are independent. Roughly speaking, two random variables are *independent* if the outcome of one random variable has no influence on the outcome of the other random variable. For example, if one has a rather high demand outcome, then that provides no information as to whether the other random variable will have a high or low outcome.

Two random variables are *correlated* if the outcome of one random variable provides information about the outcome of the other random variable. Two random variables are *positively correlated* if their outcomes tend to move in lock step: if one is high, then other tends to be high, and if one is low, the other tends to be low. Two random variables are *negatively correlated* if their outcomes tend to move in opposite step: if one is high, then the other tends to be low, and if one is low, the other tends to be high.

The correlation between two random variables can range from -1 to 1. A correlation of -1 means the two are perfectly negatively correlated: as one random variable's outcome increases, the other one's outcome surely decreases. The other extreme is perfectly positively correlated, which means a correlation of 1: as one random variable's outcome increases, the other one's outcome surely increases as well. In the middle is independence: if two random variables are independent, then their correlation is 0.

So how do we evaluate the standard deviation of X when X is the sum of two random variables that may not be independent? Use the following equation:

$$\text{Standard deviation of } X = \sigma = \sqrt{\sigma_1^2 + \sigma_2^2 + 2 \times \sigma_1 \times \sigma_2 \times \text{Correlation}}$$

where *Correlation* in the above equation is the correlation between X_1 and X_2.

Appendix B

Tables

This appendix contains the Erlang Loss Function Table and the distribution and loss function tables for the standard normal distribution and several Poisson distributions.

Erlang Loss Function Table

The Erlang Loss Function Table contains the probability that a process step consisting of m parallel resources contains m flow units, that is, all m resources are utilized. Interarrival times of flow units (e.g., customers or data packets, etc.) are exponentially distributed with mean a, and service times have a mean p (service times do not have to follow an exponential distribution).

Because there is no buffer space, if a flow unit arrives and all m servers are busy, then that arriving flow unit leaves the system unserved (i.e., the flow unit is lost). The columns in the table correspond to the number of resources m and the rows in the table correspond to $r = p / a$; that is, the ratio between the service time and the interarrival time. The following two pages include two tables, one for small values of r and one for larger values of r.

Example: Find the probability $P_m(r)$ that a process step consisting of three parallel resources must deny access to newly arriving units. Flow units arrive one every $a = 3$ minutes with exponential interarrival times and take $p = 2$ minutes to serve. First, define $r = p / a = 2/3 = 0.67$ and find the corresponding row heading. Second, find the column heading for $m = 3$. The intersection of that row with that column is $P_m(r)=0.0255$.

Note that $P_m(r)$ can be computed directly based on the following formula

$$\text{Probability}\{\text{all } m \text{ servers busy}\} = P_m(r)$$

$$= \frac{\dfrac{r^m}{m!}}{1 + \dfrac{r^1}{1!} + \dfrac{r^2}{2!} + \cdots + \dfrac{r^m}{m!}} \quad \text{(Erlang loss formula)}$$

The exclamation mark (!) in the equation refers to the factorial of an integer number. To compute the factorial of an integer number x, write down all numbers from 1 to x and then multiply them with each other. For example, $4! = 1 \times 2 \times 3 \times 4 = 24$. This calculation can be done with the Excel function FACT(x).

Erlang Loss Table

$r = p/a$	1	2	3	4	5	6	7	8	9	10
0.10	0.0909	0.0045	0.0002	0.0000	0.0000	0.0000	0.0000	0.0000	0.0000	0.0000
0.20	0.1667	0.0164	0.0011	0.0001	0.0000	0.0000	0.0000	0.0000	0.0000	0.0000
0.25	0.2000	0.0244	0.0020	0.0001	0.0000	0.0000	0.0000	0.0000	0.0000	0.0000
0.30	0.2308	0.0335	0.0033	0.0003	0.0000	0.0000	0.0000	0.0000	0.0000	0.0000
0.33	0.2500	0.0400	0.0044	0.0004	0.0000	0.0000	0.0000	0.0000	0.0000	0.0000
0.40	0.2857	0.0541	0.0072	0.0007	0.0001	0.0000	0.0000	0.0000	0.0000	0.0000
0.50	0.3333	0.0769	0.0127	0.0016	0.0002	0.0000	0.0000	0.0000	0.0000	0.0000
0.60	0.3750	0.1011	0.0198	0.0030	0.0004	0.0000	0.0000	0.0000	0.0000	0.0000
0.67	0.4000	0.1176	0.0255	0.0042	0.0006	0.0001	0.0000	0.0000	0.0000	0.0000
0.70	0.4118	0.1260	0.0286	0.0050	0.0007	0.0001	0.0000	0.0000	0.0000	0.0000
0.75	0.4286	0.1385	0.0335	0.0062	0.0009	0.0001	0.0000	0.0000	0.0000	0.0000
0.80	0.4444	0.1509	0.0387	0.0077	0.0012	0.0002	0.0000	0.0000	0.0000	0.0000
0.90	0.4737	0.1757	0.0501	0.0111	0.0020	0.0003	0.0000	0.0000	0.0000	0.0000
1.00	0.5000	0.2000	0.0625	0.0154	0.0031	0.0005	0.0001	0.0000	0.0000	0.0000
1.10	0.5238	0.2237	0.0758	0.0204	0.0045	0.0008	0.0001	0.0000	0.0000	0.0000
1.20	0.5455	0.2466	0.0898	0.0262	0.0063	0.0012	0.0002	0.0000	0.0000	0.0000
1.25	0.5556	0.2577	0.0970	0.0294	0.0073	0.0015	0.0003	0.0000	0.0000	0.0000
1.30	0.5652	0.2687	0.1043	0.0328	0.0085	0.0018	0.0003	0.0001	0.0000	0.0000
1.33	0.5714	0.2759	0.1092	0.0351	0.0093	0.0021	0.0004	0.0001	0.0000	0.0000
1.40	0.5833	0.2899	0.1192	0.0400	0.0111	0.0026	0.0005	0.0001	0.0000	0.0000
1.50	0.6000	0.3103	0.1343	0.0480	0.0142	0.0035	0.0008	0.0001	0.0000	0.0000
1.60	0.6154	0.3299	0.1496	0.0565	0.0177	0.0047	0.0011	0.0002	0.0000	0.0000
1.67	0.6250	0.3425	0.1598	0.0624	0.0204	0.0056	0.0013	0.0003	0.0001	0.0000
1.70	0.6296	0.3486	0.1650	0.0655	0.0218	0.0061	0.0015	0.0003	0.0001	0.0000
1.75	0.6364	0.3577	0.1726	0.0702	0.0240	0.0069	0.0017	0.0004	0.0001	0.0000
1.80	0.6429	0.3665	0.1803	0.0750	0.0263	0.0078	0.0020	0.0005	0.0001	0.0000
1.90	0.6552	0.3836	0.1955	0.0850	0.0313	0.0098	0.0027	0.0006	0.0001	0.0000
2.00	0.6667	0.4000	0.2105	0.0952	0.0367	0.0121	0.0034	0.0009	0.0002	0.0000
2.10	0.6774	0.4156	0.2254	0.1058	0.0425	0.0147	0.0044	0.0011	0.0003	0.0001
2.20	0.6875	0.4306	0.2400	0.1166	0.0488	0.0176	0.0055	0.0015	0.0004	0.0001
2.25	0.6923	0.4378	0.2472	0.1221	0.0521	0.0192	0.0061	0.0017	0.0004	0.0001
2.30	0.6970	0.4449	0.2543	0.1276	0.0554	0.0208	0.0068	0.0019	0.0005	0.0001
2.33	0.7000	0.4495	0.2591	0.1313	0.0577	0.0220	0.0073	0.0021	0.0005	0.0001
2.40	0.7059	0.4586	0.2684	0.1387	0.0624	0.0244	0.0083	0.0025	0.0007	0.0002
2.50	0.7143	0.4717	0.2822	0.1499	0.0697	0.0282	0.0100	0.0031	0.0009	0.0002
2.60	0.7222	0.4842	0.2956	0.1612	0.0773	0.0324	0.0119	0.0039	0.0011	0.0003
2.67	0.7273	0.4923	0.3044	0.1687	0.0825	0.0354	0.0133	0.0044	0.0013	0.0003
2.70	0.7297	0.4963	0.3087	0.1725	0.0852	0.0369	0.0140	0.0047	0.0014	0.0004
2.75	0.7333	0.5021	0.3152	0.1781	0.0892	0.0393	0.0152	0.0052	0.0016	0.0004
2.80	0.7368	0.5078	0.3215	0.1837	0.0933	0.0417	0.0164	0.0057	0.0018	0.0005
2.90	0.7436	0.5188	0.3340	0.1949	0.1016	0.0468	0.0190	0.0068	0.0022	0.0006
3.00	0.7500	0.5294	0.3462	0.2061	0.1101	0.0522	0.0219	0.0081	0.0027	0.0008
3.10	0.7561	0.5396	0.3580	0.2172	0.1187	0.0578	0.0249	0.0096	0.0033	0.0010
3.20	0.7619	0.5494	0.3695	0.2281	0.1274	0.0636	0.0283	0.0112	0.0040	0.0013
3.25	0.7647	0.5541	0.3751	0.2336	0.1318	0.0666	0.0300	0.0120	0.0043	0.0014
3.30	0.7674	0.5587	0.3807	0.2390	0.1362	0.0697	0.0318	0.0130	0.0047	0.0016
3.33	0.7692	0.5618	0.3843	0.2426	0.1392	0.0718	0.0331	0.0136	0.0050	0.0017
3.40	0.7727	0.5678	0.3915	0.2497	0.1452	0.0760	0.0356	0.0149	0.0056	0.0019
3.50	0.7778	0.5765	0.4021	0.2603	0.1541	0.0825	0.0396	0.0170	0.0066	0.0023
3.60	0.7826	0.5848	0.4124	0.2707	0.1631	0.0891	0.0438	0.0193	0.0077	0.0028
3.67	0.7857	0.5902	0.4191	0.2775	0.1691	0.0937	0.0468	0.0210	0.0085	0.0031
3.70	0.7872	0.5929	0.4224	0.2809	0.1721	0.0960	0.0483	0.0218	0.0089	0.0033
3.75	0.7895	0.5968	0.4273	0.2860	0.1766	0.0994	0.0506	0.0232	0.0096	0.0036
3.80	0.7917	0.6007	0.4321	0.2910	0.1811	0.1029	0.0529	0.0245	0.0102	0.0039
3.90	0.7959	0.6082	0.4415	0.3009	0.1901	0.1100	0.0577	0.0274	0.0117	0.0046
4.00	0.8000	0.6154	0.4507	0.3107	0.1991	0.1172	0.0627	0.0304	0.0133	0.0053

Erlang Loss Table

$r = p/a$					m					
	1	2	3	4	5	6	7	8	9	10
1.0	0.5000	0.2000	0.0625	0.0154	0.0031	0.0005	0.0001	0.0000	0.0000	0.0000
1.5	0.6000	0.3103	0.1343	0.0480	0.0142	0.0035	0.0008	0.0001	0.0000	0.0000
2.0	0.6667	0.4000	0.2105	0.0952	0.0367	0.0121	0.0034	0.0009	0.0002	0.0000
2.5	0.7143	0.4717	0.2822	0.1499	0.0697	0.0282	0.0100	0.0031	0.0009	0.0002
3.0	0.7500	0.5294	0.3462	0.2061	0.1101	0.0522	0.0219	0.0081	0.0027	0.0008
3.5	0.7778	0.5765	0.4021	0.2603	0.1541	0.0825	0.0396	0.0170	0.0066	0.0023
4.0	0.8000	0.6154	0.4507	0.3107	0.1991	0.1172	0.0627	0.0304	0.0133	0.0053
4.5	0.8182	0.6480	0.4929	0.3567	0.2430	0.1542	0.0902	0.0483	0.0236	0.0105
5.0	0.8333	0.6757	0.5297	0.3983	0.2849	0.1918	0.1205	0.0700	0.0375	0.0184
5.5	0.8462	0.6994	0.5618	0.4358	0.3241	0.2290	0.1525	0.0949	0.0548	0.0293
6.0	0.8571	0.7200	0.5902	0.4696	0.3604	0.2649	0.1851	0.1219	0.0751	0.0431
6.5	0.8667	0.7380	0.6152	0.4999	0.3939	0.2991	0.2174	0.1501	0.0978	0.0598
7.0	0.8750	0.7538	0.6375	0.5273	0.4247	0.3313	0.2489	0.1788	0.1221	0.0787
7.5	0.8824	0.7679	0.6575	0.5521	0.4530	0.3615	0.2792	0.2075	0.1474	0.0995
8.0	0.8889	0.7805	0.6755	0.5746	0.4790	0.3898	0.3082	0.2356	0.1731	0.1217
8.5	0.8947	0.7918	0.6917	0.5951	0.5029	0.4160	0.3356	0.2629	0.1989	0.1446
9.0	0.9000	0.8020	0.7064	0.6138	0.5249	0.4405	0.3616	0.2892	0.2243	0.1680
9.5	0.9048	0.8112	0.7198	0.6309	0.5452	0.4633	0.3860	0.3143	0.2491	0.1914
10.0	0.9091	0.8197	0.7321	0.6467	0.5640	0.4845	0.4090	0.3383	0.2732	0.2146
10.5	0.9130	0.8274	0.7433	0.6612	0.5813	0.5043	0.4307	0.3611	0.2964	0.2374
11.0	0.9167	0.8345	0.7537	0.6745	0.5974	0.5227	0.4510	0.3828	0.3187	0.2596
11.5	0.9200	0.8410	0.7633	0.6869	0.6124	0.5400	0.4701	0.4033	0.3400	0.2811
12.0	0.9231	0.8471	0.7721	0.6985	0.6264	0.5561	0.4880	0.4227	0.3604	0.3019
12.5	0.9259	0.8527	0.7804	0.7092	0.6394	0.5712	0.5049	0.4410	0.3799	0.3220
13.0	0.9286	0.8579	0.7880	0.7192	0.6516	0.5854	0.5209	0.4584	0.3984	0.3412
13.5	0.9310	0.8627	0.7952	0.7285	0.6630	0.5987	0.5359	0.4749	0.4160	0.3596
14.0	0.9333	0.8673	0.8019	0.7373	0.6737	0.6112	0.5500	0.4905	0.4328	0.3773
14.5	0.9355	0.8715	0.8081	0.7455	0.6837	0.6230	0.5634	0.5052	0.4487	0.3942
15.0	0.9375	0.8755	0.8140	0.7532	0.6932	0.6341	0.5761	0.5193	0.4639	0.4103
15.5	0.9394	0.8792	0.8196	0.7605	0.7022	0.6446	0.5880	0.5326	0.4784	0.4258
16.0	0.9412	0.8828	0.8248	0.7674	0.7106	0.6546	0.5994	0.5452	0.4922	0.4406
16.5	0.9429	0.8861	0.8297	0.7739	0.7186	0.6640	0.6102	0.5572	0.5053	0.4547
17.0	0.9444	0.8892	0.8344	0.7800	0.7262	0.6729	0.6204	0.5687	0.5179	0.4682
17.5	0.9459	0.8922	0.8388	0.7859	0.7334	0.6814	0.6301	0.5795	0.5298	0.4811
18.0	0.9474	0.8950	0.8430	0.7914	0.7402	0.6895	0.6394	0.5899	0.5413	0.4935
18.5	0.9487	0.8977	0.8470	0.7966	0.7467	0.6972	0.6482	0.5998	0.5522	0.5053
19.0	0.9500	0.9002	0.8508	0.8016	0.7529	0.7045	0.6566	0.6093	0.5626	0.5167
19.5	0.9512	0.9027	0.8544	0.8064	0.7587	0.7115	0.6647	0.6183	0.5726	0.5275
20.0	0.9524	0.9050	0.8578	0.8109	0.7644	0.7181	0.6723	0.6270	0.5822	0.5380
20.5	0.9535	0.9072	0.8611	0.8153	0.7697	0.7245	0.6797	0.6353	0.5913	0.5480
21.0	0.9545	0.9093	0.8642	0.8194	0.7749	0.7306	0.6867	0.6432	0.6001	0.5576
21.5	0.9556	0.9113	0.8672	0.8234	0.7798	0.7364	0.6934	0.6508	0.6086	0.5668
22.0	0.9565	0.9132	0.8701	0.8272	0.7845	0.7420	0.6999	0.6581	0.6167	0.5757
22.5	0.9574	0.9150	0.8728	0.8308	0.7890	0.7474	0.7061	0.6651	0.6244	0.5842
23.0	0.9583	0.9168	0.8754	0.8343	0.7933	0.7525	0.7120	0.6718	0.6319	0.5924
23.5	0.9592	0.9185	0.8780	0.8376	0.7974	0.7575	0.7177	0.6783	0.6391	0.6003
24.0	0.9600	0.9201	0.8804	0.8408	0.8014	0.7622	0.7232	0.6845	0.6461	0.6079
24.5	0.9608	0.9217	0.8827	0.8439	0.8053	0.7668	0.7285	0.6905	0.6527	0.6153
25.0	0.9615	0.9232	0.8850	0.8469	0.8090	0.7712	0.7336	0.6963	0.6592	0.6224
25.5	0.9623	0.9246	0.8871	0.8497	0.8125	0.7754	0.7385	0.7019	0.6654	0.6292
26.0	0.9630	0.9260	0.8892	0.8525	0.8159	0.7795	0.7433	0.7072	0.6714	0.6358
26.5	0.9636	0.9274	0.8912	0.8552	0.8192	0.7835	0.7479	0.7124	0.6772	0.6422
27.0	0.9643	0.9287	0.8931	0.8577	0.8224	0.7873	0.7523	0.7174	0.6828	0.6483
27.5	0.9649	0.9299	0.8950	0.8602	0.8255	0.7910	0.7565	0.7223	0.6882	0.6543
28.0	0.9655	0.9311	0.8968	0.8626	0.8285	0.7945	0.7607	0.7269	0.6934	0.6600
28.5	0.9661	0.9323	0.8985	0.8649	0.8314	0.7979	0.7646	0.7315	0.6985	0.6656
29.0	0.9667	0.9334	0.9002	0.8671	0.8341	0.8013	0.7685	0.7359	0.7034	0.6710
29.5	0.9672	0.9345	0.9019	0.8693	0.8368	0.8045	0.7722	0.7401	0.7081	0.6763
30.0	0.9677	0.9356	0.9034	0.8714	0.8394	0.8076	0.7758	0.7442	0.7127	0.6813
30.5	0.9683	0.9366	0.9050	0.8734	0.8420	0.8106	0.7793	0.7482	0.7172	0.6863
31.0	0.9688	0.9376	0.9064	0.8754	0.8444	0.8135	0.7827	0.7521	0.7215	0.6910
31.5	0.9692	0.9385	0.9079	0.8773	0.8468	0.8164	0.7860	0.7558	0.7257	0.6957
32.0	0.9697	0.9394	0.9093	0.8791	0.8491	0.8191	0.7892	0.7594	0.7297	0.7002

Distribution and Loss Function Tables

The Standard Normal Distribution Function Table contains the probability that the outcome of a standard normal random variable is z or smaller. The table provides z values up to two significant digits. Find the row and column headings that add up to the z value you are looking for. The intersection of that row and column contains the probability you seek, $\Phi(z)$.

Example (1): Find the probability that a standard normal random variable generates an outcome that is $z = -1.54$ or lower. First, find the row heading -1.5. Second, find the column heading -0.04, because $(-1.5) + (-0.04) = -1.54$. The intersection of that row with that column is $\Phi(-1.54) = 1.5667$.

Example (2): Find the probability that a standard normal random variable generates an outcome that is $z = 0.52$ or lower. First, find the row heading 0.5. Second, find the column heading 0.02, because $(0.5) + (0.02) = 0.52$. The intersection of that row with that column is $\Phi(0.52) = 0.1917$.

The Standard Normal Loss Function Table is organized in the same way as the Standard Normal Distribution Function Table.

The Poisson Distribution Function Table provides the probability a Poisson distribution with a given mean (column heading) is S or fewer.

The Poisson Loss Function Table provides the expected amount the outcome of a Poisson distribution with a given mean (column heading) exceeds S.

Example (3): With mean 2.25 and $S = 2$, the loss function of a Poisson distribution is 0.69795: look in the column heading for the mean 2.25 and the row with $S = 2$.

Standard Normal Distribution Function Table, $\Phi(z)$

z	−0.09	−0.08	−0.07	−0.06	−0.05	−0.04	−0.03	−0.02	−0.01	0.00
−4.0	0.0000	0.0000	0.0000	0.0000	0.0000	0.0000	0.0000	0.0000	0.0000	0.0000
−3.9	0.0000	0.0000	0.0000	0.0000	0.0000	0.0000	0.0000	0.0000	0.0000	0.0000
−3.8	0.0001	0.0001	0.0001	0.0001	0.0001	0.0001	0.0001	0.0001	0.0001	0.0001
−3.7	0.0001	0.0001	0.0001	0.0001	0.0001	0.0001	0.0001	0.0001	0.0001	0.0001
−3.6	0.0001	0.0001	0.0001	0.0001	0.0001	0.0001	0.0001	0.0001	0.0002	0.0002
−3.5	0.0002	0.0002	0.0002	0.0002	0.0002	0.0002	0.0002	0.0002	0.0002	0.0002
−3.4	0.0002	0.0003	0.0003	0.0003	0.0003	0.0003	0.0003	0.0003	0.0003	0.0003
−3.3	0.0003	0.0004	0.0004	0.0004	0.0004	0.0004	0.0004	0.0005	0.0005	0.0005
−3.2	0.0005	0.0005	0.0005	0.0006	0.0006	0.0006	0.0006	0.0006	0.0007	0.0007
−3.1	0.0007	0.0007	0.0008	0.0008	0.0008	0.0008	0.0009	0.0009	0.0009	0.0010
−3.0	0.0010	0.0010	0.0011	0.0011	0.0011	0.0012	0.0012	0.0013	0.0013	0.0013
−2.9	0.0014	0.0014	0.0015	0.0015	0.0016	0.0016	0.0017	0.0018	0.0018	0.0019
−2.8	0.0019	0.0020	0.0021	0.0021	0.0022	0.0023	0.0023	0.0024	0.0025	0.0026
−2.7	0.0026	0.0027	0.0028	0.0029	0.0030	0.0031	0.0032	0.0033	0.0034	0.0035
−2.6	0.0036	0.0037	0.0038	0.0039	0.0040	0.0041	0.0043	0.0044	0.0045	0.0047
−2.5	0.0048	0.0049	0.0051	0.0052	0.0054	0.0055	0.0057	0.0059	0.0060	0.0062
−2.4	0.0064	0.0066	0.0068	0.0069	0.0071	0.0073	0.0075	0.0078	0.0080	0.0082
−2.3	0.0084	0.0087	0.0089	0.0091	0.0094	0.0096	0.0099	0.0102	0.0104	0.0107
−2.2	0.0110	0.0113	0.0116	0.0119	0.0122	0.0125	0.0129	0.0132	0.0136	0.0139
−2.1	0.0143	0.0146	0.0150	0.0154	0.0158	0.0162	0.0166	0.0170	0.0174	0.0179
−2.0	0.0183	0.0188	0.0192	0.0197	0.0202	0.0207	0.0212	0.0217	0.0222	0.0228
−1.9	0.0233	0.0239	0.0244	0.0250	0.0256	0.0262	0.0329	0.0336	0.0351	0.0359
−1.8	0.0294	0.0301	0.0307	0.0314	0.0322	0.0329	0.0336	0.0344	0.0351	0.0359
−1.7	0.0367	0.0375	0.0384	0.0392	0.0401	0.0409	0.0418	0.0427	0.0436	0.0446
−1.6	0.0455	0.0465	0.0475	0.0485	0.0495	0.0505	0.0516	0.0526	0.0537	0.0548
−1.5	0.0559	0.0571	0.0582	0.0594	0.0606	0.0618	0.0630	0.0643	0.0655	0.0668
−1.4	0.0681	0.0694	0.0708	0.0721	0.0735	0.0749	0.0764	0.0778	0.0793	0.0808
−1.3	0.0823	0.0838	0.0853	0.0869	0.0885	0.0901	0.0918	0.0934	0.0951	0.0968
−1.2	0.0985	0.1003	0.1020	0.1038	0.1056	0.1075	0.1093	0.1112	0.1131	0.1151
−1.1	0.1170	0.1190	0.1210	0.1230	0.1251	0.1271	0.1292	0.1314	0.1335	0.1357
−1.0	0.1379	0.1401	0.1423	0.1446	0.1469	0.1492	0.1515	0.1539	0.1562	0.1587
−0.9	0.1611	0.1635	0.1660	0.1685	0.1711	0.1736	0.1762	0.1788	0.1814	0.1841
−0.8	0.1867	0.1894	0.1922	0.1949	0.1977	0.2005	0.2033	0.2061	0.2090	0.2119
−0.7	0.2148	0.2177	0.2206	0.2236	0.2266	0.2296	0.2327	0.2358	0.2389	0.2420
−0.6	0.2451	0.2483	0.2514	0.2546	0.2578	0.2611	0.2643	0.2676	0.2709	0.2743
−0.5	0.2776	0.2810	0.2843	0.2877	0.2912	0.2946	0.2981	0.3015	0.3050	0.3085
−0.4	0.3121	0.3156	0.3192	0.3228	0.3264	0.3300	0.3336	0.3372	0.3409	0.3446
−0.3	0.3483	0.3520	0.3557	0.3594	0.3632	0.3669	0.3707	0.3745	0.3783	0.3821
−0.2	0.3859	0.3897	0.3936	0.3974	0.4013	0.4052	0.4090	0.4129	0.4168	0.4207
−0.1	0.4247	0.4286	0.4325	0.4364	0.4404	0.4443	0.4483	0.4522	0.4562	0.4602
0.0	0.4641	0.4681	0.4721	0.4761	0.4801	0.4840	0.4880	0.4920	0.4960	0.5000

Standard Normal Distribution Function Table, $\Phi(z)$ (continued)

z	0.00	0.01	0.02	0.03	0.04	0.05	0.06	0.07	0.08	0.09
0.0	0.5000	0.5040	0.5080	0.5120	0.5160	0.5199	0.5239	0.5279	0.5319	0.5359
0.1	0.5398	0.5438	0.5478	0.5517	0.5557	0.5596	0.5636	0.5675	0.5714	0.5753
0.2	0.5793	0.5832	0.5871	0.5910	0.5948	0.5987	0.6026	0.6064	0.6103	0.6141
0.3	0.6179	0.6217	0.6255	0.6293	0.6331	0.6368	0.6406	0.6443	0.6480	0.6517
0.4	0.6554	0.6591	0.6628	0.6664	0.6700	0.6736	0.6772	0.6808	0.6844	0.6879
0.5	0.6915	0.6950	0.6985	0.7019	0.7054	0.7088	0.7123	0.7157	0.7190	0.7224
0.6	0.7257	0.7291	0.7324	0.7357	0.7389	0.7422	0.7454	0.7486	0.7517	0.7549
0.7	0.7580	0.7611	0.7642	0.7673	0.7704	0.7734	0.7764	0.7794	0.7823	0.7852
0.8	0.7881	0.7910	0.7939	0.7967	0.7995	0.8023	0.8051	0.8078	0.8106	0.8133
0.9	0.8159	0.8186	0.8212	0.8238	0.8264	0.8289	0.8315	0.8340	0.8365	0.8389
1.0	0.8413	0.8438	0.8461	0.8485	0.8508	0.8531	0.8554	0.8577	0.8599	0.8621
1.1	0.8643	0.8665	0.8686	0.8708	0.8729	0.8749	0.8770	0.8790	0.8810	0.8830
1.2	0.8849	0.8869	0.8888	0.8907	0.8925	0.8944	0.8962	0.8980	0.8997	0.9015
1.3	0.9032	0.9049	0.9066	0.9082	0.9099	0.9115	0.9131	0.9147	0.9162	0.9177
1.4	0.9192	0.9207	0.9222	0.9236	0.9251	0.9265	0.9279	0.9292	0.9306	0.9319
1.5	0.9332	0.9345	0.9357	0.9370	0.9382	0.9394	0.9406	0.9418	0.9429	0.9441
1.6	0.9452	0.9463	0.9474	0.9484	0.9495	0.9505	0.9515	0.9525	0.9535	0.9545
1.7	0.9554	0.9564	0.9573	0.9582	0.9591	0.9599	0.9608	0.9616	0.9625	0.9633
1.8	0.9641	0.9649	0.9656	0.9664	0.9671	0.9678	0.9686	0.9693	0.9699	0.9706
1.9	0.9713	0.9719	0.9726	0.9732	0.9738	0.9744	0.9750	0.9756	0.9761	0.9767
2.0	0.9772	0.9778	0.9783	0.9788	0.9793	0.9798	0.9803	0.9808	0.9812	0.9817
2.1	0.9821	0.9826	0.9830	0.9834	0.9838	0.9842	0.9846	0.9850	0.9854	0.9857
2.2	0.9861	0.9864	0.9868	0.9871	0.9875	0.9878	0.9881	0.9884	0.9887	0.9890
2.3	0.9893	0.9896	0.9898	0.9901	0.9904	0.9906	0.9909	0.9911	0.9913	0.9916
2.4	0.9918	0.9920	0.9922	0.9925	0.9927	0.9929	0.9931	0.9932	0.9934	0.9936
2.5	0.9938	0.9940	0.9941	0.9943	0.9945	0.9946	0.9948	0.9949	0.9951	0.9952
2.6	0.9953	0.9955	0.9956	0.9957	0.9959	0.9960	0.9961	0.9962	0.9963	0.9964
2.7	0.9965	0.9966	0.9967	0.9968	0.9969	0.9970	0.9971	0.9972	0.9973	0.9974
2.8	0.9974	0.9975	0.9976	0.9977	0.9977	0.9978	0.9979	0.9979	0.9980	0.9981
2.9	0.9981	0.9982	0.9982	0.9983	0.9984	0.9984	0.9985	0.9985	0.9986	0.9986
3.0	0.9987	0.9987	0.9987	0.9988	0.9988	0.9989	0.9989	0.9989	0.9990	0.9990
3.1	0.9990	0.9991	0.9991	0.9991	0.9992	0.9992	0.9992	0.9992	0.9993	0.9993
3.2	0.9993	0.9993	0.9994	0.9994	0.9994	0.9994	0.9994	0.9995	0.9995	0.9995
3.3	0.9995	0.9995	0.9995	0.9996	0.9996	0.9996	0.9996	0.9996	0.9996	0.9997
3.4	0.9997	0.9997	0.9997	0.9997	0.9997	0.9997	0.9997	0.9997	0.9997	0.9998
3.5	0.9998	0.9998	0.9998	0.9998	0.9998	0.9998	0.9998	0.9998	0.9998	0.9998
3.6	0.9998	0.9998	0.9999	0.9999	0.9999	0.9999	0.9999	0.9999	0.9999	0.9999
3.7	0.9999	0.9999	0.9999	0.9999	0.9999	0.9999	0.9999	0.9999	0.9999	0.9999
3.8	0.9999	0.9999	0.9999	0.9999	0.9999	0.9999	0.9999	0.9999	0.9999	0.9999
3.9	1.0000	1.0000	1.0000	1.0000	1.0000	1.0000	1.0000	1.0000	1.0000	1.0000
4.0	1.0000	1.0000	1.0000	1.0000	1.0000	1.0000	1.0000	1.0000	1.0000	1.0000

Standard Normal Loss Function Table, $L(z)$

z	−0.09	−0.08	−0.07	−0.06	−0.05	−0.04	−0.03	−0.02	−0.01	0.00
−4.0	4.0900	4.0800	4.0700	4.0600	4.0500	4.0400	4.0300	4.0200	4.0100	4.0000
−3.9	3.9900	3.9800	3.9700	3.9600	3.9500	3.9400	3.9300	3.9200	3.9100	3.9000
−3.8	3.8900	3.8800	3.8700	3.8600	3.8500	3.8400	3.8300	3.8200	3.8100	3.8000
−3.7	3.7900	3.7800	3.7700	3.7600	3.7500	3.7400	3.7300	3.7200	3.7100	3.7000
−3.6	3.6900	3.6800	3.6700	3.6600	3.6500	3.6400	3.6300	3.6200	3.6100	3.6000
−3.5	3.5900	3.5800	3.5700	3.5600	3.5500	3.5400	3.5301	3.5201	3.5101	3.5001
−3.4	3.4901	3.4801	3.4701	3.4601	3.4501	3.4401	3.4301	3.4201	3.4101	3.4001
−3.3	3.3901	3.3801	3.3701	3.3601	3.3501	3.3401	3.3301	3.3201	3.3101	3.3001
−3.2	3.2901	3.2801	3.2701	3.2601	3.2502	3.2402	3.2302	3.2202	3.2102	3.2002
−3.1	3.1902	3.1802	3.1702	3.1602	3.1502	3.1402	3.1302	3.1202	3.1103	3.1003
−3.0	3.0903	3.0803	3.0703	3.0603	3.0503	3.0403	3.0303	3.0204	3.0104	3.0004
−2.9	2.9904	2.9804	2.9704	2.9604	2.9505	2.9405	2.9305	2.9205	2.9105	2.9005
−2.8	2.8906	2.8806	2.8706	2.8606	2.8506	2.8407	2.8307	2.8207	2.8107	2.8008
−2.7	2.7908	2.7808	2.7708	2.7609	2.7509	2.7409	2.7310	2.7210	2.7110	2.7011
−2.6	2.6911	2.6811	2.6712	2.6612	2.6512	2.6413	2.6313	2.6214	2.6114	2.6015
−2.5	2.5915	2.5816	2.5716	2.5617	2.5517	2.5418	2.5318	2.5219	2.5119	2.5020
−2.4	2.4921	2.4821	2.4722	2.4623	2.4523	2.4424	2.4325	2.4226	2.4126	2.4027
−2.3	2.3928	2.3829	2.3730	2.3631	2.3532	2.3433	2.3334	2.3235	2.3136	2.3037
−2.2	2.2938	2.2839	2.2740	2.2641	2.2542	2.2444	2.2345	2.2246	2.2147	2.2049
−2.1	2.1950	2.1852	2.1753	2.1655	2.1556	2.1458	2.1360	2.1261	2.1163	2.1065
−2.0	2.0966	2.0868	2.0770	2.0672	2.0574	2.0476	2.0378	2.0280	2.0183	2.0085
−1.9	1.9987	1.9890	1.9792	1.9694	1.9597	1.9500	1.9402	1.9305	1.9208	1.9111
−1.8	1.9013	1.8916	1.8819	1.8723	1.8626	1.8529	1.8432	1.8336	1.8239	1.8143
−1.7	1.8046	1.7950	1.7854	1.7758	1.7662	1.7566	1.7470	1.7374	1.7278	1.7183
−1.6	1.7087	1.6992	1.6897	1.6801	1.6706	1.6611	1.6516	1.6422	1.6327	1.6232
−1.5	1.6138	1.6044	1.5949	1.5855	1.5761	1.5667	1.5574	1.5480	1.5386	1.5293
−1.4	1.5200	1.5107	1.5014	1.4921	1.4828	1.4736	1.4643	1.4551	1.4459	1.4367
−1.3	1.4275	1.4183	1.4092	1.4000	1.3909	1.3818	1.3727	1.3636	1.3546	1.3455
−1.2	1.3365	1.3275	1.3185	1.3095	1.3006	1.2917	1.2827	1.2738	1.2650	1.2561
−1.1	1.2473	1.2384	1.2296	1.2209	1.2121	1.2034	1.1946	1.1859	1.1773	1.1686
−1.0	1.1600	1.1514	1.1428	1.1342	1.1257	1.1172	1.1087	1.1002	1.0917	1.0833
−0.9	1.0749	1.0665	1.0582	1.0499	1.0416	1.0333	1.0250	1.0168	1.0086	1.0004
−0.8	0.9923	0.9842	0.9761	0.9680	0.9600	0.9520	0.9440	0.9360	0.9281	0.9202
−0.7	0.9123	0.9045	0.8967	0.8889	0.8812	0.8734	0.8658	0.8581	0.8505	0.8429
−0.6	0.8353	0.8278	0.8203	0.8128	0.8054	0.7980	0.7906	0.7833	0.7759	0.7687
−0.5	0.7614	0.7542	0.7471	0.7399	0.7328	0.7257	0.7187	0.7117	0.7047	0.6978
−0.4	0.6909	0.6840	0.6772	0.6704	0.6637	0.6569	0.6503	0.6436	0.6370	0.6304
−0.3	0.6239	0.6174	0.6109	0.6045	0.5981	0.5918	0.5855	0.5792	0.5730	0.5668
−0.2	0.5606	0.5545	0.5484	0.5424	0.5363	0.5304	0.5244	0.5186	0.5127	0.5069
−0.1	0.5011	0.4954	0.4897	0.4840	0.4784	0.4728	0.4673	0.4618	0.4564	0.4509
0.0	0.4456	0.4402	0.4349	0.4297	0.4244	0.4193	0.4141	0.4090	0.4040	0.3989

Standard Normal Loss Function Table, $L(z)$ (continued)

z	0.00	0.01	0.02	0.03	0.04	0.05	0.06	0.07	0.08	0.09
0.0	0.3989	0.3940	0.3890	0.3841	0.3793	0.3744	0.3697	0.3649	0.3602	0.3556
0.1	0.3509	0.3464	0.3418	0.3373	0.3328	0.3284	0.3240	0.3197	0.3154	0.3111
0.2	0.3069	0.3027	0.2986	0.2944	0.2904	0.2863	0.2824	0.2784	0.2745	0.2706
0.3	0.2668	0.2630	0.2592	0.2555	0.2518	0.2481	0.2445	0.2409	0.2374	0.2339
0.4	0.2304	0.2270	0.2236	0.2203	0.2169	0.2137	0.2104	0.2072	0.2040	0.2009
0.5	0.1978	0.1947	0.1917	0.1887	0.1857	0.1828	0.1799	0.1771	0.1742	0.1714
0.6	0.1687	0.1659	0.1633	0.1606	0.1580	0.1554	0.1528	0.1503	0.1478	0.1453
0.7	0.1429	0.1405	0.1381	0.1358	0.1334	0.1312	0.1289	0.1267	0.1245	0.1223
0.8	0.1202	0.1181	0.1160	0.1140	0.1120	0.1100	0.1080	0.1061	0.1042	0.1023
0.9	0.1004	0.0986	0.0968	0.0950	0.0933	0.0916	0.0899	0.0882	0.0865	0.0849
1.0	0.0833	0.0817	0.0802	0.0787	0.0772	0.0757	0.0742	0.0728	0.0714	0.0700
1.1	0.0686	0.0673	0.0659	0.0646	0.0634	0.0621	0.0609	0.0596	0.0584	0.0573
1.2	0.0561	0.0550	0.0538	0.0527	0.0517	0.0506	0.0495	0.0485	0.0475	0.0465
1.3	0.0455	0.0446	0.0436	0.0427	0.0418	0.0409	0.0400	0.0392	0.0383	0.0375
1.4	0.0367	0.0359	0.0351	0.0343	0.0336	0.0328	0.0321	0.0314	0.0307	0.0300
1.5	0.0293	0.0286	0.0280	0.0274	0.0267	0.0261	0.0255	0.0249	0.0244	0.0238
1.6	0.0232	0.0227	0.0222	0.0216	0.0211	0.0206	0.0201	0.0197	0.0192	0.0187
1.7	0.0183	0.0178	0.0174	0.0170	0.0166	0.0162	0.0158	0.0154	0.0150	0.0146
1.8	0.0143	0.0139	0.0136	0.0132	0.0129	0.0126	0.0123	0.0119	0.0116	0.0113
1.9	0.0111	0.0108	0.0105	0.0102	0.0100	0.0097	0.0094	0.0092	0.0090	0.0087
2.0	0.0085	0.0083	0.0080	0.0078	0.0076	0.0074	0.0072	0.0070	0.0068	0.0066
2.1	0.0065	0.0063	0.0061	0.0060	0.0058	0.0056	0.0055	0.0053	0.0052	0.0050
2.2	0.0049	0.0047	0.0046	0.0045	0.0044	0.0042	0.0041	0.0040	0.0039	0.0038
2.3	0.0037	0.0036	0.0035	0.0034	0.0033	0.0032	0.0031	0.0030	0.0029	0.0028
2.4	0.0027	0.0026	0.0026	0.0025	0.0024	0.0023	0.0023	0.0022	0.0021	0.0021
2.5	0.0020	0.0019	0.0019	0.0018	0.0018	0.0017	0.0017	0.0016	0.0016	0.0015
2.6	0.0015	0.0014	0.0014	0.0013	0.0013	0.0012	0.0012	0.0012	0.0011	0.0011
2.7	0.0011	0.0010	0.0010	0.0010	0.0009	0.0009	0.0009	0.0008	0.0008	0.0008
2.8	0.0008	0.0007	0.0007	0.0007	0.0007	0.0006	0.0006	0.0006	0.0006	0.0006
2.9	0.0005	0.0005	0.0005	0.0005	0.0005	0.0005	0.0004	0.0004	0.0004	0.0004
3.0	0.0004	0.0004	0.0004	0.0003	0.0003	0.0003	0.0003	0.0003	0.0003	0.0003
3.1	0.0003	0.0003	0.0002	0.0002	0.0002	0.0002	0.0002	0.0002	0.0002	0.0002
3.2	0.0002	0.0002	0.0002	0.0002	0.0002	0.0002	0.0001	0.0001	0.0001	0.0001
3.3	0.0001	0.0001	0.0001	0.0001	0.0001	0.0001	0.0001	0.0001	0.0001	0.0001
3.4	0.0001	0.0001	0.0001	0.0001	0.0001	0.0001	0.0001	0.0001	0.0001	0.0001
3.5	0.0001	0.0001	0.0001	0.0001	0.0000	0.0000	0.0000	0.0000	0.0000	0.0000
3.6	0.0000	0.0000	0.0000	0.0000	0.0000	0.0000	0.0000	0.0000	0.0000	0.0000
3.7	0.0000	0.0000	0.0000	0.0000	0.0000	0.0000	0.0000	0.0000	0.0000	0.0000
3.8	0.0000	0.0000	0.0000	0.0000	0.0000	0.0000	0.0000	0.0000	0.0000	0.0000
3.9	0.0000	0.0000	0.0000	0.0000	0.0000	0.0000	0.0000	0.0000	0.0000	0.0000
4.0	0.0000	0.0000	0.0000	0.0000	0.0000	0.0000	0.0000	0.0000	0.0000	0.0000

Poisson Distribution Function Table

					Mean					
S	0.05	0.10	0.15	0.20	0.25	0.30	0.35	0.40	0.45	0.50
0	0.95123	0.90484	0.86071	0.81873	0.77880	0.74082	0.70469	0.67032	0.63763	0.60653
1	0.99879	0.99532	0.98981	0.98248	0.97350	0.96306	0.95133	0.93845	0.92456	0.90980
2	0.99998	0.99985	0.99950	0.99885	0.99784	0.99640	0.99449	0.99207	0.98912	0.98561
3	1.00000	1.00000	0.99998	0.99994	0.99987	0.99973	0.99953	0.99922	0.99880	0.99825
4	1.00000	1.00000	1.00000	1.00000	0.99999	0.99998	0.99997	0.99994	0.99989	0.99983
5	1.00000	1.00000	1.00000	1.00000	1.00000	1.00000	1.00000	1.00000	0.99999	0.99999
6	1.00000	1.00000	1.00000	1.00000	1.00000	1.00000	1.00000	1.00000	1.00000	1.00000

					Mean					
S	0.55	0.60	0.65	0.70	0.75	0.80	0.85	0.90	0.95	1.00
0	0.57695	0.54881	0.52205	0.49659	0.47237	0.44933	0.42741	0.40657	0.38674	0.36788
1	0.89427	0.87810	0.86138	0.84420	0.82664	0.80879	0.79072	0.77248	0.75414	0.73576
2	0.98154	0.97688	0.97166	0.96586	0.95949	0.95258	0.94512	0.93714	0.92866	0.91970
3	0.99753	0.99664	0.99555	0.99425	0.99271	0.99092	0.98887	0.98654	0.98393	0.98101
4	0.99973	0.99961	0.99944	0.99921	0.99894	0.99859	0.99817	0.99766	0.99705	0.99634
5	0.99998	0.99996	0.99994	0.99991	0.99987	0.99982	0.99975	0.99966	0.99954	0.99941
6	1.00000	1.00000	0.99999	0.99999	0.99999	0.99998	0.99997	0.99996	0.99994	0.99992
7	1.00000	1.00000	1.00000	1.00000	1.00000	1.00000	1.00000	1.00000	0.99999	0.99999
8	1.00000	1.00000	1.00000	1.00000	1.00000	1.00000	1.00000	1.00000	1.00000	1.00000

					Mean					
S	1.25	1.50	1.75	2.00	2.25	2.50	2.75	3.00	3.25	3.50
0	0.28650	0.22313	0.17377	0.13534	0.10540	0.08208	0.06393	0.04979	0.03877	0.03020
1	0.64464	0.55783	0.47788	0.40601	0.34255	0.28730	0.23973	0.19915	0.16479	0.13589
2	0.86847	0.80885	0.74397	0.67668	0.60934	0.54381	0.48146	0.42319	0.36957	0.32085
3	0.96173	0.93436	0.89919	0.85712	0.80943	0.75758	0.70304	0.64723	0.59141	0.53663
4	0.99088	0.98142	0.96710	0.94735	0.92199	0.89118	0.85538	0.81526	0.77165	0.72544
5	0.99816	0.99554	0.99087	0.98344	0.97263	0.95798	0.93916	0.91608	0.88881	0.85761
6	0.99968	0.99907	0.99780	0.99547	0.99163	0.98581	0.97757	0.96649	0.95227	0.93471
7	0.99995	0.99983	0.99953	0.99890	0.99773	0.99575	0.99265	0.98810	0.98174	0.97326
8	0.99999	0.99997	0.99991	0.99976	0.99945	0.99886	0.99784	0.99620	0.99371	0.99013
9	1.00000	1.00000	0.99998	0.99995	0.99988	0.99972	0.99942	0.99890	0.99803	0.99669
10	1.00000	1.00000	1.00000	0.99999	0.99998	0.99994	0.99986	0.99971	0.99944	0.99898
11	1.00000	1.00000	1.00000	1.00000	1.00000	0.99999	0.99997	0.99993	0.99985	0.99971
12	1.00000	1.00000	1.00000	1.00000	1.00000	1.00000	0.99999	0.99998	0.99996	0.99992
13	1.00000	1.00000	1.00000	1.00000	1.00000	1.00000	1.00000	1.00000	0.99999	0.99998
14	1.00000	1.00000	1.00000	1.00000	1.00000	1.00000	1.00000	1.00000	1.00000	1.00000
15	1.00000	1.00000	1.00000	1.00000	1.00000	1.00000	1.00000	1.00000	1.00000	1.00000

Poisson Distribution Function Table (continued)

Mean

S	3.75	4.00	4.25	4.50	4.75	5.00	5.25	5.50	5.75	6.00	6.25	6.50
0	0.02352	0.01832	0.01426	0.01111	0.00865	0.00674	0.00525	0.00409	0.00318	0.00248	0.00193	0.00150
1	0.11171	0.09158	0.07489	0.06110	0.04975	0.04043	0.03280	0.02656	0.02148	0.01735	0.01400	0.01128
2	0.27707	0.23810	0.20371	0.17358	0.14735	0.12465	0.10511	0.08838	0.07410	0.06197	0.05170	0.04304
3	0.48377	0.43347	0.38621	0.34230	0.30189	0.26503	0.23167	0.20170	0.17495	0.15120	0.13025	0.11185
4	0.67755	0.62884	0.58012	0.53210	0.48540	0.44049	0.39777	0.35752	0.31991	0.28506	0.25299	0.22367
5	0.82288	0.78513	0.74494	0.70293	0.65973	0.61596	0.57218	0.52892	0.48662	0.44568	0.40640	0.36904
6	0.91372	0.88933	0.86169	0.83105	0.79775	0.76218	0.72479	0.68604	0.64639	0.60630	0.56622	0.52652
7	0.96238	0.94887	0.93257	0.91341	0.89140	0.86663	0.83925	0.80949	0.77762	0.74398	0.70890	0.67276
8	0.98519	0.97864	0.97023	0.95974	0.94701	0.93191	0.91436	0.89436	0.87195	0.84724	0.82038	0.79157
9	0.99469	0.99187	0.98801	0.98291	0.97636	0.96817	0.95817	0.94622	0.93221	0.91608	0.89779	0.87738
10	0.99826	0.99716	0.99557	0.99333	0.99030	0.98630	0.98118	0.97475	0.96686	0.95738	0.94618	0.93316
11	0.99947	0.99908	0.99849	0.99760	0.99632	0.99455	0.99216	0.98901	0.98498	0.97991	0.97367	0.96612
12	0.99985	0.99973	0.99952	0.99919	0.99870	0.99798	0.99696	0.99555	0.99366	0.99117	0.98798	0.98397
13	0.99996	0.99992	0.99986	0.99975	0.99957	0.99930	0.99890	0.99831	0.99749	0.99637	0.99487	0.99290
14	0.99999	0.99998	0.99996	0.99993	0.99987	0.99977	0.99963	0.99940	0.99907	0.99860	0.99794	0.99704
15	1.00000	1.00000	0.99999	0.99998	0.99996	0.99993	0.99988	0.99980	0.99968	0.99949	0.99922	0.99884
16	1.00000	1.00000	1.00000	0.99999	0.99999	0.99998	0.99996	0.99994	0.99989	0.99983	0.99972	0.99957
17	1.00000	1.00000	1.00000	1.00000	1.00000	0.99999	0.99999	0.99998	0.99997	0.99994	0.99991	0.99985
18	1.00000	1.00000	1.00000	1.00000	1.00000	1.00000	1.00000	0.99999	0.99999	0.99998	0.99997	0.99995
19	1.00000	1.00000	1.00000	1.00000	1.00000	1.00000	1.00000	1.00000	1.00000	0.99999	0.99999	0.99998

Mean

S	6.75	7.00	7.25	7.50	7.75	8.00	8.25	8.50	8.75	9.00	9.25	9.50
0	0.00117	0.00091	0.00071	0.00055	0.00043	0.00034	0.00026	0.00020	0.00016	0.00012	0.00010	0.00007
1	0.00907	0.00730	0.00586	0.00470	0.00377	0.00302	0.00242	0.00193	0.00154	0.00123	0.00099	0.00079
2	0.03575	0.02964	0.02452	0.02026	0.01670	0.01375	0.01131	0.00928	0.00761	0.00623	0.00510	0.00416
3	0.09577	0.08177	0.06963	0.05915	0.05012	0.04238	0.03576	0.03011	0.02530	0.02123	0.01777	0.01486
4	0.19704	0.17299	0.15138	0.13206	0.11487	0.09963	0.08619	0.07436	0.06401	0.05496	0.04709	0.04026
5	0.33377	0.30071	0.26992	0.24144	0.21522	0.19124	0.16939	0.14960	0.13174	0.11569	0.10133	0.08853
6	0.48759	0.44971	0.41316	0.37815	0.34485	0.31337	0.28380	0.25618	0.23051	0.20678	0.18495	0.16495
7	0.63591	0.59871	0.56152	0.52464	0.48837	0.45296	0.41864	0.38560	0.35398	0.32390	0.29544	0.26866
8	0.76106	0.72909	0.69596	0.66197	0.62740	0.59255	0.55770	0.52311	0.48902	0.45565	0.42320	0.39182
9	0.85492	0.83050	0.80427	0.77641	0.74712	0.71662	0.68516	0.65297	0.62031	0.58741	0.55451	0.52183
10	0.91827	0.90148	0.88279	0.86224	0.83990	0.81589	0.79032	0.76336	0.73519	0.70599	0.67597	0.64533
11	0.95715	0.94665	0.93454	0.92076	0.90527	0.88808	0.86919	0.84866	0.82657	0.80301	0.77810	0.75199
12	0.97902	0.97300	0.96581	0.95733	0.94749	0.93620	0.92341	0.90908	0.89320	0.87577	0.85683	0.83643
13	0.99037	0.98719	0.98324	0.97844	0.97266	0.96582	0.95782	0.94859	0.93805	0.92615	0.91285	0.89814
14	0.99585	0.99428	0.99227	0.98974	0.98659	0.98274	0.97810	0.97257	0.96608	0.95853	0.94986	0.94001
15	0.99831	0.99759	0.99664	0.99539	0.99379	0.99177	0.98925	0.98617	0.98243	0.97796	0.97269	0.96653
16	0.99935	0.99904	0.99862	0.99804	0.99728	0.99628	0.99500	0.99339	0.99137	0.98889	0.98588	0.98227
17	0.99976	0.99964	0.99946	0.99921	0.99887	0.99841	0.99779	0.99700	0.99597	0.99468	0.99306	0.99107
18	0.99992	0.99987	0.99980	0.99970	0.99955	0.99935	0.99907	0.99870	0.99821	0.99757	0.99675	0.99572
19	0.99997	0.99996	0.99993	0.99989	0.99983	0.99975	0.99963	0.99947	0.99924	0.99894	0.99855	0.99804
20	0.99999	0.99999	0.99998	0.99996	0.99994	0.99991	0.99986	0.99979	0.99969	0.99956	0.99938	0.99914
21	1.00000	1.00000	0.99999	0.99999	0.99998	0.99997	0.99995	0.99992	0.99988	0.99983	0.99975	0.99964
22	1.00000	1.00000	1.00000	1.00000	0.99999	0.99999	0.99998	0.99997	0.99996	0.99993	0.99990	0.99985
23	1.00000	1.00000	1.00000	1.00000	1.00000	1.00000	0.99999	0.99999	0.99998	0.99998	0.99996	0.99994
24	1.00000	1.00000	1.00000	1.00000	1.00000	1.00000	1.00000	1.00000	0.99999	0.99999	0.99999	0.99998

Poisson Loss Function Table

					Mean					
s	0.05	0.10	0.15	0.20	0.25	0.30	0.35	0.40	0.45	0.50
0	0.05000	0.10000	0.15000	0.20000	0.25000	0.30000	0.35000	0.40000	0.45000	0.50000
1	0.00123	0.00484	0.01071	0.01873	0.02880	0.04082	0.05469	0.07032	0.08763	0.10653
2	0.00002	0.00016	0.00052	0.00121	0.00230	0.00388	0.00602	0.00877	0.01219	0.01633
3	0.00000	0.00000	0.00002	0.00006	0.00014	0.00028	0.00051	0.00084	0.00131	0.00194
4	0.00000	0.00000	0.00000	0.00000	0.00001	0.00002	0.00003	0.00007	0.00011	0.00019
5	0.00000	0.00000	0.00000	0.00000	0.00000	0.00000	0.00000	0.00000	0.00001	0.00002
6	0.00000	0.00000	0.00000	0.00000	0.00000	0.00000	0.00000	0.00000	0.00000	0.00000

					Mean					
s	0.55	0.60	0.65	0.70	0.75	0.80	0.85	0.90	0.95	1.00
0	0.55000	0.60000	0.65000	0.70000	0.75000	0.80000	0.85000	0.90000	0.95000	1.00000
1	0.12695	0.14881	0.17205	0.19659	0.22237	0.24933	0.27741	0.30657	0.33674	0.36788
2	0.02122	0.02691	0.03342	0.04078	0.04901	0.05812	0.06813	0.07905	0.09089	0.10364
3	0.00276	0.00379	0.00508	0.00664	0.00850	0.01070	0.01325	0.01620	0.01955	0.02334
4	0.00029	0.00044	0.00063	0.00089	0.00121	0.00162	0.00212	0.00274	0.00347	0.00435
5	0.00003	0.00004	0.00007	0.00010	0.00015	0.00021	0.00029	0.00039	0.00052	0.00069
6	0.00000	0.00000	0.00001	0.00001	0.00002	0.00002	0.00003	0.00005	0.00007	0.00009
7	0.00000	0.00000	0.00001	0.00001	0.00002	0.00002	0.00003	0.00005	0.00007	0.00009
8	0.00000	0.00000	0.00001	0.00001	0.00001	0.00002	0.00003	0.00004	0.00006	0.00008

					Mean					
s	1.25	1.50	1.75	2.00	2.25	2.50	2.75	3.00	3.25	3.50
0	1.25000	1.50000	1.75000	2.00000	2.25000	2.50000	2.75000	3.00000	3.25000	3.50000
1	0.53650	0.72313	0.92377	1.13534	1.35540	1.58208	1.81393	2.04979	2.28877	2.53020
2	0.18114	0.28096	0.40165	0.54134	0.69795	0.86938	1.05366	1.24894	1.45356	1.66609
3	0.04961	0.08980	0.14562	0.21802	0.30729	0.41320	0.53511	0.67213	0.82313	0.98693
4	0.01134	0.02416	0.04481	0.07514	0.11672	0.17077	0.23815	0.31936	0.41454	0.52357
5	0.00221	0.00558	0.01191	0.02249	0.03870	0.06195	0.09353	0.13462	0.18619	0.24901
6	0.00038	0.00113	0.00278	0.00592	0.01134	0.01993	0.03270	0.05070	0.07501	0.10662
7	0.00006	0.00020	0.00058	0.00139	0.00297	0.00574	0.01026	0.01719	0.02728	0.04134
8	0.00001	0.00003	0.00011	0.00029	0.00070	0.00149	0.00292	0.00529	0.00902	0.01460
9	0.00000	0.00000	0.00002	0.00006	0.00015	0.00035	0.00076	0.00149	0.00273	0.00472
10	0.00000	0.00000	0.00000	0.00001	0.00003	0.00008	0.00018	0.00038	0.00076	0.00141
11	0.00000	0.00000	0.00000	0.00000	0.00001	0.00002	0.00004	0.00009	0.00020	0.00039
12	0.00000	0.00000	0.00000	0.00000	0.00000	0.00000	0.00001	0.00002	0.00005	0.00010
13	0.00000	0.00000	0.00000	0.00000	0.00000	0.00000	0.00000	0.00000	0.00001	0.00002
14	0.00000	0.00000	0.00000	0.00000	0.00000	0.00000	0.00000	0.00000	0.00000	0.00001
15	0.00000	0.00000	0.00000	0.00000	0.00000	0.00000	0.00000	0.00000	0.00000	0.00000

Poisson Loss Function Table (continued)

						Mean						
S	**3.75**	**4.00**	**4.25**	**4.50**	**4.75**	**5.00**	**5.25**	**5.50**	**5.75**	**6.00**	**6.25**	**6.50**
0	3.75000	4.00000	4.25000	4.50000	4.75000	5.00000	5.25000	5.50000	5.75000	6.00000	6.25000	6.50000
1	2.77352	3.01832	3.26426	3.51111	3.75865	4.00674	4.25525	4.50409	4.75318	5.00248	5.25193	5.50150
2	1.88523	2.10989	2.33915	2.57221	2.80840	3.04717	3.28804	3.53065	3.77467	4.01983	4.26593	4.51278
3	1.16230	1.34800	1.54286	1.74579	1.95575	2.17182	2.39316	2.61903	2.84877	3.08180	3.31763	3.55582
4	0.64606	0.78147	0.92907	1.08808	1.25763	1.43684	1.62483	1.82073	2.02371	2.23300	2.44788	2.66766
5	0.32361	0.41030	0.50919	0.62019	0.74303	0.87734	1.02260	1.17824	1.34362	1.51806	1.70086	1.89134
6	0.14649	0.19543	0.25413	0.32312	0.40277	0.49330	0.59479	0.70716	0.83024	0.96374	1.10727	1.26038
7	0.06021	0.08476	0.11582	0.15417	0.20052	0.25548	0.31958	0.39320	0.47663	0.57004	0.67348	0.78690
8	0.02259	0.03363	0.04839	0.06758	0.09192	0.12211	0.15882	0.20268	0.25426	0.31402	0.38238	0.45966
9	0.00778	0.01226	0.01861	0.02732	0.03893	0.05402	0.07318	0.09704	0.12620	0.16126	0.20276	0.25123
10	0.00247	0.00413	0.00662	0.01023	0.01529	0.02219	0.03136	0.04326	0.05842	0.07733	0.10056	0.12862
11	0.00073	0.00129	0.00219	0.00356	0.00559	0.00849	0.01253	0.01801	0.02528	0.03471	0.04673	0.06178
12	0.00020	0.00038	0.00067	0.00116	0.00191	0.00304	0.00469	0.00702	0.01026	0.01462	0.02040	0.02790
13	0.00005	0.00010	0.00019	0.00035	0.00061	0.00102	0.00165	0.00257	0.00391	0.00579	0.00838	0.01187
14	0.00001	0.00003	0.00005	0.00010	0.00018	0.00032	0.00054	0.00089	0.00141	0.00217	0.00325	0.00477
15	0.00000	0.00001	0.00001	0.00003	0.00005	0.00010	0.00017	0.00029	0.00048	0.00077	0.00119	0.00181
16	0.00000	0.00000	0.00000	0.00001	0.00001	0.00003	0.00005	0.00009	0.00015	0.00026	0.00042	0.00066
17	0.00000	0.00000	0.00000	0.00000	0.00000	0.00001	0.00001	0.00003	0.00005	0.00008	0.00014	0.00022
18	0.00000	0.00000	0.00000	0.00000	0.00000	0.00000	0.00000	0.00001	0.00001	0.00002	0.00004	0.00007
19	0.00000	0.00000	0.00000	0.00000	0.00000	0.00000	0.00000	0.00000	0.00000	0.00001	0.00001	0.00002

						Mean						
S	**6.75**	**7.00**	**7.25**	**7.50**	**7.75**	**8.00**	**8.25**	**8.50**	**8.75**	**9.00**	**9.25**	**9.50**
0	6.75000	7.00000	7.25000	7.50000	7.75000	8.00000	8.25000	8.50000	8.75000	9.00000	9.25000	9.50000
1	5.75117	6.00091	6.25071	6.50055	6.75043	7.00034	7.25026	7.50020	7.75016	8.00012	8.25010	8.50007
2	4.76025	5.00821	5.25657	5.50525	5.75420	6.00335	6.25268	6.50214	6.75170	7.00136	7.25108	7.50086
3	3.79599	4.03784	4.28109	4.52551	4.77090	5.01711	5.26399	5.51142	5.75931	6.00759	6.25618	6.50502
4	2.89176	3.11961	3.35072	3.58466	3.82103	4.05949	4.29974	4.54153	4.78462	5.02882	5.27395	5.51988
5	2.08880	2.29260	2.50210	2.71672	2.93589	3.15912	3.38593	3.61589	3.84863	4.08378	4.32105	4.56015
6	1.42257	1.59331	1.77203	1.95815	2.15112	2.35036	2.55532	2.76549	2.98036	3.19947	3.42238	3.64868
7	0.91016	1.04302	1.18519	1.33631	1.49597	1.66373	1.83912	2.02167	2.21087	2.40625	2.60732	2.81362
8	0.54606	0.64173	0.74671	0.86095	0.98434	1.11669	1.25777	1.40726	1.56485	1.73015	1.90277	2.08229
9	0.30712	0.37082	0.44267	0.52292	0.61174	0.70924	0.81546	0.93037	1.05387	1.18580	1.32597	1.47411
10	0.16204	0.20132	0.24694	0.29932	0.35885	0.42586	0.50062	0.58334	0.67418	0.77321	0.88047	0.99594
11	0.08031	0.10280	0.12973	0.16156	0.19876	0.24175	0.29094	0.34671	0.40936	0.47920	0.55644	0.64127
12	0.03746	0.04945	0.06427	0.08232	0.10403	0.12983	0.16013	0.19537	0.23593	0.28221	0.33454	0.39326
13	0.01648	0.02245	0.03007	0.03965	0.05152	0.06603	0.08354	0.10445	0.12913	0.15798	0.19137	0.22968
14	0.00685	0.00964	0.01332	0.01809	0.02418	0.03185	0.04137	0.05304	0.06718	0.08413	0.10422	0.12782
15	0.00270	0.00392	0.00559	0.00783	0.01077	0.01459	0.01947	0.02561	0.03326	0.04266	0.05409	0.06783
16	0.00101	0.00152	0.00223	0.00322	0.00456	0.00636	0.00872	0.01178	0.01569	0.02063	0.02678	0.03436
17	0.00036	0.00056	0.00085	0.00126	0.00184	0.00264	0.00372	0.00517	0.00706	0.00952	0.01266	0.01663
18	0.00012	0.00020	0.00031	0.00047	0.00071	0.00105	0.00152	0.00217	0.00304	0.00420	0.00573	0.00770
19	0.00004	0.00007	0.00011	0.00017	0.00026	0.00040	0.00059	0.00087	0.00125	0.00177	0.00248	0.00342
20	0.00001	0.00002	0.00004	0.00006	0.00009	0.00014	0.00022	0.00033	0.00049	0.00072	0.00103	0.00145
21	0.00000	0.00001	0.00001	0.00002	0.00003	0.00005	0.00008	0.00012	0.00019	0.00028	0.00041	0.00059
22	0.00000	0.00000	0.00000	0.00001	0.00001	0.00002	0.00003	0.00004	0.00007	0.00010	0.00016	0.00023
23	0.00000	0.00000	0.00000	0.00000	0.00000	0.00001	0.00001	0.00001	0.00002	0.00004	0.00006	0.00009
24	0.00000	0.00000	0.00000	0.00000	0.00000	0.00000	0.00000	0.00000	0.00001	0.00001	0.00002	0.00003

Appendix C

Evaluation of the Loss Function

The loss function $L(Q)$ is the expected amount a random variable exceeds a fixed value. For example, if the random variable is demand, then $L(Q)$ is the expected amount demand is greater than Q. See Appendix A, Statistics Tutorial, for a more extensive description of the loss function.

This appendix describes how the loss function of a discrete distribution function can be efficiently evaluated. (Appendix A gives one solution method, but it is inefficient.) If you need to evaluate the loss function of a continuous distribution, then convert the continuous distribution into a discrete distribution by "chopping it up" into many pieces. For example, the standard normal table is the discrete (i.e., "chopped up") version of the continuous standard normal distribution function.

Let N be the number of quantities in the distribution function and let $Q_1, Q_2, Q_3, \ldots, Q_N$ be those quantities. For example, take the empirical distribution function in Chapter 9, repeated here for convenience:

Q	F(Q)	Q	F(Q)	Q	F(Q)
800	0.0303	2,592	0.3636	3,936	0.6970
1,184	0.0606	2,624	0.3939	4,000	0.7273
1,792	0.0909	2,752	0.4242	4,064	0.7576
1,792	0.1212	3,040	0.4545	4,160	0.7879
1,824	0.1515	3,104	0.4848	4,352	0.8182
1,888	0.1818	3,136	0.5152	4,544	0.8485
2,048	0.2121	3,264	0.5455	4,672	0.8788
2,144	0.2424	3,456	0.5758	4,800	0.9091
2,208	0.2727	3,680	0.6061	4,928	0.9394
2,304	0.3030	3,744	0.6364	4,992	0.9697
2,560	0.3333	3,808	0.6667	5,120	1.0000

$F(Q)$ = Probability demand is less than or equal to the quantity Q

With this distribution function there are 33 quantities, so $N = 33$ and $Q_1 = 800$, $Q_2 = 1,184, \ldots$, and $Q_{33} = 5,120$. Furthermore, recall that we use μ to represent expected demand, which in this case is $\mu = 3,192$.

We can recursively evaluate the loss function, which means we start with $L(Q_1)$, and then use $L(Q_1)$ to evaluate $L(Q_2)$, and then use $L(Q_2)$ to evaluate $L(Q_3)$, and so forth.

The expected lost sales if we order Q_1 (which in this case is 800 units) are

$$L(Q_1) = \mu - Q_1 = 3{,}192 - 800 = 2{,}392$$

Expected lost sales if we order Q_2 are

$$L(Q_2) = L(Q_1) - (Q_2 - Q_1) \times (1 - F(Q_1))$$

$$= 2{,}392 - (1{,}184 - 800) \times (1 - 0.0303)$$

$$= 2{,}020$$

Expected lost sales if we order Q_3 are

$$L(Q_3) = L(Q_2) - (Q_3 - Q_2) \times (1 - F(Q_2))$$

$$= 2{,}020 - (1{,}792 - 1{,}184) \times (1 - 0.0606)$$

$$= 1{,}448$$

In general, the ith expected lost sales are

$$L(Q_i) = L(Q_{i-1}) - (Q_i - Q_{i-1}) \times (1 - F(Q_{i-1}))$$

So you start with $L(Q_1) = \mu - Q_1$ and then you evaluate $L(Q_2)$, and then $L(Q_3)$, up to $L(Q_N)$. The resulting table is

Q	F(Q)	L(Q)	Q	F(Q)	L(Q)	Q	F(Q)	L(Q)
800	0.0303	2,392	2,592	0.3636	841	3,936	0.6970	191
1,184	0.0606	2,020	2,624	0.3939	821	4,000	0.7273	171
1,792	0.0909	1,448	2,752	0.4242	744	4,064	0.7576	154
1,792	0.1212	1,448	3,040	0.4545	578	4,160	0.7879	131
1,824	0.1515	1,420	3,104	0.4848	543	4,352	0.8182	90
1,888	0.1818	1,366	3,136	0.5152	526	4,544	0.8485	55
2,048	0.2121	1,235	3,264	0.5455	464	4,672	0.8788	36
2,144	0.2424	1,160	3,456	0.5758	377	4,800	0.9091	20
2,208	0.2727	1,111	3,680	0.6061	282	4,928	0.9394	8
2,304	0.3030	1,041	3,744	0.6364	257	4,992	0.9697	5
2,560	0.3333	863	3,808	0.6667	233	5,120	1.0000	1

Q = Order quantity

$F(Q)$ = Probability demand is less than or equal to the order quantity

$L(Q)$ = Loss function (the expected amount demand exceeds Q)

With this empirical distribution example, the quantities differ by more than one unit, for example, $Q_2 - Q_1 = 384$. Now suppose the demand forecast is the Poisson distribution with mean 1.25. The distribution function is given in Table A.1 but is repeated here for convenience:

Q	f(Q)	F(Q)
0	0.28650	0.28650
1	0.35813	0.64464
2	0.22383	0.86847
3	0.09326	0.96173
4	0.02914	0.99088
5	0.00729	0.99816
6	0.00152	0.99968
7	0.00027	0.99995
8	0.00004	0.99999
9	0.00001	1.00000

Now we have $Q_1 = 0$, $Q_2 = 1$, and so forth. We find the expected lost sales with the same process: $L(Q_1) = 1.25 - 0 = 1.25$, and

$$L(Q_2) = L(Q_1) - (Q_2 - Q_1) \times (1 - F(Q_0))$$

$$= 1.25 - (1 - 0) \times (1 - 0.28650)$$

$$= 0.53650$$

Completing the table yields

Q	f(Q)	F(Q)	L(Q)
0	0.28650	0.28650	1.25000
1	0.35813	0.64464	0.53650
2	0.22383	0.86847	0.18114
3	0.09326	0.96173	0.04961
4	0.02914	0.99088	0.01134
5	0.00729	0.99816	0.00221
6	0.00152	0.99968	0.00038
7	0.00027	0.99995	0.00006
8	0.00004	0.99999	0.00001
9	0.00001	1.00000	0.00000

Appendix D

Equations and Approximations

This appendix derives in detail some equations and explains several approximations.

Derivation, Via Calculus, of the Order Quantity That Maximizes Expected Profit for the Newsvendor (Chapter 9)

Let the selling price be p, the purchase cost per unit be c, and the salvage revenue from left-over inventory be v. The expected profit function is

$$\pi(Q) = -cQ + p\left(\int_0^Q xf(x)dx + (1 - F(Q))Q\right) + v\int_0^Q (Q - x)f(x)dx$$

$$= (p - c)Q + \int_0^Q (p - v)xf(x)dx - (p - v)F(Q)Q$$

where $f(x)$ is the density function and $F(x)$ is the distribution function ($Prob(D = x)$ and $Prob(D<=x)$, respectively, where D is the random variable representing demand).

Via integration by parts, the profit function can be written as

$$\pi(Q) = (p - c)Q + (p - v)\left(QF(Q) - \int_0^Q F(x)dx\right) - (p - v)F(Q)Q$$

Differentiate the profit function, and remember that the derivative of the distribution function equals the density function, that is $dF(x)/dx = f(x)$

$$\frac{d\pi(Q)}{dQ} = (p - c) + (p - v)(F(Q) + Qf(Q) - F(Q)) - (p - v)(F(Q) + f(Q)Q)$$

$$= (p - c) - (p - v)F(Q)$$

and

$$\frac{d^2\pi(Q)}{dQ^2} = -(p - v)f(Q)$$

Because the second derivative is negative, the profit function is concave, so the solution to the first-order condition provides the optimal order quantity:

$$\frac{d\pi(Q)}{dQ} = (p - c) - (p - v)F(Q) = 0$$

Rearrange terms in the above equation and you get

$$F(Q) = \frac{p - c}{p - v}$$

Note that $C_o = c - v$ and $C_u = p - c$, so the above can be written as

$$F(Q) = \frac{C_u}{C_u + C_o}$$

Derivation of the Standard Normal Loss Function (Chapter 9)

We wish to derive the following equation for the standard normal loss function:

$$L(z) = \phi(z) - z(1 - \Phi(z))$$

Begin with the density function of the standard normal distribution,

$$\phi(z) = \frac{1}{\sqrt{2\pi}} e^{-z^2/2}$$

and differentiate

$$\frac{d\phi(z)}{dz} = -z \frac{1}{\sqrt{2\pi}} e^{-z^2/2} = -z\phi(z)$$

Let $L(z)$ be the expected loss function:

$$L(z) = \int_z^\infty (x - z)\phi(x)dx$$

$$= \int_z^\infty x\phi(x)dx - \int_z^\infty z\phi(x)dx$$

The first integral is

$$\int_z^\infty x\phi(x)dx = -\phi(x)|_z^\infty = \phi(z)$$

because $d\phi(x)/dx = -x\phi(x)$ and the second integral is

$$\int_z^\infty z\phi(x)dx = z(1 - \Phi(z))$$

Thus, $L(z) = \phi(z) - z(1 - \Phi(z))$.

Mismatch Cost as a Percentage of the Maximum Profit (Chapter 10)

Begin with the mismatch cost as a percentage of the maximum profit

$$\text{Mismatch cost as a \% of the maximum profit} = (C_o \times \text{Expected leftover inventory})/(\mu \times C_u) + (C_u \times \text{Expected lost sales})/(\mu \times C_u) \quad \text{(D.1)}$$

We also know the following:

$$\text{Expected leftover inventory} = (Q - \text{Expected sales})$$
$$= (Q - \mu + \text{Expected lost sales}) \quad \text{(D.2)}$$

and we can rearrange $Q = \mu + z \times \sigma$ into

$$z \times \sigma = (Q - \mu) \quad \text{(D.3)}$$

Substitute equation (D.3) into equation (D.2), then substitute that equation into equation (D.1) and simplify:

$$\text{Mismatch cost as a \% of the maximum profit} = ((C_o \times z \times \sigma) + (C_o + C_u) \times \text{Expected lost sales})/(\mu \times C_u) \quad \text{(D.4)}$$

Recall that

$$\text{Expected lost sales} = \sigma \times (\phi(z) - z \times (1 - \Phi(z)))$$
$$= \sigma \times \left(\phi(z) - z \times \frac{C_o}{C_o + C_u} \right) \quad \text{(D.5)}$$

where the second line in that equation follows from the critical ratio, $\Phi(z) = C_u/(C_o + C_u)$. Substitute equation (D.5) into equation (D.4) and simplify to obtain equation (10.2):

$$\text{Mismatch cost as a \% of the maximum profit} = \left(\frac{\phi(z)}{\Phi(z)} \right) \times \left(\frac{\sigma}{\mu} \right)$$

Exact Stockout Probability for the Order-up-to Model (Chapter 11)

Recall our main result from Section 11.3 that the inventory level at the end of the period equals S minus demand over $l + 1$ periods. If the inventory level is negative at the end of that interval, then one or more units are back-ordered. A stockout occurs in the last period of that interval if there is at least one unit back-ordered and the most recent back order occurred in that last period. Equation (11.1) in Chapter 11 acknowledges the first part of that statement (at least one unit is back-ordered), but it ignores that second part (the most recent back order must occur in the last period).

For example, suppose $l = 1$ and $S = 2$. If demand over two periods is three units, then there is one unit back-ordered at the end of the second period. As long as one of those three units of demand occurred in the second period, then a stockout occurred in the second period. A stockout does not occur in the second period only if all three units of demand occurred in the first period. Hence, the exact equation for the stockout probability is

$$\text{Stockout probability} = \text{Prob\{Demand over } l + 1 \text{ periods} > S\}$$
$$- \text{Prob\{Demand over } l \text{ periods} > S\} \times \text{Prob\{Demand in one period} = 0\}$$

Equation (11.1) is an approximation because it ignores the second term in the exact equation above. The second term is the probability that the demand over $l + 1$ periods occurs only in the first l periods; that is, there is no demand in the $(l + 1)$th period. If the service level is high, then the second term should be small. Notice that the approximation overestimates the true stockout probability because it does not subtract the second term. Hence, the approximation is conservative.

If each period's demand is a Poisson distribution with mean 0.29 and there is a two-period lead time, then the approximate and exact stockout probabilities are

	Stockout Probability	
S	Approximation	Exact
0	44.010%	25.174%
1	11.536	8.937
2	2.119	1.873
3	0.298	0.280
4	0.034	0.033
5	0.003	0.003
6	0.000	0.000

Exact Expected Fill Rate for the Order-up-to Model (Chapter 11)

The fill rate is one minus the fraction of demand not filled in a period, where

$$\text{Fraction of demand not filled in a period} = \frac{\text{Expected back orders that occur in a period}}{\text{Expected demand in one period}}$$

We know the denominator of that fraction, the expected demand in one period. We need to determine the numerator. The expected back orders that occur in a period are not quite the same as the expected back order in a period. The difference is that some of the back order might not have occurred in the period. (This is the same issue with the evaluation of the stockout probability.) For example, if the back order in a period is four units and demand in the period was three units, then only three of the four back orders actually occurred in that period; the remaining back-ordered unit was a carryover from a previous period.

Let's define some new notation. Let

$$B(l) = \text{Expected back orders if the lead time is } l$$

Hence, $B(l)$ is what we have been calling the *expected back order.*

The expected back order at the end of the $(l + 1)$th period of an interval of $l + 1$ periods is $B(l)$. If we subtract from those back orders the ones that were back-ordered at the end of the lth period in that interval, then we have the number of back orders that occurred in that last period of the interval. Hence,

$$\text{Fraction of demand not filled in a period} = \frac{B(l) - B(l - 1)}{\text{Expected demand in one period}}$$

The numerator of the above fraction, in words, is the expected back order minus what the expected back order would be if the lead time were one period faster. Our exact fill rate equation is thus

$$\text{Expected fill rate} = 1 - \frac{\text{Expected back order} - B(l - 1)}{\text{Expected demand in one period}}$$

The fill rate equation in Chapter 11 is an approximation because it does not subtract $B(l - 1)$ from the expected back order in the numerator. If the service level is very high, then $B(l - 1)$ will be very small, which is why the equation in the chapter is a good approximation.

If demand is Poisson with mean 0.29 per period and the lead time is one period, then

	Expected Fill Rate	
S	Approximation	Exact
0	−100.000%	0.000%
1	51.759	64.954
2	91.539	92.754
3	98.844	98.930
4	99.871	99.876
5	99.988	99.988
6	99.999	99.999

The approximation underestimates the fill rate, especially when the fill rate is low. However, the approximation is accurate for high fill rates.

Coordinating Buy-Back Price (Chapter 14)

If the wholesale price has been chosen, then we want to find the buy-back price that will lead the retailer to order the supply chain profit-maximizing quantity. This can be achieved if the retailer's critical ratio equals the supply chain's critical ratio, because it is the critical ratio that determines the optimal order quantity.

Let's define some notation:

p = Retail price
c = Production cost
v = Retailer's salvage value
t = Shipping cost
w = wholesale price
b = buy-back price

The supply chain's critical ratio is $(p - c)/(p - v)$ because $C_u = p - c$ and $C_o = c - v$. The retailer's underage cost with the buy-back contract is $C_u = p - w$ and its overage cost is $C_o = t + w - b$ (i.e., the shipping cost plus the amount not credited by the supplier on returned inventory, $w - b$). Hence, the retailer's critical ratio equals the supply chain's critical ratio when

$$\frac{p - c}{p - v} = \frac{p - w}{(t + w - b) + p - w}$$

If we take the above equation and rearrange terms we get equation (14.1).

Appendix E

Solutions to Selected Practice Problems

This appendix provides solutions to marked (*) practice problems.

Chapter 2

Q2.1 (Dell)

The following steps refer directly to Exhibit 2.1.

Step 1. For 2001, we find in Dell's 10-k: Inventory = $400 (in millions)

Step 2. For 2001, we find in Dell's 10-k: COGS = $26,442 (in millions)

Step 3. Inventory turns $= \dfrac{\$26{,}442/\text{Year}}{\$400} = 66.105$ turns per year

Step 4. Per-unit inventory cost $= \dfrac{40\% \text{ per year}}{66.105 \text{ per year}} = 0.605$ percent per year

Chapter 3

Q3.1 (Single Flow Unit)

The following steps refer directly to Exhibit 3.1.

Step 1. We first compute the capacity of the three resources:

$$\text{Resource 1:} \frac{2}{10} \text{ unit per minute} = 0.2 \text{ unit per minute}$$

$$\text{Resource 2:} \frac{1}{6} \text{ unit per minute} = 0.1666 \text{ unit per minute}$$

$$\text{Resource 3:} \frac{3}{16} \text{ unit per minute} = 0.1875 \text{ unit per minute}$$

Step 2. Resource 2 has the lowest capacity; process capacity therefore is 0.1666 unit per minute, which is equal to 10 units per hour.

Step 3. Flow rate = Min{Process capacity, Demand}

$\qquad\qquad$ = Min{8 units per hour, 10 units per hour} = 8 units per hour

This is equal to 0.1333 unit per minute.

Step 4. We find the utilizations of the three resources as

Resource 1: 0.1333 unit per minute/0.2 unit per minute = 66.66 percent

Resource 2: 0.1333 unit per minute/0.1666 unit per minute = 80 percent

Resource 3: 0.1333 unit per minute/0.1875 unit per minute = 71.11 percent

3.2 (Multiple Flow Units)

The following steps refer directly to Exhibit 3.2.

Step 1. Each resource can contribute the following capacity (in minutes of work per day):

Resource	Number of Workers	Minutes per Day
1	2	$2 \times 8 \times 60 = 960$
2	2	$2 \times 8 \times 60 = 960$
3	1	$1 \times 8 \times 60 = 480$
4	1	$1 \times 8 \times 60 = 480$
5	2	$2 \times 8 \times 60 = 960$

Step 2. Process flow diagram:

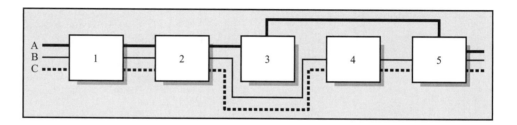

Step 3. We create a table indicating how much capacity will be consumed by the three products at the resources.

Resource	Capacity Requirement from A	Capacity Requirement from B	Capacity Requirement from C
1	$5 \times 40 = 200$	$5 \times 50 = 250$	$5 \times 60 = 300$
2	$3 \times 40 = 120$	$4 \times 50 = 200$	$5 \times 60 = 300$
3	$15 \times 40 = 600$	$0 \times 50 = 0$	$0 \times 60 = 0$
4	$0 \times 40 = 0$	$3 \times 50 = 150$	$3 \times 60 = 180$
5	$6 \times 40 = 240$	$6 \times 50 = 300$	$6 \times 60 = 360$

Step 4. Add up the rows to get the workload for each resource:

Workload for resource 1: $200 + 250 + 300 = 750$

Workload for resource 2: $120 + 200 + 300 = 620$

Workload for resource 3: $600 + 0 + 0 = 600$

Workload for resource 4: $0 + 150 + 180 = 330$

Workload for resource 5: $240 + 300 + 360 = 900$

Resource	Minutes per Day (see Step 1)	Workload per Day (see Step 4)	Implied Utilization (Step 4/Step 1)
1	960	750	0.78
2	960	620	0.65
3	480	600	1.25
4	480	330	0.69
5	960	360	0.94

Step 5. Compute implied utilization levels. Hence, resource 3 is the bottleneck. Thus, we cannot produce units A at a rate of 40 units per day. Since we are overutilized by 25 percent, we can produce units A at a rate of 32 units per day (four units per hour). Assuming the ratio between A, B, and C is constant (40:50:60), we will produce B at five units per hour and C at six units per hour. If the ratio between A, B, and C is *not* constant, this answer changes. In this case, we would produce 32 units of A and produce products B and C at the rate of demand (50 and 60 units per day respectively).

Chapter 4

Q4.1 (Empty System, Labor Utilization)

Part a

The following computations are based on Exhibit 4.1 in the book. Time to complete 100 units:

Step 1. The process will take $10 + 6 + 16$ minutes $= 32$ minutes to produce the first unit.

Step 2. We know from problem xyz that resource 2 is the bottleneck and the process capacity is 0.1666 unit per minute.

Step 3. Time to finish 100 units $= 32$ minutes $+ \dfrac{99 \text{ units}}{0.166 \text{ unit/minute}} = 626$ minutes

Parts b, c, and d

We answer these three questions together by using Exhibit 4.2 in the book.

Step 1. Capacities are

$$\text{Resource 1: } \frac{2}{10} \text{ unit/minute} = 0.2 \text{ unit/minute}$$

$$\text{Resource 2: } \frac{1}{6} \text{ unit/minute} = 0.1666 \text{ unit/minute}$$

$$\text{Resource 3: } \frac{3}{16} \text{ unit/minute} = 0.1875 \text{ unit/minute}$$

Resource 2 is the bottleneck and the process capacity is 0.1666 unit/minute.

Step 2. Since there is unlimited demand, the flow rate is determined by the capacity and therefore is 0.1666 unit/minute; this corresponds to a cycle time of 6 minutes/unit.

Step 3. Cost of direct labor $= \dfrac{6 \times \$10/\text{hour}}{60 \times 0.1666 \text{ unit/hour}} = \$6/\text{unit}$

Step 4. Compute the idle time of each worker for each unit:

Idle time for workers at resource 1 $= 6$ minutes/unit $\times 2 - 10$ minutes/unit
$= 2$ minutes/unit

$$\text{Idle time for worker at resource 2} = 6 \text{ minutes/unit} \times 1 - 6 \text{ minutes/unit}$$
$$= 0 \text{ minute/unit}$$

$$\text{Idle time for workers at resource 3} = 6 \text{ minutes/unit} \times 3 - 16 \text{ minutes/unit}$$
$$= 2 \text{ minutes/unit}$$

Step 5. Labor content $= 10 + 6 + 16 \text{ minutes/unit} = 32 \text{ minutes/unit}$

Step 6. Average labor utilization $= \dfrac{32}{32 + 4} = 0.8888$

Chapter 5

Q5.1 (Window Boxes)

The following computations are based on Exhibit 5.1.

Part a

Step 1. Since there is sufficient demand, the step (other than the stamping machine) that determines flow rate is assembly. Capacity at assembly is $\frac{12}{27}$ unit/minute.

Step 2. The production cycle consists of the following parts:

- Setup for A (120 minutes).
- Produce parts A (360×1 minute).
- Setup for B (120 minutes).
- Produce parts B (720×0.5 minute).

Step 3. There are two setups in the production cycle, so the setup time is 240 minutes.

Step 4. Every completed window box requires one part A (one minute per unit) and two parts B (2×0.5 minute per unit). Thus, the per-unit activity time is two minutes per unit.

Step 5. Use formula

$$\text{Capacity given batch size} = \frac{360 \text{ units}}{240 \text{ minutes} + 360 \text{ units} \times 2 \text{ minutes/unit}}$$
$$= 0.375 \text{ unit/minute}$$

Step 6. Capacity at stamping for a general batch size is

$$\frac{\text{Batch size}}{240 \text{ minutes} + \text{Batch size} \times 2 \text{ minutes/unit}}$$

We need to solve the equation:

$$\frac{\text{Batch size}}{240 \text{ minutes} + \text{Batch size} \times 2 \text{ minutes/unit}} = \frac{12}{27}$$

for the batch size. The batch size solving this equation is Batch size $= 960$. We can obtain the same number directly by using

$$\text{Recommended batch size} = \frac{\text{Flow rate} \times \text{Setup time}}{1 - \text{Flow rate} \times \text{Time per unit}} = \frac{\frac{12}{27} \times 240}{1 - \frac{12}{27} \times 2} = 960$$

Chapter 6

Q6.1 (Online Retailer)

Part a

We use Exhibit 6.1 for our computations.

Step 1. We collect the basic ingredients for the waiting time formula:

Activity time = 4 minutes

$$CV_p = \frac{2}{4}$$

Interarrival time = 2 minutes

$$CV_a = 1$$

Number of resources = 3

Step 2. This allows us to compute utilization as

$$p/am = 4/(2 \times 3) = 0.6666$$

Step 3. We then use the waiting time formula

$$T_q = \approx \left(\frac{4}{3}\right) \times \left(\frac{0.666^{\sqrt{2(3+1)-1}}}{1 - 0.6666}\right) \times \left(\frac{1^2 + 0.5^2}{2}\right) = 1.19 \text{ minutes}$$

Step 4. We find the

Inventory in service: $I_p = m \times u = 3 \times 0.666 = 2$

Inventory in the queue: $I_q = T_q/a = 1.19/2 = 0.596$

Inventory in the system: $I = I_p + I_q = 2.596$

Part b

The number of e-mails that have been received but not yet answered corresponds to the total inventory of e-mails. We find this to be 2.596 e-mails (see Step 4 above).

Chapter 7

Q7.1 (Loss System)

We use Exhibit 7.1 to answer parts a through c.

Step 1. The interarrival time is 60 minutes per hour divided by 55 units arriving per hour, which is an interarrival time of $a = 1.0909$ minute/unit. The processing time is $p = 6$ minutes/unit; this allows us to compute $r = p/a = 6/1.0909 = 5.5$.

Step 2. With $r = 5.5$ and $m = 7$, we can use the Erlang Loss Formula Table to look up $P_7(5.5)$ as 0.1525. Alternatively, we can use the actual loss formula (see Appendix C) to compute the probability that all seven servers are utilized:

$$\text{Prob \{all 7 servers are busy\}} = P_7(5.5) = \frac{\dfrac{5.5^7}{7!}}{1 + \dfrac{5.5^1}{1!} + \dfrac{5.5^2}{2!} + \cdots + \dfrac{5.5^7}{7!}} = 0.1525$$

Step 3. Compute the flow rate: $R = 1/a \times (1 - P_m) = 1/1.0909 \times (1 - 0.153) = 0.77$ unit per minute or 46.585 units per hour.

Step 4. Compute lost customers:

Customers lost $= 1/a \times P_m = 1/1.0909 \times 0.153 = 0.14$ unit per minute

which corresponds to 8.415 units per hour.

Thus, from the 55 units that arrive every hour, 46.585 will be served and 8.415 will be lost.

Chapter 9

Q9.1 (McClure Books)

Part a

Using Exhibit 9.3, we first find the z-statistic for 400 (Dan's blockbuster threshold): $z = (400 - 200)/80 = 2.50$. From the Standard Normal Distribution Function Table we see that $\Phi(2.50) = 0.9938$. So there is a 99.38 percent chance demand is 400 or fewer. Demand is greater than 400 with probability $1 - \Phi(2.50) = 0.0062$; that is, there is only a 0.62 percent chance this is a blockbuster.

Part b

Using Exhibit 9.3, we first find the z-statistic for 100 units (Dan's dog threshold): $z = (100 - 200)/80 = -1.25$. From the Standard Normal Distribution Function Table we see that $\Phi(-1.25) = 0.1056$. So there is a 10.56 percent chance demand is 100 or fewer; that is, there is a 10.56 percent chance this book is a dog.

Part c

Demand is within 20 percent of the mean if it is between $1.2 \times 200 = 240$ and $0.8 \times 200 = 160$. Using Exhibit 9.3, we first find the z-statistic for 240 units (the upper limit on that range): $z = (240 - 200)/80 = 0.5$. From the Standard Normal Distribution Function Table we see that $\Phi(0.5) = 0.6915$. Repeat the process for the lower limit on the range: $z = (160 - 200)/80 = -0.5$ and $\Phi(-0.5) = 0.3085$. The probability demand is between 160 and 240 is $\Phi(0.5) - \Phi(-0.50) = 0.6915 - 0.3085 = 0.3830$, that is, 38.3 percent.

Part d

Use Exhibit 9.4. The underage cost is $C_u = 20 - 12 = 8$. The salvage value is $12 - 4 = 8$ because Dan can return leftover books for a full refund (\$12) but incurs a \$4 cost of shipping and handling. Thus, the overage cost is cost minus salvage value: $C_o = 12 - 8 = 4$. The critical ratio is $C_u/(C_o + C_u) = 8/12 = 0.6667$. In the Standard Normal Distribution Function Table we see that $\Phi(0.43) = 0.6664$ and $\Phi(0.44) = 0.6700$, so use the round-up rule and choose $z = 0.44$. Now convert z into the order quantity for the actual demand distribution: $Q = \mu + z \times \sigma = 200 + 0.44 \times 80 = 235.2$.

Part e

Use Exhibit 9.8. The target is $L(z)$ is $(200/80) \times (1 - 0.95) = 0.1250$. In the Standard Normal Loss Function Table we see that $L(0.77) = 0.1267$ and $L(0.78) = 0.1245$, so use the round-up rule and choose $z = 0.78$. Now convert z into the order quantity for the actual demand distribution: $Q = \mu + z \times \sigma = 200 + 0.78 \times 80 = 262.4$.

Part f

Use Exhibit 9.9. We want to find a z such that $\Phi(z) = 0.95$. In the Standard Normal Distribution Function Table we see that $\Phi(1.64) = 0.9495$ and $\Phi(1.65) = 0.9505$, so use the round-up rule and choose $z = 1.65$. Now convert z into the order quantity for the actual demand distribution: $Q = \mu + z \times \sigma = 200 + 1.65 \times 80 = 332$.

Part g

Use Exhibit 9.7. If the in-stock probability is 95 percent, then the stockout probability (which is what we are looking for) is 1 minus the in-stock, that is, $1 - 95\% = 5$ percent.

Part h

Use Exhibit 9.5 to evaluate expected lost sales. The z-statistic for 300 units is $z = (300 - 200)/80 = 1.25$. From the Standard Normal Loss Function Table we see that $L(1.25) = 0.0506$. Expected lost sales are $\sigma \times L(1.25) = 4.05$. Use Exhibit 9.6 to evaluate expected sales, then expected leftover inventory, and then expected profit. Expected sales are $200 - 4.05 = 195.95$, expected leftover inventory is $300 - 195.95 = 104.05$, and

$$
\begin{aligned}
\text{Expected profit} &= (\text{Price} - \text{Cost}) \times \text{Expected sales} \\
&\quad - (\text{Cost} - \text{Salvage value}) \times \text{Expected leftover inventory} \\
&= (20 - 12) \times 195.95 - (12 - 8) \times 104.05 \\
&= 1151.4
\end{aligned}
$$

Part i

Use Exhibit 9.5 to evaluate expected lost sales. The z-statistic for 150 units is $z = (150 - 200)/80 = -0.63$. From the Standard Normal Loss Function Table we see that $L(-0.63) = 0.7906$. Expected lost sales are $\sigma \times L(1.25) = 63.248$. Use Exhibit 9.6 to evaluate the fill rate:

$$\text{Fill rate} = 1 - \text{Expected lost sales}/\mu = 1 - 63.248/200 = 0.6838$$

Part j

Using Exhibit 9.1 we should construct the empirical distribution function:

Book	A/F Ratio	Rank	Percentile
7	0.20	1	0.0625
1	0.27	2	0.1250
3	0.52	3	0.1875
13	0.59	4	0.2500
4	0.77	5	0.3125
14	0.79	6	0.3750
10	0.81	7	0.4375
9	0.88	8	0.5000
16	0.91	9	0.5625
15	0.97	10	0.6250
6	1.20	11	0.6875
12	1.21	12	0.7500
2	1.23	13	0.8125
11	1.34	14	0.8750
5	1.37	15	0.9375
8	1.47	16	1.0000

From part d we observed that the critical ratio is 0.6667. From the above table we see that the percentile for the A/F ratio of 0.97 is 0.6250 and the percentile for the A/F ratio of 1.20 is 0.6875. Use the round-up rule to choose the A/F ratio 1.20. Now convert that A/F ratio into an order quantity: $Q = 1.20 \times 200 = 240$.

Q9.2 (Pony Express Creations)

Part a

Use Exhibit 9.3. If they purchase 40,000 units, then they need to liquidate 10,000 or more units if demand is 30,000 units or lower. From the table provided, $F(30,000) = 0.7852$, so there is a 78.52 percent chance they need to liquidate 10,000 or more units.

Part b

Use Exhibit 9.4. The underage cost is $C_u = 12 - 6 = 6$, the overage cost is $C_o = 6 - 2.5 = 3.5$, and the critical ratio is $6/(3.5 + 6) = 0.6316$. Looking in the demand forecast table we see that $F(25,000) = 0.6289$ and $F(30,000) = 0.7852$, so use the round-up rule and order 30,000 Elvis wigs.

Part c

Use Exhibit 9.8. We want to find an order quantity that generates a 90 percent fill rate. The target lost sales are $\mu \times (1 - \text{Fill rate}) = 25,000 \times (1 - 0.90) = 2,500$. From the demand forecast table we see that $L(25,000) = 3,908$ and $L(30,000) = 2,052$, so use the round-up rule to choose $Q = 30,000$.

Part d

Use Exhibit 9.5 to evaluate expected lost sales and then Exhibit 9.6 to evaluate the fill rate. If $Q = 30,000$, then expected lost sales from the table are 2,052. The fill rate is $1 - 2,052/25,000 = 0.9179$. Hence, the actual fill rate is about 92 percent.

Part e

Use Exhibit 9.9. We want to find a Q such that $F(Q) = 0.90$. From the demand forecast table we see that $F(35,000) = 0.8894$ and $F(40,000) = 0.9489$, so use the round-up rule and order 40,000 Elvis wigs. The actual in-stock probability is then 94.89 percent.

Part f

Use Exhibit 9.5 to evaluate expected lost sales and then Exhibit 9.6 to evaluate expected leftover inventory. If $Q = 50,000$, then expected lost sales from the table are only 63 units. Expected leftover inventory $= Q - \mu + \text{Expected lost sales} = 50,000 - 25,000 + 63 = 25,063$.

Part g

A 100 percent in-stock probability requires an order quantity of 75,000 units. Use Exhibit 9.5 to evaluate expected lost sales: with $Q = 75,000$, then expected lost sales from the table are only two units. Use Exhibit 9.6 to evaluate expected sales, expected leftover inventory, and expected profit. Expected sales are expected demand minus expected loss sales $= 25,000 - 2 = 24,998$. Expected leftover inventory is $75,000 - 24,998 = 50,002$.

$$\text{Expected profit} = (\text{Price} - \text{Cost}) \times \text{Expected sales}$$
$$- (\text{Cost} - \text{Salvage value}) \times \text{Expected leftover inventory}$$
$$= (12 - 6) \times 24,998 - (6 - 2.5) \times 50,002$$
$$= -25,019$$

So a 100 percent in-stock probability is a money-losing proposition.

Q9.3 (Flextrola)

Part a

It is within 25 percent of the forecast if it is greater than 750 and less than 1,250. Use Exhibit 9.3. The z-statistic for 750 is $z = (750 - 1,000)/600 = -0.42$ and the z-statistic for 1,250 is $z = (1,250 - 1,000)/600 = 0.42$. From the Standard Normal Distribution Function Table we see that $\Phi(-0.42) = 0.3372$ and $\Phi(0.42) = 0.6628$. So there is a 33.72 percent chance demand is less than 750 and a 66.28 percent chance it is less than 1,250. The chance it is between 750 and 1,250 is the difference in those probabilities: $0.6628 - 0.3372 = 0.3256$.

Part b

The forecast is for 1,000 units. Demand is greater than 40 percent of the forecast if demand exceeds 1,400 units. Use Exhibit 9.3. Find the z-statistic that corresponds to 1,400 units:

$$z = \frac{Q - \mu}{\sigma} = \frac{1,400 - 1,000}{600} = 0.67$$

From the Standard Normal Distribution Function Table, $\Phi(0.67) = 0.7486$. Therefore, there is almost a 75 percent probability that demand is less than 1,400 units. The probability that demand is greater than 1,400 units is $1 - \Phi(0.67) = 0.2514$, or about 25 percent.

Part c

Use Exhibit 9.4. To find the expected profit-maximizing order quantity, first identify the underage and overage costs. The underage cost is $C_u = 121 - 72 = 49$ because each lost sale costs Flextrola its gross margin. The overage cost is $C_o = 72 - 50 = 22$ because each unit of leftover inventory can only be sold for \$50. Now evaluate the critical ratio:

$$\frac{C_u}{C_o + C_u} = \frac{49}{22 + 49} = 0.6901$$

Look up the critical ratio in the Standard Normal Distribution Function Table: $\Phi(0.49) = 0.6879$ and $\Phi(0.50) = 0.6915$, so choose $z = 0.50$. Now convert the z-statistic into an order quantity: $Q = \mu + z \times \sigma = 1,000 + 0.5 \times 600 = 1,300$.

Part d

Use Exhibit 9.5 to evaluate expected lost sales and then Exhibit 9.6 to evaluate expected sales. If $Q = 1,200$, then the corresponding z-statistic is $z = (Q - \mu)/\sigma = (1,200 - 1,000)/600 = 0.33$. From the Standard Normal Distribution Loss Table we see that $L(0.33) = 0.2555$. Expected lost sales are then $\sigma \times L(z) = 600 \times 0.2555 = 153.3$. Finally, recall that expected sales equal expected demand minus expected lost sales: Expected sales $= 1,000 - 153.3 = 846.7$.

Part e

Flextrola sells its leftover inventory in the secondary market, which equals Q minus expected sales (Exhibit 9.6): $1,200 - 846.7 = 353.3$.

Part f

To evaluate the expected gross margin percentage we begin with

$$\text{Expected revenue} = (\text{Price} \times \text{Expected sales})$$
$$+ (\text{Salvage value} \times \text{Expected leftover inventory})$$
$$= (121 \times 846.7) + (50 \times 353.3)$$
$$= 120{,}116$$

Then we evaluate expected cost $= Q \times c = 1{,}200 \times 72 = 86{,}400$. Finally, expected gross margin percentage $= 1 - 86{,}400/120{,}116 = 28.1$ percent.

Part g

Use Exhibit 9.6 and the results from parts d and e to evaluate expected profit:

$$\text{Expected profit} = (\text{Price} - \text{Cost}) \times \text{Expected sales}$$
$$- (\text{Cost} - \text{Salvage value}) \times \text{Expected leftover inventory}$$
$$= (121 - 72) \times 846.7 - (72 - 50) \times 353.3$$
$$= 33{,}716$$

Part h

Solectric's expected profit is $1{,}200 \times (72 - 52) = 24{,}000$ because units are sold to Flextrola for \$72 and each unit has a production cost of \$52.

Part i

Flextrola incurs 400 or more units of lost sales if demand exceeds the order quantity by 400 or more units; that is, if demand is 1,600 units or greater. The z-statistic that corresponds to 1,600 is $z = (Q - \mu)/\sigma = (1{,}600 - 1{,}000)/600 = 1$. In the Standard Normal Distribution Function Table, $\Phi(1) = 0.8413$. Demand exceeds 1,600 with the probability $1 - \Phi(1) = 15.9$ percent.

Part j

The critical ratio is 0.6901. From the graph of the distribution function we see that the probability demand is less than 1,150 with the log normal distribution about 0.70. Hence, the optimal order quantity with the log normal distribution is about 1,150 units.

Chapter 10

Q10.1 (O'Neill)

Part a

O'Neill sells each wet suit for \$180, purchases each wet suit for \$110, sells wet suits left-over at the end of the season for \$90, and can purchase additional wet suits during the season for a 10 percent premium, that is, \$121. The overage cost is $C_o = 110 - 90 = 20$, because \$20 is lost on each wet suit left at the end of the season. The underage cost is $C_u = 121 - 110 = 11$ because every unit that is ordered in the second order earns O'Neill \$11 less in profit than would have been earned had the unit been ordered in the first order. (The sales revenue is the same no matter when it is ordered; only the cost is different.) The critical ratio is $11/(20 + 11) = 0.3548$. From the Standard Normal Distribution Function Table we see that $\Phi(-0.38) = 0.3520$ and $\Phi(-0.37) = 0.3557$, so choose $z = -0.37$. Convert to Q: $Q = 3{,}192 - 0.37 \times 1{,}181 = 2{,}755$.

Part b

The maximum profit is the gross margin times expected sales: $(180 - 70) \times 3,192 = \$223,440$.

Part c

O'Neill's second order quantity equals the amount by which demand exceeds the first order quantity, which is 2,755. Hence, we need to evaluate expected lost sales with a quantity 2,755, which has a z-statistic of -0.37. From the Standard Normal Loss Function Table, $L(-0.37) = 0.6109$. Expected lost sales are then $1,181 \times 0.6109 = 722$. So TEC should expect O'Neill to order 722 units in the second replenishment.

Part d

With reactive capacity, the mismatch costs equal the cost of leftover inventory and the second order premium. Expected sales $= 3,192 - 722 = 2,470$ and expected leftover inventory $= 2,755 - 2,470 = 285$. So the cost of leftover inventory is $20 \times 285 = \$5,700$ and the cost of the second order premium is $722 \times 11 = \$7,942$. The total mismatch cost is $5,700 + 7,942 = \$13,642$. Without the second order opportunity, the mismatch cost is $\$31,680$. So mismatch costs are reduced by $1 - 13,642/31,680 = 57$ percent.

Q10.2 (Teddy Bower)
Part a

Teddy will order from the American supplier if demand exceeds 1,500 units. With $Q = 1,500$, the z-statistic is $z = (1,500 - 2,100)/1,200 = -0.5$. From the Standard Normal Distribution Function Table we see that $\Phi(-0.50) = 0.3085$, which is the probability that demand is 1,500 or fewer. The probability that demand exceeds 1,500 is $1 - \Phi(-0.50) = 0.6915$, or about 69 percent.

Part b

The supplier's expected demand equals Teddy's expected lost sales with an order quantity of 1,500 parkas. From the Standard Normal Loss Function Table, $L(-0.50) = 0.6978$. Expected lost sales are $\sigma \times L(z) = 1,200 \times 0.6978 = 837.4$.

Part c

The overage cost is $C_o = 10 - 0 = 10$ because leftover parkas must have been purchased in the first order at a cost of \$10 and they have no value at the end of the season. The underage cost is $C_u = 15 - 10 = 5$ because there is a \$5 premium on units ordered from the American vendor. The critical ratio is $5/(10 + 5) = 0.3333$. From the Standard Normal Distribution Function Table we see that $\Phi(-0.44) = 0.3300$ and $\Phi(-0.43) = 0.3336$, so choose $z = -0.43$. Convert to Q: $Q = 2,100 - 0.43 \times 1,200 = 1,584$.

Part d

First evaluate some performance measures. We already know that with $Q = 1,584$ the corresponding z is -0.43. From Standard Normal Loss Function Table, $L(-0.43) = 0.6503$. Expected lost sales are then $1,200 \times 0.6503 = 780.4$; that is, that is the expected order quantity to the American vendor. If the American vendor were not available, then expected sales would be $2,100 - 780.4 = 1,319.6$. Expected leftover inventory is then $1,584 - 1,319.6 = 264.4$. Now evaluate expected profit with the American vendor option available. Expected revenue is $2,100 \times 22 = \$46,200$. The cost of the first order is $1,584 \times 10 = \$15,840$. Salvage revenue from leftover inventory is $264.4 \times 0 = 0$. Finally, the cost of the second order is $780.4 \times 15 = \$11,706$. Thus, profit is $46,200 - 15,840 - 11,706 = \$18,654$.

Part e

If Teddy only sources from the American supplier, then expected profit would be ($22 − $15) × 2,100 = $14,700 because expected sales would be 2,100 units and the gross margin on each unit is $22 − $15 = $7.

Chapter 11

Q11.1 (Furniture Store)

Part a

Inventory position = Inventory level + On-order = 100 + 85 = 185. Order enough to raise the inventory position to the order-up-to level, in this case 220 − 185 = 35 desks.

Part b

As in part a, Inventory position = 160 + 65 = 225. Because the inventory position is above the order-up-to level, 220, you do not order additional inventory.

Part c

Use Exhibit 11.5. From the Standard Normal Distribution Function Table: $\Phi(2.05)$ = 0.9798 and $\Phi(2.06)$ = 0.9803, so choose z = 2.06. The lead time l is 2, so μ = (2 + 1) × 40 = 120 and σ = $\sqrt{2 + 1}$ × 20 = 34.64.

$$S = \mu + z \times \sigma = 120 + 2.06 \times 34.64 = 191.36$$

Part d

Use Exhibit 11.6. The target back order is $L(z)$ = (40/34.64) × (1 − 0.98) = 0.0231. From the Standard Normal Loss Function Table, $L(1.60)$ = 0.0232 and $L(1.61)$ = 0.0227, so choose z = 1.61.

$$S = \mu + z \times \sigma = 120 + 1.61 \times 34.64 = 175.77$$

Part e

Use Exhibit 11.4. The z-statistic that corresponds to S = 120 is S = (120 − 120)/34.64 = 0. Expected back order is $\sigma \times L(0)$ = 34.64 × 0.3989 = 13.82. Expected on-hand inventory is $S - \mu$ + Expected back order = 120 − 120 + 13.82 = 13.82.

Part f

Use Exhibit 11.5. The z-statistic that corresponds to S = 200 is S = (200 − 120)/34.64 = 2.31. Expected back order is $\sigma \times L(2.31)$ = 34.64 × 0.0036 = 0.12. The fill rate is 1 − 0.12/40 = 99.69 percent.

Part g

To evaluate the fill rate we need to evaluate the z-statistic. Use Exhibit 11.5 to find the z-statistic that corresponds to a 95 percent in-stock. From the Standard Normal Distribution Function Table: $\Phi(1.64)$ = 0.9495 and $\Phi(1.65)$ = 0.9505, so choose z = 1.65. Use Exhibit 11.3 to evaluate the expected back order: $\sigma \times L(1.64)$ = 34.64 × 0.0206 = 0.71. The fill rate is 1 − 0.71/40 = 98.22 percent.

Part h

From part e, on-hand inventory is 13.82 units, which equals 13.82 × $200 = $2,764. Cost of capital is 15 percent, so the cost of holding inventory is 0.15 × $2,764 = $414.60.

Q11.2 (Campus Bookstore)

Part a

Use Exhibit 11.5. Mean demand over $l + 1$ periods is $0.5 \times (4 + 1) = 2.5$ units. From the Poisson Distribution Function Table, with mean 2.5 we have $F(6) = 0.9858$ and $F(7) = 0.9958$, so choose $S = 7$ to achieve a 99 percent in-stock.

Part b

Use Exhibit 11.6. The target back order is $0.5 \times (1 - 0.99) = 0.0050$. From the Poisson Loss Function Table with mean 2.5, $L(7) = 0.0057$ and $L(8) = 0.0015$, so choose $S = 8$.

Part c

Use Exhibit 11.4. Pipeline inventory is $l \times$ Expected demand in one period $= 4 \times 0.5 = 2$ units. The order-up-to level has no influence on the pipeline inventory.

Part d

Use Exhibit 11.4. From the Poisson Loss Function Table with mean 2.5, Expected back order $= L(5) = 0.06195$. Expected on-hand inventory $= 5 - 2.5 + 0.06195 = 2.56$ units.

Part e

Use Exhibit 11.4. The fill rate is $1 - 0.06195/0.5 = 87.6$ percent.

Part f

A stockout occurs if demand is seven or more units over $l + 1$ periods, which is one minus the probability demand is six or fewer in that interval. From the Poisson Distribution Function Table with mean 2.5, we see that $F(6) = 0.9858$ and $1 - F(6) = 0.0142$; that is, there is about a 1.4 percent chance of a stockout occurring.

Part g

The store is out of stock if demand is six or more units over $l + 1$ periods, which is one minus the probability demand is five or fewer in that interval. From the Poisson Distribution Function Table with mean 2.5, we see that $F(5) = 0.9580$ and $1 - F(5) = 0.0420$; that is, there is about a 4.2 percent chance of being out of inventory at the end of any given week.

Part h

The store has one or more units of inventory if demand is five or fewer over $l + 1$ periods. From part g, $F(5) = 0.9580$; that is, there is about a 96 percent chance of having one or more units at the end of any given week.

Part i

Use Exhibit 11.5. Now the lead time is two periods (each period is two weeks and the total lead time is four weeks, or two periods). Demand over one period is 1.0 unit. Demand over $l + 1$ periods is $(2 + 1) \times 1 = 3.0$ units. From the Poisson Distribution Function Table with mean 3.0, we have $F(7) = 0.9881$ and $F(8) = 0.9962$, so choose $S = 8$ to achieve a 99 percent in-stock.

Part j

Use Exhibit 11.4. Pipeline inventory is average demand over l periods $= 2 \times 1 = 2.0$ units.

Q11.3 (Quick Print)

Part a

If $S = 700$ and the inventory position is $523 + 180 = 703$, then 0 units should be ordered because the inventory position exceeds the order-up-to level.

Part b

Use Exhibits 11.3 and 11.4. Mean demand over $l + 1$ periods is $\mu = (5 + 1) \times 100 = 600$ and the standard deviation is $\sigma = \sqrt{6} \times 65 = 159.22$. The z-statistic is $(700 - 600)/159.22 = 0.63$. $L(0.63) = 0.1606$, so expected back order is $159.22 \times 0.1606 = 25.57$. The fill rate is $1 - 25.57/100 = 74.4$ percent.

Part c

Use Exhibit 11.5. From the Standard Normal Distribution Function Table, $\Phi(2.32) = 0.9898$ and $\Phi(2.33) = 0.9901$, so choose $z = 2.33$. Convert to $S = \mu + z \times \sigma = 600 + 2.33 \times 159.22 = 971$.

Part d

Use Exhibit 11.6. The targeted expected back order is $(100/159.22) \times (1 - 0.99) = 0.0016$. From the Standard Normal Loss Function Table, $L(2.11) = 0.0063$. Convert to $S = \mu + z \times \sigma = 600 + 2.11 \times 159.22 = 936$.

Chapter 12

Q12.1 (Fancy Paints)

Part a

Assume Fancy Paints implements the order-up-to inventory model. Use Exhibit 11.6 to find the appropriate order-up-to level. The target expected back order is $1.25 \times (1 - 0.95) = 0.0625$. From the Poisson Loss Function Table with mean $(4 + 1) \times 1.25 = 6.25$, we find $L(10) = 0.1006$ and $L(11) = 0.0467$, so choose $S = 11$. Use Exhibit 11.4 to evaluate on-hand inventory, which equals $S - 6.25 + 0.0467 = 4.8$ units for each paint color. Multiply by 200 to get the total inventory $= 200 \times 4.8 = 960$.

Part b

Use Exhibit 11.6 to find the appropriate order-up-to level. The standard deviation over $(4 + 1)$ weeks is $\sigma = \sqrt{5} \times 8 = 17.89$ and $\mu = 250$. The target expected back order is $(50/17.89) \times (1 - 0.95) = 0.1397$. From the Standard Normal Loss Function Table, we find $L(0.71) = 0.1405$ and $L(0.72) = 0.1381$, so choose $z = 0.72$. Convert to $S = 250 + 0.72 \times 17.89 = 263$. Use Exhibit 11.4 to evaluate expected back order $= 17.89 \times 0.1381 = 2.47$. Expected on-hand inventory is $S - 250 + 2.47 = 15.47$. Multiply by 5 to get Total inventory $= 5 \times 15.47 = 77.35$.

Part c

The original inventory investment is $960 \times \$14 = \$13,440$, which incurs holding cost $\$13,440 \times 0.20 = \$2,688$. Repeat part b but now the target fill rate is 98 percent. The target expected back order is $(50/17.89) \times (1 - 0.98) = 0.0559$. From the Standard Normal Loss Function Table, we find $L(1.20) = 0.0561$ and $L(1.21) = 0.0550$, so choose $z = 1.21$. Convert to $S = 250 + 1.21 \times 17.89 = 272$. Use Exhibit 11.3 to evaluate Expected back order $= 17.89 \times 0.0550 = 0.98$. Expected on-hand inventory is $S - 250 + 0.98 = 22.98$. Multiply by 5 to get Total inventory $= 5 \times 22.98 = 114.9$. With the mixing machine, the total inventory investment is $114.9 \times \$14 = \$1,608.6$. Holding cost is $\$1,608.6 \times 0.2 = \$321.7$, which is only 12 percent $(312/2,688)$ of the original inventory holding cost.

Q12.2 (Burger King)

Part a

Use the newsvendor model to determine an order quantity. Use Exhibit 9.9. From the table we see that $F(3,500) = 0.8480$ and $F(4,000) = 0.8911$, so order 4,000 for each store.

Part b

Use Exhibit 9.5 to evaluate expected lost sales and Exhibit 9.6 to evaluate the expected left-over inventory. Expected lost sales come from the table, $L(4,000) = 185.3$. Expected sales are $\mu - 185.3 = 2,251 - 185.3 = 2,065.7$. Expected leftover inventory is Q minus expected sales, $4,000 - 2,065.7 = 1,934.3$. Across 200 stores there will be $200 \times 1,934.3 = 386,860$ units left over.

Part c

The mean is 450,200. The coefficient of variation of individual stores is $1,600/2,251 = 0.7108$. The coefficient of variation of total demand, we are told, is one-half of that, $0.7108/2 = 0.3554$. Hence, the standard deviation of total demand is $450,200 \times 0.3554 = 160,001$. To find the optimal order quantity to hit an 85 percent in-stock, use Exhibit 9.9. From the Standard Normal Distribution Function Table we see $\Phi(1.03) = 0.8485$ and $\Phi(1.04) = 0.8508$, so choose $z = 1.04$. Convert to $Q = 450,200 + 1.04 \times 160,001 = 616,601$.

Part d

Expected lost sales $= 160,001 \times L(z) = 160,001 \times 0.0772 = 12,352$. Expected sales $= 450,200 - 12,352 = 437,848$. Expected leftover inventory $= 616,601 - 437,848 = 178,753$, which is only 46 percent of what would be left over if individual stores held their own inventory.

Part e

The total order quantity is $4,000 \times 200 = 800,000$. With a mean of 450,200 and standard deviation of 160,001 (from part c), the corresponding z is $(800,000 - 450,200)/160,001 = 2.19$. From the Standard Normal Distribution Function Table we see $\Phi(2.19) = 0.9857$, so the in-stock would be 98.57 percent instead of 89.11 percent if the inventory were held centrally.

Chapter 13

Q13.1 (The Inn at Penn)

Part e

The booking limit is capacity minus the protection level, which is $150 - 50 = 100$; that is, allow up to 100 bookings at the low fare.

Part f

Use Exhibit 13.1. The underage cost is $C_u = 200 - 120 = 80$ and the overage cost is $C = 120$. The critical ratio is $80/(120 + 80) = 0.4$. From the Standard Normal Distribution Function Table we see $\Phi(-0.26) = 0.3974$ and $\Phi(-0.25) = 0.4013$, so choose $z = -0.25$. Evaluate $Q = 70 - 0.25 \times 29 = 63$.

Part g

Decreases. The lower price for business travelers leads to a lower critical ratio and hence to a lower protection level; that is, it is less valuable to protect rooms for the full fare.

Part h

The number of unfilled rooms with a protection level of 61 is the same as expected leftover inventory. Evaluate the critical ratio, $z = (61 - 70)/29 = -0.31$. From the Standard Normal Loss Function Table, $L(z) = 0.5730$. Expected lost sales are $29 \times 0.5730 = 16.62$ and expected leftover inventory is $61 - 70 + 16.62 = 7.62$. So we can expect 7.62 rooms to remain empty.

Part i

$70 \times \$200 + (150 - 70) \times \$120 = \$23,600$ because on average 70 rooms are sold at the high fare and $150 - 70 = 80$ are sold at the low fare.

Part j

$150 \times \$120 = \$18,000$.

Part k

If 50 are protected, we need to determine the number of rooms that are sold at the high fare. The z statistic is $(50 - 70)/29 = -0.69$. Expected lost sales are $29 \times L(-0.69) = 24.22$. Expected sales are $70 - 24.22 = 45.78$. Revenue is then $(150 - 50) \times \$120 + 45.78 \times \$200 = \$21,155$.

Q13.2 (Overbooking the Inn at Penn)

Part a

Use Exhibit 13.2. The underage cost is $120, the discount fare. The overage cost is $325. The critical ratio is $120/(325 + 120) = 0.2697$. From the table $F(12) = 0.2283$ and $F(13) = 0.3171$, so the optimal overbook quantity is 13.

Part b

A reservation cannot be honored if there are nine or fewer no-shows. $F(9) = 0.0552$, so there is a 5.5 percent chance the hotel will be overbooked.

Part c

It is fully occupied if there are 15 or fewer no-shows, which has probability $F(15) = 0.5170$.

Part d

Bumped customers equal 20 minus the number of no-shows, so it is equivalent to leftover inventory. Lost sales are $L(20) = 0.28$, expected sales are $15.5 - 0.28 = 15.22$, and expected leftover inventory/bumped customers $= 20 - 15.22 = 4.78$. Each one costs $325, so the total cost is $\$325 \times 4.78 = \$1,554$.

Q13.3 (WAMB)

Part a

First evaluate the distribution function from the density function provided in the table: $F(8) = 0$, $F(9) = F(8) + 0.05 = 0.05$, $F(10) = F(9) + 0.10 = 0.15$, and so on. Let Q denote the number of slots to be protected for sale later and let D be the demand for slots at $10,000 each. If $D > Q$, we reserved too few slots and the underage penalty is $C_u = \$10,000 - \$4,000 = \$6,000$. If $D < Q$, we reserved too many slots and the overage penalty is $C_o = \$4,000$. The critical ratio is $6,000/(4,000 + 6,000) = 0.6$. From the table we find $F(13) = 0.6$, so the optimal protection quantity is 13. Therefore, WAMB should sell $25 - 13 = 12$ slots in advance.

Part b

The underage penalty remains the same. The overage penalty is now $C_o = \$4,000 - \$2,500 = \$1,500$. Setting the protection level too high before meant lost revenue on the slot, but now at least $2,500 can be gained from the slot, so the loss is only $1,500. The critical ratio is $6,000/(1,500 + 6,000) = 0.8$. From the table, $F(15) = 0.8$, so protect 15 slots and sell $25 - 15 = 10$ in advance.

Part c

If the booking limit is 10, there are 15 slots for last-minute sales. There will be standby messages if there are 14 or fewer last-minute sales, which has probability $F(14) = 0.70$.

Part d

Over-overbooking means the company is hit with a $10,000 penalty, so $C_o = 10,000$. Under-overbooking means slots that could have sold for $4,000 are actually sold at the standby price of $2,500, so $C_u = 4,000 - 2,500 = 1,500$. The critical ratio is $1,500/(10,000 + 1,500) = 0.1304$. From the Poisson Distribution Function Table with mean 9.0, $F(5) = 0.1157$ and $F(6) = 0.2068$, so the optimal overbooking quantity is six, that is, sell up to 31 slots.

Part e

The overage cost remains the same: we incur a penalty of $10,000 for each bumped customer (and we refund the $1,000 deposit of that customer too). The underage cost is now different. If we under-overbook, we have empty slots that we must fill with standbys. Those slots could have sold for $4,000 but are actually sold at the standby price of $2,500. However, we keep the $1,000 deposit from the customer that withdrew, so $C_u = 4,000 - 2,500 - 1,000 = 500$. The critical ratio is $500/(10,000 + 500) = 0.0476$. From the Poisson Distribution Function Table with mean 4.5, $F(0) = 0.0111$ and $F(1) = 0.0611$ and so the optimal overbooking quantity is one, that is, sell up to 26 slots.

Chapter 14

Q14.1 (Buying tissues)

Part a

If orders are made every week, then the average order quantity equals one week's worth of demand, which is 25 cases. If at the end of the week there is one week's worth of inventory, then the average inventory is $25/2 + 25 = 37.5$. (In this case inventory "saw-tooths" from a high of two week's worth of inventory down to one week, with an average of 1.5 weeks.) On average the inventory value is $37.5 \times 9.25 = \$346.9$. The holding cost per year is $52 \times 0.4\% = 20.8\%$. Hence, the inventory holding cost with the first plan is $20.8\% \times \$346.9 = \$72$. Purchase cost is $52 \times 25 \times \$9.25 = \$12,025$. Total cost is $\$12,025 + \$72 = \$12,097$.

Part b

Four orders are made each year, each order on average is for $(52/4) \times 25 = 325$ units. Average inventory is then $325/2 + 25 = 187.5$. The price paid per unit is $\$9.40 \times 0.95 = \$8.93$. The value of that inventory is $187.5 \times \$8.93 = \$1674$. Annual holding costs are $\$1674 \times 20.8\% = \$348$. Purchase cost is $52 \times 25 \times \$8.93 = \$11,609$. Total cost is $\$348 + \$11,609 = \$11,957$.

Part c

P&G prefers our third plan as long as the price is higher than in the second plan, $8.93. But the retailer needs a low enough price so that its total cost with the third plan is not greater than in the second plan, $11,957 (from part b). In part a we determined that the annual holding cost with a weekly ordering plan is approximately $72. If we lower the price, the annual holding cost will be a bit lower, but $72 is a conservative approximation of the holding cost. So the retailer's purchase cost should not exceed $11,957 - \$72 = \$11,885$. Total purchase quantity is $25 \times 52 = 1300$ units. So if the price is $\$11,885/1300 = \$9.14$, then the retailer will be slightly better off (relative to the second plan) and P&G is much better off (revenue of $12,012 instead of $11,885).

Q14.2 (Returning books)

Part a

Use the newsvendor model. The overage cost is C_o = cost − salvage value = $20 − $28/4 = $13. The underage cost is C_u = price − cost = $28 − $20 = $8. The critical ratio is 8/(13 + 8) = 0.3810. Look up the critical ratio in the Standard Normal Distribution Function Table to find the appropriate z statistic = −0.30. The optimal order quantity is $Q = \mu + z \times \sigma = 100 − 0.30 \times 42 = 87$.

Part b

Expected lost sales = $L(z) \times \sigma = 0.5668 \times 42 = 23.81$, where we find $L(z)$ from the Standard Normal Loss Function Table and $z = −0.30$ (from part a). Expected sales = μ − Expected lost sales = 100 − 23.81 = 76.2. Expected left over inventory = Q − Expected sales = 87 − 76.2 = 10.8. Profit = price × Expected sales + salvage value × Expected leftover inventory − Q × cost = $28 × 76.2 + $7 × 10.8 − 87 × $20 = $469.

Part c

The publisher's profit = Q × (wholesale price − cost) = 87 × ($20 − $7.5) = $1087.5.

Part d

The underage cost remains the same because a lost sale still costs Dan the gross margin, C_u = $8. However, the overage cost has changed because Dan can now return books to the publisher. He buys each book for $20 and then returns leftover books for a net salvage value of $15 − $1 (due to the shipping cost) = $14. So his overage cost is now C_o = cost − salvage value = $20 − $14 = $6. The critical ratio is 8/(6 + 8) = 0.5714. Look up the critical ratio in the Standard Normal Distribution Function Table to find the appropriate z statistic = 0.18. The optimal order quantity is $Q = \mu + z \times \sigma = 100 + 0.18 \times 42 = 108$.

Part e

Expected lost sales = $L(z) \times \sigma = 0.3154 \times 42 = 13.2$, where we find $L(z)$ from the Standard Normal Loss Function Table and $z = 0.18$ (from part d). Expected sales = μ − Expected lost sales = 100 − 13.2 = 86.8. Expected left over inventory = Q − Expected sales = 108 − 86.8 = 21.2. Profit = price × Expected sales + salvage value × Expected leftover inventory − Q × cost = $28 × 86.8 + $14 × 21.2 − 108 × $20 = $567.

Part f

The publisher's sales revenue is $20 × 108 = $2160. Production cost is $7.5 × 108 = $810. The publisher pays Dan $15 × 21.2 = $318. The publisher's total salvage revenue on returned books is $6 × 21.2 = $127.2. Profit is then $2160 − $810 −$318 + $127.2 = $1159. Note that both the publisher and Dan are better off with this buyback arrangement.

Part g

Equation 14.1 in the text gives the buyback price that coordinates the supply chain (that is, maximizes the supply chain's profit). That buyback price is $1 + $28 − ($28 − $20) × ($28 − $6)/($28 − $7.5) = $20.41. Note, the publisher's buyback price is actually higher than the wholesale price because the publisher needs to subsidize Dan's shipping cost to return books: Dan's net loss on each book returned is $20 − (20.41 − 1) = $0.59.

Glossary

A

abandoning Refers to flow units leaving the process because of lengthy waiting times.

activity Value-adding steps in a process where resources process flow units.

activity time The duration that a flow unit has to spend at a resource, not including any waiting time; also referred to as service time.

A/F ratio The ratio of actual demand (A) to forecasted demand (F). Used to measure forecast accuracy.

Andon cord A cord running adjacent to assembly lines that enables workers to stop production if they detect a defect. Just like the jidoka automatic shut-down of machines, this procedure dramatizes manufacturing problems and acts as a pressure for process improvements.

appointment Predefined times at which the flow unit supposedly enters the process; used to reduce variability (and seasonality) in the arrival process.

assemble-to-order Also known as make-to-order. A manufacturing system in which final assembly of a product only begins once a firm order has been received. Dell Inc. uses assemble-to-order with personal computers.

assignable causes of variation Those effects that result in changes of the parameters of the underlying statistical distribution of the process. Thus, for assignable causes, a change in process performance is not driven simply by common-cause variation.

attribute-based control charts A special form of control chart that only distinguishes between defective and nondefective items. Such control charts should be used if it is not possible to capture the quality conformance of a process outcome in one variable.

authorization level For a fare class, the percentage of capacity that is available to that fare class or lower. An authorization level is equivalent to a booking limit expressed as a percentage of capacity.

availability The proportion of a time a process (single resource or buffer) is able to either process (in the case of a resource) or admit (in the case of a buffer) incoming flow units.

average labor utilization Measures the percentage of paid labor time that is spent on actual production as opposed to idle time; measures the efficiency of the process as well as the balance of work across workers.

B

back order If demand occurs and inventory is not available, then the demand can be back-ordered until inventory becomes available.

back-order penalty cost The cost incurred by a firm per back order. This cost can be explicit or implicit (e.g., lost goodwill and future business).

balancing resources Attempting to achieve an even utilization across the resources in a process. This is equivalent to minimizing idle time by reallocating work from one resource to another.

base stock level Also known as the order-up-to level. In the implementation of an order-up-to policy, inventory is ordered so that inventory position equals the base stock level.

batch A collection of flow units that are either transported together (transfer batch) or processed together (production batch).

batch flow operation Those processes where flow units are batched to benefit from scale economies of production and/or transportation. Batch flow operations are known to have long flow times.

batch ordering A firm batch orders when it orders in integer multiples of a fixed batch size. For example, if a firm's batch size is 20 cases, then the firm orders either 0, 20, 40, 60, . . . cases.

bid price With bid price control, a bid price is assigned to each segment of capacity and a reservation is accepted only if its fare exceeds the bid prices of the segments of capacity that it uses.

bid price control A method for controlling whether or not to accept a reservation. This method explicitly recognizes that not all customers paying the same fare for a segment of capacity are equally valuable to the firm.

blocking The situation in which a resource has completed its work on a flow unit, yet cannot move the flow unit to the next step (resource or inventory) downstream as there is not space available.

booking limit The maximum number of reservations that are allowed for a fare class or lower.

bottleneck The resource with the lowest capacity in the process.

buckets A booking limit is defined for a bucket that contains multiple fare class–itinerary combinations.

buffer Another word for inventory, which is used especially if the role of the buffer is to maintain a certain throughput level despite the presence of variability.

buffer inventory Allows resources to operate independent from each other, thereby avoiding blocking and starving (in which case we speak of a decoupling buffer).

buffer or suffer principle The inherent tension between inventory and flow rate. In a process that suffers from setup times or variability, adding inventory can increase the flow rate.

bullwhip effect The propagation of demand variability up the supply chain.

buy-back contract A contract in which a supplier agrees to purchase leftover inventory from a retailer at the end of the selling season.

C

capability index The ratio between the tolerance level and the actual variation of the process.

capacity Measures the maximum flow rate that can be supported by a resource.

capacity-constrained A process for which demand exceeds the process capacity.

capacity pooling The practice of combining multiple capacities to deliver one or more products or services.

channel assembly The practice in the PC industry of having final assembly completed by a distributor (e.g., Ingram Micron) rather than the manufacturer (e.g., IBM).

channel stuffing The practice of inducing retailers to carry more inventory than needed to cover short-term needs.

coefficient of variation A measure of variability. Coefficient of variation = Standard deviation divided by the mean; that is, the ratio of the standard deviation of a random variable to the mean of the random variable. This is a relative measure of the uncertainty in a random variable.

collaborative planning, forecasting, and replenishment A set of practices designed to improve the exchange of information within a supply chain.

common causes of variation Constant variation reflecting pure randomness in the process. Such causes are hence a result of pure randomness as opposed to being the result of an assignable cause.

conservation-of-matter law A law that states that, on average, the flow into a system must equal the flow out of the system, otherwise the quantity within the system will not be stable.

consignment inventory Inventory that is kept at a customer's location but is owned by the supplier.

consolidated distribution The practice of delivering from a supplier to multiple locations (e.g., retail stores) via a distribution center.

continuous process A process in which the flow unit continuously flows from one resource to the next; different from discrete process, in which the flow units are separate entities.

contract manufacturer A firm that manufactures or assembles a product for another firm. Contract manufacturers typically manufacture products from multiple competitors, they are generally responsible for procurement, but they do not design or distribute the products they assemble.

control charts Graphical tools to statistically distinguish between assignable and common causes of variation. Control charts visualize variation, thereby enabling the user to judge whether the observed variation is due to common causes or assignable causes.

control limits Part of control charts that indicate to what extent a process outcome falls in line with the common cause variation of the process versus being a result of an assignable cause. Outcomes above the upper control limit (UCL) or below the lower control limit (LCL) indicate the presence of an assignable cause.

cost of direct labor Measures the per-unit cost of labor, which includes both the labor content (the actual labor going into completing a flow unit) and the idle time that occurs across all workers per completed flow unit.

critical path A project management term that refers to all those activities that—if delayed—would delay the overall completion of the project.

critical ratio The ratio of the underage cost to the sum of the overage and underage costs. It is used in the newsvendor model to choose the expected profit-maximizing order quantity.

cross docking The practice of moving inventory in a distribution facility from the inbound dock directly to the outbound loading dock without placing the inventory in storage within the distribution facility.

cycle inventory The inventory that results from receiving (producing) several flow units in one order (batch) that are then used over a time period of no further inflow of flow units.

cycle time The time that passes between two consecutive flow units leaving the process. Cycle time = 1/Flow rate.

D

decoupling inventory See buffer inventory.

demand-constrained A process for which the flow rate is limited by demand.

demand-pull An inventory policy in which demand triggers the ordering of replenishments.

density function The function that returns the probability the outcome of a random variable will exactly equal the inputted value.

design specifications Establish how much a process outcome is allowed to vary before it is labeled a defect. Design specifications are driven by customer requirements, not by control limits.

distribution function The function that returns the probability the outcome of a random variable will equal the inputted value or lower.

diversion The practice by retailers of purchasing product from a supplier only to resell the product to another retailer.

diverters Firms that practice diversion.

double marginalization The phenomenon in a supply chain in which one firm takes an action that does not optimize supply chain performance because the firm's margin is less than the supply chain's total margin.

E

Efficient Consumer Response The collective name given to several initiatives in the grocery industry to improve the efficiency of the grocery supply chain.

efficient frontier All locations in a space of performance measures (e.g., time and cost) that are efficient, that is, have no waste.

electronic data interchange (EDI) A technology standard for the communication between firms in the supply chain.

elimination of flow units Discarding defective flow units instead of reworking them.

e-lot system A decoupling buffer that is tracked to detect any systemic variation that could suggest a defect in the process; it is thereby a way to direct managerial attention toward defects in the process that would otherwise be hidden by inventory without immediately losing flow rate.

empirical distribution function A distribution function constructed with historical data.

EOQ (economic order quantity) The quantity that minimizes the sum of inventory costs and fixed ordering cost.

erlang loss formula Computes the proportion of time a resource has to deny access to incoming flow units in a system of multiple parallel servers and no space for inventory.

expected leftover inventory The expected amount of inventory left over at the end of the season when a fixed quantity is chosen at the start of a single selling season with random demand.

expected lost sales The expected amount of demand that is not satisfied when a fixed quantity is chosen at the start of a single selling season and demand is random.

Expected Marginal Seat Analysis A technique developed by Peter Belobaba of MIT to assign booking limits to multiple fare classes.

expected sales The expected amount of demand that is satisfied when a fixed quantity is chosen at the start of a single selling season and demand is random.

exponential distribution Captures a random variable with distribution $\text{Prob}\{x<t\}=1-\exp(-t/a)$, where a is the mean

as well as the standard deviation of the distribution. If inter-arrival times are exponentially distributed, we speak of a Poisson arrival process. The exponential distribution is known for the memoryless property; that is, if an exponentially distributed service time with mean five minutes has been going on for five minutes, the expected remaining duration is still five minutes.

external setups Those elements of setup times that can be conducted while the machine is processing; an important element of setup time reduction/SMED.

F

FCFS (first-come, first-served) Rule that states that flow units are processed in the order of their arrivals.

fences Restrictions imposed on a low-fare class to prevent high-fare customers from purchasing the low fare. Examples include advanced purchase requirements and Saturday night stay over.

FIFO (first-in, first out) See FCFS.

fill rate The fraction of demand that is satisfied; that is, that is able to purchase a unit of inventory.

flow rate (R) Also referred to as throughput. Flow rate measures the number of flow units that move through the process in a given unit of time. *Example:* The plant produces at a flow rate of 20 scooters per hour. Flow rate = Min{Demand, Capacity}.

flow time (T) Measures the time a flow unit spends in the process, which includes the time it is worked on at various resources as well as any time it spends in inventory. *Example:* A customer spends a flow time of 30 minutes on the phone in a call center.

flow unit The unit of analysis that we consider in process analysis; for example, patients in a hospital, scooters in a kick-scooter plant, and callers in a call center.

forecast The estimate of demand and potentially also of the demand distribution.

forward buying If a retailer purchases a large quantity during a trade promotion, then the retailer is said to forward buy.

G

gamma distribution A continuous distribution. The sum of exponential distributions is a gamma distribution. This is a useful distribution to model demands with high coefficients of variation (say about 0.5).

Gantt chart A graphical way to illustrate the durations of activities as well as potential dependencies between the activities.

H

heijunka A principle of the Toyota Production System, proposing that models are mixed in the production process according to their mix in customer demand.

hockey stick phenomenon   A description of the demand pattern that a supplier can receive when there is a substantial amount of order synchronization among its customers.

holding cost rate   The cost incurred to hold one unit of inventory for one period of time.

horizontal pooling   Combining a sequence of resources in a queuing system that the flow unit would otherwise visit sequentially; increases the span of control; also related to the concept of a work cell.

I

idle time   The time a resource is not processing a flow unit. Idle time should be reduced as it is a non-value-adding element of labor cost.

ikko-nagashi   An element of the Toyota Production System. It advocates the piece-by-piece transfer of flow units (transfer batches of one).

implied utilization   The workload imposed by demand of a resource relative to its available capacity. Implied utilization=Demand rate/Capacity.

incentive conflicts   In a supply chain, firms may have conflicting incentives with respect to which actions should be taken.

independent arrivals   A requirement for both the waiting time and the loss formulas. Independent arrivals mean that the probability of having an arrival occur in the next x minutes is independent of how many arrivals have occurred in the last y minutes.

information turnaround time (ITAT)   The delay between the occurrence of a defect and its detection.

in-stock probability   The probability all demand is satisfied over an interval of time.

integrated supply chain   The supply chain considered as a single integrated unit, that is, as if the individual firms were owned by a single entity.

interarrival time   The time that passes between two consecutive arrivals.

internal setups   Those elements of setup times that can only be conducted while the machine is not producing. Internal setups should be reduced as much as possible and/or converted to external setups wherever possible (SMED).

inventory (I)   The number of flow units that are in the process (or in a particular resource). Inventory can be expressed in (a) flow units (e.g., scooters), (b) days of supply (e.g., three days of inventory), or (c) monetary units ($1 million of inventory).

inventory cost   The cost a process incurs as a result of inventory. Inventory costs can be computed on a per-unit basis (see Exhibit 2.1) or on a per unit of time basis.

inventory level   The on-hand inventory minus the number of units back-ordered.

inventory policy   The rule or method by which the timing and quantity of inventory replenishment are decided.

inventory position   The inventory level plus the number of units on order.

inventory turns   How often a company is able to turn over its inventory. Inventory turns = 1/Flow time, which—based on Little's Law—is COGS/Inventory.

Ishikawa diagram   Also known as fishbone diagram or cause–effect diagram; graphically represents variables that are causally related to a specific outcome.

J

jidoka   In the narrow sense, a specific type of machine that can automatically detect defects and automatically shut down itself. The basic idea is that shutting down the machine forces human intervention in the process, which in turn triggers process improvement.

just-in-time   The idea of producing units as close as possible to demand, as opposed to producing the units earlier and then leaving them in inventory or producing them later and thereby leaving the unit of demand waiting. Just-in-time is a fundamental part of the Toyota Production System as well as of the matching supply with demand framework postulated by this book.

K

kaizen   The continuous improvement of processes, typically driven by the persons directly involved with the process on a daily basis.

kanban   A production and inventory control system in which the production and delivery of parts are triggered by the consumption of parts downstream (pull system).

L

labor content   The amount of labor that is spent on a flow unit from the beginning to the end of the process. In a purely manual process, we find labor content as the sum of all the activity times.

labor utilization   How well a process uses the labor involved in the process. Labor utilization can be found based on activity times and idle times (see How-to example).

lead time   The time between when an order is placed and when it is received. Process lead time is frequently used as an alternative word for flow time.

line balancing   The process of evenly distributing work across the resources of a process. Line balancing reduces idle time and can (a) reduce cycle time or (b) reduce the number of workers that are needed to support a given flow rate.

Little's Law   The average inventory is equal to the average flow rate times the average flow time ($I = R \times T$).

location pooling   The combination of inventory from multiple locations into a single location.

loss function   A function that returns the expected number of units by which a random variable exceeds the inputted value.

M

machine-paced line   A process design in which flow units are moved from one resource to another by a constant speed dictated by the conveyor belt. There is typically no inventory between the resources connected by a conveyor belt.

make-to-order   A production system, also known as assemble-to-order, in which flow units are produced only once the customer order for that flow unit has been received. Make-to-order production typically requires wait times for the customer, which is why it shares many similarities with service operations. Dell Inc. uses make-to-order with personal computers.

make-to-stock   A production system in which flow units are produced in anticipation of demand (forecast) and then held in finished goods inventory.

margin arithmetic   Equations that evaluate the percentage increase in profit as a function of the gross margin and the percentage increase in revenue.

marginal cost pricing   The practice of setting the wholesale price to the marginal cost of production.

materials requirement planning   A system to control the timing and quantity of component inventory replenishment based on forecasts of future demand and production schedules.

maximum profit   In the context of the newsvendor model, the expected profit earned if quantity can be chosen after observing demand. As a result, there are no lost sales and no leftover inventory.

mean   The expected value of a random variable.

mismatch cost   The sum of the underage cost and the overage cost. In the context of the newsvendor model, the mismatch cost is the sum of the lost profit due to lost sales and the total loss on leftover inventory.

mixed model production   See heijunka.

MRP jitters   The phenomenon in which multiple firms operate their MRP systems on the same cycle, thereby creating order synchronization.

muda   One specific form of waste, namely waste in the form of non-value-adding activities. Muda also refers to unnecessary inventory (which is considered the worst form of muda), as unnecessary inventory costs money without adding value and can cover up defects and other problems in the process.

multiple flow units   Used in a process that has a mix of products or customers flowing through it. Most computations, including the location of the bottleneck, depend on the mix of products.

N

negative binomial distribution   A discrete distribution function with two parameters that can independently change the mean of the distribution as well as the standard deviation. In contrast, the Poisson distribution has only one parameter and can only regulate its mean.

nested booking limits   Booking limits for multiple fare classes are nested if each booking limit is defined for a fare class or lower. With nested booking limits, it is always the case that an open fare class implies all higher fare classes are open and a closed fare class implies all lower fare classes are closed.

newsvendor model   A model used to choose a single order quantity before a single selling season with stochastic demand.

nonlinear   The relationship between variables if the graph of the two variables is not a straight line.

normal distribution   A continuous distribution function with the well-known bell-shaped density function.

no-show   A customer that makes a reservation but cancels or fails to arrive for service.

O

on allocation   A product whose total amount demanded exceeds available capacity.

on-hand inventory   The number of units currently in inventory.

on-order inventory   Also known as pipeline inventory. The number of units of inventory that have been ordered but have not been received.

one-for-one ordering policy   Another name for an order-up-to policy. (With this policy, one unit is ordered for every unit of demand.)

options contract   With this contract, a buyer pays a price per option purchased from a supplier and then pays an additional price later on to exercise options. The supplier is responsible for building enough capacity to satisfy all of the options purchased in case they are all exercised.

order batching   A cause of the bullwhip effect. A firm order batches when it orders only in integer multiples of some batch quantity.

order inflation   The practice of ordering more than desired in anticipation of receiving only a fraction of the order due to capacity constraints upstream.

order synchronization   A cause of the bullwhip effect. This describes the situation in which two or more firms submit orders at the same moments in time.

order-up-to level   Also known as the base stock level. In the implementation of an order-up-to policy, inventory is ordered so that inventory position equals the order-up-to level.

order-up-to model A model used to manage inventory with stochastic demand, positive lead times, and multiple replenishments.

origin-destination control A revenue management system in the airline industry that recognizes passengers that request the same fare on a particular segment may not be equally valuable to the firm because they differ in their itinerary and hence total revenue.

out-of-stock When a firm has no inventory.

overage cost In the newsvendor model, the cost of purchasing one too many units. In other words, it is the increase in profit if the firm had purchased one fewer unit without causing a lost sale (i.e., thereby preventing one additional unit of leftover inventory).

overbooking The practice of accepting more reservations than can be accommodated with available capacity.

P

pallet Literally the platform used (often wood) by a forklift to move large quantities of material.

par level Another name for the order-up-to level in the order-up-to model.

Pareto principle Principle that postulates that 20 percent of the causes account for 80 percent of all problems (also known as the 80-20 rule).

period In the order-up-to model, time is divided into periods of time of equal length. Typical period lengths include one day, one week, and one month.

phantom orders An order that is canceled before delivery is taken.

pipeline inventory The minimum amount of inventory that is required to operate the process. Since there is a minimum flow time that can be achieved (i.e., sum of the activity times), because of Little's Law, there is also a minimum required inventory in the process. Also known as on-order inventory, it is the number of units of inventory that have been ordered but have not been received.

point-of-sale (POS) Data on consumer transactions.

Poisson distribution A discrete distribution function that often provides an accurate representation of the number of events in an interval of time when the occurrences of the events are independent of each other. In other words, it is a good distribution to model demand for slow-moving items.

Poisson process An arrival process with exponentially distributed interarrival times.

poka-yoke A Toyota technique of "fool-proofing" many assembly operations, that is, by making mistakes in assembly operations physically impossible.

pooling The concept of combining several resources (including their buffers and their arrival processes) into one joint resource. In the context of waiting time problems, pooling reduces the expected wait time.

price protection The practice in the PC industry of compensating distributors due to reductions in a supplier's wholesale price. As a result of price protection, the price a distributor pays to purchase inventory is effectively always the current price; that is, the supplier rebates the distributor whenever a price reduction occurs for each unit the distributor is holding in inventory.

priority rules Used to determine the sequence with which flow units waiting in front of the same resource are served. There are two types of priority rules: service time independent (e.g., FCFS rule) and service time dependent (e.g., SPT rule).

process Resources, inventory locations, and a flow that describe the path of a flow unit from its transformation as input to output.

process analysis Concerned with understanding and improving business processes. This includes determining the location of the bottleneck and computing the basic performance measures inventory, flow rate, and flow time.

process capability The tolerance level of the process relative to its current variation in outcomes. This is frequently measured in the form of the capability index.

process capacity Capacity of an entire process, which is the maximum flow rate that can be achieved in the process. It is based on the capacity of the bottleneck.

process flow diagram Maps resources and inventory and shows graphically how the flow unit travels through the process in its transformation from input to output.

process utilization To what extent an entire process uses its capacity when supporting a given flow rate. Process utilization = Flow rate/Process capacity.

product pooling The practice of using a single product to serve two demand segments that were previously served by their own product version.

production batch The collection of flow units that are produced within a production cycle.

production cycle The processing and setups of all flow units before the resource starts to repeat itself.

protection level The number of reservations that must always be available for a fare class or higher. For example, if a flight has 120 seats and the protection level is 40 for the high-fare class, then it must always be possible to have 40 high-fare reservations.

pull system A manufacturing system in which production is initiated by the occurrence of demand.

push system A manufacturing system in which production is initiated in anticipation of demand.

Q

quality at the source The idea of fixing defects right when and where they occur. This is a fundamental idea of the Toyota Production System. Fixing defects later on in the process is difficult and costly.

quantity discount   Reduced procurement costs as a result of large order quantities. Quantity discounts have to be traded off against the increased inventory costs.

quantity flexibility contracts   With this contract, a buyer provides an initial forecast to a supplier. Later on the buyer is required to purchase at least a certain percentage of the initial forecast (e.g., 75 percent), but the buyer also is allowed to purchase a certain percentage above the forecast (e.g., 125 percent of the forecast). The supplier must build enough capacity to be able to cover the upper bound.

queue   Another word for inventory, but used especially in the context of waiting time problems.

queuing system   A sequence of individual queues in which the outflow of one buffer/server is the inflow to the next buffer/server; also referred to as tandem queues.

Quick Response   A series of practices in the apparel industry used to improve the efficiency of the apparel supply chain.

R

R-bar charts   Track the variation in the outcome of a process. R-bar charts require that the outcome of a process be evaluated based on a single variable.

random variable   A variable that represents a random event. For example, the random variable X could represent the number of times the value 7 is thrown on two dice over 100 tosses.

range of a sample   The difference between the highest and the lowest value in the sample.

reactive capacity   Capacity that can be used after useful information regarding demand is learned; that is, the capacity can be used to react to the learned demand information.

resource   The entity of a process that the flow unit has to visit as part of its transformation from input to output.

returns policy   See buy-back contract.

revenue management   Also known as yield management. The set of tools used to maximize revenue given a fixed supply.

revenue-sharing contracts   With this contract, a retailer pays a supplier a wholesale price per unit purchased plus a fraction of the revenue the retailer realizes from the unit.

rework   An approach of handling defective flow units that attempts to invest further resource time into the flow unit in the attempt to transform it into a conforming (nondefective) flow unit.

round up rule   When looking for a value inside a table, it often occurs that the desired value falls between two entries in the table. The round-up rule chooses the entry that leads to the larger quantity.

S

safety inventory   The inventory that a firm holds to protect itself from random fluctuations in demand.

salvage value   The value of leftover inventory at the end of the selling season in the newsvendor model.

scale economies   Cost savings that can be achieved in large operations. Examples are pooling benefits in waiting time problems and lower per-unit setup costs in batch flow operations.

seasonal arrivals   Systemic changes in the interarrival times (e.g., peak times during the day, the week, or the year).

seasonal inventory   Arises if the flow rate exceeds the demand rate in anticipation of a time period when the demand rate exceeds the flow rate.

second buy   An opportunity to request a second replenishment, presumably after some demand information is learned.

service level   The probability with which a unit of incoming demand will receive service as planned. In the context of waiting time problems, this means having a waiting time less than a specified target wait time; in other contexts, this also can refer to the availability of a product.

setup cost   Costs that are incurred in production whenever a resource conducts a setup and in transportation whenever a shipment is done. Setup costs drive batching. It is important to include only out-of-pocket costs in the setup costs, not opportunity costs.

setup time   The duration of time a resource cannot produce as it is either switched from one setting to the other (e.g., from producing part A to producing part B, in which case we speak of a changeover time) or not available for production for other reasons (e.g., maintenance step). Setup times reduce capacity and therefore create an incentive to produce in batches.

setup time reduction   See SMED.

shortage gaming   A cause of the bullwhip effect. In situations with a capacity constraint, retailers may inflate their orders in anticipation of receiving only a portion of their order.

single segment control   A revenue management system in the airline industry in which all passengers on the same segment paying the same fare class are treated equally.

six-sigma   In its narrow sense, refers to a process capability of two. This means that a process outcome can fall six standard deviations above or below the mean and still be within tolerance (i.e., still not be a defect). In its broader meaning, refers to quality improvement projects that are using statistical process control.

SMED (single minute exchange of dies)   The philosophy of reducing setup times instead of just finding optimal batch sizes for given setup times.

span of control   The scope of activities a worker or a resource performs. If the resource is labor, having a high span of control requires extensive training. Span of control is largest in a work cell.

specification levels   The cut-off points above (in the case of upper specification level) and below (in the case of lower specification level) which a process outcome is labeled a defect.

SPT (shortest processing time) rule   A priority rule that serves flow units with the shortest processing time first. The SPT rule is known to minimize the overall waiting time.

standard deviation   A measure of the absolute variability around a mean. The square of the standard deviation equals the variance.

standard normal   A normal distribution with mean 0 and standard deviation 1.

starving   The situation in which a resource has to be idle as there is no flow unit completed in the step (inventory, resource) upstream from it.

stationary arrivals   When the arrival process does not vary systemically over time; opposite of seasonal arrivals.

statistical process control (SPC)   A set of statistical tools that is used to measure the capability of a process and to help monitor the process revealing potential assignable causes of variation.

stochastic   An event that is random, that is, its outcome cannot be predicted with certainty.

stockout   Occurs if a customer demands a unit but a unit of inventory is not available. This is different from "being out of stock," which merely requires that there is no inventory available.

stockout probability   The probability a stockout occurs over a predefined interval of time.

supply chain   The series of firms that deliver a good or service from raw materials to customer fulfillment.

supply chain efficiency   The ratio of the supply chain's actual profit to the supply chain's optimal profit.

supply-constrained   A process for which the flow rate is limited by either capacity or the availability of input.

T

takotei-mochi   A Toyota technique to reduce worker idle time. The basic idea is that a worker can load one machine and while this machine operates, the worker—instead of being idle—operates another machine along the process flow.

tandem queue   See queuing system.

target wait time (TWT)   The wait time that is used to define a service level concerning the responsiveness of a process.

tasks   The atomic pieces of work that together constitute activities. Tasks can be moved from one activity/resource to another in the attempt to improve line balance.

throughput   See flow rate.

tolerance levels   The range of acceptable outcomes of a process. See also design specifications.

Toyota Production System   A collection of practices related to production, product development, and supply chain management as developed by the Toyota Motor Corporation. Important elements discussed in this book are the idea of permanent improvement (kaizen), the reduction of waste (muda), inventory reduction (just-in-time, kanban), mixed model production (heijunka), and reduction of setup times (SMED).

trade promotions   A temporary price discount off the wholesale price that a supplier offers to its retailer customers.

transfer batch   A collection of flow units that are transferred as a group from one resource to the next.

trunk inventory   The inventory kept by Medtronic sales representatives in the trunk of their vehicles.

tsukurikomi   The Toyota idea of integrating quality inspection throughout the process. This is therefore an important enabler of the quality-at-the-source idea.

turn-and-earn   An allocation scheme in which scarce capacity is allocated to downstream customers proportional to their past sales.

U

underage cost   In the newsvendor model, the profit loss associated with ordering one unit too few. In other words, it is the increase in profit if one additional unit had been ordered and that unit is sold.

universal design/product   A product that is designed to serve multiple functions and/or multiple customer segments.

utilization   The extent to which a resource uses its capacity when supporting a given flow rate. Utilization = Flow rate/ Capacity.

V

value chain   See supply chain.

variance   A measure of the absolute variability around a mean. The square root of the variance equals the standard deviation.

vendor-managed inventory   The practice of switching control of inventory management from a retailer to a supplier.

virtual nesting   A revenue management system in the airline industry in which passengers on different itineraries and paying different fare classes may nevertheless be included in the same bucket for the purchase of capacity controls.

virtual pooling   The practice of holding inventory in multiple physical locations that share inventory information data so that inventory can be moved from one location to another when needed.

W

waiting time   The part of flow time in which the flow unit is not processed by a resource.

waiting time formula   The average wait time, T_q, that a flow unit spends in a queue before receiving service.

waste   An abstract word that refers to any inefficiencies that exist in the process; for example, line imbalances, inadequate batch sizes, variability in service times, and so forth. Waste can be seen as the distance between the current performance of a process and the efficient frontier. Waste is called "muda" in the Toyota Production System.

win-win   A situation in which both parties in a negotiation are better off.

work cell   A resource where several activities that were previously done by separate resources (workers, machines) are combined into a single resource (team of workers). Work cells have several quality advantages as they have a short ITAT; they are also—by definition—more balanced.

work in process (WIP)   The inventory that is currently in the process (as opposed to inventory that is finished goods or raw material).

worker-paced line   A process layout in which a worker moves the flow unit to the next resource or buffer when he or she has completed processing it; in contrast to a machine-paced line, where the flow unit moves based on a conveyor belt.

workload   The request for capacity created by demand. Workload drives the implied utilization.

X

X-bar charts   Track the mean of an outcome of a process. X-bar charts require that the outcome of a process be evaluated based on a single variable.

Y

yield management   Also known as revenue management. The set of tools used to maximize revenue given a fixed supply.

yield of a resource   The percentage of flow units processed correctly at the resource. More generally, we also can speak of the yield of an entire process.

Z

zero-sum game   A game in which the total payoff to all players equals a constant no matter what outcome occurs.

z-statistic   Given quantity and any normal distribution, that quantity has a unique z-statistic such that the probability the outcome of the normal distribution is less than or equal to the quantity equals the probability the outcome of a standard normal distribution equals the z-statistic.

References

Abernathy, F. H.; J. T. Dunlop; J. Hammond; and D. Weil. *A Stitch in Time: Lean Retailing and the Transformation of Manufacturing—Lessons from the Apparel and Textile Industries.* New York: Oxford University Press, 1999.

Anderson, E.; C. Fine; and G. Parker. "Upstream Volatility in the Supply Chain: The Machine Tool Industry as a Case Study." MIT working paper, 1996.

Anupindi, R.; S. Chopra; S. D. Deshmukh; J. A. Van Mieghem; and E. Zemel, "Managing Business Process Flows," Prentice-Hall, 1999.

Bartholdi, J. J., and D. D. Eisenstein. "A Production Line That Balances Itself." *Operations Research* 44, no. 1 (1996), pp. 21–34.

Beatty, S. "Advertising: Infinity and Beyond? No Supply of Toys at Some Burger Kings." *The Wall Street Journal,* November 25, 1996, p. B-10.

Belobaba, P. "Application of a Probabilistic Decision Model to Airline Seat Inventory Control." *Operations Research* 37, no 2 (1989), pp. 183–97.

Bohn, R. E., and R. Jaikumar. "A Dynamic Approach to Operations Management: An Alternative to Static Optimization." *International Journal of Production Economics* 27, no. 3 (1992), pp. 265–82.

Bohn, R. E., and C. Terwiesch. "The Economics of Yield-Driven Processes." *Journal of Operations Management* 18 (December 1999), pp. 41–59.

Boyd, A. "Airline Alliance Revenue Management." *OR/MS Today* 25 (October 1998), pp. 28–31.

Breyfogle, F. W. *Implementing Six Sigma.* New York: John Wiley & Sons, 1999.

Brown, A.; H. Lee; and R. Petrakian. "Xilinx Improves Its Semiconductor Supply Chain Using Product and Process Postponement." *Interfaces* 30, no. 4 (2000), p. 65.

Buzzell, R.; J. Quelch; and W. Salmon. "The Costly Bargain of Trade Promotion." *Harvard Business Review* 68, no. 2 (1990), pp. 141–49.

Cachon, G. "Supply Chain Coordination with Contracts." In *Handbooks in Operations Research and Management Science: Vol. 11. Supply Chain Management, I: Design, Coordination, and Operation* ed. T. Kok and S. Graves. Amsterdam North-Holland, 2004.

Chase, R. B., and N. J. Aquilano, *Production and Operations Management: Manufacturing and Services,* 7th ed., Irwin: 1995.

Chopra, S., and P. Meindl. *Supply Chain Management: Strategy, Planning and Operation.* 2nd ed. Upper Saddle River, NJ: Pearson Prentice Hall, 2004.

Cross, R. "An Introduction to Revenue Management." *In Handbook of Airline Economics,* ed. D. Jenkins. New York: McGraw-Hill, 1995, pp. 453–58.

Cross, R. *Revenue Management: Hard-Core Tactics for Market Domination.* New York: Broadway Books, 1997.

De Groote, X. Inventory Theory: A Road Map. Unpublished teaching note. INSEAD. March 1994.

Feitzinger, E., and H. Lee. "Mass Customization at Hewlett-Packard: The Power of Postponement." *Harvard Business Review* 75 (January–February 1997), pp. 116–21.

Fisher, M. "What Is the Right Supply Chain for Your Product." *Harvard Business Review* 75 (March–April) 1997; pp. 105–16.

Fisher, M.; K. Rajaram; and A. Raman. 2001. "Optimizing Inventory Replenishment of Retail Fashion Products." *Manufacturing and Service Operations Management* 3, no. 3 (2001), pp. 230–41.

Fisher, M., and A. Raman. "Reducing the Cost of Demand Uncertainty through Accurate Response to Early Sales." *Operations Research* 44 (1996), pp. 87–99.

Fujimoto, T. *The Evolution of a Manufacturing System at Toyota.* New York: Oxford University Press, 1999.

Gans, N.; G. Koole; and A. Mandelbaum. "Telephone Call Centers: Tutorial, Review, and Research Prospects." *Manufacturing & Service Operations Management* 5 (2003), pp. 79–141.

Gaur, V.; M. Fisher; and A. Raman. "Retail Inventory Productivity: Analysis and Benchmarking." Working paper, Stern School of Business, 2002.

Geraghty, M., and E. Johnson. "Revenue Management Saves National Rental Car." *Interfaces* 27, no. 1 (1997), pp. 107–27.

Hall, R. W. *Queuing Methods for Services and Manufacturing.* Upper Saddle River, NJ: Prentice Hall, 1997.

Hansell, S. "Is This the Factory of the Future." *New York Times,* July 26, 1998.

Harrison, M. J., and C. H. Loch, "Operations Management and Reengineering." Stanford Working Paper, 1995.

Hayes, R. H., and S. C. Wheelwright. "Link Manufacturing Process and Product Life Cycles." *Harvard Business Review,* January–February 1979, pp. 133–40.

Hayes, R. H.; S. C. Wheelwright; and K. B. Clark. *Dynamic Manufacturing: Creating the Learning Organization.* New York: Free Press, 1988.

Hillier, F. S., and G. J. Lieberman. *Introduction to Operations Research.* 7th ed. New York: McGraw-Hill, 2002.

Hopp, W. J., and M. L. Spearman. *Factory Physics I: Foundations of Manufacturing Management.* New York: Irwin/McGraw-Hill, 1996.

Jordon, W., and S. Graves. "Principles on the Benefits of Manufacturing Process Flexibility." *Management Science* 41 (1995), pp. 577–94.

Juran. J. *The Quality Control Handbook.* 4th ed. New York: McGraw-Hill, 1951.

Juran. J. *Juran on Planning for Quality.* New York: Free Press, 1989.

Karmarkar, U. "Getting Control of Just-in-Time." *Harvard Business Review* (7 September–October 1989), pp. 122–31.

Kaufman, L. "Restoration Hardware in Search of a Revival." *New York Times,* March 21, 2000.

Kimes, S. "Revenue Management on the Links I: Applying Yield Management to the Golf-Course Industry." *Cornell Hotel and Restaurant Administration Quarterly* 41, no. 1 (February 2000), pp. 120–27.

Kimes, S.; R. Chase; S. Choi; P. Lee; and E. Ngonzi. "Restaurant Revenue Management: Applying Yield Management to the Restaurant Industry." *Cornell Hotel and Restaurant Administration Quarterly* 39, no. 3 (1998), pp. 32–39.

Lee, H. "Effective Inventory and Service Management through Product and Process Redesign." *Operations Research* 44, no. 1 (1996), pp. 151–59.

Lee, H.; V. Padmanabhan; and S. Whang. "The Bullwhip Effect in Supply Chains." *MIT Sloan Management Review* 38, no. 3 (1997), pp. 93–102.

Magretta, J. 1998. "The Power of Virtual Integration: An Interview with Dell Computer's Michael Dell." *Harvard Business Review* (76 March–April 1998), pp. 72–84.

McGill, J., and G. van Ryzin. "Revenue Management: Research Overview and Prospects." *Transportation Science* 33, no. 2 (1999), pp. 233–56.

McWilliams, G., and J. White. "Others Want to Figure out How to Adopt Dell Model." *The Wall Street Journal,* December 1, 1999.

Motorola. "What Is Six Sigma?" Summary of Bill Weisz's videotape message, 1987.

Nahmias, S. 2000. *Production and Operations Analysis.* 4th ed. New York: McGraw-Hill/Irwin, 2000.

Nelson, E. "Wal-Mart Sets Supply Plan as Net Slightly Beats Forecast." *The Wall Street Journal,* November 10, 1999.

Padmanabhan, V., and I. P. L. Png. "Returns Policies: Make Money by Making Good." *Sloan Management Review,* Fall 1995, pp. 65–72.

Pasternack, B. "Optimal Pricing and Returns Policies for Perishable Commodities." *Marketing Science* 4, no. 2 (1985), pp. 166–76.

Petruzzi, N., and M. Dada. "Pricing and the Newsvendor Problem: A Review with Extensions." *Operations Research* 47 (1999), pp. 183–94.

Popely, R. "Next-Day Delivery: Cadillac Lowering Costs and Raising Satisfaction by Getting Cars to Consumers Faster." *Chicago Tribune,* April 2, 1998.

Porteus, E. *Stochastic Inventory Theory.* Palo Alto, CA: Stanford University Press, 2002.

Pringle, D. "Nokia Eschews Factories in Most Low-Cost Regions." *The Wall Street Journal,* January 3, 2003.

Ramstad, E. "Koss CEO Gambles on Inventory Buildup: Just-in-Time Production Doesn't Always Work." *The Wall Street Journal,* March 15, 1999.

Sakasegawa, H. "An Approximation Formula $L_q = \alpha\beta^\rho$ $(1 - \rho)$." *Annals of the Institute of Statistical Mathematics* 29, no. 1 (1977), pp. 67–75.

Sechler, B. "Special Report: E-commerce, behind the Curtain." *The Wall Street Journal,* July 15, 2002.

Silver, E.; D. Pyke; and R. Peterson. *Inventory Management and Production Planning and Scheduling.* New York: John Wiley & Sons, 1998.

Simchi-Levi, D.; P. Kaminsky; and E. Simchi-Levi. *Designing and Managing the Supply Chain: Concepts, Strategies, and Case Studies.* 2nd ed. New York: McGraw-Hill, 2003.

Simison, R. "Toyota Unveils System to Custom-Build Cars in Five Days." *The Wall Street Journal,* August 6, 1999.

Smith, B.; J. Leimkuhler; and R. Darrow. "Yield Management at American Airlines." *Interfaces* 22, no. 1 (1992), pp. 8–31.

Stringer, K. "As Planes Become More Crowded, Travelers Perfect Getting 'Bumped.' " *The Wall Street Journal,* March 21, 2002.

Talluri, K., and G. van Ryzin. *The Theory and Practice of Revenue Management.* Boston: Kluwer Academic Publishers, 2004.

Terwiesch, C., and C. H. Loch. "Pumping Iron at Cliffs and Associates *I: The Cicored Iron Ore Reduction Plant in Trinidad.*" Wharton-INSEAD Alliance case, 2002.

Thurm, S. "Some U.S. Manufacturers Prosper by Easing Rise of 'Virtual' Firm." *The Wall Street Journal,* August 18, 1998.

Ulrich, K., and S. Eppinger. 2004. *Product Design and Development.* 3rd ed. New York: McGraw Hill, 2004.

Upton, D. "The Management of Manufacturing Flexibility." *California Management Review* 36 (Winter 1994), pp. 72–89.

Upton, D. "What Really Makes Factories Flexible." *Harvard Business Review* 73 (July–August 1995), pp. 74–84.

Vitzthum, C. "Spain's Zara Cuts a Dash with 'Fashion on Demand.'" *The Wall Street Journal,* May 29, 1998.

Wadsworth, H. M.; K. S. Stephens; and A. B. Godfrey. *Modern Methods for Quality Control and Improvement.* New York: John Wiley & Sons, 1986.

Weatherford, L. R., and S. E. Bodily. "A Taxonomy and Research Overview of Perishable-Asset Revenue Management: Yield Management, Overbooking and Pricing." *Operations Research* 40, no. 5 (1992), pp. 831–43.

Whitney, D. *Mechanical Assemblies: Their Design, Manufacture, and Role in Product Development.* New York: Oxford University Press, 2004.

Whitt, W. "The Queuing Network Analyzer." *Bell System Technology Journal* 62, no. 9 (1983).

Zipkin, P. *Foundations of Inventory Management.* New York: McGraw-Hill, 2000.

Zipkin, P. "The Limits of Mass Customization." *Sloan Management Review,* Spring 2001, pp. 81–87.

Index of Key "How to" Exhibits

Summary of Key Notation and Equations

Chapter 2: Process Flow

$$\text{Little's Law: Average inventory} = \text{Average flow rate} \times \text{Average time}$$

Chapter 3: Capacity/Bottleneck Analysis

$$\text{Implied utilization} = \frac{\text{Capacity requested by demand}}{\text{Available capacity}}$$

Chapter 4: Labor Content

$$\text{Flow rate} = \text{Min}\{\text{Available input, Demand, Process capacity}\}$$

$$\text{Cycle time} = \frac{1}{\text{Flow rate}}$$

$$\text{Cost of direct labor} = \frac{\text{Total wages}}{\text{Flow rate}}$$

$$\text{Idle time for worker at resource } i = \text{Cycle time} \times (\text{Number of workers at resource } i) - \text{Activity time at resource } i$$

$$\text{Average labor utilization} = \frac{\text{Labor content}}{\text{Labor content} + \text{Total idle time}}$$

Chapter 5: Batching

$$\text{Capacity given batch size} = \frac{\text{Batch size}}{\text{Setup time} + \text{Batch size} \times \text{Time per unit}}$$

$$\text{Recommended batch size} = \frac{\text{Flow rate} \times \text{Setup time}}{1 - \text{Flow rate} \times \text{Time per unit}}$$

$$\text{Economic order quantity} = \sqrt{\frac{2 \times \text{Setup cost} \times \text{Flow rate}}{\text{Holding cost}}}$$

Chapter 6: Waiting Time Systems

m = number of servers

p = activity time

a = interarrival time

CV_a = coefficient of variation for interarrivals

CV_p = coefficient of variation of processing time

$$\text{Utilization } u = \frac{p}{a \times m}$$

$$T_q = \left(\frac{\text{Activity time}}{m}\right) \times \left(\frac{\text{Utilization}^{\sqrt{2(m+1)}-1}}{1 - \text{Utilization}}\right) \times \left(\frac{CV_a^2 + CV_p^2}{2}\right)$$

$$\text{Flow time } T = T_q + p$$

$$\text{Inventory in service } I_p = m \times u$$

$$\text{Inventory in the queue } I_q = T_q/a$$

$$\text{Inventory in the system } I = I_p + I_q$$

Chapter 8: Quality

$$\text{Yield of resource} = \frac{\text{Flow rate of units processed correctly at the resource}}{\text{Flow rate}}$$

Chapter 9: Newsvendor

Q = order quantity

C_u = Underage cost

C_o = Overage cost

μ = Expected demand

σ = Standard deviation of demand

$F(Q)$ = Distribution function

$\Phi(Q)$ = Distribution function of the standard normal

$L(Q)$ = Loss function

$L(z)$ = Loss function of the standard normal distribution

$$\text{Critical ratio} = \frac{C_u}{C_o + C_u}$$

$$\text{A/F ratio} = \frac{\text{Actual demand}}{\text{Forecast}}$$

$$\text{Expected actual demand} = \text{Expected A/F ratio} \times \text{Forecast}$$

$$\text{Standard deviation of actual demand} = \text{Standard deviation of A/F ratios} \times \text{Forecast}$$

$$\text{Expected profit} - \text{maximizing order quantity: } F(Q) = \frac{C_u}{C_o + C_u}$$

$$\text{z-statistic or normalized order quantity: } z = \frac{Q - \mu}{\sigma}$$

$$Q = \mu + z \times \sigma$$

$$\text{Expected lost sales with a normal distribution} = \sigma \times L(z)$$

$$\text{In Excel: } L(z) = \text{Normdist}(z,0,1,0) - z*(1 - \text{Normsdist}(z))$$

$$\text{Expected lost sales for non-normal distributions} = L(Q) \text{ (from loss function table)}$$

$$\text{Expected sales} = \mu - \text{Expected lost sales}$$

$$\text{Expected leftover inventory} = Q - \text{Expected sales}$$

$$\text{Expected profit} = [(\text{Price} - \text{Cost}) \times \text{Expected sales}]$$
$$- [(\text{Cost} - \text{Salvage value}) \times \text{Expected leftover inventory}]$$

$$\text{Fill rate} = \text{Expected sales}/\mu$$

$$\text{In-stock probability} = F(Q)$$

$$\text{Stockout probability} = 1 - \text{In-stock probability}$$

$$\text{To achieve a fill rate with normally distributed demand, } L(z) = (\mu/\sigma) \times (1 - \text{Fill Rate}),$$

$$\text{otherwise, target expected lost sales} = \mu \times (1 - \text{Fill Rate})$$

Chapter 10: Reactive Capacity

$$\text{Mismatch cost} = (C_o \times \text{Expected leftover inventory}) + (C_u \times \text{Expected lost sales})$$

$$= \text{Maximum profit} - \text{Expected profit}$$

$$\text{Maximum profit} = (\text{Price} - \text{Cost}) \times \mu$$

$$\text{Mismatch cost as a percentage of the maximum profit} = \left(\frac{\phi(z)}{\Phi(z)}\right) \times \left(\frac{\sigma}{\mu}\right)$$

$$\phi(Q) = \text{Density function of the standard normal}$$

$$\text{Coefficient of variation} = \text{Standard deviation/Expected demand}$$

$$\text{Mismatch–quantity ratio} = \frac{\text{Mismatch cost}}{Q}$$

Chapter 11: Order-up-to Model

$$l = \text{Lead time}$$

$$S = \text{Order-up-to level}$$

$$\text{Inventory level} = \text{On-hand inventory} - \text{Back order}$$

$$\text{Inventory position} = \text{On-order inventory} + \text{Inventory level}$$

$$\text{In-stock probability} = 1 - \text{Stockout probability}$$
$$= \text{Prob\{Demand over } (l + 1) \text{ periods} \leq S\}$$

$$z\text{-statistic or normalized order quantity: } z = \frac{S - \mu}{\sigma}$$

$$\text{Expected back order with a normal distribution} = \sigma \times L(z)$$

$$\text{In Excel: } L(z) = \text{Normdist}(z,0,1,0) - z*(1 - \text{Normsdist}(z))$$

$$\text{Expected back order for non-normal distributions} = L(S) \text{ (from loss function table)}$$

$$\text{Fill rate} = 1 - \frac{\text{Expected back order}}{\text{Expected demand in one period}}$$

$$\text{Expected inventory} = S - \text{Expected demand over } l + 1 \text{ periods} + \text{Expected back order}$$

$$\text{Expected on-order inventory} = \text{Expected demand in one period} \times \text{Lead time}$$

To achieve a fill rate with normally distributed demand,

$$L(z) = \left(\frac{\text{Expected demand in one period}}{\text{Standard deviation of demand over } l + 1 \text{ periods}} \right) \times (1 - \text{Fill rate}),$$

otherwise,

$$\text{Expected back order} = (\text{Expected demand in one period}) \times (1 - \text{Fill rate})$$

Chapter 12: Pooling

$$\text{Expected pooled demand} = 2 \times \mu$$

$$\text{Standard deviation of pooled demand} = \sqrt{2 \times (1 + \text{Correlation})} \times \sigma$$

$$\text{Coefficient of variation of pooled demand} = \sqrt{\frac{1}{2}(1 + \text{Correlation})} \times \left(\frac{\sigma}{\mu} \right)$$

Chapter 13: Revenue Management

$$\text{Protection level: Critical ratio} = \frac{C_u}{C_o + C_u} = \frac{r_h - r_l}{r_h}$$

$$\text{Low-fare booking limit} = \text{Capacity} - Q$$

$$\text{Overbooking: Critical ratio} = \frac{C_u}{C_o + C_u} = \frac{r_l}{\text{Cost per bumped customer} + r_l}$$

Index